SECOND EDITION

Law Enforcement
in the
21st Century

Heath B. Grant

John Jay College of Criminal Justice

Karen J. Terry

John Jay College of Criminal Justice

PEARSON

AB and

Boston   New York   San Francisco

Mexico City   Montreal   Toronto   London   Madrid   Munich   Paris

Hong Kong   Singapore   Tokyo   Cape Town   Sydney

Senior Acquisitions Editor: Dave Repetto
Series Editorial Assistant: Jack Cashman
Marketing Manager: Kelly May
Production Editor: Pat Torelli
Editorial Production Service: Modern Graphics, Inc.
Electronic Composition: Modern Graphics, Inc.
Composition Buyer: Linda Cox
Manufacturing Buyer: Debbie Rossi
Interior Design: Carol Somberg
Photo Researcher: Kate Cebik
Cover Administrator: Kristina Mose-Libon
Cover Designer: Susan Paradise

For related titles and support materials, visit our online catalog at
www.ablongman.com.

Between the time website information is gathered and then published, it is not unusual
for some sites to have closed. Also, the transcription of URLs can result in typographi-
cal errors. The publisher would appreciate notification where these errors occur so
that they may be corrected in subsequent editions.

Library of Congress Cataloging-in-Publication Data

Grant, Heath B.
    Law enforcement in the 21st century / Heath B. Grant, Karen J. Terry.—2nd ed.
        p. cm.
    Includes bibliographical references and index.
    ISBN 13: 978-0-205-54297-0
    ISBN 10: 0-205-54297-2
    1. Police—United States. 2. Law enforcement—United States. I. Terry, Karen J. II.
Title. III. Title: Law enforcement in the twenty-first century.
    HV8139.G72 2008
    363.20973—dc22

                                                                2007029578

Printed in the United States of America

10 9 8 7 6 5 4 V011 11 10 09

Credits appear on page 437, which constitutes an extension of the copyright page.

Brief Contents

Contents

part one
Law Enforcement and the Criminal Justice System

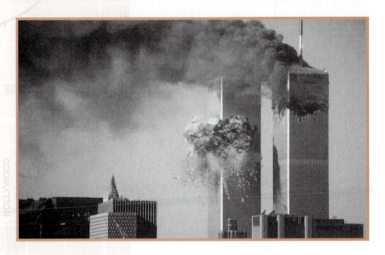

chapter 1
Law Enforcement in a Democratic Society   2

chapter 2

Origins and Development of Law Enforcement 34

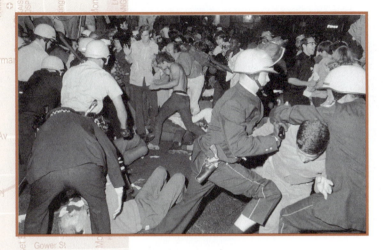

chapter 3
Traditional Policing and Police Professionalization 58

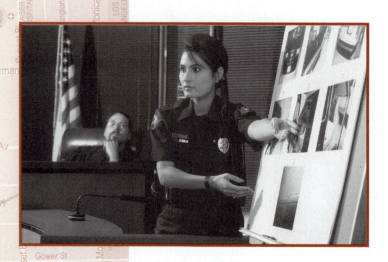

chapter 4
Law Enforcement and the Law   80

part two
Law Enforcement Organizations and Operations

chapter 5
Search and Seizure, Arrest, and Interrogation   106

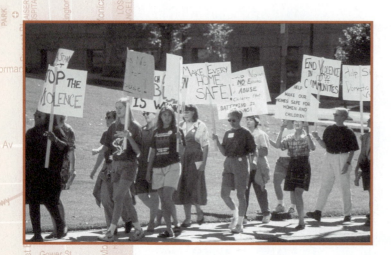

chapter 6
Policing Functions and Units   132

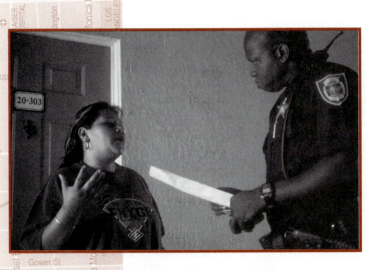

chapter 7
Patrol and Traffic 164

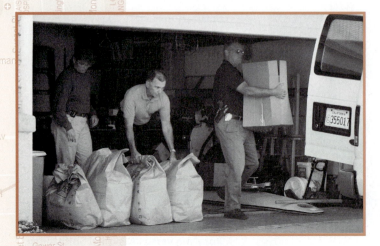

chapter 8

Investigation and Evidence Collection 190

part three
Police Conduct

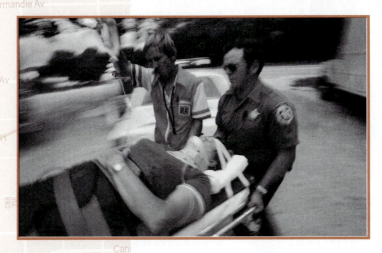

chapter 9
Policing Discretion and Behavior 212

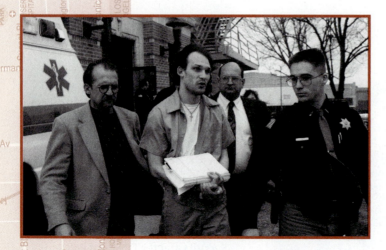

chapter **10**
Policing Multicultural Communities   240

chapter 11
Policing the Police   260

part four
The 21st Century Law Enforcement Officer

chapter 12
Community Policing and Problem Solving   286

chapter 13

Advances in Policing— New Technologies for Crime Analysis 318

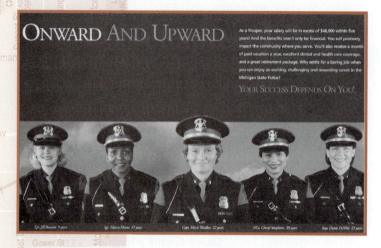

ONWARD AND UPWARD

As a Trooper, your salary will be in excess of $46,000 within five years! And the benefits won't only be financial. You will positively impact the community where you serve. You'll also receive a month of paid vacation a year, excellent dental and health care coverage, and a great retirement package. Why settle for a boring job when you can enjoy an exciting, challenging and rewarding career in the Michigan State Police?

YOUR SUCCESS DEPENDS ON YOU!

Linkages *in Law Enforcement*

Preface

Law Enforcement in the 21st Century is the first policing textbook to examine *linkage blindness*, the inability to analyze information across or within agencies, in the criminal justice system. This text also provides linkages for the reader between theories of policing and police practice, using problem-solving and crime-mapping applications.

When we conceived *Law Enforcement in the 21st Century*, our intention was to present a fresh, new approach of presenting introductory law enforcement material in a way that could be both practical for the future law enforcement officer and intellectually rewarding for the reader entering a whole new field of study. To meet these two important needs, the text provides a comprehensive overview of research and practice. In response to the many challenges facing law enforcement in the post–September 11 world, the information in this text is presented within the context of several important themes:

- The need for information sharing across law enforcement and other criminal justice agencies

- The link between law enforcement strategies and the causes of crime

- The impact of terrorism on the field of criminal justice

- Critical thinking about the role of law enforcement within our current global context, including the role of civil liberties and public security interests

Structure of the Book

This text is organized in a developmental framework:

- Part I introduces readers to law enforcement's place within the criminal justice system, the origins of policing as a profession, and traditional models of policing.

- Part II covers core aspects of police work, such as organizational structure and units, field operations, and investigations.

- Part III discusses major challenges in policing, including corruption, use of force, discretion, and multicultural policing.

- Part IV provides an overview of community policing, important technology applications that have an impact on the field of policing, and recruitment and training issues.

Thematic Pedagogy

We recognize the importance of making the material clear for the reader. Each chapter begins with a **Chapter Outline** that provides an overview of what is to come. **Chapter Objectives** lay out the specific goals for each chapter. The **Introduction** provides an example of a real case or situation so that the reader can understand what the chapter will be discussing.

Practical applications and case examples are used to introduce new material and make abstract concepts understandable. The book's **Linkages in Law Enforcement** text boxes highlight the book's central themes of inter- and intra-agency sharing, balancing public safety and individual interests, and proactive strategy developments. Practical applications related to the war on terror also are emphasized in the linkage boxes. Questions at the end of each Linkage Box challenge the reader to relate current material to earlier concepts, reinforcing the text's developmental emphasis.

Linkages in Law Enforcement

Role of Patrol in Detecting Terrorist Activities

The role of federal law enforcement agencies in combating terrorism would never have been a surprise to anyone, even prior to September 11. The need for global intelligence activities seemed well-suited for the international FBI field offices, but of little use to the local police department.

One of the most disturbing facts that resonated in the U.S. law enforcement community with the collapse of the World Trade Center was the fact that the reach of terrorism actually extended so much further than we had thought—the first responders to a terrorist act will invariably be local law enforcement, firefighters, and emergency services personnel.

On September 11, a total of 343 firefighters and 23 NYPD officers died at the World Trade Center. Dozens of firefighters and police officers went directly to the scene, and many of these first responders died (ABC News 2002). As a result, the law enforcement community has moved quickly to revise its training, deployment, and communication strategies in order to be better prepared for future terrorist attacks. In New York City, a consulting firm was contracted to review the events of that day, reviewing radio transmissions, records, and conducting dozens of interviews. As a result of the firm's findings, a significant change in deployment strategy has been controlling the number of personnel who respond at any one time to an event.

September 11 also highlighted the need for specialized knowledge within police operations, leading to the creation of special counterterrorism units in many departments. Although the FBI had created localized task forces to coordinate law enforcement resources related to terrorism, clearly information was slipping through the cracks, as noted in Chapter 1.

The importance of law enforcement being in touch with the community, a reality before September 11, is now even more important as the President Bush calls for the "vigilance" of residents to serve as the eyes and ears of law enforcement. Patrol officers are faced with renewed cultural challenges as they try to connect with Muslim segments of the community in the face of a rising tide of misunderstandings and accusations of racial profiling, particularly as the federal government has turned to the registration of people of Middle Eastern descent. However, it is only with the trust of the community that law enforcement can hope to get needed information related to suspicious activities. The reality that there are active terrorist cells in the United States cannot mean that all members of a group become suspects. This very difficult issue will be addressed further in Chapter 10.

An important issue for patrol officers is how the "war" on terrorism affects their typical response. The delicate balance remains that they still must operate within legal norms, even when military style tactics and/or assistance may be needed (White 2001). Although public safety will always be a pertinent goal with respect to dealing with terrorism, law enforcement cannot act with impunity. In some Latin American countries, semimilitary police have justified the practice of "disappearances" of suspected citizens on the basis of terrorist groups being too strong.

QUESTIONS
1. What are the most significant changes to the role of patrol officers post–September 11?
2. What specific strategies can law enforcement develop to collaborate more effectively with the Muslim community?
3. What tactics might you use to gain information on suspected terrorist cells in the community? What tactics would you consider to be going too far?

▲ Page 184 from Chapter 7, "Patrol and Traffic"

Linkages in Law Enforcement

GIS Applications to Sex Offender Management

GIS applications can also help to increase law enforcement's capacity to engage in the collaborative problem solving with other criminal justice and community agencies. The visual representation of information can be a powerful tool in coming to a common understanding of the nature of problems even across planning groups with diverse perspectives.

The authors of this text participated on a city-wide task force in New York City composed of representatives from law enforcement, probation and parole, family and criminal courts, mental health, treatment providers, and victim advocates to examine the issue of sex offender management in the community (Grant and Terry 2000). Although New York City had a large registered sex offender population at the time (over 3,000 offenders), there was as yet no comprehensive plan for the management of these offenders in the community involving collaboration between each of the key stakeholders. Building on the recognition across team members of the clear need for such a collaborative approach to sex offender management, as well as a need to better understand the dynamics of the problem through data collection, the New York City Sex Offender Management Team had tremendous momentum from the start, with agencies opening their doors to facilitate the data collection process.

Beginning at the first team meeting, the partners sought to identify a mechanism for gaining a complete understanding of the sex offender population currently residing in the community. Although it was initially suggested that each of the five district attorneys represented conduct searches on sex offenders within their own databases to form an initial population for study, it became immediately apparent that the most

Hot spots can be made readily apparent through the use of GIS density-mapping tools.

(continues)

▲ Page 329 from Chapter 13, "Advances in Policing: New Technologies for Crime Analysis"

Linkages in Law Enforcement

Posse Comitatus Today

Posse Comitatus was passed in the post–Civil War era in response to a general fear that the new federal government would interfere in state government and could use the military against its own citizens. Nevertheless, a number of exceptions to Posse Comitatus have been provided since its enactment:

- National Guard forces operating under state authority are exempt from the Act's restrictions.
- The President of the United States can use federal troops to "quell" domestic violence situations.
- Aerial photography and visual searches are allowed if for the purpose of assisting civilian law enforcement.
- An exception to the Act, created by Congress, allows the military to offer training, equipment, and advice in the "war on drugs."
- The Coast Guard is exempt from the provisions of the Act.
- The Navy can assist a Coast Guard vessel in pursuit.

In the aftermath of the September 11 attacks, further exceptions to Posse Comitatus were considered to reduce linkage blindness between military and civilian law enforcement agencies and to expedite investigations of suspected terrorists. In 2005, Whitehouse Press Secretary Scott McClellan stated that the Posse Comitatus Act of 1878 was under review, which caused a stir among journalists and legal commentators. However, later in 2005, Secretary of Defense Donald Rumsfeld stated in a meeting that the administration had no plans to make changes to the law (Plummer 2005).

In a reversal of position, PL 109-364, signed by President Bush in October of 2006, has a provision for "Use of the Armed Forces in Major Public Emergencies" (Stein 2006). The law adds "natural disaster, epidemic, or other serious public health emergency, terrorist attack or incident" to the list of conditions under which the president can command troops in the states. This allows the president to take over local authority "if domestic violence has occurred to such an extent that the constituted authorities of the State or possession are incapable of maintaining public order" (Stein 2006). Although the legislation speaks of extreme situations, it does allow the executive branch to command U.S. military personnel in a law enforcement capacity. The Posse Comitatus Act is found Appendix B.

QUESTIONS
1. How would elimination of Posse Comitatus change the balance between crime control and due process?
2. What, if any, conditions do you think could warrant such a change?
3. How would local law enforcement be helped or hindered by this change?
4. Where do you think Americans should draw the line between crime control and due process in the war on terrorism?

▲ Page 42 from Chapter 2, "Origins and Development of Law Enforcement"

At the end of each chapter, a **Chapter Summary** provides a recap of the key points. A list of **Key Terms** follows that includes the page reference where the term is introduced and defined.

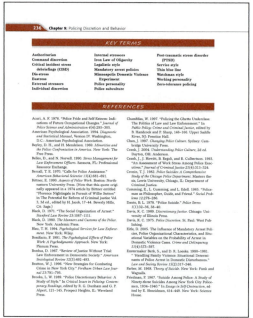

Linking the Dots exercises at the end of each chapter challenge the reader to relate current material to earlier concepts. These exercises provide yet another opportunity for readers to build their knowledge.

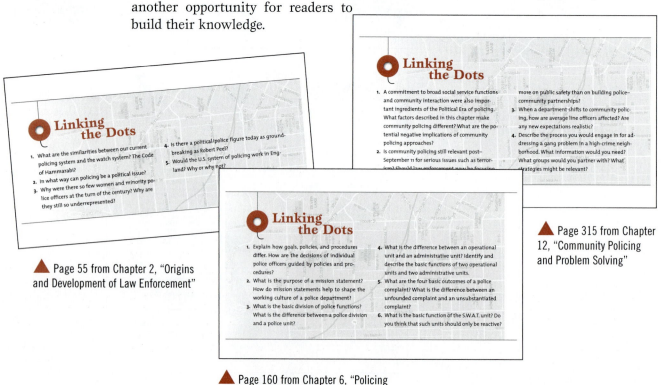

▲ Page 55 from Chapter 2, "Origins and Development of Law Enforcement"

▲ Page 160 from Chapter 6, "Policing Functions and Units"

▲ Page 315 from Chapter 12, "Community Policing and Problem Solving"

Supplementary Materials

Instructor's Resource Manual and Test Bank

This invaluable instructor resource, written by the authors of the book, includes the following tools for each chapter: the chapter-opening and chapter-ending pedagogy from the text for quick and easy reference; instructional ideas and aids; lecture launches and discussion topics; sample syllabi; handouts, and activities. The Instructor's Resource Manual is available online at www.ablongman.com.

TestGen EQ Computerized Test Bank

This computerized version of the test bank is available with Tamarack's easy-to-use TestGen software, which allows you to prepare tests to print and post online. Available for Windows and Macintosh, TestGen software allows you to fully edit and arrange the included test bank. The computerized test bank and TestGen software is available online at www.ablongman.com.

PowerPoint Lecture Presentations

These PowerPoint presentations can help to guide your class lectures and discussions. Each chapter contains between 15–25 slides and highlights important points in each chapter. The PowerPoint Lecture is available online at www.ablongman.com.

Acknowledgments

We would like to thank the reviewers of this text who helped us shape its development. We are grateful to those who reviewed and provided comments on the first edition of our text, as we tried to follow your advice as closely as possible. Those include James W. Billings, Jr., University of Southern Colorado; Greg DeLone, University of Nebraska-Lincoln; Robert Lee Edwards, Independent Judicial Commission-Bosnia; Harold A. Frossard, Moraine Valley Community College; Jack Gillen, Florida Southern College; Robert E. Grubb, Marshall University; William E. Kelly, Auburn University; Harvey Kushner, Long Island University; William E. Lanning, Guilford Technical Community College; Deborah L. Laufersweiler-Dwyer, University of Arkansas, Little Rock; Paul C. Leccese, Old Dominion University; Sharon Redhawk Love, The Penn State University; Robert W. McKenna, Roger Williams University; Susan V. Pons, Guilford Technical Community College; Chester L. Quarles, University of Mississippi, Jo Ann M. Scott, Ohio Northern University; Yolanda Scott, Roger Williams University; William C. Smith, University of South Carolina; Ivan Sun, University of Delaware; Devere Woods, Indiana State University; Kevin C. Woods, Becker College, and Jihong Zhao, University of Nebraska at Omaha.

We would like to thank many of our colleagues at John Jay College of Criminal Justice who assisted us at several points throughout the process of writing this text. In particular, thanks to Todd Clear, Joshua Freilich, Mike White, Jim Levine and Maki Haberfeld, chair of the department of Law, Police Science and Criminal Justice Administration. We also greatly appreciate the support of Jeremy Travis, Michael Steinman and Jane Bowers, whose leadership at the college is invaluable. We also offer a special thanks to Jim Fyfe, whose leadership in the field meant so much to so many, and whom we will miss greatly at John Jay.

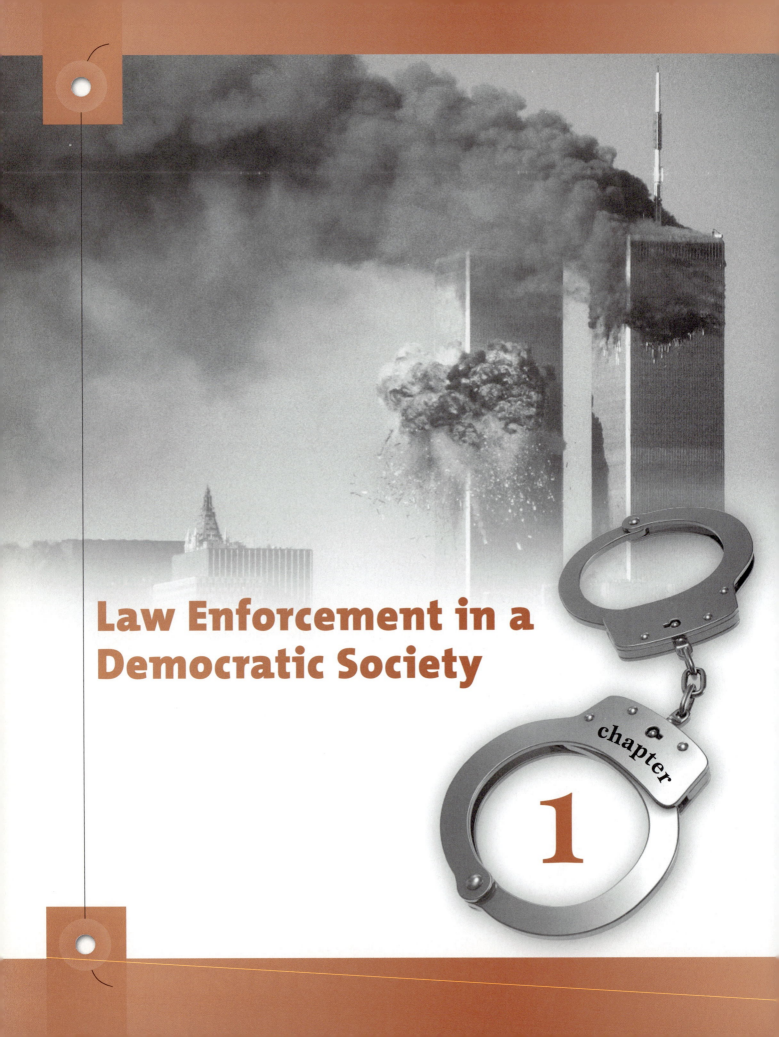

Law Enforcement in a Democratic Society

chapter

1

Chapter Objectives

- Describe the concept of linkage blindness and its importance in the criminal justice system.

- Understand the police role in maintaining social control.

- Explain why discretion is a necessary aspect of policing.

- Explain what is meant by the rule of law.

- Understand the role of law enforcement in the criminal justice system.

- Contrast the crime control and due process models.

- List the different levels of law enforcement.

- Explain how the events of September 11 changed the structure of law enforcement jurisdictions.

Introduction

Following the cataclysmic events of September 11, many people asked themselves, "How did this happen?" Despite incidents such as the 1995 bombing of the Murrah Federal Building in Oklahoma City, most Americans have viewed terrorism as a problem somewhere over there, such as in Israel, Northern Ireland, or Rwanda. People in the United States have always taken pride in the immense individual rights and freedoms they possess and that often are viewed as the fundamental premises upon which this country was built. In fact, Americans have generally disapproved of extensive domestic efforts that intrude on the ease of their day-to-day activities, preferring, for example, express check-ins at the airport over complete baggage checks.

Prior to the attacks on the World Trade Center and Pentagon, neither the average American citizen nor the government was particularly concerned with the prospect of international terrorism on United States soil. This was the case even though a number of reports, such as the Hart–Rudman Commission on National Security in the Twenty-First Century, had concluded that the U.S. government had no organizational capacity to either prevent or respond to terrorist threats (Flynn 2001). Moreover, a 1999 government report intricately profiled the leading terrorists and terrorist groups around the world, specifying the kinds of risks that existed and how future acts might occur, demonstrating that the United States intelligence community was not completely blind to the potential threat of attack (Hudson 1999). However, in the wake of the destruction of September 11, all Americans are now faced with a sense of insecurity and vulnerability that will have an impact on the delicate balance the country has always known between order and individual freedoms. This affects all aspects of public and private life, including transforming the nature and function of how we view and conduct law enforcement, the subject of this book. Federal legislation, such as the **USA PATRIOT Act of 2001**[1] and the **USA PATRIOT Improvement and Reauthorization Act of 2005**, has formally acknowledged this shift by significantly widening the investigative authority of law enforcement agencies across the country. The USA PATRIOT Act is discussed in detail in Chapter 7. An abridged version of the Act is offered in Appendix B.

Despite federal, state, and local inquiries, law enforcement and criminal justice experts argue that blame for the failure to anticipate the September 11 attacks cannot be attributed to any single agency. Given the complexity of both the intelligence and law enforcement communities and their many overlapping jurisdictions, it was inevitable that key information would slip through the cracks between agencies. The inability to analyze and link critical information across (or even within an agency) is referred to as **linkage blindness** and will be a major theme throughout this book. In part, the Homeland Security Act of 2002, the USA PATRIOT Act of 2001, and its reauthorization in 2005 were executive and legislative responses to the problem of linkage blindness by organizing diffuse and autonomous law enforcement agencies and strengthening the government's abilities to obtain information. Stephen Flynn (2001) provides a useful illustration of this critical law enforcement problem, referring to the arrival of a hypothetical ship with questionable cargo and a crew on an intelligence watch list for potential terrorist ties:

> The Coast Guard would be likely to know about the scheduled arrival of a tanker carrying hazardous cargo. The Customs Service might have some advance cargo manifest information. The INS might or might not know much about the crew, depending on the kinds of visas the sailors are holding and the timeliness with which the shipping crew faxed the crew list. None of the front-line inspectors in these agencies, meanwhile, are likely to have access to national security intelligence from the Federal Bureau of Investigation or the Central Intelligence Agency.[2] (p. 190)

Although Flynn was referring to linkage blindness prior to the governmental reorganization after September 11, this problem continues to exist. Because of the elusive nature of terrorism and the apparent ease with which terrorists can slip across U.S. borders, federal to local agencies are requesting increased law enforcement investigative authority. The September 11 attacks offered evidence that even with a threat of transnational origins, the front-line responders are local law enforcement and fire departments. Thus, terrorism is not simply within the domain of the federal government and military. What has been exposed is the need to build adequate mechanisms of information sharing across levels of government in an area that is traditionally rife with issues of territoriality and rivalry. This need led to the formation of the Department of Homeland Security, the largest government reorganization in over fifty years.

The Themes of the Book

Many myths and stereotypes surround policing, including the ever-prevalent image of a law enforcement officer as crime fighter engaging in a "war on crime" (Bittner 1980). However, the average officer rarely makes a felony arrest, and most do not fire their firearms during their careers. However, by definition, the term **law enforcement** suggests that the enforcement of existing legislation or rules of society is central to the role of the police. This rather simplistic view of law enforcement ignores the tremendous complexities in agencies, missions, and functions across levels of government (federal, state, and local) or jurisdiction in the United States. More important, such a definition fails to take into account the evolving nature of policing as a strategy (Kelling and Moore 1989). This book explores the changing dynamics and nature of policing within its larger contexts. Although the terms are utilized interchangeably on occasion, the emphasis on *law enforcement* as opposed to *policing* reflects the larger scope and focus of the book.

A central theme of this text is the linkages across law enforcement jurisdictions and the struggle to develop a coordinated approach to information sharing and strategy development in the face of any crime, including terrorism. Additionally, the text explains the connections between law enforcement and the rest of the criminal justice system. Moreover, the importance of information sharing and collaboration across the criminal justice system agencies (and thus, the relevance of linkage blindness in this context as well) also is woven throughout relevant chapters of the book. New technologies to combat linkage blindness are highlighted in Chapter 13.

Another central theme of this text is the changing paradigm of policing throughout its history, highlighting the movement from reactive to proactive management models. A major philosophical and practical shift in the field of law enforcement came when Herman Goldstein (1979) pioneered the principles of problem-oriented policing. Law enforcement agencies continue to use problem-solving approaches in community-oriented policing to address quality-of-life concerns. This central element of problem solving and proactive policing is relating underlying causes to strategy, which is yet another theme revisited throughout the text.

This book is divided into four sections. The first section lays out the framework of the law enforcement field for the reader, establishing common definitions and tracing

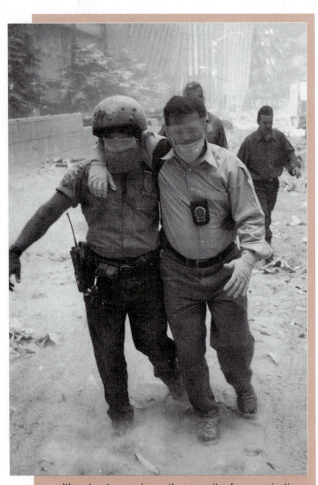

Although not a new issue, the necessity of communication across all levels of law enforcement (federal, state, and local) became all too apparent following the tragic events of September 11. Coordination and collaboration with respect to homeland security need to occur both before and immediately after a terrorist attack. Recognition of this fact has led to the formation of the Department of Homeland Security.

the origins and developments of the field up to the end of the professionaliza-tion movement. The second section of the book presents the more traditional functions and operations of law enforcement (i.e., structure and operations) in a way that prepares the reader for changing dynamics to encompass evolving policing models and demands. The legal underpinnings of police work briefly introduced in the first section will be expanded on, with particular attention to the challenges to precedents evident in the new threat of terrorism and related legislation, such as the USA PATRIOT Act of 2001. The third section examines current challenges in policing, such as the role of discretion and the demands of policing minority communities. Special attention is paid here to the changing demographics of the country, as well as the impacts of a post–September 11 world. The reader is thus exposed to the major issues, challenges, and functions of policing in a developmental manner. The final section challenges readers to analyze the future directions and trends in law enforcement.

Throughout the text, Linkages and Law Enforcement features are pre-sented that challenge readers to relate concepts and issues presented in a cur-rent chapter to earlier material or current events, thereby encouraging a developmental learning approach. A major theme tracked in this format is the challenges of balancing the concerns of public safety with those of individual freedoms or due process.

The Police Function: Social Control and the Use of Force

Most of us are relatively familiar with the general operations of the three major components of the criminal justice process—police, courts, and corrections—as well as the important roles of federal and state governments in creating and modifying laws through the legislative process. What we are often unable to an-swer, however, is what it is about these institutions that makes them work as agents of social control. What is it about them that works (or does not work) in achieving order in society?

Informal social control refers to the influences of parents, families, peers, and the community in training individuals about the norms, rules, and customs of a locality in an attempt to compel conformity (this process also is called **so-cialization**). Informal social control occurs when the influential party reacts to **deviance**, or violations of social rules. Deviance can refer to a range of actions, from something minor, such as getting a tattoo, all the way up to acts of murder and rape (see Figure 1.1). Once an act of deviance occurs in which a law is

FIGURE 1.1

Spectrum of Deviance

| Asserting individuality | Misbehaving (home) | Formal sanction (rule) | Law violation (fine) | Serious criminal act |

broken, as in the case of murder, it is the responsibility of **formal social control** agents, such as law enforcement officers, to enforce the law.

Many criminal justice practitioners and scholars have argued that the use of force is the principal way in which order is achieved in society: "Institutions of law and government maintain order and control deviant behavior primarily through force, through the forcible apprehension and incarceration of others" (Eisenhower 1970, p. 6). Law enforcement usually is at the forefront when it comes to the application of force and apprehension.

According to Manning (1977), *policing* literally means "controlling, monitoring, tracking, and altering, if required, public conduct" (p. 27). Given the many competing expectations of the police, Klockars (1985) has argued that the meaning of *police* can be found in what they are supposed to do rather than on what exactly is done in a given situation. An officer writing traffic citations is still a police officer, as is another speaking at a community meeting. To Klockars (1985), the core of policing is identified by its relation to the potential use of force.

However, in the examples just given (i.e., traffic citation, community meeting), force is not an element of the policing function. How then can **coercive force** be the defining feature of policing? Egon Bittner's (1970) classic work argues that it is the fact that the police are authorized to use force in a number of social situations in response to a variety of social problems that forms the basis of our interactions with police.

Returning to our examples, although a citizen may be equally capable of writing traffic citations, only a police officer will be able to force an individual

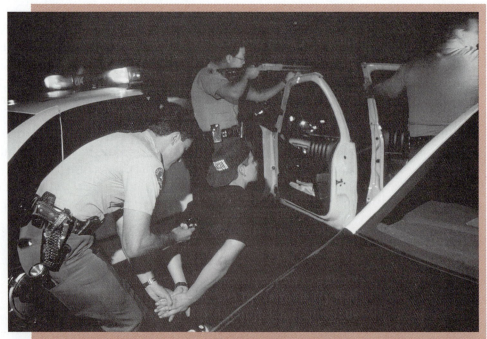

The legal authority to use force is considered the defining characteristic of law enforcement even though in reality it is used only rarely. Some studies have found force to be used in only 4.10 of every 10,000 incidents.

to comply, if necessary (e.g., if the vehicle's operator had failed to pull over, and so on). Similarly, community residents often involve the police in community meetings discussing even minor quality-of-life issues (e.g., noise disturbances, littering), because they will ultimately be able to resort to force if all other options of problem resolution are not successful.

Although the importance of force in defining policing is clear, it alone cannot achieve the public order to which the police often are held accountable. Because the police cannot possibly be omnipresent, enforcing all deviations from the law, there must also be both a commitment and willingness on the part of the majority of citizens to respect the laws and institutions of society. Without this **culture of lawfulness**, law enforcement would be inundated and unable to carry out its functions effectively (Godson 2000). To achieve this, the average citizen must recognize the legitimacy of the law and its enforcement as an effective means of controlling the behavior of all members of society, from the richest government official to the poorest laborer. Much of this respect will come from the degree to which the government operates within the rule of law and decisions are not arbitrarily made at the hands of its officials or enforcers, a topic we turn to now.

Policing Within the Rule of Law: The Challenges of Discretion

Agents at every level of the criminal justice system have a significant level of individual **discretion**, particularly law enforcement officers. Agents are said to have discretion when they have the freedom to make decisions—legal or otherwise—based on their own judgment and are not bound by formal, inflexible rules. It was in the 1950s, when the American Bar Foundation (ABF) conducted the first field observations of police work, that the central role of discretion in law enforcement was first "discovered" (Walker 1992). Many studies have since validated the significance of discretion in the criminal justice system, but at no point has it ever been officially "recognized" with legislation acknowledging its functional role in police decision making.

Matters such as arrest and charge are, for example, subject to varying degrees of police discretion, as are issues relating to the collection and presentation of evidence. Officers do not receive "official" training on how to use discretion, but legal factors provide a guide in some instances. For the most part, discretion exists to ensure that agents within the criminal justice system are free to respond to the particular circumstances and challenges presented by each new case and each new crime. Because each offense is different, flexibility is needed to ensure that justice prevails. Moreover, it is not possible for officers to enforce every violation they encounter, making discretion a practical and necessary reality in law enforcement.

In many instances, however, the decisions of individual police officers are not transparent or open to scrutiny. The police are not monitored 24 hours a day or required to justify themselves every time they stop someone on the street or in their car. As a consequence, there is a danger that agents within the criminal justice system may make decisions that are not in full accordance with the law or that infringe upon the rights of suspects, offenders, or prisoners.

How can we be sure then that two individuals who committed similar crimes would not be treated differently by separate officers or because of **extra-legal factors** (factors outside of the legal parameters of an offense), such as differences in skin color or socioeconomic status? It is because of the perception of inequality in law enforcement that discretion can play a divisive role in the community. Discretion can be the result of numerous community, organizational, and individual influences outside of the formal legal codes, a subject we will return to in Chapter 9.

Although there is no simple way to ensure that discretion is exercised fairly in each and every case, principal decisions made by individuals within the criminal justice system are meant to be governed by a set of ideals known as the **rule of law**. Developed over many years through case law, statutes, and scholarly writings, the rule of law can be stated simply as follows (National Strategy Information Center 1999):

- All people in society have the opportunity to participate in establishing the law;

- The rules apply equally to everyone; and

- The rules protect individuals as well as society.

The rule of law was developed in an effort to constrain kings and rulers who regarded themselves as above the law. At its heart is a commitment to the fundamental idea that equality before the law and justice are inseparable. Regardless of their position or responsibilities, all agents within the criminal justice system are bound by the rule of law, and they are required to exercise their discretion according to the limits it prescribes. Of course, in practice not every decision meets the high standards required by the rule of law. Much of its significance, however, derives from its status as an *ideal*; it is a standard which guides individuals and agencies within the system, and which—in theory at least—binds them together through a shared commitment to justice and the law.

 # The Delicate Balance: Crime Control versus Due Process

Although the "delicate balance" between public safety and individual freedoms has always been a struggle for law enforcement, these issues are particularly salient in the post–September 11 climate. During a lecture immediately following the September 11 attacks, then U.S. Supreme Court Justice Sandra Day O'Connor remarked that "we're likely to experience more restrictions on our personal freedom than has ever been the case in this country" (Greenhouse 2001, B5). Despite protestations otherwise by former Attorney General John Ashcroft that "we'll not be driven to abandon our freedoms by those who would seek to destroy them," some fear the potential "slippery slope" of giving expansive powers to law enforcement (Hentoff 2001).

One of the most influential frameworks for explaining the differing views and values of justice has been the crime control/due process model first expounded upon by the sociologist Herbert Packer in the 1960s. According to

Packer (1968), agents within the criminal justice system can be broadly divided into two camps depending on the strength of their support for either strong law enforcement or protection of civil liberties. For those who see the criminal justice system in terms of **crime control**, the overriding aim is to ensure that suspects are processed as quickly and efficiently as possible. Typically, advocates of this approach emphasize the importance of attempting to distinguish between the innocent and the guilty at the precharge stage. Though the adversarial system is based on the assumption that an individual is innocent until proven guilty, advocates of the crime control model assume that once a suspect has been formally charged, the suspect can be processed on the basis of an informal "presumption of guilt." Guilty pleas are preferred over lengthy hearings and trials, and informal methods of disposal are preferred over legalistic procedures. Perhaps unsurprisingly, the police and other law enforcement agencies are the most vocal supporters of a crime control approach to criminal justice. Extensive police powers, limited rights for suspects, and greater emphasis on pretrial processes are all seen as vital to the effective functioning of the system. The danger lies in the extent to which this favoring of crime control undermines the rule of law, and thus potentially the legitimacy of law enforcement and the criminal justice system in society (Skolnick 1994).

In contrast, supporters of a **due process** approach argue that the criminal justice system must strive to protect the rights of the innocent and ensure that only the guilty are punished. Although recognizing that the primary aim of the system is to reduce and prevent crime, adherents of the due process model maintain that safeguards are necessary to protect individual rights and to ensure that the number of wrongful convictions is kept to a minimum. "Better that ten guilty men go free than one innocent man be punished" is an idea that is central to the due process approach. Advocates of this model favor considerable restrictions being placed on the police, are suspicious of informal processes, and view the criminal trial as the most reliable method of determining guilt. With the due process model, the civil rights and liberties of citizens outweigh the information needs of law enforcement. Key features of both models are summarized in Table 1.1.

Historically, considerable tension has existed between these two different approaches to crime and the criminal justice process. During the 1960s, the civil

TABLE 1.1

Key Features of the Crime Control and Due Process Models

Crime Control Model	Due Process Model
• Suppression of crime is the overriding aim of the criminal justice system.	• Justice and fairness are the overriding aims of the criminal justice system
• Cases need to be disposed of quickly and efficiently, even if this means ignoring suspects' rights.	• Cases need to be dealt with according to formal procedures that protect suspects' rights.
• Emphasis is on pretrial processes and encourages guilty pleas.	• Emphasis is on the trial process and the determination of legal guilt.
• Authority of the criminal justice system derives from the legislature.	• Authority of the criminal justice system derives from the judiciary.

rights movement helped to increase public awareness of individual rights and placed considerable pressure on the criminal justice system to expand basic due process protections. Responding to the mood of the times, the Supreme Court under Justice Warren—in cases such as *Escobedo v. Illinois* (1964),[3] *Miranda v. Arizona* (1966),[4] and *Terry v. Ohio* (1968)[5]—moved to specify the powers of the police, emphasizing the need for the criminal justice system to recognize and protect the rights of suspects. Due process concerns also were addressed in the landmark case of *Gideon v. Wainwright* (1963),[6] which extended the right to counsel to indigent individuals who would otherwise have been unable to exercise their Sixth Amendment rights.

As crime rates began to rise through the 1970s and 1980s, however, there was a gradual but significant shift toward an emphasis on crime control. Although the largest increase in crime was for the possession and sale of drugs, the rate of serious violent crime—including murder, rape, and robbery—also increased dramatically during this period. In the eyes of many policy makers and the general public, the criminal justice system was clearly failing. Proponents of the crime control model argued that the rise in crime was the direct result of an overemphasis on suspects' rights and called for increased police powers and an easing of due process restrictions on law enforcement agencies.

Throughout the 1990s, the crime control model continued to dominate policy making in the United States. Mandatory sentencing for repeat offenders, zero-tolerance policing, and the gradual lowering of the age of criminal responsibility for juveniles all grew from a desire to make the criminal justice system more efficient and effective. At the same time, however, several high-profile incidents of police brutality,[7] police corruption,[8] and racial profiling[9] helped to remind the public of the need for due process protections and the respect for civil liberties.

In the first decade of the twenty-first century, crime control values still prevail, yet there is a continuing tension between the two models first identified by Packer in the 1960s. In light of the past fifty years of criminal justice history, as well as the U.S. government's war on terrorism, there can be little doubt that the struggle between advocates of crime control and due process will continue to shape the development of criminal justice policy throughout the coming century.

The Levels of Law Enforcement

The current system of law enforcement in the United States is as complex as it is varied, in many ways reflecting the tensions between the crime control and due process models, as well as an overriding fear of too much power being placed in the hands of a centralized, federal law enforcement entity. Representing the largest segment of the criminal justice system, with over 1 million employees in 1996 (Reaves and Goldberg 1998), contemporary law enforcement agencies operate on a variety of levels within local, state, and federal **jurisdictions**, or areas of responsibility. Although the boundaries across levels would appear to be straightforward, since each enforces the laws of its respective level, in practice the boundaries often are more of a gray tint than a black-and-white tone. There is no direct order of authority with respect to these jurisdictions. For example, in most cases federal law enforcement cannot exert authority over local matters unless requested to do so by local authorities. Each level of law enforcement has its own jurisdiction. These difficulties are, of course, further fueled by the territorial nature of many law enforcement agencies.

Municipal Agencies

The United States had 12,656 municipal police jurisdictions in 2003 (Bureau of Justice Statistics 2006a), varying in size from large city departments [e.g., New York Police City Police Department with 40,435 officers in 2000 (Bureau of Justice Statistics 2004)] to local departments with a few officers (the majority). In 2000, there were 501 municipal police departments with 100 or more full-time sworn personnel, but of these, only 60 (11 percent) had 1,000 or more full-time sworn personnel that included 500 or more officers responding to calls for service (Bureau of Justice Statistics 2004). Most departments have a small number of officers who have jurisdiction over largely rural or suburban landscapes.

Municipal police departments unquestionably represent the greatest number of law enforcement officers in the United States and will thus be the primary focus of this text. In 2000, large municipal departments (those with at least 100 officers) employed 312,201 full-time employees, compared with 31,945 in county departments, 154,384 in sheriff's departments, and 87,028 in state law enforcement agencies (Bureau of Justice Statistics 2004).

Large local law enforcement agencies often are responsible for investigating serious violent and property crimes in their jurisdictions, compared to half of state agencies (Bureau of Justice Statistics 2000). Local agencies also are more likely to handle fingerprint processing (81 percent); however, state agencies often provide the needed support for crime lab services and ballistic testing (Bureau of Justice Statistics 2000).

The city government is usually responsible for appointing police chiefs, who are responsible for running departments with general law enforcement authority within its boundaries. Most police chiefs are appointed at the discretion of the mayor or city manager and lack contracts protecting them from unjustified termination. As a result, the average tenure of most police chiefs is only three to six years (Swanson et al. 2001).

Although for the most part similar in nature to municipal police departments, **township police departments** can vary greatly with regard to law enforcement powers and authority. Well-developed townships often operate with responsibilities close to those of municipal police departments. The United States has approximately 1,600 township police departments (Bureau of Justice Statistics 2004).

County Agencies

Although the primary agency at the county level is the sheriff's office, with 3,061 sheriff's departments across the country (Bureau of Justice Statistics 2006b), in some jurisdictions this office is dissolved into a county police force that functions much the same as municipal police. County police departments usually surface in areas where the workload is too large for the sheriff's department. The local context greatly influences the nature and scope of responsibilities for the sheriff's department. In some jurisdictions, the sheriff's office is entirely law enforcement focused, with no other responsibilities, whereas in others the principal responsibilities involve carrying out court orders and summons or operating the county jail. The majority of sheriff's departments involve some combination of all three responsibilities (Brown 1979). In large cities with populations of over one million, the sheriff's office will only serve correctional functions; those serving very small populations usually are the chief law enforcement agents of that jurisdiction (Senna and Siegal 2001).

In all but two states, sheriffs are elected for a two- to four-year term. Because they are elected, sheriffs often have a degree of freedom from local city officials, unlike the relationship between the police chief and mayor or city manager in many large cities. However, because it is an elected term, additional forms of accountability and scrutiny can transform the dynamics of the role.

In some jurisdictions, there are county-level courts that maintain limited jurisdiction as described by statute in civil matters, such as the performance of marriages and hearings for minor criminal offenses. Referred to as **Justice's courts**, they are under the responsibility of **justices of the peace**, or magistrates of lesser rank than in the higher courts. It should be noted, however, that the trend has been to dissolve the Justice's courts and transfer their power to other municipal courts of limited jurisdiction (Nolan and Nolan-Haley 1990).

State Agencies

Most states have police agencies in addition to agencies within specific municipalities, townships, or counties. The first state to establish a police agency was Texas in 1835, with the creation of the Texas Rangers. Massachusetts implemented a state police agency shortly thereafter in 1865, though this is often credited as the first modern state law enforcement agency. The state agency in Pennsylvania is credited with being a model agency for other states, viewed as the archetype of modern policing when it was created in 1905.

The power of most state agencies includes the ability to arrest an individual for an offense committed in the presence of the officer, as well as the ability to execute a search warrant. In addition to the state police, some states have established a Highway Patrol with jurisdiction over traffic laws on interstate roads. These patrols have the authority to enforce traffic laws as well as investigate traffic accidents on highways and freeways. Hawaii is the only state without a state law enforcement agency.

Federal Agencies

The first federal agency to be established by the U.S. government was the U.S. Marshall Service, which was founded in 1789. Since that time, the U.S. government has created eight additional government departments with twenty-one agencies dealing with issues of law enforcement. Additionally, several of these eight departments contain dozens of smaller offices and bureaus. It is important to note that federal agencies only have the power to enforce federal laws and mandates. The Attorney General, for example, cannot simply call a governor to dictate a certain policy on the part of the state police unless a constitutional violation of some kind has occurred. Otherwise, the Tenth Amendment of the Constitution reserves powers over local matters to the various local law enforcement agencies. Prior to September 11, two federal departments were most involved in law enforcement: the Department of Justice (DOJ) and the Department of the Treasury. The Homeland Security Act of 2002 reorganized many federal law enforcement agencies under the new Department of Homeland Security (DHS). Presently, the DHS and the DOJ are the two most important federal departments involved with law enforcement. However, other federal departments (e.g., the Food and Drug Administration) have certain law enforcement functions within their mandates.

Department of Justice   The Department of Justice (DOJ) was established in June 1870 and is headed by the Attorney General (AG) of the United States. As of the writing of this text, Alberto Gonzalez is the Attorney General. The AG is appointed by the president and represents the United States in legal matters. The AG is also responsible for supervising and directing the administration and operation of the offices, boards, divisions, and bureaus that make up the DOJ, as well as assisting the president, the president's cabinet, and the heads of the executive departments and agencies of the federal government in legal matters.

The DOJ is the federal agency responsible for conducting and coordinating investigations, both those by the DOJ as well as those being conducted by other departments. The DOJ has thirty-eight components, and those most relevant to law enforcement are described in the following sections. The primary responsibilities of the agency are enforcing U.S. law; protecting citizens against criminals; ensuring healthy competition among business; safeguarding consumers; enforcing drug, immigration, and naturalization laws; and protecting citizens through effective law enforcement (U.S. Department of Justice 2001).

U.S. Marshal Service. The passage of the Judiciary Act in Congress in 1789 established the first formal law enforcement agency under the federal government, the office of the United States Marshal. The current structure of the **U.S. Marshal Service (USMS)** was established in 1969. The USMS has a variety of duties, including the execution of warrants for the federal courts and the handling of federal suspects and prisoners (i.e., transporting them, arresting fugitives).

Federal Bureau of Investigation. The **Federal Bureau of Investigation (FBI)** is the main investigative agency in the federal government. It currently has over 10,000 agents. The agency was created in 1908, and by 1909 was named the Bureau of Investigation, with its present name designated by Congress in 1935. The principal responsibility of the FBI is to investigate violations of federal criminal law and to assist local agencies in investigations. The FBI has jurisdiction over particular offenses, such as kidnapping, auto theft, organized crime, civil rights violations, and internal security (espionage). It also has the authority to locate and apprehend fugitives who have violated specified federal laws.

The U.S. Attorney General designated the FBI as primary agency in charge of investigating acts of domestic and international terrorism. Coordination of information exchange has become a priority given this role. **Joint Terrorism Task Forces (JTTFs)** were established in FBI field offices prior to 2001. By 2004, the number of JTTFs had increased from 36 to 84. These task forces, which are located within FBI field offices, are composed of representatives of local and state law enforcement, FBI agents, and teams from other federal agencies. A report by the RAND Corporation found that 95 percent of state law enforcement agencies had coordinated with a JTTF. However, only one-third of local law enforcement agencies had coordinated with the FBI (Riley et al. 2004).

In addition to its investigative responsibilities, the FBI also has responsibility for publishing the Uniform Crime Reports (UCRs) (U.S. annual crime statistics, discussed in Chapter 3) and the *Law Enforcement Bulletin*. It is also responsible for conducting personnel investigations (background checks) for those applying for employment within the DOJ and other government agencies, as requested.

The FBI has developed training programs for law enforcement personnel at the local, state, federal, and international levels in order to assist others in the development of new approaches and law enforcement techniques. Several departments within the FBI, such as the FBI Crime Lab, can aid in criminal investigations or provide technical assistance in mass disasters.

Drug Enforcement Administration. In an attempt to control the supply of dangerous drugs, the Harrison Narcotics Act was passed in 1917. At the time, it was established as a branch of tax law, and as such fell under the responsibility of the Department of the Treasury. In 1930, the Treasury Department created the Bureau of Narcotics, which was reorganized in 1968 to become the Bureau of Narcotics and Dangerous Drugs under the DOJ.

The **Drug Enforcement Administration (DEA)** as we know it today was created in 1973 with the merging of the Bureau of Narcotics and Dangerous Drugs, the Office for Drug Abuse Law Enforcement, the Office of National Narcotics Intelligence, some U.S. Customs officials, and the Narcotics Advance Research Management Team. The DEA, which is responsible for investigating both domestic and international drug violators and traffickers, uses both control and prevention techniques to stop the flow of drugs from their manufacture through sales.

The primary responsibility of the DEA is to investigate and prepare evidence for the prosecution of major violators of controlled substances laws both domestically and internationally. It is also involved in the collection and analysis of information regarding drug use and trafficking and is responsible for developing strategic plans aimed at eliminating such activities. It has the authority to use nonenforcement methods of drug elimination, such as crop eradication, and it also has the authority to seize assets that are in any way related to drug trafficking.

U.S. Bureau of Alcohol, Tobacco, and Firearms. The **U.S. Bureau of Alcohol, Tobacco, and Firearms (ATF)** is primarily concerned with the licensing, investigation, and control over its three components as well as explosives. However, it was originally established as a tax-collecting agency, which is why it is located in the Treasury Department rather than the DOJ. Employees of the ATF include many forensic experts as well as law enforcement experts, including chemists, document analysts, latent print specialists, and firearms and toolmark examiners who are trained in forensic skills relating to arson, explosives, and criminal-evidence examination. The ATF works closely with the FBI in federal investigations requiring both areas of expertise. A well-known case that came to the attention of the public was the involvement of the two agencies with David Koresh's Branch Davidian cult in Waco, Texas. It was the ATF that was originally called to the Koresh compound, beginning the standoff that led to the death of 71 individuals.

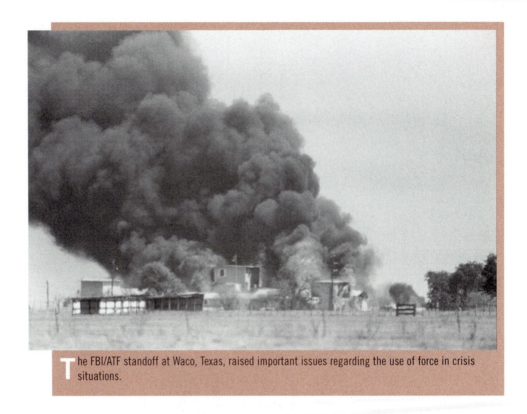

The FBI/ATF standoff at Waco, Texas, raised important issues regarding the use of force in crisis situations.

Department of Homeland Security   On July 26, 2002, the U.S. Congress approved the creation of the **Department of Homeland Security (DHS)** in the largest government reorganization of federal agencies in fifty years (Firestone 2002). The aim of this reorganization was to better coordinate the intelligence and law enforcement resources of the U.S. government in the war on terror by attempting to eliminate the problems of linkage blindness. DHS assumed many of the law enforcement functions previously performed by the Department of the Treasury and other federal agencies. DHS's twenty-two domestic agencies employ about 180,000 people, making it one of the largest federal departments. DHS includes over 87,000 different governmental jurisdictions at the federal, state, and local levels, with the overall goal of developing a connected system of information exchange and law enforcement with an emphasis on combating terrorism (DHS 2007a). After the formation of DHS, President Bush selected former Pennsylvania Governor Tom Ridge as the first Director of Homeland Security, though he has since been replaced.

In addition to the twenty-two agencies, DHS is composed of five *directorates* and other agency components that fulfill a myriad of responsibilities. Each directorate is a large oversight body in charge of fundamental and broad elements of the department's old and newly formed federal agencies. The five directorates are (1) Preparedness, (2) Science and Technology, (3) Management, (4) Office of Policy, and (5) the Federal Emergency Management Agency (DHS 2007b). Figure 1.2 shows the current structure of the DHS.

Immigration and Customs Enforcement.   The Department of Homeland Security reorganization effort transferred the U.S. Customs Service functions

FIGURE 1.2

Department of Homeland Security Organizational Chart

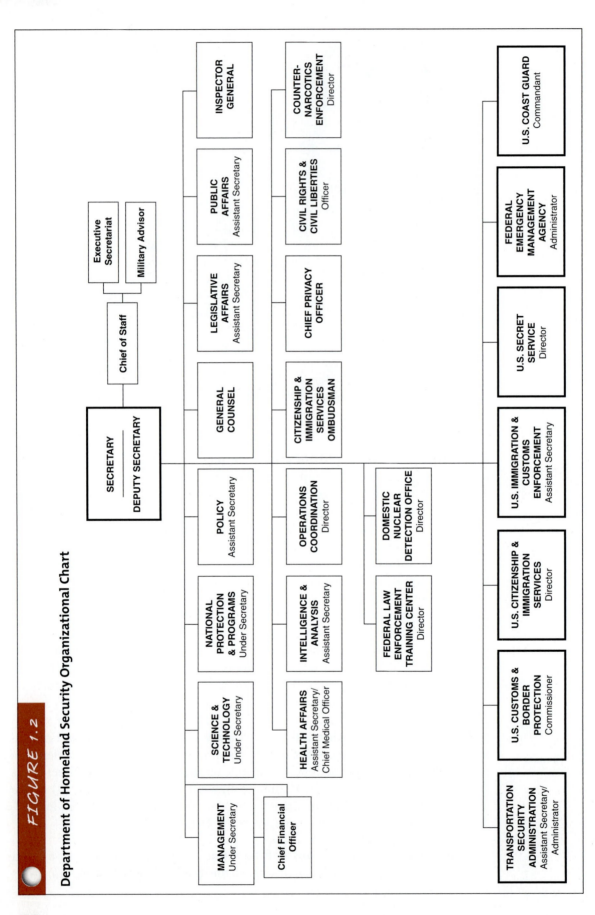

Source: Department of Homeland Security, 2007.

from the Department of the Treasury and the former Immigration and Naturalization Service's enforcement functions from the Department of Justice to the newly created **Immigration and Customs Enforcement (ICE)** agency. This agency is the largest investigative branch of the DHS. ICE is responsible for enforcing immigration and customs laws and protecting the United States from terrorist activity. ICE also targets gang organizations by disrupting their movement across U.S. borders. The agency seeks out illegal workers in critical areas such as power plants or airports to prevent potential terrorist activity. ICE detects and investigates fraudulent immigration documents and investigates those who produce them. ICE also investigates the illegal export of U.S. munitions and technology and cross-border human trafficking. The agency is also responsible for the management of deportation. ICE also attempts to find and close illicit channels for the movement of money by organized crime (ICE 2007).

The ICE's **Law Enforcement Support Center (LESC)** assists in the provision of information and assistance to federal, state, and local law enforcement. The primary beneficiaries of the LESC are state and local law enforcement officers seeking information about foreign nationals they encounter in their jurisdictions.

U.S. Customs and Border Protection. U.S. Customs and Border Protection (CBP) is a combination and unification of the former U.S. Customs Bureau,[10] functions of the U.S. Immigration and Naturalization services,[11] the Animal and Plant Health Inspection Service, and the U.S. Border Patrol. The agency guards over 7,000 miles of land border that the U.S. shares with Canada and Mexico as well as 2,000 miles of coastal waters around California and Florida (CBP 2007b). In 2005, the agency arrested over 1.1 million illegal aliens and seized around 1.7 billion dollars worth of drugs (CBP 2007a). The CPB is also responsible for the inspection and collection of tariffs for over 1.4 trillion dollars worth of imported goods, including cargo moved by sea container, representing most of the material goods moved in and out of the United States. The CPB shares responsibility for the security of U.S. ports with the **U.S. Coast Guard** (also under DHS) and the local or state port authority who manages or maintains the seaport, airport, or bus terminal (CBP 2007c). The CBP screens visitors by air using law enforcement databases that "verify identity, determine admissibility and prevent terrorists from entering the country" (CBP 2007b).

Transportation Security Administration. The **Transportation Security Administration (TSA)** was transferred to DHS from the Department of Transportation, where it was placed after its creation in September of 2001. The TSA is responsible for the security of all modes of U.S. transportation. It is responsible for security officers for all commercial airports and for the screening of luggage for explosives. The primary law enforcement entity within the TSA is the **Federal Air Marshal (FAM) Service**. Several thousand Air Marshals ensure the safety of U.S. domestic and international flights. Air Marshals fly an average of 5 hours a day and 900 hours per year (TSA 2007).

U.S. Secret Service. The **U.S. Secret Service** was transferred to the DHS from the Department of the Treasury on March 1, 2003. Although the Secret Service was originally established to suppress counterfeit currency, by 1901 its duties were modified to include protecting the president, the vice president, and the families of each. Congress believed that this was necessary in light of the assassination of President William McKinley. By 1902, the Secret Service assumed full-time responsibility for protection of the president. Presidents who were elected into office prior to January 1, 1997, receive lifetime protection from the Secret Service; however, those elected after this time will receive Secret Service protection for 10 years. The Secret Service is also responsible for the investigation of all access device fraud, financial-institution fraud, identity theft, computer fraud, and computer-based crimes involving the U.S. financial, banking, and telecommunications infrastructure (Secret Service, 2001).

Federal Law Enforcement Training Center. Another agency of the DHS is the **Federal Law Enforcement Training Center (FLETC)**. The FLETC is an interagency law enforcement training organization, serving over 80 different federal agencies. It provides training to state, local, and international law enforcement agencies. Under the direction of DHS, the FLETC trains federal officers from the Department of Justice and the DHS. It trains personnel from the following agencies: ATF, FBI, U.S. Marshals, U.S. Border Patrol, U.S. Coast Guard, U.S. Immigration and Customs Enforcement, and the U.S. Secret Service.

Additional Programs Under DHS. The **Joint Regional Information Exchange System (JRIES)** enables the exchange of law enforcement information over the Internet. Through this system, the Department of Defense has access to information pertinent to terrorist activity on U.S. citizens, resident foreigners, and others that is collected by local and state police agencies. This program was created by the **Defense Intelligence Agency (DIA)** in 2002 and then moved to the DHS in 2004. Many members of the law enforcement community sit on the executive board, including representatives from DHS and from police departments in New York City, New York state, Washington D.C., Pennsylvania, and Louisiana. Some police officials have characterized the JRIES as more effective than the local JTTFs. Some concerns have been raised by the collection of information on political, nonterrorist, groups (Rood 2004).

The **Office of State and Local Government Coordination (SLGC)** facilitates and coordinates DHS programs with state, local, and tribal governments. The program enables DHS to exchange information with state, local, and tribal homeland security personnel. The DHS identifies homeland security practices and processes at the federal, state, local, or regional levels and uses this information to ensure that opportunities for improvement of information sharing (DHS 2007).

The DHS's **Commercial Equipment Direct Assistance Program (CEDAP)** has provided $32 million in material to "rural and smaller communities" for hardware such as weaponry and heavily armored transport vehicles (DHS 2006).

Department of the Treasury   The Treasury Department has traditionally had several important law enforcement functions, most of which have now been transferred to the DHS or DOJ. Now, the primary law enforcement agency of importance within the Department of the Treasury is the Internal Revenue Service (IRS).

Internal Revenue Service. The **Internal Revenue Service (IRS)** is the largest agency within the Treasury Department. Its roots date back to 1862, when President Abraham Lincoln and Congress decided to enact an income tax to pay for expenses related to the Civil War. Though the income tax was ruled unconstitutional ten years later, Congress once again enacted an income tax in 1913 after the states ratified the Sixteenth Amendment. The IRS was established in 1862 and is designed to regulate compliance with tax laws and investigate tax evasion and fraud.

The IRS has many divisions, including Appeals, Chief Counsel, Communications and Liaison, and Criminal Investigation. Though most people associate criminal investigations with the FBI, the IRS's Criminal Investigation division is responsible for, among other things, enforcing tax laws and identifying money laundering individuals and organizations. The IRS is the primary agency responsible for enforcing the Racketeer Influenced and Corrupt Organizations (RICO) statutes. In fact, was the IRS was responsible for investigating and convicting organized crime figure Al Capone.

U.S. Postal Service   In the past, the average person reading this text might have questioned why the **U.S. Postal Service (USPS)** would be included in a listing of federal law enforcement agencies. However, following the series of anthrax attacks in the United States in the fall of 2001, most would now appreciate the significance of law enforcement activities related to USPS functions. The approximately 2,200 postal inspectors stationed throughout the United States are responsible for the enforcement of over 200 federal laws affecting the U.S. mail and postal system (USPS 2002).

Postal inspectors are law enforcement officers; they can carry firearms, make arrests, and serve federal search warrants and subpoenas (USPS 2002). The Inspection Service also maintains five forensic crime laboratories stationed throughout the United States to carry out its investigative functions. Some examples of laws under Postal Service enforcement jurisdiction include:

- Assaults or robberies of postal service employees
- Bombs
- Distribution of child pornography
- Distribution of controlled substances
- Money order crimes
- Theft of mail

Tribal Agencies

At present, 556 tribal entities in 31 states are recognized by the Bureau of Indian Affairs (BIA) as Native American tribes. More tribes are located in the Southwest than any other area of the United States, and the largest of these is the Navajo Nation in Arizona. Native American tribes are unique in that they are self-governed. Although they must abide by federal regulations, they have their own sovereignty. Tribal agencies face many problems that are either more extreme or unique to tribal entities. For instance, tribes have a higher rate of unemployment, a lower level of educational achievement, and a higher rate of suicide than states. They also have an extremely high crime rate, particularly in terms of substance abuse. Because most tribes live in remote areas and are small

Linkages *in Law Enforcement*

An Introduction to the Linkage-Blindness Phenomenon

One of the consequences of having a complex and interlocking system of laws and law enforcement institutions is the problem of *linkage blindness*. When different institutions operate within overlapping areas of specialization and jurisdiction, they inevitably duplicate information amongst themselves and become interested in the same individuals, organizations, and problems. For example, a suspect wanted by the FBI for drug offenses may also be the subject of a local police investigation for an entirely different offense. Because these two institutions may not readily share information, however, it is possible that evidence held by the FBI and crucial to the particulars of the police investigation is never made available to officers on a local level, and vice versa.

Linkage blindness arises, in part, from the failure of different institutions to recognize areas of mutual interest (Egger 1990)—they are in effect blind to the important connections between them. One of the key challenges for law enforcement agencies in the United States in the twenty-first century is to find ways of overcoming this problem and making the best use of all available information in their efforts to reduce and prevent crime. Linkage blindness surfaced as a visible problem following the terrorist attack on the United States on September 11, 2001. Section 4 of this text will provide technological advances and strategies designed to address the problem of linkage blindness.

QUESTIONS

1. How might linkage blindness affect domestic terrorism (i.e., blowing up an abortion clinic)?

2. How might linkage blindness affect international terrorism?

3. How might linkage blindness affect the following crimes: kidnapping, distribution of child pornography, burglary?

---

in number, they often are required to enforce the law on their own relatives. All of these issues create challenges for tribal police agencies.

The goal of law enforcement services for Native American tribes is to provide quality investigative and police services and technical expertise specifically designed for Native American tribes. Tribally operated law enforcement programs receive assistance from the BIA's law enforcement program. The BIA aims to create a system of training for criminal investigators specific to the needs of the tribal entities, as well as an internal tracking process to monitor the efficiency of police responses to incidents on tribal land. Few monitoring systems exist to assess the quality and rate of completion of investigations, nor the maintenance of a professional and cooperative working relationship with tribal and federal prosecutors and other law enforcement agencies.

A number of programs train tribal law enforcement personnel, such as the Indian Police Academy in Artesia, New Mexico. Such programs are designed to teach Native American police recruits and other law enforcement personnel the basics of policing, investigative techniques, and justice administration principles to law enforcement personnel who will be working in Native American communities.

Linkages *in Law Enforcement*

Coordination and Information Sharing Between Law Enforcement and the Rest of the Criminal Justice System

Communication is an important issue within and across law enforcement jurisdictions; it is also important for the rest of the criminal justice system. Broadly speaking, the **criminal justice system** is a collection of agencies and institutions that enforce criminal law and work to reduce and prevent crime. In the United States, the criminal justice system consists of three main components: the police and other law enforcement agencies; the courts; and correctional services, such as prison and probation programs. Each of these institutions plays a role in the criminal justice process and has particular areas of responsibility, as determined by law. The police, for example, are entrusted with the task of investigating crimes and apprehending criminal suspects. They do not—in theory at least—make decisions about an alleged offender's guilt or innocence or hand down punishments. Instead, these functions are carried out by the courts. Equally, the courts do not play a role in the gathering of evidence, but instead rely on the police to bring cases before them.

The police, the courts, and the correctional services are collectively referred to as the *criminal justice system* because they are organizationally linked and serve a common purpose. In an ideal world, all three would work in harmony, apprehending suspects, determining guilt, and punishing offenders efficiently and in full accordance with the law. In practice, however, the criminal justice system does not always operate in a smooth or structured fashion. In part, this is due to the fact that each branch works according to its own distinct rules, organizational culture, and history. Although the police, the courts, and correctional services are required to work together as partners, different organizational styles or institutional priorities can make interagency cooperation difficult. For instance, information possessed by police is not always readily available to other law enforcement agencies; correctional services may not have the resources to imple-

ment recommendations made by the courts; and efforts to implement system-wide changes may be undermined by the desire of each branch to maintain existing working practices.

In addition to these institutional and cultural factors, decisions made by individuals also affect the workings of the criminal justice system and in some instances may undermine the distinction between its different branches. The police and other law enforcement agencies do not, for example, always restrict themselves to investigating crimes or apprehending suspects. Summary punishments in the form of physical beatings or unwarranted detention in police cells are all examples of the police going beyond their boundaries and assuming the powers of the courts and the correctional service. It is not just the police, however, who at times exceed their authority within the criminal justice system. For instance, in the judiciary, prosecutors may overcharge a suspect in order to encourage the suspect to accept a plea bargain (thus reducing the charge to the original act committed). In the correctional system, prison officials—through the granting or restriction of informal privileges—may influence the way in which an inmate's sentence is carried out, or even its eventual length. Although the powers and responsibilities of agents within the system are defined by law, at every stage of the criminal justice process individuals make decisions that affect how the system operates *in practice*. As a consequence, in order to understand how the criminal justice process works, it is important to remember that although the system has a formal structure, much of its operation depends on the values, informal rules, and decision making that characterizes each of its component parts.

The criminal justice process, which can be broken down into a series of distinct, but interrelated, stages, begins with the initial police investigation and concludes with an inmate's release from correctional services. As individuals move through the process, they are gradually transformed—from

(continues)

suspect to defendant to offender—as the police, the courts, and correctional services each discharge their particular responsibilities. Figure 1.3 outlines the formal structure of a typical state criminal justice process. In addition to demonstrating the flow of cases through the system, the chart highlights relevant issues facing law enforcement at each stage.

FIGURE 1.3

The Criminal Justice Process

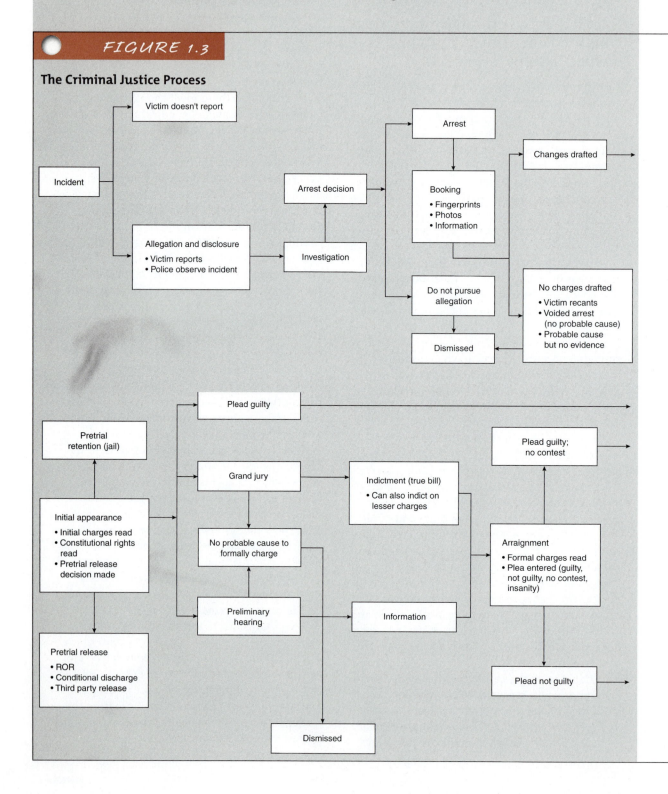

From Suspect to Charge: The Role of the Police

The police are responsible for investigating crime, apprehending and arresting suspects, taking them into custody, and charging them. Once a crime has been committed, it generally comes to the attention of the police in one of two ways: either a member of the public reports it or the police themselves observe it. Although the police undertake

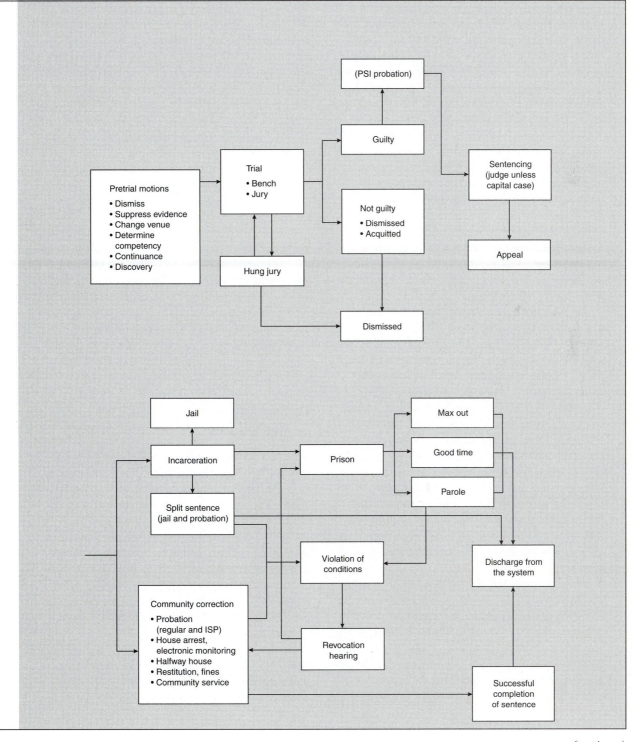

(continues)

regular patrols and carry out various forms of surveillance, most of their information about crime in the community comes from the public. As a result, despite the fact that police officers occupy a unique position in society, they rely heavily on the support and cooperation of the public.

When police observe a crime taking place, they can immediately **arrest** those they have cause to believe are responsible and take them into custody for questioning. In those instances in which a crime is reported by a member of the public, however, depending on the plausibility of the report and the seriousness of the alleged offense, the police can choose either to simply record the report or begin a criminal investigation. The purpose of a criminal investigation is to identify those responsible for the commission of a crime and to gather evidence that proves their guilt. In most cases, once the police have identified a likely suspect they can either ask the person to come to the police station in order to answer questions or—when a suspect is unwilling to cooperate or is believed to be dangerous—arrest the person and hold him or her in custody while a case is prepared.

Because the police possess limited powers of arrest, in certain situations it is necessary for them to obtain a warrant of arrest from a magistrate or a judge. In such circumstances, it is necessary for the police to demonstrate **probable cause**. Probable cause exists when the police have evidence capable of convincing a reasonable person that a crime has been committed and that the person they intend to arrest is responsible for that crime. In principle, the requirement of probable cause serves to restrict the power of the police, ensuring that they do not abuse their powers of arrest. In practice, however, the need for probable cause does not always prevent the police from using arrest as a means of exercising authority over individuals and controlling suspect populations.

Once arrested, the suspect is taken into police custody, booked, and interrogated. **Booking** refers to the process of recording a suspect's entry into detention after arrest. At this time, the police record the suspect's personal details (name, birth date, address, etc.) and take his or her photograph and fingerprints. The suspect is also required to sign a form stating that his or her constitutional rights have been read and they are understood.

Prior and subsequent to arrest, the police are responsible for conducting an **investigation** to gather evidence about the crime and the suspect. This is one of the most important steps in the criminal justice system, because evidence gathered at this time is used throughout the pretrial and adjudication processes. The police often are required to conduct a search, and strict constitutional standards must be adhered to for this procedure (these standards are discussed in detail in Chapter 5). There are different types of searches; the least intrusive is a stop and frisk, where the police can pat down an individual if there is **reasonable suspicion** that the person is in possession of a weapon or is carrying drugs. Reasonable suspicion is a lower legal standard than probable cause, and probable cause is required for any full-scale search of persons, their residence, their automobile, or their personal possessions.

The Fourth Amendment is perhaps the most important safeguard of individual rights against police powers because it protects individuals from illegal searches and seizures. Several landmark cases have established safeguards for individual rights by limiting the powers of the police at this stage of the criminal justice process. These safeguards are detailed in Chapters 4 and 5.

Determining Guilt: The Role of the Courts

Once the suspect has been booked and informal charges have been pressed, the police are required to bring the suspect before a court for an **initial appearance**. In order to ensure that the police do not hold suspects in custody without due cause, the police must ensure that an initial appearance takes place within 24 hours or risk being held liable for false imprisonment. During the initial appearance, the defendant is informed of his or her rights by the judge and formal charges are considered. At this stage, the individual ceases to be a suspect and becomes a defendant. In addition, at the initial appearance an attorney is assigned to indigent defendants if desired or needed and a pretrial release decision is made. In deciding whether to release the defendant on bail or re-mand him or her in custody, the judge will typically consider such factors as the nature and seriousness of the crime, the likelihood that the defendant will voluntarily return for trial, and the safety of the general community.

Bail concerns can seriously affect the level of confidence in the police and a corresponding willingness to report crimes to the police in some high-crime neighborhoods. For example, during one of the author's tour of a high-gang-density housing project in Knoxville, Tennessee, many residents informed him that they would not report gang members or activity because "they are just going to get right back out again." The fear for personal safety, even when formal charges have been laid against an offender, can severely hamper the criminal justice process given the importance of victim testimony in the successful resolution of many cases (Grant 1996).

After the initial appearance, formal charges are then filed against the defendant. At this time, the case is given to the prosecutor, who in most jurisdictions is the District Attorney (DA). The prosecutor has the discretion to determine whether there is probable cause to formally charge the defendant and, if so, what the charges are going to be. Policing practices and enforcement standards can be impacted greatly by a prosecutor's enforcement policies, because the two initially come into contact during the formal complaint process. If a department feels that certain types of violations are consistently not pursued, they will very likely divert their enforcement resources to other areas (Swanson et al. 2001).

If the prosecutor decides to proceed, the case will be brought before either the grand jury or the bench (in a preliminary hearing) to determine whether there are grounds for a trial. Whether there is a preliminary hearing or the case is brought before the grand jury depends on the jurisdiction and the crime committed, although both produce the same result: a formal charge against the defendant and committal for trial. As Swanson et al. (2001) point out, relations between the prosecutor and police can be severely weakened whenever the prosecutor's office chooses to formally charge a local law enforcement officer.

During the preliminary hearing, the defendant has the option of attending the preliminary hearing with counsel or waiving the hearing and allowing it to continue in the defendant's absence.[12] Unlike the grand jury, the preliminary hearing is open to the public and the press, and the defendant has the right to the use of hearsay evidence. When both a grand jury and a preliminary hearing are available, the prosecutor has the discretion to decide which is more appropriate in the particular case. Generally, more serious offenses are brought before the grand jury; misdemeanors and less serious felonies tend to be brought before the bench in a preliminary hearing. In some jurisdictions, a preliminary hearing occurs prior to the grand jury proceeding.

The testimony of the investigating police officer will often be crucial in this stage of the process, requiring the presence of the officer or even the subpoena of the officer's field notes. The importance of strong field notes will be apparent to the officer the first time he or she is on the stand and is required to remember specifics rather than simply generalities (Adams 2001).

Once there is a formal charge, the defendant enters the first stage of the adjudication process, the **arraignment**. At this stage, the formal charges against the defendant are read and the defendant enters a plea.

The decision of the judge to suppress evidence during **pretrial motions** can lead to an extreme frustration on the part of an individual officer or an entire department. This is particularly true in cases where the suppressed evidence is perceived to be an unjustifiable technicality that could damage the entire case. As with the case of the prosecutor discussed above, if judges make it clear the courts are **voiding** certain categories of arrest continually, decisions may be made to no longer enforce those specific types of offenses.

If the defendant elects to have a jury trial—which is available for more serious crimes that carry a potential sentence of six months or more imprisonment—then jurors must be selected prior to the trial.[13] Defendants who choose not to exercise their Sixth Amendment right to a trial by jury can have a bench trial, the outcome of which is decided by a judge.

At the trial, it is the responsibility of the prosecutor to prove **beyond a reasonable doubt** that the defendant committed the crime in question, otherwise the defendant must be acquitted. If

(continues)

the prosecution can prove the case, then the accused is found guilty and the case moves on to the sentencing phase of the adjudication process. Occasionally, juries cannot come to a unanimous or a majority decision, in which case a **hung jury** is declared. In such circumstances, the prosecutor has the discretion to retry the case or dismiss it. Because trials are costly and time consuming, the majority of cases that result in a hung jury are dropped.

Although the trial is the cornerstone of the criminal justice system, the majority of criminal cases never actually come to trial. Instead, approximately 90 percent of cases are resolved through the process of plea bargaining at the arraignment stage of the process. **Plea bargains**, which are arranged between the prosecutor, defense attorney, the defendant, and the judge, are negotiations of guilty pleas in exchange for reduced charges or lenient sentences.

Historically, the police have been strongly opposed to plea bargaining. Having spent time and valuable resources apprehending the suspects and collecting evidence against them, the police often feel that plea bargaining devalues their work and provides offenders with an opportunity to "escape justice." Indeed, plea bargaining is one of the key sources of tension between the police and the courts within the criminal justice system. Despite these problems and concerns, because it provides a mechanism for disposing of cases quickly and efficiently, plea bargaining remains a vital part of the criminal justice process.

Offenders who plead guilty or are found guilty at trial continue on to the sentencing phase of the adjudication process. Before making a determination of an appropriate sentence for the offender, a **presentence investigation (PSI)** is conducted by the office of probation to investigate the offender's background, which helps the judge to determine what type of sentence is appropriate, within legislated parameters.

Although the corrections stage of the criminal justice process begins after sentencing, sentencing does not necessarily mark the end of the adjudication stage. The offender can appeal either the decision of the trial court or the conditions of custody by filing a **writ**, or a formal document requesting an appeal. If the decision is appealed, the facts of the case are not retried, but the legal procedures and decisions from arrest through the trial are reviewed by the appellate court. Although each state has a different appellate court system, most states have an intermediate appellate court and a "court of last resort." The highest appellate court for any case, on a state or federal basis, is the U.S. Supreme Court. Offenders can appeal to have their case reviewed by the Supreme Court by filing a **writ of certiorari**; however, the Court is very selective about cases it reviews. Generally, only cases that raise serious constitutional or human rights issues are reviewed at this level.

Administering Punishment and Reforming the Offender: The Role of Corrections

Once a defendant has been found guilty, a variety of sentencing options are available to the courts, including the death penalty, prison, jail, split sentences, boot camp, probation, residential centers (halfway houses, furloughs), house arrest, electronic monitoring, community service, fines, and restitution. Typically, the most significant decision made by the judge during the sentencing process is whether to hand down a community sentence (usually probation) or a sentence of imprisonment. Some offenses require mandatory prison sentences; for example, the Rockefeller drug laws in New York require that any person convicted of selling two ounces of a narcotic or in possession of four ounces of the narcotic receive a minimum prison sentence of fifteen years to life (Lindesmith Center 1999). Nonetheless, in the vast majority of cases the judge has discretion as to the type of sentence and its length.

Offenders can be incarcerated or given a community sentence irrespective of whether they commit a felony or a misdemeanor. If incarcerated for a misdemeanor, the offender will be sentenced to a year or less in jail. **Jail** is a local county or city institution for temporary detention of persons who are awaiting indictment, arraignment, trial, or sentencing, or for people serving short-term sentences for misdemeanors. Offenders incarcerated for felonies will be sentenced to **prison**, which is a state or federal correctional facility that houses offenders serving sentences of a year or more.

There are three main ways in which offenders can be released from prison. They can serve their entire sentence in prison, or **max out**, at which time the state is required to release them. Offenders who abide by the prison rules and receive only positive reports from correctional services may be released prior to their maximum sentence with **good time**. Offenders in most states may also be released early with **parole**, which allows for supervision from a field agent once the offender is living in the community for the remainder of the sentence. Some states have abolished parole, whereas others have abolished parole for violent offenders and **recidivist**, or repeat, offenders, typically on the grounds that parole undermines the judicial stage of the criminal justice process and leads to inconsistency in the administration of punishment.

Alternative sanctions, also called *subincarcerative sanctions* or *community corrections*, are sentences in which the offender serves part or the entire sentence in the community (e.g., **probation**, intensive supervision probation, house arrest and electronic monitoring, and community service). All of these forms of alternative sanctions are cost-effective, help to reduce the problem of overcrowding in prison, and result in similar rates of recidivism as for offenders who were incarcerated. Some, such as intensive supervision probation

(ISP), even result in lower rates of recidivism. However, there are problems with these sanctions that need to be addressed. As technologies such as electronic monitoring become more sophisticated, so do the offenders who are supervised in such a way.

For community corrections to be effective, the various criminal justice agencies involved must cooperate. This is one example of how the system functions successfully with an interdependence of agencies involved. The recent successes of police-probation partnerships in Boston (Berren and Winship 1999) and Baton Rouge, Louisiana (Sheppard et al. 2000), demonstrate how increased information sharing and collaboration between law enforcement and corrections can lead to reductions in recidivism through a combination of increased surveillance and a greater understanding of the needs of the probationer, and thus an ability to place the probationer into needed services. The importance of increased communication related to sex offender registration will be detailed in the final section of the text.

QUESTIONS

1. Where do you think linkage blindness occurs most in the criminal justice process?

2. Should information about suspects, defendants, and offenders be available to all actors in the criminal justice system? Why or why not?

Chapter Summary

- The concept of linkage blindness is a central theme throughout the book. *Linkage blindness* refers to the lack of communication between different agencies or even within agencies. The terrorist attacks on September 11 were largely a result of linkage blindness; various law enforcement agencies or divisions of agencies had information on the known terrorists, but they did not share the information with the correct sources.

- The primary duty of the police is to maintain social control within the community. What distinguishes the police from other individuals is their ability to use coercive force if necessary to control a situation.

- *Discretion*, which is the freedom for an individual to make a decision based on his or her personal judgment, is a necessary aspect of policing. Although police officers must respond to situations within the parameter of the law, they should have the freedom to make a decision based upon the circumstances of a particular case. Also, it is impossible for an officer to respond to every violation of the law; therefore, discretion is a necessary component of law enforcement.

- The *rule of law* refers to the ideal that equality and justice are inseparable and that laws are applied equally to everyone. It is a standard that is used to guide decision making throughout the criminal justice system.

- All of the agencies within the criminal justice system are interlocked and must work together to ensure justice. The three components of the criminal justice system are the police, the courts, and corrections. The police are the first agents within the criminal justice process. Once a crime occurs, the police are in charge of taking a report, investigating the crime, arresting a suspect, and booking the suspect. The methods by which the police investigate crimes will have an impact on whether and how the case proceeds through the criminal justice system and often whether there is a conviction in the case.

- The crime control model emphasizes the support for law enforcement over individual rights. Advocates of this approach emphasize extensive police powers, limited rights for suspects, and a quick and speedy process. The due process model emphasizes individual rights with restrictions on police power. It focuses on civil liberties and the quality of arrests over the quantity of arrests.

- The six levels of law enforcement are federal, state, county, municipal, township, and tribal. The largest is municipal, with nearly 13,000 municipal jurisdictions.

- In the aftermath of the terrorist attacks on September 11, 2001, the federal government restructured many agencies so that they could better coordinate intelligence and law enforcement resources in the war on terrorism. This reorganization resulted in the formation of the Department of Homeland Security and a restructuring of the agencies within the Department of Justice and the Department of the Treasury.

Linking the Dots

1. What are the benefits of the government's reorganization of departmental agencies within the Department of Justice, the Department of Homeland Security, and the Department of the Treasury? Are there any drawbacks?

2. Should the police be bound by due process constraints when investigating terrorism?

3. What role does the police ability to use force play in their interactions with the community?

4. Do the police curtail their discretion according to the ideal of the rule of law? Explain.

5. How might information sharing be enhanced within and across law enforcement jurisdictions? With the rest of the criminal justice system?

KEY TERMS

Alternative sanction   29
Arraignment   27
Arrest   26
Beyond a reasonable
    doubt   27

Booking   26
Coercive force   8
Commercial Equipment Direct
    Assistance Program
    (CEDAP)   20

Crime control   11
Criminal justice system   23
Culture of lawfulness   9
Defense Intelligence Agency
    (DIA)   20

REFERENCES

Adams, T. 2001. *Police Field Operations*, 5th ed. Upper Saddle River, NJ: Prentice Hall.

Berren, J., and C. Winship. 1999. "Lessons Learned from Boston's Police-Community Collaboration." *Federal Probation* 63(2):25–32.

Bittner, E. 1980. *The Functions of the Police in Modern Society*. Cambridge, MA: Olgeschlager, Gunn, and Hain.

Brown, L. 1979. "The Role of the Sheriff." In *The Future of Policing*, edited by A. Cohn, 227–247. Beverly Hills: Sage.

Bureau of Justice Statistics. 1997. *Sheriffs Departments, 1997*. Washington, D.C.: Bureau of Justice Statistics.

Bureau of Justice Statistics. 2000. *Law Enforcement Management and Administrative Statistics: Data for Individual State and Local Agencies with 100 or More Officers*. Washington, D.C.: Bureau of Justice Statistics.

Bureau of Justice Statistics. 2001. *Local Police Departments, 1999*. Washington D.C.: Bureau of Justice Statistics.

Bureau of Justice Statistics. 2003. *Law Enforcement Statistics*. Available at www.ojp.usdoj.gov/bjs/lawenf.htm.

Bureau of Justice Statistics. 2004. *Law Enforcement Management and Administrative Statistics, 2000: Data for Individual State and Local Agencies with 100 or More Officers*. Washington, D.C.: Bureau of Justice Statistics.

Bureau of Justice Statistics. 2006a. *Local Police Departments, 2003*. Washington, D.C.: Bureau of Justice Statistics.

Bureau of Justice Statistics. 2006b. *Sheriff's Offices, 2003* (No. NCJ 211361): Washington, D.C.: Bureau of Justice Statistics.

Customs and Border Protection. 2007a. *Fact Sheet: Securing America's Borders*. Available at www.cpb.gov.

Customs and Border Protection. 2007b. *Immigration and Travel*. Available at www.cpb.gov.

Customs and Border Protection. 2007c. *Fact Sheet: Securing U.S. Ports*. Available at www.cpb.gov/xp/cgov/newsroom/fact_sheets/port_security/securing_us_ports.xml.

Department of Homeland Security. 2006. *Commercial Equipment Direct Assistance Program (CEDAP)*. Available at www.ojp.usdoj.gov/odp/equipment_cedap.htm.

Department of Homeland Security. 2007. *Homeland Security*. Available at www.dhs.gov/xnews/releases/press_release_0785.shtm.

Egger, S. A. 1990. *Serial Murder: An Elusive Phenomenon*. Westport, CT: Praeger.

Eisenhower, M. 1970. *The Rule of Law—An Alternative to Violence: A Report to the National Commission on the Causes and Prevention of Violence*. Nashville, TN: Aurora Publishers.

Firestone, D. 2002. "Traces of Terror: the Reorganization." *New York Times*, July 26, A1.

Flynn, S. 2001. "The Unguarded Homeland: A Study in Malign Neglect." In *How Did This Happen: Terrorism and the New War*, edited by J. Hodge and G. Rose, 183–197. New York: Public Affairs Press.

Godson, R. 2000. "Guide to Developing a Culture of Lawfulness." Paper prepared for the Symposium on the Role of Civil Society in Countering Organized Crime: Global Implications of the Palermo, Sicily, Renaissance, Palermo, Italy, December 2000.

Goldstein, H. 1979. "Improving Policing: A Problem-Oriented Approach." *Crime and Delinquency* 25(2):236–258.

Grant, H. 1996. Unpublished video documentary of a gang needs assessment in Knoxville, Tennessee.

Greenhouse, L. 2001. "A Nation Challenged: The Supreme Court; in New York Visit, O'Connor Foresees Limits on Freedom." *New York Times*, September 29, B5.

Hentoff, N. 2001. "Has the U.S. Attorney Read the Constitution." *Jewish World Review*, November 19, 2001. Available at www.restoringamerica.org/archive/constitution/has_ashcroftjead.html.

Hudson, R. 1999. *Who Becomes a Terrorist and Why: The 1999 Government Report on Profiling Terrorists*. Guilford, CT: Lyons Press.

Immigration and Customs Enforcement. 2007. *Fact Sheet*. Available at www.ice.gov/about/index.htm.

Kelling, G., and M. Moore. 1989. *The Evolving Strategy of Policing*. Vol. 4 of *Perspectives on Policing*. Washington, D.C.: Government Printing Office.

Klockars, C. 1985. *The Idea of the Police*. Beverly Hills, CA: Sage.

Lindesmith Center, Drug Policy Foundation. 1999. "The Rockefeller Drug Laws and the Second Felony Offender Law." Available at www.Lindesmith.org/focal8/html.

Manning, P. 1977. *Police Work: the Social Organization of Policing*, 2d ed. Prospect Heights, IL: Waveland.

National Strategy Information Center. 1999. *School-Based Education to Counter Crime and Corruption*. Washington, D.C.: National Strategy Information Center.

Nolan, J., and J. Nolan-Haley. 1990. *Black's Law Dictionary*, 6th ed. St. Paul, MN: West Publishing.

Packer, H. 1968. *The Limits of the Criminal Sanction*. Stanford, CA: Stanford University Press.

Reaves, B. A., and A. L. Goldberg. 1998. *Census of State and Local Police Departments, 1996*. Washington, D.C.: U.S. Government Printing Office.

Riley, K. J., L. M. Davis, G. Ridgeway, J. Pace, S. K. Cotton, P. S. Steinberg, K. Damphousse, and B. L. Smith. 2004. *When Terrorism Hits Home: How Prepared Are State and Local Law Enforcement?* Los Angeles: RAND Corporation.

Rood, J. 2004. *Pentagon Has Access to Local Police Intelligence Through Office in Homeland Security Department*. Congressional Quarterly Homeland Security. Available at http://page15.com/2004/07/pentagon-has-access-to-local-police.html.

Senna, J., and L. Siegel. 2001. *Essentials of Criminal Justice*. Belmont, CA: Wadsworth.

Sheppard, D., H. Grant., W. Rowe, and N. Jacobs. 2000. "Fighting Gun Crime." *OJJDP Bulletin in Brief*. Washington, D.C.: U.S. Government Printing Office.

Skolnick, J. 1994. *Justice Without Trial: Law Enforcement in a Democratic Society*, 3d ed. New York: Macmillan College Publishing.

Swanson, C., L. Territo, and R. Taylor. 2001. *Police Administration: Structures, Processes, and Behavior*. 5th ed. Upper Saddle River, NJ: Prentice Hall.

Transportation Security Administration. 2007. *Federal Air Marshal Service*. Available at www.tsa.gov/lawenforcement/people/index.shtm.

U.S. Postal Service. 2002. Available at www.consumer.gov/postalinspectors/aboutus.htm.

Walker, S. 1992. "Origins of the Contemporary Criminal Justice Paradigm: the American Bar Foundation Survey, 1953–1969." *Justice Quarterly* 9(1):47–76.

NOTES

1. Uniting and Strengthening America by Providing Appropriate Tools Required to Intercept and Obstruct Terrorism Act (Public Law 107-56).
2. Although this quote is useful in illustrating the concept of linkage blindness, it should be noted that there have been changes in the structure of governmental agencies since the time that Flynn made this statement.
3. *Escobedo v. Illinois*, 378 U.S. 478 (1964).
4. *Miranda v. Arizona*, 384 U.S. 436 (1966).
5. *Terry v. Ohio*, 392 U.S. 1 (1968).
6. *Gideon v. Wainwright*, 372 U.S. 335 (1963).
7. The case of Rodney King is an example of this. This incident involved the beating of a black man by four white officers after a car chase. It would not have come to the attention of the public had a citizen not been videotaping the incident.
8. An example of this is the Rampart CRASH officers scandal in the Los Angeles Police Department, which involved a number of officers engaging in

criminal misconduct, including working off-duty for Death Row Records, robbing banks, stealing cocaine, falsifying testimony, and beating suspects. At the height of the scandal, two officers shot, framed, and testified against a known gang member. The gang member was rendered paralyzed from the shooting.

9. An example of this is the investigation of New Jersey State Troopers, sparked by an incident in 1998 where two state troopers stopped a van of African American men on the New Jersey Turnpike. During the stop, the van began rolling backwards. The state troopers thought that the driver was trying to run them over, so they began shooting the passengers. Three of the men were wounded. This incident led to a full investigation of state troopers in New Jersey, and a board found that the troopers regularly practiced racial profiling in their stops.

10. The Bureau of Customs was created as a response to the need for revenue shortly after the United States declared independence and was nearly bankrupt. It was established after the passage of the Tariff Act of 1789, which authorized the collection of duties on imported goods. The primary duty of Customs was to ensure that all imports and exports complied with U.S. laws and regulations. It collected and protected the revenue, guarded against smuggling, and was responsible for investigation of these activities. It had the authority to interdict and seize contraband, detect and apprehend any person who circumvented Customs and related laws, and protect intellectual property rights.

11. The Bureau of Immigration was first established in 1891 within the Treasury Department, but by 1903 it was transferred to the Department of Commerce and Labor. In 1906, this organization became know as the Immigration and Naturalization Service (INS), which was transferred to the Department of Justice in 1940. The primary responsibility of the INS was to determine the admissibility of persons seeking entry into the country, ensure appropriate documentation at entry, and control the status of aliens in the country during their stay. It was also responsible for accepting and processing applications from any person petitioning for naturalization or citizenship. The INS worked to both control and reprimand those who were in the country illegally and prevent future acts of illegal entry.

12. *Coleman v. Alabama,* 389 U.S. 22 (1967).

13. In most jurisdictions, defendants charged with serious offenses can choose between a jury trial and a bench trial, though some states require that all defendants who can receive 6 months or more imprisonment are subject to a jury trial.

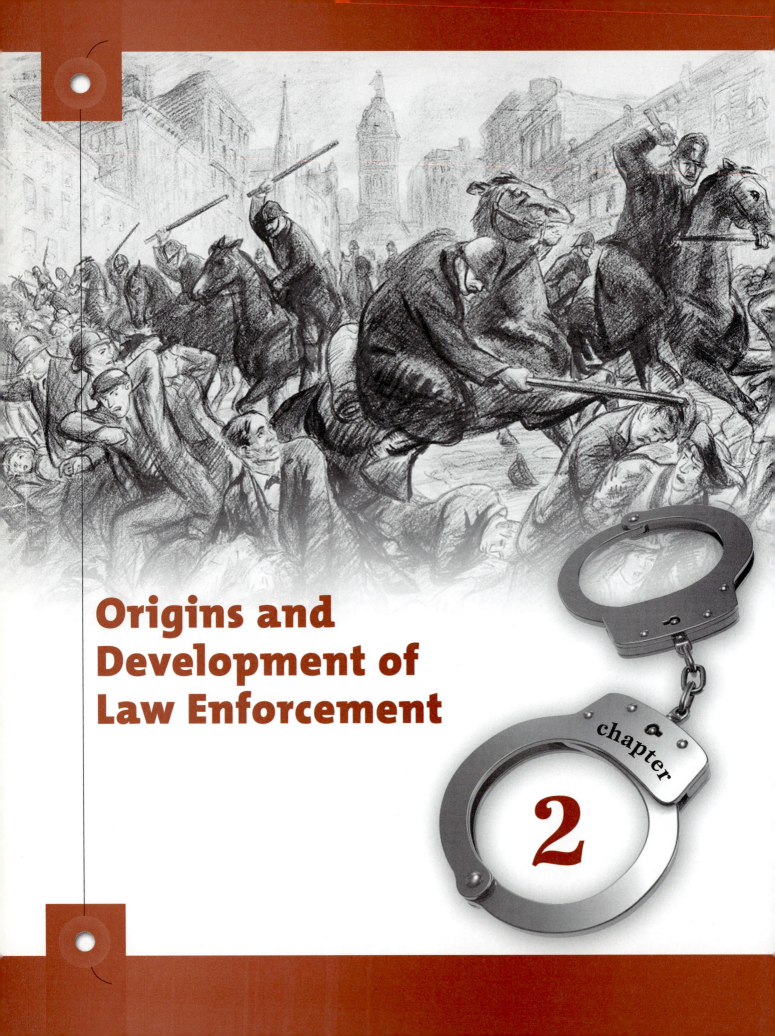

Origins and Development of Law Enforcement

chapter

2

Chapter Objectives

● Explain the origins and meaning of social control.

● Trace the development of informal policing in England and the United States.

● Analyze the impact of the London Metropolitan Police.

● Explain regional differences in the development of law enforcement, such as slave patrols and Jim Crow laws.

● Identify Kelling and Moore's eras of policing and describe key events in the Political Era.

● Discuss key elements of the Reform Era, including its origin, types of reforms, and the individuals responsible for implementing the reforms.

● Describe the early role of women and minorities in policing.

Introduction

"Happily for English liberty there has never existed in this country any police force at the disposal of the central government, powerful enough to coerce the nation at large. Our national police have always been of the people and for the people" [London, 1901] (Lee 1901, quoted in Reiner 1994, p. 61).

"After the classical precipitating incident of a fatal fight between a black civilian and a white policeman, rampaging crowds moved up and down Eighth and Ninth avenues beating Negros. Policemen swarmed over the area, cracking the heads of Negroes and doing nothing to restrain the Irish mob. That the Negroes were bitter is hardly surprising seeing that the police not only did not protect them, did not arrest any of the whites involved, but also indulged in gratuitous clubbing" [New York City, 1901] (quoted in Silver 1984).

These two quotes, both made the same year in London and New York, highlight the importance of political and cultural contexts in the development of law enforcement. Although New York City set out to replicate the English model of policing, the realities of implementation were far different. Political challenges, including the United State's recent history of slavery, played a significant role in the development and character of its early policing systems.

This chapter examines how formal systems of policing have developed throughout the centuries. Although any society governed by law must at some point address the question of how best to enforce those laws, the idea that law enforcement should be the responsibility of a permanent, professional police force is a modern one.

Up until the last two hundred years, most societies relied on individual citizens and communities to ensure that laws were upheld and criminals apprehended. With the arrival of the Industrial Revolution and rising levels of poverty, crime, and public disorder, however, governments in Europe and elsewhere were forced to develop new and more effective ways of enforcing the law and maintaining order. First in Britain and then the United States, law enforcement eventually passed out of the hands of the ordinary citizen and became the direct responsibility of professional law enforcers: the police.

This chapter traces the historical development of law enforcement and the emergence of the modern, professional police force and examines how the idea of "policing" has changed from ancient times to the present. Despite the fact that the modern police officer faces challenges that are very different from those that confronted local sheriffs in feudal England or the Bow Street Runners in eighteenth-century London, much contemporary thinking about law enforcement is rooted in traditions that have changed little over time.

Understanding how different societies have, throughout history, sought to combat crime and enforce the law is an important step toward understanding many of the key issues that now face police forces in the twenty-first century.

Early Origins of Social Control

Any society, if it wishes to survive, needs to develop some system of ensuring that the norms and values of that society are upheld and that members of the community can live free from harm. Prior to the emergence of formal governments and states, early societies were regulated by systems of informal rules and traditions that dictated how members of the society should behave and how conflicts should be resolved. In prehistoric societies, these rules were extremely basic and aimed to ensure that everyone worked together for the survival of the group. Acts such as stealing and murder were prohibited because they created division and distrust and led to conflicts that could threaten the welfare of the community as a whole. Within these early societies, justice was typically an individual matter. The victim of a wrong was responsible for punishing the alleged wrongdoer. Punishment, usually based on the simple notion of an "eye for an eye" (**lex talionis**), was meted out by the victim or the victim's family, with the result that justice was frequently swift, bloody, and final.

As societies became more complex and systems of law emerged, however, these informal methods of social control gave way to more organized systems of law enforcement. In addition to setting out the law to be followed by all citizens, some of the original systems of law also prescribed specific penalties for particular types of wrong. One of the earliest known systems, the **Code of Hammurabi** (2200 BC), originated in the kingdom of Babylon in Mesopotamia (the geographic area that is now Iraq). Although in this system individuals remained responsible for ensuring that the law was followed, under the Code of Hammurabi they were not permitted to impose their own punishments. The Code made the enforcement of law more consistent and established a clear relationship between the type of crime committed and the punishment that could be expected.

Centuries later, the city fathers of Rome established an early system of military policing by assigning responsibility for protecting the Emperor's palace and patrolling the city to the Praetorian Guard and the Urban Cohort. It is the Emperor Augustus, however, who is most frequently credited with establishing the first civilian police force—known as the *vigiles*—shortly before the birth of Christ. Drawn from the general citizenry of Rome, the *vigiles* were originally intended to serve as firefighters, but soon took on the role of law enforcers as well. Unlike the Praetorian Guard or the Urban Cohort, the *vigiles* were given general powers to keep the peace and investigate crime. They patrolled the streets of Rome dressed in ordinary clothes,

The Roman emperor Augustus is frequently credited with establishing the first civilian police force, known as the *vigiles*. Although this early model of policing would reach England, it would collapse with the progression of the Dark Ages.

keeping a watch over the general public. Renowned for their ruthlessness and for handing down severe punishments, the *vigiles* soon became despised by the people and were regarded by many as no better than state-sponsored spies and informants. Although the system of *vigiles* eventually came to an end with the fall of Rome, the word **vigilante**—a person who takes the law into his or her own hands—finds its origin in this early form of community policing. These informal styles of law enforcement soon found their way into England, which was under Roman rule during the time of Augustus, and similar systems were established in place of more traditional, tribal forms of social control.

It should be noted that throughout the ancient world there was considerable resistance to the idea of organized enforcement of laws. In Egypt, where soldiers and temple officials were responsible for enforcing the law, these early enforcement officers of the aristocracy were seen by many as simple servants of the Pharaoh and other members of the ruling elite, concerned only with protecting the property of the wealthy. In Greece, the philosopher Aristotle (384–322 BC) maintained that the existence of a permanent police force was contrary to the very idea of democracy, arguing that the people should be directly responsible for enforcing their own laws. Interestingly, this same argument was raised again some two thousand years later in England by those concerned about the plans for the establishment of the first modern police force. While many centuries may have passed since the time of the ancient Greeks and Romans, the people of London nevertheless found themselves confronted with the questions about who should be responsible for enforcing the law: the police or the people themselves.

Development of Formal Policing in England

Following the fall of Rome and end of the Roman occupation of Britain, traditional forms of law enforcement based on individual and tribal justice reemerged throughout England. As in ancient times, each community adhered to its own rules and punishments, leaving law enforcement in the hands of the individual. As the Dark Ages progressed, powerful landholders and rulers began to assert themselves and establish a hold over large areas of the country. Victims and their families, however, remained responsible for pursuing and punishing perpetrators within their communities. As a consequence, the administration of justice and punishment was inconsistent and there was no organized system of policing.

Punishments during this time were typically severe, frequently resulting in the death of the offender. In cases where the truth of the accusation was disputed, the accused was given the opportunity to prove his or her innocence by undergoing some form of predetermined ordeal or trial. Ironically, the process of proving one's innocence could often be as painful as the punishment that accompanied a finding of guilt.

From Tithings to Posse Comitatus

Toward the end of the Dark Ages, the gradual merging of Roman, Germanic, and Anglo-Saxon traditions and the emergence of the monarchy gave rise to the general acceptance of two ideas that were to provide the basis for a more unified and consistent approach to law enforcement. The first of these was the concept of the "king's peace," which held that any crime against an individual was also a crime against the king. This meant that the crown could claim to have a legitimate interest in the enforcement of the law, even if no offence had been directly committed against the king or his agents.

The second idea was the notion that all of the king's subjects were also his property. Accordingly, anyone who caused harm to any citizen was potentially liable to pay compensation to the crown. These two ideas provided the basis for the legal principle that a criminal act represented a crime against the state as well as the individual and that the state had a direct interest in ensuring that the laws were upheld and enforced. This principle remains at the heart of criminal law in both England and the United States and provides the basic justification for the existence of the police in both countries. Although the law continued to be enforced according to local tradition, the end of the Dark Ages opened the way for a more centralized approach to the problem of law enforcement.

By the middle of the ninth century, the majority of the English population lived in established towns and cities, each with its own system of rules and organization. During the reign of Alfred the Great (849–899 AD), however, a new system of social organization was imposed. In an effort to make the collection of taxes and the maintenance of the king's peace easier, Alfred divided England into regions known as **shires**. Each shire, which was similar to the American county, consisted of geographic units known as "hundreds"—so named because each contained 100 families. Each of the hundreds was composed of ten **tithings**, and a tithing consisted of ten families. Under this new arrangement, every citizen was tied to a particular tithe and was jointly responsible with all other members of his or her group for the payment of taxes and the maintenance of order (Stead 1985). As a result, a crime committed by one person was held to be a crime committed by his or her entire community, with the punishment to be borne by the group as a whole. In essence, Alfred's aim was to make communities self-regulating when it came to the payment of taxes and the enforcement of law. **Shire reeves**, precursors to modern-day sheriffs, were the leaders of the shires and were appointed by the king. They were given the task of ensuring that law and order was maintained throughout their region. Drawing on the assistance of locally elected **constables**, shire reeves frequently organized villagers and other members of the community into **posses** that would track down and apprehend offenders.

Although by modern standards the system of policing established by Alfred the Great might appear to be crude, the introduction of shire reeves and local constables revolutionized the way in which laws were enforced throughout medieval England. In the space of a few decades, the administration of justice was taken out of the hands of individuals and made the responsibility of particular communities and their appointed leaders. Law enforcement ceased to be a private matter and became associated with the king and his agents.

Some three centuries later, this system was formalized by the Statute of Winchester (1285), which increased the power of the constables and made them responsible for organizing local watchers. In addition, under the Statute all men between the ages of fifteen and sixty were required to bear arms in defense of the crown and the king's peace and to assist their local constable in the pursuit of offenders. Failure to heed the constable's call for help—known as the **hue and cry**—was a punishable offense under the new law, and anyone who did not help to apprehend criminals risked being tried with them as associates.

It was also around this time that the first justices of the peace began to emerge, who acted as judges and presided over local trials. Typically country gentlemen and members of the aristocracy, these justices were central to the administration of justice throughout the shires, and, like the constables, were also entrusted with the task of keeping the king's peace.

This system of justices and constables was to change little over the next four hundred years in England. Although the criminal law expanded considerably during this time, law enforcement remained the responsibility of local officials answerable to the king. By the eighteenth century, however, the system had begun to fail. In many regions, justices and constables had become corrupt and unaccountable, frequently using their considerable powers to enhance their own positions and wealth. More importantly, the steady processes of industrialization and urbanization had also made local peace keeping more and more difficult. As the population grew, informal methods of policing based on collective responsibility and local ties became unwieldy and ineffective. Lawlessness and disorder became more widespread, with many members of the upper class employing guards to protect them and their property from attack. Faced with the possibility of anarchy, it became clear that something had to be done.

After various efforts failed to rejuvenate the existing system of constables, the government eventually granted the London magistrate, Henry Fielding, permission to found a group of organized law enforcement agents. Known as the **Bow Street Runners**, these men were given the task of apprehending criminals and recovering stolen goods within London. They were paid, in part, out of city funds. Because they also had the duty to solve crimes, the Runners were essentially the first paid detectives (Howe 1965). They failed to stem the rising tide of crime in the city, however, and they were eventually disbanded some years later. The Runners did enjoy a limited degree of success. Many individuals were impressed by their organization and effectiveness, and they had the reputation of being incorruptible and determined (Howe 1965). Soon the idea of maintaining a permanent, salaried police force began to gain wider acceptance.

Another driving force behind the push for the foundation of a professional police force was the public outrage following the **Peterloo massacre of 1819** in which a political protest turned riotous after the military was brought in to break it up. This incident left eleven dead and hundreds injured, as well as a lingering fear in the minds of many of the dangers of relying on the military to handle public order. In the United States, the **Posse Comitatus Act** (18 U.S. Code, Section 1385) was signed in 1878 to separate military functions from local law enforcement. The original intent of this act was to prohibit the use of federal troops in the policing of state elections; however, in effect, it also prohibits the military from serving as a domestic police force. The act bans the Army, Navy, Air Force, and Marines from participating in arrests, evidence search and seizure, or any other conventional policing activity on U.S. soil.

The Formal System of Policing

The term *police* entered into the English language in the mid-fifteenth century from the middle-French word *porice*, meaning "public order assured by the state" (*Oxford English Dictionary* 1996). The modern usage of *police* as "the civil force responsible for maintaining public order and enforcing the law" came into recorded usage in the English language in 1798, when the Marine Police were established to protect merchant shipping on the River Thames in London. The law enforcement entity established in London in 1828 was sometimes called the New Police (*Oxford English Dictionary* 1996).

 Linkages *in Law Enforcement*

Posse Comitatus Today

Posse Comitatus was passed in the post–Civil War era in response to a general fear that the new federal government would interfere in state government and could use the military against its own citizens. Nevertheless, a number of exceptions to Posse Comitatus have been provided since its enactment:

- National Guard forces operating under state authority are exempt from the Act's restrictions.

- The President of the United States can use federal troops to "quell" domestic violence situations.

- Aerial photography and visual searches are allowed if for the purpose of assisting civilian law enforcement.

- An exception to the Act, created by Congress, allows the military to offer training, equipment, and advice in the "war on drugs."

- The Coast Guard is exempt from the provisions of the Act.

- The Navy can assist a Coast Guard vessel in pursuit.

In the aftermath of the September 11 attacks, further exceptions to Posse Comitatus were considered to reduce linkage blindness between military and civilian law enforcement agencies and to expedite investigations of suspected terrorists. In 2005, Whitehouse Press Secretary Scott McClellan stated that the Posse Comitatus Act of 1878 was under review, which caused a stir among journalists and legal commentators. However, later in 2005, Secretary of Defense Donald Rumsfeld stated in a meeting that the administration had no plans to make changes to the law (Plummer 2005).

In a reversal of position, PL 109-364, signed by President Bush in October of 2006, has a provision for "Use of the Armed Forces in Major Public Emergencies" (Stein 2006). The law adds "natural disaster, epidemic, or other serious public health emergency, terrorist attack or incident" to the list of conditions under which the president can command troops in the states. This allows the president to take over local authority "if domestic violence has occurred to such an extent that the constituted authorities of the State or possession are incapable of maintaining public order" (Stein 2006). Although the legislation speaks of extreme situations, it does allow the executive branch to command U.S. military personnel in a law enforcement capacity. The Posse Comitatus Act is found Appendix B.

QUESTIONS

1. How would elimination of Posse Comitatus change the balance between crime control and due process?

2. What, if any, conditions do you think could warrant such a change?

3. How would local law enforcement be helped or hindered by this change?

4. Where do you think Americans should draw the line between crime control and due process in the war on terrorism?

By the early 1800s, London had over 450 paid police officers working throughout the city. Despite this, there was still no centrally organized system of law enforcement. In 1828, however, the Home Secretary **Sir Robert Peel** set about establishing what was later to be called the London Metropolitan Police. Having served in Ireland for many years and successfully organized the Royal Irish Constabulary, Peel was keen to reform the way in which the law was enforced in England and create a new police force for the city of London. Parliament was initially resistant to Peel's ideas, largely because they feared the introduction of a military-style force along French lines. They eventually passed the London **Metropolitan Police Act** in 1829, providing funds for the establishment of a 1,000-officer force governed by strict standards of conduct and discipline. Early developments in policing through the creation of the Metropolitan Police are outlined in Table 2.1.

Initially under the command of two magistrates (who later became known as *commissioners*), this new Metropolitan Police force differed markedly from previous efforts at law enforcement in England. Most important, the officers were organized along military lines and subject to clear chains of command and rules of conduct. To encourage accountability and professionalism, officers were required to wear uniforms, making them easily identifiable in public, and to carry badges with their identification number inscribed upon it. In addition, officers were direct employees of the state, as opposed to being private citizens charged by law to assist in the apprehension of offenders. In these respects, Peel's Metropolitan Police were the first modern police force. Indeed, many forces around the world continue to be organized around the same basic rules and principles contained in Peel's **Principles of Policing** (reproduced in Table 2.2).

Initially, British citizens did not embrace the concept of a formal governmental police force. They feared that the police would be a pawn of the government and act as an occupying army in their towns. However, the sentiment towards the police changed in 1833 with the riots in Cold Bath Fields. One riot resulted in the violent death of Police Constable Culley, and at trial a jury returned a verdict of justifiable homicide for his killer.[1] After a newspaper account

---

TABLE 2.1

Key Dates in the History of Law Enforcement

2200 BC	Code of Hammurabi standardizes laws and punishments in Babylon.
1340 BC	Nile River Police established in Egypt.
510 BC	Romans establish the Praetorian Guard and Urban Cohort.
27 BC	Roman system of *vigiles* instituted by Augustus.
400–800	Law enforcement in England based on traditional notions of individual justice and punishment.
899	System of shires, hundreds, and tithes established by Alfred the Great.
1285	Statute of Winchester establishes the watch-and-ward system in England.
1326	Justices of the Peace first appointed by the king in England.
1748	Formation of the Bow Street Runners in London.
1829	Creation of the London Metropolitan Police.

TABLE 2.2

Sir Robert Peel's Principles of Policing (1829)

1. The police must be stable, efficient, and organized along military lines.
2. The police must be under government control.
3. The absence of crime will best prove the efficiency of the police.
4. The distribution of crime news is essential.
5. The deployment of police strength both by time and area is essential.
6. No quality is more indispensable to a policeman than a perfect command of temper; a quiet determined manner has more effect than violent action.
7. Good appearance commands respect.
8. The securing and training of proper persons is at the root of efficiency.
9. Public security demands that every police officer be given a number.
10. Police headquarters should be centrally located and easily accessible to the people.
11. Policemen should be hired on a probationary basis.
12. Police records are necessary to the correct distribution of police strength.

L ondon bobbies with Robert Peel, founder of the Metropolitan Police Force in London.

published the story of the officer's widow, citizens began to show public support for the police and their efforts to stem crime in the city.

After witnessing the effectiveness of the London Metropolitan Police, several other professional forces were established throughout England along similar lines by 1856. As the recruitment and training methods developed by Peel spread, interest in crime prevention grew and the idea of local "policemen"—called **bobbies** after their founder—as the central law enforcement figures in the community gained wide acceptance.[2]

Development of Formal Policing in the United States

During the early years of colonization, law enforcement in America developed along English lines. Towns and villages appointed constables and sheriffs with powers very similar to their English counterparts. Additionally, they organized watch systems that were an adaptation of those that had existed for centuries in England. As time went on, and as English policing became increasingly centralized, its development began to deviate from the pattern that was being established in the United States. There, following law enforcement traditions brought with them from Europe, citizens were made responsible for helping to maintain the peace, and although in larger towns, such as Boston and Philadelphia, laws were passed requiring the public to help officials in the apprehension of criminals, victims of crime could not always rely on the authorities or the community to bring criminals to justice.

Early Watch Systems

As in England, the first system of policing in the United States was an informal one where individuals within a community protected each other. This informal system consisted of numerous positions, including a justice of the peace, a sheriff, constables, and a night watch. The role of the sheriff was strictly confined to law enforcement and the apprehension of criminals, serving warrants and subpoenas and maintaining the local jails. Although initially the sheriff was an appointed position, over time it evolved into an elected position. The sheriff's responsibilities eventually expanded beyond law enforcement to include collecting taxes and monitoring the system of cattle branding. Although the main duty of the sheriff continued to be law enforcement oriented, this was a reactive role without any general crime-prevention functions.

As the population in cities began to grow, it became increasingly difficult for sheriffs and local marshals (similar to the English constables) to maintain order. Consequently, cities such as New York, Boston, and Philadelphia began to experiment with **watch systems**. These watches, which consisted of volunteer citizens, were based on the concept of *community responsibility*. Members of the community were required by local law enforcement officers to undertake patrols of their neighborhood under the guidance of local marshals or constables. The purpose of these patrols was to watch for signs of criminal activity, though the powers of the watchmen were limited only to arrest and holding individuals suspected of wrongdoing.

Although watchmen occasionally averted criminal acts, the watch system was fraught with problems. Night watchmen were unpopular, largely as a result of their lack of enthusiasm, lack of competency, and frequent state of drunkenness. Their weaknesses were most apparent in situations of large-scale disorder, such as riots. By the mid-1840s, most large cities came to regard the night watch system as inefficient and more harmful than beneficial. As a result, this informal system of night watchmen drawn from the community evolved into a system whereby the patrols were undertaken by full-time, paid watchmen. The changeover between volunteer and paid watchmen was gradual, and for many years in some cities (e.g., Philadelphia during the 1830s) the two systems coexisted in a hybrid structure of paid day watchmen and volunteer night watchmen.

Cities were not the only areas experiencing difficulties with law enforcement during the colonial era. Outside of the major towns and cities, lawlessness was often widespread. Vast distances and the absence of communal ties in the frontier made it difficult for individual sheriffs to impose their authority on citizens. As a result, vigilantism was common. In many jurisdictions **vigilante committees** composed of area residents wishing to actively fight crime would take on all law enforcement duties, from pursuing offenders to trying them and punishing them. Individual landholders often employed these vigilantes to protect them, and in many cases the threat of violence was the only effective deterrent to potential offenders.

Slave Patrols and the Jim Crow Laws

While cities in the North developed a night watch system, law enforcement in the South tended to focus on the control and discipline of slaves. **Slave patrols** were first established in the South during the mid-1740s, with officers being given broad powers to punish slaves who committed offenses or who refused to submit to their masters. The slave patrols at this time were coordinated by property owners who, individually, had difficulty controlling the slave population and ensuring that they did not defy their masters. As with the night watch system, slave patrols were based on a form of citizen obligation whereby members of a community would watch over other citizens' slaves to ensure their obedience. Although informal initially, slave patrols evolved into an organized system with a chain of command and organizational structure (Wood 1984). In fact, they were generally considered the precursor to modern police forces in the United States despite their extremely narrow and clearly racist focus (Williams and Murphy 1990). By 1837, South Carolina, which had instituted particularly infamous slave codes, had one of the largest police forces in the country, with over 100 officers on slave patrol (Conser and Russell 2000).

A BOLD STROKE FOR FREEDOM.

Considered the precursor to modern police forces in the United States, slave patrols emerged in the South out of fear of possible slave insurrection. Slave patrols enforced slave codes prohibiting such things as literacy, commerce, and the possession of weapons by slaves.

Slaves in most states were deemed incapable of exercising the rights of ordinary citizens. Often mounted on horseback and carrying whips, the slave patrols enforced laws that prohibited literacy and commerce amongst slaves. The slave patrols also made sure that slaves were not in possession of weapons or ammunition, and they had the power to search "Negro houses" to ensure that such laws were not being violated. Even though the slaves were not considered full citizens, they were capable of being held criminally responsible for their "crimes," particularly actions such as being away from their masters without carrying passes.

When the slave codes were abolished after the Civil War, a number of states, mainly in the South, adopted "Black Codes" that set out the responsibilities of newly freed slaves through a complex system of laws and judicial conventions. The Civil Rights Act in 1866 helped to improve the position of blacks, and subsequently Congress enacted the Civil Rights Act of 1871 as a method of remedy for persons whose civil rights were violated. This Act followed the ratification of the Thirteenth and Fourteenth Amendments, which abolished slavery and ensured due process rights to all U.S. citizens. This was sometimes called the Ku Klux Klan Act, because the violent and obstructive conduct of the Ku Klux Klan prompted Congress to enact this legislation (Kappeler 1997). (The Civil Rights Act of 1871 is discussed in greater detail in Chapter 4).

Although such legislation was meant to give more rights to blacks, many states in the 1880s enacted **Jim Crow Laws**. These codes, examples of which are shown in Table 2.3, enforced segregation between whites and blacks in schools, parks, restrooms, public transportation, sports teams, and most other public facilities. Interracial marriage was prohibited, and employers were required to have separate facilities for their white and black workers. Some states

---

TABLE 2.3

Examples of the Jim Crow Laws[4]

Issue	Law
Interracial marriage	Marriage between a Caucasian person and a Negro, or an individual with any Negro blood, is prohibited.
Buses	All bus stations must have separate waiting rooms and ticket windows for Caucasians and Negros. All buses must have separate sections in which the Caucasians and Negros can sit.
Restrooms	Employers, schools and recreational facilities must provide separate toilet facilities for Caucasians and Negros.
Restaurants	It is prohibited to serve food to Caucasians and Negros in the same room, unless they are separated by a partition.
Education	Caucasian and Negro children will be educated in separate buildings.
Housing	It is a crime for Caucasians to rent rooms in a dwelling to Negros, and vice versa. Caucasians and Negros must not dwell within the same building.
Juvenile detention	Caucasian and Negro children in juvenile detention facilities shall be kept completely separated.
Prisons	Caucasian and Negro convicts will eat and sleep separately.
Sports	Particularly baseball, Caucasian and Negro players must have separate teams, fields, and equipment.
Leisure activities (e.g., theaters)	All individuals operating leisure activity centers (e.g., cinemas, pubic halls, theatres, etc.) must have separate facilities for Caucasians and Negros.

even required separate facilities for whites and blacks in prisons and mental hospitals. The Supreme Court deemed segregation constitutional in 1896 by setting out a "separate but equal" doctrine in *Plessy v. Ferguson*.[3]

Because the police were required to enforce the Jim Crow laws, the black community came to view them essentially as agents of an oppressive legal system that treated them as second-class citizens rather than equal to whites. Much of the tension between the police and minority communities that ensued throughout the early twentieth century resulted from their enforcement first of the slave codes and subsequently the Jim Crow laws. Even after such codes were abolished, many in the black community viewed the police as "slave patrols in disguise," with police behavior towards minorities still derisive. The relationship between the police and minority communities has been wrought with friction and hostility since the abolishment of the last Jim Crow laws in the 1960s, and this tension—discussed at length in Chapter 10—is still present in many respects today.

The Eras of American Policing

Kelling and Moore (1991) describe American policing as having progressed through three distinct eras—the Political Era, the Reform Era, and the Community Era—each characterized by its own organizational structure, tactics, and primary focus. The remainder of this chapter examines the Political Era; Chapter 3 focuses on the Reform and Community Eras. Table 2.4 summarizes the characteristics of each era.

TABLE 2.4

Kelling and Moore's Eras of Policing

The Political Era (1840–1930)	Authority is derived primarily from politicians. Primary police function is to respond to citizens and politicians, satisfy their needs. Organization is decentralized. Intimate relationship with the community. Much use of foot patrol. Significant amount of corruption.
The Reform Era (1930–1980)	Authority is primarily derived from the law. Primary police function is crime control. Organization is centralized and efficient. Professional, but remote, relationship with the community. Use of motorized patrol; rapid response to emergency calls. Poor relationship with the community.
The Community Era (1980–present)	Authority is derived from both law and the community. Primary police function is community service and crime control. Organization is decentralized with special units. Intimate relationship with the community. Use of problem-oriented policing, foot patrol, and public relations. Improve citizen's quality of life, but reliance on officer as a social worker.

Source: "From Political to Reform to Community: The Evolving Strategy of the Police." G. L. Kelling and M. H. Moore in *Community Policing: Rhetoric or Reality*. J. R. Greene and S. D. Mastrofski (eds.). Copyright © 1991 by Praeger. Reproduced by permission of Greenwood Publishing Group, Inc. Westport, CT.

Political Era (1840–1930)

As in England, industrialization in the United States during the late eighteenth and early nineteenth century brought with it rising levels of urban crime and public disorder. As immigration and internal migration led to rapid increases in urban populations—particularly in cities such as New York, Boston, Chicago, and Philadelphia—a new underclass of urban poor emerged. Food riots, labor strikes, and the growing threat of widespread civil disturbance led many local politicians and industrialists to conclude that a new system of law enforcement was needed if the social fabric of the country was to be maintained. However, many were wary of allowing the government to establish a permanent police force, particularly given that Americans had fought the American Revolution to free themselves from just such control by the British. Eventually, however, formal police forces were established, and by the end of the nineteenth century professional policing and law enforcement had become a fact of American life.

Boston was the first city to establish a formal night watch system in 1801, supplemented by a day watch in 1838. The first city to formally employ both day and night watchmen was Philadelphia, though it was New York City that established what is considered the first modern police force given that the day and night watchmen were under the supervision of one police chief. The force—loosely modeled on the London Metropolitan Police—was organized along military lines, but, unlike their counterparts in London, the New York Police derived their authority not from an Act of Parliament, but rather from the support of local politicians. As a consequence, from the outset they were vulnerable to political interference and external pressure.

To exacerbate the problem, early police organizations tended to be highly decentralized. Local stations and officers were rarely supervised or held accountable by anyone except their immediate superiors. During the nineteenth century, most police officers actively worked to further the interests of the local politicians who placed them in power and gave them their resources and authority. These politicians were almost all upper-middle-class white males who worked within a **spoils system**, appointing people to civil service jobs predominately based on patronage, political affiliation, or in return for monetary payments. In addition, they often rewarded their associates by giving them key positions in police departments, and the politicians, in turn, used the police to help them maintain their political positions. As a result, policing was rife with corruption. Toward the end of the nineteenth century, many public leaders became convinced that something needed to be done to combat increasing levels of corruption and political favoritism resulting from the spoils system. It was at this point that the police began a period of major reform, aimed primarily at making them more professional and less susceptible to outside pressures.

The Pendleton Civil Service Act of 1883   One of the most significant developments at the end of the nineteenth century was the passage of the **Pendleton Act**, whose primary purpose was to abolish the spoils system. The Pendleton Act was a federal bill, and its main goal was to reduce the level of corruption endemic with the federal administration of Ulysses S. Grant (*The Columbia Encyclopedia* 2001). Because it was a federal act, it only applied to federal employees. However, it set in motion a series of similar proposals at the state and local levels calling for the reform of hiring and promotion standards for civil servants in local governments.

Because it established objective criteria for hiring public officials and made it unlawful to dismiss civil employees for political reasons, the Act led to a wave of reforms. Before the Act, most government positions were political appointments. Although the Act did not entirely eliminate the influence of politicians, it was an important first step towards regulating the influence of politicians in hiring decisions. For instance, under the Act politicians were prevented from hiring members of the same political party, but instead were required to hire equally across all parties. This resulted in less power being vested in individual parties and, thus, less corruption. Note that corruption was ever more difficult to combat during this period, given that the police forces were not particularly **legalistic**, or oriented toward the strict enforcement of the letter of the law. Instead, police forces focused on **order maintenance** and the status quo.

In addition to regulations on hiring and firing of employees, the Pendleton Act also established regulations for promotions. The second clause of section two of the Act states that competitive exams must be given to all those applying for a promotion and that the person with the highest exam score will be promoted. This reform was intended to ensure that promotion was based on an objective evaluation of performance in police departments in hopes that the best person for the position would be selected. The same section goes on to state that "no person in said service has any right to use his official authority or influence to coerce the political action of any person or body," once again establishing a fair system whereby no one from a particular party is favored or punished. As a whole, the Act did not directly address the sources of corruption; however, it did provide honest officers with some degree of protection from political pressure and a degree of job security.

Wickersham Commission   The turn of the century brought with it significant social change in the United States. The Industrial Revolution was causing vast urban growth, which coincided with a rise in anonymity within the cities and an increase in crime. It also brought forth different types of crime. Not only were juveniles and women being picked up by the police more than ever before, but there was also an increase in organized crime. This was aggravated in 1920 with the passage of the Eighteenth Amendment, or Prohibition.

In hopes of finding solutions for these and other social ills, Herbert Hoover organized the **Wickersham Commission** in 1929. The purpose of the Commission was to address growing concerns with prohibition, the increasing crime rate, and problems with the juvenile justice and adult criminal justice processes (National Commission on Law Observance and Enforcement 1931). Hoover also recognized the need for evaluation of governmental agencies; many individuals were calling for a reduction in civil liberties and increased police powers in order to reduce the crime rate. At the same time, however, he recognized that there was an increasing social awareness of problems between police and minority communities and that police abuse of power over minorities needed to be addressed.

Though its findings were not remarkable, the Wickersham Commission has come to be regarded as a turning point in the history of policing. The primary reason for this is that it undertook the first large-scale study of the U.S. criminal justice system. Additionally, it was critical of the police in its findings, calling for significant police reforms. In particular, the commission focused on police misconduct, spurring leaders in the policing community to develop systems whereby citizens could register complaints against the police and implementing internal mechanisms for the investigation of police misconduct. Although the main focus of the Wickersham Commission was on issues other than the police, it served as an important precursor to future Commissions.

Women and Minorities in Early Policing.

It is important to note that although many police forces in the United States were modelled along English lines, America's past meant that these new police officers faced a number of challenges different from those that confronted their counterparts in England. Perhaps most significant was the question of how the police were to deal with issues relating to race and the continuing effects of slavery. The Political Era of policing was not particularly concerned with the recruitment of women and minorities. Instead, where this did it occur, it was based on a narrow view of their potential uses in policing.

African American officers were almost unheard of in the early days of policing. A consequence of this was accusations of racial bias by the police. The first known African American police officer served in Washington, D.C., in 1861 (Sullivan 1989). In the 1870s, the New Orleans police force was the first to actively recruit African Americans. New Orleans had a large African

The first documented policewoman was Alice Stebbins Wells, who joined the Los Angeles police department in 1910. However, it was not until the 1960s that women and minority officers began to take on equal roles within law enforcement.

American community at this time, and black police officers were hired to police predominantly black areas. Three African American officers were even appointed to the police board. Despite these developments, Williams and Murphy (1990) contend that the Supreme Court's decision in *Plessy v. Ferguson* "completed the quarter-century-long process of standing the law established by the reconstruction amendments on its head." In New Orleans, the number of African American police officers dropped from 177 in 1870 to 27 in 1880. By 1910, there were no African American police officers in New Orleans, and the city remained without one until 1950 (Williams and Murphy 1990). It was not until the second half of the next century that forces across the country began to deal directly with the issue of law enforcement and race.

Like ethnic minorities, women also were nearly nonexistent in early police forces. When women were first hired by the police, it was as police matrons in the 1880s. The police matrons, who were for the most part upper-middle-class white women, performed duties such as visiting the sick, making lunches for the male officers, searching female and juvenile suspects, escorting and supervising women in precinct detention facilities, and going to houses of prostitution, amusements, theatres and dance halls, as needed, to reform the wayward women. The first documented policewoman was Alice Stebbin Wells, who joined the Los Angeles Police Department in 1910. The duties of policewomen, like the matrons, focused on social service activities such as preventive and protection programs for women and children. Not surprisingly, the appointment of minority policewomen lagged behind that of whites. The first black female to be hired by the police was Georgia Robinson, who began working for the Los Angeles Police Department in 1916 as a matron and was then promoted to policewoman in 1919 (Schulz 1995).

In 1926, it was estimated that there were around 500 policewomen working in 175 cities across the United States. Salaries were an issue, because nearly all policewomen earned less money than their male counterparts. By 1945, a government publication, based on the U.S. Census, put the number of policewomen at around 3,000. Despite the increase in numbers, women still performed duties oriented toward social service roles. In the era of professional policing, crime fighting, not social services, was the hallmark of a typical police officer (Schulz 1995).

Though the hiring of policewomen increased during World War II, women were still significantly underrepresented in the police. Demonstrating its position as a both a barometer and enforcer of the external social forces in which it is situated, it was not until the civil rights movement and equal employment opportunity legislation in the 1960s that women and minority officers began to take on equal roles within law enforcement, themes that will be developed throughout this book.

Origins of the Reform Era

Looking back over the history of policing, both in England and the United States, it is possible to see that many of the basic concerns about accountability, independence, and effectiveness that occupied the minds of the first law enforcers are still issues today. The extent to which police officers should be a part of the communities they police and the role that the public ought to play in the task of law enforcement remain important questions. In an effort to "correct" some of the negative influences in law enforcement, such as entrenched practices of corruption and brutality, reform efforts sought to create a more objective, legalistic profession driven by the rule of law.

Faces of Reform: Early Leaders in Law Enforcement Reform

Although a number of individuals have had a significant influence on policing throughout the century, three in particular were at the forefront of police change during the Reform Era. August Vollmer, O. W. Wilson, and J. Edgar Hoover all helped to transform law enforcement from a corrupt organization into a respectable profession at the local, state, and federal levels.

August Vollmer: The Father of Police Professionalism　**August Vollmer** is perhaps best well known for linking education to police training, establishing the first police training school in the United States by drawing on the resources of universities in and around Berkeley. Having served as the chief of police in

August Vollmer was a pioneer of police professionalism during the Reform Era, battling corruption through improved recruitment, selection, and training standards.

Berkeley, California, from 1905 to 1932, August Vollmer is considered a pioneer of police professionalization and reform. He also helped to develop the School of Criminology at the University of California at Berkeley, which would become a model for law and criminal justice education throughout the United States.

Vollmer is credited with, among other things, introducing the use of intelligence and psychological testing to officer-selection procedures. He also led the move toward greater use of the scientific method in police investigations, establishing a forensic laboratory in Berkeley. Vollmer viewed police officers as "social workers dealing with a range of societal problems which manifested themselves in crime and disorder. In his view, policemen should become college-educated professionals akin to doctors and lawyers" (Repetto 1978, p. 243). To this end, he was one of the founders of the professional association that later would become the American Society of Criminology.

O. W. Wilson: The Protégé   A protégé of Vollmer, **O. W. Wilson** stands as one of the most influential writers on the subject of policing during the twentieth century. He is the author of the first two books on police management, one of which is described by some authors as being "the Bible of policing for decades" (Dempsey 1999, p. 16).

During his tenure as head of the Wichita, Kansas, police department, Wilson conducted the first systematic study of the effectiveness of one-officer police squad cars. His results showed that they are as efficient and effective as two-person cars, contrary to popular opinion at the time. During his time in Kansas, Wilson would make major reforms to police training, implementing many of the ideas of his mentor, August Vollmer.

Wilson viewed managerial efficiency as central to police administration, believing that police departments should "maximize patrol coverage by replacing foot patrols with one-person auto patrols" (Dempsey 1999, p. 16). Moreover, he saw rapid response to calls as being the best means of measuring the effectiveness of police departments. As such, he developed workload formulas to measure calls for service versus reported crimes on each beat to guide deployment. Both of these views became leading principles guiding police management throughout the Reform Era.

J. Edgar Hoover: The FBI.   Even today, the name **J. Edgar Hoover** is synonymous with that of the FBI in the minds of many Americans. A firm believer in the need for professional law enforcement agencies, Hoover was largely responsible for developing the FBI National Academy in 1935, which is responsible for training police officers from around the country in specialized policing and investigation techniques. Hoover also was responsible for establishing the FBI Crime Laboratory, which, despite controversy surrounding the lab in the 1990s, is generally regarded as one of the best such laboratories in the world.[5] Hoover's other key achievements include the introduction of the FBI Uniform Crime Reports; the hiring of accountants and lawyers to serve as special agents; and the development of the FBI's Ten Most Wanted Criminals program.

Although Hoover is well regarded as a reformer and advocate of police professionalism, his reputation since his death has suffered considerably. There are many reasons for this, both professional and personal. On a professional note, Hoover has been accused of harassing alleged Communists, using domestic surveillance by the FBI during his time as head of the Bureau, suppressing information from the Warren Commission (the Commission that investigated the murder of John F. Kennedy), protecting individuals involved in organized crime from investigations, and mishandling royalty funds from books and movies (Gentry 1991).

On a personal level, there were many rumors about his sexual proclivities, including his possible homosexuality (despite his vehement opposition to homosexual relationships) and cross-dressing (Theoharis 1995). Some biographers speculate that his protection of organized crime families was the result of indecent photos they possessed of him and his sexual activity (Summers 1993). It might be beneficial to consider Hoover's harassment of alleged Communists and improper use of surveillance as we consider limits to law enforcement freedoms today in investigating alleged terrorists.

Chapter Summary

- The origins of social control date back to at least 2200 BC. The earliest known formal law is the Code of Hammurabi, which was the first set of laws to establish punishments for specific acts.

- Both England and the United States had informal systems of policing until the nineteenth century. The informal systems were based upon the concept of community responsibility. Neighbors would take turns watching each other's houses for protection. In the United States, there were vigilante committees in the frontier, composed of citizens who wanted to actively fight crime.

- The first formal police organization was the London Metropolitan Police, formed by Sir Robert Peel when he signed the Metropolitan Police Act 1829. This organization was governed by strict standards of conduct and discipline that were laid out in Peel's Principles of Policing. Many forces worldwide followed the military-like structure of the Metropolitan Police.

- Throughout the South (and in some Northern cities) policing focused on slave patrols. The primary purpose of these was to ensure that slaves did not escape from their masters and followed the rules. Once the slave codes were abolished, Jim Crow laws were formed. These required that a number of institutions, such as schools and parks, have "separate but equal" areas for blacks and whites.

- Kelling and Moore describe three eras of policing: the Political Era (characterized by corruption, decentralized structure, and an intimate relationship with the community); the Reform Era (characterized by professionalism, centralized structure, rapid response to calls, and poor relations with the community); and the Community Era (characterized by a focus on service to the community, going back to a decentralized force, and the use of foot patrols and problem-oriented policing).

- Policemen and policewomen have traditionally held very different roles (though their roles are now equal). Policewomen were originally hired as matrons and worked only with women and juveniles. Their roles were similar to that of a social worker, and their primary concern was the welfare of women and children in the community.

- In an effort to professionalize law enforcement and remove the political influences fueling corruption, the reform movement was born. August Vollmer, O. W. Wilson, and J. Edgar Hoover were at the forefront of these reform efforts.

Linking the Dots

1. What are the similarities between our current policing system and the watch system? The Code of Hammarabi?
2. In what way can policing be a political issue?
3. Why were there so few women and minority police officers at the turn of the century? Why are they still so underrepresented?
4. Is there a political/police figure today as groundbreaking as Robert Peel?
5. Would the U.S. system of policing work in England? Why or why not?

KEY TERMS

Bobbies 44	Order maintenance 50	Spoils system 49
Bow Street Runners 41	Sir Robert Peel 43	Tithings 40
Code of Hammurabi 38	Pendleton Act 49	Vigilante 39
Constables 40	Peterloo massacre of 1819 41	Vigilante committees 45
J. Edgar Hoover 53	Posse Comitatus Act 41	*Vigiles* 38
Hue and cry 41	Posses 40	August Vollmer 52
Jim Crow laws 47	Principles of Policing 43	Watch systems 45
Legalistic 50	Shire reeves 40	Wickersham Commission 50
Lex taliones 38	Shires 40	O. W. Wilson 53
Metropolitan Police Act 43	Slave patrols 46	

REFERENCES

The Columbia Encyclopedia, 6th ed. 2000. Farmington Hills, MI: Gale Group.

Conser, J. A., and G. D. Russell. 2000. *Law Enforcement in the United States*. Gaithersburg, MD: Aspen Publishers.

Dempsey, J. 1999. *An Introduction to Policing*. Belmont, CA: Wadsworth.

Gentry, C. 1991 J. *Edgar Hoover: The Man and the Secrets*. New York: W. W. Norton & Company.

Howe, R. 1965. *The Story of Scotland Yard*. New York: Horizon.

Kappeler, V. E. 1997. *Critical Issues in Police Civil Liability*, 2d ed. Prospect Heights, IL: Waveland Press.

Kelling, G. L., and M. H. Moore. 1991. "From Political to Reform to Community: The Evolving Strategy of the Police." In *Community Policing: Rhetoric or Reality*, edited by J. R. Greene and S. D. Mastrofsky. New York: Praeger.

National Commission on Law Observance and Enforcement. 1931. *Report on Lawlessness in Law Enforcement*. Washington, D.C.: National Commission on Law Observance and Enforcement.

Oxford English Dictionary. 1996. *Police*. Oxford: Oxford University Press.

Palmer, S. H. 1988. *Police and Protest in England and Ireland 1780–1850*. Cambridge: Cambridge University Press.

Plummer, A. 2005. "Bush Said 'Maybe' at the Time, but Rumsfeld Says 'No' on Posse Comitatus." *CQ Today*.

Reiner, R. 1994. *The Politics of the Police*, 2d ed. New York: Harvester.

Reppetto, T. A. 1978. *The Blue Parade*. New York: Free Press.

Schulz, D. M. 1995. *From Social Worker to Crime Fighter: Women in United States Municipal Policing*. Westport, CT: Praeger.

Silver, A. 1984. "The Demand for Order in Civil Society: A Review of Some Themes in the History of Crime, Police and Riot." In *The Police: Six Sociological Essays*, edited by D. Bordua, 1–24. New York: Wiley.

Stead, P. J. 1985. *The Police of Britain*. London: Macmillan Publishing Company.

Stein, J. 2006. "Fine Print in Defense Bill Opens Door to Martial Law." *CQ Homeland Security*. Available at http://public.cq.com/public/2006/201_homeland.html.

Sullivan, P. 1989. "Minority Officers: Current Issues." In *Critical Issues in Policing: Contemporary Readings*, edited by R. Dunham and G. Alpert, 331–345. Prospect Heights, IL: Waveland.

Summers, A. 1993. *Official and Confidential: The Secret Life of J. Edgar Hoover*. New York: Orion Publishing Group.

Tanner, A. R. 2003. "Crime Labs Stained by a Shadow of a Doubt." *LA Times*, July 13, AIS.

Theoharis, A. G. 1995. *J. Edgar Hoover: Sex and Crime*. Chicago: Ivan R. Dee, Inc.

Williams, R., and P. V. Murphy. 1990. *The Evolving Strategy of Police: A Minority View*. Washington, D.C.: U.S. Department of Justice.

Wood, B. 1984. *Slavery in Colonial Georgia*. Athens, GA: University of Georgia Press.

NOTES

1. See, e.g., www.met.police.uk/index.shtml.
2. For a thorough analysis of the history of British policing, see Palmer, S. H. (1988), *Police and Protest in England and Ireland 1780–1850*. Cambridge: Cambridge University Press.
3. *Plessy v. Ferguson*, 163 U.S. 537 (1896).
4. Jim Crow laws differed in each state. These are general examples of requirements of Jim Crow laws and are not specific to a particular state. For a summary of many laws by state, see www.nps.gov/malu/documents/jim_crow_laws.htm.
5. Contaminated evidence from the FBI Lab has been used to convict individual of serious violent crimes. See Tanner, A. R. 2003. "Crime Labs Stained by a Shadow of a Doubt." *LA Times*, July 13, A18.

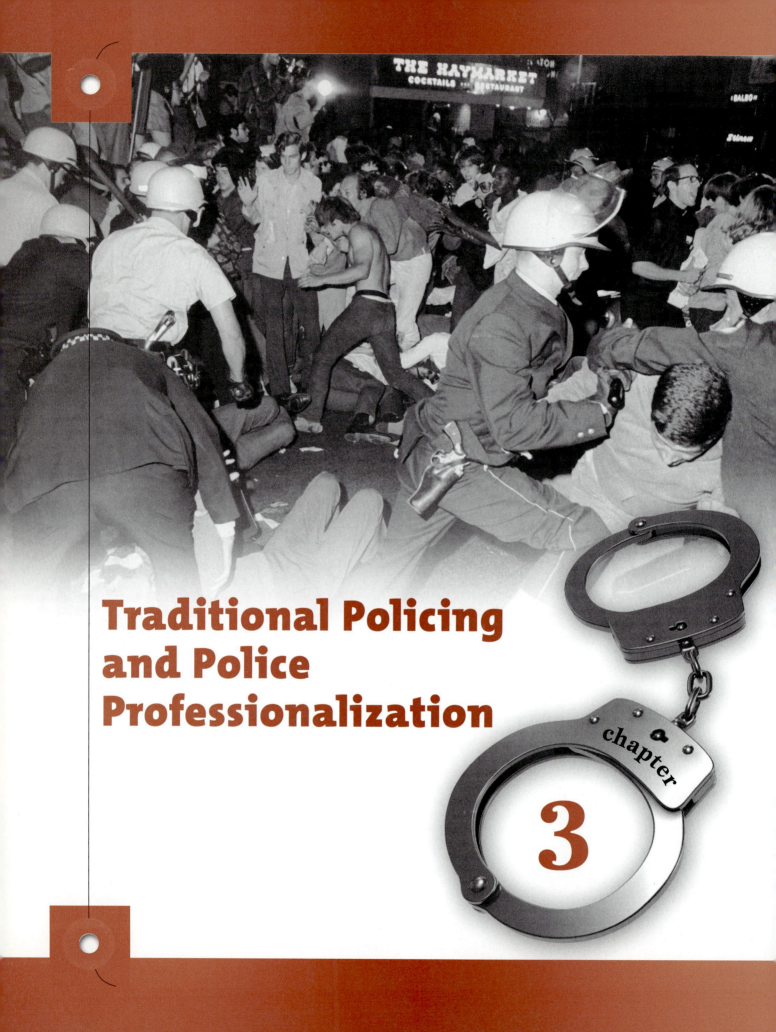

Traditional Policing and Police Professionalization

Chapter Objectives

- Discuss policing as a profession.

- Explain the effect of the Reform Era on crime rates, resource deployments, and police–community relations.

- Describe the UCR, analyze its limitations, and identify other instruments for counting crime.

- Compare the UCR and NIBRS in terms of similarities, differences, and effectiveness.

- Evaluate the effectiveness of the traditional model of policing that emerged from the Reform Era.

Introduction

> To the middle classes, the police wish to symbolize crime control (of the lower classes), while their actions toward the middle classes are in accord with the middle classes' general moral and social position (that is, they maintain good police/community relations). On the other hand, to the lower classes, the police wish to symbolize, at least on occasion, and as long as it is expedient (as long as there are federal dollars to support the programs), police/community relations, while their conduct is actually crime-repression oriented. (Manning 1977, p. 360)

This quote from the late 1970s emphasizes the new problems that arose from the reform movement in policing during the Reform Era. By the end of the Political Era, significant enthusiasm for reform had grown within policing circles. In an effort to correct the mistakes of the past, a new professionalism would be born that would take policing well into the twentieth century. But as with any new movement, even those fueled by a well-intentioned desire for change, there can be a danger of "throwing the baby out with the bathwater." In the desire to create an impartial and independent law enforcement profession that was truly "ruled by the law" and not the corruptive influences of the spoils system, the Reform Era sought to distance the officer from the political machine. An unfortunate by-product of these efforts involved an increasing alienation of the profession from the public, thereby affecting the very core of the Peelian Principles upon which modern policing was born.

As the quote by Manning suggests, the success of the reform movement in taking officers off the streets and into motor vehicle patrol would only serve to alienate segments of the community in the long run. As the focus of policing turned toward crime fighting, policing fell victim to the racial divide and political unrest of the tumultuous 1960s and 1970s. This led to violent clashes between the police and citizenry, and, ultimately, a need to reexamine the very foundations upon which the Reform Era was built.

This chapter examines the advances of the Reform Era, technological and otherwise, as well as their long-term effects on the policing profession. The reader is introduced to the birth of social science applications on policing policy and practice. Most important, the chapter provides readers with an analytical basis to learn from the lessons of policing's history and gain an understanding of what a twenty-first century police force should look like—a topic to which Section 4 is devoted.

The Rise of the Professional Model of Policing

Although paid professional police forces existed in the United States from 1844 onward, early attempts to professionalize the police benefited greatly from the work of August Vollmer, who was discussed in Chapter 2. According to Abadinsky and Winfree (1992), the key features of a professional police force, as imagined by the early reformers such as Vollmer, were as follows:

- Replacement of patronage systems with civil service
- Job security for police administrators and leaders
- Centralized policing and recordkeeping

Each of these principles represented positive attempts to move policing out of the political domination that had consumed its early developmental years. In fact, it is as a result of the efforts made by pioneers such as Vollmer that policing truly began to be capable of being considered a **profession** in the modern sense of the word. Although definitions vary somewhat, the following seven criteria must be met in order to qualify as a profession (Swanson et al. 2001, pp. 3–4):

1. An organized body of theoretically grounded knowledge
2. Advanced study
3. A code of ethics
4. Prestige
5. Standards of admission
6. A professional association
7. A service ideal

We will use these criteria to detail the successes of the Reform Era in modifying police practices.

Advanced Study

As described in Chapter 2, Vollmer began to include law, criminology, and police administration in police training as early as 1908. He also began to actively recruit people with college experience to the police force. Moreover, in a variety of ways he tried to advance the field through social science applications to policing, a path that O. W. Wilson would continue. To this end, he created the first scientific crime laboratory, mobile patrol, and lie detector. He also began to routinely conduct beat analysis.

In the 1960s, police departments began to require a high school degree or GED as a minimum entrance requirement. Some even began to require a college degree or credits toward one. The federal government also joined the push for more educated officers in 1964 with the funding of the **Law Enforcement Education Program (LEEP)**. Although LEEP would ultimately be phased out over time, it helped provide the impetus for police-related training/courses in academic institutions across the country by offering financing for criminal justice professionals seeking postsecondary educational opportunities.

The **National Institute of Justice (NIJ)** was created in 1960 as a research entity specifically targeting advanced study in the areas of policing and other areas of criminal justice. A part of the U.S. Department of Justice, its mission is to advance scientific research, development, and evaluation to enhance the administration of public safety both within the United States and internationally (U.S. Department of Justice, n.d.). Despite changing political and social contexts in law enforcement and criminal justice, NIJ continues to fund important law enforcement research.

The logic behind a push for higher education standards was based on the premise that educated officers would be better problem-solvers. In addition, community relations would be improved through officers' greater exposure to and appreciation for diversity as a result of the college experience, and corruption would decline. Some studies have demonstrated that officers with higher levels of education have in fact been associated with fewer citizen complaints and overall better performance than their non-college-educated counterparts (Bowker 1980; Sanderson 1977). Higher education has also been linked to fewer physical force allegations (Cascio 1977), as well as decreased incidence of citizen complaints, greater acceptance of minorities, and decreased use of discretionary arrests (Bowker 1980). Similar results have been reported with respect to ethical decision making and the influence of a college education, with the correlation between ethical decisions and a higher education being twelve times greater for police officers than a control group (Tyre and Braunstein 1992).

As evidence of the success of early reform efforts on the field of law enforcement, a recent national study of the educational levels of police officers in 3,000 state and local departments found that although only 1 percent of depart-

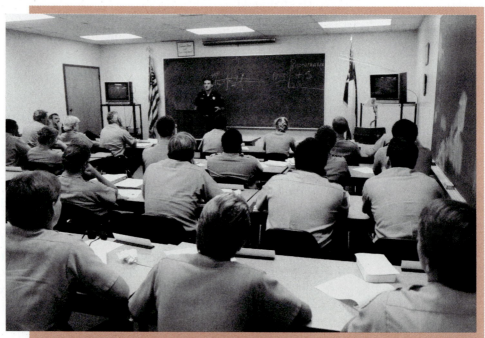

Police departments nationally are implementing higher educational standards for officers, and about one-third of officers nationally have some college education.

ments required a four-year college degree, 18 percent of departments required at least some college education. Nationally, 33 percent of officers were employed in a department with a college requirement. Moreover, 98 percent of departments had some form of an educational requirement; 81 percent required a high school diploma (Bureau of Justice Statistics 2006). Although some critics initially argued that higher educational standards would pose unfair additional barriers on minority recruits, this has not proven to be the case. Programs, such as the Cadets, continue to encourage the higher education of officers by paying for schooling with the promise of at least two to three years of committed service following degree attainment.

Code of Ethics

Beginning in the Reform Era, police departments began to recognize the need to create codes of ethics that could assist in educating officers about the organizational value systems and accountability mechanisms guiding behavior in the organization (Pollack 1993). Codes of ethics include provisions related to the service orientation of an agency, as well as statements formulated much like oaths of office related to corruption, integrity, and the use of force (see Figure 3.1 on page 64).

Although it is clear that formal codes of ethics assist departments in establishing appropriate accountability and education mechanisms, the formal code of conduct can be very different from the subcultural values of its officers, an issue discussed further in Chapter 9. In addition to individual codes of ethics developed by departments, in 1992 the International Association of Chiefs of Police (IACP) created a Law Enforcement Code of Ethics and the Police Code of Conduct to guide departments in the creation of their own.

Prestige

Prestige refers to the degree to which a profession is seen as desirable for employment or worthy of respect. Although prestige will clearly vary significantly from jurisdiction to jurisdiction, depending on factors such as the nature of police–community relations, educational requirements of officers, and local salary of sworn officers, some evidence indicates that the U.S. public views policing as an honest and desirable profession in comparison to others. In a 1995 poll of ethics and various professions, police received an 88 percent positive approval rating (Maguire and Pastore 1995). Business executives, lawyers, U.S. Senators, bankers, journalists, and numerous other professions ranked lower than law enforcement officers, thereby defying the premise that a high level of prestige is associated with a high salary. Such levels of support do, however, vary consistently by race, indicating an important need for concern, particularly where minority recruitment is seen as desirable. Fraternal organizations within police departments often seek to enhance the prestige of the profession within their communities to assist recruitment efforts.

Following explosive events involving the excessive use of force, studies have shown an unfortunate demoralizing effect of the resulting negative media coverage on officer morale. In contrast, some evidence suggests that the tragic events of September 11 led to an increase in the perceived prestige of law enforcement careers, leading to massive surges in applicants for criminal justice programs and agencies (Tyre 2001).

FIGURE 3.1

Example Codes of Ethics

Anaheim, California, Code of Ethics

As a law enforcement officer, my fundamental duty is to serve mankind; to safeguard lives and property; to protect the innocent against oppression or intimidation, and the peaceful against violence or disorder; and to respect the constitutional rights of all men to liberty, equality, and justice.

I will keep my private life unsullied as an example to all; maintain courageous calm in the face of danger, scorn, or ridicule; develop self-restraint; and be constantly mindful of the welfare of others. Honest in thought and deed in both my personal and official life, I will be exemplary in obeying the laws of the land and the regulations of my department. Whatever I see or hear of a confidential nature or that is confided to me in my official capacity will be kept ever secret unless revelation is necessary in the performance of my duty.

I will never act officiously or permit personal feelings, prejudices, animosities, or friendships to influence my decisions. With no compromise for crime and with relentless prosecution of criminals, I will enforce the law courteously and appropriately without fear or favor, malice or ill will, never employing unnecessary force or violence and never accepting gratuities.

I recognize the badge of my office as a symbol of public faith, and I accept it as a public trust to be held so long as I am true to the ethics of the police service. I will constantly strive to achieve these objectives and ideals, dedicating myself before God to my chosen profession—Law Enforcement.

—Adopted 1956

Mobile, Alabama, Code of Ethics

All sworn officers will abide by the following Law Enforcement Code of Ethics:

As a Law Enforcement Officer, I do solemnly swear that my fundamental duty is to serve the community; to safeguard lives and property; to protect the innocent against deception, the weak against oppression or intimidation, and the peaceful against violence or disorder; and to respect the Constitutional rights of all people to liberty, equality and justice.

I will keep my private life unsullied as an example to all and behave in a manner that does not bring discredit to me or to my agency. I will maintain courageous calm in the face of danger, scorn or ridicule; develop self-restraint; and be constantly mindful of the welfare of others. Honest in thought and deed in both my personal and official life, I will be exemplary in obeying the laws of the land and the regulations of my department. Whatever I see or hear of a confidential nature or that is confided to me in my official capacity will be kept ever secret unless revelation is necessary in the performance of my duty.

I will not act officiously or permit personal feelings, prejudices, political beliefs, aspirations, animosities or friendships to influence my decisions. With no compromise for crime and with relentless prosecution of criminals, I will enforce the law courteously and appropriately, without fear or favor, malice or ill will, never employing unnecessary force or violence and never accepting gratuities.

I recognize the badge of my office as a symbol of public faith, and I accept it as a public trust to be held so long as I am true to the ethics of the police service. I will never engage in acts of corruption or bribery, nor will I condone such acts by other officers. I will cooperate with all legally authorized agencies and their representatives in the pursuit of justice.

I know that I alone am responsible for my standard of professional performance and will take every reasonable opportunity to enhance and improve my level of knowledge and competence.

I will constantly strive to achieve these objectives and ideals, dedicating myself before God to my chosen profession . . . law enforcement.

I do further swear that I will support the Constitution of the United States and the Constitution of the State of Alabama, that I will faithfully enforce the laws of this state and ordinances of the City of Mobile, and perform the duties of a police officer to the best of my ability. I will obey the rules and regulations of the department and carry out all orders which may be lawfully given me by my superior officers.

I do further swear that I accept this oath as a police officer subject to all the limitations, conditions, and restrictions imposed by the City of Mobile, the ordinances of the City of Mobile, and the regulations or the Police Department.

Source: Reprinted from Law Enforcement Code of Ethics. Copyright held by the International Association of Chiefs of Police, 515 North Washington Street, Alexandria, VA 22314 USA. Further reproduction without express written permission from IACP is strictly prohibited. Reprinted by permission of the IACP and the Mobile Police Department.

Standards of Admission

In addition to an increase in minimum educational levels during the Reform Era, departments began to conduct thorough character and background investigations as part of the selection process, including the use of psychological testing. The logic for such reforms is of course that a professional force requires high-caliber applicants. Over time, these requirements have seen modifications to the extent that high-quality candidates were being disproportionately excluded from the force based on standards of admission that had no meaningful relationship to on-the-job performance. Chapter 14 details the recruitment and selection process; Figure 3.2 lists common standards of admission.

Professional Associations

One of the first attempts to professionalize the police came with the creation of a professional society known as the **International Association of Chiefs of Police (IACP)**. The group's first meeting was held in Chicago in 1893 and was attended by 51 police chiefs. Initially calling itself the National Chiefs of Police Union, it changed its name to IACP in 1902. From the outset, IACP was devoted to the creation of a professional police force bound by civil service conventions and rules and free from political control and corruption.

Policewomen also founded their own organization around this time. In 1915, Alice Stebbin Wells, appointed in 1910 as the first policewoman in the

FIGURE 3.2

Standards of Admission

Requirements vary from state to state and from jurisdiction to jurisdiction. However, most recruitment standards have provisions for the following characteristics:

Minimum age: Eighteen at time of first application and 21 at time of hire.

Minimum education: High school graduation or G.E.D. equivalency and two or more college courses by date of hire or two years of experience in military police.

Citizenship: U.S. citizenship (at hire or in some states within two years of hire).

Background: No felony or misdemeanor convictions (other than traffic violations) that would make it illegal to carry a gun or that involve perjury, false statement, moral turpitude, or domestic violence. No history of criminal or improper conduct. No poor employment, military, or driving record that would affect law enforcement work. Valid driver's license. Responsible financial history. Good moral character.

Health: Good health with no conditions that would restrict ability to perform all aspects of police work. Vision and hearing must be tested and successfully corrected, if necessary; color blindness can be disqualifying. Weight must be proportional to height. There is no height requirement.

Tests: Written civil service examination, medical examination, psychological examination, test of physical fitness or agility, voice stress analysis or polygraph test, drug tests. Background and character investigation. Interview. Employment often is conditional on further testing during the periods of orientation, training, and probation as a police recruit.

Residency: Becoming a resident in the jurisdiction of hire is a requirement. (The range of residency boundaries can very significantly by jurisdiction.)

United States, founded the **International Association of Policewomen (IAP)**. Wells and other policewomen formed the IAP out of the National Conference of Charities and Correction (NCCC) in order to address issues of police professionalism and the work of policewomen in the social services (Schulz 1995). One of the primary purposes of the IAP was to promote higher educational entry standards and higher work standards in the field. Although some male police chiefs, such as August Vollmer, supported the idea of higher entry standards for men and women alike, other police chiefs disagreed, and as a result women had higher educational entry standards than men until 1972. After a surge of economic and social momentum from 1924 to 1928, the IAP eventually disbanded in 1932, and the IACP was the sole national organization for police managers.[1]

Although the IACP was initially established to serve as a voluntary organization for police managers, it soon began to provide specific support services, such as technical assistance and training for local police, and a central clearinghouse for criminal identification records (Abidinsky and Winfree 1992). To this day, IACP remains one of the leading police organizations in the United States, but it is now joined by other police research entities such as the Police Executive Research Forum (PERF) and the Police Foundation.

Also essential in the process of "professionalizing" the police was the establishment of the **Commission for the Accreditation of Law Enforcement Agencies (CALEA)**. CALEA standards stress the importance of the law enforcement agencies being run according to the traditional criteria for professionalization: centralization, tall hierarchies, and narrowed discretion (Swanson et al. 2001). The core foundation across the CALEA standards is accountability; in part, accreditation can actually serve as a shield to a department under some civil liability issues. The procedure for becoming accredited first involves the agency conducting its own self-assessment, prior to a site visit review by the CALEA. Individual officers can also now be accredited in much the same way as their agency through the National Law Enforcement Credentialing Board (NLECB) (Hill 1999).

Today, many professional organizations are available to police officers. Figure 3.3 provides just a sample of these.

A Service Ideal

Although the professionalization movement stressed a focus on crime control rather than the service to the community ideals that are characteristic of the Community Era, policing still had a strong service ideal, albeit with a different focus. As outlined years earlier in the work of O. W. Wilson, an agency would measure the quality of its service according to the speed of its response time and the efficiency with which an incident was handled. Chapter 6 discusses the impact of response time on criminal justice outcomes. By the 1980s, however, clashes between the police and community made it clear that having a true service ideal, in which professionalism includes the provision of services outside of the traditional crime control focus of law enforcement, became apparent. As a result, police–community relations programs became more prominent throughout the late 1970s and early 1980s until police leaders began to argue that these only served a very basic public relations mechanism that would ultimately do little for reducing crime over the long term or even significantly enhancing police relations with the community. Despite the successes of so-called crime preven-

FIGURE 3.3

Police Professional Organizations

The Bellingham, Washington, Police Department belongs to the following professional organizations (www.cob.org/police/source/htm/pro_orgs.htm):

- International Association of Chiefs of Police (IACP)
- Western States Hostage Negotiators Association (WSHNA)
- American Polygraph Association (APA)
- National Tactical Officers Association (NTOA)
- Washington State Tactical Officers Association (WSTOA)
- Washington Law Enforcement Explorer Advisors
- International Association of Bomb Technicians and Investigators (IABTI)

The following list shows examples of national professional organizations and associations that law enforcement officers can choose to participate in independently of their police or sheriff's departments. Similar professional organizations exist for law enforcement officers in specific regions, states, counties, and cities, as well as for other specialties within law enforcement, such as juvenile officers, narcotics officers, and specialists in forensic investigation and analysis.

- American Criminal Justice Association
- American Jail Association
- Fraternal Order of Police
- Association of Certified Fraud Specialists
- International Association of Undercover Officers
- International Union of Police Associations
- Ranger
- Police Athletic League
- Patrolmen's Benevolent Association
- National Sheriff's Association

tion units and media campaigns in some jurisdictions, creating a special unit with the responsibility for effective community relations had four adverse consequences, according to Moore (1992, p. 135):

- Isolating the special unit made it vulnerable to organizational ridicule.
- The presence of the unit created the perception amongst others in the department that they were free from the responsibility of enhancing community relations.
- Even where such units might gain important information about community concerns it would be difficult to make this heard in the rest of the department.
- The organization becomes stagnant and refrains from seeking other new and innovative ways to improve police–community relations.

Police leaders and scholars began to argue for increased partnerships with the community in enhancing the quality of life, a mandate that would be met with varying successes as the profession entered the Community Era, which is discussed in the remaining chapters of the text, primarily in Section 4.

Crime Control as a Focal Concern: Implications for Resource Deployment

As noted, with professionalization and the development of new policing models police departments began to have a narrow focus on crime control, believing that department policy should be driven strictly by the enforcement of the law as measured by the reduction of crime rates. The fear of corruption resulting from officers becoming too close to the community residents they serve resulted in emphasis being taken away from foot patrol and redirected to random motor vehicle patrol, made possible by increasing automotive and communications technology throughout this era of policing. Incident response time became a central focus of concern with what would later be named **traditional policing**, leading to the development of **reactive models** for resource deployment. Criminal investigation and **clearance rates** also are important priorities in the traditional professional model of policing. Clearance rate refers to the ratio of solved to unsolved cases that are reported to a particular law enforcement agency. Given the tremendous impact crime measurement had on law enforcement beginning in this era, significant attention will now be paid to the evolution of how crime is measured.

Counting Crime: The Uniform Crime Reports

Traditional policing emphasized crime reduction or the elimination of crime in a jurisdiction; therefore, another important measure of departmental effectiveness is the police's ability to reduce crime within the jurisdiction, in addition to always getting to the call quickly. Measuring and tracking crime trends became possible during the Reform Era through the creation of the **Uniform Crime Reports (UCR)**.

The seeds for the UCR were planted in the 1920s when the IACP created a committee to study crime records in the United States (O'Brien 1985). By the end of the 1920s, the FBI began to compile data given to them by local police departments, and in the mid-1930s Congress passed a bill requiring the FBI to compile national crime statistics. To address this responsibility, the UCR was born. With its emphasis on crime data measurement and mechanisms for comparing the rates of law enforcement jurisdictions nationally, police departments began to use crime statistics as a key organizational performance measure throughout the Reform Era, again contributing to the redefinition of law enforcement agencies as being strictly about crime control.

Response Rate   The UCR is compiled annually by the FBI and today contains data from approximately 17,000 local police departments, covering 97 percent of the total population (Maltz 1999). This is a significantly high response rate given the fact that it is voluntary for law enforcement agencies to report their data to the FBI. For the "gap" data, or that which is not reported, the FBI uses various estimates and proxies.

Structure of the UCR   The UCR divides offenses into two major categories: **Part I Index Crimes** and **Part II Index Crimes**. Part I offenses include four **violent personal crimes**—murder, rape, robbery, and aggravated assault—and four **property crimes**—burglary, larceny, motor vehicle theft, and arson. These offenses and their definitions are outlined in Table 3.1.

Part II offenses include all other crimes, including forgery, fraud, embezzlement, vandalism, weapons (carrying/possession), gambling, sex offenses (other than forcible rape, prostitution), drug abuse, disorderly conduct, and so on. Generally speaking, the more serious offenses as determined by legislatures, fear of crime, and public opinion have been classified as Part I crimes. However, some serious offenses, such as kidnapping, are classified as Part II offenses for the purposes of the UCR.

The UCR includes information about all offenses known to the police, including those cleared by arrest or exceptional means. **Cleared crimes** are those for which an arrest has been made or a person charged. Cleared crimes also are referred to as being "solved," although they may not have been adjudicated yet. **Exceptional clearance** refers to a situation whereby the offender's identity has been established and there is enough information to support an arrest, but for some reason the suspect has not been or cannot be arrested (e.g., the suspect has died).

Calculating Crime Indices   Given the tremendous diversity in size of jurisdictions across departments, the annual data contained in the UCR could not be meaningfully compared across locations without the calculation of **crime indices**. The crime index for a given crime in any jurisdiction is calculated by dividing the total reported crimes by the total population of the reporting area,

TABLE 3.1

UCR Index Offenses

Offense	Description
Crimes Against Persons—Violent Crime	
Murder	Willful killing of a human by another human.
Aggravated Assault	Severe bodily harm; a weapon often is involved.
Rape	Having sexual intercourse with a female through the use or threat of force.
Robbery	Stealing or taking anything of value from the care, custody, or control of a person by force or threat of force.
Crimes Against Property	
Burglary	Unlawful entry into a building to commit theft or another felony.
Larceny/theft	Unlawful taking and removing another's personal property with the intent of permanently removing it.
Motor vehicle theft	Unlawful taking or stealing of a motor vehicle without the authority or permission of the owner.
Arson	Intentionally damaging or destroying or attempting to damage or destroy by means of fire, with or without the intent to defraud.

then multiplying by a 100,000 (the index). For instance, if 50 robberies occurred in one year in a city of 10,000 people, the crime rate would be 500 robberies per 100,000 people. This rate could then be compared to robberies in a city of any size (see Figure 3.4).

Limitations of the UCR as a Measure of Crime   When the UCR was established, it appeared to be the most effective method by which general crime data could be analyzed. However, by the end of the 1970s it was clear that the UCR needed to be completely revised to provide analysis of emerging issues such as domestic violence and hate crimes. The eight summary index offenses used by

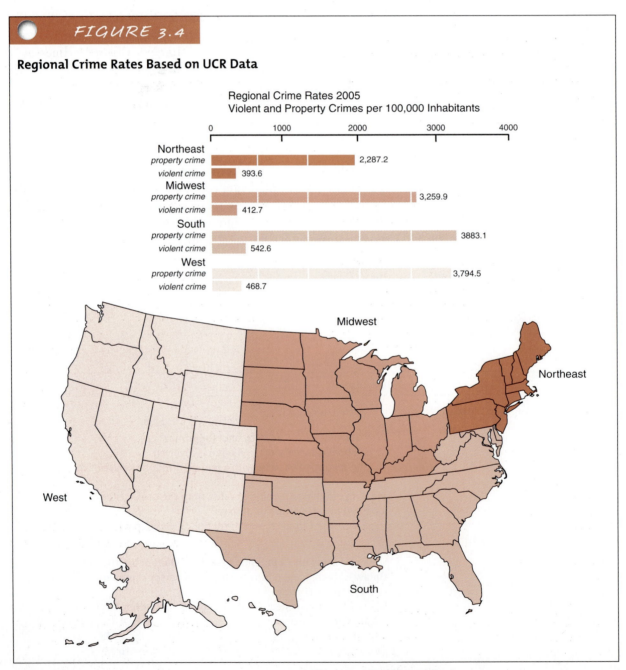

FIGURE 3.4

Regional Crime Rates Based on UCR Data

Regional Crime Rates 2005
Violent and Property Crimes per 100,000 Inhabitants

Northeast
property crime — 2,287.2
violent crime — 393.6

Midwest
property crime — 3,259.9
violent crime — 412.7

South
property crime — 3883.1
violent crime — 542.6

West
property crime — 3,794.5
violent crime — 468.7

Source: UCR data at www.fbi.gov/ucr/05cius/offenses/standard_links/regional_estimates.html

the UCR were not able to show the complexities of crimes, particularly with regard to issues such as domestic terrorism, and the UCR no longer seemed capable of capturing the changing trends in crime. In order to address these inadequacies, the FBI and the Bureau of Justice Statistics began a reevaluation of the UCR in 1982. They produced a report in 1986 based upon their evaluation, called the *Blueprint for the Future of the UCR Program*, which set out suggestions for a new design and additional reporting requirements.

One major limitation of the UCR as a measure of total crime is its reliance on officially **reported crime**, or crimes brought to the attention of the police. A crime must be reported to the police in the form of a compliant or a call for service to be compiled by the UCR (U.S. Department of Justice 2004). As such, it will always underestimate the total volume of crime, because crime is significantly underreported.

The UCR is also limited by the application of the **hierarchy rule**. In a multiple-offense situation where more than one offense is committed at the same time and place, the UCR only scores the highest-ranking offense and ignores all others, regardless of the number of victims or offenders. So if a man were to break into a house, rape a woman who lives there, and steal her purse, only the rape would be reported (and not the burglary). Justifiable homicide, motor vehicle theft, and arson are the only exceptions to the hierarchy rule; they can be counted along with the other most serious offenses within an incident.

The UCR is also limited by the fact that the offense definitions used in the report often do not correspond with federal and state statutes. For example, many states acknowledge that a man can be the victim of rape, but according to UCR definitions, such a case would be classified as a Part II sexual offense (i.e., a less serious assault) instead of a Part I forcible rape. Also important is the role that discretionary error can play in limiting the accuracy of UCR data. The police report could classify an offense incorrectly or the departmental data clerk may make an error in coding the data. Although many departments have greatly enhanced their data collection/analysis capacities in recent years, for many departments the UCR coding process remains a manual effort coded from the original police report.

The Dark Figure of Crime

The UCR has been a primary resource for law enforcement professionals for many years, but given the limitations just outlined it is clear that it alone does not provide a completely accurate picture of total crime in the country. Crime data from law enforcement agencies, such as those reported by the UCR, require that an incident has first made it to the attention of the police. Crimes are not reported for a variety of reasons, such as poor trust of police in minority communities, shame associated with offenses such as rape or domestic violence, a perception that the police cannot do anything, and so on. The level of unreported crime is referred to as the **dark figure of crime**.

To gain a closer understanding of the magnitude of the dark figure of crime, beginning in 1972 the Bureau of Justice Statistics (BJS), in collaboration with the Census Bureau, began to conduct an annual survey of a representative sample of approximately 49,000 households for respondents over twelve years old. Referred to as the **National Crime Victimization Survey (NCVS)**, the survey

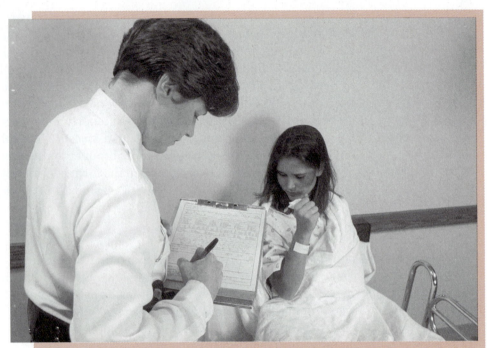

In an effort to understand more about which crimes are underreported, why, and by how much, researchers from the Bureau of Justice Statistics conduct the National Crime Victimization Survey.

collects self-report data on all crimes against individuals or households, regardless of whether they were reported to the police.

Of importance is the amount of incident-level data, or crime details, that can be collected, such as victim and offender age, race, ethnicity, sex, marital status, the involvement of substance use, victim-offender relationship, use of weapons, time and place, and so on. The NCVS indicates that only about 41 percent of all crime is reported to the police (Bureau of Justice Statistics 2005).

Of course, the NCVS is not without its own limitations, not the least of which is the reliability of self-reported data. Because the survey asks respondents to report all crimes that have occurred in their lives within the last 6 months, **telescoping** might occur in which serious incidents might be remembered as more recent to the victim than they really are, leading to an over-reporting in the data. The opposite could be true, too. In addition, self-reporting can lead to misidentification of certain crimes (e.g., a rape victim who does not realize that anal penetration can be classified as rape in some jurisdictions may misreport the offense as an assault or some less serious offense).

The FBI also is trying to improve the UCR to obtain a more accurate picture of the volume and nature of crime in the United States. In so doing, it has created the **National Incident Based Reporting System (NIBRS)**. It is meant to replace the UCR eventually. Police departments, however, have been very slow to switch over to the more detailed format of the NIBRS.

Measuring the Effectiveness of the Traditional Model of Policing

The Reform Era brought with it many important lasting advances, such as technological developments, greater use of research findings, and an improvement in the status and representation of women and minorities in police departments

Linkages *in Law Enforcement*

Incident-Based Reporting and the National Incident-Based Reporting System (NIBRS)

The FBI first implemented the National Incident-Based Reporting System (NIBRS) in 1989 as a means of improving existing statistical reporting and crime analysis standards nationally (Grant 2005). Unlike the UCR, NIBRS is an incident-based reporting system. NIBRS reporting guidelines define an *incident* as "one or more offenses committed by the same offender or group of offenders *acting in concert*, and *at the same time and place*." This broad definition allows for the calculation of multiple offenses, multiple victims, multiple offenders, and multiple arrests within a single incident, as well as counting completed and attempted crimes. In defining "same time and place," the NIBRS requires that the time and distance between incidents be minimal. "Acting in concert" requires that each of the perpetrators be actively involved in the commission of the crime or assistance in it. If *all* offenders are not involved in the commission of *all* the offenses in the series, then more than one incident is said to be involved. This definition requires that all actions be counted in crime statistics, thereby abolishing the hierarchy rule used in the UCR.

To calculate crime rates, NIBRS utilizes detailed data on offenders, victims, locations, properties, and arrests on each single crime incident. NIBRS data are divided into two categories: Group A and Group B crimes. Group A is made up of twenty-two offense categories, with forty-six specific crimes; Group B is composed of arrest data for eleven additional offense categories. Because of the level of detail in the data, NIBRS offers law enforcement, legislators, and policy makers increased understanding of national crime trends. Unlike the UCR, NIBRS can offer insight into offenses such as gang-related crimes, domestic violence, weapons violations, drug offenses, elder abuse, and bias crimes.

One of the most basic modifications from the old system to the new *Blueprint* was a recognition that a crime data analysis system should be incident based, because incident-based crime analysis is integral to proactive police management. Without an incident-based system, police managers would be hampered in their tactical decision making, strategic planning, and research based on the specific characteristics of the offender, victim, property stolen, and location of the crime. In order to address some of the problems with the UCR's summary reporting format, the FBI created NIBRS. Despite the enhanced benefit of having a standardized incident-based reporting system, NIBRS is complicated due to the addition of offense types and incident-based reporting and has taken a long time to implement.

Despite difficulties with its implementation, NIBRS is a significant improvement over the UCR in accuracy of statistics and understanding of crime. Unlike with the UCR summary format, NIBRS data are collected on individual offender and victim characteristics for all Group A offenses, not just homicide and rape. This allows for the calculation of offending and victimization rates by the type of offense involved. Additionally, annual changes in the number of offenders and victims are now possible rather than simply raw counts of offenses.

The most important result of the implementation of NIBRS is that it allows for a detailed analysis at the incident level, thereby creating a common denominator of information that can be shared between agencies. This will create opportunities for regional and local law enforcement agencies to implement for proactive strategic and tactical planning and problem identification. Thus, NIBRS offers far greater practical information and may be used as an additional tool against linkage blindness.

QUESTIONS

1. Explain the benefits of NIBRS in understanding sexual offenses, homicide, and hate crimes.

2. What are the key obstacles in fully implementing NIBRS? Explain how the obstacles can be overcome.

(detailed in Chapters 10 and 14). However, despite such achievements, several important challenges surfaced during this period that revealed a serious need for the law enforcement profession to reanalyze itself and its direction, possibly returning to previous policies and strategies while at the same time working to integrate these with the important things the field had gained/learned through the process of professionalization.

Rising Crime Rates

Law enforcement agencies had a rejuvenated sense of their role as crime fighters during the Reform Era, moving away from simply "trying to keep a handle on things," or the **order maintenance** that was characteristic of the Political Era. As such, a great deal of attention was paid to overall trends in crime, made possible through the use of such mechanisms as the UCR. Although the period included many tumultuous events out of the immediate control of the police, such as the civil rights movement and the Vietnam War, crime rates continued to rise dramatically throughout the period, demonstrating that if law enforcement agencies wanted to hold themselves accountable for crime reductions they would have to move from a reactive to a more **proactive** stance (e.g., act before the problem occurs) and develop new strategies and collaborative partnerships. This theme will be explored throughout the remaining sections of this text, laying the groundwork for the shift to the Community Era.

Traditional Strategies

Much patrol work was carried out behind the wheel of a car during the Reform Era, based on the belief that random patrol could deter crime by its presence alone. This strategy also seemed perfectly suited to the police need to always be available to respond quickly to incoming calls for service. However, despite the central role that random patrol played in policing throughout this period, the now famous Kansas City Preventive Patrol Experiment found that it made no significant difference to crime reduction, fear of crime, or even response time (Kelling et al. 1974). This study, its implications, and limitations will be detailed in Chapter 6.

Just a year after the Kansas City Experiment, the traditional policing model took another serious blow with the Rand Corporation's finding that much of the investigative function is ineffectual, and that the patrol function may actually be more responsible for clearances than the investigative units (Chaiken et al. 1975). Given the traditional model's reliance on the criminal investigative function, here, too, was another major study that left police administrators and academics looking for new solutions to old problems. The Rand Study will be a focal point of Chapter 8.

Both the Kansas City and the Rand study challenged a reactive mode of thinking that had dominated the law enforcement field for decades. However, getting the bureaucracy of law enforcement to accept a paradigm shift can be a slow process, which we will document throughout the remainder of the text's chapters.

Police–Community Relations

It has been argued that during the Reform Era officers became more remote and "independent" from the community, and as a result the relationship between law enforcement and the community became increasingly hostile. This is the period of civil disobedience with the Vietnam War protests and the race riots of Detroit, Watts, Harlem, and Newark. It was readily apparent that the police

---

FIGURE 3.5

Time Line for the Reform Era

1893	First meeting of the National Association of Chiefs of Police.
1905–1932	Police reformer August Vollmer in Berkeley, CA.
1924–1973	J. Edgar Hoover is Director of the FBI.
1930s	The FBI National Academy, Crime Laboratory, and *Uniform Crime Reports* are founded.
1950; 1957	*Police Administration* and *Police Planning* by Vollmer's protégé O. W. Wilson become classics in law enforcement.
1950s and 1960s	Civil Rights protests; race riots in Detroit, Watts, Harlem, Newark.
1960	National Institute of Justice (NIJ) is founded.
1964	Law Enforcement Education Program (LEEP) is funded.
1960s and 1970s	Anti-Vietnam War protests and War on Drugs.
1974	Results of the Kansas City Preventive Patrol Experiment are presented.
1975	Results of the Rand Study of Detectives are released.
1980s	Crack epidemic hits major urban areas.

---

were not considered to be "of the people and for the people," particularly in certain neighborhoods. The analogy of there being "two America's" was a reality for the law enforcement officer. Moreover, because the civil rights and war protests brought the police into clashes with even middle class youths and families, there became an even stronger call for change and collaboration with the community. Chapter 12 will expand on these issues and the development toward a return to Peelian principles of "community policing." However, it should be noted here that evidence indicates serious flaws in the traditional model of policing.

Back to Basics—The Beginnings of the Community Era of Policing

In the Reform Era, policing in the United States evolved into the paramilitary structure that we know today. The origins of the centralized, hierarchical departmental structures common throughout the country are found in a desire to create professional, accountable models for law enforcement. With varying degrees of success, this was achieved. Moreover, the technological advances of the era, such as crime data collection, sophisticated calls for service mechanisms, automobile patrol, and communication improvements, helped to drive a law enforcement emphasis based on quick response to crime incidents and decreasing crime rates.

This chapter opened with the argument that with the desire for reform in any profession, there can be a tendency to "throw the baby out with the bathwater." In this case, the police officer of the Political Era was embedded in the political contexts of his beat, often even residing in the same area he policed. As such, policing had a much greater service orientation with respect to community needs. However, this orientation came with a serious price in the tremendous opportunities it created for corruption and brutality.

Community-policing advocates argued for a return to decentralized policing, sending officers into the community so that they would once again "be of the people" and focus on community service needs. With this call for a community-based approach, policing once emphasized the foot patrol. Some argued that policing had to "return to its roots." The remainder of this text will discuss ways in which this movement occurred.

However, note that the same risks of "throwing the baby out with the bathwater" can be true of Community Era reforms as well. Turning policing into a proactive force seeking to address the underlying causes of crime in collaboration with the community is an important and useful emphasis of the Community Era. Improving police–community relations is an essential ingredient of truly being able to accomplish professional law enforcement goals. However, at the same time, the lessons gained and structures created with respect to accountability and technology should be drawn upon and reformed, rather than thrown out altogether. In calls for decentralization and increased officer discretion, the realities of corruption and brutality should be factored into any implementation. Foot patrol and the response needs and mobility issues of the motor vehicle patrol must be balanced.

The Community Era offers tremendous potential in its ability to draw upon the best of both eras. Even with a changing global context, whereby public safety needs once again rise to the surface, proactive policing models that are in touch with the community offer the greatest chance for a safe environment while maintaining fair and effective law enforcement.

Chapter Summary

- During the Reform Era, law enforcement was increasingly viewed as a profession. An organization is considered to be a profession if it meets the seven-prong test of professionalism. A profession has an organized body of theoretically grounded knowledge, advanced study, a code of ethics, prestige, standards of admission, a professional association, and a service ideal.

- Key reformers were August Vollmer (called the father of police professionalism, leading the way with studies using the scientific method); O. W. Wilson (Vollmer's protégé, credited as one of the most influential writers

- on policing); J. Edgar Hoover (he professionalized the FBI and made it a respectable organization).

- Though the police became more professional during the Reform Era, crime rates actually increased. Additionally, police–community relations became strained due to the lack of communication between the police and the community.

- The primary source of criminal statistical data is the UCR. However, the UCR has two serious limitations. First, it only measures reported crime; and, crime is seriously underreported. Second, it conforms to the hierarchy rule, meaning that only the most serious offense is calculated if more than one offense is committed at a given time by one person.

- The focus of the Reform Era was to professionalize the police, taking them out of the community and putting them in motorized patrol. During the Political Era, police officers conducted foot patrols and had an intimate relationship with the community. Though the intimate relationship with the community was beneficial, it also led to corruption. In order to reduce corruption and increase efficiency, officers were removed from the beat, and police–community relations were strained further.

Linking the Dots

1. Despite its weaknesses, what are the benefits of analyzing UCR statistics?

2. Compared to professions such as law, medicine, and accounting, do you consider policing to be a profession? Why or why not? What criteria do you use to make your determination?

3. Studies indicate that patrol does not reduce crime or fear of crime. Why do you suppose that is the case?

4. How can police officers improve their relationship with the public while avoiding the corruption that was rampant during the Political Era?

KEY TERMS

Clearance rate   68
Cleared crimes   69
Commission for the Accreditation of Law Enforcement Agencies (CALEA)   66
Crime indices   69
Dark figure of crime   71
Exceptional clearance   69
Hierarchy rule   71
International Association of Chiefs of Police (IACP)   65

International Association of Policewomen (IAP)   66
Law Enforcement Education Program (LEEP)   61
National Crime Victimization Survey (NCVS)   71
National Incident-Based Reporting System (NIBRS)   72
National Institute of Justice (NIJ)   62
Order maintenance   74

Part I Index Crimes   69
Part II Index Crimes   69
Proactive   74
Profession   61
Property crimes   69
Reactive model   68
Reported crime   71
Telescoping   72
Traditional policing   68
Uniform Crime Reports (UCR)   68
Violent personal crimes   69

REFERENCES

Abadinsky, H., and L. Thomas Winfree, Jr. 1992. *Crime and Justice: An Introduction*. Chicago: Nelson Hall Publishers.

Bowker, L. 1980. "A Theory of Educational Needs of Law Enforcement Officers." *Journal of Contemporary Criminal Justice* 1(4):17–24.

Bureau of Justice Statistics. 2003. *Reporting Crime to the Police, 1992–2000*. Washington, D.C.: U.S. Department of Justice, Office of Justice Protection.

Bureau of Justice Statistics. 2005. *Criminal Victimization in the United States*. Washington, D.C.: U.S. Department of Justice, Office of Justice Programs.

Bureau of Justice Statistics. 2006. *Local Police Departments, 2003*. Washington, D.C.: Bureau of Justice Statistics.

Cascio, W. 1977. "Formal Education and Police Officer Performance." *Journal of Police Science and Administration* 5(1):89–96.

Chaiken, J., P. Greenwood, and J. Petersilia. 1975. "The Rand Study of Detectives." *Journal of Policy Analysis and Management* 3(2):187–217.

Grant, H. 2005. "The National Incident-Based Reporting System." In *Encyclopedia of Law Enforcement*, edited by L. Sullivan, D. M. Schulz, and M. Haberfeld. Thousand Oaks, CA: Sage.

Hill, S. 1999. "The Significance of Credentialing." *Police* 23(8):40–42.

Kelling, G., T. Pate, D. Diekman, and C. Brown. 1974. *The Kansas City Preventive Patrol Experiment: A Summary Report*. Washington, D.C.: The Police Foundation.

Maguire, K., and A. Pastore, eds. 1995. *Sourcebook of Criminal Justice Statistics—1995*. Washington, D.C.: National Institute of Justice.

Maltz, M. D. 1999. *Bridging Gaps in Police Crime Data: A Discussion Paper from the BJS Fellows Program*. Washington, D.C.: U.S. Department of Justice.

Manning, P. 1977. *Police Work: Essays on the Social Organization of Policing*. Cambridge, MA: MIT Press.

Moore, M. H. 1992. "Problem-solving and Community Policing." In *Modern Policing*, edited by M. Tonry and N. Morris, 293–338. Chicago: University of Chicago Press.

O'Brien, D. M. 1985. *Civil Rights and Civil Liberties*, vol. 2. New York: W. W. Norton & Company.

Pollack, J. 1993. *Ethics in Crime and Justice: Dilemmas and Decisions*, 3rd ed. Belmont, CA: Wadsworth.

Sanderson, B. 1977. "Police Officers: The Relationship of a College Education to Job Performance." *Police Chief* 44(11):62.

Schulz, D. M. 1995. *From Social Worker to Crime Fighter: Women in the United States Municipal Policing*. Westport, CT: Praeger.

Swanson, C., L. Territo, and R. Taylor. 2001. *Police Administration: Structures, Processes, and Behavior*, 5th ed. Upper Saddle River, NJ: Prentice Hall.

Tyre, P. 2001. "Turning John Jay into Terrorism U." *Newsweek*, November 12, 52.

Tyre, M., and S. Braunstein. 1992. "Higher Education and Ethical Policing." *FBI Law Enforcement Bulletin*, June, 6–10.

U.S. Department of Justice. 2000. *National Incident-Based Reporting System: Vol. 1: Data Collection Guidelines*. Washington, D.C.: U.S. Department of Justice.

U.S. Department of Justice. n.d. *National Institute of Justice: About NIJ* Available at www.ojp.usdoj.gov/nij/about.htm.

U.S. Department of Justice. 2004. *Uniform Crime Reporting Handbook*. Washington, D.C.: Federal Bureau of Investigation.

NOTE

1. See Schulz (1995) for a detailed overview of the history of women in policing.

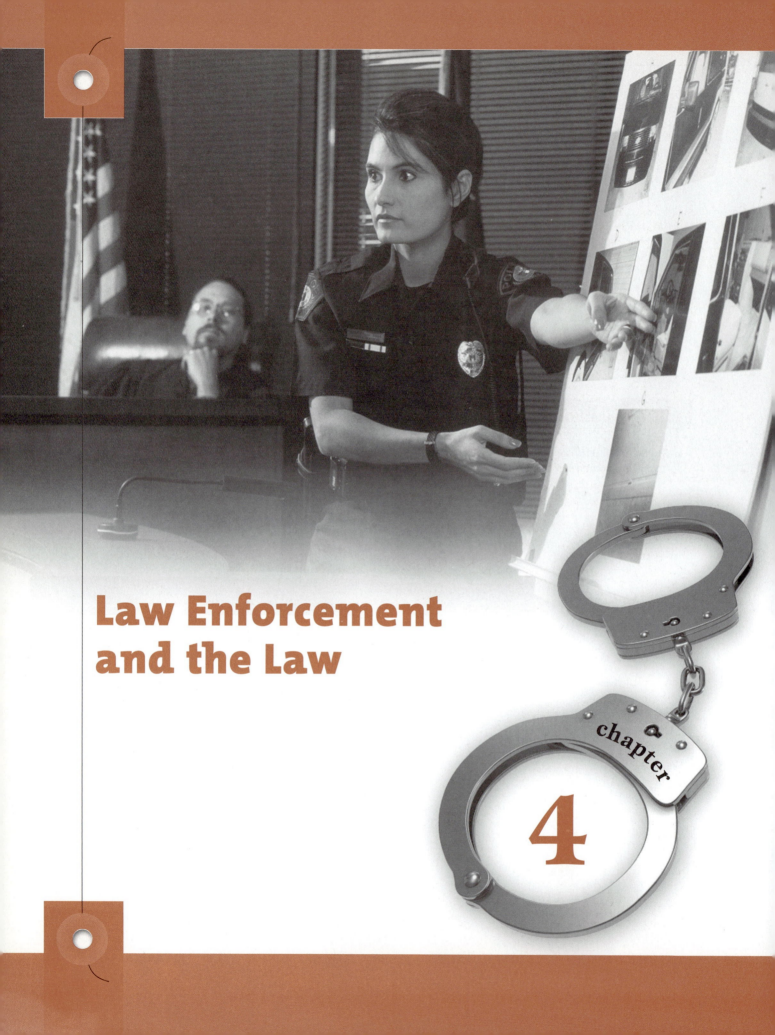

Law Enforcement and the Law

chapter

4

Chapter Objectives

- Understand how constitutional, criminal, and civil law differ and their importance to law enforcement.

- Understand the significance of the order of authority.

- List the civil rights and liberties guaranteed in each Amendment of the Bill of Rights.

- Distinguish between substantive and procedural law.

- Classify criminal law.

- Identify and understand the components of crime.

- Understand the significance of the Civil Rights Act (section 1983) to law enforcement and the types of civil liability law enforcement can face.

In *Sorichetti v. City of New York*,[1] Mrs. Sorichetti received an order of protection against her abusive spouse that required that he stay away from the house. He was, however, granted visitation rights to see his daughter on the weekends as long as she was picked up and delivered at the precinct house. After threatening his wife and child on the first visit, Mrs. Sorichetti asked the precinct desk officer to arrest her husband for violating the order of protection, but the officer refused. The following day, Mrs. Sorichetti repeated her plea, but even though the desk officer was told of Mr. Sorichetti's violent history by a fellow officer, he still denied her request for her husband's arrest. That same day, Mr. Sorichetti violently attacked the child, leaving her with permanent physical damage. He was charged with attempted murder. Mrs. Sorichetti filed a civil suit against the New York City Police Department for damages (Sullivan 2000).

The legal question raised in *Sorichetti* is the degree to which an officer or agency can be held liable for failing to protect an individual. In this case, Mrs. Sorichetti received a $2 million reward. Although there is generally no liability for failure to protect an individual (be-cause the police duty is to protect the public rather than each individual), liability may arise if a **special relationship** is found to exist to the claimant (Sullivan 2000). In this case, the court found that the elements of a special relationship were met as a result of the order of protection, the knowledge of the father's violent history, Mrs. Sorichetti's "reasonable expectation of protection," and the police's failure to respond to her request for help (Sullivan 2000).

This case underscores the importance of law enforcement practitioners and scholars having a suitable understanding of the basics of civil, constitutional, and criminal law. Although some students may wonder why they should care when first introduced to these basic legal principles, this knowledge provides the foundations for both understanding the field of law enforcement and for preparing to enter the field as an officer.

As described in Chapter 1, law enforcement officers act as frontline agents of the law, often serving as the first interpreters as to whether a crime has been committed (**criminal law**). One of their most important duties is to acquire sufficient evidence during the course of an investigation in order to be able to prove all elements of the offense in a court of law. Similarly, officers must also ensure that their handling and treatment of potential suspects is in accordance with the civil rights and liberties guaranteed to each citizen (**constitutional law**), and that any evidence against them is obtained lawfully. Finally, officers must be careful not to expose either themselves or their department to civil actions for damages or compensation from aggrieved members of the public, victims of crime, or the offenders themselves, as in the *Sorichetti* case (**civil law**). This chapter will examine various aspects of constitutional, criminal, and civil law, focusing on their application to law enforcement situations.

In order to understand the role of the police in enforcing the law, it is important to understand the position of law enforcement in the legal system and how it has attained this position. The central function and purpose of the police is to enforce laws; the power of the police is derived from the U.S. Constitution, Supreme Court rulings, statutes, and local ordinances. These sources give the police their powers, including the ability to use force as necessary. However, these sources also limit these powers based on the parameters outlined in the U.S. Constitution.

As discussed in Chapter 1, the problem of enforcing the law while simultaneously maintaining respect for civil rights and liberties is often referred to as a "delicate balance" (O'Brien 1991). The phrase **civil rights** refers to the rights of citizens not to have their legitimate interests interfered with by the government (i.e., with regard to freedom of speech, religion, etc.). In contrast, **civil liberties** refer to an individual's freedom to act in pursuit of those interests. Striking a balance between the need to respect and protect rights and liberties and the need for effective law enforcement can be inherently problematic. Some commentators argue, for example, that with too many checks and balances, the police cannot adequately protect the public; others instead point out that without enough restrictions on police power, there is a danger that our fundamental rights and freedoms may be threatened or restricted.

Order of Authority

The Constitution is the ultimate law of the United States. It was designed to enshrine within the law a respect for certain fundamental principles of justice and to ensure a proper balance between the rights of the individual and power of the government. It is the document that separates the legislative, executive, and judicial branches of the government, as shown in Figure 4.1.

In order to guarantee a separation of powers, the framers of the Constitution sought to ensure that no one branch of government could ever become so powerful as to threaten the independence and workings of any of the other branches. Having fought to free themselves from what they saw as the tyranny and injustice of British rule, the Founding Fathers of the United States were unwilling to entrust any one branch of government or entity with too much power. By developing a system of government in which independent bodies were charged with creating, interpreting, and enforcing the law, the framers of the Constitution also aimed to ensure that the laws themselves could continue to evolve as society itself expanded and changed. This early philosophy of **equity** recognizes that, at times, the underlying spirit or principles of the law are sometimes more important than the actual "letter of the law."

However, in its original form the **Constitution** did not include many of the personal guarantees and rights we now recognize today, and as a result many of the states initially refused to ratify it. Eventually, a compromise was reached whereby ten Amendments—referred to collectively as the **Bill of Rights**—were added, and the Constitution was accepted. In addition, although states and localities were left to craft their own individual constitutions and pass their own laws, an **order of authority** was established so that conflicts between different federal, state, and local laws could be resolved. In essence, a hierarchy of legal

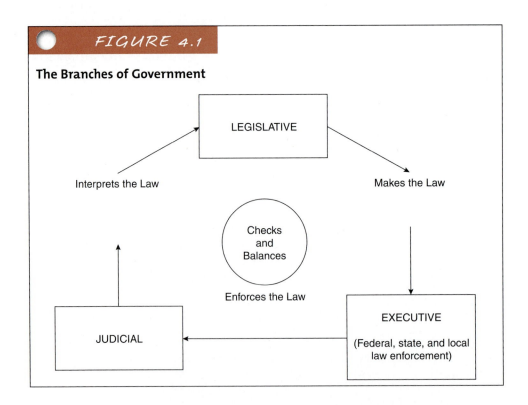

FIGURE 4.1

The Branches of Government

LEGISLATIVE

Interprets the Law

Makes the Law

Checks and Balances

Enforces the Law

JUDICIAL

EXECUTIVE

(Federal, state, and local law enforcement)

The U.S. Constitution was the product of the Constitutional Convention of 1787. However, it was not ratified until 1789. Not until 1791 were the ten Amendments added that would become known collectively as the Bill of Rights, following resistance on the part of the states to the lack of guarantees exhibited in the original draft of the Constitution. This document provides the basis of the power and duties of law enforcement.

authority was established, with the Constitution at the top as the ultimate and final form of the law.

Federal legislation is framed under the U.S. Constitution, state legislation is framed under state constitutions, and local ordinances reflect the immediate public safety and regulatory needs of local jurisdictions. Underlying the application of written law at all levels is the interpretative function of the judiciary, which has led to the development of **case law** intended to guide future decision making (see Figure 4.2 on page 86). Although lower levels of authority cannot contradict one another, each level has its own unique jurisdiction in certain manners. For example, interstate transport laws are always within the domain of federal government and federal law enforcement, whereas laws related to common theft or robbery within a single jurisdiction are found within state **penal codes**. Moreover, whereas statutory case law must abide by at least the level of rights guaranteed in the U.S. Constitution, states are free to, and sometimes do, grant greater rights and liberties to citizens than those the Supreme Court has developed based on the Constitution.

Law Enforcement and Constitutional Law

Consisting of seven articles and twenty-six Amendments, the purpose of the Constitution is to provide a structure for the federation of states, to regulate the relationship between the federation and the member states, and to explain

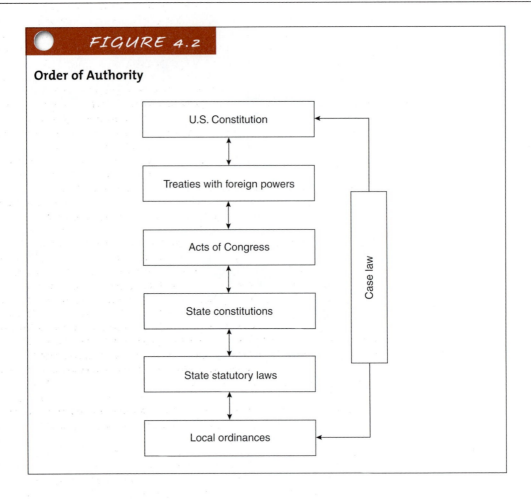

FIGURE 4.2

Order of Authority

the rights of individuals subject to state authority. The strength of constitutional law and politics rests in the power of **judicial review** given to the Supreme Court and the federal judiciary in *Marbury v. Madison* (1803)[2] to "consider and overturn any congressional and state legislation or other official governmental action deemed inconsistent with the Constitution, Bill of Rights, or federal law" (O'Brien 1991, p. 25). However, the very separation of powers and the principles of federalism described above as strengths, given the underlying goal of checks and balances, can also lead to ongoing political struggles and debates about enduring constitutional principles as they are interpreted over time by the Supreme Court (O'Brien 1991).

One of the central goals of law enforcement is to protect the civil rights and liberties of U.S. citizens. In addition to policing within constitutional parameters, this also requires ensuring that individuals do not infringe the civil rights of others. Figure 4.3 presents the Bill of Rights and the Fourteenth Amendment of the Constitution.

First Amendment

The First Amendment encompasses freedom of religion, freedom of peaceable assembly, freedom of petition, freedom of speech, and freedom of the press.

Freedom of Religion   Under the **establishment of religion clause**, a clear separation is made between church and state.[3] Because a large number of early

FIGURE 4.3

The Bill of Rights and the Fourteenth Amendment

Amendment I	Congress shall make no law respecting an establishment of religion, or prohibiting the free exercise thereof; or abridging the freedom of speech, or of the press; or the right of the people peaceably to assemble, and to petition the government for a redress of grievances.
Amendment II	A well-regulated militia, being necessary to the security of a free state, the right of the people to keep and bear arms, shall not be infringed.
Amendment III	No soldier shall, in time of peace be quartered in any house, without the consent of the owner, nor in time of war, but in a manner to be prescribed by law.
Amendment IV	The right of the people to be secure in their persons, houses, papers, and effects, against unreasonable searches and seizures, shall not be violated, and no warrants shall issue, but upon probable cause, supported by oath or affirmation, and particularly describing the place to be searched, and the persons or things to be seized.
Amendment V	No person shall be held to answer for a capital, or otherwise infamous crime, unless on a presentment or indictment of a grand jury, except in cases arising in the land or naval forces, or in the militia, when in actual service in time of war or public danger; nor shall any person be subject for the same offense to be twice put in jeopardy of life or limb; nor shall be compelled in any criminal case to be a witness against himself, nor be deprived of life, liberty, or property, without due process of law; nor shall private property be taken for public use, without just compensation.
Amendment VI	In all criminal prosecutions, the accused shall enjoy the right to a speedy and public trial, by an impartial jury of the state and district wherein the crime shall have been committed, which district shall have been previously ascertained by law, and to be informed of the nature and cause of the accusation; to be confronted with the witnesses against him; to have compulsory process for obtaining witnesses in his favor, and to have the assistance of counsel for his defense.
Amendment VII	In suits at common law, where the value in controversy shall exceed twenty dollars, the right of trial by jury shall be preserved, and no fact tried by a jury, shall be otherwise reexamined in any court of the United States, than according to the rules of the common law.
Amendment VIII	Excessive bail shall not be required, nor excessive fines imposed, nor cruel and unusual punishments inflicted.
Amendment IX	The enumeration in the Constitution, of certain rights, shall not be construed to deny or disparage others retained by the people.
Amendment X	The powers not delegated to the United States by the Constitution, nor prohibited by it to the states, are reserved to the states respectively, or to the people.
Amendment XIV (section 1)	All persons born or naturalized in the United States and subject to the jurisdiction thereof, are citizens of the United States and of the State wherein they reside. No State shall make or enforce any law which shall abridge the privileges or immunities of citizens of the United States; nor shall any State deprive any person of life, liberty, or property, without due process of law; nor deny to any person within its jurisdiction the equal protection of the laws.

settlers to the United States immigrated to escape government-enforced support of churches, the framers saw a need for such a clear division. No state or federal government can establish a church, and no law or tax can be passed that favors or recognizes one religion over another. This also includes legislation designed to promote a particular dogma or viewpoint within the school system.[4]

Although the First Amendment guarantees the **free exercise of religion**, this does not include exemptions from generally applicable laws,[5] such as the use of illegal drugs or sacrifice of animals. There can never be a private right to ignore general laws.

Freedom of Peaceable Assembly   People are free to assemble in groups for religious, political, or social activities for **expressive purposes** or protests. However, the right to associate for expressive purposes is not absolute: "Infringements on that right may be justified by regulations adopted to serve compelling state interests, unrelated to the suppression of ideas, that cannot be achieved through means significantly less restrictive of associational freedoms."[6]

The right to peaceable assembly can place law enforcement agencies and officers in precarious situations, such as having to protect the right of groups they may fundamentally disagree with to assemble (i.e., an African American officer at a Klu Klux Klan march that has a legal permit). This can include citizen protests against the police themselves! There are, however, practical limits on the right of assembly. Although a crowd of people protesting peacefully in front of police headquarters is within the guidelines of the First Amendment, for example, this right is eliminated as soon as the entrance is blocked. It is constitu-

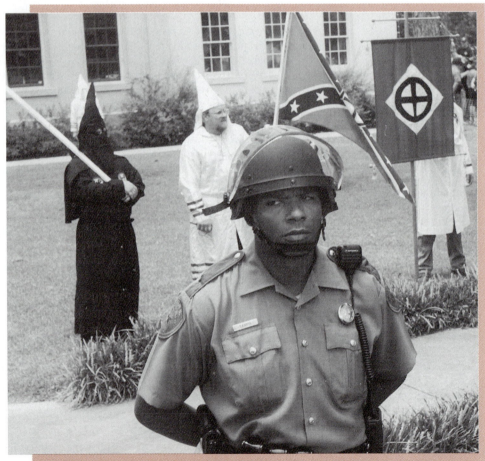

The right to peaceable assembly can place law enforcement in precarious situations, such as having to protect the rights of groups with which they fundamentally disagree.

tional for law enforcement officers to remove people by force if necessary in such a situation, because they are violating the rights of others to freely enter and leave the building. It also is constitutional for municipalities to require permits for official assemblies, provided it is for regulatory purposes only and is not disproportionately applied to some groups over others.

Freedom of Petition   As part of the democratic political process, people are free to communicate with the government without obstruction. Such a right only holds, however, until such communications reach the level of threat or stalking. The Secret Service monitors such communications with the President of the United States, using professional threat assessors to determine whether a serious risk is involved.

Freedom of Speech   The ability to express one's opinions and perspectives without the fear of censorship is at the core of American life. **Pure speech**, or words that are not accompanied by an action, are protected by the U.S. Constitution. Such protections also extend to the area of **symbolic speech**, whereby expression takes place through tangible items, such as signs, buttons, or flags.

Such protections have even been extended to include antigovernment protests in the form of burning the American flag.[7] In *Texas v. Johnson*, the Court held that it is "not simply the verbal or nonverbal nature of the expression, but the governmental interest at stake, that helps determine whether or not a restriction on that expression is valid." Freedom of speech is not absolute, but a "compelling governmental interest" must always be demonstrated before intrusion or restriction is justified.

For example, the landmark case of *Schenck v. United States* (1919)[8] established the **clear and present danger doctrine**, which restricts expression in situations when there is a significant likelihood that it will lead to an action or result that the government has the right to prevent (e.g., danger to other citizens, direct obstruction of government military interests in times of war, etc.). Similarly, **fighting words**, or speech that "may have all the effect of force,"[9] are not protected by the Constitution, due to the likely resulting violence.

Linkages *in Law Enforcement*

Freedom of Speech, Assembly, and Religion and the War on Terror

The War on Terror has brought with it many challenges for local law enforcement. In addition to the need to be better prepared as potential first responders to terrorist incidents, conflicts in Afghanistan and Iraq have led to protests throughout the country. At these protests, public safety concerns are heightened due to the increased likelihood of terrorist attacks.

QUESTIONS

1. Should law enforcement be able to arrest a person who burns the American flag during a legal protest? Base your answer on the First Amendment cases discussed in this chapter.

2. To what extent should federal law enforcement be able to track Internet usage, book purchases, and religious affiliations of U.S. citizens? Again, base your answers upon the First Amendment. What about for nonresident legal aliens?

Speech-plus conduct includes activities such as peaceful picketing, boycotts, and demonstrations. Although these activities may receive some First Amendment protection, they do not receive the same protection as pure speech (O'Brien 1991). When engaging in such conduct, individuals remain subject to generally applicable laws, such as trespass, resisting arrest, inciting riots, and blocking traffic (O'Brien 1991). In such circumstances, it is legally permissible for police to disperse the group without violating the First Amendment.

Freedom of the Press   People can now access information 24 hours a day via news channels, the radio, and the Internet. The importance of the freedom of the press within this information age cannot be underestimated. Law enforcement representatives investigating major cases are often made to hold press conferences or offer press releases throughout the course of an investigation.

Access to information throughout an ongoing investigation, however, can have a price. At some point, the constant release of new investigative leads can hamper an ongoing investigation, just as war reporting can in some cases compromise military action. In *New York Times v. United States* (1971),[10] the Court stated that the courts cannot "make" a law restricting freedom of the press in the name of presidential or national security. Even in a circumstance involving the guarding of military and diplomatic secrets, "to find that the President has the inherent power to halt the publication of the news by resorting to the courts would wipe out the Constitution and destroy the fundamental liberties and security of the very people the government hopes to make 'secure.' " Thus, although law enforcement and government officials may choose to not release information about an investigation or military action to the public, once such information is "released" a Department of Justice injunction against the publication of findings would be very difficult to justify.

In addition to affecting the possible integrity of an investigation, the desire for a free press can conflict with the criminal justice system's interests in ensuring that suspects receive a "fair" in addition to "public" trial. Although the case of *Sheppard v. Maxwell* (1966)[11] recognized that a person can be tried in the media in especially sensitive cases, and thus overturned the conviction due to the taint of media, the continued use of gag orders by courts following the case was vigorously contested by the press as a First Amendment violation. As a result, in the later ruling of *Nebraska Press Association v. Stuart* (1976),[12] the Supreme Court acknowledged the difficulties inherent in balancing the right to a fair trial according to the Sixth Amendment and the First Amendment freedom of the press. Refusing to ban courtroom orders outright, the Court did "not rule out the possibility of showing the kind of threat to fair trial rights that would justify such restraint." However, such a restriction on the press's access to a court would be very difficult to justify particularly given how difficult it is to predict how media exposure might affect the interests of the accused. The Supreme Court also stressed that even pervasive pretrial publicity may not inevitably prevent the holding of a fair trial.

Second Amendment

The right of the people "to keep and bear arms" continues to be a source of controversy in the United States today. Many are quick to note that over 70,000,000 guns are in private hands, a situation that is not going to go away without highly intrusive measures to limit gun ownership (Walker 2001). In addition, it can be argued that efforts at gun control may only result in restricting access to firearms by legitimate owners rather than making a significant dent in the use of guns by criminal entrepreneurs. Others look at the drastically lower violent crime rates in countries with greater gun control restrictions, such as Canada, Japan, and the United Kingdom, where the homicide rate is 530 percent lower than in the United States (Zimring 1995), as major examples of the positive effects such legislation can have. Research has shown that cities in states with licensing and registration requirements have a lower proportion of crime with guns purchased in their own state (Vernick, Webster, and Hepburn 2001). Other research contends that gun ownership can significantly deter certain types of crime (Lott and Mustard 1997).

In its original design, as with many elements of the Bill of Rights, the Second Amendment reflected a fear of federal dominance of the states following confederation. As such, the intention of the Second Amendment was to give the states the right to maintain an armed militia to protect their own interests. The Supreme Court itself confirmed this interpretation of the Second Amendment in *United States v. Cruickshank* (1876),[13] ruling that federal gun control legislation was constitutional unless an individual could demonstrate a correlation between possession of an illegal firearm according to federal laws, and the ability to maintain a well-armed militia. Cases following this precedent have continued to support the fact that the right to bear firearms is a collective rather than individual right (Kirkland 2003).

Although both the federal government and the states have the authority to regulate gun ownership, the federal government does not have the jurisdiction to compel state law enforcement agencies to implement federal regulatory procedures related to firearms (such as the 1993 Brady Bill's national five-day waiting period for handgun purchases and mandatory background checks).[14] This is because regulatory procedures are the jurisdiction of the states. A 1998 modification to the Brady Bill now allows for immediate clearance to purchase a gun, with police agencies being able to receive FBI clearance via computer, should they have the technological capabilities.

Many states have since introduced both zero-tolerance and other innovative approaches aimed at reducing firearms demand and supply. For example, the **Massachusetts Bartley-Fox laws** mandate a one-year jail term for individuals caught carrying a handgun outside of the home without a permit. These laws are particularly strict, because they make no provision for either probation or parole. It is important to note, however, that the right to own a gun in the home is not challenged.

Beginning in Richmond, Virginia, in 1997, **Project Exile** represents a coordinated approach to gun control. The U.S. Attorney's office works alongside an Assistant Commonwealth Attorney to review cases involving "felons with guns, drug users with guns, guns used in drug trafficking, and gun domestic violence referrals" (Office of Juvenile Justice and Delinquency Prevention 1999). Such cases are tried in federal court where possible, resulting in longer sentences for convicted felons in possession of firearms and/or repeat violent offenders. Moreover, when an officer finds a gun, a Bureau of Alcohol, Tobacco, and Firearms (ATF) agent can be immediately paged; representatives from the Richmond Police Department, ATF, and U.S. Attorney's office may also be involved. Other comprehensive models for firearms reduction have also proven effective, combining similar zero-tolerance gun control approaches with community

The controversy over the Second Amendment reflects deeply entrenched values in U.S. history, particularly with regards to fears of the power of a strong, centralized government. In examining the wording of the Amendment, and given the context in which it was framed, do you feel that it refers to an individual right to bear arms, or is it referring to the collective power of the state?

mobilization and offender intervention strategies (Sheppard, Grant, and Rowe 1999).

Despite the increased focus on gun control, more than half of the states have adopted **concealed-carry handgun statutes**, which allow ordinary citizens to apply for a permit to carry a concealed weapon. The increase comes primarily in **shall-issue statutes**, whereby the state creates a list of criteria for obtaining a concealed weapon permit and if the individual meets the criteria the state is required to issue the person a permit. Twelve states have discretionary issue permits, whereby the state can use discretion in determining whether to issue a permit. Only seven states do not allow individuals to apply for a permit to carry a concealed weapon (Andrus 2000). Some researchers suggest that concealed carry handgun statutes are correlated to a reduction in violent crime (Andrus 2000; Lott 1998); others contend no empirical evidence is available to support such claims (Ludwig 2000). Thus, the issue of gun control and concealed weapons laws remains a controversial issue.

Fourth Amendment

The Fourth Amendment restrictions on "unreasonable searches and seizures" and its explicit requirement of "probable cause" for the issuance of warrants has perhaps had the greatest impact on the day-to-day activities of law enforcement agencies in the United States. Intended to protect citizens from unwarranted governmental intrusions, the Fourth Amendment has produced a body of case law on the subject of **search and seizure** that is integral to law enforcement practice. As a result, the Fourth Amendment is detailed at length in Chapter 5 with only basic information presented here.

According to the exact wording of the Fourth Amendment, an individual's home or person cannot be searched unless a **warrant** based upon **probable cause** is issued. However, a literal interpretation of the Amendment would make many routine law enforcement activities extremely difficult to carry out. Accordingly, Fourth Amendment case law reflects the need to balance the rights of individuals to be free from unwarranted search with the practicalities of law enforcement.

Ideally a warrant should be obtained before an arrest is made to ensure that probable cause (facts or proof that a crime has been committed and that the identified individual committed the act) has been judicially determined. If a crime is committed in the immediate presence, or **plain view**, of an officer, the person can be taken into custody without a warrant. As soon as probable cause sufficient for an arrest has been established, the officer is permitted to search the individual, as well as the immediate area within the suspect's control.[15]

If an officer is simply suspicious of an individual's activities and can offer "specific and articulable reasons to justify a stop," the officer has **reasonable suspicion** and is allowed to stop a suspected individual. If a reasonable police officer would believe (in light of his experience) that a situation is dangerous, then that officer may **frisk** the suspect, searching the outside of a suspect's clothing for weapons.[16] Given the mobile nature of traffic situations, officers are also able to ask all passengers to step out of the car.[17] In such a situation, if there is probable cause to believe that contraband is in the car, the officer can search the entire car and its compartments.

Even words can be "seized," as case law on **wiretapping** and **electronic surveillance** indicate.[18] Warrants usually are required for wiretaps and electronic surveillance, with some exceptions. In the wake of September 11, sweeping new antiterror legislation—the USA PATRIOT Act—was passed into law in October 2001. This legislation was reauthorized by Congress in January 2006 in the USA PATRIOT Improvement and Reauthorization Act of 2005. Under the USA PATRIOT Act and its reauthorization, investigators are able apply for court orders approving "roving bugs" to tap any phone a suspected terrorist might use rather than a single phone. In addition, the government can acquire "records and tangible things from custodians," which encompasses educational and financial records, information from Internet service providers, or even from library records (Herman 2006).

To deter police abuse of Fourth Amendment rights, the **exclusionary rule** states that any evidence obtained in violation of the Amendment will be inadmissible in a court of law. Building on federal precedent from 1914,[19] this rule was extended to include the states in 1961.[20]

Fifth Amendment

The Fifth Amendment is of fundamental importance to the criminal justice system in general, and law enforcement in particular, as it ensures due process and the right against self-incrimination and double jeopardy.

Due Process   Due process of law, which is broadly defined as protection from arbitrary or unfair proceedings against individuals by the criminal justice system, is guaranteed by the Fifth, Sixth, and Fourteenth Amendments. Although it is the Fourteenth Amendment that makes due process binding on the states, it does so by duplicating the wording of the Fifth Amendment, which states that "no person . . . shall be deprived of life, liberty, or property without due process of law." The concept of due process is central to the Bill of Rights, because it mandates equal protection for all individuals within the United States. For instance, during a trial the judge must be impartial, the defendant must be able to present evidence on his or her own behalf, and the defendant must be presumed innocent until proven guilty based upon the evidence presented.

Because the meaning of due process is not specifically defined within the Constitution, the courts have sought to provide guidance on this issue. According to case law, judges are required to interpret the law in accordance with constitutional provisions set out in the Bill of Rights, and the Supreme Court has described the limits of judicial interpretation as "vague contours of the due process clause." The two types of due process are **substantive**, which protects against arbitrary or unfair laws, and **procedural**, which protects individuals from arbitrary and unfair application of the laws. The majority of due process cases heard by the courts relate to issues of procedural due process, such as police entrapment, questions relating to the composition of lineups, and pretrial motions requesting suppression of evidence by the defense. For instance, the Supreme Court stated that the lineup procedure in *Stovall v. Denno* (1967)[21] violated due process of law because the defendant was the only black man in the line presented to the victim. The Court said this procedure was "unnecessarily suggestive and conducive to irreparable mistaken identification" and thus denied the defendant due process of law. As described by *Palko v. Connecticut* (1937),[22] the fundamental purpose of the Bill of Rights is to protect basic values "implicit in the concept of ordered liberty."

Double Jeopardy   The Fifth Amendment not only requires due process of law, but also protects individuals against double jeopardy. **Double jeopardy** means that an individual should not be tried twice in either a federal or state court for the same crime once a verdict is given, regardless of whether the person is acquitted or convicted. Double jeopardy does not apply, however, if there is a mistrial, some type of trial error, or if there is a hung jury (no verdict is reached). Additionally, the defendant can be tried in a state and federal court on different charges resulting from the same crime (i.e., if the conduct of the accused violates both state and federal laws). In addition, the accused can be tried in a criminal court for a crime and in civil court to determine liability. These two different trials proceed without violation of the double jeopardy clause. The O. J. Simpson case exemplifies this point; Simpson was acquitted by a criminal court but a civil court held him accountable for the wrongful deaths of his ex-wife and her friend.

Self-incrimination   The Fifth Amendment also protects against **self-incrimination**; a person does not have to say anything in a court of law that may implicate his or her guilt. This rule is applicable from the moment an individual is arrested and continues to operate through the entire judicial proceedings. The current interpretation of the Fifth Amendment was established during the 1960s when the Supreme Court considered a number of cases involving civil liberties violations. For example, the case of *Miranda v. Arizona* (1966)[23] established the rule that suspects must be warned of their rights prior to their custodial interrogation. This decision built on the reasoning in previous cases such as

Brown v. Mississippi (1936),[24] where the defendants were coerced into confessing to a crime without counsel present. In this case, the convictions rested solely on the defendants' confessions, which were extorted through "brutality and violence." The Court held that this violated both due process rights (from the Fourteenth Amendment) and the right against self-incrimination.

Following the decision in *Miranda*, the concept of self-incrimination was gradually refined by the courts. In *Brewer v. Williams* (1977),[25] for example, the defendant was indirectly coerced into confiding to police where he had dumped the body of a ten-year-old girl, whom he had abducted on Christmas Eve. Although he was represented by an attorney and had been warned of his *Miranda* rights, a detective transported him by car and began speaking about how the family deserved to give their daughter a Christian burial during the holidays. The detective never directly questioned him, though the Court still considered the defendant's statement to amount to a confession obtained through surreptitious means, because the defendant was a religious man. The Court stated that "there can be no doubt that Detective Leaming deliberately and designedly set out to elicit information from Williams just as surely as—and perhaps more effectively than—if he had formally interrogated him." Despite the ruling in *Brewer*, the courts have increasingly allowed the police to use deception, along with broad definitions of custody and interrogation, thereby making exceptions to the *Miranda* rule (Lunney 1999).

The Court also has examined other types of self-incrimination and in later cases stated that interrogation refers only to speech and does not include blood samples, handwriting, or voice tests. In *Schmerber v. California* (1966)[26], for example, the defendant was driving while intoxicated and crashed his vehicle. The responding police officer took a blood sample to determine the defendant's blood alcohol content. Although the defendant claimed that this violated his right to due process and privilege from self-incrimination, the Court rejected the argument, finding that driving offered implied consent to such measures.

Sixth Amendment

The Sixth Amendment is the basis for a number of rights, including the right to a speedy trial, a trial by jury, a public trial, the right to confront witnesses, and the right to counsel. This final right is particularly important for the police; an officer cannot interrogate a suspect without informing the person of his or her rights (as a result of the *Miranda* decision), one of which is the right to counsel.

The right to counsel is a fundamental right, yet the Supreme Court has heard many cases questioning the **critical stage** at which counsel is necessary. The Supreme Court has stated that the critical stage begins when a defendant's rights may be lost or waived, privileges may be lost or waived, or beyond which point the outcome of the case may be otherwise substantially affected. This is a particularly contentious topic in terms of indigent defendants who are unable to afford counsel. Over time, the Court has extended the notion of the critical stage of counsel from application to capital cases (*Powell v. Alabama*[27]) to felony cases (*Gideon v. Wainwright*[28]) to cases that may result in more than six months imprisonment (*Argesinger v. Hamlin*[29]) to the appeals process (*Douglas v. California*[30]) and back to lineups (*Escobedo v. Illinois*[31]).

It was only after *Powell v. Alabama* in 1932 that an indigent defendant was allowed to exercise the constitutional right to counsel even in a capital case, though in the 1942 case of *Betts v. Brady*[32] the Court stated that indigency alone did not necessitate court-appointed counsel, because the appointment of counsel is not a fundamental right. However, the 1963 case of *Gideon* extended the right of counsel to indigent defendants for all felony cases. This was a landmark case, and one of the most important changes to the criminal justice system brought about during Warren Era. The Court unanimously held that such a rule is necessary in order to establish procedural and substantive safeguards to ensure fair trials, with the judges agreeing that the decision in *Betts* was "an anachronism when handed down."

Eighth Amendment

The Eighth Amendment contains key constitutional provisions for the criminal justice system, though these relate primarily to the adjudication process and field of corrections. The Eighth Amendment establishes two further individual safeguards for those accused of a crime: (1) that bail, if specified, must not be excessive and (2) that punishment cannot be cruel and unusual.

Bail   **Bail** is a specified amount of money that the defendant is ordered to pay the court on release from custody to ensure his or her return to court for trial. The purpose of bail, which is paid prior to the trial, is not meant to be punishment, and this has been the subject of a number of court cases. In *Stack v. Boyle* (1951),[33] the Court ruled that a person arrested for a noncapital offense is entitled to bail. Because the purpose of bail is not punishment, if the amount set is higher than reasonably necessary to accomplish this goal, it is considered to be excessive, and therefore unconstitutional. According to the Supreme Court, bail is not a device for keeping people in jail, but rather to enable them to stay out of jail.

In *United States v. Salerno* (1984),[34] however, the Court held that no absolute right to bail exists under the Eighth Amendment. The defendants in this case were involved in organized crime activities, including drug trafficking and violence, and it was assumed that if they were given bail they would be a substantial flight risk. The Bail Reform Act (1984) states that if no release conditions "will reasonably assure the safety of any other person and the community, bail pretrial release can be denied." Although the defendants called this punishment before trial, the decision was upheld.

Cruel and Unusual Punishment   Many issues come up under this clause of the Eighth Amendment, including the type and length of punishment given and prisoners' rights once they are incarcerated. Prisoners' rights often are an issue of contention in the courts. Under the Eighth Amendment, prisoners have the right to decent conditions, including access to medical care and religious services, although the Court has also considered whether further conditions beyond this are necessary. The Court established in *Estelle v. Gamble* (1976)[35] that prisoners not only have the right to medical care, but also that it is unconstitutional for prison officers to show a deliberate indifference to the health-care needs of prisoners.

The death penalty is a particularly controversial punishment imposition that was declared "cruel and unusual" under the Eighth Amendment and disallowed in *Furman v. Georgia* (1972),[36] only later to be reinstated in *Gregg v. Georgia* (1976).[37] In *Furman*, the court looked at whether capital punishment was *unusual* because it was seldom imposed, and often imposed disproportionately, and whether it was *cruel* because it involved the intentional taking of a human life in ways that were unpredictable to potential recipients. In *Gregg*, the Court set out a number of standards for the application of the death penalty, including the establishment of a bifurcated trial system (for the trial and sentencing phases of the case); application only to crimes that are proportionate (e.g., murder, but not rape[38]); the existence of aggravating circumstances (e.g., premeditated murder, murder of an officer); and the absence of arbitrary application of the punishment (e.g., it should not be applied disproportionately to individuals of a particular race). Though capital punishment has historically been accepted as constitutional, the Court has provided room for reconsideration in terms of American society's evolving standards of decency.

Tenth Amendment

Although it often receives less attention than other constitutional guarantees, the Tenth Amendment plays a critical role in the United States through its transference of all remaining powers not covered in the Constitution to the states. Law enforcement thus derives much of its power through the Tenth Amendment's explicit recognitions of state sovereignty.

Fourteenth Amendment

The notion that "all people are created equal" is embodied in the language of the Fourteenth Amendment through the **equal protection clause**, which makes it unconstitutional for states to create arbitrary distinctions between the rights and privileges of different groups of people. As noted earlier, prior to the Fourteenth Amendment the Bill of Rights was applicable only to the states. In duplicating the language of the Fifth Amendment, the Fourteenth Amendment ensured that all of the rights and protections afforded citizens by federal agencies could not be avoided simply by a government's turning to a state court for refuge.

Law Enforcement and Criminal Law

For a crime to be committed, a written law passed by a legislature, also referred to as **statutory law**, must be violated. Statutory laws frequently are combined to form the penal code of states and the federal government, within which there are two types of written law: **substantive law**, which defines the specific elements of the crime committed, as well as the parameters available for punishment; and **procedural law**, which specifies how the criminal justice system should deal with violations of the substantive laws in a manner that is both efficient and fundamentally fair (in accordance with the civil rights and liberties described within the Constitution).

The principle that an orderly society needs to be governed by written laws in such a precise and fair manner is known as the **rule of law**, which was discussed in Chapter 1. According to the rule of law, everyone should be held accountable to the same laws, including politicians as high up as the President of the United States. However, differences in interpretation or enforcement of the law can be found at all levels of the criminal justice system.

In order to provide consistency in the interpretation of laws, judges follow precedent from case law (previous trial and appellate decisions). Once a judge makes a decision in a case, it becomes precedent, and all courts of an equal or lower level faced with subsequent cases with similar facts have to follow that decision. This concept is embodied in the principle of *stare decisis* (to stand on decided cases). This is the recognition that previous cases should guide future deliberations, thus ensuring predictability in the enforcement of laws. Precedents can, however, be overturned with new case decisions by higher courts, allowing the justice system to adapt existing laws to changing social and cultural conditions.

Classification of Criminal Laws

Within penal codes, crimes are classified according to their perceived seriousness and the type of punishment prescribed by the legislature. The two primary categories of criminal offenses are felonies and misdemeanors.

Felonies **Felonies** are serious crimes punishable with at least one year in a state prison or federal penitentiary. Depending on the laws of a particular state, certain felony crimes can also be punishable by death. Conviction for a felony offense results in the loss of many rights, such as the right to hold public office and the right to own a firearm. The range of felonies is vast, and as a result some states and the federal government now have different degrees, or classes, of felonies. Whereas the federal government assigns felony scores based on the severity of the offense, states tend to designate the most serious felonies as either Class A or Class 1 felonies.

Misdemeanors **Misdemeanors** are relatively minor crimes subject to fines or brief confinement in a location other than prison (e.g., county jail) (Garner 1999). Most individuals convicted of misdemeanors, however, are given suspended sentences, fines, or a form of community sentence, such as community service.

An important point to note is that the police may make warrantless arrests for both felonies and misdemeanors committed in their presence, which are referred to as **public offenses**. Warrantless arrests also can be made for felony offenses not committed in the presence of the officer, but for which there is probable cause.

Violations **Violations** are lesser wrongs, such as not obeying a municipal ordinance, that are rarely considered to be part of the criminal law and usually result in fines. An example of a violation is an illegally parked car. Rather than making an arrest, the police are likely to give the violator a traffic ticket with a specified fee to be paid by a particular date.

The Components of Crime

For an act to be considered a crime, it must include three specific elements: *actus reus, mens rea,* and *corpus delecti*. First, there must be some act or omission, known as the **actus reus**. This is the commission of a wrongful act in violation of written statutory law. The specific statutory elements must clearly define the conditions necessary for the criminal act or omission to have occurred. Acts do not always have to be completed, however, for a crime to occur; attempts also are criminal offenses. For example, if a man attempts to murder a woman by stabbing her to death, the man can be prosecuted for attempted murder even if she does not die. Incomplete crimes are sometimes referred to as **inchoate offenses** and may also be prosecuted. Perhaps the most commonly prosecuted inchoate offense is conspiracy, which can be prosecuted in many cases purely on the basis of two or more persons' intent and agreement that at least one person intends to commit a crime.

The second component of a crime is *mens rea*, or a guilty mind, and in most cases a crime can only occur if *actus reus* and *mens rea* are formed simultaneously. *Mens rea* refers to whether there was intent to commit an offense. **Intention** is said to exist when the accused intends to commit the act in question or to bring about a certain consequence. It does not matter to the formation or determination of intent why the act was committed, that is, what the defendant's **motive** may have been.

The four levels of culpability or blameworthiness as described by the Model Penal Code are (1) purposely (the act was premeditated, demonstrating a conscious decision to engage in certain conduct or to cause a certain result); (2) knowingly (the actor is practically certain that his or her conduct will produce such a result); (3) recklessly (an actor consciously disregards a substantial and unjustified risk or greater risk than is reasonable of harm caused by his or her conduct); and (4) negligently (the actor should know of a substantial and unjustified risk that a harm will result from his or her conduct) (American Law Institute 2001).

If both the *actus reus* and the *mens rea* occur, then there is a body of crime referred to as **corpus delecti**. For example, the *corpus delicti* of the offense of robbery would include proving that property was taken by force or threat, that the suspect was the same person who took the property by force or threat, and that the suspect had the requisite intention to commit a criminal act.

In addition to the specific requirements of *actus reus* and *mens rea*, a number of guiding principles govern the interactions between the various elements of a crime. There must be **concurrence**, meaning that both the act (*actus reus*) and intent (*mens rea*) must occur at the same point in time for a crime to have been committed (except in the case of strict liability offenses, where no culpable mental state is ever required, such as with routine traffic violations or statutory rape). In most instances, a legal connection must exist between the act committed and the harm caused (**causation of harm**), though this does not necessarily mean that the two have to occur closely in time and space. An individual can be held criminally responsible for murder even if the death resulting from the injuries occurs months later. All that needs to be proven is that the death is the direct result of the criminal act committed.

If a crime does occur, the accused can raise a number of defenses in court. **Defenses** are arguments raised by the accused at trial that either attempt to prove that the prosecution's arguments are flawed and that law enforcement has not collected enough evidence to establish that all elements of a crime were committed or that the wrongful conduct is not necessarily criminal (as in the case of self-defense). Defenses fall into three broad categories: (1) reasonable doubt (a denial that the prosecution demonstrated one or more of the necessary elements of the offense); (2) excuses (the defendant admits that his or her conduct was wrong, but that he or she is not blameworthy because of some condition that affected the

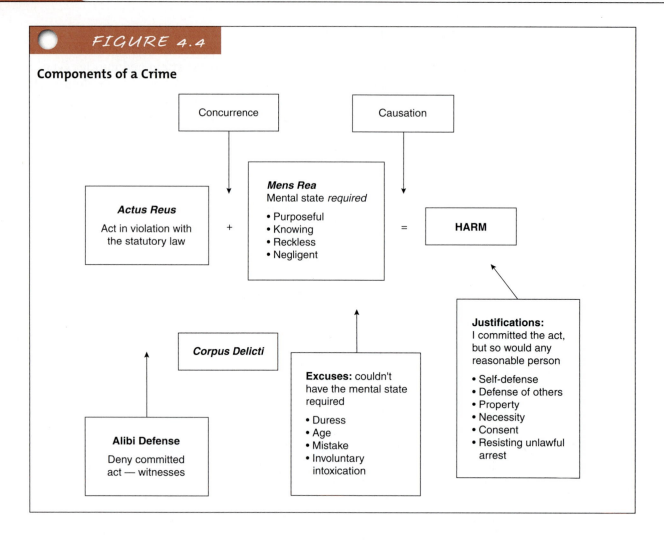

FIGURE 4.4

Components of a Crime

defendant at the time of the act); and (3) justifications (the defendant admits that the act was committed, but that the act was not wrong because any reasonable person would have acted the same way; for example, self-defense).

Figure 4.4 illustrates the components necessary to be proven in order for a crime to have occurred and their relationship to different defense strategies. It is the job of law enforcement to collect the necessary evidence to prove all necessary elements of the criminal act or omission.

Law Enforcement and Civil Law

Noncriminal restrictions placed on the freedom of individuals are referred to as **torts** rather than crimes and fall under the jurisdiction of civil law. In contrast to crimes, torts deal with civil wrongs against a person rather than the public, and proceedings are initiated both by and for the privately wronged individual. Torts include situations where one person causes injury to the person or property of another in violation of a legal duty imposed by law.

Rather than seeking a person's incarceration, in civil cases the victim seeks restitution or compensation, usually in the form of monetary damages. Typically, civil cases look at the outcome of the situation rather than the intent do harm. Unlike the standard of proof required in criminal proceedings (beyond a reasonable doubt), civil cases must be proved according to a standard of **preponderance of the evidence**, meaning that the weight of the evidence must be in favor of the complainant. A person charged with a crime can be tried in a civil court without violation of the double jeopardy clause outlined in the Fifth Amendment. This is often the case with situations involving medical malpractice, in which the patient sues the doctor following any criminal proceedings for criminal negligence or assault.

In some cases, the same set of facts can give rise to both civil and criminal proceedings. The rule against double jeopardy is not violated because the private individual initiates civil proceedings, whereas criminal proceedings are initiated by the state. Additionally, damages received in a civil proceeding are not seen as punishment. As such, civil forfeiture, or seizure of stolen goods or assets following a criminal conviction, is constitutional.[39]

In order to protect themselves from the possibility of civil litigation resulting from an admission or guilty plea in criminal proceedings, many defendants plead *nolo contendere*, or no contest, at criminal arraignment, a plea that initiates the sentencing proceedings of the criminal justice system but that cannot be used against that same individual in civil proceedings.

Mechanisms for Civil Liability and Law Enforcement

The **Civil Rights Act of 1871 (section 1983)** states that:

> . . . every person who, under the color of any statute, ordinance, regulation, custom, or usage, of any state or authority, subjects, or causes to be subjected, any citizen of the United States or other persons within the jurisdiction thereof to the deprivation of any rights, privileges, or immunities secured by the Constitution and laws, shall be liable to the party injured in an action at law, suit in equity, or other proper preceding at redress.

In other words, if a plaintiff is deprived of his or her constitutional right by law enforcement officers or public officials acting in the context of their duties, a lawsuit can be filed for redress.

In the landmark case of *Monroe v. Pape* (1961),[40] the Court established that a section 1983 lawsuit provided a remedy for a greater portion of actions by the police that violate a person's rights under the U.S. Constitution. In this case, the rights of the Monroe family were violated during the course of a search of Mr. Monroe's home. The Court reasoned that the Act was meant to provide a remedy for persons whose rights are violated by officials acting "under the color of law," or in a capacity of authority. Previously, when officers acted outside of the rules of law proscribed by the government, they were not considered to have acted under the authority of the government. With this decision, the Supreme Court enabled people whose constitutional rights were violated to sue government officials when they act outside the rules of the government's law (Kappeler 1997).

Civil Liability and Law Enforcement: Intentional versus Negligent Wrongs

Over the past three decades, the number of civil rights cases filed against law enforcement agencies has grown exponentially. In 1966, only one civil liability case resulted in an award exceeding $1 million, but by 1983 over 350 awards exceeding this amount had been made (del Carmen 1991). Despite the large number of cases filed, however, less than one-quarter go to trial, and fewer than one in five result in judgment for the plaintiff. Common allegations include both intentional and civil wrongs, with the greatest damages offered in brutality cases, such as the case against the New York City Police Department (NYPD) following the attack on Abner Louima.

Intentional torts are torts in which the officer intended to engage in the conduct that led to the injury (note that harm caused by the officer does not have to be found to be intentional) (Kappeler 1997). However, with regard to law enforcement agents, these cases typically involve situations in which an officer engaged in conduct that was substantially certain to cause harm. Examples of intentional torts that can be committed by law enforcement agents include the excessive use of force, false arrest and imprisonment, assault and battery, wrongful death, intentional infliction of emotional or mental distress, misuse of legal procedure, invasion of privacy, illegal electronic surveillance, defamation, and malicious prosecution (del Carmen 1991; Kappeler 1997).

The breach of a common law or statutory duty to act reasonably toward those who may be harmed by an officer's conduct are liable to be tried in a civil court as **negligent wrongs**. Examples of possible negligent wrongs include negligent operation of a motor vehicle, negligent failure to protect an individual or personal property, and negligent failure to respond to calls. Thus, in the case of law enforcement agents, civil litigation can result from omissions or failure to discharge one's duty. For example, if an officer failed to take into custody an individual clearly driving while under the influence of alcohol, the failure to intervene could qualify as a constitutional violation for which the department and/or individual could be held accountable for the resulting harm caused by the drunk driver.

Damages Awarded for Torts and Individual Officer Responsibility

Three types of damages can be awarded to plaintiffs who bring forth a civil action. The first is **nominal**, whereby the court acknowledges that the plaintiff proved his or her allegation, but suffered no actual injury. As a result, no significant monetary contribution is provided. The second type of damages awarded is **actual**, whereby damages are provided for actual injuries to the victim. Damages can cover medical bills, lost wages, or other such costs. A third type of damages is **punitive**, which is most often sought in cases against law enforcement officials. In this case, the intent of the award is to punish or make an example of the wrongdoer; thus, significant monetary awards often are given.

Civil liabilities may result in restitution to the plaintiffs, as with the three categories of damage awards. However, when **criminal liabilities** are involved individual officers can be punished. Violations of proper departmental procedure constitute **administrative liabilities** and may result in dismissal, demotion, transfer, or reprimand. In some cases, officers may be held accountable for liabilities in all three of these areas.

Although damage claims can be pursued against individual law enforcement officers or officials, officers should not be held liable in certain situations that trigger immunity. Absolute immunity rarely applies to police officers, because it pertains to judicial roles (e.g., officers are immune from civil liability for perjury). Qualified immunity is a more common form of immunity claimed by police officers. This type of immunity recognizes that many officers' duties require discretion and must be immune from liability to enable effective police work. In such cases, courts employ a specific test to determine whether a police officer's duties were discretionary. Probable cause applies most often in claims of false arrest or unlawful search. If an officer can demonstrate that there was probable cause to make an arrest or perform a search, then the court will find the officer immune from liability. **Good faith immunity** is form of immunity applicable when an officer could not reasonably know that his or her conduct was illegal or unconstitutional (Kappeler 1997).

In the case of *Monell v. Department of Social Services* (1978),[41] the Court ruled that municipalities can be held liable for their official actions if a constitutional violation was the result of an official policy or recognized and established custom. In this circumstance, the policy or custom must impel the officer or official to act in violation of a person's constitutional rights; in addition, these policies or customs must be the consequence of decisions by a top policy maker. Policies and procedures that may be held responsible include negligent recruitment, negligent deployment or retention, negligent supervision, and negligent training (Kappeler 1997). Each of these potential sources of liability will be detailed throughout this book, particularly in Part 4.

Chapter Summary

- The three types of law discussed in this chapter are criminal law (an individual commits a wrong against the state); constitutional law (civil rights and liberties guaranteed to all individuals); and civil law (also called a tort, a wrong committed against the person).

- When considering the order of authority with regard to the federal, state, and local governments, the highest form of authority is always the U.S. Constitution. The Constitution ensures a proper balance between individual rights and the powers of the state.

- The civil rights and liberties guaranteed in the Bill of Rights are the right to due process; the right to equal protection under the law; the right to be presumed innocent until proven guilty in a court of law; the right to petition, assemble, and choose your own religion; the right to bear arms; the right against unreasonable searches and seizures; the right against arrest without probable cause; the right against self-incrimination and double jeopardy; the right to an attorney; the right to a speedy trial and a trial by jury; the right to speak to and cross-examine witnesses;

- the right to know the charges against you; the right against excessive bail or fines; and the right against cruel or unusual punishment.

- The two components of statutory criminal law are substantive and procedural law. Substantive law defines the specific elements of the crime committed; procedural law specifies how the criminal justice system should deal with an offender.

- The two main classifications of criminal law are felonies and misdemeanors. A felony is a serious crime subject to death or at least one year in prison. A misdemeanor is a relatively minor crime subject to a fine or less than one year in a local jail. A person may also receive a violation, such as a parking ticket, which does not fall under either of the two classifications.

- The Civil Rights Act (section 1983) is significant to law enforcement because it allows the public to sue public officials who deprive people their constitutional rights. Police officers can be held liable if they act negligently, recklessly, knowingly, or purposely when they harm someone.

Linking the Dots

1. How would policing be different if we didn't have the Bill of Rights?

2. Offer an example of how a person could be tried in both criminal and civil courts.

3. Why isn't police use of force cruel and unusual punishment under the Eighth Amendment?

4. Why is it necessary to classify criminal laws?

5. In what type of case might a civil suit be more appropriate than a criminal charge?

6. Should individual officers be held civilly accountable for their actions or their departments? Explain.

KEY TERMS

Actual damages   102
Actus reus   98
Administrative liability   102
Bail   96
Bill of Rights   84
Case law   85
Causation of harm   99
Civil law   83
Civil liability   102
Civil liberties   83
Civil rights   83
Civil Rights Act of 1871 (section 1983)   101
Clear and present danger doctrine   89
Concealed-carry handgun statutes   92
Concurrence   99
Constitution   84
Constitutional law   83
Corpus delicti   99
Criminal law   82
Criminal liability   102
Critical stage   95
Defenses   99
Double jeopardy   94

Electronic surveillance   93
Equal protection clause   97
Equity   84
Establishment of religion clause   86
Exclusionary rule   93
Expressive purposes   88
Felony   98
Fighting words   89
Free exercise of religion   88
Frisk   93
Good faith immunity   103
Inchoate offense   99
Intention   99
Intentional tort   102
Judicial review   86
Massachusetts Bartley-Fox laws   91
Mens rea   99
Misdemeanor   98
Motive   99
Negligent wrong   102
Nolo contendere   101
Nominal damages   102
Order of authority   84
Penal code   85

Plain view   93
Preponderance of the evidence   101
Probable cause   93
Procedural due process   94
Procedural law   97
Project Exile   91
Public offense   98
Punitive damages   102
Pure speech   89
Reasonable suspicion   93
Rule of law   97
Search and seizure   92
Self-incrimination   94
Shall-issue statutes   92
Special relationship   82
Speech-plus conduct   90
Stare decisis   98
Statutory law   97
Substantive due process   94
Substantive law   97
Symbolic speech   89
Torts   100
Violation   98
Warrant   93
Wiretapping   93

REFERENCES

American Law Institute. 2001. *Model Penal Code, Section 2.02.* New York: Aspen Law and Business.

Andrus, R. S. 2000. "The Concealed Handgun Debate and the Need for State-to-State Concealed Handgun

Permit Reciprocity." *Arizona Law Review* 42(1): 129–156.

del Carmen, R. 1991. *Civil Liabilities in American Policing*. Englewood Cliffs, NJ: Prentice Hall.

Garner, B. A. (ed.). 1999. *Black's Law Dictionary*, 7th ed. St. Paul, MN: West Group.

Herman, S. N. 2006. "The USA PATRIOT Act and the Submajoritarian Fourth Amendment." *Harvard Civil Rights-Civil Liberties Review* 41(1):67–132.

Kappeler, V. E. 1997. *Critical Issues in Police Civil Liability*, 2d ed. Prospect Heights, IL: Waveland Press.

Kirkland, M. 2003. "Court Rejects Second Amendment Case." United Press International. Available at www.washtimes.com/upi-breaking/2003201-1053337-9133r.htm.

Lott, J. R. 1998. "The Concealed-Handgun Debate." *Journal of Legal Studies* 27(1):221–243.

Lott, J. R. and D. B. Mustard. 1997. "Crime, Deterrence, and Right-To-Carry Concealed Handguns." *Journal of Legal Studies* 26(1):1–68.

Ludwig, J. 2000. "Gun Self-Defense and Deterrence." *Crime and Justice: A Review of Research*, edited by M. Tonny. Chicago: University of Chicago Press, 363–417.

Lunney, L. A. 1999. "The Erosion of Miranda: *Stare Decisis* Consequences." *Catholic University Law Review* 48:727–861.

O'Brien, D. 1991. *Constitutional Law and Politics: Civil Rights and Civil Liberties*, vol. 2. New York: W. W. Norton and Company.

Office of Juvenile Justice and Delinquency Prevention. 1999. *Promising Strategies to Reduce Gun Violence*. Washington, D.C.: Author.

Sheppard, D., H. Grant, and W. Rowe. 1999. *Fighting Juvenile Gun Violence*. Washington, D.C.: Office of Juvenile Justice and Delinquency Prevention.

Sullivan, J. 2000. *Civil Liabilities of N.Y. Law Enforcement Officers*, 4th ed. Flushing, NY: Looseleaf Law Publications.

Vernick, J. S., D. W. Webster, and L. M. Hepburn. 2001. "Relationship Between Licensing, Registration, and Other Gun Sales Laws and the Source State of Crime Guns." *Injury Prevention* 7:184–189.

Walker, S. 2001. *Sense and Nonsense about Crime and Drugs: A Policy Guide*. Belmont, CA: Wadsworth.

Zimring, F. E. (1995). "Guns and Violence Symposium." *Journal of Criminal Law & Criminology* 86(1): 1–9.

NOTES

1. *Sorichetti v. City of New York*, 69 N.Y. 2d 255 (1987).
2. *Marbury v. Madison*, 1 Cranch 137 (1803).
3. *Everson v. Board of Education*, 330 U.S. 1 (1947).
4. *Edwards v. Aguillard*, 482 U.S. 578 (1987)
5. *Employment Division, Department of Human Resource of Oregon v. Smith*, 110 S. Ct. 1595 (1990).
6. *Roberts v. United States Jaycees*, 486 U.S. 609 (1984).
7. *Texas v. Johnson*, 109 S.Ct. 2533 (1989).
8. *Schenck v. United States*, 249 U.S. 47 (1919).
9. *Gompers v. Buck's Stove and Range*, 221 U.S. 418 (1911).
10. *New York Times v. United States*, 403 U.S. 713 (1971).
11. *Sheppard v. Maxwell*, 385 U.S. 333 (1966).
12. *Nebraska Press Association v. Stuart*, 427 U.S. 539 (1976).
13. *United States v. Cruickshank*, 92 U.S. 542 (1876).
14. *Printz v. United States*, 521 U.S. 898 (1997).
15. *Chimel v. California*, 395 U.S. 752 (1969).
16. *Terry v. Ohio*, 392 U.S. 1 (1968).
17. *Maryland v. Wilson*, 519 U.S. 408 (1997).
18. *Katz v. United States*, 389 U.S. 347 (1967).
19. *Weeks v. United States*, 232 U.S. 383 (1914).
20. *Mapp v. Ohio*, 367 U.S. 643 (1961).
21. *Stovall v. Denno*, 388 U.S. 293 (1967).
22. *Palko v. Connecticut*, 302 U.S. 319 (1937).
23. *Miranda v. Arizona*, 384 U.S. 436 (1966).
24. *Brown v. Mississippi*, 297 U.S. 278 (1937).
25. *Brewer v. Williams*, 430 U.S. 387 (1977).
26. *Schmerber v. California*, 384 U.S. 757 (1966).
27. *Powell v. Alabama*, 287 U.S. 45 (1932).
28. *Gideon v. Wainwright*, 372 U.S. 335 (1963).
29. *Argesinger v. Hamlin*, 407 U.S. 25 (1972).
30. *Douglas v. California*, 372 U.S. 535 (1963).
31. *Escobedo v. Illinois*, 378 U.S. 478 (1964).
32. *Betts v. Brady*, 316 U.S. 455 (1942).
33. *Stack v. Boyle*, 342 U.S. 1 (1951).
34. *United States v. Salerno*, 481 U.S. 739 (1987).
35. *Estelle v. Gamble*, 429 U.S. 97 (1976).
36. *Furman v. Georgia*, 408 U.S. 238 (1972).
37. *Gregg v. Georgia*, 428 U.S. 153 (1976).
38. This was reinforced in *Coker v. Georgia*, 433 U.S. 584 (1977).
39. *United States v. Ursery*, 518 U.S. 267 (1996).
40. *Monroe v. Pape*, 365 U.S. 167 (1961).
41. *Monell v. Department of Social Services*, 436 U.S. 658 (1978).

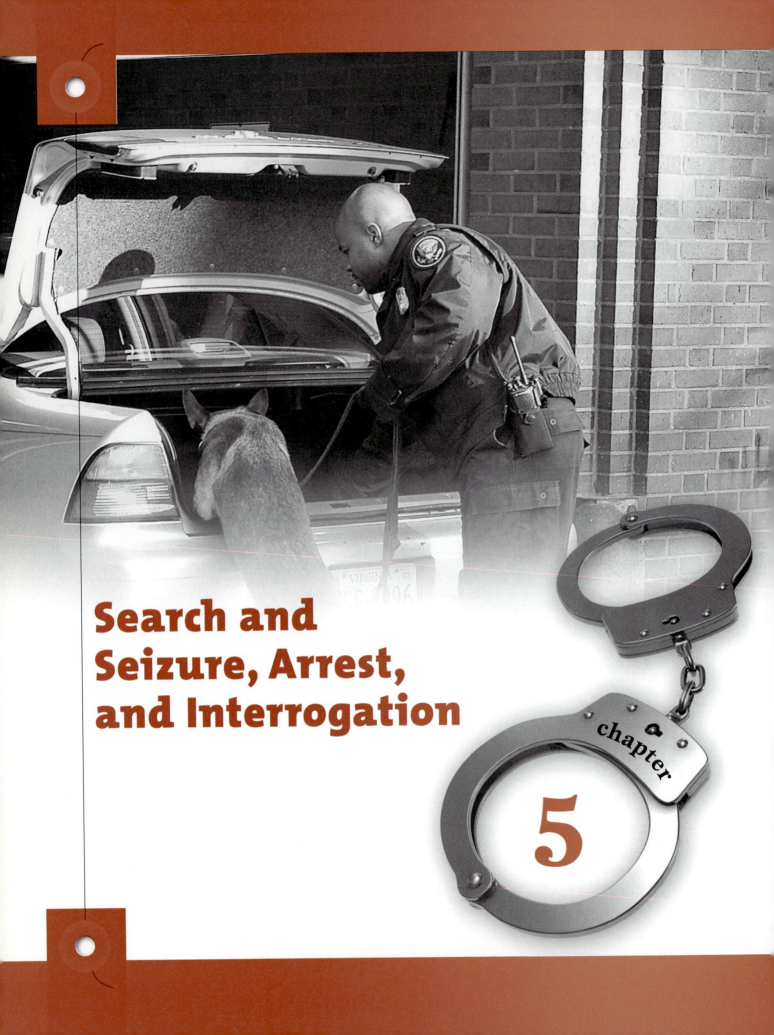

Search and Seizure, Arrest, and Interrogation

chapter

5

Chapter Objectives

- Understand the rights guaranteed by the Fourth and Fifth Amendments.

- Know the different types of searches and the requirements for those searches.

- Understand *Miranda*, the role of this case in arrest and interrogation, and its limitations.

- Know the different standards of proof and understand what is necessary for various types of searches.

- Be familiar with case law relating to the search, seizure, arrest, and interrogation and understand how it has shaped the role of the police in these processes.

Introduction

On February 4, 1999, a bus driver en route from Florida to Michigan allowed three plainclothes police officers to board the bus and conduct a search for weapons and drugs. The search was voluntary, and the officers asked each individual passenger to consent to the search. On the bus, the officers stood so that they were not blocking the door or the aisle to assure passengers that they could leave at any time. One officer approached two passengers, Clifton Brown, Jr., and Christopher Drayton, identified himself as a police officer, and asked if he could search them and their luggage. The passengers consented to the search, and the officer found packets of drugs. Both passengers were led from the bus, arrested, and charged with conspiring to distribute cocaine and possessing cocaine with intent to distribute it. Though convicted, the passengers argued that they did not realize they could refuse the search. The Court, looking at the totality of the circumstances, upheld the conviction and said that although they may not have realized they could refuse to cooperate, the passengers' consent to this suspicionless search was nevertheless voluntary. The Court found that a reasonable person in similar circumstances, would have understood that he or she was free to refuse the search, and the search was therefore not coercive. Thus, the search was constitutional under the Fourth Amendment.[1]

The Supreme Court found that the searches of Brown and Drayton were constitutional. But what is a constitutional search and, subsequently, seizure, under the Fourth Amendment? This is one of the most complicated issues in law enforcement, as will be shown in this chapter. There are numerous types of searches, and case law is constantly evolving in this area. In our post–September 11 environment, the Court may allow the police more leniency as to who is searched, despite the constitutional requirement that people have a right to "be secure in their persons, houses, papers and ef-fects, against unreasonable searches and seizures." The question is: What is reasonable, and how has this definition changed?

Search and Seizure

The Fourth Amendment is critical to policing because it structures how police investigate crimes and suspects. During the Warren Court era of the 1960s, the Court began to put systemic restrictions on the police and to promote the ideal of human rights. The Court refused to accept confessions that were coerced or evidence that was obtained improperly. It also recognized that the police routinely violated the rights of individual suspects and that in order for a court to function democratically it must curb the power of the state.

In order to conduct a search, police officers must have probable cause. **Probable cause** is an ambiguous concept that is difficult to define. A literal definition from *Black's Law Dictionary* states that *probable cause* is "a set of probabilities grounded in the factual and practical considerations which govern the decisions of reasonable and prudent persons and is more than mere suspicion but less than the quantum of evidence required for conviction" (p. 1201). The Court has decided several cases that relate to a definition of probable cause, dating back to *Locke v. United States*[2] in 1813. However, the often-accepted definition of probable cause comes from *Carroll v. United States*,[3] which was later solidified in *Brinegar v. United States*.[4] Procedurally, the Court defined probable cause as existing where "the facts and circumstances within their [the officers'] knowledge and of which they had reasonably trustworthy information [are] sufficient in themselves to warrant a man of reasonable caution in the belief that an offense has been or is being committed."[5] In *Draper v. United States*,[6] the Court devised a definition of probable cause that is still relevant today. The Court's definition stated that probable cause was more than suspicion, requiring the existence of facts that would lead a person of reasonable caution to believe that a crime has been committed, yet not requiring proof of guilt.

Though the courts still refer to the definition set out in *Draper*, they have since further clarified the definition. The Supreme Court set out a two-pronged test in *Spinelli v. United States*[7] that required verification of information and its source to establish probable cause; however, the Court has since provided a less rigid conception of probable cause. In *Illinois v. Gates*,[8] the Court defined probable cause as "a fair probability that contraband or evidence of a will be found in a particular place." The Court's opinion in this case emphasized that police work inevitably deals with probabilities; the weighing of information is done best by law enforcement professionals whose experience can aid them to make judgments about information based on a totality of the circumstances. The Court held that the rigid test laid out in *Spinelli* overly hindered the interests of law enforcement. In this case, the Court applied this reasoning to allow the use of anonymous informants.

Officers can discern whether probable cause exists in a number of different ways. Oftentimes, probable cause may result from information received from reliable and well-known informants, victims, witnesses, police bulletins and broadcasts, or other independent sources (with confirmation). Evidence from consensual searches and interviews may establish probable cause, as can weapons or evidence seized during the course of a stop. Further, items in plain view may establish probable cause for a search or seizure if it is immediately apparent that these items are contraband or evidence. Finally, an officer's experience, special training, and expertise allow him or her to make limited inferences in decisions about persons, circumstances, or evidence to establish probable cause (*Georgetown Law Journal* 2006). Chapter 10 will discuss the fine, and at times difficult, line between relying on experience and using stereotypes. However it is attained, probable cause must exist before a full-scale search can take place.

Stop and Frisk

In some cases, police officers must make stops and perform limited searches for the interest of the public good and for their own safety. In such cases and under specific conditions, probable cause is not required. After 1968 and the Court's decision in the landmark *Terry v. Ohio*[9] case (discussed below), police officers often refer to "*Terry* stops." *Terry* stops are situations where concern for public safety, crime prevention, or criminal apprehension and an officer's own safety lead to a **stop and frisk**.

An officer may stop an individual when there is reasonable and articulable suspicion that a crime has occurred or is about to occur. In other words, an officer must be able to specifically explain the reasons for stopping an individual. Officers cannot rely on intuition or hunches to stop individuals. Any time an officer uses physical force or his or her authority to prevent a person from leaving a space, a seizure of that person has occurred. After an individual has been stopped, an officer must reasonably determine that there is a possibility that the person has a weapon in order to perform a particular kind of search. In this case, the officer may **frisk** the outside of a person's clothing in search of a weapon. The officer can ask the individual to take off any outer clothes, such as a jacket, but the officer cannot reach into the clothing for any contraband other than a weapon, unless the officer, without added manipulation, simultaneously recognizes the item is not a weapon and is contraband (Plain Feel Doctrine). In everyday practice, the requirement to stop and the requirement necessary to frisk a person will not be distinct. However, it is possible that an officer's stop of an individual does not then justify a frisk.

As long as there have been professional police officers, officers have conducted **field interrogations**. These range from casual questions and conversations to specific discussions and information gathering about a crime or criminal. In these situations, there is no seizure of the person, and the person must reasonably believe he or she is free to leave at any time. If the officer wishes to detain a person, however briefly, against his or her will while using force or authority, probable cause must exist.

Police officers can conduct field interrogations and stop and frisks based upon **reasonable suspicion**. Like probable cause, reasonable suspicion is an ambiguous term, and the courts have wavered in their definition of it though the Court articulated a standard for reasonable suspicion in *Terry*. Cleveland police detective Martin McFadden, a thirty-nine-year veteran of the police force, observed two men who he perceived to be "casing" a store. After they walked back and forth past the store twenty-four times, they briefly met with a third man. Officer McFadden approached the men, identified himself as a police officer, and asked them for identification. Based on his experience as a police officer, he assumed that they would have weapons if they were, in fact, casing the store, so he frisked them. The Court upheld this stop, despite the fact that no crime had taken place and the officer only had his expertise to rely upon. The judge not only said that McFadden conducted the search properly—making sure

Stop and frisk is one of the most common and controversial investigative techniques available to the patrol officer.

that the search was minimally intrusive and served only to determine if the men were armed—but that it would have been irresponsible *not* to stop them based on his expertise.

Other cases since *Terry* have supported a standard of reasonable suspicion in order to conduct a minimally intrusive stop or frisk. In *United States v. Arvizu*,[10] the Court allowed an investigatory stop of a vehicle by Border Patrol officers based on reasonable suspicion. However, the Court emphasized that race alone does not constitute reasonable suspicion.[11] The Court has also addressed the issue of drug courier profiles and whether these are sufficient in order to establish reasonable suspicion for a field interrogation. In the *United States v. Sokolow*,[12] the Court explained that based on the totality of the circumstances it was acceptable to use such a profile. The Court has also confirmed that fleeing at the sight of police officer does not, in itself, constitute reasonable suspicion, even if the person is fleeing in a high-crime area.[13]

The Exclusionary Rule

The Fourth Amendment places considerable restriction on police power and **seizure**, because if evidence is obtained improperly during any type of search it is excluded in a court of law. Searches can be conducted prior to, incident to, or after an arrest. Whenever the search occurs, officers must follow specific procedures, and they are usually required to obtain a search warrant stipulating what they are to search and what they are searching for. The **exclusionary rule**, which prohibits the admission of illegally obtained evidence in court, was established on a federal level in 1914.[14] This includes any physical or verbal evidence that was obtained while violating an individual's Fourth, Fifth, or Sixth Amendment rights.

The exclusionary rule was established federally in 1914 and was applied to the states in 1961. However, in 1952 the Court did put some restrictions on improper seizure of evidence in the case of *Rochin v. California*.[15] After a tip that an individual was selling narcotics, police officers went to question him and illegally entered his home. At this time, the suspect put two capsules of morphine in his mouth. The officers attempted to forcefully extract the capsules, but the suspect swallowed them. The police handcuffed the suspect, took him to a hospital, and had a doctor pump his stomach against his will. He initially was convicted based upon this "seizure" of evidence. The U.S. Supreme Court later overturned the finding, saying, "We are compelled to conclude that the proceedings by which this conviction was obtained do more than offend some fastidious squeamishness or private sentimentalism about combating crime too energetically. This is conduct that shocks the conscience. . . . This course of proceeding by agents of government to obtain evidence is bound to offend even hardened sensibilities."[16]

The "shocks the conscience" standard remained the only check on police search and seizure powers in state cases until 1961, when the exclusionary rule became applicable on a state level with the case of *Mapp v. Ohio*.[17] In this case, the police illegally entered Mapp's home because they thought she was harboring a fugitive. While in the house, they found and seized a trunk full of obscene material. The Court claimed that this material was inadmissible because the search was not conducted following proper police procedures. The judge said, "nothing can destroy a government more quickly than its failure to observe its own laws."[18]

All illegally obtained evidence is excluded from a court of law, as is anything that an officer seizes as a result of the tainted evidence or search. For instance, if a police officer conducts an illegal interrogation and violates an individual's Fifth Amendment right against self-incrimination, that confession would be thrown out. If, based on that confession, the suspect tells the police where the weapon is that he used to kill his victim, the weapon also would be excluded during the trial because the police learned about the weapon through illegal means. The weapon would be considered **fruit of the poisonous tree**. The fruit of the poisonous tree doctrine was established in *Wong Sun v. United States*,[19] in which the Court explained that police misconduct does not require the entire case to be dismissed, but only the tainted evidence, or "fruit," resulting from that misconduct.

The most common fruits are derived from an interrogation that has been conducted improperly, during which the suspect discloses information about evidence relating to the offense. The Court explained in *Michigan v. Tucker*,[20] however, that when a suspect's *Miranda* rights are violated, this does not automatically result in the exclusion of the fruits from that confession. The case of *New York v. Quarles*[21] supported this decision, creating a public safety exception to the exclusionary rule. In *Quarles*, a woman approached two officers and told them that an individual with a gun had just raped her. She also pointed out the supermarket into which her assailant had fled. Upon entering the store and finding the alleged perpetrator, they frisked him and found only an empty holster. Out of concern for public safety, the officer asked where the gun was. The suspect told him, and that statement was later used against the suspect in court. Because the officers had not yet read him his *Miranda*

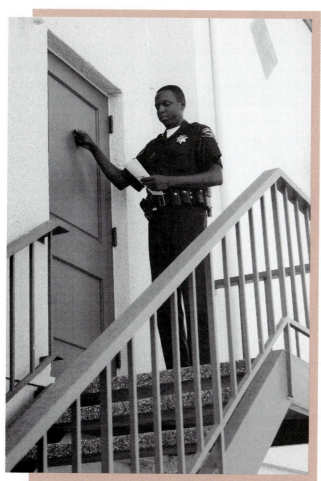

Officers usually are required to first obtain a warrant prior to searching individuals or homes according to the Fourth Amendment. However, the practical realities of law enforcement make many exceptions necessary.

rights, the trial court excluded the statement under the exclusionary rule and the gun as a "fruit of the poisonous tree." However, the Supreme Court allowed both the statement and the gun to be entered as evidence, explaining that public safety takes precedence over individual rights when there is an imminent danger to life or limb.

Although the exclusionary rule remains an important check on police powers, there are exceptions to it. The **good faith exception**, established by *United States vs. Leon*,[22] establishes that if officers believe, in good faith, that their actions are authorized by warrants that turn out to be defective, the evidence should still be admissible. In *Leon*, the Court claimed that the exclusionary rule should not be applied as a blanket solution to improper searches and should not serve to deter reasonable law enforcement activity. In *Massachusetts v. Sheppard*,[23] the court affirmed this position and ruled that technical judicial errors were not cause for the exclusion of evidence.

Another exception to the exclusionary rule is **inevitable discovery**, which holds that evidence obtained illegally can be admitted if the police could have legally found it anyway. This occurred in the case of *Nix v. Williams*,[24] where the defendant was accused of murdering a ten-year-old girl. The police drove the suspect from Davenport to the police station in Des Moines. The suspect explained that, on advice of counsel, he wanted to invoke his Fifth Amendment right to remain silent. During the three-hour drive, the officers spoke to each other about the case and how badly the family feels that they wouldn't be able to give their daughter a proper Christian burial. Although they never asked him directly about the offense, he confessed to the killing and explained where he buried the body. The Court said that the officer's "Christian burial" speech was tantamount to interrogation and the evidence (the child's body) was considered the fruit of an illegal search. However, the Court also later found that the police would have found the child's body through legal means even without Williams' confession, and it was therefore admissible. Such after-the-fact justifications illustrate the sometimes difficult balance between crime control and due process concerns discussed in Chapter 1. The Supreme Court was justifiably concerned about asking law enforcement agencies to "turn the other way" with respect to the body of a little girl, despite apparent improper actions on the part of a detective.

Search of Persons and Premises

Full-scale searches of premises generally require a warrant. Searches can be done either before or after arrest, depending on the circumstances. In order to get a **search warrant**, the officer must prepare an affidavit for a judge that contains information on the area to be searched, what is being searched for, and the facts establishing probable cause. The judge can then issue a warrant for the police to search for specific property in a particular area, seize it, and return it to the court.

When searching a house with a warrant, officers are generally required to **knock and announce**, knocking on the door and announcing their presence. The Fourth Amendment protects against unannounced police entry. This concept dates back to 1756 (*Curtis' Case*), at which time the Supreme Court stated that "peace-officers, having a legal warrant to arrest for a breach of the peace, may break open doors, after having demanded admittance and given due notice of their warrant."[25] Most warrants will be secured for a daytime search; however, searches may be legal at night if the officers believe that there will be either an imminent consumption or movement of the evidence or the officer's safety is in jeopardy during the day. If the officer perceives the situation to be dangerous or that the suspect may not cooperate with the search procedure, the normal knock-and-announce procedure does not need to be followed. The knock-and-announce rule was held as a part of the reasonableness requirement of the Fourth Amendment by the Court in *Wilson v. Arkansas*.[26] The Court confronted the rule again in 1997 and held that to justify a "no knock" entry the police must have a reasonable suspicion to believe that knocking and announcing would be dangerous to themselves or lead to the destruction of evidence (*Richards v. Wisconsin*[27]). This is often the case when the police raid the residence of a suspected drug dealer, though the Court has said there is no blanket dismissal of knock-and-announce procedures for such cases. Moreover, in *Hudson v. Michigan*[28] the Court held that an illegal entry into a house because of a failure to knock and announce was not grounds for the exclusion of evidence.

The police do not always need warrants to search premises. When there are **exigent circumstances**, or emergency circumstances, the officers can search premises without a warrant. There are several types of exigent circumstances, the most common being that evidence is about to be destroyed. When in question, the Court will almost always uphold the individual's right to be free from unwarranted searches over the power of the police if there is a question about the legitimacy of the exigency. A search without a warrant will be considered illegal if there was no probable cause or if the officers had time to secure a warrant.

For instance, in *Kirk v. Louisiana*[29] the Supreme Court claimed that the police erred in searching the petitioner prior to securing a warrant because there were no obvious exigent circumstances. The police had received an anonymous complaint that drug sales were occurring in an apartment, and so they placed the apartment under surveillance. The police witnessed what they thought were several drug transactions and stopped an individual leaving the premises. After finding illegal drugs on the individual, they immediately knocked on the door, found Kennedy Kirk in possession of drugs and money, and saw contraband in plain view in the apartment. The officers arrested Kirk and called for a search warrant before searching the rest of the house. The Court found, however, that their original entrance into the house was not legal, and that they should not have searched Kirk without a warrant because there were no seemingly exigent circumstances. A similar error occurred in the case of *Payton v. New York*[30] in which the officers suspected Payton of a homicide and conducted a warrantless search of his home. The Court declared this search illegal and the evidence seized as poisonous fruit, even though the evidence was in plain view.

Warrantless entry is justified in a few other particular situations. In *United States v. Santana*,[31] the Court justified a search without a warrant because the police were in **hot pursuit** of a suspect. The Court has held that hot pursuit is a standard broad enough to justify the apprehension of a fleeing suspect. Any form of chase when the suspect may escape without immediate police action, however mundane, is a pursuit of a suspect (as opposed to a dramatic, high-speed car chase) that may constitute hot pursuit. In the case of fire or explosion, the police may search areas where they reasonably believe hazardous items are located (*Michigan v. Tyler*[32]; *Michigan v. Clifford*[33]).

If evidence is in plain view, it can be seized without a warrant. The **plain view doctrine** states that evidence of criminal activity can be seized if it is "immediately apparent" and the officer has a legal right to be in the place where the contraband is viewed. It is also necessary for the contraband to be immediately recognizable. In a similar vein, the Court allows evidence to be seized if it is in "plain smell" or an officer experiences "plain feel." In the case of *Minnesota v. Dickerson*,[34] the Court upheld the concept of plain feel but said that the officer did not immediately recognize the contraband. Rather, when an officer did a *Terry* frisk on Dickerson and realized that there was no weapon, he felt a lump in his pocket and determined that it was a narcotic substance. The Court rejected this evidence, because the officer had to manipulate the substance with his fingers in order to determine what the substance was; therefore, the substance was not immediately recognizable.

Another type of search is one of voluntary consent. Officers can ask a person for consent to search his or her house; if the person agrees, the search is legal without a warrant. The consent must be knowing, free, and voluntary and not a result of deceit or trickery. The only individuals who can give consent to search a residence are the adults who live there, including roommates, a spouse, or an individual who is temporarily staying at the residence.[35] Guests, juveniles, and landlords cannot legally give consent to search a dwelling.

A search of premises can also involve sense-enhancing technology, namely, thermal imaging. With **thermal imaging**, a device is used to determine the amount of heat emanating from the premises. Thermal imaging can be used to detect body heat, but it is more likely to be used to detect lights that give off a particularly high level of heat and that are used to grow marijuana plants. In the case of *Kyllo v. United States*,[36] the petitioner questioned the use of a thermal-imaging device on his home, which he claimed was intrusive and violated his Fourth Amendment rights. The Court stated that the use of thermal imaging would be constitutional within the confines of a legal search. However, as used in *Kyllo*—at 3 AM, aimed at a private home from a public street, and without a warrant—thermal imaging is unconstitutional. The Court said this search turned up information that the police could not have otherwise found without a physical intrusion into the home.

In addition to searching premises, the police can search a person **incident to arrest**, or at the time of arrest, as well as the area that is in the immediate arm span (reach) of the suspect. *Chimel v. California*[37] set this precedent. In this case, officers arrested Chimel for the burglary of a coin shop. The officers searched Chimel's three-bedroom house at the time of his arrest and seized evidence, including coins, that were admitted into evidence and that helped to convict him. Though the appellate court upheld his conviction because the search was incident to a lawful arrest, the Supreme Court overturned the decision because the search of the defendant's home went far beyond the immediate area of the suspect in which he might have been able to obtain a weapon or destroy evidence. The Court said that without a search warrant there was no constitutional jurisdiction to search beyond the immediate area, and the search was therefore unconstitutional.

If, however, an officer believes that the suspect poses a danger, the officer can conduct a protective sweep of the immediate surroundings. A protective sweep is limited and can only last as long as is necessary to secure the immediate area and dispel the suspicion of danger. In *Maryland v. Buie*,[38] the Court held that a warrantless protective sweep of a house was allowable if the officer reasonably believes that there is an individual in the house who may harm the officer or others.

Another case involving search of a person is *Schmerber v. California*.[39] Schmerber was pulled over while driving under the influence of alcohol. The police officer required that blood be drawn from Schmerber, which Schmerber later claimed was an improper "seizure" of his person. The Court disagreed, claiming that so long as experienced medical personnel drew the blood that this is an acceptable seizure of evidence.

Thermal imaging is one example of technological advancements in policing. A thermal-imaging device can be used to assist in the search of a premises as long as it is within the confines of a legal search.

Search of Motor Vehicles

As with searching premises and persons, police officers must have probable cause in order to search an automobile. However, unlike other full-scale searches, officers generally do not need a warrant to search automobiles, and they can search all areas of the car, including the trunk and glove compartment. The reason that officers do not need a warrant to search cars follows the idea of mobility: In the time that it would take to obtain a warrant, the driver can move the car and possibly destroy evidence. The concept of mobility was introduced in 1924 in *Carroll v. United States*[40] and further supported in many subsequent cases. In *Chambers v. Maroney*,[41] the Court extended the concept of mobility to include cars that have been impounded. The Court determined that the warrantless search of a car after it had been taken to the police station did not violate the petitioner's Fourth Amendment rights because a car can maintain its mobility even when impounded. If there is probable cause, an automobile, because of its mobility, may be searched without a warrant in circumstances that would not justify a warrantless search of a house or office. However, the police do not have a blanket ability to search impounded cars. The Court in *Coolidge v. New Hampshire* claimed that mobility only applies if there is a danger the car will be moved.[42]

The protection of an automobile is not as stringent as that of a home. Whereas "a man's home is his castle" and will be protected to the utmost, the Court is more lenient on officers searching cars and the passengers within. In *Michigan v. Long*,[43] the Court held that a warrantless search of the passenger compartment of a car was permissible (limited to areas where a weapon may be hidden) when an officer reasonably believes that the situation is dangerous or that the suspect may have immediate access to a weapon. The Court has also upheld a warrantless search of the passenger compartment and any containers within as valid incident to an arrest (*New York v. Belton*[44]). Further, if officers have legitimately stopped a vehicle and have probable cause to believe that there is contraband hidden within the car, they may search it (*United States v. Ross*[45]). It is constitutional to seize a car from a public place without a warrant as well, as happened in *Florida v. White*,[46] when officers seized White's car in order to search it for narcotics. Because the warrantless seizure of the car was deemed constitutional, the narcotics found in the car were not fruits of a poisonous tree. When conducting a stop of a vehicle, an officer can ask both the driver and the passenger to step out of the car in order to ensure that evidence is not

Motor vehicle stops are among the most common, yet potentially hazardous, police–citizen interactions.

destroyed.[47] Although the majority of searches on cars are considered legal once stopped, considerable debate continues about what constitutes a legal stop.

In addition to warrantless searches of a vehicle based upon mobility, the Court has also decided that warrantless searches are constitutional when the car is used in the commission of a felony.[48] At this time, everything in the car may be searched, including closed containers.[49]

Pretextual Stops

Many searches of autos arise from pretextual stops. A **pretextual stop** occurs when an officer ostensibly stops a vehicle for a traffic violation (e.g., a broken taillight or speeding) and proceeds to use that stop to conduct a full-scale search of the car.[50] The Court has upheld pretextual stops, calling them a constitutionally acceptable policing tactic. The first formal acknowledgement of pretext stops occurred in 1996 in the case of *Whren v. United States*.[51] A police officer pulled Whren over for a vehicular violation, though the true intention of the stop was to investigate drug-dealing activity. The officer saw drug-related contraband in plain view when he approached the car. The Court said that this stop was constitutional, even though the traffic violation was only a pretext to the real reason for the stop. The Court said the stop was reasonable because the officers had probable cause to believe that the petitioner had violated the traffic code. Therefore, the seizure of the evidence was constitutional and admissible in court. The Court went on to say that the law could not be selectively enforced, because to do so would violate the Equal Protection Clause of the Constitution. However, it would not violate the Fourth Amendment search and seizure laws; the pretext stop was therefore constitutional on those grounds.

Because so many people could conceivably be pulled over for a violation, it is likely that officers may use race, or racial profiling, as a factor to decide whom they will pull over. At the center of the racial profiling controversy is the allegation that police officers exercise their discretionary power to stop based upon race, and this is used primarily against African Americans and Latinos (American Civil Liberties Union Special Report 1999). Litigation against police agencies in New Jersey, Illinois, and Maryland has occurred because of alleged racial disparities in stops (Gibbons 2003). Following the terrorist attacks on September 11, renewed justifications have surfaced with respect to Arab Americans, particularly in the context of airports. We will return to this very difficult issue in Chapter 10.

Systematic Stops and Searches

The police are allowed to stop and search individuals without probable cause for **systematic stops**, or if there is a set method to the searches. One method by which this is done is through roadblocks for either border patrol areas or sobriety checkpoints. The Court has ruled that temporary roadblocks are constitutional and a reasonable law enforcement tool based on the fact that 1.5 percent of the drivers stopped at sobriety checkpoints were legally drunk.[52] Additionally, these checkpoints are not aimed at a particular group of people, but rather follow a systemic method as to who is stopped (e.g., every fifth car). The key to systematic searches is that there is no reasonable suspicion or probable cause that a particular individual has committed an offense. Rather, the purpose of these stops is to prevent crime. Such justifications again illustrate the need to balance individual liberties and public safety concerns. In this case, the Court found the intrusion to be minor while at the same time providing a significant benefit to society.

Another type of systematic search is similar to that described in the chapter's opening case, where the police boarded a bus and asked the passengers to voluntarily consent to a search. Police officers can board any form of public transportation to conduct searches of luggage and passengers for weapons or illegal contraband. Similarly, individuals at an airport can be stopped prior to boarding a plane or upon landing and their luggage can be checked. As with roadblocks, this is constitutional so long as it follows a systematic method by which airport personnel choose individuals to be stopped and searched. The stops must be random, and race cannot be a determining factor as to who is stopped and searched.[53]

Whereas random sobriety checkpoints are legal, random drug checkpoints are not. The Court declared these unconstitutional in *City of Indianapolis v. Edmond*, calling them an unconstitutional means to a justified end. The Court recognized that drug use, particularly while driving, may be dangerous, but to allow such roadblocks would set a precedent for interrogating people about any illegal activity. The Court claimed that this would be intrusive and unconstitutional under the Fourth Amendment.

Search of Public Places

The key concept of the Fourth Amendment is privacy. However, it only protects **reasonable expectations of privacy**. Common land, or that which is open to the public, can be searched without a warrant, because there is no reasonable expectation of privacy. Generally, a reasonable expectation of privacy exists within the **curtilage**, or the immediate area, surrounding the residence. However, some areas are not easily defined as either private or public; for example, public telephone booths, garbage, driveways, and vacated hotel rooms.

The courts have decided many cases that have helped to define what is considered to be private. The case that determined the recognized standard of reasonable expectation of privacy was *Katz v. U.S.* as it set boundaries for **wiretapping**.[54] Katz used a public telephone booth to wager money on a gambling deal. Police officers had wiretapped this booth and introduced the evidence from Katz's conversation into the court. Katz claimed that he should have a reasonable expectation of privacy in a phone booth and that the evidence should therefore be inadmissible. The Supreme Court agreed, and set forth a two-prong test in order to determine privacy in future case. First, the individual must show that he or she expected privacy. Second, that expectation should be reasonable.

Although driveways fall within the general definition of curtilage, garbage that is placed out on the street does not. In *California v. Greenwood*,[55] the Court stated that Greenwood did not have a reasonable expectation of privacy with his garbage when he put the garbage in front of his house. Investigators who looked through the garbage to determine whether Greenwood was involved in drug trafficking did not violate Greenwood's right to privacy. Similarly, individuals do not have a reasonable expectation of privacy with regard to abandoned property—such as vacated hotel rooms—and the police can search this without violating an individual's Fourth Amendment rights.

Linkages *in Law Enforcement*

Searches and Terrorism: The USA PATRIOT Improvement and Reauthorization Act of 2005

On October 26, 2001, the USA PATRIOT Act of 2001 was signed into law, expanding all four traditional tools of surveillance—wiretaps, search warrants, pen/trap orders, and subpoenas. The USA PATRIOT Improvement and Reauthorization Act of 2005 reaffirmed the expansion of these surveillance powers. Powers under the Foreign Intelligence Surveillance Act (FISA), which applies to spying within the United States by foreign intelligence agencies, also were expanded (Electronic Frontier Foundation 2001). A major purpose of these acts was to facilitate law enforcement's ability to investigate terrorist activities in the interest of public safety.

The following are some of the key provisions of the USA PATRIOT Improvement and Reauthorization Act of 2005:

- The FBI and CIA can now conduct nationwide roving wiretaps. Law enforcement is no longer limited to specific phones or specific computers. Instead, the government can issue one wiretap order that will extend a search to different phones and computers without having to prove in court that the information being accessed is specifically relevant to the investigation.

- The government can now receive all "noncontent" information voluntarily given to them by an Internet Service Provider (ISP) without the need for a court order or subpoena. Additionally, court order review is not required to access records of session times and durations and means and source of payments.

- Simply by telling any single judge in the United States that the information collected would be relevant to an ongoing criminal investigation, the government can now spy on people's Web surfing activity, including key terms entered into search engines, regardless of whether the person being monitored is the target of the investigation.

The following are some of the key provisions of FISA:

- The FISA has increased powers, including a lower standard for spying on American citizens.

- Where the standard of probable cause is not met for domestic surveillance, the Attorney General can obtain an FISA wiretap for the monitoring of an American citizen. All information from the search can subsequently be shared with the FBI.

- The Act addresses money laundering and includes RICO-style provisions for the seizure of property and assets.

QUESTIONS

1. No one can argue with the public safety concerns raised by September 11. Do these concerns warrant increased law enforcement powers to combat terrorism?

2. Which of the provisions of the USA PATRIOT Improvement and Reauthorization Act of 2005 do you feel "water down" civil liberties beyond the public safety justifications noted in the previous question? What are the risks involved?

3. Should FISA be used against U.S. citizens? What are the implications of this?

4. Research the 1974 spying revelations against the FBI and foreign intelligence agencies. What precipitated the concerns? How does the current climate differ?

Arrest

If a police officer has probable cause to believe that an individual has committed a criminal act, the officer can arrest the individual. An **arrest** occurs when an officer takes a person suspected of criminal activity into custody. Officers are allowed to use coercive force when arresting an individual. Although the force cannot be excessive, police officers are allowed to use the minimum amount of force necessary to ensure the arrest and control the situation.

Arrests versus Stops

An arrest is more intrusive upon civil liberties than a stop. During a stop, an individual is not in custody and can leave at any time. An arrest is generally defined as the point at which a suspect is taken into custody and detained or the point at which a reasonable person believes that he or she is not able to leave. As noted earlier, any such situation that involves "significant deprivations of freedom of movement" (*Terry*) is considered a seizure under the meaning of the Fourth Amendment's "search and seizure" provision. Several cases have supported the opinion that an individual is in custody and has been "seized" when he or she does not perceive the ability to leave as opposed to being in the physical custody of the police. This was the argument of Clifton Brown, Jr. and Christopher Drayton, the case discussed at the beginning of the chapter. They argued that the police officers conducted a stop that was custodial in nature, thereby exceeding the legality of a stop and voluntary search. Though the court disagreed in this particular case, several other cases have deliberated over the perception of a custodial condition. They can be summed up by the decision in *Florida v. Bostick*,[56] in which the Court explained that a stop does not become custodial as long as a reasonable person would be free to leave the situation. This supports the concept of custody discussed in *Miranda v. Arizona*,[57] in which the Court described custody as being psychologically rather than physically oriented.

The Arrest Warrant

An arrest can occur with or without a warrant. Generally, an officer is supposed to obtain a warrant if the suspect is not yet in police custody. The process for obtaining an arrest warrant is similar to that of a search warrant, because both require a set of facts indicating probable cause to believe the person committed the act. The Court in *Wong Sun* stated that an arrest must stand upon firmer ground than mere suspicion, although it is not necessary to prove guilt at this stage.[58]

It is actually more common for officers to arrest suspects without a warrant than with one. To make a warrantless arrest of a suspect who has committed a misdemeanor, the officer must be present during the commission of the crime. Otherwise, the arrest would not be valid. An arrest for a felony can be made without a warrant if the officer witnesses a crime, has probable cause to believe that an individual committed a crime that the officer knows was committed, or if there are exigent circumstances. Exigent circumstances for warrantless arrests are similar to those discussed in regard to searches. Exigent circumstances may involve a suspect who is armed, violent, threatening, or destroying evidence. If any of these circumstances exists, officers do not need to announce their presence before entering the premises to arrest the suspect.

The Court has deliberated upon several cases in order to determine the validity of a suspect's warrantless arrest. In the *People v. Ramey*,[59] officers made an arrest without a warrant in the absence of exigent circumstances. The Court invalidated the arrest and the subsequent search (as a fruit of an invalid arrest). The Court further supported this decision in *Payton v. New York*,[60] claiming that officers can only make a warrantless arrest in a dwelling if there are exigent circumstances. Once a legal arrest has been made, the officer must inform the suspect of his or her rights before an interrogation.

Interrogation

Upon arrest, the police must question the suspect about the crime that they believe the suspect has committed. This goes beyond the field interrogation, which only requires the police to have a reasonable suspicion that a crime is afoot. Field interrogations require cooperation between the police and the suspect, whereas an interrogation is not voluntary. The suspect in an interrogation does not have the right to leave. Before the police can conduct an **interrogation**, or a questioning of the suspect after an arrest, they must inform the suspect of his or her rights. Although nearly all police departments in the United States use the rights enumerated in *Miranda v. Arizona*[61] (also referred to as **Miranda rights**), they are not required to use the Court's specific list of rights and their explanation. Most departments do so to ensure that they fulfill their constitutional obligation without threat of losing a conviction on appeal. Most people in the United States know the *Miranda* rights well, because they have been documented in police dramas on television and in movies since the late 1960s. The *Miranda* rights and waiver state:

> You have the right to remain silent. If you give up that right, anything you say can and will be used against you in a court of law. You have the right to speak with an attorney and to have the attorney present during questioning. If you so desire and

A suspect is interrogated by a police officer while in custody.

cannot afford one, an attorney will be appointed for you without charge and before questioning. Do you understand each of these rights I have read to you? Having these rights in mind, do you wish to give up your rights as I have explained them to you and talk to me now?

The common perception, based on television docudramas, is that the police read individuals their rights as they are handcuffing them and taking them into custody. Such a dramatic occurrence is unlikely; the rights must only be read prior to interrogation.

So how did these rights come to being, and what is their significance?

Miranda v. Arizona

Ernesto Miranda was arrested in Phoenix, Arizona, in 1963 on charges of kidnapping and rape. He was identified by the victim in a lineup, arrested, and subsequently interrogated for two hours without being advised of his right to remain silent and right to counsel. He confessed to the crimes, and this statement was later admitted into evidence. He was convicted of the offenses, but the conviction was later overturned because the Supreme Court recognized that *Miranda*'s constitutional rights had been violated.

The basis of *Miranda* is that coerced confessions are unconstitutional and may not be true. To avoid coerced confessions, the Court suggested specific steps for the police officers to follow prior to interrogation. It is necessary for the police to explain to each suspect the right not to incriminate him or herself under the Fifth Amendment, as well as the right to counsel under the Sixth Amendment. Though many suspects waive their rights and speak to the police, the waiver must be knowing and voluntary. For a suspect to waive his or her *Miranda* rights, the suspect must agree orally or in writing to speak without counsel present. If the suspect indicates that he or she wants a lawyer present, the police must stop the questioning immediately. However, they can later ask the suspect again whether he or she wants to waive the *Miranda* rights. It is important to note, however, that the request to waive rights cannot be made every day and cannot be made if the suspect has asked to speak to a lawyers, unless at the initiation of the suspect.

Problems can arise, however, if the suspect does not understand the *Miranda* rights or does not waive them voluntarily. For instance, the suspect may not understand English, may be intoxicated, may be under the control of substances, or even be mentally ill. An alternative version of the *Miranda* warnings is used in some jurisdictions to determine whether an officer is dealing with a mentally ill offender incapable of comprehending his or her rights. The police must be careful in such a situation, because any confession must be voluntary and knowing in order to be admissible in court. If it is not, then the confession (and any of the fruits resulting from it) is excluded.

The police are allowed to use cunning tactics to work around *Miranda* rights and get a suspect to confess. For example, upon the recommendation of an offender profiler (see Chapter 8), an interrogator left pictures of the victim and crime scene in the room an offender was being held in to make the suspect feel guilty and perhaps more likely to confess (Douglas 1994).

However, the police must respect the suspect's right to counsel if so asked. In the case of *Brewer v. Williams*[62] (see the rehearing of *Nix v. Williams*, discussed earlier, for inevitable discovery doctrine), the police officers tricked

FIGURE 5.1

Alternative *Miranda* Warning

1. You have the right to remain silent.
   "You do not have to talk to anyone.
   Tell me in your own words what I just said."

2. Anything you say can and will be used against you in a court of law.
   "If you talk, I can tell others what you said. Tell me in your own words what I just said."

   "What you say can get you in trouble. Tell me in your own words what I just said."

3. You have the right to talk to a lawyer and have him present at any time during questioning.
   "You can talk to a lawyer. Tell me in your own words what I just said."

   "Your lawyer can be with you if you talk to anyone. Tell me in your own words what I just said."

4. If you cannot afford a lawyer, one will be appointed for you without cost.

   "If you cannot pay for a lawyer, the judge will get you one for free. Tell me in your own words what I just said."

Williams into confessing where he buried the body of the girl he killed. Because the police were driving Williams to a police station three hours away, he was essentially "in custody" while in the car. This, combined with the fact that he asked for counsel immediately, invalidated the confession that he made about the body. The confession was thrown out in the trial; however, the girl's body was admitted as evidence due to inevitable discovery.

When *Miranda* Rights Must Be Read

The police are required to inform a suspect of his or her rights prior to interrogation. This usually occurs when the police take the suspect into custody, but the definition of *custody* is not always clear. Although indirect, the discussion between the police and Williams was considered an interrogation. In his opinion in *Miranda*, Chief Justice Warren stated that a custodial interrogation can be psychological as well as physical, and that coercion can be mental as well as physical. This was also clear in *Williams*, because the tactic used by the police was to make Williams feel guilty. They convinced him that the morally correct thing to do was to lead them to the body so that her parent's could organize a Christian burial. This psychological tactic, while "in custody" in the police car, was considered to be equivalent to a custodial interrogation, and the confession was thereby invalidated because Williams had asked for counsel.

In the absence of an arrest or an interrogation, it is not necessary for the police to read a suspect his or her *Miranda* rights. It is not necessary to read *Miranda* warnings during a traffic stop, a stop and frisk, or when the suspect volunteers information to the police prior to an arrest. The police also can use voluntary information that a suspect tells an acquaintance, but they cannot encourage the acquaintance to extract such information for investigative purposes. If the suspect does not directly ask for questioning to cease and requests a lawyer, the police do not have to grant one.

The Court has debated the necessity of *Miranda* on several occasions, but upheld its requirement in *Dickerson v. United States*[63] in 2000. In *Dickerson*, the Court deemed that statutes that conflict with *Miranda* (specifically, 18 USCS 3501) are invalid. Prior to *Dickerson*, a number of cases allowed for exceptions to *Miranda*. For example, *New York v. Quarles*, discussed earlier, established that a confession given prior to *Miranda* rights being read is valid and admissible if there is a necessary public safety exception. In another case, *Arizona v. Fulminante*,[64] the Court held that a coerced confession can be considered a fruit of the poisonous tree, but that it does not automatically require a conviction to be overturned. Although these cases may diminish *Miranda*'s worth through the establishment of their many exceptions, the warnings are still "embedded in routine police practice to the point where the warnings have become part of our national culture . . . If anything, subsequent cases have reduced *Miranda*'s impact on legitimate law enforcement while reaffirming the decision's core ruling."[65]

Privacy and the Internet

The Internet has spawned a new type of crime—cyber crime. A **cyber crime** is any offense that occurs via the Internet as opposed to in the real world. This is not the same as computer crime, which is any wrongful act occurring on or directed against a computer, although it can include cyber crime. The emergence of cyber crime has challenged traditional law enforcement in many ways, ranging from creating problems of jurisdiction to difficulties in investigation. It has also produced new rules and regulations on information that can be searched and seized and the search methods that can be used without violating an individual's right to privacy.

How private is information generated by the Internet? What information can law enforcement officers retrieve from a person's computer or a company's computer server (e.g., America Online)? How can they legally monitor a person's time on the Internet? Who has jurisdiction over cyber space? These are questions that are just now being answered in the courts.

Cyber Offenses

A number of different types of offenses can be committed in cyber space. Many of these offenses are not new, but are now being committed via the Internet. Cyber crimes include, but are not necessarily limited to, cyber stalking, cyber fraud, cyber theft (including identity theft), cyber terrorism, hacking, cyber money laundering, pirating intellectual property, online gambling, and child pornography (Gaines and Miller 2003). These offenses are difficult to investigate, and laws against cyber crimes are difficult to enforce. Over 600 million people use the Internet, which makes it difficult to regulate. **Cyber sleuths**, individuals who monitor Internet use and enforce cyber laws, focus their

Technological advances have changed the way police conduct investigations and searches. Is this enhanced protection or a violation of privacy?

attention on certain serious crimes. One of the most important crimes to track over the Internet is the possession and distribution of child pornography.

Child Pornography Investigations

Child pornography is the depiction of sexually explicit behavior involving a minor, including actual or simulated intercourse; oral or anal intercourse; bestiality (sexual behavior involving animals); masturbation; sexual sadism and masochism; penetration of the vagina or rectum digitally or with foreign objects; exhibition of the genitals, pubic, or rectal area for the purpose of sexually stimulating the viewer; excretory functions performed in a lewd manner; and lascivious exhibition of the genitals. Images also are considered pornographic if the child is the focal point of a sexually suggestive setting, is in an unnatural pose or inappropriate attire, is depicted suggesting coyness or willingness to engage in sexual activity, or if the depiction is intended to elicit a sexual response in the viewer (Terry 2006). Despite the benefits of the Internet, it is unfortunately responsible for an increased circulation of child pornography (and adult pornography, which is, for the most part, legal).

Another issue of contention is that of "virtual" child pornography. With "virtual" child pornography, images appear to depict minors engaging in sexual activity, but the images are produced by some means other than the use of real children (such as computer-generated images of children or images of adults who look like children). Virtual, or fictitious, children are not protected by the Child Pornography Prevention Act of 1996, and several court cases have upheld this Act in order to protect free speech. In the case of *Ashcroft v. Free Speech Coalition*,[66] the Supreme Court said that acts banning virtual child pornography are overbroad and violate the First Amendment. Although the Court recognized the dangers of allowing such material to be produced, it also acknowledged that virtual images are not fundamentally related to the sexual abuse of children.

Legal Implications of Cyber Crime

Because of the anonymity of the Internet, investigating cyber crime is very difficult. In many cases, the jurisdiction as to who should be investigating particular offenses is unclear. Jurisdiction generally relates to physical geography, but there is no geographical boundary for the World Wide Web. Although local agencies have some duties to investigate cyber crimes, jurisdiction usually falls upon federal agencies. This is because most cyber crime crosses state, and even international, boundaries, and is therefore often cross-jurisdictional. With cyber crime, problems of linkage blindness can intensify even further.

Cyber crime generates little physical evidence. Cyber sleuths must target offenders through their "conversations" and electronic "fingerprints." Any computer, computer system, computer network, or any software or data, owned by the suspect that is used during the commission of any public offense involving pornography (or any other cyber crime) or that which is used as a repository for the storage illegal software is subject to forfeiture. A suspect does not have to be convicted for his or her computer to be seized; rather, there must be probable cause to show that the material is obscene. When officers do seize a computer, they must show that the removal is reasonable, and they must return anything that is not evidence. That said, few established boundaries exist as to how cyber searches can legally take place and what type of searches would be considered constitutional under the Fourth Amendment.

One way to conduct cyber searches is through wiretaps. Although similar to telephone wiretaps, it is not as difficult to obtain warrants to tap electronic sources so long as the order is issued where the interception occurs. There can also be consensual wiretaps, although the party must consent, not the service provider. The service provider can monitor information, however, if it is necessary for the protection of the provider. Additionally, the provider can disclose information that it inadvertently came across if the information pertains to a crime.

In terms of the Fourth Amendment, computers are equivalent to "containers"; the user does not have a special expectation of privacy, even though data can be erased.[67] As with a container, the officer must have probable cause to search the computer, which usually requires a warrant specifying exactly what is to be searched and what the officer is searching for. Once the officers look for material beyond the scope of their specified search, they violate the individual's Fourth Amendment rights. For instance, in the case of *United States v. Carey*,[68] the officers had a warrant to search the suspect's computer for drug-related information. Upon finding images of child pornography, the officers continued to search for pornographic images in the .jpeg files. The Court invalidated the search, claiming that the officers should have stopped the search and obtained a warrant once they found the pornographic images.

Chapter Summary

- Many different types of searches are possible, including stop and frisk, search of persons, search of premises, search of vehicles, search of public places, and plain view searches. In order to conduct a search, the officer must have probable cause to believe that a particular person committed a crime.

- Officers usually need a warrant to conduct a search. However, under exigent circumstances a warrant is not necessary. Additionally, officers usually do not need a warrant to search a car because of the issue of mobility. Other times that officers do not need a warrant are when the suspect consents to a search, when searching public places, when there is a systematic search, or searching incident to arrest.

- A frisk is a type of search, though it is less invasive than a full search. It is only a pat down for weapons, and an officer needs reasonable suspicion rather than probable cause to believe that crime is afoot in order to stop and frisk an individual.

- After arrest and prior to custodial interrogation, the police must warn suspects that they have the right to remain silent and they have the right to counsel. This precedent, established in *Miranda v. Arizona*, helps to reduce the likelihood of coerced confessions.

- A new and challenging type of search is one conducted via the Internet. These are more difficult than searches in the "real world" because of jurisdictional issues, the changing nature of cyber crime, and the anonymity of the Internet.

Linking the Dots

1. What are the most important cases that have resulted in limiting police powers with regard to illegal searches and seizures?

2. Should police officers be able to make pretextual stops of vehicles? What are the costs and benefits of this practice?

3. Do officers have to tell individuals during systematic searches that they are free to leave? Should they be required to explain to the individuals that this type of search is consensual?

4. What are the most significant challenges of investigating the possession and distribution of child pornography on the Internet?

5. How do investigations in the real world differ from those in the virtual world? How are they similar?

KEY TERMS

Arrest 120
Child pornography 126
Curtilage 119
Cyber crime 125
Cyber sleuths 125
Exclusionary rule 111
Exigent circumstances 114
Field interrogation 110
Frisk 110
Fruit of the poisonous tree 112

Good faith exception 113
Hot pursuit 115
Incident to arrest 115
Inevitable discovery 113
Interrogation 122
Knock and announce 114
Miranda rights 122
Plain view doctrine 115
Pretextual stops 118
Probable cause 109

Reasonable expectations of privacy 119
Reasonable suspicion 110
Search warrant 114
Seizure 111
Stop and frisk 110
Systematic stops 118
Thermal imaging 115
Wiretapping 119

REFERENCES

American Civil Liberties Union. 1999. *An American Civil Liberties Union Special Report: Driving While Black: Racial Profiling on Our Nation's Highways.* New York: American Civil Liberties Union.

Black's Law Dictionary. 1990. St. Paul, MN: West Publishing.

Douglas, J. 1994. *Mind Hunter.* New York: Scribner.

Electronic Frontier Foundation. 2001. "EEF Analysis of the Provisions of the USA Patriot Act." Available at www.eff.org/Privacy/Surveillance/Terrorism_militias/20011031_eff_us_patriot_analysis.php.

Gaines, L. K., and R. L. Miller. 2003. *Criminal Justice in Action*, 2d ed. Belmont, CA: Wadsworth.

Georgetown Law Journal. (2006). Annual Review of Criminal Procedure. *Georgetown Law Journal Annual Review* 35 Crim. Proc. 3.

Gibbons, M. 2003. "Profiling-More than a Euphemism for Discrimination: Legitimate Use of a Maligned Investigative Tool." In *Policing and Minority Communities: Bridging the Gap*, edited by D. J. Jones-Brown and K. J. Terry, 36–51. Upper Saddle River, NJ: Prentice Hall.

Terry, K. J. (2006). *Sexual Offenses and Offenders: Theory, Practice and Policy.* Belmont, CA: Wadsworth.

NOTES

1. *United States v. Drayton*, 122 S. Ct. 2105 (2002).
2. 11 U.S. 339 (1813). Probable cause in this case is defined vaguely as prima facie evidence, which is less than that which would justify condemnation.
3. 267 U.S. 132 (1925).
4. 338 U.S. 160 (1949).
5. *Carroll v. United States*, 267 U.S. 132 (1925) at 162, n.15; *Brinegar v. United States*, 338 U.S. 160 (1949) at 175–176.
6. 358 U.S. 307 (1959).
7. 393 U.S. 410 (1969).
8. 462 U.S. 213 (1983).
9. 392 U.S. 1 (1968).
10. 534 U.S. 266 (2002).
11. *United States v. Brignoni-Ponce*, 422 U.S. 873 (1975).
12. 490 U.S. 1 (1989).
13. *Illinois v. Wardlow*, 528 U.S. 119 (2002).
14. *Weeks v. United States*, 232 U.S. 383 (1914).
15. 342 U.S. 165 (1952).
16. Ibid, at 210.
17. 368 U.S. 871 (1961).
18. If there is a question at all as to the legality of a police officer's actions in terms of a search, the judge will exclude the evidence seized. For example, when a New York City police officer saw a suspect toss a bag of marijuana onto the floor of his car—which was illegally parked in front of a fire hydrant in a well-known drug neighborhood—he approached him to ask some questions. When the suspect mumbled, the officer pinched his cheeks until the drugs he put in his mouth fell out. The judge excluded the four bags of marijuana from the trial, stating that forcing the suspect to open his mouth was unnecessarily intrusive. See *New York v. Cooper*, 2002 NY Slip Op 50399U. Cited *Schmerber v. California*, 384 U.S. 757 (1966), the judge said there was no "clear indication" that the officer would find evidence through such actions.
19. 371 U.S. 471 (1963).
20. 417 U.S. 433 (1974).
21. 467 U.S. 649 (1984).
22. 468 U.S. 897 (1984).
23. 468 U.S. 981 (1984).
24. 430 U.S. 387 (1977).
25. Originally from *Curtis' Case*, Fost. 135, 168 Eng. Rep. 67 (1756), the Court cited this decision in *Ker v. California*, 374 U.S. 23 (1963). This was further supported in *Wilson v. Arkansas*, 514 U.S. 927 (1995), where the Court cited the necessity of an officer to knock and announce unless there are exigent circumstances.
26. 514 U.S. 927 (1995).
27. *Richards v. Wisconsin*, 520 U.S. 385 (1997).

28. 547 U.S. ____ (2006).

29. 122 S. Ct. 2458 (2002).

30. 445 U.S. 573 (1980).

31. 427 U.S. 38 (1976).

32. 436 U.S. 499 (1978).

33. 464 U.S. 287 (1984).

34. 508 U.S. 366 (1993).

35. *United States v. Matlock* (1974), which states that a roommate can give consent to search the common areas of the residence; *People v. Cosme* (1979), which states that either the husband or the wife can give consent; *Illinois v. Rodriguez* (1990), which states that an individual who by all appearances is staying at the residence, even if they are not living there permanently, can give consent. This does not, however, include overnight guests (*Minnesota v. Olsen*, 1989).

36. 533 U.S. 27 (2001).

37. 395 U.S. 752 (1969).

38. 494 U.S. 325 (1989).

39. 384 U.S. 757 (1966).

40. 267 U.S. 132 (1924).

41. 399 U.S. 42 (1970).

42. 403 U.S. 443 (1971).

43. 463 U.S. 1032 (1983).

44. 453 U.S. 454 (1981).

45. 456 U.S. 798 (1982).

46. 526 U.S. 559 (1999).

47. *Maryland v. Wilson* 519 U.S. 408 (1997).

48. *United States v. Ross* 456 U.S. 798 (1982).

49. *California v. Acevedo*, 500 U.S. 565.

50. The Court in *Knowles v. Iowa*, 525 U.S. 113 (1998), confirmed that the police can legally conduct a full-scale search of the car even if they pull over the individual for a traffic citation.

51. 517 U.S. 806 (1996).

52. *Michigan Department of State Police v. Sitz* (1990).

53. Randomized searches of passengers prior to boarding a plane is different from the stop and search of those who fit a drug courier profile discussed in the previous section. With drug courier profiles, race can be one factor, although not the sole factor for a stop.

54. 389 U.S. 347 (1967).

55. 486 U.S. 35 (1988).

56. 501 U.S. 429 (1991).

57. 384 U.S. 436 (1966).

58. *Wong Sun v. United States*, supra n. 20.

59. 16 Cal. 3d 263 (1976).

60. 445 U.S. 573 (1980).

61. 384 U.S. 436 (1966).

62. 430 U.S. 387 (1977).

63. 530 U.S. 428 (2000).

64. 499 U.S. 279 (1991).

65. *Dickerson v. United States*, supra note 36 at 419–420.

66. 122 S. Ct. 1389 (2002).

67. *Commonwealth of Pennsylvania v. Copenhefer*, 587 Atl. 2d 1353 (Pa. 1991).

68. 172 F.3d 1268 (1999).

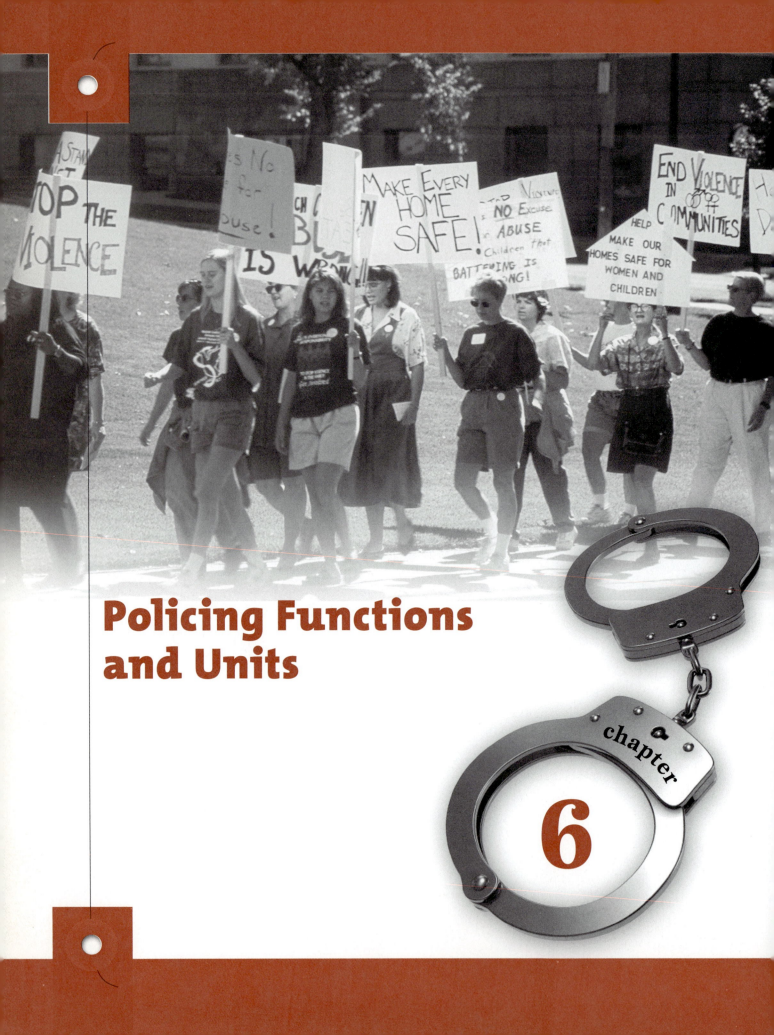

Policing Functions and Units

Chapter Objectives

- Understand the relationship between policing goals, policies, and procedures, and how they interact within a department to influence policing practices.

- Understand the key features of the quasi-military model of policing.

- Become familiar with the structure and operation of police administrative units.

- Identify some of the most important police special units and understand how they operate within the overall policing structure.

Terrorism has provided a significant impetus for organizational restructuring and increased cross-agency information sharing nationwide. However, in our use of this issue to highlight key trends in law enforcement in the twenty-first century, it is important not to lose sight of the fact that linkage blindness has existed since the early days of law enforcement. Linkage blindness has severe implications for all criminal activity, not simply the most heinous or recent in our minds; however, throughout the history of criminal justice it has often taken such events to catalyze major reforms or change. A good example of this is found in the case of Daniel Funk in Dutchess County.

Despite the fact that the owner of the Little Tikes Day Care Center in the Town of Poughkeepsie reported to the Dutchess County Child Protective Services that his employees strongly suspected that Daniel Funk was being abused, he was allowed to remain in the care of his mother and her live-in boyfriend (Farmer 2002). As a result, the two-year-old boy later died after receiving a severe beating from the couple. One of the central reasons this was able to occur was the lack of information sharing between the Department of Child Protective Services and law en-forcement. Due to confidentiality concerns, the agency did not feel it was able to share such information with law enforcement.

As a result of the incident, a multi-disciplinary fatality review team, modeled on other fatality teams around the nation, was developed for dealing with cases of child abuse in the county. The bottom line for the success of this model has been the establishment of information-sharing mechanisms that put the safety of the child first. The National Center for Child Fatality Review (NCCFR) investigates cases of "intentional and preventable deaths" and shares its findings with local fatality review teams. The aim is to prevent future deaths through this shared knowledge base (OJJDP 2001).

Before it used to be that "one agency may know about domestic violence in the home, another may be aware of a history of mental illness with a parent and yet another may know of past injuries suffered by the child" (Farmer 2002, p. 1). Thus, it is only with the sharing of information across agencies that such tragic events can hope to be stopped.

This chapter examines the goals of law enforcement agencies in this country, highlighting the important role that organizational structure can play in attaining these goals. Although September

11 clearly exposed the raw wound in relation to the poor history of cross-agency information sharing in modern law enforcement, such problems have existed for a long time and are not made any easier by the complex bureaucracies of such agencies, as well as the entrenched cultures of territoriality and interagency rivalry. It will also be stressed that even within a large agency with many specialized units and functions, linkage blindness can be as significant a barrier as across agencies.

Although such communication barriers can be reduced through advances in technology (a subject of Chapters 8 and 13), the organizational structure itself can be modified to ensure that information reaches all relevant parties bearing on a particular problem. The creation of the Department of Homeland Security represented the most significant organizational restructuring in years at the federal level. Through such modifications at the federal, state, and local levels, it is hoped that cases similar to that of Daniel Funk will be less likely to occur.

Goals of Policing

Every police department, regardless of its size or location, will have an established set of **policing goals** that aim to provide that department with a sense of purpose and direction. Reflecting the underlying values and assumptions of the department, these goals help to inform the development of policing plans and strategies, the allocation of departmental resources, and even the exercise of discretion by individual police officers. Although the precise objectives will vary from department to department, some commonly stated policing goals (in no particular order) include:

- The prevention of crime and protection of life
- To uphold and enforce the law
- To combat public fear of crime
- To promote community safety
- To control traffic
- To encourage respect for the law
- To protect the civil rights and liberties of individuals

Order Maintenance versus Law Enforcement

Policing goals are significant because they help to shape the organizational culture of a police department. Looking back to our discussion of the police function in earlier chapters, we can see that there is an important relationship between ideas about the proper role of the police and the determination of policing goals, policies, and procedures. During the Political Era, order-maintenance goals dominated; police departments were more concerned about maintaining the status quo with respect to existing political power structures. However, with the advent of professionalization and reform, law enforcement agencies tended to restrict their focus to "upholding and enforcing the law." As we have seen, however, fear of crime may not be connected to the actual rate of crime in an area, making it another important goal of policing. Fear of crime will not simply "go away" as a result of the more traditional crime control techniques. Reducing crime requires additional service activities that engage the police in interactions with the community, a topic discussed in Chapter 7. In this manner, the goals of an organization will directly influence particular decisions with respect to resource deployments.

Police departments can be torn by what might seem to be conflicting goals or demands. Promoting community safety and enforcing the law seem like essential goals from which to drive an agency's decision making. However, to what extent should these goals be sacrificed to the important goal of protecting the civil rights and liberties of individuals? Where these goals clash, which should hold more weight in guiding police managers' decision making? Similarly, how does a department "encourage respect for the law" at the same time that it engages in aggressive zero-tolerance tactics that may alienate the community? Such approaches can have important merit for ultimately maintaining long-term reductions in crime; that is, meeting the goal of crime prevention."

Police officers have many duties, including to protect and maintain order in all communities.

Law enforcement operates within the political and social forces in which it is embedded. To view the police department as a closed organization driven solely by the need to attack crime will lead to direct conflicts with the community, as witnessed throughout the Reform Era. However, the extent to which community priorities should drive policy will remain difficult as larger public safety needs, such as those resulting from the threat of terrorism, rise to the surface. Striking this balance will be the focus of the rest of this book.

Translating Goals into Mission Statements and Policy

Goals often will be stated in writing, either as part of a general **mission statement** or in the form of specific **police policies**. Typically short and designed to be easily understood and remembered, a mission statement is an expression of a department's overall purpose; it will usually be accompanied by a list of **values** that summarize the core beliefs and concerns of the department (see Figure 6.1). Ideally, a good mission statement encourages feelings of loyalty and commitment amongst officers and helps to shape the day-to-day operations of the department. In addition, a mission statement sends a powerful message to the public, fostering confidence in the police and a better understanding of their role in society.

A policy is a specific statement of principle that aims to guide individual decisions and ensure that those decisions reflect the overall objectives of the department. An example of a police policy might be a written directive or **interim order** to all patrol officers prohibiting them from asking witnesses or victims of a crime about their nationality or immigration status or from

FIGURE 6.1

NYC Police Department's Mission Statement and List of Values

Mission

The mission of the New York City Police Department is to enhance the quality of life in our City by working in partnership with the community and in accordance with constitutional rights to enforce the laws, preserve the peace, reduce fear, and provide for a safe environment.

Values

In partnership with the community, we pledge to:
Protect the lives and property of our fellow citizens and impartially enforce the law.
Fight crime both by preventing it and by aggressively pursuing violators of the law.
Maintain a higher standard of integrity than is generally expected of others because so much is expected of us.
Value human life, respect the dignity of each individual and render our services with courtesy and civility.

Source: Used with permission of the New York City Police Department. © 2001. New York City Police Department. All rights reserved..

sharing information with the Department of Homeland Security (via Immigrations and Customs Enforcement) without the permission of their supervisor. In such a case, the aim of the policy may be to promote trust between the police and the immigrant community or to clarify the responsibilities of officers when dealing with suspected illegal aliens. It is important to note, however, that such policies do more than simply provide a guide for individual decision making and the use of police discretion. In addition, they also help to maintain consistency of practice within the department and provide the basis for police accountability and external scrutiny of police activities.

Organizational Structure and Accountability

An **organizational chart** reflects the formal structure of a police department, in terms of both task and authority, that is required to "get a job done." In policing, "getting a job done" refers to the operations of the department, manifested in terms of the patrol, traffic, and investigations divisions, in addition to any other specialized units required to meet the specific needs of a given jurisdictional context.

Small, rural departments (representing the majority of law enforcement agencies in the United States) exhibit far less diversification or specialization across units. Instead, individual officers are likely to be **generalists**; that is, responsible for carrying out all operations functions. Officers in rural settings respond to different crime problems and are usually more acquainted with the people they encounter during their day-to-day duties. In addition to acting as general practitioners of law enforcement, rural officers often are called upon to serve a wider variety of services (Wells and Weisheit 1995). Police agencies in these environments will have very different, often less structured, organizational structures.

Organizational charts can be organized across many different criteria, including location (i.e., precinct, division, or other jurisdictional boundary), time (i.e., shift structure), and, most typically, **hierarchy**.

Rising out of the political turmoil of the late nineteenth/early twentieth centuries, law enforcement organizations across all levels of government sought to create **chains of command** to create professional, accountable agencies. To accomplish this, most departments turned to the military model as an example of efficiency and accountability. As a consequence, the vast majority of police departments are organized along rigidly hierarchical, **quasi-military** lines. Typically depicted as a pyramid with power and control emanating from the top (see Figure 6.2), the quasi-military model is characterized by strict adherence to formal chains of command and the clear division of personnel into ranks. **Command** and administrative responsibilities are placed in the hands of the chief and his or her deputy chiefs, who exercise direct control over both **middle management**—captains and lieutenants—who in turn are responsible for supervising the day-to-day police work undertaken by **line personnel**, such as patrol officers, who are themselves immediately supervised by the rank of sergeants. Administrative personnel (e.g., human resources, fiscal, etc.) within the department generally are considered line personnel and may be supervised by sworn commanding officers according to the above rank structure or higher-level civilian staff, depending upon the jurisdiction.

Adopted as a replacement for the political patronage model, the quasi-military approach has been favored by the police in part because divisions of responsibility are clearly defined. In principle at least, this division of responsibility helps to ensure that police resources are used effectively and efficiently by helping to avoid duplication of effort and jurisdictional overlap and that individuals within the hierarchy can be held accountable for their decisions. Furthermore, the division of officers according to rank tends to foster order and discipline within the department. Line officers are constantly aware that there is

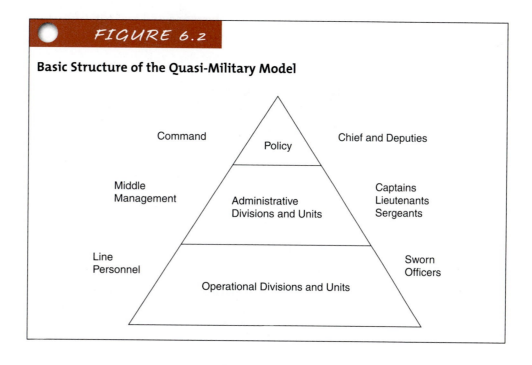

FIGURE 6.2

Basic Structure of the Quasi-Military Model

Command — Policy — Chief and Deputies

Middle Management — Administrative Divisions and Units — Captains Lieutenants Sergeants

Line Personnel — Operational Divisions and Units — Sworn Officers someone above them in the hierarchy monitoring their performance, just as members of middle management are closely supervised by police command. Because power is concentrated at the top of the organization, police departments tend to be "tall" bureaucracies; that is, there are large numbers of intermediary ranks between the top and bottom levels of the pyramid. For this reason, chains of command are extremely important to the police, because they ensure that changes in policy and procedure dictated by police command eventually flow down to the line personnel who are expected to implement them.

Although the quasi-military model, the key features of which are shown in Table 6.1, has many strengths, some critics of the police have argued that this commitment to military principles leads to serious organizational and cultural problems. Bittner (1970) claimed that military organization discourages reward or disapproval of police service and activities outside the officially recognized duties. Moreover, administrators hesitate to recognize such behavior because it may damage the administrator's relationship with those officers who perform well according to officially recognized occupational protocol.

According to Goldstein (1977), the use of military-style uniforms and language and a strong institutional focus on the value of discipline and solidarity encourages officers to see themselves as a tightly knit group, bound together by a common commitment to fighting crime and apprehending the "enemy." Acutely aware of their organizational uniqueness and convinced that only other police officers can ever truly "understand the job," officers soon learn to protect one another and maintain the "Blue Wall of Silence" as a means of deflecting outside scrutiny and criticism of police activities (see Chapter 9). In addition, because it favors career advancement based on length of service and rank, the quasi-military style of organization also has a tendency to mismatch jobs and officer skills. As officers advance up the hierarchy, they frequently take on senior positions within divisions to which they are either unfamiliar or possibly unsuited. For this reason, despite its emphasis on promotion according to competency, the quasi-military model can actually prevent skilled officers from advancing and make it difficult for senior management to reform working practices.

TABLE 6.1

Key Features of the Quasi-Military Model

- Centralized command structure
- Clearly defined hierarchy of authority and chains of command
- Rigid adherence to rank
- Use of military terminology
- Division of labor according to function and specialization
- Selection and promotion according to merit and competence
- Strictly enforced rules and disciplinary procedures

Source: R. Sheehan and G.W. Cordner. 1989. *Introduction to Police Administration,* 2nd ed. pp. 14–15. Cincinnati: Anderson Publishing.

Flat Organizations—Decentralized Policing

Although centralized policing models have the advantage of accountability brought about by the tall bureaucracy, they also have a downside: They create an environment in which information can more easily slip through the cracks, resulting in linkage blindness. For example, lower-level line officers often are the most in tune with the day-to-day realities of policing within their beat and are thus more likely to have access to information that might have important strategy or policy implications. However, because of the rigid chain of command, important, sometimes time-sensitive, information might become dated or meaningless by the time it filters its way to the appropriate commanding officer who actually has the authority to act on the information.

The information blockage that occurs through the chain of command is a product of **vertical differentiation**, or the levels of formal power in an organization. Organizations with many layers in the chain of command are referred to as **tall organizations** (Figure 6.3). Such organizations are generally characterized by a small **span of control**, which is the number of people reporting to one commanding officer.

Reducing the excessive bureaucracy of the chain of command by eliminating ranks is known as **flattening** the organization (see Figure 6.4).

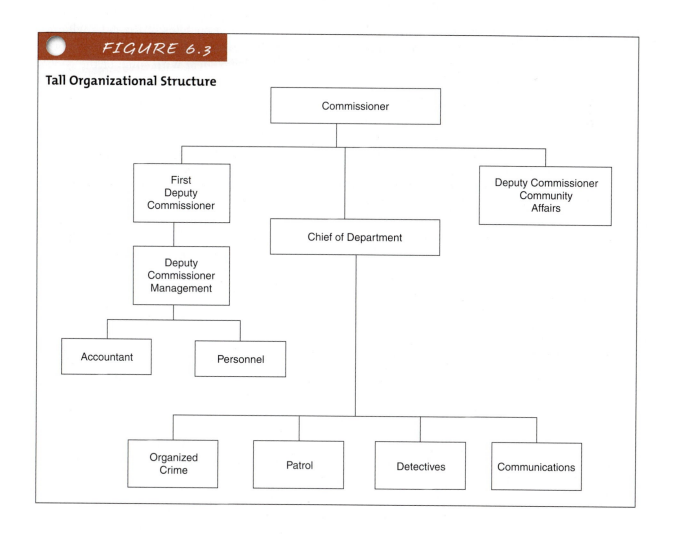

FIGURE 6.3

Tall Organizational Structure

FIGURE 6.4

Flat Organizational Structure

Information sharing also can be hampered by **horizontal differentiation**. This is particularly true in large, urban police departments. Many departments have become highly specialized in order to develop a knowledge base in a particular area and to maintain efficiency. However, although such differentiation is in many ways desirable and practical for large departments, it, too, can lead to linkage blindness if not monitored closely. For example, a gang resource officer may have collected important information about youths involved in local drug sales, including developing a rapport with associates of the gang who are always willing to let him know what is going on. At the same time, the narcotics division might be trying to put together a case to deal with some of the gang's criminal activities, but has proven unable to break through in terms of gaining key witnesses. Meanwhile, detectives are investigating a murder in the area that they believe to be gang related based upon its modus operandi (the manner in which it was committed), but they have no major investigative leads to go on. Although such an extreme lack of communication has been presented for illustrative purposes and is unlikely to occur in reality, it highlights the importance of building proper information-sharing mechanisms even within one agency.

To break down some of these barriers, several organizational structure changes have been advocated and piloted in various forms. **Functional structures** (see Figure 6.5) try to overcome this issue by making specific units that overlap in purpose (such as intelligence) responsible to a variety of other commanders. In this manner, the sharing of information is promoted at the same time as competing loyalties are diminished. An unfortunate downside of such a structure, however, is the possibility of creating conflict for the unit by having to be responsive to several commanders. As a result, functional structures are seldom used.

Another model that attempts to address linkage blindness is the matrix structure, which was used in early attempts at team policing. **Matrix structures** (see Figure 6.6) create a team problem-solving environment in which members of different divisions (e.g., detective bureau, patrol, vice/narcotics) are assigned to specific problem areas, such as counterterrorism, organized crime, and so on. Matrix structures are like the task force model and are generally time limited and focused on a particular problem. Members return to their respective units upon completion of the project.

To facilitate the exchange of information across ranks, some departments have tried to create flat organizations, eliminating unnecessary layers of com-

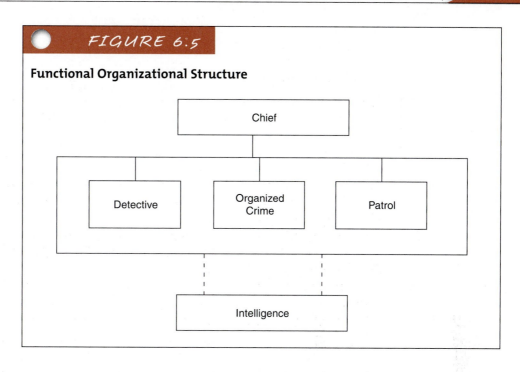

FIGURE 6.5

Functional Organizational Structure

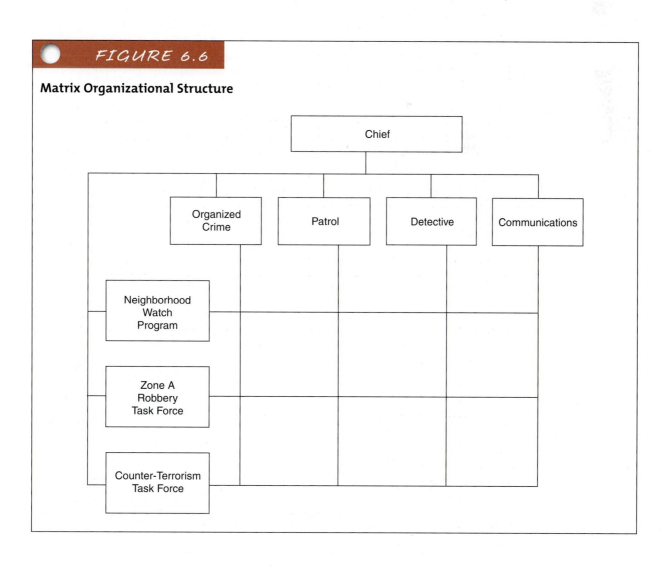

FIGURE 6.6

Matrix Organizational Structure

Implications of Cross-Agency Cooperation for Organizational Structure

The challenges of interagency communication, particularly across levels of government are best served through the task force, or matrix structure, design. Such an approach has been successful with crimes as diverse as organized crime, drug trafficking, serial murder, and terrorism (see Figure 6.7). However, task forces may become ends in themselves, with participants coming to the meeting table to gripe and stall, and nothing meaningful ever being accomplished as a result. Early FBI Counterterrorism Task Forces were one such example. To this extent, sound proactive leadership is required that helps the diverse groups to focus on the data speaking to the issue at hand and to develop and implement sound strategy. Additional examples of this model will be the subject of Chapter 12.

FIGURE 6.7

Public Safety Fact Sheet: A Publication of the Washington County Antiterrorism Advisory Committee

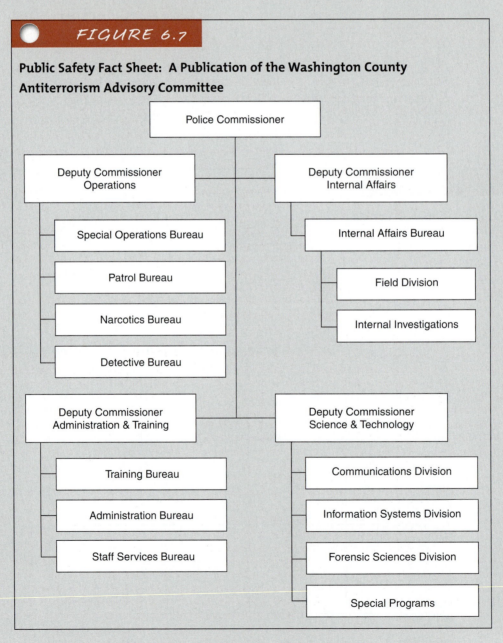

Source: Reprinted by permission of the City of Philadelphia Police Department.

mand. Although the realities of creating truly flat organizations in large, urban departments are limited, there have been a number of successful attempts in flattening organizations. Former New York City Police Commissioner William Bratton accomplished this to a degree with the CompStat model detailed in Chapter 13. To ensure that departments are tied to community needs and information, **decentralizing** commands and increasing discretion within the precinct unit have also been implemented with varying degrees of success. The implications of both flattening and decentralization on community policing models will be returned to in the following chapter.

Divisions and Units

Within the overall quasi-military model, the two most common organizational structures used by the police are the **division** and the **unit**. Generally speaking, a division is a group of police personnel who share responsibility for a particular policing function. For example, members of a department's vice division will all be involved with the prevention of prostitution and other forms of organized sexual exploitation, as well as the enforcement of local gaming laws. Typically, in large departments each division is commanded by a high-ranking commanding officer who answers directly to the deputy chief. Higher-level command positions can vary in title depending on the department, but commonly include such categories as inspector or assistant superintendent.

Within a division, staff may then be organized into smaller groups—known as *units*—that deal with a specific aspect of the division's overall function. Depending on the size of the police department, a vice division may include a specialized unit that only handles problems associated with illegal gambling and

One of the key activities for a police department is roll call, when line officers are given instruction as to daily priorities and information about changing crime in their areas.

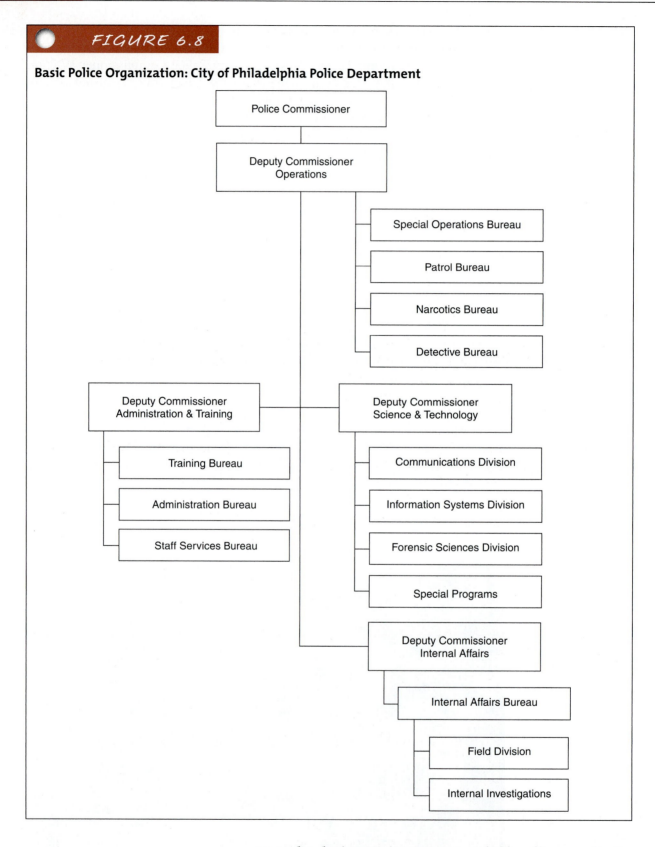

FIGURE 6.8

Basic Police Organization: City of Philadelphia Police Department

gang-related crime. Units are commanded by officers under the rank of inspector who report through their divisional commander to the deputy chief. In many small and medium-sized police departments, the distinction between divisions and units is not always maintained. In such departments, functions will usually be assigned at the unit level, with unit commanders reporting to the deputy chief or some other senior police officer below the rank of chief. Once again, the extent of differentiation in a department will depend upon its size and setting (i.e., urban versus rural). A sample organizational chart is shown in Figure 6.8.

Administrative Services

Most basic police functions can be classified according to whether they are **operational** or **administrative** in nature (see Table 6.2). Operational divisions and units are engaged in activities performed in direct assistance to the public, such as police patrol and traffic, and are typically staffed by sworn police officers. In contrast, administrative units are responsible for providing support and assistance for the police organization as a whole. Sometimes also referred to as *support services*, administrative units manage such diverse functions as hiring and training of police personnel, maintaining police records, planning and research, and running internal affairs. Typically, administrative units are staffed by a mixture of sworn police officers and civilian employees and are housed in the central police headquarters. In the following sections, we will examine some of the more common police administrative units, before turning to examine a number of special police units, such as internal affairs, and police tactics.

Personnel The personnel unit or division is responsible for the selection and hiring of staff (officer and civilian), managing the promotion process, and overseeing all aspects of employee performance and welfare. As a result, the personnel unit will typically be in charge of:

- Officer recruitment
- Setting entry-level and promotional examinations
- Maintaining personnel records
- Establishing and monitoring standards of employee performance
- Administering employee health, safety, and benefits programs

TABLE 6.2

Police Organization by Function

Operational Units	Administrative/Auxiliary Units
• Patrol	• Clerical
• Traffic	• Finance
• Crime Prevention	• Personnel
• Criminal Investigations	• Training
• Juvenile Service	• Records
• Community Services	• Public Information
• Vice and Narcotics	• Planning and Analysis
• Organized Crime	• Intelligence
• Intelligence and Undercover	• Internal Affairs
• Special Operations	

Source: R. Sheehan and G.W. Cordner. 1989. *Introduction to Police Administration,* 2nd ed. pp. 14–15. Cincinnati: Anderson Publishing.

- Processing applications for transfers and jobs within the department
- Processing applications for extended leaves of absence
- Ensuring that the department adheres to applicable employment and labor laws

In most large police departments, the personnel division will be divided into a number of individual commands, each of which is responsible for managing different aspects of the human resource function. Given that policing is an extremely "human focused" occupation, personnel units play a crucial role in the day-to-day operation of even the smallest police departments. As we shall see in Chapter 9, police work can place great stress on individual officers; ensuring that police employees are treated fairly by the department is often essential to maintaining staff morale.

Records   Record keeping is an essential aspect of all forms of law enforcement activity. In order to do their job effectively, the police must be able to access and cross-reference large quantities of information about past crimes and ongoing investigations quickly and efficiently. The records unit is responsible for storing the vast amounts of information accumulated by the police and ensuring that these records are kept up-to-date and accessible. Because most interactions between the police and the public are documented as a matter of procedure, the variety and volume of records handled by the records department of even a medium-sized police department can be enormous. As a consequence, in many large departments records are computerized as much as is practicable. The following list offers a sample of the types of records typically maintained by the records unit:

- Arrest reports
- Incident reports
- Accident reports
- Juvenile reports
- Field interrogations
- Witness statements
- Suspect interviews
- Photographic records
- Fingerprint files
- M.O. (modus operandi) files
- Warrant files
- Property damage reports
- Police vehicle damage report
- Public complaints
- Internal investigation reports

Research and Planning   Closely connected to the records division is the research and planning unit. Because the police do not have unlimited resources or perfect information, police managers need to develop and implement law enforcement strategies that address existing patterns of crime and anticipate future crime trends and problems of disorder. Research and planning units provide the police with information about local social, economic, and political conditions that can be used as the basis for such strategies, as well as with assessments of past law enforcement initiatives and predictions about the likely success of future programs. In addition, the research and planning unit also is responsible for ensuring that the police take advantage of developments in the area of law enforcement techniques and new equipment and for providing the training unit with information that can be used to improve existing policing methods.

Public Information   The public information unit is responsible for communicating with the media and making information about policing activities available to the public. Depending on the size of the police department, this task may either be carried out by a separate unit within the administrative services division or managed by staff from some other unit, such as the clerical/secretarial unit. Maintaining public confidence is of vital importance to the police, particularly given that they are extremely dependent on public for information and assistance. Furthermore, in a democracy it is essential that the activities of the police are open to scrutiny by the media, politicians, and the public at large. The information unit ensures that the public is kept informed about such matters as changing crime rates, new policing strategies, and the progress of high-profile investigations. The intense media coverage of the Virginia Tech shootings on April, 16, 2007, illustrates the difficult task of balancing the public's right to know with the need to keep certain information confidential at times.

Internal Affairs

In many police departments, the task of handling public complaints against the police is the responsibility of the **internal affairs unit**, sometimes called the *office of professional standards*. These units typically investigate noncriminal allegations of police misconduct—for example, when an officer is accused of breaching departmental rules or standards—and make recommendations to senior police management as to the appropriate punishment or disciplinary action. In some departments, these units also act proactively, working to uncover police corruption and other forms of serious crime committed by serving officers.[1]

Although internal affairs units typically are staffed by sworn police officers, some departments also employ civilian investigators in an effort to reassure members of the public that their complaints are being taken seriously. In addition, a minority of police departments deliberately locate their internal affairs units away from the main police headquarters, in the hope that a less-intimidating setting will help to encourage citizens to come forward with their complaints. Not surprisingly, internal affairs units are often regarded with suspicion and even hostility by other police officers, and as a result officers who work for internal affairs can face many of the same problems that confront outsiders who attempt to penetrate the "Blue Wall of Silence" (Thrasher 2001).

Once a complaint has been filed with the internal affairs unit, various steps are taken to determine whether the complaint should be investigated and ultimately upheld. Although the procedures used for internal investigations vary from department to department, most follow the key stages set out in Table 6.3,

TABLE 6.3

Key Phases in the Investigation of Complaint Against the Police

1. Initial review and establishment of grounds for complaint.

2. Collection of witness and complainant evidence.

3. Collection of all other additional relevant evidence, such as police reports and medical records.

4. Background check on complainant to establish character and reliability.

5. Background check on accused officer, including a review of any prior complaints and past disciplinary actions.

6. Interview and take statements from all other departmental personnel involved in the complaint.

Source: S. D'Arcy. 1990. *Internal Affairs Units Guidelines*. San Jose, CA: San Jose Police Department. Reprinted by permission of the City of San Jose.

depending on the degree to which civilian oversight is built into the process. The process of investigating civilian complaints will be detailed further in Chapter 11. Possible punishments and disciplinary outcomes are detailed in Table 6.4 on page 151.

Special Units and Divisions

In addition to operational and administrative divisions, many police departments maintain a number of specialized units to handle matters beyond the skills and competency of ordinary police officers. Among the most common specialized units are undercover operations, special weapons and tactics, juvenile policing, and police dog (K9) units.

Undercover/Intelligence In addition to more traditional forms of investigation, many police departments also engage in **covert**, or **undercover**, **operations**. During a covert operation, a police officer will assume a false identity—that is, go "undercover"—in order to obtain evidence of criminal activity or gain access to a suspect or known fugitive (Miller 2001; Dumont 2000). In some cases, undercover officers may also work in conjunction with an ongoing police surveillance operation, helping the police establish the reliability of an informant, prevent a crime from being committed, or make an arrest (Bennet and Hess 2001; Jacobs 1993; Miller 1987).

Although undercover work often is portrayed as glamorous and exotic in television dramas and in movies—with undercover officers frequently posing as criminals in order to gain access to a gang or some tight-knit criminal organization—in reality many covert operations are far more mundane. As Hess and Wrobleski (2002) have observed, undercover officers often pass themselves off as utility workers or phone company employees in order to enter a suspect's home or pretend to be a newspaper reporter or photographer in order to gather evidence without arousing suspicion.

This is not to say, however, that undercover work cannot be extremely dangerous. Every year, large numbers of undercover police officers—particularly those involved in the investigation of drug-trafficking and drug-related

TABLE 6.4

Punishments and Disciplinary Outcomes (in decreasing order of seriousness)

Punishment	Outcome
Termination of employment	Officer is forced to permanently leave the department, losing all salary and benefits.
Loss of rank	Officer is demoted to a lower rank, usually resulting in a fall in salary and some loss of benefits. In most cases, demotion is likely to affect the officer's chances of future promotion.
Punitive suspension	Officer is forced to take unpaid leave for a set period, typically between one and four weeks, during which time they are also prohibited from undertaking other law enforcement–related employment.
Punitive probation	Officer remains on duty with full salary and benefits, but risks termination if he or she commits any further acts of misconduct during the probation period.
Reassignment	Officer is removed from his or her current unit or assignment and moved to another division or location within the department.
Mandatory training	Officer is required to receive training designed to help the officer understand why his or her behavior was unacceptable and to teach the officer how best to prevent future instances of misconduct.
Reprimand	Officer receives a formal, written warning from his or her commanding officer, setting out details of the complaint and reprimanding the officer for their behavior. This warning is placed in the officer's personnel file and may be referred to when making decisions about the officer's career and any future disciplinary actions.
Supervisory counseling	Officer is required to discuss his or her behavior with either a police counselor or a senior officer within the department, with a view to developing ways of avoiding future instances of misconduct. The least punitive of all of the possible outcomes, counseling is not intended to act as a formal punishment and is rarely noted in an officer's personnel file.

Source: D. Carter. 1994. "Police Disciplinary Procedures: A Review of Selected Police Departments," in *Police Deviance,* 3rd ed., edited by T. Barker and D. Carter, 351–372. Cincinnati: Anderson Publishing..

crime—are either injured or killed while on assignment, often as a result of having their cover "blown" and being exposed as a police officer (DeBlanc and Redman 2000).

Covert operations can take a number of different forms, each with its own unique threats and legal challenges. With **sting operations** undercover agents pose as buyers of illegal goods or services. For example, in a sting operation of the Stanislaus County Sheriff's Department Special Investigations Unit, an undercover agent entered a convenience store and struck up a conversation with one of its employees, telling him that he had some stolen cigarette cartons and liquor he was looking to sell them at a discounted price. After agreement by the employee, the undercover deputies returned on two other occasions and purchased some of the "stolen" goods now on the rack for sale. Arrests were subsequently made for the buying and selling of stolen goods (Stanislaus County Sheriff's Department 2002).

In sting operations to identify retail establishments that sell to minors, a minor (always in the presence of a sworn officer) is instructed to dress age appropriately and attempt to purchase alcoholic beverages. In these operations, the minor is told to be polite and truthful to the sales clerk if asked about his or her age (Texas Alcoholic Beverage Commission 2002). If the minor is sold the goods, an arrest can be made.

Undercover agents also may engage in **reverse sting operations** in which officers pose as drug dealers and arrest those who buy drugs from them.

A **decoy operation** involves an officer assuming the identity or physical appearance of a victim or potential victim of a crime with the objective of apprehending a suspect in the commission of a crime. For example, undercover agents might pose as the drivers of livery cabs in an area where livery cab robberies are a major problem. Alternatively, a department might use decoy vehicles similar to those targeted for theft. These vehicles might be used to apprehend individuals committing crimes against the vehicle or to locate possible "chop shops" if it is stolen.

Finally, **blending** operations pose the most significant threat to an undercover agent in that they require the officer to assimilate into the surrounding activities or culture. The penetration of an agent into organized crime entities or gangs would be examples of undercover blending activities.

The Fine Line Between Entrapment and Encouragement. Although undercover operations can be an extremely effective method of gathering evidence and apprehending criminals, the use of covert investigative techniques by the police raises a number of difficult ethical issues. Because an undercover officer often is required to lie to members of the public in order to conceal his or her true identity, the question arises as to how such lies can be justified and under what circumstances. For example, should officers only be allowed to deceive the public and use undercover methods when investigating major crimes, such as racketeering and drug dealing, or are such practices also permissible when it come to the investigating less serious crimes, such as shoplifting and petty theft? According to Klockars (1985), the answer to such questions is relatively straightforward: If the use of deception means that the police are able to achieve their goals without recourse to the use of force, then the lies are morally justifiable. However, other considerations should be taken into account in addition to the desirability of avoiding force. As Marx (1995; 1992) has pointed out, the line between legitimate and illegitimate goals is not always clear, and there is always a danger that were the use of undercover tactics to become more widespread, that police may come to view such methods as a way of circumventing due process controls and engaging in illegal, undirected surveillance of the public. Furthermore, it can be argued that greater police reliance on undercover operations might seriously undermine their moral authority in the eyes of the public and erode their position of trust within the community.

Traditionally, undercover operations have not been subject to strict controls, although in recent years many police departments have taken steps to ensure that the use of covert tactics is regulated and that undercover officers are subject to close supervision (Marx 1988). In addition, the Commission on Accreditations for Law Enforcement Agencies (CALEA 1999, see Chapter 3) currently requires all police departments to have "written procedures for conducting vice, drug, and organized crime surveillance, undercover, decoy, and raid operations." As Walker and Katz (2002) note, these procedures must specifically address issues relating to the use of false identities and credentials by officers and establish a system of effective supervision for all officers working undercover or engaged in covert surveillance. The legal standard for **entrapment**, or **agent provocateur**, is when the agent incites or counsels another to commit a crime that that person would not otherwise have committed; thus, the line between entrapment and encouragement can be very fine indeed.

Unique Stressors and Dangers. In recent years, a number of studies have examined the effects of undercover work on police officers and other law enforcement agents (Marx 1988, 1995; Pogrebin and Poole 1993). According to the findings of a self-report survey of 271 federal undercover agents administered by Girodo (1991a, 1991b) in the early 1990s, undercover agents are likely to experience a variety of social and psychological problems as a result of spending long periods in the field. In particular, Girodo found that those working undercover assignments frequently had problems with drug and alcohol abuse, as well as difficulties with impulse control, discipline, and maintaining interest in the job. These results mirrored the findings of an earlier study by Farkas (1986) of undercover officers in Hawaii, which found that more than one-third of those surveyed experienced problems in their relationships with friends and family, often as a result of being unable to discuss their work with those closest to them. In addition to the psychological effects of covert work, undercover police officers also run the risk of being exposed to friendly fire or assaults from other police officers unaware of their true identity. One particularly tragic incident of such a shooting occurred in New York during the early 1990s, when a black undercover officer who was holding a suspect at gunpoint was shot and killed by white officers who mistakenly believed that a robbery was in progress (McFadden 1992; Marx 1995). Incidents such as this have led some police officer groups—particularly those representing officers from racial minorities—to encourage their members to refuse plainclothes assignments and undercover work (Marx 1995). Based on the unique conditions of undercover work, most officers in local departments are not allowed assignments longer than two to three years.

Special Weapons and Tactics (S.W.A.T.) Units In addition to regular patrol units and other field divisions, many police departments now maintain paramilitary units that specialize in the use of force and aggressive policing techniques. Most commonly referred to as **S.W.A.T. (Special Weapons and Tactics) teams**, these units are responsible for handling high-risk law enforcement situations that are beyond the capabilities of ordinary patrol officers. Such situations typically include the following (Dulin 2005; Gaines and Kraska 2003; Kraska and Kappeler 1997):

- Apprehension of barricaded suspects
- Resolution of hostage situations
- Warrant service when narcotics are the subject of the warrant or when there is a chance of violent confrontation
- Arrest or incapacitation of armed or dangerous suspects
- Provision of security for visiting dignitaries and politicians

Fitted with body armor and equipped with a variety of specialized weapons—including submachine guns, sniper rifles, and tear gas grenades—members of S.W.A.T. teams receive extensive training in a diverse range of skills and are expected to maintain levels of fitness considerably higher than those of regular police officers. Although in some large police departments, such as the

NYPD and the LAPD, officers are assigned to S.W.A.T. units on a full-time basis, in most departments it is a **co-lateral assignment**. In such departments, teams are made up of officers who continue to work regular police assignments and serve as S.W.A.T. members as and when required. Table 6.5 identifies a number of key areas of S.W.A.T. training.

The Origins of Police S.W.A.T. Teams. Although the military use of specialized sharpshooter and tactical units can be traced back as far as the Revolutionary War, the first S.W.A.T. teams were established in the United States in the late 1960s. They were initially established in response to a number of high-profile sniper attacks against police and civilians, the most notable of which occurred in Austin, Texas, in 1966. During this particularly shocking episode—sometimes referred to as the "Texas Tower Incident"—Charles Whitman, former Marine sharpshooter, climbed to the top of the University of Texas Tower with a rifle and proceeded to murder fifteen people and wound an additional thirty-one others before eventually being killed by two Austin police officers. Following this incident, many police departments across the country concluded they were ill-prepared to handle such situations and moved to develop specialized teams trained to deal with similar emergencies.

The LAPD is now generally credited with having established the first dedicated special weapons and tactics unit, which consisted of fifteen four-man teams made up of volunteers drawn from regular police assignments, many of whom either had prior military experience or were familiar with special weapons operations. These teams, originally referred to as *station defense teams*, received regular monthly training in special weapons handling and tactics and were expected to respond whenever an situation emerged that was beyond the capabilities of normal police personnel.

In 1969, the newly formed LAPD station defense team was called to its first major incident. In the course of attempting to carry out a search for illegal weapons at the Los Angeles headquarters of the Black Panther Movement, a gun battle broke out between the police defense team and members of the Panthers.

TABLE 6.5

Key Areas of S.W.A.T. Training

Tactical planning

Incident management and intelligence gathering

Emergency and rapid deployment

Building search and clearing

Vehicle repossession and hostage rescue

Basic rappel techniques

Advanced handgun skills

Advanced close-quarter battle skills

Live-fire training

Source: Adapted from the James A. Neal Public Safety Training Center (Georgia) SWAT I-III Curriculum (http://jamesanealtraining.com).

In addition to receiving advanced weapon and tactics training, S.W.A.T. officers also are required to maintain high levels of fitness and preparedness.

During the ensuing siege of the headquarters—which lasted over four hours—three Black Panthers and three police officers were wounded and thousands of rounds of ammunition were fired before the Panthers eventually surrendered. Remarkably, no one was killed in the shootout. The LAPD was praised widely for its handling of what was an extremely charged and dangerous situation. By 1971, the volunteer system was abandoned by the LAPD and officers were placed on full-time assignment to the teams, which were renamed Special Weapons and Tactics (S.W.A.T.).

Over the past three decades, hundreds of police departments have established their own special weapons and tactics units, many of them based on the original LAPD model. According to recent studies, approximately 77 percent of all medium- and large-sized police departments (i.e., those policing areas with populations over 25,000) now maintain S.W.A.T. teams or similar special units. Small jurisdictions saw a 157 percent increase in S.W.A.T. units between 1985 and 1995 (Kraska and Cubellis 1997). Although the acronym S.W.A.T. is commonly used, alternative names for such units include Special Response Teams (S.R.T.) and Emergency Response Teams (E.R.T.).

New Trends and Controversies. Although the use of S.W.A.T. teams often is viewed as an essential part of modern policing, some commentators have raised concerns about growing use of such specialized units. According to Kraska and Cubellis (1997), for example, in 1995 alone there were a total of 29,929 paramilitary deployments by the police and other law enforcement agencies, more than nine times the number of similar deployments recorded in 1980. Although it has been suggested that this increase in activity can be attributed to similar increases in the rate of violent crime over the same period, this argument is rejected by Kraska and Cubellis (1997). Instead, they claim that S.W.A.T. teams and other special police units have become increasingly proactive in recent years, gradually moving away from their original emergency role and becoming more akin to specialized search and patrol units. Moreover, they argue that the increasing reliance on specialized, essentially paramilitary units is indicative of a return to the military models that dominated policing for much of the first half of the twentieth century and a shift away from a commitment to the ideals of community policing. According to Kraska and Cubellis (1997):

> [W]e find strong support for the thesis that the military model is still a powerful force guiding the ideology and activities of the American police. This should not be surprising considering the war/military paradigm remains an authoritative framework for crime-control thinking and action by politicians, bureaucrats, the media, and much of the public. (p. 622)

If it is true that S.W.A.T. teams are being used more proactively, then the question arises as to whether these units should continue to be regarded as special units or instead be treated as a form of specialized patrol. Finally, in the wake of September 11 some commentators have argued that there is a need for local police S.W.A.T. units to be more involved in national antiterrorism operations. In large cities such as New York and Los Angeles—cities particularly at risk from terrorist attack—police administrators have already begun to take steps to expand existing special operations training programs to include a greater emphasis on antiterrorist tactics and strategies.

In summary, it should also be stressed that although the military style of S.W.A.T. teams has been emphasized throughout this chapter, most units also are trained in **hostage negotiation techniques** to minimize the likelihood of having to resort to lethal force measures where possible. For example, during a hostage situation during a bank robbery situation trained hostage negotiators will try to persuade the suspect to release the hostages and/or surrender without bursting on the scene and risking more lives.

Juvenile Units In recent years, the police have become increasingly aware of the need to provide young children and juveniles with special care and protection (Krisberg and Austin

Policing juveniles requires officers to employ a range of skills and to be ready to work with vulnerable young people at risk of committing crimes.

1993). In most states, juvenile offenders do not have the same rights as adult offenders and are processed by specialized institutions (such as Youth Courts) within the criminal justice system. As a consequence, many police departments around the country now maintain dedicated juvenile crime units that only handle juvenile offenders and victims and that ensure that children who come into contact with the law receive specialized attention (Bittner 1976; National Institute for Juvenile Justice and Delinquency Prevention 1997; Kobetz and Borsage 1973). In addition to dealing with cases of juvenile crime and investigating crimes against children, one of the key functions of these units is to work with schools, social services, child welfare services, and voluntary organizations to develop strategies for protecting children and keeping young people out of the criminal justice system.

In many instances, these units will include officers who specialize in particular aspects of juvenile crime and victimization, such as homelessness, gang violence, child prostitution, and juvenile drug use. Some juvenile units also employ **school liaison officers** (also referred to as *school resource officers* in some jurisdictions), who are permanently assigned to local high schools to investigate juvenile crime and serve as a resource to school staff and students. School liaison officers provide students and teachers with direct access to police services as well as information, counseling, and referrals. They frequently assist with such activities as:

- Juvenile offender counseling
- Counseling of juvenile offender's family members
- Placement of juvenile offenders into drug/alcohol treatment programs
- Voluntary fingerprinting of juveniles, toddlers, and infants at the request of parents
- Lectures to schools and youth groups on drug/alcohol awareness and detection

Although most juvenile units exist primarily to investigate crimes, an increasing amount of police time and resources are spent on youth education and crime prevention programs. In recent years, for example, many juvenile crime units have become actively involved in the **D.A.R.E. (Drug Abuse Resistance Education)** program, which consists of a series of officer-led series of classroom lessons designed to teach children and young people how to avoid becoming involved in drugs, gangs, or violence. Founded in 1983 by the Los Angeles Police Department and the Los Angeles Unified School District, the program is now run in almost 75 percent of schools and is taught from kindergarten through the twelfth grade (DARE America 1996). Although a number of recent studies have questioned the program's effectiveness, the program is widely regarded as one of the most successful collaborations between the police and the community ever devised in the United States (Rosenbaum and Hanson 1998; LaFree et al. 1995; Sigler and Talley 1995). The D.A.R.E. program can now be found in national and even international contexts in countries such as Mexico.

As mentioned, a number of scholars have criticized the actual preventive success of D.A.R.E. programming. In contrast, recent evaluation studies have demonstrated the promise of a similar model targeting youth involvement in gangs. Called **Gang Resistance Education and Training (GREAT)**, this

In large departments, officers who specialize in juvenile crime and victimization have become an important resource, offering activities ranging from investigation and counseling to crime prevention classes, such as the well-known D.A.R.E. program.

model, which puts officers into the classroom to discuss the negative implications of gang involvement, has been shown to have a significant effect on youth behavior several years after participation in the program. Future study and replication is of course necessary.

Canine (K9) Units   The use of police dogs is now widespread throughout the United States, with **canine (K9)** units being deployed in a vast array of situations and emergencies ranging from public-order incidents to drug investigations and the tracking of suspects.[2] Although dogs were regularly used by the police in Europe from the end of the nineteenth century (most notably in Belgium and Holland), it wasn't until the early 1900s that a small number of U.S. police departments began to look into the feasibility of establishing dedicated K9 units. New York is now generally credited with setting up the first dedicated police dog unit in 1907, although almost from the outset the unit was regarded as a mixed success and was eventually disbanded in 1951. Between the World War I and World War II, numerous other police departments experimented with the use of dogs, but as in the case of New York, these units were frequently plagued by problems of inadequate funding, a shortage of competent trainers, and difficulties finding suitable animals. In addition, K9 units initially were regarded with considerable suspicion by members of the public, many of whom feared that the police might begin to use dogs for such things as crowd control and disabling suspects who resisted arrest.

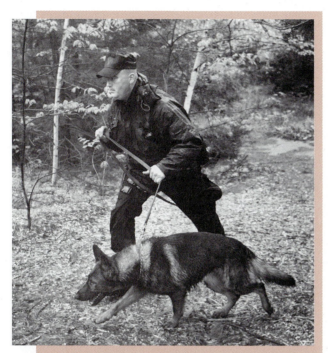

Over time, police handlers develop extremely close relationships with their dogs.

During the 1950s, however, police and public attitudes toward K9 units began to change. Rising crime rates led a number of departments to reevaluate the use of police dogs. In 1957, the Baltimore Police Department established a highly effective K9 unit. Its success in combating certain types of crime prompted numerous cities to follow their example. By 1970, over 80 police departments were employing dogs as part of their patrol force, with most departments favoring the use of breeds such as the German Shepherd, Doberman, and Labrador. As drugs began to become an increasing problem in many major cities, K9 units expanded their operations beyond the use of dogs for public order and police protection and developed sophisticated training programs designed to teach dogs how to identify certain types of narcotics and other prohibited substances.[3] Today, it is rare to find a police department that doesn't either keep trained dogs or have ready access to them, if needed (ACLU of Southern California 1992; Stitt 1991; Bird 1996).

K9 units can be used for the following activities:

- Tracking of suspects
- Area, building, and vehicle searches
- Drug identification
- Officer backup

Given the degree of injury a dog can inflict upon a suspect (including even lethal levels of force), K9 officers are taught to command their charges according to the same principles governing the use of all other types of force detailed in Chapter 11. Failure to exercise proper command over a police dog can itself be a civil liability concern for the department.

Chapter Summary

- Every police department will have a set of organizational goals and values that provide officers with a sense of direction and purpose. These goals are often framed in the form of a mission statement and form the basis of police polices and rules.

- Traditionally, police departments in the United States have been organized along quasi-military lines and have favored hierarchical bureaucracy based on clear chains of command and the division of police personnel into ranks.

- Police units and divisions can be classified according to whether they are operational or administrative. Typical operational units include police patrol, traffic, and criminal investigation; administrative units include personnel, records, research and planning, and public information. In addition, many police departments now have specialized units that deal either with specific crimes or certain types of offenders.

- According to some commentators and researchers, the increasing importance being placed on special units like S.W.A.T. by police departments in the United States may be indicative of a shift to a more proactive style of policing, away from the community policing strategies that have been popular for the past three decades.

Linking the Dots

1. Explain how goals, policies, and procedures differ. How are the decisions of individual police officers guided by policies and procedures?

2. What is the purpose of a mission statement? How do mission statements help to shape the working culture of a police department?

3. What is the basic division of police functions? What is the difference between a police division and a police unit?

4. What is the difference between an operational unit and an administrative unit? Identify and describe the basic functions of two operational units and two administrative units.

5. What are the four basic outcomes of a police complaint? What is the difference between an unfounded complaint and an unsubstantiated complaint?

6. What is the basic function of the S.W.A.T. unit? Do you think that such units should only be reactive?

KEY TERMS

Administrative unit 147
Agent provocateur 152
Blending 152
Canine (K9) units 158
Chains of command 139
Co-lateral assignment 154
Command 139
Covert (undercover) operations 150

D.A.R.E. (Drug Abuse Resistance Education) 157
Decentralizing 145
Decoy operation 152
Division 145
Entrapment 152
Flat organizations 141
Flattening 141
Functional structures 142

Gang Resistance Education and Training (GREAT) 157
Generalists 138
Hierarchy 139
Horizontal differentiation 142
Hostage negotiation techniques 156
Interim order 137
Internal affairs unit 149

REFERENCES

ACLU of Southern California. 1992. *Analysis and Recommendations: Los Angeles Police Department K9 Program.* Los Angeles, CA: NAACP Legal Defense Fund, Police Watch.

Bennett, W. W., and K. M. Hess. 2001. *Criminal Investigation,* 6th ed. Belmont, CA: Wadsworth.

Bird, R. C. 1996. "An Examination of the Training and Reliability of the Narcotics Detection Dog." *Kentucky Law Journal 85*(2):405–433.

Bittner, E. 1970. "The Quasi-Military Organization of the Police." In V. E. Kappeler (Ed.), *The Police and Society.* Prospect Heights, IL.: Waveland Press.

Bittner, E. 1976. "Policing Juveniles: The Social Context of Common Practice." In *Pursuing Justice for the Child,* edited by M. K. Rosenheim, 351–372. Chicago: University of Chicago Press.

Carter, D. 1994. "Police Disciplinary Procedures: A Review of Selected Police Departments." In *Police Deviance,* 3d ed., edited by T. Barker and D. Carter, 351–372. Cincinnati: Anderson Publishing.

Chapman, S. G. 1990. *Police Dogs in North America.* Springfield, IL: Charles C. Thomas.

Commission on Accreditations for Law Enforcement Agencies (CALEA). 1999. *Standards for Law Enforcement Agencies,* 4th ed. Fairfax, VA: Author.

D'Arcy, S. 1990. *Internal Affairs Units Guidelines.* San Jose, CA: San Jose Police Department.

D.A.R.E. America. 1996. *The Official D.A.R.E. Website: D.A.R.E. America.* Available at www.dare.com/home/default.asp.

DeBlanc, D., and W. Redman. 2000. "Officer Safety for Undercover Violence." *The Law Enforcement Trainer 15*(4):34–35.

Dulin, A. 2005. "Special Weapons and Tactics Teams." *TeleMasp Bulletin: Texas Law Enforcement Management and Administrative Statistics Program, 12*(3):1–12.

Dumont, L. F. 2000. "Minimizing Undercover Violence." *Law and Order 48*(10):103–109.

Farkas, G. 1986. "Stress in Undercover Policing." In *Psychological Services for Law Enforcement,* edited by J. T. Reese and H. A. Goldstein, 433–440. Washington, D.C.: U.S. Government Printing Office.

Farmer, A. 2002. "Law Fosters Interagency Cooperation: Evidence of Abuse Not Always Shared." *Poughkeepsie Journal,* April 7. Available at www.poughkeepsiejournal.com/projects/cps/1_040703.shtml.

Gaines, L. K., and P. B. Kraska. 2003. *Drugs, Crime and Justice: Contemporary Perspectives.* Prospect Heights, IL: Waveland Press.

Girodo, M. 1991a. "Drug Corruption in Undercover Agents: Measuring the Risk." *Behavioral Sciences and the Law 9*(3):361–370.

Girodo, M. 1991b. "Personality, Job Stress, and Mental Health in Undercover Agents: A Structural Equation Analysis." *Journal of Social Behavior and Personality 6*(3):375–390.

Goldstein, H. 1977. "Directing Police Agencies Through the Political Process." In *Policing a Free Society,* edited by H. Goldstein, 131–156. Cambridge, MA: Ballinger.

G.R.E.A.T. n.d. 200S *Plan: No Violence is Great.* Available at www.aff.gov/grat/2000/htm.

Grennan, S. 2001. "Historical Perspective of Police Corruption in New York City." In *Police Misconduct: A Reader for the 21st Century,* edited by M. Palmiotto, 117–131. Upper Saddle River, NJ: Prentice Hall.

Hart, L. A., and R. L. Zasloff. 2000. "The Role of Police Dogs as Companions and Working Partners." *Psychological Reports 86*(1):190–202.

Hess, K. M., and H. M. Wrobleski. 2002. *Police Operations: Theory and Practice,* 3d ed. Belmont, CA: Wadsworth.

Jacobs, B. 1993. "Undercover Deception Clues." *Criminology 31*(2):281–299.

Klockars, C. 1985. *The Idea of Police.* Beverly Hills, CA: Sage Publications.

Kobetz, R., and B. Borsage. 1973. *Juvenile Justice Administration.* Gaithersburg, MD: International Association of Police Chiefs (ICAP).

Kraska, P. B., and L. J. Cubellis. 1997. "Militarizing Mayberry and Beyond: Making Sense of American Paramilitary Policing." *Justice Quarterly* 14(4):607–629.

Kraska, P. B., and V. E. Kappeler. 1997. "Militarizing American Police: The Rise and Normalization of Paramilitary Units." *Social Problems* 44(1):1–18.

Krisberg, B., and J. Austin. 1993. *Reinventing Juvenile Justice.* Newbury Park, CA: Sage.

LaFree, G., C. Birkbeck, and N. Wilson. 1995. *Policemen in the Classroom: Albuquerque Adolescents' Opinions About the Drug Awareness and Resistance Education Program.* Albuquerque, NM: New Mexico Criminal Justice Statistical Analysis Center.

Marx, G. T. 1988. *Undercover: Police Surveillance in America.* Berkeley: University of California Press.

Marx, G. T. 1992. "Under-the-Covers Undercover Investigations: Some Reflections on the State's Use of Sex and Deception in Law Enforcement." *Criminal Justice Ethics* 11(1):13–24.

Marx, G. T. 1995. "Recent Developments in Undercover Policing." In *Punishment and Social Control: Essays in Honor of Sheldon Messinger*, edited by T. Blomberg and S. Cohen, 88–101. New York: Aldyne de Gruyler.

McFaddan, R. D. 1992. "Darkness and Disorder in Subway: Questions Swirl in Police Shooting." *New York Times*, November 20, A1.

Miller, C. 2001. "The Art of the Ruse: Does Winning a Battle Mean Losing a War?" *Law Enforcement Technology* 18(1):26–32.

Miller, G. 1987. "Observations on Police Undercover Work." *Criminology* 25(1):27–46.

National Institute for Juvenile Justice and Delinquency Prevention. 1997. *Police–Juvenile Operations: A Comparative Analysis of Standards and Practices*, Vol. 2. Washington, D.C.: Government Printing Office.

Office of Juvenile Justice and Delinquency Prevention. 2001. *The National Center on Child Fatality Review*.

Washington, D.C.: Department of Justice, Office of Juvenile Justice and Delinquency Prevention.

Pogrebin, M., and E. Poole. 1993. "Vice Isn't Nice: A Look at the Ethics of Working Undercover." *Journal of Criminal Justice* 21(4):383–394.

Rosenbaum, D. P., and G. S. Hanson. 1998. "Assessing the Effects of School-based Drug Education: A Six-year Multilevel Analysis of Project D.A.R.E." *Journal of Research in Crime and Delinquency* 35(4):381–412.

Sheehan, R., and G. W. Cordner. 1989. *Introduction to Police Administration*, 2d ed. Cincinnati: Anderson Publishing.

Sigler, R. T., and G. B. Talley. 1995. "Drug Abuse Resistance Education Program Effectiveness." *American Journal of Police* 14(3/4):111–121.

Stanislaus County Sheriff's Department. 2002. "Sheriff's Undercover Unit Has Many Faces." Available at www.stanislaussheriff.com/pub_info/2002/n021102. Accessed February 11, 2002.

Stitt, B. G. 1991. "Practical, Ethical, and Political Aspects of Engaging 'Man's Best Friend' in the War on Crime." *Criminal Justice Policy Review* 5(1): 53–65.

Texas Alcoholic Beverage Commission. 2002. "Minor Sting Operations." Available at www.tabc.state.tx.usl enforce/minor.htm.

Thrasher, R. 2001. "Internal Affairs: The Police Agencies' Approach to the Investigation of Police Misconduct." In *Police Misconduct: A Reader for the 21st Century*, edited by M. Palmiotto, 396–408. Upper Saddle River, NJ: Prentice Hall.

Walker, S., and C. Katz. 2002. *Police in America: An Introduction*, 4th ed. Boston: McGraw-Hill.

Wells, L. E., and R. A. Weisheit. 1995. *Crime and Policing in Rural and Small Town America: An Overview of the Issues* (Research Report). Washington, D.C.: National Institute of Justice.

NOTES

1. A good example of an internal affairs unit that has been successful in helping to combat police corruption is the NYPD Internal Affairs Bureau (IAB). See Grennan (2001).

2. For a good overview of the role played by police dogs, see Chapman (1990) and Hart and Zasloff (2000).

3. For a more detailed discussion of the history of police dogs units, see the City of Toronto Police Department website at www.torontopolice.on.ca/pds/histdog1.html.

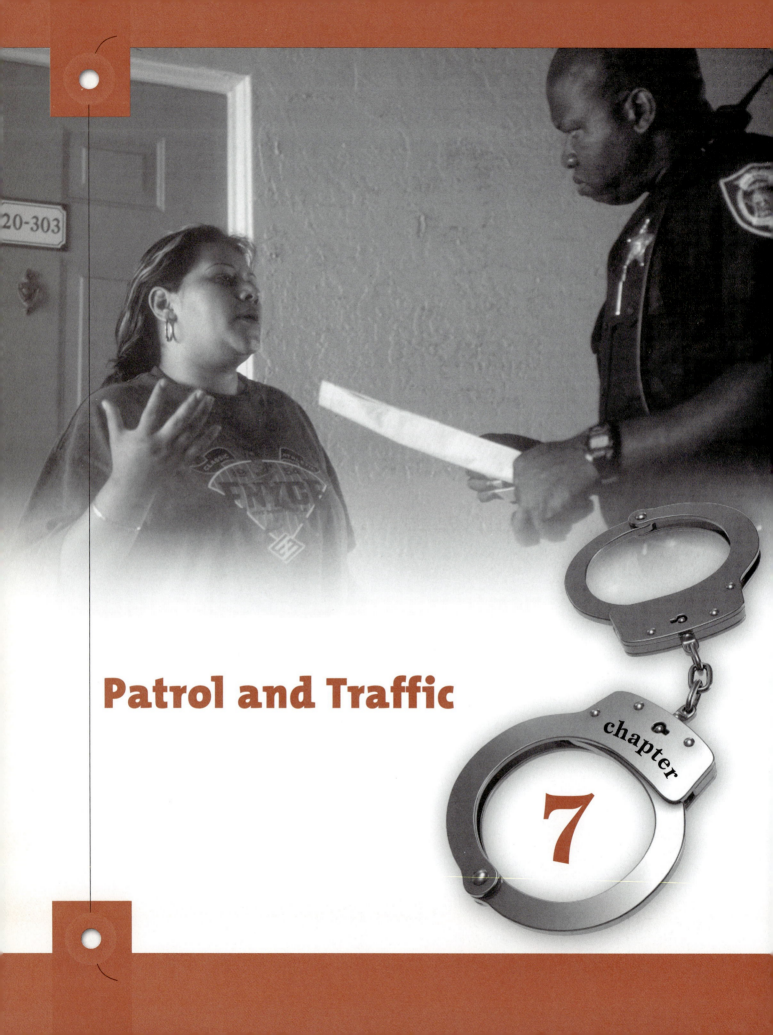

Patrol and Traffic

chapter 7

Chapter Objectives

- Appreciate the nature of patrol work and be familiar with empirical data related to the use of time by patrol officers and officer productivity.

- Become familiar with various types of patrol, including random, directed, and aggressive patrol.

- Understand the implications of the Kansas City Patrol Experiment for the traditional model of policing and recognize the experiment's weaknesses.

- Articulate the various types of patrol deployments, as well as studies related to their effectiveness.

- Know the nature and importance of the traffic function and its unique dangers.

Introduction

In Akron, Ohio, two women were attacked within two months of each other. Only one of these women survived. The first attack took place in May 2002, and the victim had an order of protection against her ex-husband. Despite the order forbidding him to contact her or come within 100 yards of her, Karen Hunter's ex-husband decided to pay her an unfortunate visit.

A neighbor saw Karen's ex-husband dragging her into the home and called 911 immediately upon hearing her scream. Unfortunately, the police did not arrive at the home until 40 minutes after the 911 call, finding the victim stabbed to death on the kitchen floor.

The Akron Police Department did not react to this incident lightly. They made all domestic violence calls involving a court order a higher priority. In July 2002, the police responded to an incident similar to that of Karen and her ex-husband. Within minutes after receiving an emergency call, the police arrived at the house of Tracy Stoyer. Upon arriving at the scene, the responding officers heard screams, leading them to kick down the door and enter the home. When they reached Mrs. Stoyer, they found her bruised and bloody with impressions of fingers on her neck, but she was alive. In this case, Mrs. Stoyer claimed that the police's response time had saved her life (Associated Press 2002).

Police response time to emergencies has traditionally been viewed as a central measure of departmental effectiveness. Although the patrol officer can make the life-saving difference in cases such as the example above, the realities of patrol are such that, more often than not, a quick response time will not make a significant difference in the outcome of the incident.

This chapter examines the essential role of patrol within policing, often referred to as the "backbone of policing" given its predominance within the overall designation of departmental resources (Walker 2002). In 2000, for example, 60 percent of all sworn officers were assigned to patrol duty (Bureau of Justice Statistics 2002).

Patrol officers are the most visible ambassadors for the police department. The nature of police–community relations can be shaped by citizen interactions with the patrol division more than any other part of the department. Even with the best-intentioned police chief, if departmental controls do not significantly affect patrol officer behavior, individual policies will fail. Moreover, citizen interactions with patrol are often used to frame an analysis of departmental priorities and policies.

This chapter will examine the critical role of patrol in contemporary policing. Although patrol plays such a significant role in the department, very few large-scale evaluations of its effectiveness have been carried out. Despite this, we know a great deal more about what works related to patrol than in the past, thanks to an explosion of police research throughout the 1970s and 1980s.

The Realities of Patrol

When the average person envisions a career in law enforcement, he or she is usually thinking of the patrol function as depicted on television: high-speed pursuits, chasing offenders through back alleys and crowded nighttime streets, or arriving at the scene of a robbery in progress to arrest and bring in the "bad guy." Also common is for aspiring law enforcement professionals to have a glamorized version of the FBI, CIA, or CSI roles based upon media imagery. Although such activities do not represent the day-to-day realities of the patrol function, patrol officers are the most visible symbol of the law and must conduct themselves in a manner that inspires confidence and respect in the law.

Use of Time by Patrol Officers

Despite our perceptions about the nature of policing, empirical evaluations of the patrol function have consistently demonstrated that responding to crime is not the primary activity engaged in by officers on patrol. Some studies have suggested that only about 20 percent of all assigned calls involve active Part I and Part II offenses, as defined by the UCR (see Chapter 3) (Boydstun et al. 1977). Of these calls involving more serious offenses, 15 percent involved officers taking reports of crimes that had already occurred, and 8 percent involved checking on suspicious circumstances or individuals (Boydstun et al. 1977).

In the **Police Services Study (PSS)**, officers from twenty-four departments were observed to determine how they spent their time and their interactions with citizens in sixty residential neighborhoods. The PSS found that, on average, two-thirds of an officer's shift was "unassigned" (Whitaker 1982).

Although required to be both reactive and proactive, officers typically spend considerable time dealing with routine administration arising from patrol.

Most of this time was spent patrolling the beat and engaging in officer-initiated contacts with citizens; more often than not, these citizen encounters involved traffic-stop situations. In support of Boydstun et al.'s (1977) findings, the PSS found that only 38 percent of all observed encounters involved crime as the primary problem (Whitaker 1982).

Overall, officers engaged in information gathering more than any other activity. This included helping citizens and controlling offenders. Despite the central role of force discussed in Chapter 1, the PSS found that actual force was only used in 5 percent of all encounters, and this usually involved taking suspects by the arm or handcuffing them (Whitaker 1982). The threat of force, however, was more common, occurring in up to 14 percent of all encounters (Whitaker 1982). Interestingly, arrests occurred in only one out of every twenty PSS encounters. Other studies have found that officers can sometimes go months without ever reporting an arrest. One such study of officers in Washington, D.C., found that 46 percent made no arrests in a year (Forst et al. 1978)!

Productivity Measures

In light of the studies just described, one obvious question that emerges is how officer productivity should be measured. Are arrest quotas a sufficient gauge of an officer's average job performance given that so little of their time is spent dealing with crime problems? In the absence of other indicators, how should command staff evaluate line officers? Despite the reported successes of the NYPD's CompStat model, a significant number of reports have been published about the demoralizing effects the "pressure to produce" arrests play on the average officer (see Chapter 13). We will return briefly to the question of quotas as it relates to traffic enforcement at the end of this chapter.

Response time to calls for service has also been used as a measure of officer effectiveness, but here, too, one can run into some difficulties in practice. Although the public is generally thought to desire a quick response to their calls, the reality is that most of the time the speed of the officer's arrival will make little difference to the outcome of the incident. Obviously a speedy response is a necessity in situations where the crime is in progress, such as the example at the beginning of this chapter. However, according to a PERF study, only 25 percent of cases involve an ongoing confrontation between a victim and an offender (Skogan and Attunes 1979). In most situations, particularly property offenses, the chance of case clearance is almost nonexistent if adequate information is not provided to the officer. If a patrol officer's time might be better spent engaged in meaningful interactions with the community, should response time be such a significant determinant of performance?

Some departments, such as the Indiana State Police, no longer use arrest or ticket quotas as measures of officer performance. Instead, district commanders work with their troopers to craft performance goals that include community activities that most departments do not use as performance measures, such as interactions with the community and evidence of problem solving (Niederpruem 2000).

In sum, productivity or performance measures can be used to evaluate the effectiveness of police agencies. However, they should be based on an understanding not only of *what* the police actually do, but also what the police *should* do (Fridell 2000). According to Moore (1999), agencies should identify "what matters" for the purposes of performance evaluation by considering overall accountability needs from the perspective of both internal command structures, as well as from the vantage point of citizen needs and those of other **external authorizing environmental stakeholders**.

Future research into performance measures should examine the following:

- How to link performance evaluation to accountability mechanisms within the department

- How best to incorporate the needs and expectations of community residents and external agencies into the performance evaluation system

- How to determine the impact of performance evaluation systems on departmental achievement of goals and objectives

Community policing activities require significant resource expenditure on tasks not captured by traditional performance measures. For example, collaborative problem-solving efforts can require attendance at community meetings, outreach to other city agencies/businesses, and addressing "noncrime" community problems. Community police officers often complain about the conflicting demands upon them to meet arrest quotas at the same time that they are engaged in these types of activities (Moore 1999). Even in departments where community police officers are excluded from regular response to calls for service, they may be the focus of resentment or ridicule from the regular patrol line officers, resulting in the loss of morale among such officers.

The Patrol Function

Whatever the incident, from the minor squabble between a cab driver and a patron to a serious domestic assault, an officer is generally the first to arrive at the scene, highlighting how the job can turn from mundane to life threatening within the blink of an eye. Given this wide range of possible daily interactions, the patrol officer serves many functions, including crime fighter, mediator, social worker, and service provider. Adams (2001) identifies several objectives of police field operations or patrol (Adams 2001):

- Protection and defense of lives and property
- Repression of criminal and delinquent behavior
- Identification, apprehension, and conviction of offenders
- Traffic flow and collision reduction
- Maintenance of order and public safety

In a newly developed training curriculum for both recruit and in-service officers, Kenney et al. (2002) categorize central patrol functions into three non-mutually exclusive types of interactions:

- Information gathering
- Conflict resolution
- Maintenance/restoration of control

As noted by Bittner (1990), at some level policing is always going to be about force or control, even when an officer is engaging in simple information-gathering activities. Conflict resolution also is a regular component of an officer's interactions; therefore, good communication and problem-solving skills also are crucial to success. In many situations, such skills will also allow the officer to maintain control without having to resort to the use of force. However, once physical force becomes necessary, it can safely be said that the officer has lost control of the situation (not necessarily as a fault of their own actions), and the range of possible options for problem resolution has narrowed significantly (Kenney et al. 2002).

Types and Effectiveness of Patrol

Although the image of a police vehicle cruising slowly through a neighborhood is what we most often think of as patrol activity, police commonly use several different types of patrol, each with varying degrees of effectiveness.

Random, or Routine, Patrol

When engaged in **random**, or **routine**, **patrol**, officers assigned to a specific area move around in an "unsystematic" way (usually by motor vehicle) (Cordner and Trojanwicz 1992). The goals of this type of patrol are to detect crimes in progress and to deter crime through police presence. Because of the presumed deterrence effect, this type of patrol often is referred to as *preventive*

One of the most significant technological development of the twentieth century, the invention of the automobile revolutionized policing and gave officers the ability to respond to incidents both quickly and efficiently.

patrol. Random patrol is said to be **incident driven**, or reactive, in that officers are responding to crimes only after they occur, either through rapid response to calls for service or to a violation or call in progress. Because officers are constantly moving while awaiting calls, the logic of random patrol dictates that they will be ready to respond to 911 calls, thereby lessening the time between call and response. The specific activities an officer engages in while on random patrol vary significantly across officers, times, locations, and departments, because much of the time spent on patrol is officer initiated.

Directed Patrol

Directed patrol focuses patrol resources on targeted hot spots, crime problems, and/or offenders. Crime statistics are used to assess crime patterns for strategic purposes. In addition to using data to isolate high-crime areas and peak times, directed patrol addresses the problem-identification component of the problem-solving process detailed in Chapter 12. Sometimes a directed patrol can occur on an informal level, with an experienced officer self-initiating "directed" patrol by regularly driving past hot spots during random wanderings. Parking the squad car in a specific location when writing reports and using the toilet in the back of a 7-Eleven that has been the source of problems are examples of such informal, directed activities.

To the extent that it attempts to target problems rather than simply respond to them, directed patrol can be viewed as a form of **proactive patrol**. Cordner (1981) notes that although directed patrol can have an immediate effect on certain crimes (i.e. gun crimes, street robberies), over time there may be a point of diminishing returns in terms of factors such as police–community relations. Additionally, it remains unclear whether such activities only serve to displace crime activities. Table 7.1 presents a comparison of random and directed patrol.

Freeing Up Resources for Directed Patrol—Differential Response A major downside to directed patrol is its significant costs. Directing greater police resources to one specific location and/or time often means taking them away from somewhere else or replacing them through overtime provisions and so on. To run directed patrol operations extensively, departments often have to engage in **differential response** strategies. Differential response involves the more effi-

---

TABLE 7.1

Differences Between Random and Directed Patrol

Random Patrol	Directed Patrol
Random—Patrol officers begin their shift by driving randomly throughout their sector in the hopes of detecting crimes in progress and deterring crime through their presence.	**Proactive**—Focuses on hot spots, targeted locations, problems, and people (e.g., gun crimes).
	Puts more officers in peak areas at times when crime committed.
Incident driven—Reactive	
Rapid response to calls for service	

cient screening of calls for service at dispatch. Rather than treating all calls as deserving of the same priority, dispatchers screen incidents based on need for immediate response time. Some possible options involved in differential response include:

- Provide the caller with an estimate of how long it will take the patrol officer to respond.
- Have civilian personnel or a dispatcher take a report over the phone or have the complainant submit it via fax or over the Internet.
- Have a civilian, rather than a sworn officer, respond to the scene for less serious or cold cases.

Although we are often quick to judge the police based on how quickly they respond to our needs, the empirical research is somewhat mixed regarding the degree to which this affects overall dissatisfaction with police services. Although it is true that response time plays a part in overall satisfaction, researchers have found that such an evaluation is more closely related to civilians' expectations of how quickly the police should arrive rather than just the actual response time (Percy 1980). Thus, departments that cannot afford the significant resources it would take to improve response time may be better served by a community relations campaign that stresses realistic arrival expectations for certain types of offenses. This also can be a component of differential response strategies.

Aggressive Patrol

Often considered a form of directed patrol, **aggressive patrol** refers to the use of high-profile patrol activities, such as frequent traffic stops and regular field interrogations. Aggressive patrol often involves crackdowns aimed toward drawing media attention in the hope that this will enhance any deterrent effect (Cordner and Trojanwicz 1992). For example, the targeting of known "crack rows" for the apprehension of offenders and later cleanup usually bring significant media attention. Strategies such as closing down street access to high drug trafficking locations have proven successful, such as the NYPD's Model Block Program or similar efforts by many Weed and Seed programs by departments nationwide (Grant 2000; Grant and Jacobs 1998).

Sheppard et al. (2000) point to the need for community collaboration when engaging in aggressive patrol activities because of the seemingly disproportionate affect such strategies can have on certain segments of the population. In this case, a zero-tolerance program for gun violence in a predominantly lower-class African American community in Baton Rouge, Louisiana, was implemented successfully after receiving community approval from clergy leaders and organizations, such as 100 Black Men (Sheppard et al. 2000). The degree to which such aggressive tactics successfully target offenders rather than average citizens can go a long way towards reducing community dissatisfaction (Boydstun 1975).

The results of the **Kansas City Gun Experiment**, in which intensive patrols targeted an 80-block, high-crime area with traffic stops and field interrogations, revealed that aggressive patrol can significantly reduce gun crimes, such as drive-by shootings and homicides. Most important, no displacement effects were observed (at least in the short term of the study) (Sherman et al. 1995).

Saturation Patrol

Placing extremely high levels of patrol within a narrowly defined geographic area is referred to as **saturation patrol**. Although empirical findings are mixed, some evidence indicates that saturation patrol can reduce crime (Wilson 1975), but that the suppressive effect may be limited to certain times of day (Carr et al. 1980) and depends on reaching a certain "tipping point" in terms of number of officers. In the latter case, increases from one to two officers in a beat made no difference, but as more were added there were increasingly greater effects on crime (Bright 1969).

The Effectiveness of Patrol

Different types of patrol will be more effective depending on the specific crime and location being targeted. An **integrated patrol**, combining random patrol with any of the other more intensive tactics, might be successful in suppressing open-air activities, but the degree to which this lasts over time or leads to crime displacement is difficult to gauge. What we do know, however, based on patrol studies from the 1970s and 1980s, is that random patrol on its own does not significantly affect criminal activity. The study most responsible for bringing this point home to the police community and forcing a reconsideration of the role of random patrol as a policing strategy was the **Kansas City Patrol Experiment**.

The Kansas City Patrol Experiment   At the request of the Kansas City Police Department, and funded by the Police Foundation, the Kansas City Patrol Experiment was conceived of in 1972 as a means of evaluating the true ability of random patrol to reduce crime and fear of crime. Random patrol's ability to meet these two goals had been accepted on faith rather empirical research prior to this time.

To conduct the quasi-experiment, researchers divided fifteen patrol beats in the south side of the city into three types of intervention activities (Kelling et al. 1974) (Figure 7.1). In the **reactive beats**, all random patrol activity was suspended; patrol officers only responded to calls for service in the area and then would quickly retreat. Normal levels of patrol were maintained in the **control beats**, allowing patrol to function as it had prior to the intervention. Finally,

FIGURE 7.1

The Three Experimental Areas in the Kansas City Patrol Experiment

Reactive Beats
• No RP

Control Beats
• Normal level of RP

Proactive Beats
• Tripled the level of RP

proactive beats were established that had three times the level of random patrol activity.

Over the course of the study, between 1972 and 1973, the researchers closely monitored whether displacement effects were occurring or if the pattern of crime was significantly changing in the reactive beats. Should this have occurred, as many Kansas City officers and personnel predicted, the experiment would have been called off immediately for ethical reasons.

However, this never occurred. In fact, no significant differences were found between the three areas in terms of either crime, fear of crime, or even attitudes toward the police. The assumption by experts that random patrol had a deterrent effect appeared to be faced with its first real challenge. Varying the levels of random patrol appeared to have no effect on crime. The authors of the study were quick to point out that the findings in no way suggested that patrol was unnecessary or could operate effectively with significantly fewer resources (Wilson 1975).

In the years since the study was completed, some critics have questioned the experiment's central findings. For example, it has been argued that a visible presence was inadvertently maintained in the reactive area by specialized units not participating in the experiment, as well as a higher incidence of such activities as siren use and more than one unit responding to a call for service (Larson 1975). Some authors claim that heightened perception of presence also resulted in residual deterrence, in which people believe patrol is working in their area because they had seen the police recently, either responding to a call the previous day or in another beat of the city (Sherman 1990).

Walker (2001) argues that the Kansas City Experiment could only meaningfully serve as an evaluation of the level of patrol. Whether certain types of patrol are more effective than others was not examined. For example, officers engaging in activities outside the "traditional box" of patrol might see greater reductions in both fear of crime and/or actual crime. In fact, some of the studies discussed in this chapter with respect to aggressive, saturation, and directed patrol would indicate that there is some validity to this statement.

Others argue that the analysts in the study only looked at overall numbers in the experimental areas rather than factoring different styles of policing (Cordner and Trajanwicz 1992). That "aggressive" order maintenance and hot-spot policing have been associated with decreased criminal activity offer some support for these assertions. Despite such challenges to the study's validity and implications, the results of the Kansas City Preventive Patrol Experiment have largely been accepted by the law enforcement community. Few efforts have since attempted to verify or refute its findings. It is important to use caution in generalizing from any one study to all areas without being aware of all factors involved in the study and their related reliability and validity concerns.

However, the challenges these findings present to the traditional model of policing propagated during the Reform Era cannot be underestimated. In many ways, later developments related to community and problem-oriented policing reflect a sentiment that innovations are necessary if policing is ever able to contribute meaningfully to crime or fear reduction in the community. As Goldstein (1990) notes:

> Upon discovering that their traditional methods were not as effective as previously assumed, the police realized the need to enlist the community in preventing crime.

But it was clear that this would not be accomplished simply by renewing the old campaigns. The police were going to have to cultivate an entirely different type of relationship with the people that they served. (p. 23)

These findings thus went a large way toward laying the foundations of the community-policing movement detailed in Chapter 12.

Patrol Methods

Many methods of patrol are in use today. The particular method used depends greatly upon the terrain being covered and the jurisdiction's specific needs. However, unquestionably the two most common patrol methods are automobile and foot patrol.

Automobile Patrol

Automobile patrol is by far the most common patrol method used, encompassing 84 percent of all patrol activities in 1997 (Bureau of Justice Statistics 1999). Probably the greatest reason for the predominance of this method of patrol is the significant mobility and flexibility offered to the patrol officer. Not only does the method allow for wider coverage, especially with improvements in communication and information technology, but it also offers quick response to calls for service. Moreover, it is far easier to transport suspects back to the precinct in an automobile. In areas without accessible or manageable roads, such as beaches, some jurisdictions rely heavily on alternatives to the automobile, such as ATVs and dirt bikes.

The method is not without its limitations, however. For example, officer vision is significantly restricted during automobile patrol, and unless an officer gets out of the car, he or she is unable to view many activities taking place on the street. Moreover, as demonstrated by the Kansas City Preventive Patrol Experiment, random patrol by automobile alone has a limited deterrent effect. Part of this may be due to the fact that a great number of Part I crimes occur indoors, outside of the scope of motor vehicle patrol efforts (Walker 2001). Some experts also argue that although there might be an initial deterrent effect resulting from random automobile patrol, crime will either be displaced from regularly patrolled areas or simply return as soon as the vehicles have passed.

As noted in Chapter 3, a major problem with an overreliance on automobile patrol is the distancing of law enforcement from the community it serves. Although this may have had the benefit of "professionalizing" the police, removing many of the corruptive influences associated with the intimate connection to the community prevalent during the Political Era, it has also contributed to a great divide between law enforcement and their beats. Police officers no longer know the specific contexts and issues, as well as politics and personality dynamics, that they had when they were on their feet interacting with the community each shift.

Safety concerns also have arisen due to the fact that the majority of automobile patrol activities consist of **one-officer cars**. A central reason for departmental preference for one as opposed to **two-officer cars** is the overall cost-efficiency of this approach. One-officer deployments can cover twice as much area and respond to twice as many calls as a two-officer deployment system (Walker 2001). Although many patrol officer unions have protested against departmental shifts from two-officer to one-officer systems on safety grounds, a Police Foundation study found that one-officer cars were actually involved in fewer assaults and fewer arrest incidents than two-officer cars (Boydstun et al. 1977).

Of course, such a finding can be explained by other factors than that one-officer cars are simply equally safe. For example, one-officer cars might be less likely to observe crimes in progress or more reticent to get involved before first calling for back up. In response to such a claim, Boydtson et al. (1977) note that in only 2.8 percent of all incidents did one-officer cars call for back-up following arrival to the scene.

Foot Patrol

Although there has been a significant push for a return to foot patrol following the Kansas City Preventive Patrol Experiment, and with the corresponding impetus for community policing and problem-solving models, it only represents roughly 4 percent of all patrol activities (Bureau of Justice Statistics 1999). Foot patrol seriously limits the area an officer can cover on his or her shift. Similarly, although communications technology (e.g., radios and cellular phones) has significantly improved interactions between the foot patrol officer and precinct, response time is generally slower with foot patrol officers for obvious reasons.

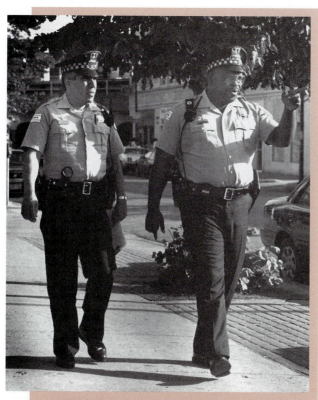

Foot patrol offers less mobility than automobile patrol, but it has important benefits in terms of monitoring and identifying crimes in building or places that would not be readily visible from behind the wheel of a cruiser.

However, despite the challenges of limited mobility, patrol officers are better poised to monitor and identify crimes in progress within buildings or in areas that would be out of the visual path of a passing cruiser.

Patrol studies following the Kansas City Patrol Experiment have also identified an additional significant advantage to foot patrol: the ability to influence fear of crime in the community. Using a design similar to that used in Kansas City with random patrol, researchers who conducted the **Newark Foot Patrol Experiment** found that, as with earlier patrol studies, increased foot patrol did not appear to have a significant effect on overall crime levels in the community (Police Foundation 1981). However, citizens in the intensive foot patrol beats reported significantly more positive attitudes toward the police as well as reductions in fear of crime (Police Foundation 1981). Such findings led to a resurgence in the use of foot patrol officers in many pilot community-policing programs throughout the 1980s and early 1990s.

Motorcycle and Bicycle Patrols

Foot patrol is generally limited to small, clearly defined areas that automobile patrol cannot access. However, where patrol officers need to cover greater distances than would be possible on foot, many departments offer the use of

At the core of the community-policing philosophy, police–citizen interactions provide the police with vital information and can greatly improve their responsiveness to local problems.

motorcycles and bicycles. **Motorcycles** are particularly useful in traffic enforcement activities given their ability to negotiate heavy traffic situations (Adams 2001). Motorcycles also are indispensable in cases of high-profile police escorts and parades.

In tighter areas, such as pedestrian-only streets, malls, or parks, patrol officers may use **bicycles** (Adams 2001). The use of bicycles maintains the foot patrol's benefits of high visibility and approachability while at the same time increasing the officer's mobility.

Horse Patrols

Similarly, but used far less frequently, **horse patrol** offers mobility to officers in places inaccessible to automobiles or even motorcycles, such as parks and wild terrain. Even in urban crowd settings, such as during a parade or protest, the horse patrol can offer officers greater visibility of the masses of people in crowd control situations due to the overall stature of the horse.

Water and Helicopter Patrols

Harbor or **water patrol** is a necessity for jurisdictions bordering shorelines, beaches, or lakes given the tremendous amount of illegal activity that can begin on the water. Because "the smuggling of people and contraband from coastal waters into inland harbor areas is a constant problem . . . investigation and apprehension can be accomplished only with the aid of boats and helicopters" (Adams 2001, p. 129).

Patrol Deployment

As evidenced throughout the chapters so far, **patrol deployment** practices have developed considerably since the earliest days of law enforcement in the United States. The reliance on up-to-date statistics to inform decision making related to patrol deployment and resource distribution enables departmental planners to have a greater chance to understand and resolve crime-related problems across diverse contexts. In addition to methods of patrol, patrol deployment has provided us with insight into the effective use of military troops in occupation circumstances.

Rotating versus Assigned Shifts

Rotating shifts were developed during the Reform Era as a means of combating police corruption. **Rotating shifts** refers to the rotation of officers across either different working hours or different divisions within the department. In contrast, **assigned shifts** involve officer assignment to the same shifts and/or areas for extended periods of time.

Time of Day and Shift Hours

Most jurisdictions have a three-shift structure, sometimes referred to as *tricks* or *watches*. For example, the NYPD organizes its shifts across three eight-hour periods:

- 7 AM to 3 PM (watch)
- 3 PM to 11:30 PM (swing watch)
- Midnight (11 PM to 7 AM) (dog watch)

If a department utilizes a rotating shift structure for working hours, an officer will gradually progress through each of the shift periods. For example, an officer might work the swing watch, progress to dog watch, and finally day watch, staying on each shift generally for a period of a few weeks.

The most popular shift plan is an **eight-hour shift structure**. With an eight-hour plan, officers generally work five days a week for eight hours and then get two days off. Following an additional five days, the officer will receive four days off. Some jurisdictions utilize a **twelve-hour plan** where officers work three 12-hour days and then have the next four days off.

Fatigue

Fatigue is a problem with shift work. PERF has conducted a series of studies to measure the effects of officer fatigue on job performance. In addition to the obvious health costs, it has been found that fatigue can lead to severe impairment of cognitive and motor coordination, thereby lowering productivity and/or leading to accidents (Vila 2000).

The important role of discretion in policing was emphasized in Chapter 1. Given the discretionary powers of officers, and the fact that they may at any time be called upon to use force, the potential dangers of officer fatigue cannot be underestimated.

Not surprisingly, the problems of fatigue need to be considered when deciding on the appropriate shift structures in patrol, both in terms of rotating versus assigned shifts and the length of each shift. Unfortunately, only a limited amount of research in this area has been conducted (Vila 2000); the majority of empirical studies related to fatigue are in the fields of nursing and public health. Constantly rotating officers through each of the three shifts can ultimately take a toll on an officer's health, ability to manage stress, interpersonal relationships, and daily functioning (Vila 2000). Anyone who has ever flown an international flight across time zones knows how difficult it can be to adjust to significant changes in one's sleep patterns. Research on our internal biological clocks, or **circadian rhythms**, supports the claim that at least six months are required to adjust to changes in sleep patterns. Rotating shifts thus alter circadian rhythms with long-term negative consequences (Milia and Bowden 2007). The toll rotating shifts can have on one's family life is also worth mentioning. The many other stressors related to shift work and the nature of policing are detailed in Chapter 9.

Some research indicates that officers on an eight-hour shift structure can be more sleep deprived than those on twelve-hour shifts (Vila 2000). The likely reason for this finding is that following a three-day work week, officers in the twelve-hour structure have the next four days off to rejuvenate. However, before taking these findings as indicative of a need to change departmental shifts to twelve hours (which would be a significant move given that most departments follow an eight-hour system), an important word of caution is necessary: Toward the end of a twelve-hour shift officers also exhibit signs of sleep deprivation, thereby diminishing their effectiveness and productivity (Vila 2000).

Personnel Allocation

Proactive police departments make decisions about level and target of patrol deployments based on a review of all available data sources (Thibault et al. 2001). Peak times and areas thus receive proportionately larger numbers of patrol officers per shift. In some cases, deployment decisions might be made on the basis of a specific crime problem or issue rather than overall rates.

However, the collaborative effort and proactive problem solving required by community-policing models requires more than simply directing resources to an area or specific time. An intimate knowledge of the community is essential for true problem solving to occur, an issue that will be detailed at length throughout Chapter 12. Part of this intimate knowledge includes an acquaintance with key leaders in the community who might be important collaborators in addressing the issues at hand. As such, many departments opt for assigned shifts in which officers patrol the same beat and time period for extended periods of time. Working the same shifts is important in that a community can change significantly depending on the time of day, as can the influence of key players in the community. Thus, officers on assigned shifts may be more acquainted with the concerns of their beat.

Some departments have taken lessons from the corporate model, providing officers with a wide range of experiences across divisions that can help them as they move toward advancement in the agency. Following rotation across divisions, officers are returned to patrol in a senior status, such as **field training officers** for new recruits (Thibault et al. 2001).

Foot Patrol versus Automobile Patrol Assignments

In most departments, police officers are assigned a sector each shift at roll call, which is called a **tour**. Interestingly, in many departments rookie officers are assigned to foot patrol. Although in many small and medium-sized departments foot patrol is a desired assignment, some large departments need to work to remove the stigma that foot patrol is undesirable and to be avoided. However, some research has demonstrated that officers on foot patrol or who have the opportunity to interact frequently with the community actually have higher levels of job satisfaction (Grant and Jacobs 1998). These officers report a sense of accomplishment from their interactions, learning that even in the most high-crime areas the majority of citizens are respectable and law abiding.

Balancing the Proactive and Reactive Models—Integrated Patrol

As noted earlier, automobile patrol has important benefits that will continue to make it essential to patrol division activities, even if it cannot reduce crime or fear of crime by itself. The need to cover large distances in a short amount of time is critical in emergency situations. Additionally, note that the vast majority of municipal police departments are small agencies covering large, rural areas with as few as ten officers on staff. Under such circumstances, foot patrol is not even a practical option.

The finding that foot patrol can play an important role in reducing fear of crime and enhancing police–community interactions has made it an important element of community-policing models. The **1994 Violent Crime Control and Law Enforcement Act** provided funding for an additional 100,000 officers nationally to increase the availability of officers for foot patrol and other community-policing functions.

Traffic Goals and Enforcement

Traffic enforcement is arguably the most undervalued division within law enforcement in terms of status, primarily because it does not fit into the traditional "crime enforcer" image many members of the public hold. Moreover, most members of the public feel resentment when interacting with officers engaged in the traffic function, because such interactions often result in a ticket and corresponding fine. However, the importance of the professional handling of a traffic stop, even in the face of an irritable public, cannot be underestimated in that this is the most common interaction the average citizen has with law enforcement. The nature of the interaction can thus carry weight in terms of police–community relations.

Public safety on streets and highways is the overarching goal of traffic enforcement. The majority of state and municipal law enforcement agencies have responsibility for the enforcement of traffic regulations, or **moving violations**, to ensure this safety (Dempsey 1999).

Thibault, Lynch, and McBride (2001) outline a number of the more important functions performed by the traffic division:

- Eliminating accident causes and congestion
- Identifying potential traffic problems and hazards

- Regulating parking on street and municipal facilities

- Investigating property damage and personal-injury automobile accidents

- Directing public awareness toward the proper use of automobiles, bicycles, and motorcycles

- Arresting offenders

Another important function of traffic patrol is to route traffic around special events, such as parades and protests. Note that although the largest police departments in the country have specialized traffic patrol functions, these duties are covered by regular patrol in the majority of small to medium-sized departments.

Traffic enforcement became a very important part of American law enforcement in the early urban environment of cities such as New York and Chicago. Johnson (1981) notes how the movement of people and goods throughout cities was constantly jeopardized by massive disorder:

Horsecar drivers frequently raced one another through the streets, paying no attention to the discomfort of their passengers or the danger to pedestrians. Wagon drivers and coachmen often disputed rights-of-way, sometimes to the point of assaulting one another. Pedestrians wandered haphazardly across the streets. At busy intersections, it was every man for himself as dozens of drivers sought to force their way through a maze of competing vehicles. (p. 36)

In order to eliminate such disorder, cities created numerous ordinances to regulate proper traffic behavior through fines and penalties. However, as Johnson stresses, compliance was not an instantaneous development with "thousands of people unaccustomed to these kinds of laws provid(ing) enough work to keep as much as one-third or more of the city's police busy writing citations" (Johnson 1981, p. 39).

Traffic enforcement became even more complicated with the advent of automobiles, particularly as they moved from being "toys for the wealthy" to cheap and commonly owned following the introduction of the Ford Model T. With such developments, law enforcement had to evolve. For example, as travel outside of the city became more popular for the average citizen and criminals alike, state police had to evolve to meet a changing, increasingly mobile enforcement context.

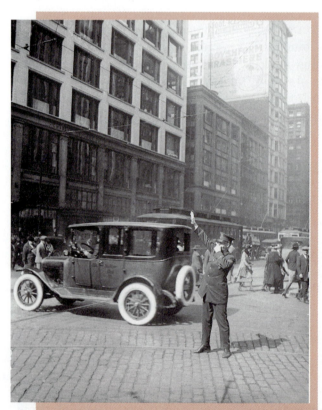

Traffic enforcement became an important means of reducing the severe disorder in the early urban environment of cities such as New York and Chicago.

The multi-agency investigation of the Washington, D.C., area sniper case highlights the important use of automated traffic surveillance technology in attempts to identify offenders' vehicles.

The Dangers of Traffic Stops

The dangers inherent to traffic stops are often not fully appreciated by members of the public. However, many officers are killed each year, and thousands more injured in the course of traffic stops gone wrong. In 1999, over half the officers killed in the line of duty were killed in a traffic-related incident (Onder 2002). From 1996 through 2005, 48 percent of all officers killed in the line of duty were killed in traffic-related incidents, including 18 percent of those who were killed feloniously (U.S. Department of Justice 2006). When traffic stops require the use of officers' weapons, the percentage of officer fatalities increases significantly (Onder 2002).

What might start out as a **routine traffic stop** for a minor violation can very quickly escalate when an officer learns that he or she is dealing with a wanted offender, an impaired driver, a car containing contraband, and so on. Under such circumstances, an officer might face a desperate (and potentially armed) offender. The fact that many major offenders in U.S. law enforcement history (e.g., Timothy McVeigh, Ted Bundy, Randall Kraft) were captured as a result of a routine traffic stop should drive this point home to the reader.

High-risk traffic stops are those where the officer is aware that the driver has committed a felony. Such stops often are the finale to a high-speed pursuit. In these cases, the vehicle may have been identified as stolen or people in the car are suspected of being involved in a serious offense, such as murder, rape, or robbery. The fact that such stops are extremely dangerous needs little explanation.

Linkages *in Law Enforcement*

Role of Patrol in Detecting Terrorist Activities

The role of federal law enforcement agencies in combating terrorism would never have been a surprise to anyone, even prior to September 11. The need for global intelligence activities seemed well-suited for the international FBI field offices, but of little use to the local police department.

One of the most disturbing facts that resonated in the U.S. law enforcement community with the collapse of the World Trade Center was the fact that the reach of terrorism actually extended so much further than we had thought—the first responders to a terrorist act will invariably be local law enforcement, firefighters, and emergency services personnel.

On September 11, a total of 343 firefighters and 23 NYPD officers died at the World Trade Center. Dozens of firefighters and police officers went directly to the scene, and many of these first responders died (ABC News 2002). As a result, the law enforcement community has moved quickly to revise its training, deployment, and communication strategies in order to be better prepared for future terrorist attacks. In New York City, a consulting firm was contracted to review the events of that day, reviewing radio transmissions, records, and conducting dozens of interviews. As a result of the firm's findings, a significant change in deployment strategy has been controlling the number of personnel who respond at any one time to an event.

September 11 also highlighted the need for specialized knowledge within police operations, leading to the creation of special counterterrorism units in many departments. Although the FBI had created localized task forces to coordinate law enforcement resources related to terrorism, clearly information was slipping through the cracks, as noted in Chapter 1.

The importance of law enforcement being in touch with the community, a reality before September 11, is now even more important as President Bush calls for the "vigilance" of residents to serve as the eyes and ears of law enforcement. Patrol officers are faced with renewed cultural challenges as they try to connect with Muslim segments of the community in the face of a rising tide of misunderstandings and accusations of racial profiling, particularly as the federal government has turned to the registration of people of Middle Eastern descent. However, it is only with the trust of the community that law enforcement can hope to get needed information related to suspicious activities. The reality that there are active terrorist cells in the United States cannot mean that all members of a group become suspects. This very difficult issue will be addressed further in Chapter 10.

An important issue for patrol officers is how the "war" on terrorism affects their typical response. The delicate balance remains that they still must operate within legal norms, even when military-style tactics and/or assistance may be needed (White 2001). Although public safety will always be a pertinent goal with respect to dealing with terrorism, law enforcement cannot act with impunity. In some Latin American countries, semi-military police have justified the practice of "disappearances" of suspected citizens on the basis of terrorist groups being too strong.

QUESTIONS

1. What are the most significant changes to the role of patrol officers post–September 11?

2. What specific strategies can law enforcement develop to collaborate more effectively with the Muslim community?

3. What tactics might you use to gain information on suspected terrorist cells in the community? What tactics would you consider to be going too far?

Unlike the routine traffic stop situation, the danger of stopping such a vehicle is known in advance.

The Supreme Court has recognized the inherent dangers involved in traffic stops, granting officers the right to order all passengers out of the car for officer safety concerns (see *Maryland v. Wilson*,[1] discussed in Chapter 5).

Automated Traffic Enforcement

One of the most interesting developments in the area of traffic control and traffic policing has been the growing use of automated tracking technology. Typically consisting of a system of cameras (positioned at or near cross-streets) fitted with sophisticated motion detectors, these systems are able to monitor traffic flow and provide traffic authorities with accurate information on road usage. Where these cameras also are linked to some form of video-monitoring system, they can be used by law enforcement agencies to conduct searches for particular types of vehicles or even individual suspects. Even small municipalities may find this equipment to be affordable; manufacturers are utilizing a fee system in which free equipment and installation is offered, with a percentage of all revenue generated through tickets paid to the company.

A good example of such a system is currently in operation in New York City. Originally established to help improve traffic flows on Manhattan Island, the system is now used by the police for such things as monitoring street sellers, searching for stolen vehicles, and policing public demonstrations. Indeed, the use of such systems by the police has led some civil libertarians to complain that such monitoring threatens individual privacy, particularly in light of the fact that this form of police surveillance activity is almost completely unregulated.

The potential uses of such technology have been demonstrated is some high-profile cases. For example, during the five-jurisdiction search for D.C. snipers John Allen Muhammad and Lee Boyd Malvo, who killed ten individuals and injured two more over a period of twenty-three days in 2002, hundreds of hours of traffic surveillance tapes were reviewed at locations and times near to each of the crime scenes (where such cameras are located) to try and identify the sniper's vehicle and license plate. Although the surveillance tapes were not ultimately involved in the suspects' capture, the use of these tapes demonstrates the need to better integrate such technologies into the routine and daily work of large police departments.

Chapter Summary

- Despite common perceptions of the patrol function, responding to crime is not the primary activity engaged in by patrol officers. The majority of an officer's time is spent "unassigned" or patrolling. Force is rarely used, and arrests are infrequent. Patrol observation studies, such as the Police Services Study (PSS) played an important role in aiding our understanding of patrol operations.

- Response time to calls for service only makes a significant difference in involvement crimes, which a PERF study indicates are only about 25 percent of all incidents.

- Police utilize several types of patrol. Random patrol involves officers driving "unsystematically" around their assigned beats looking for crimes in progress, waiting for calls for service, or deterring crimes through presence.

Random patrol is an incident-driven or reactive form of patrol. Directed patrol involves targeting patrol resources on hot spots, crime problems, and/or offenders, usually based upon an analysis of crime trends. Aggressive patrol refers to the use of high-profile activities, such as intensive traffic stops and field interrogations. Finally, saturation patrol is when a department places extremely high numbers of patrol in a very narrowly defined area.

- The Kansas City Gun Experiment and other studies indicate that directed, aggressive, and saturation patrols can have immediate effects on crime. However, the effectiveness of such strategies can reach a point of diminishing returns.

- Given the finding that not all calls require equal response times and the need to free up patrol resources for more proactive or directed patrol activities, many departments use differential response strategies. In such cases, dispatchers will either take the report over the phone, send a civilian to take the report, or explain to the caller that a sworn officer will be there in a specified (but longer) period of time.

- The Kansas City Preventive Patrol Experiment found that random patrol used alone has no significant effect on crime, fear of

crime, or even attitudes toward the police. This finding was significant given the reliance on this type of patrol at the time, forcing the law enforcement community to reexamine its methods. The movement toward proactive community-policing models began following this and a series of other key findings.

- Although foot patrol represents only a small proportion of total patrol resources, studies such as the Newark Foot Patrol Experiment have found that it can have a significant effect on residents' fear of crime, even if it does not significantly reduce crime itself.

- Decisions related to shift structure (i.e., rotating versus assigned; number of hours) need to be made cautiously. Studies have demonstrated the serious effects fatigue can play on officers' cognitive and motor skills, which could possibly lead to serious mistakes on the job. The type and structure of patrol can also impact the success of community-policing models in an area.

- The traffic division is often underestimated. It can be one of the most dangerous patrols for officers, regardless of whether they are dealing with a routine or high-risk (felony) stop situation. Recent Supreme Court decisions have recognized the importance of officer safety in traffic stop situations.

Linking the Dots

1. Explain the significance of the Kansas City Preventive Patrol Experiment to policing. How did it help shift policing from reactive to proactive strategies?

2. What productivity measures should be used to evaluate the effectiveness of patrol officers?

3. How can a patrol officer's job be affected by issues of linkage blindness within the department?

4. Explain the role of foot patrol in community policing. What other patrol deployment and shift-structure decisions should a department wishing to implement community policing consider?

KEY TERMS

REFERENCES

ABC News. 2002. "Report Recommends FDNY Response Changes." August 19, 1992. Available at abcnews.go.com/sections/us/DailyNews/homefront 020819.htm.

Adams, T. 2001. *Police Field Operations*, 5th ed. Upper Saddle River, NJ: Prentice Hall.

Associated Press. 2002. "Response Time Proves Crucial When Protection Order Violated." August 25. Available at www.wkyc.com/news/morelocal/akron/020825dispatch.asr.

Bittner, E. 1990. *Aspects of Police Work*. Boston: Northeastern University Press.

Boydstun, J., M. Sherry, and N. Moelter. 1977. *Patrol Staffing in San Diego*. Washington, D.C.: The Police Foundation.

Boydstun, J. E. 1975. *San Diego Field Interrogation: Final Report*. Washington, D.C.: The Police Foundation.

Bright, J. A. 1969. *Beat Patrol Experiment*. London: Home Office.

Broughton, M. 2000. *Circadian Rhythms and Shift Work*. Available at www.ifpo.org.

Bureau of Justice Statistics. 1999. *Law Enforcement Management and Administrative Statistics, 1997*. Washington, D.C.: Bureau of Justice Statistics.

Bureau of Justice Statistics. 2002. *Census of State and Local Law Enforcement Agencies, 2000*. Washington, D.C.: Bureau of Justice Statistics.

Carr, A. F., J. F. Schnelle, and J. F. Kirchner. 1980. "Police Crackdowns and Slowdowns: A Naturalistic Evaluation of Changes in Police Traffic Enforcement." *Behavioral Assessment* 2:33–41.

Cordner, G. 1981. "The Effects of Directed Patrol: A Natural Quasi-Experiment in Pontiac." In *Contemporary Issues in Law Enforcement*, edited by J. Fyfe, 37–58. Beverly Hills, CA: Sage.

Cordner, G. W., and R. C. Trojanwicz. 1992. "Patrol." In *What Works in Policing? Operations and Administration Examined*, edited by G. W. Cordner and D. C. Hale, 3–18. Cincinnati, OH: Anderson Publishing.

Dempsey, J. 1999. *An Introduction to Policing*. Belmont, CA: Wadsworth Publishing.

Department of Justice. 2006. *Law Enforcement Officers Killed and Assaulted, 2005*. Washington, D.C.: Federal Bureau of Investigation.

Forst, B., J. Lucianovic, and S. Cox. 1978. *What Happens After Arrest?* Washington, D.C.: U.S. Government Printing Office.

Fridell, L. 2000. *Measuring What Matters: Designing, Implementing and Evaluating a Comprehensive Model of Police Performance.* Unpublished manuscript, Police Executive Research Forum.

Goldstein, H. 1990. *Problem-oriented Policing.* Boston: McGraw-Hill.

Grant, H. 2000. "The Buffalo Weed and Seed Program." In *Comprehensive Strategies to Reduce Juvenile Gun Violence.* Washington, D.C.: Office of Juvenile Justice and Delinquency Prevention.

Grant, H., and N. Jacobs. 1998. *The Brooklyn North Neighborhood Safety Project.* Washington, D.C.: Office of Community-Oriented Policing Services.

Johnson, D. 1981. *American Law Enforcement: A History.* St. Louis: Forum Press.

Kelling, G., T. Pate, D. Dieckman, and C. E. Brown. 1974. *The Kansas City Preventive Patrol Experiment: A Summary Report.* Washington, D.C.: The Police Foundation.

Kenney, D., H. Grant, and N. Allen. 2002. *Policing a Diverse Society: Curriculum II.* Washington, D.C.: Policy Lab.

Larson, R. C. 1975. "What Happened to Patrol Operations in Kansas City? A Review of the Kansas City Preventive Patrol Experiment." *Journal of Criminal Justice* 3(4):267–297.

Milia, L. D., and B. Bowden. 2007. Unanticipated Safety Incomes: Shiftwork and Drive-in, Drive-out Workforce in Queenland's Bowen Basin. *Asia Pacific Journal of Human Resources* 45(1):100–112.

Moore, M. 1999. *Recognizing and Realizing Public Value in Policing: The Challenge of Measuring Police Performance.* Unpublished manuscript, Kennedy School of Government.

Niederpruem, K. 2000. "Downplaying Patrols and Embracing Communities, the State Police Sets Its Sights on Being a Force of Change." *Indianapolis Star,* January 9.

Onder, J. 2002. "Traffic Safety." Available at www .sussexcountysheriff.com/traffic_safety.htm.

Percy, S. L. 1980. "Response Time and Citizen Evaluation of Police." *Journal of Police Science and Administration* 8(1):75–86.

The Police Foundation. 1981. *The Newark Foot Patrol Experiment.* Washington, D.C.: Author.

Sheppard, D., H. Grant, W. Rowe, and N. Jacobs. 2000. *Fighting Gun Crime.* Washington, D.C.: U.S. Department of Justice.

Sherman, L. 1990. "Police Crackdowns: Initial and Residual Deterrence." In *Crime and Justice: A Review of Research*, edited by M. Tonry and N. Morris, 1–49. Beverly Hills: Sage.

Sherman, L., J. Shaw, and D. Rogan. 1995. *The Kansas City Gun Experiment*. Washington, D.C.: U.S. Government Printing Office.

Skogan, W., and G. Attunes. 1979. "Information, Apprehension, and Deterrence: Exploring the Limits of Police Productivity." *Journal of Criminal Justice* 7(3):217–241.

Thibault, E., L. Lynch, and R. McBride. 2001. *Proactive Police Management*, 5th ed. Upper Saddle River, NJ: Prentice-Hall.

Vila, B. 2000. *Tired Cops: The Importance of Managing Police Fatigue*. Washington, D.C.: Police Executive Research Forum.

Walker, S. 2001. *Police in America: An Introduction*. Boston: McGraw-Hill.

Whitaker, G. 1982. "What Is Patrol Work?" *Police Studies* 4(2):13–22.

White, J. 2001. *Terrorism*, 3d ed. Belmont, CA: Wadsworth Publishing.

Wilson, J. Q. 1975. *Thinking About Crime*. New York: Basic Books.

NOTE

1. 519 U.S. 408 (1997).

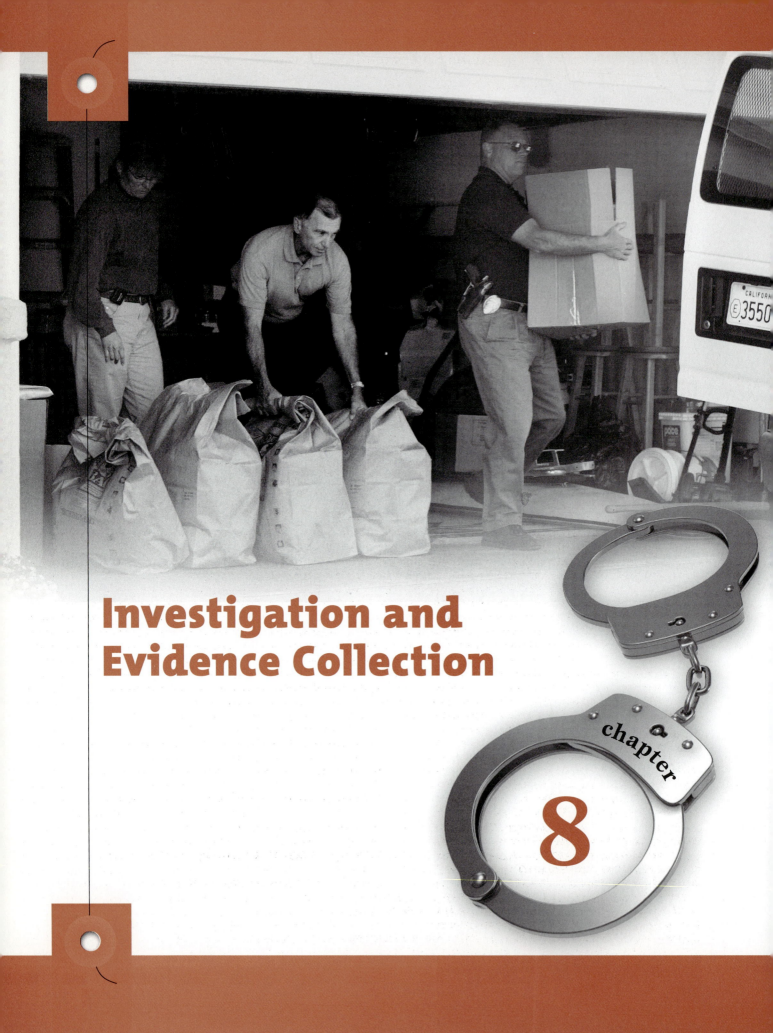

Investigation and Evidence Collection

chapter

8

Chapter Objectives

- Learn about the development and evolution of the investigative function.

- Understand the Locard exchange principle and its importance to investigations.

- Know the different types of evidence and how they affect an investigation.

- Understand the concept of behavioral profiling and how police officers can use it to identify a perpetrator.

- Know how new technologies are being used to solve investigations.

- Learn about different counterterrorism models at the local, state, and federal levels.

- Appreciate the challenges and issues involved in police–prosecutor collaboration.

Early on the morning of February 2, 2002, seven-year-old Danielle van Dam disappeared from her bedroom in San Diego, California. David Westerfield, who lived two houses away from the Van Dams, quickly emerged as a suspect following the abduction. The prosecutors obtained warrants enabling them to search for child pornography and any DNA evidence linking Danielle to his house or vehicles. Westerfield was arrested nearly three weeks later and charged with murder, kidnapping, and possession of child pornography. At the time of his arrest, Danielle's body had not yet been found.

The prosecution referred to evidence found in Westerfield's home during these initial searches as the "smoking gun" linking him to Danielle's abduction and suspected murder. Such evidence included fiber, hair, and fingerprint samples found in his motor home and a small amount of her blood on his jacket. Even though the body was not found until four days after Westerfield's arrest, the trace evidence found in the searches was used to form the probable cause necessary for his arrest. In addition to this physical evidence, investigators also brought to trial circumstantial evidence linking Westerfield to the death, such as his collection of child pornography, his 600-mile meandering trip immediately following her abduction, and his unusual actions, such as cleaning all of his bed linen and profuse sweating while the police searched his house.

Even in cases where investigators have strong reason to believe in the potential guilt of a suspect, incidental evidence such as the strange behavior of David Westerfield after the abduction of Danielle Van Dam is not enough. The criminal justice system requires an establishment of credible evidence to meet the standards of probable cause necessary for an arrest and full search. The case of David Westerfield is an example of this. The investigators were able to demonstrate Danielle's connection to the Westerfield motor home through fingerprints, blood, hair, and fibers, which was enough to obtain an arrest warrant even in the absence of finding the body. In addition to thorough physical evidence, however, behavioral evidence can help solidify a case, helping to ultimately sway jurors toward a guilty verdict. This chapter will introduce readers to the investigative process, highlighting key issues and topics in this very central function of the law enforcement process.

The Development of the Investigative Function

As discussed in Chapter 2, Henry Fielding's Bow Street Runners were a significant first step in the movement toward the creation of the London Metropolitan Police, or law enforcement as we know it today. In London during this time period, thieves were the central criminal figures, with individuals and families turning to theft as a profession when access to the industry-sector jobs proved to be more elusive than the initial promise. In the face of this perceived crime wave, the constable system proved inadequate, leaving local businesses and residents responsible for crime prevention or even the recovery of stolen property. Those individuals who could afford the service would often hire a **thief catcher** to aid in finding lost property. Similar to a law enforcement officer who moonlights as a security guard in modern times, the thief catcher was also often a constable in his primary job. However, even where successful in finding stolen property, thief catchers were unable to reduce general crime levels in a seemingly besieged city (Emsley 1996).

Taking on the position of London Magistrate in a city bereft with crime and disorder, Fielding sought to revitalize the government's crime-fighting arsenal by appointing a group of parish constables to his court. This group quickly began to demonstrate effective thief-catching functions as a result of implementing key criminal investigative activities, such as using informants for their close ties with the criminal underworld. Despite these successes, which led to them being acclaimed as the leading law enforcement agency in the metropolitan London area (Johnson and Wolfe 1996), the Bow Street Runners would also face issues of corruption and abuse (Osterburg and Ward 1997). In 1790, the Runners became an officially recognized force of trained and paid detectives who continued to fight criminal behavior for nearly fifty years—ten years after the Metropolitan Police Act.

It was not long after the disbandment of the Runners that Sir Robert Peel recognized the need to create an investigative division within the Metropolitan Police. Recruited directly from the patrol ranks, Peel sought to encourage foot patrol (beat) officers to develop the observational skills and intelligence networks important for promotion to the detective role. Housed in Scotland Yard, these officers were soon dubbed the "detective force" (Osterburg and Ward 1997). Johnson and Wolfe (1996) note that this method of selecting officers is very similar to contemporary police practices.

In the United States, the detective function also was recognized as a necessity early on. Thomas Byrnes was appointed as the first detective bureau chief for the New York City Police Department in 1880. However, as was the case with Fielding's Bow Street Runners, Byrnes' close ties to the underworld often led him to walk a fine ethical line. Theodore Roosevelt would force Byrnes out of the role immediately upon taking over the position of President of the Board of Police Commissioners in 1895.

The detective function, as with law enforcement in general, saw increased professionalism with the application of science and technology over time. Part of this professionalization also involved a shift of the detective role from being intimately tied to the underworld to one that is principally undertaken by a police officer, even where the use of criminal informants would always remain an important tool.

The Realities of Investigation

When one thinks of an investigation, a number of things might come to mind. One might think of Sherlock Holmes and his skills of deduction—meticulously taking seemingly meaningless elements of a crime scene and then brilliantly using them to take us from the "what" to the "why" and ultimately to the "who." Or, perhaps one thinks of the television show *CSI*, in which detectives evaluate forensic evidence from crime scenes and are nearly always able to use it to identify violent perpetrators. And no one can forget the chilling "quid pro quo" exchange in *Silence of the Lambs* between Hannibal Lector and the newly recruited FBI agent, Clarice Starling, ultimately leading to her honing in on a killer who had eluded teams of law enforcement agents. In fact, it is such portrayals of detectives in movies, books, and television that have the public equating investigation with policing itself, despite that fact that about 60 percent of departmental resources are dedicated to patrol and only 15 percent to investigation (Bayley 1994). Popular crime dramas such as *Law and Order* focus on the detectives chasing down the suspects through a combination of intellect and physical prowess; they do not focus on the officer on patrol offering directions or writing reports. Detectives also have a certain special status within many police departments, receiving higher salaries than ordinary officers and having the freedom to choose their own hours and not wear a uniform (Bayley 1994).

As noted in Chapter 6, the **Kansas City Response Time Study** suggested that citizens take longer to report crimes to the police than it takes the police to respond (Kansas City Police Department 1977). Additionally, the likelihood of arrest is more significantly related to the citizen's time to report than police response time. Given that 75 percent of crimes are **discovery crimes**, in which the police respond well after the crime was committed, how significant a role can investigation play in solving the majority of offenses? **Involvement crimes**, in which the police arrive during the commission of the offense, account for only 25 percent of all cases (Wrobleski and Hess 2002).

Researchers first examined the realities of investigation in a study by the Rand Corporation in 1975. They examined how serious crimes such as rape, robbery, murder assault, theft, and burglary were solved, using a variety of data sources from 153 jurisdictions na-

As glamorous and exciting as media portrayals of investigation may be, the reality of investigation for many detectives and agents is far more mundane and routine.

tionwide serving populations over 100,000 (Greenwood and Petersilia 1975). Seeking to understand the contribution that investigation ultimately makes to the resolution of crimes, the researchers examined clearance rates by organizational structure, technology, and departmental role.

Clearance rate refers to the ratio of successful identification and apprehension of offenders to unsolved crimes. The results of the Rand study had a similar impact on thinking about investigation as the Kansas City Preventive Patrol Experiment had on patrol (see Chapter 7). Figure 8.1 pre-sents the percentage of Part I crimes that can be attributed to traditional detective work.

Less than 3 percent of all Part I crime clearances can be attributed to special investigation techniques. Thus, 97 percent of all cleared crimes will be cleared, regardless of what the investigators do. Of course, that 2.7 percent often includes the most interesting and publicly visible crimes, such as homicides (Greenwood and Petersilia 1975). Recent research on homicide clearance rates in New York City shows a decrease in clearance rates over the past 40 years, despite the increased testing of forensic evidence (Schroeder 2007).

How can this be? In reality, patrol officers are responsible for most clearances. Thirty percent of all clearances are the result of pickup arrests by patrol officers responding to the scene of the crime. These are the "smoking gun" situations in which the offender has not left the immediate crime area when the first responding officer arrives at the scene. Such cases are obvious examples of the involvement crimes discussed earlier in which fast law enforcement response to the scene is critical (Greenwood and Petersilia 1975).

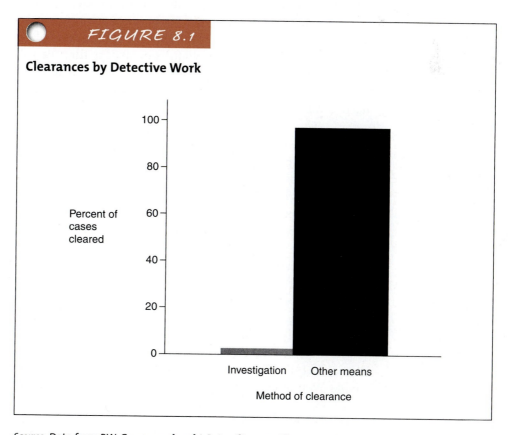

FIGURE 8.1

Clearances by Detective Work

Source: Data from P.W. Greenwood and J. Petersilia. 1975. *The Criminal Investigative Process,* Vol. 1, *Summary and Policy Implications.* Santa Monica, CA: RAND Corp.

In 50 percent of cleared cases, the offender was already known when the crime report was taken at the scene. Greenwood and Petersilia (1975) offer three examples of such cases:

- The offender was arrested at the scene.
- The victim and/or other witnesses identified the offender by name and address.
- Unique evidence, such as a license plate, identified a perpetrator.

In these instances, no amazing sleuth work is necessary to solve the crime. Instead, the principal efforts of the investigation will be pulling together enough facts for the successful prosecution of the case and locating the offender to take him or her into custody. Although this leaves a remaining 20 percent of cleared crimes that could still potentially be solved by good "detective work," the reality remains that a good number of these actually are solved by patrol officers or members of the public later revealing critical information. In other cases, simple clerical work plays the central role in identifying the perpetrator. In his seminal study on homicide, Wolfgang (1958) attributed the high clearance rate to general police functions—taking eyewitness statements, eyewitness identifications, and confessions. Other surprising findings revealed in the Rand study included that although crimes such as homicide, rape, and suicide certainly receive some investigative attention, over half of all serious offenses received only superficial investigative work. Organizational changes related to staffing, workload, or even training appeared to have no effect on the clearance rates.

Does this mean that investigative units are unnecessary? No. The quality of investigative work can still affect the clearance rates of homicide, robbery, and commercial theft. However, what is evident is that the role of the patrol officer conducting the preliminary investigation needs to be given important consideration; the patrol officer's role in initially documenting the crime scene evidence needed for the legal resolution of a case is indispensable.

The Preliminary Investigation

The first uniformed officer (usually a patrol officer) to arrive at the crime scene conducts a **preliminary investigation**. Duties involved upon arrival at the scene include determining whether the offender is at the scene or in the area, responding to the victim's needs, and ensuring the general safety of anyone in the immediate vicinity. The statistics presented earlier demonstrate the importance of the first officer's training and professional response given that what initially occurs at a scene can determine whether the crime will eventually be cleared.

As such, initial crime scene processing and the recording of relevant evidence and information are critical. In addition to securing the scene from possible contaminants, detailed and methodical note and record keeping are essential in order to document everything exactly as it was found. Some departments even have sophisticated computer software available in laptops to assist in this process, making it easy to produce a true-scale drawing for even the most artistically challenged investigator.

Contaminants are anything that can alter a crime scene. This can involve taking something from the scene, leaving something behind, or moving things from their original position. Because the elements of a crime scene can be critical to the **reconstruction** of the crime scene, that is, determining exactly what happened and by whom, the introduction of any foreign items to the scene can send the investigation in many wrong (and time-consuming) directions. For example, if an officer enters a murder scene, picks up three kitchen chairs that had been knocked over and casually smokes a cigarette, the investigators might make some false initial conclusions. Rather than seeing the obvious signs of a struggle, the investigator might see a scene that was calm and methodical, to the point where the offender even took the time to smoke a cigarette immediately following the event, not to mention the fact that the cigarette will be sent into the crime lab for costly testing.

The patrol officer who first arrives at the scene will pass a report to the detective unit regarding all evidence found at the scene. Based on **solvability factors**, a decision is made whether to assign a follow-up investigation by investigative services. Solvability factors are anything that can potentially affect the probability of successfully concluding the case (e.g., presence of witnesses and/or physical evidence) (Skogan and Attunes 1979).

The Follow-up Investigation

The Rand study showed that more than half of serious reported crimes do not receive full investigative attention (Greenwood and Petersilia 1975), and when full attention is given, it may only involve a reading over of the incident report. Although crimes such as homicide, rape, and suicide are almost guaranteed to

Based on the evidence available at the crime scene or solvability factors, important decisions will be made as to whether or how to proceed with an investigation. As such, the careful securing of a crime scene and documentation of all conditions are essential to the investigative process.

get some subsequent investigative activity, less than half of reported felonies will not, with many receiving less than a day of investigative work (Greenwood and Petersilia 1975).

Types of Crime Scenes

What do we mean by the phrase *crime scene*? A **crime scene** is the area from which the majority of the physical evidence associated with the crime is obtained (Lee et al. 2001). This is often, although not always, the starting point for an investigation. Lee et al. (2001) identifies two types of possible crime scenes. The **primary crime scene** is where the original crime took place. Any subsequent scene is referred to as a **secondary crime scene**. See Figure 8.2 for a graphic illustration of the two crime scene types.

The Danielle van Dam case introduced at the beginning of this chapter demonstrates the difference between primary and secondary crime scenes. Although the little girl's body was found wrapped in a blanket in the desert, this would be classified as a secondary scene. Any trace evidence located in the car used to transport her from the site of her death (Westerfield's motor home) to the dump site would also be classified as a secondary scene. The motor home itself would be classified as the primary scene, because that is where Westerfield allegedly raped and killed her, leaving behind the majority of evidence. Hair, fingerprints, and blood were found on the bed and walls in the bedroom. Blood was found on Westerfield's jacket. Even though Danielle was originally abducted from her own home, this would also likely not be classified as a primary scene given the lack of evidence and the fact that most of the serious action took place once Westerfield transported her to his own quarters. To the extent possible, investigators need to make an effort to find the primary scene, because that is where the bulk of the evidence will be. As will become clear in the following text, the lack of trace evidence is what makes dumping scenes so difficult to investigate.

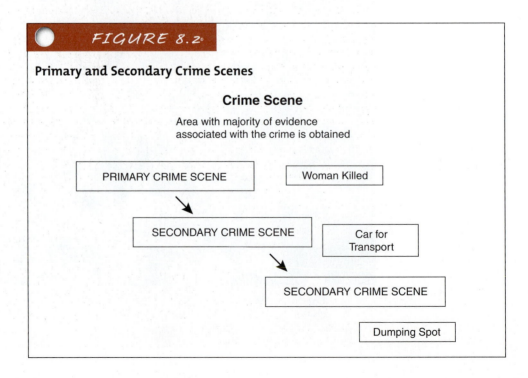

FIGURE 8.2

Primary and Secondary Crime Scenes

Crime Scene

Area with majority of evidence
associated with the crime is obtained

PRIMARY CRIME SCENE   Woman Killed

SECONDARY CRIME SCENE   Car for Transport

SECONDARY CRIME SCENE

Dumping Spot

Making the Case: Linking the Offender to a Crime Scene

The most effective way to prosecute a case is to collect reliable and sufficient evidence linking an offender to a crime scene; thus the need for crime laboratories that are capable of examining evidence in a scientific manner. Edmond Locard established the first "crime laboratory" in Lyon, France, in 1910, followed by others in the 1920s and 1930s. Since the 1930s, there has been an explosion in the number of crime laboratories operating in the United States, so much so that it is difficult to find a major city without such a facility.

Named after the founder of the first crime lab, the **Locard exchange principle** recognizes that it is simply impossible for anyone to enter a location without changing it in some way, either by bringing something to it or removing something from it (see Figure 8.3). This principle is essential to linking an offender and weapon to a crime scene (e.g., through blood, carpet fibers, soil, etc.). It also explains why it is crucial to shield the scene from possible contaminants and why the importance of detailed, meticulous note taking throughout all phases of the investigative process cannot be overemphasized.

The crime scene is usually photographed, measured, and sketched in great detail. The photographs need to show the scene as it was found, taken in a series to reconstruct the crime. Scale and dimension are critical, which is why computer programs, photographs, and even videotaping are all used.

The importance of strict procedures guiding the investigation process was never more apparent than during the O. J. Simpson trial. The bulk of testimony in Simpson's trial focused on the admissibility and relevance of DNA evidence. The accusations against detective Mark Fuhrman in that case highlighted the need to maintain a chain of evidence as soon as the first officer enters the scene through the initial collection of physical evidence and continuing on to its analysis and presentation in court. **Chain of evidence** refers to the meticulous documentation and tracking of all physical evidence taken from a crime scene. Sometimes this process is called the **chain of custody**. Evidence may change hands many times in the journey from investigation to trial or to the final legal phase. Investigators must track and document all the persons, locations, and specific times that evidence have been outside of their control. Specifically, these records should include (Buckwalter 1984):

- When and to whom evidence is given

- Why the evidence was given to that person or department

- Who returned the evidence and when it was returned

FIGURE 8.3

Locard Exchange Principle

CRIME SCENE ⟶ OFFENDER
⟵

Physical evidence links offender
to crime scene—chain of evidence thus is crucial

- The conditions and location in which the evidence was kept leading into a criminal trial

To ensure the integrity and usefulness of evidence at trial, investigators must limit the exchange of evidence between persons and departments. This procedure ensures that evidence has not been tampered with and is intact for presentation in the final legal proceeding (Buckwalter 1984).

Establishing a Physical Link

Obtaining physical evidence is a central function of the investigation. Remember Locard's principle of exchange: Physical evidence links an offender and weapon to the crime scene. In property crimes, the investigator will generally look for signs of forcible entry, such as marks on doors from an implement used to pry the door open. Physical evidence in a violent crime may include blood, hair, fibers, fingerprints, and weapons. Depending on the type of offense, investigators may also expect to find evidence such as semen or bite marks on the victim. Table 8.1 offers some examples of several types of physical evidence.

Associative evidence is a nonlegal term for the laboratory work used to link the crime scene, the victim, and the offender (Osterburg and Ward 1997). **Criminalistics** encompasses the application of scientific technology to the minute details of a crime scene used to reconstruct what happened, as well as to establish connections between people, places, and things (Saferstein 1995).

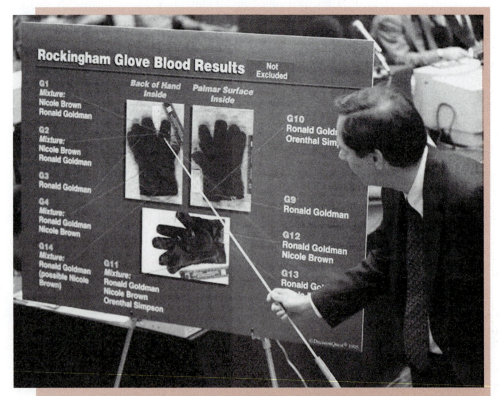

The chain of evidence documenting the whereabouts of evidence from the early moments of the preliminary investigation to its admission in court is essential. Failure to do so can mean the difference between conviction and reasonable doubt.

TABLE 8.1

Types of Physical Evidence

Physical Evidence	Investigative Significance
Fingerprints	• No two people have the same fingerprints. Eight possible patterns are possible. When a person grasps an item with reasonable pressure, grease oozing form the pores under the ridges leave **latent fingerprints.** • In the past, matches were performed manually. Now, automated fingerprint identification systems (AFIS) are used.
Blood Saliva Semen Skin	• DNA profiling uses genetic material to identify individuals. No two people have the same DNA structure, except for identical twins. • The **National DNA Index System (NDIS) is** a database of approximately 600,000 offenders. It enables states to exchange profiles and comparisons. • Legal? Yes. Federal law allows states to take blood samples from convicted felons.
Weapon	• When a weapon is fired, the bullet picks up tiny imperfections of the bore as it passes through. Scratches are caused by the imperfections in the lands and grooves placed in the barrel at the time of manufacture and caused through use. These marks enable experts to determine which rounds are fired by the same gun. The science of ballistics deals with the motion of bullets. • The make of a weapon, determined by riflings (spiral grooves) in the barrel, varies from manufacturer to manufacturer.

Behavioral Evidence—Signature versus Modus Operandi

In addition to **physical evidence,** investigators also rely on interrogating suspects who they believe to be connected with the crime, relying on **nonverbal cues** (e.g., tone, pitch, inflection) and **kinesics** (body language) to support or confirm statements. Consider the nonphysical evidence used in the van Dam case: Westerfield's strange behavior following the disappearance, his meandering journey, his sweating, and his obsessive need to clean all of his bed linen.

However, reliance on nonverbal cues can also be misleading when the investigator or police officer comes from a different culture than the suspect. Nonverbal cues can actually vary across cultures, leading some authors to refer to them as cultural cues (Kenney et al. 2002). **Cultural cues** are the alternative meanings of nonverbal cues that can vary by culture. For example, the inability to make eye contact is often viewed by investigators as a clear sign of suspiciousness or guilt. However, in some Asian cultures a lack of eye contact (a form of kinesics) can actually mean deference to authority (National Crime Prevention Council 1999). Automatically jumping to conclusions based on one's cultural framework may lead an investigation in the wrong direction. Law enforcement officers should receive diversity training as a means of helping them to recognize potentially misleading cues, a subject we return to in Chapter 10.

Criminal profiling involves the use of behavioral evidence found at the scene to predict what type of person committed the crime. Profiling is based on past experience with patterns identified in similar crimes. Despite the mythological presentation of profiling in the media, it can never replace true investigative work. Profiling should only be viewed as an additional tool in the arsenal of the investigator to narrow the field of investigation, particularly in cases where there is no connection between victim and offender. In the end, even with the most accurate criminal profile, it will take investigative skills to identify a perpetrator.

In determining a behavioral profile, it is helpful for the investigator to ascertain whether the perpetrator follows a particular modus operandi or has an identifiable signature. Though sometimes discussed interchangeably, these are different, but equally important, concepts in establishing a behavioral profile.

Modus operandi (MO) refers to "how" a crime is committed. Although MO analysis is useful in linking crimes by the same suspect, this must be done with caution (Gerbeth 1996). For example, sexual homicide can involve the escalation of acts as the offender becomes more comfortable with his behavior. What starts out as being an act of voyeurism may progress into burglary, rape, and ultimately homicide. Where an offender is in this cycle can influence the commonalities in MO across crime scenes. Moreover, it may not be the type of weapon that is important to the offender, but some other fantasy element that is difficult for an untrained investigator to detect. Sex offender registries are a useful medium for monitoring and controlling such suspects. Police agencies are now keeping computerized records containing descriptions, addresses, and MOs of local offenders to, among other things, help in the investigation of new offenses and pinpoint emerging patterns in a geographic area.

Signature refers to the "what" instead of the "how" at a crime scene. Specifically, the offender's signature is what the offender needs or takes from a crime scene (Douglas and Munn 1992). FBI agent John Douglas has referred to this as the "behavioral fingerprint" of the offender, because it is directly tied to his or her fantasy element regarding the crime. Though the fantasy may evolve over time, this element is likely to remain consistent from scene to scene and is therefore more reliable than the MO (Douglas and Munn 1992). For example, one rapist's signature may be to have his victims say, "I love you," during the act, whereas another rapist may enjoy torturing and humiliating his victims (Hazelwood 1987). These indicate two very different types of individuals and may give investigators a clue as to the type of perpetrator for whom they are searching.

Following a now classic, but hotly contested, study of sexual homicide offenders, FBI agents John Douglas and Robert Ressler developed a typology to guide and classify the examination of physical evidence at a sexual homicide (also referred to as *lust murders*) crime scene (Douglas et al. 1985). Correlating crime scene elements with key personality characteristics is a key function of the **organized–disorganized typology**, as described in Table 8.2.

The organized offender takes great care in the planning of his or her offense, ensuring that little or no evidence remains at the crime scene (Holmes and Holmes 1999). As a result, the weapon of choice will usually be brought to the scene by the offender and taken away following the completion of the act. The victim is likely to be targeted by the offender, eliminating the connection between victim and offender that increases the likelihood of getting caught. Victims tend to be selected opportunistically, and as such may include prostitutes, hitchhikers, and others with "deviant" or "risky" lifestyles. This leads to a minimal risk of the killer being caught (Gerbeth 1996).

TABLE 8.2

The Organized–Disorganized Crime Scene Typology

A. Organized Offender

Crime Scene Indicators	Personal Characteristics	Postoffense Behavior	Interview Techniques
Planned offense	High intelligence	Returns to crime scene	Use direct strategy
Targeted stranger	Socially adequate	Volunteers information	Be certain of deaths
Personalizes victim	Sexually competent	Police groupie	Be aware that
Controlled conversation	Lives with partner	Anticipates	offender will admit
Controlled crime scene	High birth order	questioning	to only what he
Submissive victim	Harsh discipline in	May move body	must
Restraints used	childhood	May dispose of body to	
Aggressive acts	Controlled mood	advertise crime	
Body moved	Masculine image		
Weapon taken	Charming		
Little evidence	Situational cause		
	Geographically mobile		
	Occupationally mobile		
	Follows media		

B. Disorganized Offender

Crime Scene Indicators	Personal Characteristics	Postoffense Behavior	Interview Techniques
Spontaneous event	Below average	Returns to crime scene	Show empathy
Victim unknown	intelligence	May attend victim's	Introduce
Depersonalizes victim	Socially inadequate	funeral	information
Minimal conversation	Unskilled worker	May change job	indirectly
Chaotic crime scene	Low birth order status	May have personality	Use counselor
Sudden violence	Father's work unstable	change	approach
No restraints	Lives alone	May turn to religion	Interview at night
Sex after death	Lives/works near scene	May keep diary or news	
Body not moved	Nocturnal	clippings	
Weapon left	Poor personal hygiene		
Physical evidence	High school dropout		

Source: Adapted from Ronald M. Holmes, *Profiling Violent Crimes: A Practical Tool for Homicide Investigation.* Copyright © 1989 by Sage Publications. Reprinted by permission of Sage Publications, Inc.

In contrast, disorganized offenders often engage in a chaotic, unplanned style of attack in which substantial amounts of evidence are left behind at the crime scene. Although the victims also are likely to be strangers, they are less likely to be selected based on a likelihood of being caught. In fact, with disorganized offenders the victims tend to be distant acquaintances, such as residents in the same building. Unlike the organized offender, who is more likely to have traveled great distances to the scene, the spontaneous nature of a disorganized killer's act makes him or her more likely to either live or work within their original zone of comfort (Rossmo 2000).

Holmes and Holmes (1999) argue for the maintenance of the FBI's original distinction between the organized **nonsocial offender** and disorganized **asocial offender** due to their closer match to the specific profile characteristics suggested by the typology. The organized nonsocial offender is likely to meet the classification of a **psychopath**, one who is able to charm his victims but who has a complete void of empathy that is often manifested in sadistic sexual pleasure. Control of the victim and the scene is the central signature element for many organized offenders. The disorganized asocial offender is closer in profile to a **schizoid personality**, or someone who is withdrawn from society. The inability to relate to others can explain the reliance on sudden attack for such offenders, as well as the disordered nature of their crime scenes.

The ability to use crime scene information to suggest personality type is controversial. Even those who subscribe to the possibilities of profiling are quick to refute the organized–disorganized dichotomy (Turvey 2001), largely because offenders rarely fit into such mutually exclusive categories. Few meaningful evaluations of the effectiveness of either the organized–disorganized typology or profiling in general have been completed to date, and many studies now tend to focus on "thematic" frameworks rather than a simple dichotomous characterization of personality. For example, Salfati (2000) notes that offenders can be classified into either an "expressive" or "instrumental" theme.

Information, Clearance Rates, and Investigation

As described earlier, clearance rates vary significantly from crime to crime. Only crimes involving some level of interpersonal vigilance have at least some chance of positive resolution. Some of this has to do with factors related to the circle of investigation. The **circle of investigation** is the pool of possible suspects in a crime (Skogan and Attunes 1979). Crimes involving personal contact and/or acquaintanceship with the victim have a much narrower circle of investigation, and, consequently, a greater chance of clearance.

Although people expect the police to dust their homes for fingerprints following a burglary, the unfortunate reality is that such crimes are very rarely solved. When they are, it is often due to the confessions of an offender caught during the commission of another crime. The solution of any particular property crime has been referred to as "a chance event, insensitive to the amount of investigation conducted" (Greenwood 1970, p. 37).

Skogan and Antunes (1979) correctly note that the low level of solvability of property crimes clearly demonstrates the importance of information in policing. Without adequate information being obtained by the first patrol officer responding to the scene, the likelihood of successful clearance can be dramatically reduced. As a result of such findings, many departments began to alter their perceptions of the patrol officer role during the 1970s. Training procedures for patrol began to emphasize the importance of gathering all pertinent information at the scene. However, Greenwood and Petersilia (1975) point out that the departmental practice of creating long checklists of crime scene data for officers to wade through and record can actually be a hindrance. Too much information can be as bad as too little; the key to collecting information is to only collect that which is likely to be useful in the resolution of the immediate offense. The selection of information is related to "case construction," a factor that can be related to police attitudes. For example, police often emphasize or downplay pieces of information depending on whether it fits with their preconceived ideas about the crime and offender, a fact that for obvious reasons could significantly throw off the course of an investigation.

Linkages *in Law Enforcement*

Role of Technology in Reducing Linkage Blindness

Many factors related to investigations can contribute to linkage blindness, the inability to analyze and link critical information across or within an agency. Specific concerns include the many overlapping jurisdictions between and even within organizations that can lead to inadequate communication and coordination. Linkage blindness occurs in most cases where two or more jurisdictions are investigating the same crime from different perspectives, but are not sharing information. This inability to "connect the dots" can stop certain crimes from being solved or prevent the linking of incidents to recognize larger problems. For example, the Bridgeport, Connecticut, Police Department might have an open murder case that has been under investigation for years. If they ran ballistics tests on spent shell casings found at the scene and then shared this information with the NYPD, they may find that the same weapon had been involved in an assault case in that jurisdiction. The NYPD knows the identity of the weapon's owner. If the Bridgeport department knew this information, they would be able to solve the case. National efforts to reduce linkage blindness through technological advancements have been developed and are constantly evolving.

National Crime Information Center

The **National Crime Information Center (NCIC)** is a national, computerized, shared system run by the FBI. It contains items such as a fingerprint database, a list of individuals on supervised release (parole), and a sex offender database. Officers in the field can call in to operators in their department to run checks on stopped individuals for wanted persons, stolen guns, stolen vehicles, and so on (FBI 1999). This would, for example, allow an officer in California to know that the person pulled over on a highway is wanted for a felony offense in Connecticut, thereby allowing the individual to be arrested and cleared.

Violent Criminal Apprehension Program

In response to fears of serial murders and child kidnappings in the 1980s, the FBI created the **Violent Criminal Apprehension Program (VICAP)** to help identify national homicide patterns. VICAP is a comprehensive database of solved and unsolved violent crimes that includes significant details related to crime scenes, victim characteristics, and offender characteristics (where known). In practice, VICAP is meant to draw connections between similar incidents, even if they take place in opposite parts of the country. For example, a series of prostitute murders occurring in Seattle, Washington, might be linked to a similar series that had occurred two years previously in New York City. By drawing this connection, the two police departments can now share information they would not have previously, perhaps through the establishment of a joint investigative task force. It may be that each department is holding different pieces of the puzzle, which when put together can lead to the successful apprehension of the offender. The usefulness of VICAP has been limited, however, by the unwillingness of departments to regularly submit their cases to the FBI.

National Integrated Ballistic Information Network

NIBIN, the **National Integrated Ballistic Information Network**, is a firearms identification program run by the department of Alcohol, Tobacco, and Firearms (ATF). Since 2000, the network has catalogued over 926,000 pieces of crime-scene evidence and over 12,500 matches have been made by investigators using the system. Nationally, 182 federal, state, and local law enforcement agencies use the system. The technology enables firearms analysts to obtain digital images of markings made by a firearm on bullets and cartridge casings that may then be analyzed through automated comparison. Developed jointly by the FBI and the ATF to replace the incompatible Drugfire System,[1] the

(continues)

Integrated Ballistic Information System (IBIS) is the administrative and networking system of technology that gives law enforcement agencies access to NIBIN (ATF 2007).

Automated Fingerprint Identification Systems

A significant advance beyond the days when **latent fingerprint** matches had to be done by comparing manual cards, **automated fingerprint identification systems (AFISs)** involve the digitized matching of fingerprints found at different crime scenes. AFISs are linked to the **integrated automated fingerprint identification system (IAFIS)**, which is maintained by the FBI. IAFIS is a national fingerprint and criminal history system under the FBI's Criminal Justice Information Services (CJIS) Division. This system enables "automated fingerprint search capabilities, latent searching capability, electronic image storage, and electronic exchange of fingerprints and responses, 24 hours a day, 365 days a year" (FBI 2007b) Agencies can acquire electronic responses to criminal fingerprint inquiries within two hours. (See Chapter 13 for a more detailed explanation of this technology).

National DNA Identification System

Operated by the FBI, the **National DNA Identification System (NDIS)** database includes the DNA of over 600,000 felons. This system is a part of the **Combined DNA Index System (CODIS)**, which is a structured database with local, state, and federal levels. The NDIS is the highest level of the CODIS system; it enables the exchange and comparison of DNA evidence on a national level (FBI 2007a). As with the other systems, NDIS is able to make computerized matches between the DNA profiles of hair, blood, semen, and saliva found at one scene as compared to another. If there is a successful "hit" in the database, then a successful identification is made.

QUESTIONS

1. What are the strengths of these technologies in eliminating linkage blindness? What are their weaknesses?

2. Which technology could best be adapted to communicate to a patrol officer in a routine traffic stop that the individual in the car is on an FBI terrorist watch list?

3. Should all American citizens be required to submit DNA and fingerprint samples for storage in AFIS and NDIS systems? Why or why not? Should owners of firearms be required to submit ballistics samples for a national Drugfire expansion system? What opposition will law enforcement face in implementing such policies?

Ultimately the research shows that, contrary to public perception, the responsibility for resolving crime lies in the hands of the community as much or more than it does on the police. This citizen responsibility is reflected in both the initial reporting of crime and providing adequate information about the crime and perpetrator to the responding officers. This is one reason why barriers to police–community communications may have a detrimental effect on the police, even as it relates to such measures as arrest productivity and clearance rates. This is an issue we will return to in Chapters 10 and 12.

Investigating Terror: Models of Counterterrorism

The task force concept, introduced earlier, brings together multiple agencies from different jurisdictions to come to bear on a problem. Task forces are very important in counterterrorism efforts. Each major jurisdiction in the United States had a counterterrorism task force in place even prior to September 11. For instance, several incidents of violence from the Puerto Rican Armed Forces for National Liberation (FALN) in the late 1970s to early 1980s led to the creation of the New York Terrorism Task Force, which included agencies at the federal, state, and local levels. The New York Terrorism Task Force successfully investigated and charged key members of FALN who were involved in the murder of an armored truck driver and two law enforcement officers. Its central post-September task is to revitalize such efforts and increase their effectiveness. (See Chapter 6 for more on task force structures).

Terrorism investigations involve the same techniques used to investigate other crimes; there are no techniques that are specific to the investigation of terrorism (Dyson 2001). Dyson (2001) identifies a number of key factors in a successful terrorism investigation:

- The task force concept;
- The recognition of terrorism as a specialty;
- Focusing on people committing crimes rather than those exercising their constitutional rights; and
- Exercising great care with respect to gathering evidence

Because local law enforcement officers often are the first responders to the scene of a terrorist act, it is essential that they be adequately trained to recognize the incident as being the result of terrorism. In addition, they must be able to understand and deal with the use of possible weapons of mass destruction and adequately document the crime scene. Problems in identifying the true significance of the 1993 World Trade Center bombing may have contributed to a time delay in successfully resolving the case. Moreover, it was not until much later that connections were made between this event and the worldwide efforts of the Al Qaeda network (White 2001).

The blurring of jurisdictional boundaries caused by the global nature of terrorism is evident by the NYPD's recent deployment of officers to Israel shortly after September 11 to learn firsthand how to respond to terrorist activity. NYPD officers now scan newspapers around the world to gain a handle on global trends and issues, a task previously thought to be only within the domain of the FBI or CIA (Grant 2000). Departments across the country are being forced to reexamine their practices, creating specialized counterterrorism units and revising training procedures.

Challenges of Police–Prosecutor Collaboration

As noted throughout this chapter, the importance of successfully documenting a crime scene and maintaining a sound chain of evidence cannot be underestimated. Failure to do so can lead to the outright dismissal of a case by the time it gets to the prosecutor. The inability of a responding officer to write sound, descriptive reports can play a major role in a detective's decision not to proceed to a follow-up investigation, or to waste valuable time re-interviewing witnesses, an effort that more often than not will prove to be futile (Skogan and Attunes 1979).

A lack of communication or collaboration between the prosecutor and police department might also lead to a significant number of dismissals and voided arrests. In such cases, police organizational practice can be affected. For example, if the chief perceives that the district attorney consistently does not prosecute a certain type of crime, he or she may divert enforcement efforts and resources elsewhere (Swanson et al. 2001).

Although the prosecutor is technically the chief law enforcement officer under the statutes of some states, he or she does not have overall responsibility for supervision. However, close collaboration between the agencies over chain of evidence in investigation required. One needs only to look at the problems evidenced in such cases as the O. J. Simpson trial for this point to be driven home. In some jurisdictions postarrest investigations are handled by the prosecutor's office to avoid tensions and conflict. Tensions between the prosecutor and the police can be particularly salient when there are indictments against the police for criminal acts such corruption or excessive use of force. Similar tensions also can arise as a result of judicial practices. For example, sometimes a motion to suppress will be granted by a judge who believes a case should not be prosecuted because it is too minor. These practices may confuse officers, leading them to stop enforcing laws in similar cases in the future (Swanson et al. 2001).

Chapter Summary

- The investigative function evolved out of the success of Henry Fielding's Bow Street Runners. The Bow Street Runners would last until Sir Robert Peel created Scotland Yard following the creation of the London Metropolitan Police Force.

- As with patrol, the realities of the investigation function are not as they are portrayed in the media. In fact, most clearances are the result of patrol and victim activities at the scene of the crime, according to a pivotal Rand study.

- Although the patrol officer conducts the preliminary investigation, it is usually up to the detective whether to proceed to a follow-up investigation. The majority of cases will be lost here. Detectives will make a decision as to whether to investigate further based on solvability factors.

- Meticulous detail and a sound chain of evidence are essential to ensure that no contaminants have entered a crime scene, potentially throwing off the credibility of the entire case. The Locard exchange principle recognizes that just as an offender can never leave a crime scene without taking some part of it with him or leaving a part of him behind, a sloppy investigator could destroy or alter physical evidence.

- Criminalistics are used to establish the physical link between victim and offender; profiling often relies on behavioral evidence to identify the "type" of offender likely to have committed a particular offense.

- Technological advances have played a significant role in reducing linkage blindness, such as AFIS, NDIS, VICAP, NCIC, and Drugfire. One method of investigating terrorist activities and reducing linkage blindness on federal, state, and local levels is through the creation of task forces. Training local law enforcement officers is key to counterterrorism efforts, since they are almost always first responders to terrorist activity.

- Lack of communication and collaboration between police and prosecutors may lead to a dismissal of cases of voided arrests. Tensions between the two groups are particularly high in cases in which police officers are on trial.

Linking the Dots

1. Explain the importance of the Locard exchange principle as a justification for creating sound investigation policies.

2. What were the key findings of the Rand Study? How are they similar or different from those of the Kansas City Preventative Patrol Experiment?

3. What factors might influence an investigator's decision to pursue a follow-up investigation? How might these vary by crime scene? How might these vary based on the reader's own personal characteristics?

KEY TERMS

Asocial offender   203
Associative evidence   200
Automated fingerprint identification system (AFIS)   206
Behavioral evidence   201
Chain of evidence (custody)   199
Circle of investigation   204
Clearance rate   195
Combined DNA Index System (CODIS)   206
Contaminants   196
Crime scenes   198
Criminal profiling   201
Criminalistics   200
Cultural cues   201
Discovery crimes   194

Integrated automated fingerprint identification system (IAFIS)   206
Integrated Ballistic Information System (IBIS)   206
Involvement crimes   194
Kansas City Response Time Study   194
Kinesics   201
Latent fingerprints   206
Locard exchange principle   199
Modus operandi (MO)   202
National Crime Information Center (NCIC)   205
National DNA Identification System (NDIS)   206
National Integrated Ballistic

Information Network (NIBIN)   205
Nonsocial offender   203
Nonverbal cues   201
Organized–disorganized typology   202
Physical evidence   201
Preliminary investigation   196
Primary crime scene   198
Psychopath   204
Reconstruction   197
Schizoid personality   204
Secondary crime scene   198
Signature   202
Solvability factors   197
Thief catcher   193
Violent Criminal Apprehension Program (VICAP)   205

REFERENCES

Bayley, D. 1994. *Police for the Future*. New York: Oxford University Press.

Buckwalter, A. 1984. *The Search For Evidence*. Stoneham, MA: Butterworth Publishers.

Bureau of Alcohol, Tobacco, and Firearms. 2007, January 17. *National Integrated Ballistic Information Network*. Washington, D.C.: Author.

Cassidy, J. 2000. Personal interview by Grant on June 6, 2000.

Douglas, J., and C. Munn. 1992. "Violent Crime Scene Analysis: Modus Operandi, Signature and Staging." *FBI Law Enforcement Bulletin 61*(2):1–10.

Douglas, J., R. Ressler, A. Burgess, and C. Harman. 1985. "Criminal Profiling from Crime Scene Analysis." *Behavioral Sciences and the Law 4*(3): 401–421.

Dyson, W. 2001. *Terrorism: An Investigator's Handbook*. Cincinnati, OH: Lexis Nexis.

Emsley, C. 1996. *The English Police: A Political and Social History*. Harrow: Addison Wesley Longman.

Federal Bureau of Investigation. 1999. *NCIC Operating Manual*. Washington, D.C.: Author.

Federal Bureau of Investigation. 2007a. *CODIS-Mission Statement and Background*. Available at www.fbi.gov/hq/lab/codis/index1.htm.

Federal Bureau of Investigation. 2007b. *Integrated Automated Fingerprint Identification System*. Available at www.fbi.gov/hq/cjisd/iafis.htm.

Gerberth, V. 1996. *Practical Homicide Investigation: Tactics, Procedures and Forensic Techniques*, 3d ed. Boca Raton, FL: CRC Press.

Grant, H. 1996. *Evaluation of the Bridgeport Youth Firearms Violence Initiative*. Washington, D.C.: Office of Community Oriented Policing Services.

Greenwood, P. 1970. *An Analysis of the Apprehension Activities of the New York City Police Department*. New York: Rand Institute.

Greenwood, P. W., and J. Petersilia. 1975. *The Criminal Investigative Process: Summary and Policy Implications*, Vol. 1. Santa Monica, CA: RAND Corp.

Hazelwood, R. 1987. *Practical Aspects of Rape Investigation: A Multidisciplinary Approach*, 3d ed. Boca Raton, FL: CRC Press.

Holmes, R., and S. Holmes. 1999. *Profiling Violent Crimes*. Thousand Oaks, CA: Sage.

Johnson, H., and N. T. Wolfe. 1996. *History of Criminal Justice*, 2d ed. Cincinnati, OH: Anderson Publishing Company.

Kansas City Police Department. 1983. *Response Time Analysis*. Washington, D.C.: The Police Foundation.

Kenney, D. H., H. Grant, and T. Allan. 2002. *Policing in a Diverse Society*. Washington, D.C.: Bureau of Justice Assistance.

Lee, H., T. Palmback, and M. Miller. 2001. *Henry Lee's Crime Scene Handbook*. San Diego, CA: Academic Press.

National Crime Information Center. 2001. *When Law and Culture Collide*. Washington, D.C.: Author. National Crime Prevention Council. 1999. *When Law and Culture Collide: Handling Conflicts Between U.S. Laws and Refugees' Cultures*. Washington, D.C.: NCPC.

Osterburg, J. W., and R. H. Ward. 1997. *Criminal Investigation: A Method for Reconstructing the Past*, 2d ed. Cincinnati, OH: Anderson Publishing Company.

Rossmo, K. 2000. *Geographic Profiling*. Boca Raton, FL: CRC Press.

Saferstein, C. 1995. *Criminalistics*. Englewood Cliffs, NJ: Simon and Schuster.

Salfati, G. 2000. "Profiling Homicide: A Multidimensional Approach." *Homicide Studies 4*(3):265–293.

Schroeder, D. 2007. False Hope? DNA Evidence and Homicide Clearance. New York: John Jay College dissertation (unpublished).

Skogan, W., and G. Attunes. 1979. "Information, Apprehension, and Deterrence: Exploring the Limits of Police Productivity." *Journal of Criminal Justice 7*(3):217–241.

Swanson, C., L. Territo, and R. Taylor. 2001. *Police Administration: Structures, Processes, and Behavior,* 5th ed. Upper Saddle River, NJ: Prentice Hall.

Turvey, B. 2001. *Criminal Profiling: An Introduction to Behavioral Evidence Analysis*. San Diego: Academic Press.

White, J. 2001. *Terrorism*, 3d ed. Belmont, CA: Wadsworth.

Wolfgang, M. (1958). Patterns in Criminal Homicide. Philadelphia: University of Pennsylvania.

Wrobleski, H. M., and K. Hess. 2002. *Introduction to Law Enforcement and Criminal Justice*. St. Paul, MN: West Publishing.

1. Drugfire was a pilot project that established a digital database of shell casings to match guns used in crimes across different jurisdictions. Departments wishing to participate in Drugfire had to first demonstrate a forensic examiner capacity for dealing with firearms (Grant 1996). Some senators (e.g., Chuck Schumer of New York) sought to have data from all new, legally purchased firearms entered into such a system so that matches would not have to rely on whether the gun was used in two separate incidents. The database would contain a "ballistic fingerprint" for each gun, to which they could match spent shell casings.

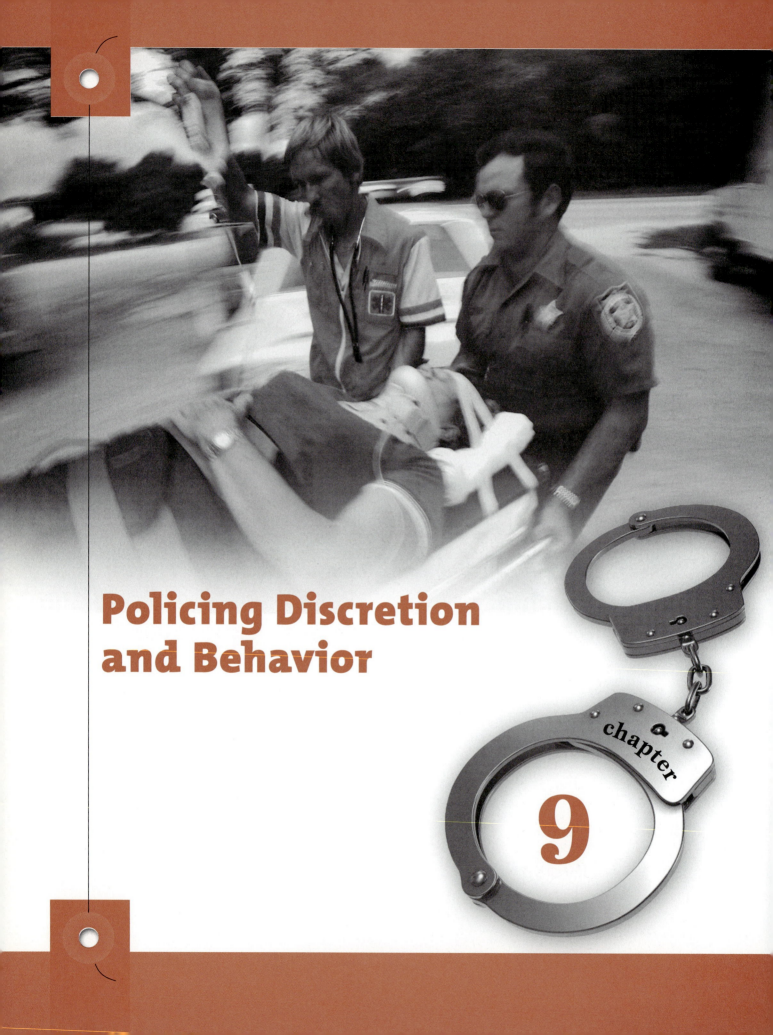

Policing Discretion and Behavior

chapter

9

Chapter Objectives

- Understand what is meant by the term *police discretion*.

- Identify and examine the factors that influence police decision making and the exercise of discretion.

- Examine different theories of police behavior and address the question of whether there is such a thing as a "police personality."

- Become familiar with Wilson's three styles of policing and explore the relationship between police organization and the behavior of individual officers.

- Examine the causes of police stress and police suicide.

Maria Teresa Macias lived in fear. After separating from her husband, she continued to be terrorized and abused by him as a result of repeated stalking and harassment, despite having successfully obtained a restraining order against him. On April 15, 1996, the abuse finally ended when her husband showed up at her home for the last time, ultimately shooting and killing her. What raises many questions is that in the year and a half leading up to her death, Maria Macias had contacted the Sonoma County Sheriff's Department on more than twenty-two occasions for help in dealing with her husband, including making them aware of his repeated threats to kill her. According to expert testimony, "the Sheriff's Department brushed Teresa off at every turn" (Women's Justice Center n.d.).[1]

Despite the husband's known violent history, and the escalating seriousness and fear on the part of Maria Macias, the Sheriff did not come to her aid. Expert testimony in the $15 million federal civil rights wrongful death lawsuit filed by the Macias family claimed that the failures of the Sheriff's office to respond, and in many incidents properly investigate the seriousness of occurrences, contributed to the escalation of violence as the suspect was sent the message that he could continue his actions, and that Macias' life was expendable. Sergeant Anne O'Dell testified that "long gone are the days when the criminal justice system has to speculate on how and why people are murdered" (Women's Justice Center n.d.). Domestic violence homicide is often preventable. O'Dell went on to cite that in many jurisdictions responding officers no longer have complete discretion to treat domestic incidents as "family affairs," formerly common practice in law enforcement. As a result, domestic violence homicides have decreased more than 50 to 60 percent (Women's Justice Center n.d.).

In the case of domestic violence, then, practices to reduce officer discretion might appear to make sense. However, in reality, discretion can never completely be eliminated in policing, given its complex realities, just as it will always play a central role within the courts and correctional agencies across this country as well. Even with domestic violence, the answer is not always as simple as **mandatory arrest policies**. Studies such as the **Minneapolis Domestic Violence Experiment** have pointed to a more cautious interpretation of such policy; mandatory arrests might decrease the escalating violence of those males who have a lot to lose by criminal justice attention, such as the employed or political figures in a community. For others, however, such a practice can lead to further anger and ultimately aggression (Worthington 1991).

The good news in the case of Maria Macias is ultimately its legacy. After an initial dismissal of the case by the Ninth District court judge on grounds that there was not a "direct causal link" between the murder and the response of the Sheriff's Department, the U.S. Ninth Circuit Court of Appeals ruled to reverse the dismissal, finding that women have the constitutional right to nondiscriminatory protection. Although not eliminating the complexities of officer discretion in domestic violence altogether, even with mandatory arrest policies the Macias case evidences that "proper care" in such cases on the part of law enforcement will be a standard to follow for jurisdictions nationally in the future.

The Role of Discretion in Policing

Along with the right to use force, one of the defining characteristics of policing as a profession is the amount of **discretion** given to individual officers, as introduced in Chapter 1. Although the organizational structure of most police departments follows a traditional bureaucratic model—power concentrated at the top of a hierarchal pyramid and clear lines of accountability running up from the base—police organizations differ from many other public institutions in that low-ranking individuals are given considerable decision-making power, much of which is unsupervised. Although it is senior police management that makes decisions about police strategy, departmental policy, and the allocation of police resources (called departmental or **command discretion**), the great majority of day-to-day policing decisions are in fact made by ordinary officers (**individual discretion**). These police officers decide whom to stop, whom to question, and whom to arrest, as well as how best to deal with public concerns and complaints.

In this sense, the formal organization of traditionally oriented police departments offers support for the Iron Law of Oligarchy proposed by Michels (1966). The **Iron Law of Oligarchy** suggests that the formal organization of bureaucracies inevitably leads to oligarchy, in which even organizations that originally proposed to be based upon democratically oriented philosophies eventually come to be dominated by a small, self-serving group of people who have achieved positions of power. Over time, this group will become more distant from the needs and realities of the rank and file. The depersonalizing effect of police bureaucracies has often been cited as a major contributing factor to the development and maintenance of a distinct police subculture.

Because so much power is concentrated in the hands of officers, no matter how rigid the formal bureaucracy of a department, how and why they exercise their discretion continues to be a source of great interest to policy makers, researchers, and the media. Studying police discretion is, however, problematic. Many important police decisions are made on the job and on the street, and as a consequence are not open to easy scrutiny. For example, although police departments record all of the arrests made by their officers, they rarely if ever keep track of police–public interactions that do not lead to arrest or some other type of formal response. Police officers do not inform their superiors every time they decide to let a speeding motorist off with a warning or choose to overlook some minor incident of public disorder or illegality. For this reason, criminologists and sociologists interested in police discretion have tended to concentrate their efforts on identifying those factors most likely to influence the exercise of police discretion, especially as it relates to the power of arrest and the use of force.

Defining Police Discretion

Although a number of writers have attempted to define *police discretion*, one of the most widely accepted definitions is that used by Kenneth Culp Davis in his book *Discretionary Justice* (1969). According to Davis:

> A police officer or police agency may be said to exercise discretion whenever effective limits on his, or her, or its power leave the officer or agency free to make choices among possible courses of action or inaction.[2] (p. 4)

Put another way, a police officer is said to have discretion when he or she has a choice over how to respond to a specific problem or situation.[3] In the majority of cases, officer discretion is expressly provided for by the law or police procedure. For example, although NYPD officers are given the power to arrest citizens for jaywalking by the city's Traffic Rules and Regulations, they are not required by the statute to make an arrest in every case.[4] As a consequence, an officer can exercise discretion when dealing with a pedestrian who has broken the law and choose whether to arrest that individual or issue a warning or some other verbal reprimand. In other cases, police discretion exists because the law does not expressly cover the situation facing the officer. As Bittner (1990, p. 249) notes in his famous article on the function of the police, officers frequently find themselves in the role of society's problem solvers of last resort, called in to deal with situations that "ought not to be happening and about which someone had better do something now!"[5]

According to early studies by LaFave (1965) and Davis (1969), police officers may choose not to arrest for a number of different reasons. In many cases, police officers will not arrest a suspected offender either because they believe that the legislature did not intend the law in question to be enforced in all cases or because they feel that the general community would not be in favor of the arrest. As both LaFave and Davis observe, laws that officers feel are out of date, ambiguous, or overly harsh are often not enforced, particularly if those laws deal with questions of community standards or "victimless crimes." Equally, because the police are aware of the need to maintain good relations with the public, where strict enforcement of an unpopular law may lead to serious conflict with the community, the police may choose to use less formal means of discouraging the unlawful behavior. In addition, police officers may choose not to enforce a certain law because it would mean drawing time and resources away from other more important tasks. The police cannot arrest everyone who breaks the law, and as a result they have to make choices about which laws they enforce and under what circumstances. Time spent arresting jaywalkers could, for example, be spent preventing or investigating more serious crimes such as assaults and burglaries.

Discretion is regarded as an essential aspect of policing because individual police officers are required to deal with a vast range of problems and situations, many of which are not precisely regulated by the law. Indeed, so important is the exercise of discretion to police work that it is hard to imagine what policing would be like without it. In a world in which individual police officers had no discretion, every type of possible police–public interaction would have to be governed by clear policies, guidelines, and rules, which the officer would then be required to follow precisely and without deviation. Police officers would walk the streets with a book of laws and rules that they would enforce without exception, irrespective of their own personal judgments or feelings. This is hardly a model of policing that many would regard as either realistic or desirable.

Although such extreme examples help to highlight the importance and necessity of discretion, "nondiscretionary" policing tactics are sometimes employed in real-world situations. **Zero-tolerance policing**, for example, often is used by the police as a means of combating certain forms of minor crime, such as urinating in public, aggressive begging, and fare dodging. When zero-tolerance policies are in effect, police officers are required to stop anyone they see committing such offenses, with little or no discretion as to whether to arrest. According to advocates of zero-tolerance policing, limiting or removing police discretion in this way is justified because strict enforcement of the law sends a powerful deterrent message to potential offenders and increases public confidence in the police (Bratton 1996; Greene 1999; Kelling and Coles 1996). Critics, however, argue that such policies rarely have a lasting effect on crime rates and can cause considerable harm to fragile police–public relations (Harcourt 1998).[6] Ironically perhaps, these critics argue that it is the existence of police discretion that protects the public from abuse and helps to ensure that the police respect the rights of citizens.

Factors Affecting the Exercise of Officer Discretion

Over the past fifty years, a large number of studies have examined police decision making to identify factors that influence the exercise of officer discretion (see, for example, Black 1971; Davis 1975; Klinger 1995; Reiss 1968; Worden 1995). Broadly speaking, these factors can be grouped as follows (also see Figure 9.1).

Type and Seriousness of Offense   According to research undertaken by Black in the late 1960s and early 1970s, one of the most important factors that police officers take into consideration when deciding whether to arrest a suspect is the seriousness of the alleged offense (Black 1971).[7] As might be expected, the police are far more likely to arrest an individual they believe to have committed a major crime, such as assault or robbery, than one who has committed a relatively minor offense, such as ignoring parking regulations or littering. In Black's study, for example, the police chose to arrest a suspect in 58 percent of all felony cases, as opposed to only 44 percent of all misdemeanors (Black 1971).[8] More recent statistics on arrest rates also appear to bear out this basic relationship. As

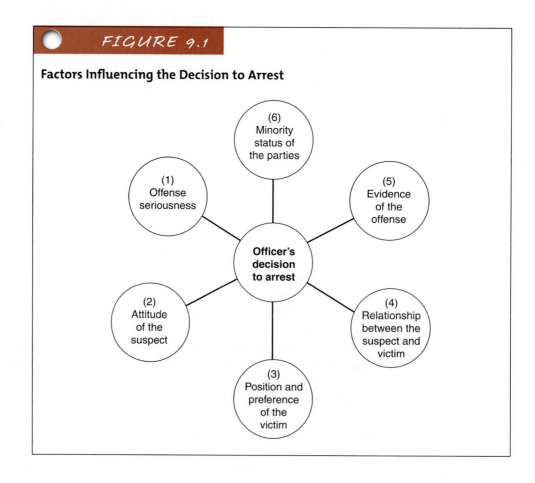

FIGURE 9.1

Factors Influencing the Decision to Arrest

(6) Minority status of the parties

(1) Offense seriousness

(5) Evidence of the offense

Officer's decision to arrest

(2) Attitude of the suspect

(4) Relationship between the suspect and victim

(3) Position and preference of the victim

Roberg et al. (2000) observe, approximately half of all violent crimes result in an arrest, as compared with less than a quarter of all property offenses. Other factors related to offense seriousness that may influence officer decision making include the use or presence of weapons and the type of property concerned (where the offense is property related).

There are, of course, obvious reasons for this. Given that one of the primary aims of the police is to maintain order and promote public safety, arrest is one way in which the police can incapacitate a suspect and ensure that he or she does not have an opportunity to re-offend. In addition, from the perspective of both the police and the public, arresting those suspected of committing serious crimes is far more important than apprehending those responsible for minor offenses and misdemeanors. Yet there are, however, other reasons why serious offenses are more likely to lead to an arrest. Many instances of violent crime, for example, involve an identifiable victim who can serve as both a complainant and a witness to the offense, increasing the likelihood that arrest will lead to prosecution and eventually conviction of the suspect. Furthermore, as Black and others have observed, the decision to arrest is frequently based on questions of probable cause, which is generally easier for an officer to establish in the case of a serious crime (Black 1980).

Certain types of offenses might have differential rates of arrest as well, particularly crimes such as domestic violence. Domestic violence represents approximately 20 percent of all violent crime committed against women (Eitle 2005). Thirty years ago police agencies had policies in place that discouraged arrest in cases of domestic violence (Klinger 1995). These policies have gradually been eliminated, but many advocates and scholars claim that police are still less likely to arrest men in cases of domestic violence and more likely than in cases involving women as suspects or other persons in others kinds of violent encounters. This claim has been called the *leniency thesis*.

Despite the advent of mandatory arrest polices, the results of studies are not clear as to the practice of police officers in domestic violence situations. Klinger (1995) found that although officers were unlikely to arrest in cases of domestic violence, the police were equally as unlikely to make arrests in other violent incidents. A 2005 study found that in states with mandatory arrest policies the chance of arrest was 50 percent, whereas in those without mandatory arrest policies the chance was 45 percent (Eitle 2005). Klinger et al. (1997) found support for the leniency thesis, finding arrests in only 13 percent of domestic violence cases. However, the study found a strikingly low overall arrest rate—28 percent—for violent encounters. The role of discretion is undeniable. Even in the face of widespread policy changes, decisions made by individual officers still determine who is arrested and who is not.

Attitude of the Suspect How a suspect reacts to being stopped and questioned by the police can also have a significant effect on an officer's decision to arrest, particularly if the suspect appears aggressive or disrespectful. As Black (1971) notes, "disrespect in a police encounter is much the same as 'contempt' in a courtroom hearing" (p. 1092) in that it represents a challenge to the position and authority of the police officer. Just like a judge in the courtroom, the police need to maintain the public's respect in order to do their job, and as a result they can be expected to vigorously defend that authority when threatened. Some authors have referred to this attitude as **contempt of cop (COC)**.

Studies of police discretion also have found that the demeanor of the suspect is an important factor in the police decision to use force. Research by Reiss (1968) in the late 1960s found, for example, that police officers were far more likely to use physical force against suspects who they felt had not shown the proper amount of respect to them either as individuals or to the police in general. Similarly, a later study by Worden (1995) suggested that disrespect was a key factor in the decision to use force, as was the perception that the suspect was being uncooperative or attempting to resist arrest. The conclusions drawn by both Reiss and Worden, have, however, been the subject of some debate. According to Klinger (1994), for example, in many cases disrespect and friction between the police and the suspect emerges after the arrest has taken place, and as a result such behavior cannot be said to have influenced the initial decision to arrest. However, later studies have found the opposite: that disrespect is not a key predictor of behavior with respect to force (Terrill and Mastrofsky 2002).

Characteristics, Position, and Preference of the Victim

Although offense seriousness and suspect demeanor appear to play an important part in the decision to arrest, research also has shown that the characteristics of the victim may be significant. In his study of police attitudes toward rape victims, LaFree (1989) found evidence to suggest that officers may be less likely to arrest a suspected offender when they disapprove of the victim or her lifestyle in some way. Furthermore, when the victim of a crime does not want the suspect to be arrested, the police are likely to take this into account, particularly if the victim is the sole witness to the crime. Of course, many studies have demonstrated that the presence of a witness (or willingness to report of a witness) is a key factor

Given the many complexities inherent to police work, officer decision making on the street can be influenced by numerous factors that are often difficult to control through departmental hierarchy, policy, or training strategies. Ultimately, discretion will remain a core force in police work.

influencing discretionary decisions to pursue an allegation or incident (Black 1971; Greenwood and Petersilia 1975). Officers are far more likely to arrest/cite the offender if witnesses are present.

Relationship Between the Suspect and the Victim   Another factor that can have an effect on a police officer's decision to arrest is the relationship between the suspect and the victim. In situations in which the parties are close—for example, when the suspect and victim are husband and wife—the officer may feel that there is little chance that the victim will be willing to testify against the suspect in court, and as such an arrest is unlikely to lead to a conviction (Enstermaker et al. 1980–1981).[9] In such cases, the officer may choose to regard the incident as a "private matter" and simply decide to issue the suspect a warning (Black 1971). An officer may choose not to arrest when the relationship between the suspect and complainant is close for a number of reasons, including:

- The officer believes the complainant does not actually want the suspect arrested, but merely wants to "teach them a lesson" by calling in the police.

- In suspected cases of domestic violence, the officer believes there is a strong possibility that suspect may re-offend as a way of punishing the victim for making the complaint.

- The officer believes the arrest would deprive a family of its major income earner ("breadwinner").

Evidence of the Offense   According to work by Black and others, police officers are more likely to arrest a suspect when there is clear evidence of wrongdoing. In cases in which there is little or no physical evidence, or where the only evidence available to the police is the testimony of the complainant or victim, the officer must decide whether there is enough evidence for there to be a reasonable chance of conviction if the case goes to court (Black 1971).

Minority Status of the Parties to the Offense   Of all the factors that can influence an officer's decision to arrest, questions of race and gender are by far the most controversial. Based on studies of racial profiling and the impact of race on police decision making, many criminologists and police researchers now believe that a suspect's race is an important factor in the decision to arrest. Although Black (1971) did not find any clear evidence of racial discrimination in his study of police discretion, subsequent work by Maurer (1993) and Chambliss (1997) indicate that African American suspects are not only more likely to be stopped and arrested than whites, but that they are also more likely to be subjected to police use of force.

In their efforts to explain these findings, some criminologists (Worden 1995) have suggested that this difference in treatment may not simply be a product of police racism, but rather a consequence of poor police–minority relations or miscommunication between white officers and African American suspects. It is also worth noting that although there may be a broad consensus regarding the existence of racial profiling and gender bias, considerable disagreement exists over the relative importance that police officers attach to race when making the decision to arrest. Is, for example, a suspect's race more important than their attitude or the seriousness of the alleged offense? Are officers more likely to take a victim's complaints if they are members of an ethnic or racial majority? To what extent does race outweigh or "trump" other considerations?

In contrast to the issue of race, very few studies have examined the impact of a suspect or victim's gender on the decision to arrest. One widely held belief is that male police officers are generally more lenient when it comes to dealing with women and have a tendency to act out of a sense of "chivalry" when dealing with female victims or complainants. Research by Visher (1983), however, suggests that the level of chivalry extended depends largely on whether the woman's appearance, demeanor, and behavior conforms to the male officer's traditional gender stereotypes and conception of how a woman "ought to behave." In those cases in which the woman does not conform to the ideal image, she may in fact be treated more severely than a man on the basis that she is "doubly deviant"—that is, she has offended both the law and the officer's idea of what constitutes normal female behavior. Although many police departments in the United States continue to be dominated by men, the evidence suggests that women are no more (or less) likely to be stopped or arrested by the police than men (Martin 1980).[10] Perhaps the one exception to this general finding, however, is in relation to traffic violations. According to a study undertaken by Kappeler et al. (1994), attractive young women are more likely stopped for traffic offenses by male police officers than men, in many cases simply because the male officer is looking to initiate personal contact with the female driver in question.[11]

Finally, research suggests that individual factors also affect the exercise of police discretion. According to a number of studies, female officers tend to be less aggressive when dealing with suspects than their male counterparts, particularly when it comes to the use of force (Grennan 1988; Martin 1990). Some of this difference has been attributed to the greater tendency of female officers to use more developed mediation skills in tense situations, as compared to their male counterparts. In contrast, evidence indicates that African American officers are stricter when dealing with the African American community than they are with other racial and ethnic groups and are more likely to arrest African American suspects than whites or Hispanics (Brooks 1989).

The devalued status of other minority groups has also historically been said to influence police decision making, as will be discussed further in Chapter 10. Depending on the degree of tolerance of the responding officer, he or she may have difficulties dealing with members of the Gay Lesbian Bisexual or Transgendered Community (GLBT). One particularly disturbing example of such differential treatment is how two officers responded to a bleeding, disoriented Laotian boy on the streets of Milwaukee after receiving a call from a disturbed neighborhood resident. After learning that the fifteen-year-old boy was gay, the officers dismissed the incident as a "lover's quarrel" and returned him to the apartment of Jeffery Dahmer, now widely known as a depraved serial killer. The taped communications of the two responding officers revealed horrible references to needing to "delouse" following contact with the "gay couple."

The Importance of Police Behavior

Since the early 1960s, researchers in the United States have become increasingly interested in police behavior and the possibility that there may be a distinct **police personality**. According to a number of prominent sociologists and criminologists, including Goldstein (1968), Neiderhoffer (1969), and Skolnick (1966), it is possible to identify certain core beliefs, values, and behavioral traits that are common to many police officers and that help to explain how individual officers exercise their discretion and how they deal with members of the public as well as how police organizations function. Many studies argue for the existence of a police subculture with distinct traits, such as cynicism, authoritarianism, and suspiciousness of the general public, and that these traits often affect the way in which the police deal with particular groups, such as women and racial minorities (Leftkowitz 1973; 1975).

In their efforts to explain how the police personality and subculture develops and why certain beliefs are more prevalent than others, researchers have tended to favor one of four main theories or explanations. Broadly speaking, they can be summarized as follows:

- **Psychological theories.** These theories argue that core attitudes are formed *before* the individual enters the police force and are a function of such things as family background, social status, and prior education.

- **Educational theories.** These theories state that core attitudes are acquired during police training and early years on the street and are passed on to recruits by older, more experienced police officers.

- **Sociological theories.** These theories state that police attitudes are shaped by the daily demands of police work and reflect the "working culture" of policing.

- **Organizational theories.** These argue that police attitudes and values are shaped by the organizational and working culture of policing and the demands placed upon officers by their police colleagues.

Before moving into a discussion of these theories, however, it is important to note that idea of the police personality, or subculture, remains extremely controversial. Many of the key studies in this area were conducted during the 1960s and 1970s, and as a result their relevance to policing today must be questioned. Although most criminologists and sociologists appear to accept that the police are indeed more conservative than the average citizen, many remain unconvinced that the police are necessarily more authoritarian or more prone to racism and sexism (Worden 1995).

Psychological Explanations: Predisposition and Police Behavior—Police Personality or Culture?

As noted by Bonifacio (1991), most predisposition theories focus on the reasons why people join the police and whether particular personality patterns common to police applicants distinguish them from members of the general public. In an effort to identify these patterns, a number of researchers have looked at the reasons why people join the police in an effort to determine whether a link exists between the motivation to join and certain key personality traits. For example, various studies have suggested that most people who apply to become police officers do so either because they want to help society or because they want a job that offers them challenge and excitement (Lester 1983). According to work by Arcuri (1976), Lester (1983), Reiser (1973), and Stratton et al. (1984), such individuals tend to see themselves as "brave" and "powerful" and are more conservative and **authoritarian** in their thinking than the average person. In addition, it has also been argued that because many police recruits are drawn from traditional working-class backgrounds, they are naturally more inclined towards conservative attitudes. Work by Bayley and Mendelson (1969), however, has found that working-class recruits were no more or less authoritarian than those drawn from other social backgrounds.

The emerging consensus in the research literature indicates that career socialization is a stronger influence than preexisting differences in temperament (Wiederhoffer 1969; Worden 1995). However, famed police personality researcher Lefkowitz (1975) found that although police do not differ from other groups in terms of psychological disorders or intelligence, a constellation of traits/attitudes does significantly merge with officers, such as authoritarianism, suspiciousness, conservatism, loyalty, secretiveness, physical courage, and self-assertiveness. These traits are likely more influenced by the strong influence of a **police subculture** than a predisposed personality type. For example, one of the key elements stressed in the police subculture literature is the sense of mission felt by police that corresponds with each of the cluster traits noted by Lefkowitz. This sense of mission is characterized by the perception that the police are a **thin blue line** between anarchy and order in a society (Reiner 1992). The peer solidarity and loyalty so often noted in the literature also are seen as outcomes of this sense of mission and the type of work that police do (Waddington 1999).

Chan (1997) argues that the majority of the academic literature related to police culture is too simplistic. Instead, she argues that police culture is the result of history and learned dispositions (socialization), which both mold the police officer's sense of what constitutes suspicious activities, and thus police work itself. These sociological processes have been categorized within educational, sociological, and organizational domains, depending upon the background of the researcher.

Educational Explanations: Police Recruits and the Effects of Police Training

According to traditional educational theories of police personality, the character traits typically observed in serving police officers are the direct result of the process of police training and early experiences "on the job." Perhaps the most well-known and influential advocate of this explanation of police attitudes is Arthur Niederhoffer. In a study that attempted to measure levels of job satisfaction and cynicism amongst recruits and serving police officers, Niederhoffer (1963) found that after less than three months, levels of cynicism amongst serving recruits rose dramatically. For example, in Niederhoffer's study, nearly half of all first-day recruits polled believed that the average police superior was "very interested in the welfare of his subordinates." Two months later, the number of recruits who still believed this to be true had fallen to just 13 percent. Similarly, nearly 80 percent of first day recruits believed that their department was an "efficient, smoothly operating organization." Two months later, less than a third of experienced recruits held that same opinion. Lastly, nearly three-quarters of all new recruits questioned believed that police training does "a very fine job of preparing the recruit for life in the precinct." Two months later, less than a quarter of the experienced recruits believed that was the case.[12] It is important to note that such cynicism may be a result of psychological shielding against the realities faced by officers on a regular basis.

Based on these results, Niederhoffer concluded that the quasi-military style of police training caused police recruits to become cynical about themselves, others, and the department they were joining. A parallel study undertaken later by Van Maanen (1997) returned similar results. For his study, Van Maanen sought to determine how much a recruit's feelings about the department changed during the course of the police training process. To test this, Van Maanen developed a questionnaire to measure the motivational level and organizational commitment of recruits. Note that Van Maanen also did participant observation, thus lending greater weight to his final results. According to of Van Maanen's finding, as recruits' careers progressed, their attitudes and beliefs changed significantly. Recruit motivation declined significantly, as did organizational commitment.

In summary, these studies suggest that the person who completes police training is clearly different from the person who begins it. At the outset of the training experience, the recruit identity is embraced. A few months later, however, the typical recruit is disenchanted with the recruit role and the department. In light of the changes that have taken place in police training practices since the 1960s and 1970s, however, these findings need to be treated with caution.

Sociological Explanations: Skolnick's "Working Personality"

In contrast to the approach taken by Neiderhoffer and others, some sociologists, most notably Jerome Skolnick, have sought to explain various aspects of police behavior in terms of the relationship between individual officers and the police organization. One of the most influential writers on the subject of police personality, Jerome Skolnick, published his first book, *Justice on Trial* (1966), at the height of the American civil rights movement, at a time when the public was becoming increasingly concerned about the issue of racial bias in law enforcement and the problem of police brutality. Having examined the subculture of policing and police deception in his book, Skolnick came to the conclusion that there were "distinctive cognitive tendencies in police as an organizational grouping" and that it was possible to identify a number of elements that combine to form a police officer's "working personality," most notably danger and authority.

According to Skolnick (1966), because police officers are constantly faced with dangerous, sometimes life-threatening situations, many officers tend to become suspicious when dealing with members of the public. In addition to danger, the public nature of police work and the resulting constant observation by the citizenry have an isolating effect. Officers are taught to regard civilians as potential offenders or even as threats to their personal safety, and they have difficulty trusting anyone other than their own police colleagues or forming friendships with people outside the department. As a consequence, police officers show an exceptionally high degree of work-related solidarity and tend to socialize together.

Skolnick proposes that police officers have a "perceptual shorthand" with which they come to perceive certain attitudes, movements, and styles of dress as cues of potential trouble. Individuals are stereotyped by the police as sources of danger, grouped into a mental category as "symbolic assailants." Just as their sense of isolation is worsened by their exclusive association with other officers, their detachment from those they police is increased by their classifications of these individuals. Even though officers may speak the slang of those they police efficiently, it is only a function of their ability to remember the properties of these "symbolic assailants."

Additionally, the qualities that enable officers to deal with danger efficiently do not lend themselves to stringent moral behavior. Whereas the public expects men or women of flawless character, police officers seem normally predisposed to even more of the imperfections and vices common within the population. This provides another reason for officers to associate closely with fellow officers; to avoid public scrutiny of indiscretions that persons would otherwise deem harmless or common (e.g., drunkenness, colorful language, etc.). This unusual solidarity leads to a sense of dependence and a system of watchfulness or protection of other officers. Along with danger and authority, isolation and solidarity lead many officers to conclude that the only way for the police to protect themselves from the outside world is to be loyal to one's fellow officers, even if this means lying or covering up acts of police misconduct.

Drawing on this account of the police **working personality**, Skolnick argues that police behavior and many undesirable police practices can be explained by reference to the emphasis on solidarity within police culture. From the police perspective, lying to protect another officer is seen as acceptable, even if this means deliberately deceiving one's superiors or police investigators. As Skolnick (2000) notes, new police officers quickly learn to back up their fellow officers when dealing with the authorities, and expect to be backed up in return. Equally, officers who do not support their fellow officers are regarded as "rats" who are not to be trusted and deserve to be excluded from the group.

Although Skolnick's work has had an enormous influence on thinking about the police and police working culture over the past thirty years, he has not been without his critics. In 1967, for example, the criminologist David Bordua (1967) argued in a review of *Justice on Trial* that Skolnick's account of police behavior was somewhat misleading and overly negative. Although agreeing with many of Skolnick's conclusions, Bordua believes that Skolnick's concern with the police work ethic leads him to understate the positive effect professionalism has had on police efficiency and formal legality. On a similar note, the John Birch Society has continued to argue since the 1960s that it is important to recognize that the same subculture that Skolnick sees as the source of police deception and brutality also provides individual officers with the support they need to do their job effectively and with confidence (Grant 1995).

Organizational Explanations: Wilson's Three Styles of Policing

In addition to these various sociological and psychological theories of individual officer behavior, attempts have also been made to explain police attitudes in terms of the history of the policing function and changes in the organization of policing in the United States. By the beginning of the 1960s, most theories of police management focused primarily on the importance of bureaucracy, hierarchy, and authoritarianism.[13] According to this view, the police were almost exclusively concerned with the task of law enforcement and crime control, a fact reflected in the militaristic organization of police departments and the strict emphasis placed on formal chains of command. In the 1970s, however, this view of policing began to give way to new theories of police organization. These theories, sometimes referred to as *behavioral management theories*, emphasized the importance of looking at what police officers actually do and acknowledging just how complex the modern police department had become. Research during the 1960s had revealed, for example, that the less than 20 percent of police time was devoted to law enforcement, with police officers being more likely to spend their days engaged in community service activities than arresting criminals or preventing crimes (Bercall 1970; Cummings et al. 1965; Goldstein 1968). Furthermore, researchers had observed that while many police departments were organized along similar lines, they often adopted very different approaches to basic policing problems and their relationship with the public. These findings prompted a number of police researchers—most notably, the American criminologist James Q. Wilson (1978)—to reexamine existing ideas about the police function, to develop new theories about how police organizations worked, and to look for new explanations of individual officer behavior.

According to Wilson (1978), all police departments were faced with two fundamental but different types of problems: problems of law enforcement and problems of order maintenance. Law enforcement problems typically involved illegal conduct that could lead to an arrest, whereas order maintenance problems involved less serious behavior that in many cases could be dealt with informally by the police. Based on a study of eight police departments, Wilson concluded that police organizations could be divided into one of three basic categories depending on how they approached these problems: the watchman style, the legalistic style, and the service style (see Table 9.1). The key features of each of these policing styles are as follows.

The Watchman Style Based primarily on the use of the uniformed police patrol, this approach places great emphasis on order maintenance and individual officer discretion. Because most policing activity takes place on the street, officers are less concerned with law enforcement than keeping the peace in their patrol areas, with the result that minor infractions of the law are generally overlooked. According to Lundman (1980), for example, one of the defining characteristics of the **watchman style** of policing is the tendency of officers to "avoid trouble" and to rely on informal, nonlegalistic means of resolving conflicts. Police departments adopting this style rarely engage in research or systematic planning and tend to suffer from problems of discriminatory arrests and

TABLE 9.1

Key Features of Wilson's Typology of Policing

Watchman Style	Legalistic Style	Service Style
Policing as order maintenance	Policing as law enforcement	Policing as public service
Few policies and procedures	Emphasis on legal rules	Emphasis on community relations
Individual approach to problems	Formal resolution of problems	Informal resolution of problems
Emphasis on "curbside" justice	Commitment to professionalism	Commitment to public service

Source: J.Q. Wilson. 1978. *Varieties of Police Behavior.* Cambridge, MA: Harvard University Press, p. 33.

The style of policing exhibited by a department can be seen as a reflection of the history of the police function in society, moving from watchman to legalistic to service style models. What will be the most dominant model post–September 11?

corruption, because there are few effective restraints on the activities of individual officers. In Fyfe et al.'s (1997) study of domestic violence, the police department observed displayed a remarkably low rate of arrest in violent encounters. The authors speculate that the selection of departments by academics and the demeanor of those departments (given their cooperation) are probably not representative of most municipal police agencies. They surmise that the "declining blue-collar city" (whose data was acquired by court order) was more representative of Wilson's watchman style of policing, and they suggest that this style is more representative of most police agency's operations.

The Legalistic Style   This style of policing emphasizes the importance of law enforcement and maintaining clear and impartial legal standards for both the police and public alike. Police departments organized along legalistic lines tend to be bureaucratic, use performance indicators as a means of promoting professional standards, and place considerable importance on research and planning. In addition, individual officers are less inclined to exercise curbside discretion, preferring instead to refer to the law and make arrests. Corruption—at least at the operational level—is far less pervasive and discrimination less institutionalized than under the watchman model. Looked at historically, the **legalistic style** of policing tends to replace the watchman approach as the police become more professional, technologically advanced, and more proactive.

The Service Style   According to Wilson's typology, the **service style** of policing sees the police primarily as servants of the community. Although law enforcement and order maintenance remain priorities, emphasis is placed on maintaining good police–public relations and on the use of informal policing methods aimed at keeping offenders out of the criminal justice system. As a consequence, service-style departments tend to favor strategies that are proactive and heavily oriented toward crime prevention, with individual officers preferring to avoid reference to the law when dealing with the public. As Lundman (1980) has observed, service-style police departments are most likely found in affluent, middle-class communities style.[14]

By dividing police organizations according to these typologies, Wilson was able to explain the differences he observed in terms of both police functions and individual officer behavior. In addition, one of the great strengths of Wilson's approach was that he did not abandon previous theories of police organization, but instead argued that the "legalistic model" favored by many departments in the 1960s and early 1970s was better understood as a stage in the overall development of policing. Although elements of all three styles can be found in most police departments, according to Wilson as society becomes more complex and begins to demand more of its police, police organizations tend to go through stages of evolution, moving more closely toward the service-style model.

Reconciling the Theories

Attempting to account for and explain why police officers appear to share certain values and personality traits, criminologists, sociologists, and psychologists have approached the subject of police personality from a variety of angles. Clearly, the reality is that all of the factors and influences identified in this section play a part in shaping how police officers think, behave, and exercise their discretion. One thing that is apparent from this section is that there is a pressing need for more work to be done in this area and for many of the seminal studies, such as those by Niederhoffer and Skolnick, to be updated to account for the very real changes that have taken place in policing over the past thirty years.

Police Stress

In addition to being interested in how police officers behave, police researchers have also devoted considerable time examining how individual officers are affected by the demands of police work and how police officers deal with stress. It is generally accepted by the public that policing is one of the most stressful occupations in contemporary society. Many police officers deal with potentially dangerous situations on a daily basis and are required to handle a wide range of different and challenging tasks as a matter of routine. Furthermore, because they occupy a unique position in relation to the public they exist to serve and protect, the police are required to maintain high standards and are frequently subjected to intense scrutiny and criticism from the media and the public at large.

Although police work is clearly stressful, research suggests that policing may not be the most stressful profession. According to a study conducted by Pendleton (1983) in the 1980s, police work can be extremely stressful, but members of many other occupations, including emergency medical personnel and correctional service officers, face stress levels at least equal to and in many cases in excess of those confronting police officers (Patterson 1992). Regardless of whether policing is any more or less stressful than other forms of work, however, stress and its consequences for the health and well-being of individual officers is a serious problem for many police departments across the country.

Sources of Police Stress

Police officers experience stress for a variety of reasons.[15] There are two categories of occupational stress: **eustress** (stress that is normal and good, even providing on-the-job motivation) and **disstress** (stress that is outside of the normal range and very harmful over time). Often referred to as *stressors*, the causes of police stress can be broadly categorized according to the source of the stress, that is, whether the cause is produced by the police organization itself or by the on-the-job pressures of actual police work.

Internal and External Organizational Stressors   These include stress factors that stem either from the relationship between the individual police officer and his or her department (**internal stressors**) or from outside pressures place on the police as a group by the criminal justice system or the community at large (**external stressors**):

External Stressors

- Lack of interagency cooperation or community support
- Ineffective criminal justice system
- Overly lenient courts
- Political interference in police policy and decision making
- Overly critical media coverage of police actions
- Poor police–minority relations

Internal Stressors

- Overly tough supervision
- Absence of promotional opportunities
- Troublesome or offensive internal policies and procedures
- Excessive paperwork
- Poor or substandard equipment

Work-Related Stressors   These include stress factors that result from the day-to-day work done by police officers. Although these stressors often affect officers who are not engaged in routine patrol or investigative work, they are most likely to have a negative impact on officers on the street or otherwise engaged in more "traditional" policing tasks such as public order maintenance and crime prevention. These stressors include, but are not limited to:

- Work fatigue
- Rotating shift patterns
- Having to maintain conflicting roles in the community (i.e., as both law enforcer and public servant)
- Persistent fear and danger associated with police work
- Dealing with victims and the families of victims
- Lack of control over the progress of cases within the department
- Internal review boards and ongoing performance assessments

In terms of the relative importance of individual stress factors, research by Violanti and Aron (1995) found that the single most stressful event a police officer is ever likely to face in the course of his or her career is killing someone in the line of duty. Closely behind this was the death of a fellow police officer, and then being subjected to injury or physical attack. Although the majority of officers are rarely, if ever, forced to deal with such events, the fact that they are all incidents that occur on the job reinforces the point that policing is an inherently dangerous and stressful profession.

How police officers respond to these different forms of stress will vary according the personality of the individual concerned; the level of support they receive from friends, family, and their department; and other factors, such as their level of experience on the job, years of service, ability to develop effective coping strategies, and the nature of the stressful event itself. According to an early study by Niederhoffer (1969), most police officers respond to stress by withdrawing into themselves and becoming more cynical.

Police Suicide

In recent years, police suicide has become a major concern for many departments throughout the United States. Although it is difficult to get an accurate picture of the problem, most studies suggest that suicide rates among serving police officers are considerably higher than those of the general population. In one of the first studies of the problem, Guralnick (1963) compared suicide rates for police officers with those of 130 other occupations and found that police officers were almost twice (1.8 times) as likely to take their own lives as members of the general public. These results were later confirmed by a similar study conducted by Richard and Fell in 1975, which concluded that policing had the third-highest suicide rate of any profession.[16] Although more recent studies by Heiman (1979), Terry (1981), Allen (1986), Ivanoff (1994), Violanti (1996), and Hoenig and White (2000) have returned marginally different results, in each case police officers were found to be more likely to commit suicide than almost any other group. Perhaps even more disturbing, Violanti (1996) found that more police officers—over 8.3 times more—die at their own hands than at the hands of criminals or in the line of duty.

As disturbing as such figures are, there is reason to believe that the problem of police suicide is far more pervasive than these studies suggest. According to Violanti (1996), many officer suicides are intentionally misclassified by police departments as "accidental," either to protect the reputation of the individual officer or the department as a whole. For example, police investigators may deliberately misclassify an apparent gun-related suicide as a result of careless weapon handling or instead conclude that the gun had misfired while the officer was cleaning his or her weapon. Such misclassification allows the deceased officer to be treated as having died in the line of duty, entitling him or her to burial with police honors and the officer's surviving family to full insurance and benefits (Bonifacio 1991). Alternatively, a suspected suicide may be misclassified in an effort to protect the officer's department from criticism, particularly regarding the provision of mental health services and officer support. Although the courts have ruled that police

Linkages *in Law Enforcement*

Post-traumatic Stress Disorder Following Response to Stress— Law Enforcement and Other Emergency Workers

Although police work often involves its share of mundane activities, such as report writing or having to respond to minor disputes, there can be no question that the job always holds the threat of difficult and dangerous situations. In addition to the often insular nature of the profession (Blau 1994), many officers often feel alone when they have to work in a "thankless" environment, that is, a community that does not support their efforts. Moreover, police often have to see the very worst in people or communities, more often responding to the violent or disturbed elements of a community than having a chance to meaningfully interact with those that are truly supportive.

In the course of their duties, patrol officers may have to confront highly disturbing or stressful situations, such as responding to a particularly gruesome accident, taking testimony from a sexually abused child, or having had their own personal encounter with serious injury. In situations where officers have had to use lethal force, the months afterwards can be filled with sorrow and second-guessing one's own actions. The response of police officers, firefighters, and other emergency workers in the horrific events of domestic and international terrorism evidenced in the Oklahoma City Bombing and the attacks of September 11 demonstrate both the courage of so many in these professions, as well as the gravity of situations they can be called upon to face in the course of their duties.

Post-traumatic Stress Disorder (PTSD)

In some cases, traumatic incidents can lead to the development of **post-traumatic stress disorder (PTSD)** in law enforcement or other emergency personnel. The diagnostic criteria for PTSD are as follows:

- The person experiences a traumatic event that involved the actual or threatened death or injury to self or others;

- The traumatic event is persistently re-experienced through recurrent and intrusive recollections or dreams, acting or feeling as though the event were reoccurring; and

- Intense psychological distress and physiological reactivity upon exposure to internal or external cues resembling an aspect of the traumatic event.

In some cases, there may not be one single traumatic event, but rather a cumulative weight of numerous stressors. Officers develop numerous coping mechanisms for dealing with these stressors, including the isolation of feelings, use of seemingly callous humor, and shutting off of the outside world characteristic of the insular police subculture (Blau 1994). In many cases, however, these coping and defense mechanisms are not enough, requiring more formal intervention services. Some of these interventions might consist of a day-long workshop; other officers may require more intensive services.

Strategies for Dealing with PTSD and the Patrol Officer

Because of the negative stereotype within law enforcement that accompanies accessing mental health services, interventions are usually referred to as **critical incident stress debriefing (CISD)** (Belles and Norvell 1990). CISD is a "structured intervention designed to promote the emotional processing of traumatic events" through the discussion and normalization of reactions, as well as preparing officers to be able to cope with other possible traumatic events in the future (Miller 1999). CISD has seven phases (Miller 1999):

1. Introduction: A debriefing in a group setting about the CISD approach.

2. Fact phase: Group discussion as to the facts surrounding exactly what happened during the traumatic event.

3. Thought phase: Group members begin to discuss what was going through their minds during the event.

4. Reaction phase: Group members begin to comprehend the emotional consequences of the event, highlighting what the worst part of the event was for them.

5. Symptom phase: Group members work past the incident to begin to deal with their experiences since the event occurred.

6. Education phase: Information is provided to the group as to the stress response and the related psychological and physiological symptoms.

7. Reentry phase: Coping strategies are provided to prepare members for the eventuality of future traumatic events.

In order to prevent the possibility of group participants being subpoenaed as witnesses, it is rec-

ommended that the CISD process not begin until after the initial investigation and collection of formal statements in the case of officer-involved shooting investigations.

QUESTIONS

1. In your opinion, what are the most stressful aspects of police work? Have these stressful conditions changes since September 11? Why or why not?

2. What intervention might a police manager introduce to help police officers deal with stress?

3. What characteristics/background in new recruits might indicate a better ability to cope with stress?

Officers in a Group Therapy Setting

departments are responsible for ensuring that all police personnel are psychologically fit, many departments do not have the resources to effectively monitor the mental health of their officers (Meredith 1984). As a result, there is a strong incentive for departments to "cover up" the problem of police suicide, both to protect themselves from possible legal actions and external investigations that may harm the department's reputation. In either case, there is reason to believe that many police suicides go unreported. According to an FBI study of Chicago Police Department (Cronin 1982), it was possible that as many as 67 percent of all police suicides in Chicago had been misclassified, a finding that suggests reported police suicide rates may seriously underestimate the extent of the problem.

Over the past forty years, researchers have advanced a number of theories of police suicide in attempts to explain why police officers kill themselves in such numbers. One of the earliest explanations can be found in the work of Friedman (1967), who looked at incidences of police suicide in the NYPD between 1934 and 1940. Having examined 93 individual cases, Friedman concluded that while approximately two-thirds of the officers who committed suicide could be said to have had "passive" personalities, the remaining one-third could be classified as "overtly aggressive, impulsive, and reckless" in nature. This led Friedman (1967) to conclude that police suicide is primarily the result of emotional displacement, with officers turning their aggressive impulses onto themselves in an effort to deal with feelings of frustration or inadequacy:

> The policeman is permitted to kill and receives praise from his superiors, peers, and even the public for carrying out these acts. The aggressive and controlling drives, which are no doubt the primary motivations for his choice of occupation, are often in collision with the command to refrain and repress, therefore causing tremendous conflict within him. (p. 430)

This explanation—sometimes referred to as the *displaced aggression theory*— was later challenged by Farber (1968), Heiman (1977), and Danto (1978), all of whom argued that it was too simplistic and failed to adequately explain why officers in the "passive" category also took their own lives. More recently, theories of police suicide have sought to explain the problem in terms of stress, substance abuse, and the personal lives of officers. Based on their examination of police suicides in Buffalo between 1950 and 1990, for example, Violanti and Vena (1995) concluded that many officers commit suicide because of work-related stress and problems with their social and marital relationships. Violanti and Vena also found, like Cronin (1982) and Wagner and Brzeczek (1983) before them, that the majority of officers who committed suicide had a history of alcohol abuse.[17] In contrast, while Ivanoff's 1994 study of police suicide in New York also found that many of the deceased officers had abused alcohol, there was little evidence to suggest that job-related stress was a major cause of police suicide. Instead, Ivanoff concluded that personal problems, such as depression and marital difficulties, were far more likely to result in feelings of depression among officers than the challenges they faced on the job.

Chapter Summary

- One of the key features that distinguish the police and other criminal justice agencies from other public institutions and organizations is the extent to which serving police officers possess and exercise discretion. Although efforts can be made to reduce officer discretion, such as zero-tolerance or mandatory arrest policies, the complexities of police work will ensure that discretion will always remain a central ingredient in policing.

- Police decision making can be influenced by many factors related to the officer's own disposition or the nature of the act itself. Factors commonly cited in the literature as influencing police discretion include offense seriousness, attitude of the suspect, characteristics of the victim, relationship between the suspect and victim, evidence of the offense, and the minority status of the parties to the offense.

- Whether officers exhibit similar personality traits and the extent to which these are caused by predisposing factors or a socialization into the police culture is the subject of many diverse explanations: psychological, educational, sociological, and organizational. The influence of historical factors on officer perceptions of suspiciousness must also be considered in discussing the origins of police culture. Police are in many ways a reflection of the larger societal force in which they are embedded.

- The nature of police work can bring with it many serious stressors requiring complex coping mechanisms that themselves can contribute to the maintenance of police culture. However, following particularly serious traumatic incidents, officers can develop post-traumatic stress disorders, requiring serious intervention strategies to minimize.

Linking the Dots

1. Why do police officers need to use discretion? Where is the majority of discretionary power concentrated in the typical police department?

2. What is zero-tolerance policing? Why do some commentators believe that limiting police discretion can damage police–public relations?

3. Identify four factors that may influence an officer's decision to arrest. Which factor do you think should be given the most weight by the officer? Which should be given the least weight? (Explain your reasons in each case.)

4. Explain the difference between the predispositional and socialized theories of police behavior.

Which of these theories do you find to be most convincing?

5. What are the major causes of police stress? Do you think that limiting the amount of discretion given to individual police officers would help to reduce stress levels?

6. Can you think of any reforms that could help to lower the stress suffered by police officers? Do you think that limiting the amount of discretion possessed by officers would help to reduce the strain of daily police–public interactions?

KEY TERMS

Authoritarian 224

Command discretion 216

Critical incident stress
    debriefings (CISD) 232

Contempt of cop (COC) 219

Disstress 229

Eustress 229

External stressors 230

Individual discretion 216

Internal stressors 230

Iron Law of Oligarchy 216

Legalistic style 228

Mandatory arrest policies 214

Minneapolis Domestic Violence
    Experiment 214

Police personality 222

Police subculture 224

Post-traumatic stress disorder
    (PTSD) 232

Service style 228

Thin blue line 224

Watchman style 227

Working personality 226

Zero-tolerance policing 217

REFERENCES

Acuri, A. F. 1976. "Police Pride and Self-Esteem: Indications of Future Occupational Changes." *Journal of Police Science and Administration* 4(4):295–305.

American Psychological Association. 1994. *Diagnostic and Statistical Manual*, Version IV. Washington, D.C.: American Psychological Association.

Bayley, D. H., and H. Mendelson. 1969. *Minorities and the Police: Confrontation in America*. New York: The Free Press.

Belles, D., and N. Norvell. 1990. *Stress Management for Law Enforcement Officers*. Sarasota, FL: Professional Resource Exchange.

Bercall, T. E. 1970. "Calls for Police Assistance." *American Behavioral Scientist* 13(4):681–691.

Bittner, E. 1990. *Aspects of Police Work*. Boston: Northeastern University Press. (Note that this quote originally appeared in a 1974 article by Bittner entitled "Florence Nightingale in Pursuit of Willie Sutton" in The Potential for Reform of Criminal Justice, Vol. 3, 3d ed., edited by H. Jacob, 17–44. Beverly Hills, CA: Sage.)

Black, D. 1971. "The Social Organization of Arrest." *Stanford Law Review* 23:1087–1111.

Black, D. 1980. *The Manners and Customs of the Police*. New York: Academic Press.

Blau, T. H. 1994. *Psychological Services for Law Enforcement*. New York: Wiley.

Bonifacio, P. 1991. *The Psychological Effects of Police Work: A Psychodynamic Approach*. New York: Plenum Press.

Bordua, D. 1967. "Review of Justice Without Trial: Law Enforcement in Democratic Society." *American Sociological Review* 32(3):492–493.

Bratton, W. J. 1996. "New Strategies for Combating Crime in New York City." *Fordham Urban Law Journal* 23:781–795.

Brooks, L. W. 1989. "Police Discretionary Behavior: A Study of Style." In *Critical Issues in Policing: Contemporary Readings*, edited by R. G. Dunham and G. P. Alpert, 121–145. Prospect Heights, IL: Waveland Press.

Chambliss, W. 1997. "Policing the Ghetto Underclass: The Politics of Law and Law Enforcement." In *Public Policy: Crime and Criminal Justice*, edited by B. Handcock and P. Sharp, 146–166. Upper Saddle River, NJ: Prentice Hall.

Chan, J. 1997. *Changing Police Culture*. Sydney: Cambridge University Press.

Crank, J. 2004. *Understanding Police Culture*, 2d ed. Dayton, OH: Anderson.

Crank, J., J. Hewitt, B. Regoli, and R. Culbertson. 1993. "An Assessment of Work Stress Among Police Executives." *Journal of Criminal Justice* 21(4):313–324.

Cronin, T. J. 1982. *Police Suicides: A Comprehensive Study of the Chicago Police Department*. Masters thesis, Lewis University, Chicago, IL: Department of Criminal Justice.

Cumming, E., L. Cumming, and L. Edell. 1965. "Policeman as Philosopher, Guide, and Friend." *Social Problems* 12:276–286.

Danto, B. L. 1978. "Police Suicide." *Police Stress* 1(1): 32–36, 38–40.

Davis, K. C. 1969. *Discretionary Justice*. Chicago: University of Illinois Press.

Davis, K. C. 1975. *Police Discretion*. St. Paul: West Publishing.

Eitle, D. 2005. The Influence of Mandatory Arrest Policies, Police Organizational Characteristics, and Situational Variables on the Probability of Arrest in Domestic Violence Cases. *Crime and Delinquency* 51(4):573–597.

Enstermaker Berk, S., and D. R. Loeske. 1980–1981. "Handling Family Violence: Situational Determinants of Police Arrest in Domestic Disturbances." *Law and Society Review* 15(2):317–346.

Farber, M. 1968. *Theory of Suicide*. New York: Funk and Wagnalls.

Friedman, P. 1967. "Suicide Among Police: A Study of Ninety-three Suicides Among New York City Policemen, 1934–1940." In *Essays in Self-Destruction*, edited by E. Shneidman, 414–449. New York: Science House.

Friedrich, R. J. 1980. "Police Use of Force: Individuals, Situations, and Organizations." *The Annals 452* (November):82–92.

Goldstein, H. 1968. "Police Response to Urban Crisis." *Public Administration Review 28* (July–August):417–418.

Goldstein, J. 1998. "Police Discretion Not to Invoke the Criminal Justice Process: Low Visibility Decisions in the Administration of Justice." In *The Criminal Justice System: Politics and Policies*, 7th ed., edited by G. F. Cole and M. G. Gertz, 85–103. Belmont, CA: Wadsworth Publishing.

Greene, J. A. 1999. "Zero Tolerance: A Case Study of Police Policies and Practices in New York City." *Crime and Delinquency 45*(2):171–187.

Grennan, S. A. 1988. "Findings on the Role of Officer Gender in Violent Encounters with Citizens." *Journal of Police Science and Administration 15*(1):78–85.

Guralnick, L. 1963. "Mortality by Occupation and Cause of Death Among Men 20–64 Years of Age." *Vital Statistics Special Reports 53.* Bethesda, MD: Department of Health, Education, and Welfare.

Harcourt, B. 1998. "Reflecting on the Subject: A Critique of the Social Influence Conception of Deterrence, the Broken Windows Theory, and Order Maintenance Policing New York Style." *Michigan Law Review 97*(2):291–389.

Harcourt, B. 2001. *Illusion of Order: The False Promise of Broken Windows Policing.* Cambridge, MA: Harvard University Press.

Heiman, M. F. 1975. "Police Suicide." *Journal of Police Science and Administration 3*(3):267–273.

Hoenig, A., and E. White. 2000. "By Their Own Hand." *The Police Chief 67*(10):156–161.

Ivanoff, A. 1994. *The New York City Police Suicide Training Project.* New York: Police Foundation.

Kappeler, V. E., R. D. Sluder, and G. Alpert. 1994. *Forces of Deviance: Understanding the Dark Side of Policing.* Prospect Heights, IL: Waveland Press.

Kelling, G. L., and C. Coles. 1996. *Fixing Broken Windows.* New York: The Free Press.

Klinger, D. A. 1994. "Demeanor or Crime? Why 'Hostile' Citizens Are More Likely To Be Arrested." *Criminology 32*(3):475–493.

Klinger, D. A. 1995. "Policing Spousal Assault." *Journal of Research in Crime and Delinquency 32*(3):308–324.

Klinger, D., J. J. Fyfe, and J. Flavin. 1997. "Differential Police Treatment of Male-On-Female Spousal Violence." *Criminology 35*(3):455–473.

Kroes, W. 1976. *Society's Victim, The Policeman: An Analysis of Job Stress in Policing.* Springfield, IL: Charles C. Thomas.

LaFave, W. 1965. *Arrest: The Decision to Take a Suspect into Custody.* Boston: Little, Brown and Company.

LaFree, G. 1989. *Rape and Criminal Justice.* Belmont, CA: Wadsworth.

Leftkowitz, J. 1973. "Attitudes of Police Towards Their Job." In *The Urban Policeman in Transition*, edited by R. J. Snibbe and H. M. Snibbe, 203–232. Springfield, IL: Charles C. Thomas.

Leftkowitz, J. 1975. "Psychological Attributes of Policemen: A Review of Research and Opinion." *Journal of Social Issues 31*(1):3–26.

Lester, D. 1983. "Why Do People Become Police Officers: A Study of the Reasons and Their Predictions of Success." *Journal of Police Science and Administration 11*(2):170–174.

Lord, V. 1996. "An Impact of Community Policing: Reported Stressors, Social Support, and Strain Among Police Officers in a Changing Police Department." *Journal of Criminal Justice 24*(6):503–522.

Lundman, R. J. 1980. *Policing the Police.* New York: Holt, Reinhart, and Winston.

Manning, R. 1977. *Police Work: The Social Organization of Policing.* Prospect Heights, IL: Waveland Press.

Martin, S. E. 1980. *Breaking and Entering: Policewomen on Patrol.* Berkeley: University of California Press.

Martin, S. E. 1990. *On the Move: The Status of Women in Policing.* Washington, D.C.: Police Foundation.

Maurer, M. 1993. *Young Black Men and the Criminal Justice System: A Growing National Problem.* Washington, D.C.: U.S. Government Printing Office.

Meredith, N. 1984. "Attacking the Roots of Police Violence." *Psychology Today 18*(1):20–26.

Michels, R. 1966. *Political Parties.* New York: The Free Press.

Miller, L. 1999. *Law Enforcement Traumatic Stress: Clinical Syndromes and Intervention Strategies.* Available at www.aaets.orglarts/art87.htm.

Niederhoffer, A. 1963. *A Study of Police Cynicism.* Garden City, NY: Doubleday.

Neiderhoffer, A. 1969. *Behind the Shield.* Garden City, NY: Doubleday.

Niederhoffer, A. 1977. *The Police Family: From Station House to Ranch House.* Lexington, MA: Lexington Books.

Niederhoffer, A. 1985. *The Ambivalent Force: Perspectives on the Police.* New York: Holt, Rinehart, and Winston.

Patterson, B. 1992. "Job Experience and Perceived Job Stress Among Police, Correctional, and Probation/Parole Officers." *Journal of Criminal Justice and Behavior 19*(3):260–285.

Pendeleton, M. 1983. *Police Stress: Value Disparity, Self-esteem and Occupational Strain.* Unpublished dissertation, University of Washington.

Reiner, R. 1992. *The Politics of the Police*, 2d ed. Oxford: Oxford University Press.

Reiser, M. 1973. *Practical Psychology for Police Officers.* Springfield, IL: Charles C. Thomas.

Reiss, A. 1968. "Police Brutality—Answers to Key Questions." *Transactions 5*(8):10–19.

Richard, W., and R. Fell. 1975. "Health Factors in Police Job Stress." In *Job Stress and the Police Officer*, edited by W. W. Kroes and J. J. Hurrell, 172–185. Washington, D.C.: U.S. Government Printing Office.

Roburg, R., J. Crank, and J. Kuykendall. 1999. *Police and Society*. Los Angeles, CA: Roxbury.

Roburg, R., J. Crank, and J. Kuykendall. 2000. *Police and Society*, 2d ed. Los Angeles, CA: Roxbury.

Skolnick, J. H. 1966. *Justice Without Trial*. New York: John Wiley & Sons.

Skolnick, J. H. 2000. "Code Blue." *The American Prospect 11*(10):49.

Smith, B. 1960. *Police Systems in the United States*, 2d ed. New York: Harper and Row.

Solomon, R. 1995. "Critical Incident Stress Management in Law Enforcement." In *Innovations in Disaster and Trauma Psychology: Applications in Emergency Services and Disaster Response*, edited by G. S. Everly, 123–157. Elliott City, IA: Chevron.

Stratton, J. G., D. A. Parker, and J. R. Snibbe. 1984. "Posttraumatic Stress: Study of Police Officers Involved in Shootings." *Psychological Reports 55*(7): 127–131.

Terrill, W. and S. Mastrofski. 2002. "Reassessing Situational and Office-Based Determinants of Police Coercion." *Justice Quarterly 19*(2):215–248.

Terry, W. C. 1981. "Police Stress: The Empirical Evidence." *Police Science and Administration 9*(1):61–75.

Van Maanen, D. 1997. "Making Rank: Becoming an American Police Sergeant." In *Critical Issues in Policing: Contemporary Readings*, 3d ed., edited by R. G. Dunham and G. P. Alpert, 167–183. Prospect Heights, IL: Waveland Press.

Violanti, J. 1996. *Police Suicide: Epidemic in Blue*. Springfield, IL: Charles Thomas.

Violanti, J., and F. Aron. 1995. "Police Stressors: Variations in Perceptions Among Police Personnel." *Journal of Criminal Justice 23*(2):280–291.

Violanti, J. M., and J. E. Vena. 1995. "Epidemiology of Police Suicide." Washington, D.C. NIMH Grant MH47091-02.

Visher, C. A. 1983. "Gender, Police Arrest Decisions, and Notions of Chivalry." *Criminology 21*(I):5–28.

Waddington, P. 1999. *Policing Citizens: Authority and Rights*. London: UCL Press.

Wagner, M., and R. J. Brzeczek. 1983. "Alcoholism and Suicide: A Fatal Connection." *FBI Law Enforcement Bulletin 52*(3):8–15.

Wilson, J. Q. 1978. *Varieties of Police Behavior*. Cambridge, MA: Harvard University Press.

Wilson, O. W. 1950. *Police Administration*. New York: McGraw-Hill.

Women's Justice Center. N.D. Available at www.justicewomen.com/witness.htm1.

Worden, R. E., and A. A. Pollitz. 1984. "Police Arrest in Domestic Disturbances: A Further Look." *Law and Society Review, 18*(1):105–119.

Worden, R. E. 1995. "The 'Causes' of Police Brutality: Theory and Evidence on Police Use of Force." In *And Justice for All*, edited by W. A. Geller and H. Toch, 31–60. Washington, D.C.: Police Executive Research Forum.

Worthington, R. 1991. "Value of Mandatory Arrest for Women Beaters Questioned." *Chicago Tribune*, November 19, 5.

NOTES

1. The story of Maria Macias is summarized from the presentation of the expert testimony of retired San Diego Police Sergeant Anne O'Dell found on the Women's Justice Center website, www.justicewomen.com/witness.html.

2. For a more condensed account of Davis' thinking about the issue of police discretion, see also Davis, K. C. (1975). *Police Discretion*. St. Paul: West Publishing.

3. Another excellent definition is provided by Goldstein, who argues that discretion is the decision not to impose a sanction in a situation where a sanction is available to the police. See Goldstein, J. (1998). "Police Discretion Not to Invoke the Crimi-

nal Justice Process: Low Visibility Decisions in the Administration of Justice." in G. F. Cole and M. G. Gertz (eds.), *The Criminal Justice System: Politics and Policies*, 7th ed. Belmont, CA: Wadsworth Publishing, 85–103.

4. New York City Traffic Rules and Regulations 2002, Section 4-04(c).

5. Note that this quote originally appeared in an article by Bittner entitled "Florence Nightingale in Pursuit of Willie Sutton" in Jacob, H. (1974). *The Potential for Reform of Criminal Justice Vol. 3*, 3d ed. Beverly Hills: Sage.

6. For a more detailed critique of zero-tolerance policing, see also Harcourt, B. (2001). *Illusion of Order: The False Promise of Broken Windows Policing*, Cambridge MA: Harvard.

7. See also Black, D. (1980). *The Manners and Customs of the Police.* New York: Academic Press.

8. See also Friedrich, R. J. (1980). "Police Use of Force: Individuals, Situations, and Organizations." *Annals 452*:82–97.

9. See also Worden, R. E. and Pollitz, A. A. (1984). "Police Arrest in Domestic Disturbances" in G. P. Whitaker (ed.), *Understanding Police Agency Performance*. Washington D.C.: Government Printing Office.

10. See also Martin, S. E. (1989). "Female Police Officers on the Move?" in R. G. Dunham and G. P. Alpert (eds.), *Critical Issues in Policing: Contemporary Readings*. Prospect Heights, IL: Waveland Press; Martin, S. E. (1990). *On the Move: The Status of Women in Policing*. Washington, D.C.: Police Foundation.

11. See also Roburg, R., Crank, J. and Kuykendall, J. (1999). *Police and Society*, Los Angeles: Roxbury.

12. See also Niederhoffer, A. (1977). *The Police Family: From Station House to Ranch House.* Lexington, MA: Lexington Books; and Niederhoffer, A. (1985). *The Ambivalent Force: Perspectives on the Police.* New York: Holt, Rinehart, and Winston.

13. Two of the most important books on police management at this time were both firmly rooted in the "classic" tradition. See: Wilson, O. W. (1950). *Police Administration*, New York: McGraw-Hill; and Smith, B. (1960). *Police Systems in the United States*, 2d ed. New York: Harper and Row.

14. See also Manning (1977).

15. Some of the more notable studies of police stress in recent years include: Kroes, W. (1976). *Society's Victim, The Policeman: An Analysis of Job Stress in Policing.* Springfield: C. Thomas; Crank, J., Hewitt, J. Regoli, B. and Culbertson, R. (1993). "An Assessment of Work Stress among Police Executives." *Journal of Criminal Justice 21*:310–321; Lord, V. (1996). "An Impact of Community Policing: Reported Stressors, Social Support, and Strain Among Police Officers in a Changing Police Department." *Journal of Criminal Justice 24*:503–522.

16. Richard, W., and Fell, R. (1975). "Health Factors in Police Job Stress." in W. W. Kroes and J. J. Hurrell (eds.). *Job Stress and the Police Officer*. Washington D.C.: U.S. Government Printing Office.

17. Cronin, T. J. (1982). *Police Suicides: A Comprehensive Study of the Chicago Police Department*, Masters Thesis, Lewis University (cited in Roburg, R., Crank, J. and Kuykendall, J. (1999). *Police and Society*. Los Angeles: Roxbury, 484); Wagner, M. and Brzeczek, R. J. (1983). "Alcoholism and Suicide: A Fatal Connection." *FBI Law Enforcement Bulletin 52*:8–15.

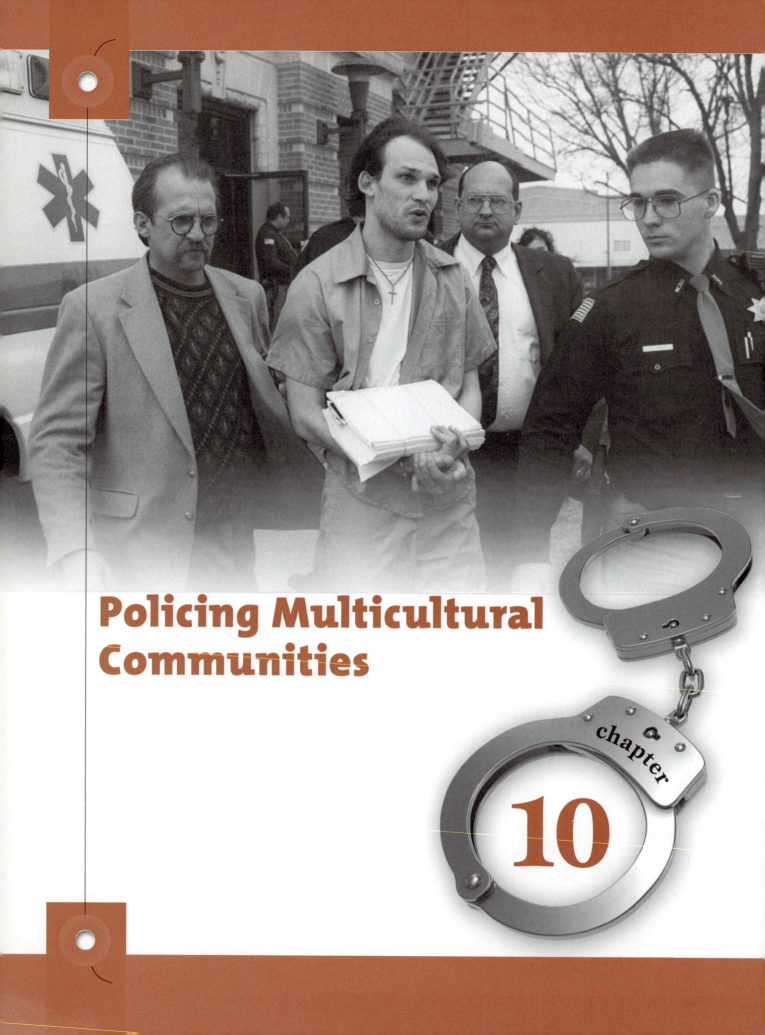

Policing Multicultural Communities

chapter

10

Chapter Objectives

- Become familiar with the state of relations between the police and racial and ethnic minorities in the United States.

- Identify some of the key challenges facing the police in their efforts to provide law enforcement services to diverse communities.

- Examine the problem of police racism and understand the current debate over the use of racial profiling by the police and other law enforcement agencies.

- Consider some of the ways in which police departments in the United States have attempted to improve their relations with immigrant and other minority communities and understand what is meant by the phrase "cultural diversity in policing."

Brandon Teena lived the life of many troubled youths, compulsively forging checks in order to win the affections of his girlfriends, leading to a series of convictions for forgery and theft by 1993 (Reardon 2000). However, there was one important difference: Brandon Teena was originally born as Teena Brandon. Feeling that his gender by birth did not correspond with his perception of himself as a male, he changed his name to Brandon Teena as a teenager and began a full-time life as a man. Brandon's frustration at being remembered as a female, particularly within his growing number of petty theft records, led to his decision to move away from his home town for a future as an unknown in Falls City, Nebraska. Although quickly finding love prospects in Lana Tisdel, as well as the acceptance and friendship of her ex-convict male companions, Brandon's luck was soon to run out. Brandon was arrested again when he resorted back to stealing to support himself, leading to the revelation of his true female identity to the small town he now called home. This revelation would enrage his new companions, John Lotter and Tom Nissen, leading both to violently rape and beat Brandon for his deception. Police investigating the attack on Brandon were more preoccupied with his true identity than with apprehending his attackers and thus preventing him from future harm. One week later he was dead when Lotter and Nissen fatally shot him on New Year's Eve 2003.

In another case, plaintiffs of the Mohawk Indian reservation alleged that the New York State police failed to provide protection on the reservation from the violent actions of a private security force for illegal casinos. The situation was complicated by the fact that, according to the New York state police, the tribe exercised a considerable amount of self-governance. The state police felt that the violence on the reservation put their officers at risk, and thus they did not intervene. The court of appeals denied the claim, finding that a claim under the equal protection clause for discriminatory denial of police protection does not depend on whether it can be demonstrated that other "similarly situated individuals" received better protection, or even that it involved an express racial classification. Rather, what must be demonstrated is a "discriminatory motivation for the denial" (*Pyke v. Cuomo*[1]).

Providing effective policing for minority communities is one of the greatest challenges facing law enforcement agencies in the United States today. Language barriers, racial stereotyping, and cultural differences are all factors that can prevent minorities from gaining access to justice or taking advantage of important criminal justice services. In addition, the failure of certain groups—such as recent immigrants—to report crimes to the police means that many minority communities in the United States currently receive inadequate levels of funding for local crime control and law enforcement initiatives.

Today, a key question for the police and public is how to improve relations between the police and the various racial, ethnic, and other cultural communities that make up the United States. Unfortunately, highly publicized incidents of police misconduct and brutality have done little to improve matters, and, in some cases—as in the mishandling of the Brandon Teena case—have made them considerably worse. Nor are these high-profile cases always an accurate reflection of the true sensitivity or concern for cultural issues of police nationally or even within one jurisdiction. This chapter explores some of the issues surrounding the policing of diverse communities and examines some of the ways in which the police are trying to improve relations between themselves and minority communities in the United States. Although the picture that emerges is not always a positive one, it is clear that significant, if perhaps slow, progress is being made toward ensuring that all citizens—regardless of race or ethnic background—receive equal protection from the police and other law enforcement agencies.

Key Problems and Sources of Tension

Ever since the first organized police forces were established during the second half of the nineteenth century, the police have been faced with the challenge of providing law enforcement services and protection to a vast range of different racial and ethnic communities. Frequently called upon to uphold laws seen by many as racist and discriminatory, such as the Jim Crow laws discussed in Chapter 2, and often accused by critics of engaging in racist tactics and behavior themselves, the police have repeatedly found themselves drawn into some of the most divisive racial struggles in American history. According to many historians, police involvement in the suppression of black riots during the 1930s and 1940s and open clashes with civil rights activists in the 1960s severely damaged police–minority relations in America, leaving many convinced that the police exist to protect the interests of only white communities. Furthermore, although the problems of police racism and poor police-minority relations have had a long history, many commentators have begun to argue that there is now an even greater need to address these issues than ever before.

According to the most recent national census, between 1990 and 2000 the total population of the United States increased by 13.2 percent, and while the majority white population, representing 75.1 percent of the total, increased by 5.9 percent during this period, the African-American and Hispanic communities increased by more than 15 and 50 percent, respectively (U.S. Census Bureau 2001a).[2] If Census Bureau predictions prove to be accurate, within the space of a few generations, no single racial or ethnic group will hold a clear majority in the United States. Instead, the country will be made up of a collection of significant "minorities," namely black, white, and Hispanic. In certain communities across the United States (particularly on the West coast), Asian and Pacific Islander communities also continue to see significant growth. (See Table 10.1.)

Despite the fact that police departments across the country have worked hard to improve their relations with minority communities in recent years, research suggests that many racial and ethnic minorities continue to encounter considerable difficulties in their dealings with the police and the criminal justice system in general. In the following sections, we look briefly at some of the major sources of tension that currently exist between the police and minorities in the United States, including problems stemming from the use of racial profiling and difficulties arising from **linguistic** and **cultural barriers** between the police and many **minority communities**.

TABLE 10.1

Projected Ethnic Composition of the United States

Year	White	Black	Hispanic	Asian	Minority Total
1980	80.0%	11.5%	6.4%	1.5%	19.4%
1995	73.9	12.0	10.2	3.3	25.5
2030	60.5	13.1	18.9	6.6	38.6
2050	52.8	13.6	24.5	8.2	46.3

Source: United States Census Bureau (2001). *Census 2000 Projections of the Resident Population by Race, Hispanic Origin, and Nativity.* Populations Projections Program. Washington, DC: U.S. Census Bureau.

Police Racism and Racial Profiling

One of the most common explanations offered for the poor state of police–minority relations in the United States is **racism** on the part of individual officers. Generations of racial minorities throughout the United States have repeatedly complained of being treated more harshly than whites, and although it is notoriously difficult to measure the importance of race on police behavior, figures released by the Department of Justice suggest that racial profiling and police discrimination continue to be significant problems (Rennison 2001). As Tables 10.2 and 10.3 show, blacks and Hispanics are more likely to be searched, handcuffed, and arrested during traffic stops than whites, and minorities in general are more likely to be subjected to the threat or actual use of force in contacts with the police. Blacks and other minorities also experience higher rates of victimization than whites—particularly for violent crime and theft—leading some to conclude that the police are less concerned with protecting minorities and are unwilling to devote necessary resources to the policing of minority communities (Rennison 2001).

In light of these figures, it is perhaps unsurprising that surveys within minority communities reveal a widespread belief that differential treatment by the police is simply a fact of life (Morin and Cottman 2001). According to public opinion polls commissioned by the Bureau of Justice Statistics, only 58 percent of blacks said that they held a favorable opinion of the police (as compared with 81 percent of whites), and only 38 percent reported having "a great deal or quite a lot of confidence in the police" (Langan et al. 2001). Perhaps even more disturbing, however, is the extent to which conflict with the police is regarded as unavoidable by many minorities. For young black men in particular, a dangerous and sometimes fatal encounter with the police has almost come to be seen as a rite of passage, while within the larger black community comments about being stopped for the offense of DWB ("driving while black") frequently hide considerable resentment and hostility towards the police (Wycliff 1987).

According to some critics of the police, police officers routinely discriminate against members of racial minorities because they regard them as second-class citizens, unworthy of the same legal protections and rights enjoyed by members of the majority white community. In support of this view, critics of the police

TABLE 10.2

Police Actions During Traffic Stops by Race and Ethnicity of Stopped Drivers (1999)*

Race/Ethnicity of Stopped Driver	Ticketed the Driver	Driver or Vehicle Searched	Driver Searched	Vehicle Searched	Handcuffed the Driver	Arrested the Driver	Used Force Against the Driver	Used Excessive Force Against the Driver
White	51.8%	5.4%	3.5%	4.3%	2.5%	2.6%	0.6%	0.4%
Black	60.4	11.0	8.0	8.5	6.4	5.2	1.5	1.0
Hispanic	65.6	11.3	7.0	9.7	5.0	4.2	1.4	1.4
Other	61.9	6.5	3.2	5.4	1.7	2.1	0	0

*Percentages may not sum to 100 due to rounding.

Source: P.A. Lagan et al. (2001). *Contacts between Police and the Public: Findings from the 1999 National Survey,* Washington, DC: U.S. Department of Justice, Bureau of Justice Studies.

TABLE 10.3

Experience of Force by Race and Ethnicity (1999)*

Race/Ethnicity	Percentage of All Police Contacts	Percentage of Persons Experiencing Force in Contact with the Police	Experience of Force as a Percentage of *All* Contacts with the Police
White	78.25%	58.9%	0.72%
Black	10.56	22.6	2.06
Hispanic	8.10	15.5	1.85
Other	3.08	3.0	0.90

*Percentages may not sum to 100 due to rounding.

Source: P. A. Lagan et al. (2001). *Contacts between Police and the Public: Findings from the 1999 National Survey,* Washington, DC: U.S. Department of Justice, Bureau of Justice Studies.

point out that the vast majority of police officers are white and typically drawn from some of the more conservative sections of the community. Armed with racist attitudes before they enter the force, once these individuals become police officers, they are free to harass and discriminate against minorities without fear of reprisals or censure from their presumably like-minded colleagues. In contrast, other critics contend that it is the police **socialization process** that plays a critical role in promoting racist attitudes and cultural insensitivity among serving officers (Shusta et al. 2002). As a number of researchers have observed, one of the key characteristics of police working culture is the use of **stereotypes** when dealing with members of the public (Goldstein 1990; Walker 1992). New officers quickly learn from their colleagues how to "recognize" actual or potential offenders and to discriminate between those citizens who are regarded as generally law-abiding and those who are not. Where these stereotypes are informed by ideas about race and criminality—for example, a belief that black people are more prone to violence than whites—racist attitudes can be passed from one generation of officers to the next in the guise of received wisdom or operational knowledge, although there is no evidence of truth to such stereotypes.

Both of these views of police behavior are, however, overly simplistic, and there is now a vast body of research to suggest that police racism is an extremely complex phenomenon. As Blakemore et al. (1995, p. 79) have observed, police prejudices are often based on "a lifetime of personal and professional experience, along with a multiplicity of ideological influences." Both **predisposition** and **socialization** play major roles in the formation and promotion of racist attitudes within the police, but understanding how they affect actual police behavior and decision making is extremely difficult, in part because officers may be motivated by reasoning that is subconscious and essentially unknown even to themselves (Lumb 1995).

Police officers are given considerable discretion when making decisions about whether to stop, search, or arrest individual citizens. Although in principle they are expected to exercise this discretion without regard to extra-legal factors such as class, race, gender, or age, in practice all of these factors have a bearing on how individual officers deal with members of the public. Police discrimination can also be the result of **fundamental attribution errors** on the part of serving officers and police managers. According to Winkel (1991), there is a tendency for police officers to explain criminal behavior in terms of "internal factors"—such as race or membership of a particular ethnic group—rather than by reference to external or situational factors, such as poverty or marginal social position. Often based on a genuine misunderstanding of the causes of crime, this type of reasoning frequently lies behind the practice of racial profiling and is used by officers who do not otherwise consider themselves or their conduct to be racist. Fundamental attribution errors can also be compounded by ignorance of minority cultures. In Das' (1993) study of the Canadian police and their views on the policing of minorities, for example, officers complained about what they perceived to be the "poor upbringing" of minority children and of the disregard shown by immigrants from "Third World" countries for traffic regulations and other minor laws.

Complaints like these often mask mistaken assumptions—such as the belief that individuals from certain cultures are inherently less law-abiding—that arise from a lack of cultural understanding on the part of the police. Such assumptions can soon become part of the **operating stereotype** used by officers when dealing with members of particular minority communities. Again, although officers holding such views may not consider themselves to be racist, such stereotypes can provide the basis for unwitting but serious discrimination on the grounds of race or ethnicity. Finally, it is important to remember that few, including even the most critical, researchers have suggested that the majority of police officers hold racist or discriminatory views. Indeed, most of the studies cited in this section point to the fact that although police racism is a serious problem, the vast majority of police officers are sensitive to issues of race and the need to treat all citizens equally. Unfortunately however, as the cases of Rodney King and Abner Louima demonstrate, incidents of police misconduct are not only more likely to receive attention than proper behavior, but also to have a significant effect on minority attitudes toward and images of the police.

Linkages *in Law Enforcement*

Terrorism, Racial Profiling, and the Arab Community

Although polls provide conflicting results, some have indicated that as many as 70 percent of Americans believe that some form of racial profiling of the Arab American community is necessary, and acceptable, to ensure public safety (Davis 2001). This is compared to 80 percent of Americans being opposed to the practice prior to September 11 (Davis 2001). Other polls have indicated that respondents are more suspicious of people of Arab descent, making special identification cards for this population acceptable.

QUESTIONS

1. Do you feel that the post–September 11 global climate justifies racial profiling of Arab Americans? Justify your argument with respect to the concepts and cases covered throughout Chapter 5.

2. What are the potentially negative consequences of racially profiling persons of Arab descent?

3. In what specific ways do you feel that the practice of racial profiling actually helps law enforcement keep society safe?

Linkages *in Law Enforcement*

Myths About Immigrant Communities and the Criminal Justice System

One of the most prevalent myths about immigrants in the United States is that they are more likely to commit crimes than native-born American citizens. In the past, this assumption has driven the police and other law enforcement agencies to adopt particularly aggressive tactics when dealing with these communities, often at the expense of building good relations, despite the fact that many immigrant communities are in desperate need of more effective policing. When compared to the population at large, however, there is little evidence to suggest that immigrants are any more criminal than native-born residents. Indeed, recent studies appear to show that immigrants—far from being "inherently criminal"—are in fact more law-abiding than members of the general population (Aronson 1997).

According to research undertaken at Harvard's Kennedy School of Government, immigrant men are far less likely to be in correctional institutions than native-born residents and rates of imprisonment for recent immigrants are considerably lower than those for earlier arrivals (Butcher and Piehl 1998).[3] Data compiled by the Immigration and Naturalization Service (INS) also suggested that recidivism rates for immigrant offenders are considerably lower than those for the population at large. According to INS figures for the late 1990s, of the 35,318 immigrant offenders released from custody during the period October 1994 to May 1999, 11,605 went on to re-offend (Goold 2002). This puts the rate of recidivism for immigrants at approximately 37 percent, some 30 percent lower than the 66 percent rate for U.S. criminal population as a whole. Far from being major contributors to the U.S. "crime problem," it appears that immigrants are less likely to offend or re-offend than many other groups, a fact that is being increasingly focused upon by the police in their efforts to improve relations with these communities.

QUESTIONS

1. Why have many Americans throughout history associated immigrant populations with crime? Is this justified?

2. What are the positive and negative impacts of aggressive policing tactics in immigrant communities?

3. To what extent should local law enforcement be in partnership with federal agencies such as ICE?

Aggressive Patrol Tactics and Minority Communities

Related to the issue of racial profiling is the use of aggressive patrolling techniques in minority communities. As discussed in Chapter 7, **aggressive patrolling** is designed to reduce crime in a given neighborhood or area by raising the immediate police presence, sending a signal to offenders in the community that a failure to obey the law will no longer be tolerated. Although welcome in many neighborhoods that have experienced persistently high crime rates, the use of this technique of policing in minority communities has attracted some criticism. Aggressive patrolling can reduce crime. However, it necessarily increases the likelihood of cultural misunderstandings and possible conflicts between the police and certain minority groups, such as recent immigrants. More significantly, when aggressive patrolling is directed at an area that contains a mixture of communities, there is a danger of the police being perceived to favor one group over another, subjecting the police to accusations of racism and harassment.

As a consequence, although aggressive patrolling is extremely effective at bringing down the overall level of crime in an area in certain situations, the police need to be aware of the concerns of all of the residents affected by such tactics and ensure that law enforcement is being carried out in an even-handed and unbiased manner. Failure to do so can lead to an increase in police–community tensions and discrimination against minority groups.

Policing Diversity: Cultural and Linguistic Barriers to Communication

Although much of the research on police–minority relations has tended to focus on the problem of police racism and the use of discriminatory policing tactics, cultural and linguistic barriers can also have a profound effect on dealings between the police and racial and ethnic minorities. Gardenswartz and Rowe (1998) argue that **diversity** includes all ways that human beings are both the similar and different; these factors create the commonalities we feel with others, as well as areas in which we can conflict.

Many minority communities in the United States have—for a variety of historical and social reasons—developed and continue to maintain cultures that are unique to them and often significantly different from those of the general community. A typical example of this can be found in **immigrant communities**. Because many immigrants continue to observe the cultural beliefs and practices of the native country after they settle in the United States, officers working in immigrant communities often are confronted with the task of maintaining order and providing protection for groups of people whose behavior and basic values may be unfamiliar to them. In extreme cases, these cultural differences between the police and the communities they serve can lead to serious misunderstandings and accusations of bias or lack of concern. Immigrants who have come to the United States to escape political persecution may, for example, view the police with suspicion based on experiences in their home country (Vrij et al. 1991). As one police officer interviewed by Das (1993) observed, minorities were often "afraid of the police as they carried at the back of their minds their conception about the police from their countries of origin" (p. 142). Similarly, for recent arrivals from countries where police corruption and malpractice is rife, such as parts of Eastern Europe and the former Soviet Union, trusting the police to help them rather than make their problems worse may be extremely difficult. In either case, interactions between these individuals and local police officers are likely to be colored by these beliefs, and possibly fraught with peril as a result.

In addition to the need to be aware of potential cultural differences, the police are also regularly confronted with the perennial problem of language. In an effort to solve this problem, almost every major police department in the United States has, at one time or another, experimented with short language courses for patrol officers (Taft 1982). Research has consistently shown, however, that requiring police officers to undergo intensive language training, typically in the form of so-called "crash courses," frequently does little more than provide them with a few key words and phrases. Although useful, knowing how to tell a suspect to "Put your hands up" is unlikely to help an officer whose primary concern

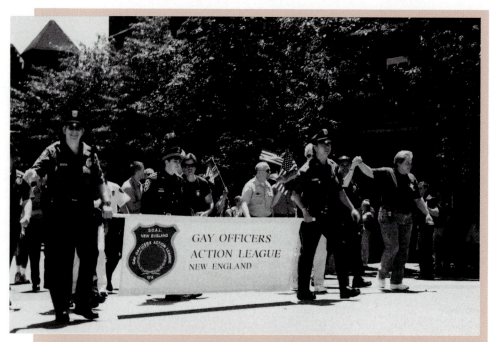

Attendance by law enforcement representatives at key cultural events can be an important first step toward positive police–minority interactions, thereby enhancing police–community relations.

is not with asserting authority, but rather with establishing trust. Being able to speak to ethnic minorities and recently arrived immigrants in their own language not only improves the ability of the police to gather information and carry out investigations, but, more importantly, it demonstrates a commitment to the community in question and a willingness to at least try to understand their culture. Furthermore, in many cases linguistic barriers do more than simply make it difficult for officers and minorities to communicate with each other. They also undermine the ability of the police officer to assert his authority through the use of spoken commands and gestures.

Making things even more complex, according to Kenney et al. (2002), police have to be able to perform their duties professionally when interacting with groups that are cross-cultural in nature. **Cross-cultural populations** include many layers of diversity that can be viewed as enriching, but at the same time pose their own unique challenges. Examples of such groups in the community include the deaf and hearing-impaired community; the mentally ill; and the Gay, Lesbian, Bisexual, and Transgendered (GLBT) communities.

Policing the Deaf and Hearing-Impaired Community   "You lose a lot of the impact of surprise, a lot of your knowledge, a lot of your gut feelings. You lose all of your years of experience working through an interpreter" [Lt. William Lamb, Miami Beach Police Department, quoted in Taft (1982, p. 14)]

Contrary to popular belief, the deaf and hearing-impaired community represents a diverse community in terms of individual's ability to hear and communicate vocally. The **profoundly deaf** are incapable of any hearing; those who are **hearing impaired** have some ability to hear and often try to hide their inability to hear through reliance upon lip-reading or closed captioning (Stolba and Sliman 2002). Encounters with the deaf population can be potentially dangerous for officers who are not informed about signs that indicate that they are interacting with a member of this population, because they may misperceive the situation at hand. For example, Stolba and Sliman (2002) note the following difficult encounters:

- A deaf person who has not seen an officer approach or not seen his or her lips move when issuing a command might appear to the officer to be disregarding a direct order.

- It is a misperception that written warnings from law enforcement will be a suitable substitute, because the average deaf person in the United States writes at near fourth-grade level.

- Police officers may misperceive communication among deaf individuals as other activity, as was the case of a Chicago police officer who arrested a group of teenagers at a bus stop on the grounds that they were making gang signals when, in fact, they were using **American Sign Language (ASL)**.

Deaf individuals themselves can benefit from an understanding of the precautions officers need to take in their interactions so that misunderstandings might be avoided. Although officer understanding of ASL is of course desirable, it is entirely impractical to believe that the average officer will ever have enough training to be competent in this complex language. As a result, new efforts in cultural diversity training seek to educate officers about the signs to recognize when dealing with a deaf or hard of hearing individual and offer interpretation services and alternative strategies as necessary.

Policing the Mentally Ill   People mistakenly tend to perceive the mentally ill as being violent and uncontrollable (Durham 1989). This being said, officers must be familiar with a variety of techniques for dealing with the mentally ill, recognizing the tremendous scope of the population. Police officers need to recognize that responding to a call for an emotionally disturbed or mentally ill individual will often require a significant amount of time and patience and in some cases may require the transfer of the individual to a hospital (Glenn and Hadfeild 2002). Education may play a part in the skills necessary to successfully navigate these situations. A 2003 study found that college education played a role in whether an individual was referred for treatment by an officer (La Grange 2003). The officer must understand that in many circumstances the assistance of a specially trained mental health professional may be necessary.

It is for this reason that many police departments, such as those in Los Angeles, Memphis, and Houston, have created special crisis intervention teams with specially trained officers to respond to calls involving the mentally ill. However, these agencies also offer a condensed recruit and in-service training so that officers generally are better able to respond to the unique needs of this population, and thereby prevent situations from escalating needlessly.

Policing the Gay, Lesbian, Bisexual, and Transgendered Community (GLBT)
The history of police relations with the GLBT population is not a very positive one, with police interactions with the community often focusing on the invocation of laws against disorderly conduct, public lewdness, and solicitation to

arrest GLBT individuals, including gay men hitting on individuals in public bars and even, on occasion, private parties in homes (D'Emilio 1983). It is in large part because of this history that many GLBT individuals do not feel comfortable reporting their victimizations to the police, even though many reports indicate that gays and lesbians continue to be among of the most stigmatized and victimized minorities in the United States (Leinen 1993).

Homophobia can greatly increase the effects of domestic violence from a partner due to the reluctance of community members to come forward for fear of a homophobic reaction from police. Even where called, however, responding to domestic violence incidents can pose even greater complexities in ascertaining who the primary aggressor is in cases involving a GLBT couple.

Few police departments have attempted to develop strategies aimed specifically at combating hate crimes directed at homosexuals or improving police handling of victims of such crime. Furthermore, it is rare for police departments to classify the GLBT community as an identifiable minority, and as a result diversity programs designed to improve police–minority relations often focus on issues of race and ethnicity rather than sexual identity and orientation.

The Underreporting of Crime

Similar to the challenges noted in the GLBT community, one of the major challenges facing the police is how to increase the reporting of crime in minority and immigrant communities. There is good reason to believe, for example, that immigrant victims are far less likely to report crimes than other victims, despite the fact that immigrants are victimized at rates comparable with those of the population at large. Although it is notoriously difficult to measure the extent of underreporting, based on a national survey of police chiefs, prosecutors, and court administrators, researchers have concluded that the underreporting of serious crimes, such as sexual assault and gang violence, is particularly endemic in communities of recent immigrants (Davis and Erez 1998).

Aside from the fact that underreporting means that many crimes go unpunished and offenders are left free to re-offend (often against the same victim), underreporting also has serious implications for the allocation and use of resources within the criminal justice system as a whole. As noted by approximately one-third of the officials surveyed by Davis and Erez (1998), underreporting leads to the undercounting of crimes in immigrant communities, with the result that these communities often receive inadequate levels of policing and other law enforcement resources. This is not a problem that can be solved simply by

Police outreach materials in languages representative of the community are an essential means of providing information and breaking down barriers.

putting more officers on the streets or improving levels of cultural awareness or linguistic competence. As many commentators have noted, underreporting stems from two main sources: (1) internal cultural pressures within immigrant communities that discourage individuals from seeking police help, and (2) a general lack of trust in the police and other law enforcement agencies.

For example, what most Americans might call a crime, members of a particular immigrant community may consider tradition, or if it is a crime, it is a "family matter" that does not require outside interference. In this view, police are not supposed to supplant patriarchal authority in resolving disputes, however evident that the "conflict" in question seems to call for it (Horowitz 2001).

Although underreporting has made it difficult for both the police and independent researchers to develop an accurate and detailed picture of crime in minority communities, in recent years it has become increasingly clear that violent crime is an especially serious problem for immigrants. Researchers from the UCLA School of Public Health found that although immigrants make up approximately 17 percent of the overall population in California, between 1970 and 1992 they accounted for roughly 23 percent of all recorded homicides (Roback 1996). As Susan B. Sorenson, one of the chief authors of the report notes, these findings "demonstrate the urgent need to establish violence-prevention programs geared specifically towards immigrant groups. . . . We need to find ways to intervene early to keep immigrants from becoming victims of violence" (Chu and Sorenson 1996, p. 120).

Underrepresentation of Racial Minorities in the Police

Finally, it is important to acknowledge that the state of police–minority relations has not been helped by the fact that police departments have, until recently, been slow to acknowledge and eliminate racial discrimination in their own hiring practices. Although the numbers of African American officers rose from 1975 to 1985, a 1989 study suggested that those increases were best predicted by the appointment of an African American mayor or police chief or by an affirmative-action initiative (Lewis 1989). From 1970 to 2006, the number of African American officers increased from around 6 to 18 percent in the nation's 300 largest police departments (Sklansky 2006). In cities with populations over 250,000, the percentage of Latino officers has increased by 9 percent (Sklansky 2006). However, both groups together still only represent just over 20 percent of the total number of officers in service (Bureau of Justice Statistics 2006).

Minority officers also are not promoted as often as white police officers. Although it is true that considerable variations exist across different police departments—in Chicago and Detroit, for example, black officers are far more likely to hold supervisory positions than in New York or Philadelphia—only some of this disparity can be explained by reference to differences in local demographics. What is clear is that some degree of racial bias continues to play a part in determining what opportunities are available to minorities within the police. As has already been noted earlier in this chapter, fostering trust is an essential precursor to the development of good police–community relations. According to some minority leaders, this trust will only result once the police and other law enforcement agencies demonstrate that they are open to **minority recruitment**, and that they are aware of the importance of being representative of the communities they are charged with serving and protecting.

Finding Solutions: Cultural Diversity and Policing

Despite the fact that the state of police–minority relations in the United States remains a source of concern, over the past three decades many police departments across the country have worked extremely hard to address the issues raised throughout this chapter. As a result of a growing emphasis on the need for greater cultural diversity in police training and recruitment policies, considerable progress has been made in a number of major cities, including New York and Los Angeles, which have historically suffered from poor police–minority relations, and in many other cities and towns with significant minority and immigrant populations. In addition, positive changes to police complaints procedures have also helped to build trust and instill greater levels of confidence in the police.

Training and Education: Cultural Diversity Training

Of the various efforts that have been made to improve police–minority relations in the United States over the last fifty years, perhaps the greatest amount of reform has come in the area of police training and education. As Blakemore et al. (1995) have observed, "the preparation of police officers for work in a multicultural society has become a major concern for police departments, local governments, and the general community" (p. 71), with the result that most city and state police departments now provide some form of ongoing cultural diversity training for their officers. The emergence of community policing as the dominant philosophy in contemporary law enforcement has also led to an increased emphasis on diversity training, on the assumption that "to achieve better relationships, knowledge of people, their motivations, beliefs and behaviors are necessary complements to officer training and increased understanding" (Lumb 1995, p. 42).

Though it has increased, the police approach to cultural diversity training and education has not changed dramatically since the 1960s (Blakemore et al. 1995). Generally speaking, the approach to cultural diversity training has been based on two key assumptions. First, police officers can be more effective social control agents if they are able to secure community support through better communication skills. Second, police officers will be more responsive to all members of the community and less likely to be abusive if they have an understanding of marginalized groups. Furthermore, this thinking has been underpinned by a particularly pragmatic approach to the problem of transforming attitudes and beliefs. Although many programs attempt to explain to officers how cultural stereotypes develop and go to great lengths to present principled arguments against prejudice, most accept that one of the best ways to promote change is to convince officers that they also stand to benefit from improved police–minority relations (Barlow and Barlow 1993).

Today, police cultural diversity training programs typically include substantial sections on such issues as race, culture, and interethnic relations; migration, minority integration, and cultural evolution; the dynamics of prejudice; group traditions, values, and attitudes; police intervention strategies; human rights; and police ethics and behavior (Lumb 1995; Normandeau and Leighton 1990). Although diversity training aims to challenge police prejudices and assumptions about minorities, sophisticated programs also strive to bring about organiza-

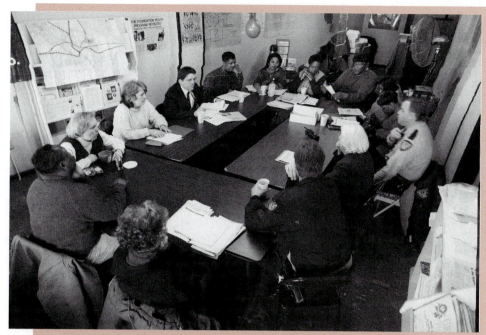

Cultural diversity training for law enforcement makes officers aware of the practical implications of cultural boundaries; immediate attitude change is generally not a practical expected outcome on its own—emphasis on awareness, human dignity, and sensitivity is.

tional and institutional changes and to fundamentally reorient police–minority relations (Lumb 1995).

Improving the Representation of Minorities in the Police

In addition to attempting to change police culture and combat discriminatory attitudes through education and officer training, many police departments have also begun to take steps towards ensuring that minorities are better represented within departments. It is now generally accepted by most policy makers and police administrators that part of community policing involves "making the police as representative of the community as possible" (Cox 1990, p. 169). According to some commentators, if we are committed to the idea that policing should be a community-based activity, then it follows that the police should strive to represent the society they are sworn to serve and protect (Lumb 1995). Perhaps even more fundamentally, however, it can be argued that the very legitimacy of the police depends on the extent to which they are representative of society at large.

In keeping with the recommendations of the National Advisory Commission's *Report on Police* (1973), most U.S. police departments have sought to increase the number of minority police officers through the use of **affirmative action** policies. According to some estimates, almost two-thirds of all police departments in the United States now have affirmative action employment policies in place. As a number of commentators have argued, however, there is a danger that the practice of hiring or promoting minorities without proper regard to individual qualifications is ultimately detrimental to the officers themselves, their colleagues, and the community at large (Alpert and Dunham 1992). According to Cox (1990):

> Only when all new police recruits meet the same, basic qualifications will there be any chance that race and gender will cease to be the controversial issues that they have traditionally been in American law enforcement (which simply reflects the larger society). If, and only if, this happens, will the difficulties in recruiting qualified women and minorities be eased and the goal of a community police partnership which includes all segments of the community be achievable. (p. 176)

Regardless of whether one accepts such objections to affirmative action in police recruitment, it is clear much remains to be done before the police manage to achieve a ratio of minority group employees that approximates its proportion in the larger population (National Advisory Commission 1973). As has already been noted, despite the fact that significant progress has been made in terms of the recruitment and promotion of minorities, it remains true that African Americans, Hispanics, and other ethnic minorities remain underrepresented in police departments at both the local and state levels. To ensure that the police continue to become more representative over time, it is necessary for departments to continue to reassess their hiring and promotion policies and that all officers are treated equally irrespective of their race or ethnic background. In addition, such attempts at reform need to be accompanied by a range of other proactive measures aimed at improving levels of diversity and encouraging understanding within the department. Simply hiring more minority officers is not enough; personnel practices, officer evaluation methods, and disciplinary procedures must all be examined and restructured to ensure that institutional biases and discriminatory polices are eliminated. These issues will be elaborated upon in Chapter 14.

Chapter Summary

- Providing effective policing for minority communities is one of the greatest challenges facing law enforcement agencies in the United States today. Despite the fact that police departments across the country have worked hard to improve their relations with minority communities in recent years, research suggests that many minorities continue to encounter considerable difficulties in their dealings with the police and the criminal justice system in general.

- One of the most common explanations offered for the poor state of police–minority relations in the United States is lack of multicultural knowledge on the part of individual officers and the use of racial profiling in police decision making. In support of this

view, critics of the police point out that the vast majority of police officers are white and typically drawn from some of the more conservative sections of the community.

- Cultural and linguistic barriers to communication can also pose a problem for police working in minority communities and can hinder the development of good police–minority relations. In recent years, the police have devoted considerable resources to overcoming these problems, and many departments across the country have well-established language and cultural diversity programs that attempt to address these issues.

- Although the numbers of minorities entering careers in law enforcement has been rising steadily, many racial and ethnic groups are still significantly underrepresented within policing. The number of African American and Hispanic officers has been rising steadily since the 1960s, yet both groups together still comprise less than 20 percent of the total number of officers in service. Evidence suggests that minority officers still do not receive the same promotional opportunities as white officers, a fact that has led some to argue that racial bias plays a significant part in determining what opportunities are available to minorities within the police.

- Despite police efforts, the underreporting of crime continues to be a problem in many minority communities. According to a number of recent studies, recent immigrants are particularly reticent about reporting crime to the police, in part because many fear contact with the authorities and because of the "closed" nature of their communities.

Linking the Dots

1. How have critics of the police sought to explain the phenomena of police racism? What steps can police departments take to eliminate racism within their ranks?

2. What is meant by the term *racial profiling*? Do you think that racial profiling is a legitimate police tactic? Are there any circumstances under which racial profiling can *never* be justified? Explain.

3. Why do many minority leaders object to the use of aggressive patrol tactics? What sorts of communities are most likely to be affected by the use of such police tactics?

4. Can you think of an example of a common cultural barrier that might provide difficulties for police officers working in a minority or immigrant community?

5. Aside from taking language courses, what can individual police officers do to overcome the problem of linguistic barriers?

6. Why is the underreporting of crime a problem? Why are certain minority communities particularly prone to underreporting? What can the police do to combat this problem?

7. Do you believe that the police in your city or town are representative of the entire community? Do you think that affirmative action recruitment policies are appropriate in policing and law enforcement?

8. What is *cultural diversity training*? What sorts of topics are typically covered in such programs?

9. What do you think is the greatest challenge currently facing the police in the efforts to improve relations with minority communities?

KEY TERMS

Affirmative action   255
Aggressive patrolling   248
American Sign Language (ASL)   251
Cross-cultural populations   250
Cultural barriers   244
Diversity   249

Fundamental attribution errors   246
Hearing impaired   250
Immigrant communities   249
Linguistic barriers   244
Minority communities   244
Minority recruitment   253
Operating stereotype   247

Police–minority tensions   244
Predisposition   246
Profoundly deaf   250
Racism   245
Socialization   246
Socialization process   246
Stereotype   246

REFERENCES

Alpert, G. P., and R. G. Dunham. 1992. *Policing Urban America*, 2d ed. Prospect Heights, IL: Waveland Press.

Aronson, D. 1997. "Immigration and the Criminal Justice System." *Research Perspectives on Migration* 1(5):1–14.

Barlow, D. E., and M. H. Barlow. 1993. "Cultural Diversity Training in Criminal Justice: A Progressive or Conservative Reform?" *Social Justice* 20(1):69–85.

Barlow, D. E., and M. H. Barlow. 1994. "Cultural Sensitivity Rediscovered: Developing Training Strategies for Police Officers." *Justice Professional* 8(1):97–116.

Blakemore, J. L., D. Barlow, and D. L. Padgett. 1995. "From the Classroom to the Community: Introducing Process in Police Diversity Training." *Police Studies* 18(1):71–83.

Bureau of Justice Statistics. 2006. *Local Police Departments, 2003*. Washington, D.C.: Bureau of Justice Statistics.

Butcher, K. F., and A. M. Piehl. 1998. "Cross-City Evidence on the Relationship Between Immigration and Crime." *Journal of Policy Analysis and Management* 17(3):457–493.

Chu, L. D., and S. Sorenson. 1996. "Trends in California Homicide, 1970 to 1993." *Western Journal of Medicine* 165:119–125.

Cox, S. M. 1990. "Policing into the Twenty-first Century." *Police Studies* 13(2):168–177.

D'Emilio, J. 1983. *Sexual Politics, Sexual Communities: The Making of a Homosexual Minority in the United States*. Chicago: University of Chicago.

Das, D. K. 1993. "Canadian Police Perception of Minority Problems." *Police Studies* 16(2):138–146.

Davis, N. 2001. "The Slippery Slope of Racial Profiling." *Color Lines*, December 13, 2001. Available at www.arc.org.

Davis, R. C., and E. Erez. 1998. "Immigrant Populations as Victims: Toward a Multicultural Criminal Justice System." *Research in Brief*, May 1998. Washington, D.C.: National Institute of Justice.

Durham, M. 1989. "The Impact of Deinstitutionalization on the Current Treatment of the Mentally Ill." *International Journal of Law and Psychiatry* 12(1):117–131.

Gardenswartz, L., and M. Barlow. 1993. *Managing Diversity: A Complete Desk Reference and Planning Guide*. New York: McGraw-Hill.

Glenn, J., and K. Hadfield. 2002. *Policing Persons with Mental Illness*. Washington, D.C.: Bureau of Justice Assistance.

Goldstein, H. 1990. *Problem-Oriented Policing*. New York: McGraw-Hill.

Goold, B. 2002. *Policing Immigrant Communities*. Washington, D.C.: Bureau of Justice Assistance.

Hagan, J., and A. Palloni. 1998. "Immigration and Crime in the United States." In *The Immigration Debate: Studies on the Economic, Demographic, and Fiscal Effects of Immigration*, edited by J. P. Smith and B. Edmonston, 367–387. Washington D.C.: National Academy Press.

Horowitz, C. 2001. *An Examination of U.S. Immigration Policy and Serious Crime*. Washington, D.C.: Center for Immigration Studies.

Kenney, D., H. Grant, and T. Allen. 2002. *Policing a Diverse Society*. Washington, D.C.: Bureau of Justice Assistance.

Lagan, P. A., et al. (2001). *Contacts Between Police and the Public: Findings from the 1999 National Survey*. Washington D.C.: U.S. Department of Justice, Bureau of Justice Statistics.

La Grange, T. C. 2003. "The Role of Police Education in Handling Cases of Mental Disorder." *Criminal Justice Review* 28(1):88–112.

Langan, P. A., L. A. Greenfeld, S. K. Smith, M. R. Durose, and D. J. Levin. 2001. *Contacts Between Police and the Public: Findings from the 1999 National Survey*. Washington, D.C.: Bureau of Justice Statistics.

Leinen, S. 1993. *Gay Cops*. New Brunswick, NJ: Rutgers University Press.

Lewis, W. G. 1989. "Toward Representative Bureaucracy: Blacks in City Police Organizations." *Public Administration Review* 49(3):257–268.

Lumb, R. C. 1995. "Policing Culturally Diverse Groups: Continuing Professional Development Programs for Police." *Police Studies* 18(1):23–43.

Morin, R., and M. H. Cottman. 2001. "Discrimination's Lingering Sting: Minorities Tell of Profiling, Other Bias." *The Washington Post*, June 22, 6.

National Advisory Commission on Criminal Justice. 1973. *Report on Police. Standards and Goals*. Washington, D.C.: U.S. Government Printing Office.

Normandeau, A., and B. Leighton. 1990. *A Vision of the Future of Policing in Canada: Police Challenge 2000*. Ottawa: Minister of Supply and Services Canada.

Rennison, C. M. 2001. *Criminal Victimization 2000: Changes 1999–2000 with Trends 1993–2000*. Washington, D.C.: Bureau of Justice Statistics.

Roback, W. 1996. "Immigrants More Likely to be Victims of Homicide." *UCLA School of Public Health Web Bulletin*. January 26, 1996. Available at www.ph.ucla.edu/sph/pr/wr038.html.

Shusta, R., D. Levine, P. Harris, and H. Wong. 2002. *Multicultural Law Enforcement*. Upper Saddle River, NJ: Prentice Hall.

Sklansky, D. A. 2006. "Not Your Father's Police Department: Making Sense of the New Demographics of Law Enforcement." *Journal of Criminal Law & Criminology* 96(3):1209–1243.

Stolba, C., and M. Stilman. 2002. *Policing the Deaf and Hard of Hearing Community*. Washington, D.C.: Bureau of Justice Statistics.

Taft, P. B. 1989. "Policing the New Immigrant Ghettos." In *Crime and the New Immigrants*. H. Launer and J. Palenski, eds., pp. XX–XX. Springfield, IL: Charles C. Thomas.

U.S. Census Bureau. 2001a. *Census 2000 Projections of the Resident Population by Race, Hispanic Origin, and Nativity*. Washington, D.C.: U.S. Census Bureau.

U.S. Census Bureau. 2001b. *Census 2000 Redistricting Data*. Washington, D.C.: U.S. Census Bureau.

U.S. Census Bureau. 2001c. *Census 2000: Overview of Race and Hispanic Origin*. Washington, D.C.: U.S. Census Bureau.

Vrij, A., F. W. Winkle, and F. Willen. 1991. "Encounters Between the Dutch Police and Minorities: Testing the Noncooperation Hypothesis of Differential Treatment." *Police Studies* 14(1):17–21.

Walker, S. 1992. *The Police in America*. New York: McGraw-Hill.

Winkel, F. W. 1991. "Interaction Between the Police and Minority Group Members: Victimization Through the Incorrect Interpretation of Nonverbal Behavior." *International Review of Victimology* 2(1):15–27.

Wycliff, D. 1987. "Blacks and Blue Power." *New York Times*, February 8.

NOTES

1. F.3d (2110 WL 822327, 2d Cir., 2001).
2. See also U.S. Census Bureau (2001a, 2001b).
3. See also Hagan and Palloni (1998).

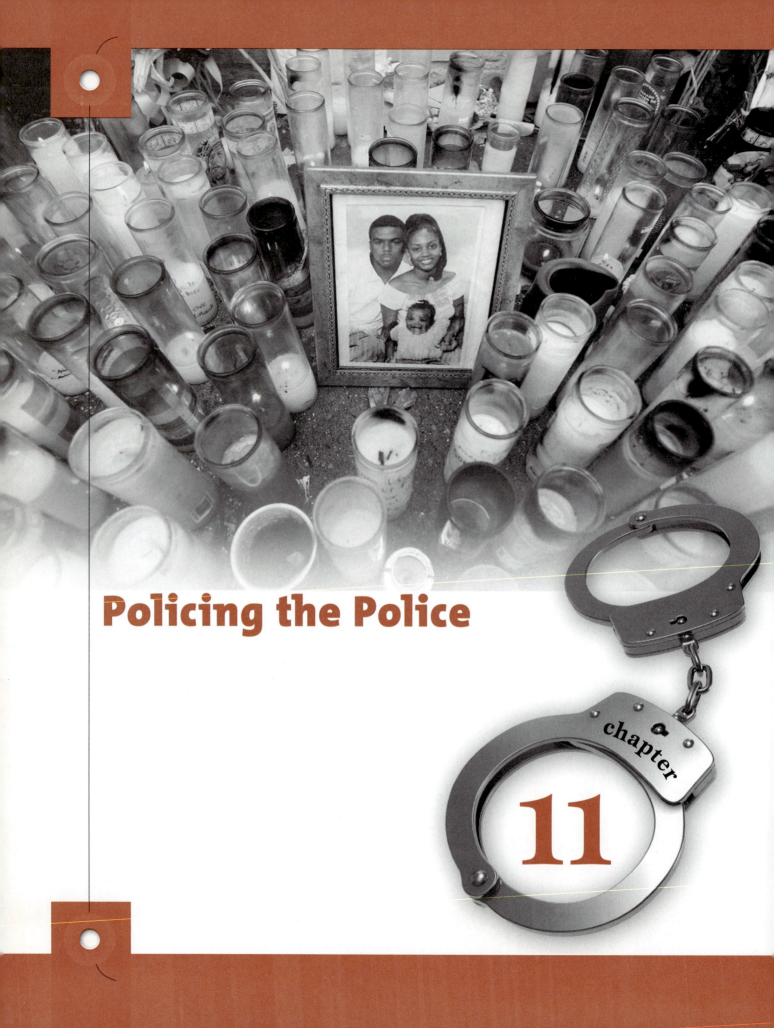

Policing the Police

chapter

11

Chapter Objectives

- Understand the continuum of force and recognize when legitimate force becomes excessive force.

- Explain when deadly force is legitimate and the guidelines by which officers can use it.

- Understand the differences among force, brutality, and corruption.

- List the types of oversight for police officers and explain which is best in a particular situation.

- Recognize the common problems that lead to police corruption and know the recommendations that have been made to combat it.

On November 25, 2006, Sean Bell was celebrating his impending wedding with a bachelor party at the Kalua Cabaret, a strip club in Queens, New York. Unbeknownst to Bell and his friends, Kalua was being investigated for numerous violations related to prostitution, drugs, noise, and liquor laws. On the night of his bachelor party, undercover detectives who were part of the "Club Enforcement Initiative" were investigating Kalua. At about 3:30 AM, a group of men, including Bell and his friends, began arguing outside the club. The argument seemed to center around a woman who had said she would not have sex with all the men. One of the undercover officers thought he heard Joseph Guzman, one of Bell's friends, state that he was going to get a gun and saw him gesture as though he had one. As the group dispersed, Bell and his two friends got into his car, and at that time some of the officers approached the group (Rashbaum and Baker 2006).*

A series of events then unfolded that left Sean Bell dead on his wedding day and his two friends seriously injured. Exactly how and why this happened is not clear. The detectives said that they approached the car with their badges out, identified themselves as police officers, and asked the occupants of the car to show their hands. However, Bell drove toward them, hitting one of the officers and then an officer's minivan, so the officers opened fire. Bell's friends stated that the detectives did not identify themselves, and they thought they were being ambushed by individuals with guns. In total, the officers fired fifty shots. Bell and his friends were unarmed (Rashbaum and Baker 2006).

Was this use of deadly force justified? Was this shooting of three unarmed men by the police a crime? Police officers are unique in that they are not only justified in using the amount of force reasonably necessary to control a situation, but that that force can be deadly. The question is: Did the officers reasonably believe that deadly force was necessary to control this situation? Charges were filed against the officers, and a grand jury indicted three of the officers involved (two for manslaughter, one for lesser charges).

This case is similar to others in which deadly force was used, most notably the shooting death of Amadou Diallo. In both cases, an unarmed black man was shot by police officers, raising issues of racial stereotyping. However, Diallo was shot by four white undercover agents, and the officers involved in the Bell case were of mixed races and ethnicities (two officers were black, one was white, one was Middle Eastern, and one was biracial; the first officer to fire a shot was black). Both the mayor and governor at the time said that the shooting of Bell was excessive, particularly since one officer fired thirty-one shots. The officers who shot forty-one bullets at Amadou Diallo were all acquitted of criminal charges. Despite established guidelines on the use of force, in many cases it is difficult to determine whether force was justified, and if so, whether it was reasonable or excessive. This chapter discusses controversial issues such as the use of force and explains the guidelines that exist for situations such as the unfortunate one involving Sean Bell.

Use of Force

As discussed in Chapter 1, the use of force is central to the role of the police (Klockars 1985). The police are authorized to use coercive force to control a variety of situations, and this authority defines the police role (Bittner 1970). Although the police are allowed to use coercive force, there are limits to how much force an officer can legitimately use. Use of force is **legitimate** if it is the minimum amount of force necessary to control a situation. Yet, the word *necessary* is ambiguous and is certainly subject to the discretion of any officer who responds to a situation.

The Force Continuum

Officers are not always justified in using force, and for the use of force to be legitimate they must abide by a number of criteria. Officers are only allowed to use force to protect themselves and others around them. However, research indicates that officers may disproportionately use force in certain situations. A study by Manz et al. (2003) that investigated the relationship between the type of call for service and the force used by police against a suspect found an unusual trend. The average amount of force applied during calls for service involving property offenses was higher than the average level of force used in calls for service that typically involved violence, specifically domestic violence (Manz et al. 2003). As discussed in Chapter 9, domestic violence situations are prevalent and often involve serious cases of assault. Although each call an officer responds to is different, a uniform method must be available for an officer to determine the type of reaction that is appropriate to differing levels of suspect resistance and hostility.

The **force continuum** is used to guide an officer's reaction and to focus his or her perception of risk (Figure 11.1 on page 266). The officer's observations of suspect behavior should correspond to an awareness and understanding of an appropriate level of coercive force. The sequence laid out by models of the force continuum must represent a logical chain of cause and effect. This rational explanation, through repetition, can help an officer use reasoned judgment in determining the type of force to be applied (Graves and Connor 1992).

The Federal Law Enforcement Training Center (FLETC) has designed a nationally recognized force continuum. This agency is responsible for training officers from many federal law enforcement agencies. FLETC has developed its own model for the application of force that color codes appropriate officer perceptions based on a suspect's level of resistance and the appropriate level of force, including the necessary tactics associated with each level.

The FLETC's force model depicts the force continuum as a set of adjacent steps. These steps indicate that the use of force is both progressive with the suspect's resistance and causally linked to the suspect's actions (Graves and Connor 1992). At the blue level, or *professional perception*, are normal, day-to-day law enforcement activities and interactions with the community. In most cases, conversations or verbal commands are located at this perceptual level. At the *tactical perception* level, which is color-coded in green, suggestive physical tactics, such as taking hold of a suspect, are appropriate responses to an officer's increased sense of the threat of confrontation. At this level, suspects are engaged in passive resistance, especially nonresponsive behaviors. The *threshold threat*, color-coded yellow, indicates that the officer perceives a serious situation that requires significant use of force, such as chemical sprays or application holds to pressure points, to subdue physical resistance. This is also known as **less-than-lethal force**. The orange level, or *harmful threat perception*, is when a suspect physically assaults an officer. In such instances, the officer should respond both defensively and decisively with striking maneuvers, using the hands or a baton. This is another example of less-than-lethal force. The final and most serious level of force is reserved for when the officer perceives a *lethal threat*, which is coded red. The red level requires "absolute and immediate tactics," such as the use of a firearm (Graves and Connor 1992), which is also referred to as **lethal force**.

A number of researchers have examined the use of force. One study employed a measurement termed the "force factor." If the force continuum is conceived as a series of ordered levels, then one may assign an ordinal value to both the suspect's resistance and the officer's response. The difference between the suspect's resistance and the applied force should, ideally, equal zero. In cases where too much or too little force has been applied, a positive score (too much force) or a negative score (too little force) will reflect that situation. However, there are problems with classifying each level of force distinctly, and research has sought to develop a more detailed and complex approach to measuring the use of force (Alpert et al. 2003).

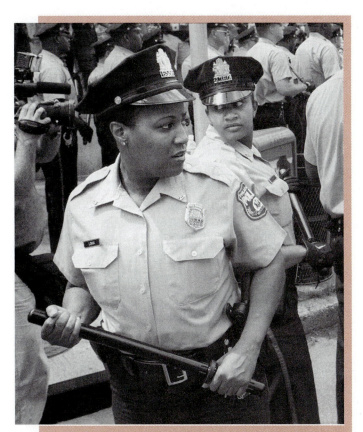

The use of force is a central, though often complex, function of the police role in society.

To better understand the complexities of the force continuum, take the example of Gideon Busch (Marzulli and Hoyle 2003). Police officers responded to a complaint that a mentally disordered man from Brooklyn was acting "strangely." The police arrived to find the 6′4″ Gideon Busch wielding a hammer, screaming incoherently, and threatening neighbors and the police with the hammer. Four officers surrounded him and shouted at him to put down the hammer. He did not respond to the verbal force, so they used pepper spray in an attempt to subdue him. Rather than its intended effect, the pepper spray appeared to agitate him, and he reportedly began hitting a police sergeant with the claw hammer. After exhausting the verbal and less-than-lethal means of force, the four officers shot him a total of twelve times. The family filed a wrongful death suit, but the courts came back with a finding that the officers did not use unreasonable force. So, how much force is reasonable? This chapter introduces the standards governing law enforcement use of force in the United States.

FIGURE 11.1

The Force Continuum

Level of threat

(1) Compliant (level I)

(2) Passive resistance (level II)

(3) Active resistance (level III)

(4) Assaultive with the potential for bodily harm (level IV)

(5) Assaultive with the potential for serious bodily harm or death (level V)

Corresponding force

Communication, such as verbal commands

Low-level physical tactics, such as grabbing a suspect's arm

Use of come-along holds, pressure points, and chemical sprays

Defensive tactics, such as striking maneuvers with the hands or a baton

Deadly force

Source: FLETC.

Objective Reasonableness: *Graham v. Connor*

Reasonable is an ambiguous term. How much force is reasonable in any given situation? Without precise definitions, it is difficult to explain when an officer has used coercive force legitimately, or when the force is excessive. The Court attempted to define legitimate use of force in the case of *Graham v. Connor*.[1]

Dethorne Graham was diabetic and had an insulin reaction. He asked a friend to drive him to a convenience store to buy a carton of orange juice to counteract the effect of the insulin. He quickly walked into the store, saw a long line, and then quickly walked back out to the car and asked his friend to drive him elsewhere. After witnessing this strange behavior, police officer Connor pulled over the vehicle and asked Graham and his friend to step out of the car. Confusion ensued, and the officers (Connor had called backup officers to the scene) handcuffed Graham, told him to shut up, and withheld orange juice from him, while waiting to find out what Graham had done at the store. Upon receiving information that he had not done anything wrong, the officers drove him home. Graham sustained several injuries, including bruises, cuts, and a broken foot, and he subsequently claimed excessive use of force.

The Court had to determine whether Connor's behavior, based on what he had witnessed, was reasonable under the Fourth Amendment. Though he acknowledged using force, he claimed that Graham's erratic behavior justified the need to detain him in a forceful manner. The Court agreed, explaining that reasonableness could not be specifically defined and that the Court would be required to look at the issue of reasonableness on a case-by-case basis. The Court found that Connor used force appropriate under the circumstances, and that force was used for the purpose of securing a potentially volatile scene rather than for the purpose of causing harm. **Objective reasonableness**, then, is based on the circumstances of the case. The Court is required to judge whether the force used is legitimate based on the perspective of a "reasonable officer" on the scene who is required to make quick decisions on the amount of force that may be necessary to use to control a situation.

Excessive Force: The Road to Brutality

Officers sometimes use more than the minimum amount of force necessary to control a situation, and that is when legitimate force becomes **excessive force**. There is no clear line between behavior that is acceptable and that which is too aggressive. In many cases, force that appears to be excessive may, in fact, be required in a particular situation. That is why the Court must apply the objective reasonableness standard on a case-by-case basis. Did the officers use excessive force against Sean Bell? Did the officers use excessive force against Rodney King?

Although police officers partake in some behavior that is questionably reasonable, other behavior is clearly a violation of an individual's human rights. For instance, compare the cases of Rodney King and Abner Louima. In 1991, the country watched an amateur videotape of four Los Angeles police officers beating Rodney King after he had allegedly violated traffic laws and led the police on a high-speed pursuit.[2] The police claimed that King, a 25-year-old black male, was driving 115 miles per hour in his Hyundai. After stopping him, they claimed that he appeared to be on PCP and of "superhuman" power. They beat him with nightsticks and their fists, and eventually hit him with tasers. He sustained skull fractures and broken bones in his face, and the officers knocked out some of his teeth. The officers in the case claimed that King threatened them, and that, combined with the reaction to the alleged drugs, is why they used such a high degree of force.

The case of Abner Louima was for all intents and purposes more severe than the King beating. Louima, a Haitian immigrant, was arrested on charges that he assaulted a police officer outside a nightclub. After the police took him into custody, Louima claims that two officers took him in to the precinct bathroom and one sodomized him with the broken handle of a toilet plunger while the other held him down.[3] Louima had been doing nothing to provoke such an attack; he was not even verbally abusing the officers. Yet officer Justin Volpe, angered by Louima's earlier outburst outside the nightclub, brutally committed an act of torture, causing Louima's rectum to rupture, injuring his bladder, and requiring him to be hospitalized for several weeks. Additionally, Volpe lied about the attack and said that Louima likely sustained such injuries as a result of homosexual activity that night, claiming he was afraid to tell his wife so he made up the story of abuse. Later, with the weight of evidence against him, Volpe pleaded guilty to the offense.

The case of Rodney King shows an excessive use of force by police officers. Anyone who witnessed the videotaped beating would likely agree. Although coercive force was arguably justified, King's eleven skull fractures and broken facial bones lead one to believe that the level of force was unreasonable. The case of Abner Loiuma, however, clearly goes beyond excessive force and would be considered police brutality. People often equate excessive use of force with police brutality, but the most common type of excessive force is actually pushing or grabbing by the officer (Bureau of Justice Statistics 2001). In contrast, **brutality** is when officers express malicious intent to harm. Generally, brutality can be defined as the intent to cause physical harm, as in the case of Abner Louima. However, officers can also use verbal brutality, or the use of words to harm. This harassment may be psychologically, if not physically, damaging.

It is not clear what causes an officer to go from law-abiding rookie officer to a ruthless oppressor. Perhaps it is the development of a police personality, discussed in Chapter 9, that might lead some officers into a life of stress, cynicism, and authoritarianism. As these police officers develop an "**us versus them**" attitude toward members of the community, the members of the community that the officers abuse often develop the same attitude toward them. Unfortunately, such behavior does not usually come to the attention of the police manager until it is too late. After the Rodney King beating, the Christopher Commission was formed to investigate excessive force within the LAPD. Even though Chief Darryl Gates said it was an isolated incident, they found that the excessive use of force was widespread.

Deadly Force

The police rarely use **deadly force**, and most officers do not even draw their guns in their career. However, many highly trained officers, such as SWAT team members (see Chapter 6), are far more likely to use their guns. The police are allowed to use deadly force, but only if it is the minimum amount of force necessary to control a situation. Because deadly force is the ultimate ban on a person's civil liberties, the courts have regulated use of deadly force and consider it to be reasonable only as an absolute last resort.

Deadly force is most often used in high-crime, urban areas. In fact, because of the prevalence of deadly force incidents in New York City in the mid-1980s, then-mayor Mario Cuomo appointed a Deadly Force Task Force to review all cases in which police used their firearms. The duty of this task force was to investigate the causes of deadly force and the effect this had on the community. The task force determined that minorities were more likely to be victims of deadly force than whites, negatively impacting police–community relations (Condon 1986).

The Fleeing-felon Rule

Elsewhere, there was also little regulation on police use of deadly force until the mid-1980s. Until 1985, the police could legitimately shoot a fleeing felon—an individual suspected of committing a felony who is fleeing the scene of the crime—in twenty-three states. In 1985, however, the U.S. Supreme Court invalidated the **fleeing-felon rule** and imposed a set of uniform rules governing the use of deadly force that reflected their ruling in *Tennessee v. Garner*.[4]

One evening the police were called to investigate the presence of a prowler in a Memphis, Tennessee, neighborhood. They came upon an individual who ran away from them after they told him to halt. Obeying the fleeing-felon laws, the police officer shot and killed the suspect. However, the suspect turned out to

Police officers can use deadly force when it is reasonable to believe it is the minimum amount of force necessary to protect themselves or others in the immediate area.

be a fifteen-year-old boy, Edward Garner. In court, the officer testified that he did not think the boy was armed, but he shot him so that he would not get away. The officer stated that he could not have caught the suspect any other way, because he was old and overweight. Moreover, the officer claimed that he believed that Garner was an adult. The Supreme Court called the shooting of felons to prevent their escape constitutionally unreasonable under the Fourth Amendment. The Court explained that deadly force is unjustified when the suspect poses no immediate danger to the officer or public.

As a result of *Garner*, the federal government and most states established guidelines on the acceptability of deadly force. Generally, the police can only use deadly force when

- An individual commits a felony and uses deadly force or a threat of deadly force during the commission of a felony (i.e., the suspect has committed an armed robbery and is threatening to use deadly force)

- The officer reasonably believes there is a substantial imminent risk that the person to be arrested will cause death or serious bodily harm to the officer or to another person in the vicinity

- Such force must be used to prevent the escape of a prisoner from prison[5]

- They need to suppress a riot after sufficient warning has been given

High-Speed Pursuits as Deadly Force

High-speed vehicle pursuits are dangerous to the police, the public, and the suspect who is fleeing from the police. A **pursuit** can be defined as a situation in which an officer attempts to initiate a stop, but the suspect flees and the officer pursues the suspect (Welch 2002).

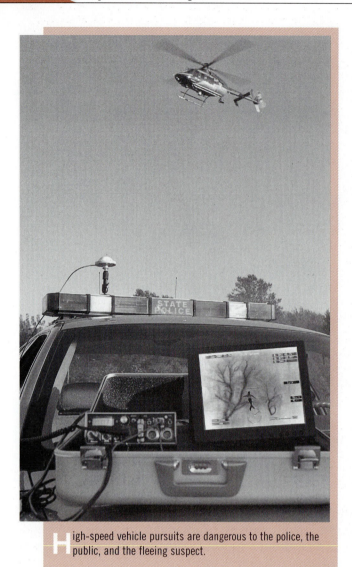

High-speed vehicle pursuits are dangerous to the police, the public, and the fleeing suspect.

Suspects may flee officers who are initiating a stop for a number of reasons. For instance, they may have stolen the car, have an outstanding arrest warrant, or are leaving a crime scene (Dunham et al. 1998). Or, they may be fearful of the police and not want a confrontation for some other reason (e.g., they are illegal immigrants). Whatever the reason, pursuits constitute a high risk, and approximately one in five individuals who initiates a pursuit is seriously injured (Dunham et al. 1998).

High-speed pursuits most often end in one of four ways. First, the suspect can voluntarily stop the pursuit and surrender to the police. Second, the police can damage the fleeing suspect's car or tires so that he or she is forced to stop (e.g., by planting spikes on the road or by shooting the tires). This is more common than the first option, though this may be dangerous, and the suspect may try to flee from the vehicle. The most common method by which vehicle pursuits end, however, is when the fleeing suspect crashes the vehicle into an inanimate object (e.g., a tree or light pole) or into another motorist. When the pursuit ends this way, it can result in serious injury or death to both the suspect and the other individual into whom he or she crashes. For this reason, many police departments have policy guidelines governing high-speed pursuits (Rayburn 2001). A fourth way in which high-speed pursuits end is that the police officer terminates the pursuit because it is endangering the lives of others. More police departments are beginning to adopt the policy that when the public safety risk outweighs the risk of the fleeing offender getting away, the pursuit must stop.

Though they are dangerous, high-speed pursuits are not unconstitutional. In the case of *County of Sacramento v. Lewis*,[6] the Court ruled that high-speed pursuits, though dangerous, do not constitute a deliberate indifference or a reckless disregard for human life.[7] The Court reviewed whether such pursuits, when they end in death, violate the Fourteenth Amendment due process clause of the Constitution. In *Lewis*, the Court claimed that liabilities for injuries resulting from high-speed pursuits arise only if the officer involved in the pursuit intended to harm the suspect physically. The Court claimed that the majority of high-speed pursuits do not go as far as to "shock the conscience," and they are therefore constitutional. Despite this fact, cases have continued to come before the Court to test this concept.[8] As of yet, no cases have overridden the important precedent set in *Lewis*.

Corruption

Police corruption, or the misuse of authority by a police officer, has been a concern in policing since the time of the watch system. Corruption involves a range of actions encompassing an officer's misuse of his or her authority for personal gain. These actions can include both passive and active behaviors on the part of the officer. Many types and levels of corruption are possible, but the Knapp Commission (see Commissions, below) described corruption by placing corrupt officers into one of two categories: grass eaters and meat eaters. **Grass eaters** are officers who accept gifts or favors from individuals, but they do not actively seek out or demand such activities. In contrast, **meat eaters** aggressively demand bribes in exchange for protection (or lack of) for the person from whom they are seeking the favor. Studies have shown that in environments where meat-eater activity is allowed to persist with impunity, a greater number of grass eaters will be the inevitable result (Swanson et al. 2000).

Investigative Commissions: From Wickersham to Christopher

One way to investigate corruption or brutality in a department is to form a commission. A **commission** is a group of individuals, generally appointed by a governor, mayor, or the president, who come together to investigate misconduct.

Serpico remains an important symbol in the fight against police corruption.

Since the 1930s, many investigative commissions have been appointed to investigate allegations of police abuse of power. The purpose of such commissions is to find the source of misconduct and hold the police, either individually or collectively, accountable for their actions. The commissions then offer recommendations for improving the accountability of the police. A review of commission recommendations indicates that the formation of commissions and their recommendations are cyclical in nature.

Commission reports have three recurring themes: improve recruitment and training, improve police–community relations, and improve the existing police complaints system (Terry and Grant 2004). However, commissions are formed as a reaction to specific incidents of misconduct, and their recommendations tend to lack any recognition of the underlying issues that caused the triggering incident. As a result, the changes are rarely effective in the long-term.

The first commission to fully analyze police conduct (and misconduct) was the Wickersham Commission in the 1930s. Since that time, the most influential commissions to investigate police conduct include the Kerner Commission, the Knapp Commission, the Mollen Commission, and the Christopher Commission.

Commissions are not only an American phenomenon, however. In England, the McPherson Report was written in response to an inquiry into the police investigation of the death of Stephen Lawrence, a black teenager, at the hands of four white teenagers. Specifically, the inquiry sought to determine whether the British police showed a systemic racial bias in their investigative duties. The report indicated that Lawrence's death was not only racially motivated, but that the police response was grossly inadequate and that the police need to implement long-term, systemic changes in order to combat such problems in the future (McPherson 1999). The inquiry investigated several of the same issues as the American commissions, and the findings were surprisingly analogous.

The Wickersham Commission (1931)

In the late 1920s, the United States was facing a number of social and criminal problems, such as crime stemming from Prohibition, a rise in organized and juvenile crime, and discord between the police and the community. In 1929, President Herbert Hoover organized the Wickersham Commission to investigate these problems. The Wickersham Commission produced a total of fourteen volumes of reports analyzing the social problems and the criminal justice system's response to those problems.

In terms of police abuse of power, the Commission examined the interrogation toll called the "third degree" (National Commission on Law Observance and Enforcement 1931).[9] The **third degree** was a technique whereby officers would inflict pain upon the suspect in order to elicit a confession (Walker et al. 1996). At this point in time, state police could still legally get coerced confessions.[10] However, the report contained a scathing analysis of such techniques, which soon fell into disuse.

The Wickersham Commission provided the first national analysis of police misconduct, and for the first time police reform leaders formed a system whereby civilians could register complaints against the police. These were internal systems, consisting of specialized officers whose sole duty was to investigate misconduct by fellow officers. Though there were problems with the system, it was the first true system of accountability of the police.

The Kerner Commission (1965)

The 1960s was an era of civil unrest in the United States. Many cities experienced riots, stemming largely from the deteriorating relationship between the police and the community—particularly minority communities. Police misconduct was rampant, and there was still no adequate way to hold police accountable for their actions. The police routinely violated the constitutional rights of individuals, and the Court finally took notice. Under the leadership of Chief Justice Earl Warren, the Supreme Court decided a number of landmark cases during the 1960s that limited the powers of the police and held them accountable for their actions.[11] Individuals were registering complaints with the police in record numbers, but the only means by which these complaints were investigated was by the police themselves. To the community, this was not acceptable.

As a result of community discord, riots, and increasing reports of police misconduct, the government sponsored the formation of a number of commissions. President Lyndon Johnson formed the Kerner Commission in 1965. The Kerner Commission reported widespread racial injustices by the police and general dissatisfaction with the internal review procedures of police practices (Morris and Hawking 1970).

The Kerner Commission's final report suggested many reforms (National Advisory Commission on Civil Disorder 1968). Similar to those before and after it, the report suggested the need to eliminate aggressive policing tactics (which largely targeted minorities), to implement effective mechanisms of police accountability, to increase minority recruitment for and promotion within the police, and to improve police relations with the community through the establishment of community policing programs. Despite the implementation of many of the suggestions, as well as the Court's curb on police power, there was no long-term reduction of police brutality or corruption (Bureau of Justice Statistics 2001).

The Knapp Commission (1972)

In the 1970s, the police were embroiled in a number of corruption scandals. The alleged "blue wall of silence" kept officers from testifying against the corrupt practices, though in 1972 that silence was broken. Frank Serpico, a plainclothes officer from the Bronx in New York City, exposed the widespread corruption within the NYPD and testified against his fellow officers in the resulting Knapp Commission (Knapp Commission Report 1972). The Knapp Commission found significant forms of police misconduct at all levels of the NYPD, including corruption, bribery, and participation in illegal activities, such as gambling and prostitution.

The Knapp Commission recognized that the system of police accountability was inadequate. Though the NYPD had an Internal Affairs Division (IAD), it was ineffective and needed to be reorganized. Additionally, the Commission stated that police officers should be criminally prosecuted for any type of misconduct. As with the Kerner Commission, these recommendations were implemented, but were largely ineffective, with the post of special prosecutor dissipating by 1990.

The Mollen Commission (1994)

After the scandal of the Knapp Commission findings, the NYPD vowed to reform its organizational structure, crack down on misconduct, and eliminate corruption. Yet, just over 20 years later, they were embroiled in yet another scandal. Six NYPD officers were arrested on drug charges in 1992, prompting another inquiry into police misconduct. The Mollen Commission, formed to investigate the new revelations of abuse, found that corruption was still widespread and that the types of misconduct were more serious that those found by the Knapp Commission. The many crimes included protecting narcotics traffickers, conducting illegal searches and seizures, falsifying records, and committing crimes such as robbery and drug trafficking (Mollen Commission 1994). The Mollen Commission found a link between corruption and brutality, and that this was particularly prevalent in minority communities. The misconduct had continued for an extended period of time, and it was able to continue again because of the code of silence amongst officers. It was apparent at all levels of the NYPD, from top managers to rank-and-file officers, and there was no system to adequately address complaints.

Like the Knapp Commission before it, the Mollen Commission suggested sweeping changes to both structure and practice within the NYPD. Although the reports of both commissions recommended increased accountability, the Mollen Commission specifically suggested the implementation of a system of external oversight. It recognized that the Internal Affairs Department was not sufficient to combat the problems within the department, and that the managerial officers in charge of the department were themselves corrupt. Although the NYPD has not yet formed any more commissions since the Mollen Commission, it has still perpetrated acts of misconduct and brutality. The case of Abner Louima is an example of how police misconduct can escalate to severe cases of brutality, according to some officers, the most severe case of brutality the department had ever witnessed.

The Christopher Commission (1992)

The Los Angeles Police Department, like the NYPD, has also been subject to independent review by a commission. In 1991, the world witnessed four white officers beating Rodney King, a black motorist, who was allegedly on PCP and displaying "superhuman" powers. This case was highly publicized because a civilian videotaped the beating and sent the tape to a television station.[12] The Christopher Commission was formed as a result of the King beating. It subsequently found evidence of racism and bias rampant within the LAPD. It also noted the department's lack of accountability to the community and suggested extensive reforms, such as changes in structure, recruitment, and accountability mechanisms (Christopher Commission 1992). The Commission also found that police management was poor and officers were rarely reprimanded for complaints about excessive force.

Recommendations from the Commissions

The commissions have all offered similar recommendations: minority recruitment, educational and residency requirements, and police accountability (specifically, civilian oversight of the police). Despite their cyclical nature, the reforms are rarely implemented and, when they are, they rarely result in the sweeping changes suggested. See Table 11.1 for a summary of the cyclical nature of these commission reports.

TABLE 11.1

Major Commission Findings and Recommendations

Commission/Task Force	Precipitating Incident	Underlying Problem	Recommendations
Wickersham	Prohibition, increasing crime rate, need to reevaluate juvenile justice, evaluate the adult criminal justice process	Increasing crime rate, particularly organized crime; need for evaluation of governmental agencies; and adequacy of the criminal justice process	• Social awareness of problems between police and minority communities • Establish a complaints system
Kerner	Riots of the 1960s, complaints by minorities about police abuse of power	Police misconduct, lack of accountability to all citizens, no oversight of police procedures	• Better recruitment and training standards • Accountability to the community • Establish mechanisms for registering complaints
Knapp	Widespread corruption and bribery, particularly among undercover units in New York City	Lack of oversight of police procedures, decreasing hierarchical accountability, identification of "blue wall of silence"	• Reorganize Internal Affairs Department • Civilian oversight of the police • Create post of state special prosecutor
Deadly Force Task Force	Numerous cases of police use of deadly force, disproportionate against minorities	Deteriorating police–community relations, increasing crime rate, increasing interaction between police and citizens	• Create a fair and impartial mechanism by which citizens can register complaints against the police • Enhanced police–community understanding • Expanded minority recruitment
Christopher	Excessive use of force by the police against a black motorist, subsequent riots and inability of the LAPD to adequately control the situation	Lack of accountability, lack of repercussions for misconduct, concealment of brutality	• Implement structural changes in recruitment, selection, training, and evaluation • Establish a new system for handling complaints and improve civilian oversight • Implement a community-based policing model
Mollen	Corruption scandal in specific undercover units, linking of corruption and brutality	Lack of accountability in undercover units, concealment of corruption and brutality by officers and management	• Improve screening, recruitment, and training (for new and in-service officers) • Increase and improve supervision • Reform internal/external oversight • Enhance sanctions for brutality and corruption

The most significant recruitment push resulting from investigative commissions has been toward greater representation of both ethnic minorities and women in law enforcement agencies. Despite this push, as discussed in Chapter 10, representation of minorities on the police force continues to be disproportionate. Racial and ethnic minorities represented about one-fifth of local police department personnel in 1997 (Bureau of Justice Statistics 2001). This constitutes a significant increase from the previous decade, but it is still not representative in urban areas such as Los Angeles and New York City.

Educational and residency requirements are other topics frequently touched upon by commissions. Many police departments have educational standards whereby officers are required to have either a college degree or a certain number of college credits toward a degree in order to join a police force. Although the majority of departments still do not require college credits, just over one-quarter of all departments require some college education for entry-level positions, a number double what it was in the 1980s (Terrill 1991).

In addition to education requirements, some departments have residency requirements mandating that officers live within the jurisdiction in which they are policing. This recommendation has surfaced from many of the commissions in the hopes that by living in the communities they police, officers will be better equipped to understand, and thereby interact with, its citizenry. The commissions were most adamant about their recommendations for accountability. Specifically, they called for a system of civilian oversight so that the police could be held accountable for their actions.

Models of Civilian Oversight

Prior to the 1960s, only one body reviewed complaints against the police: the police. This internal investigation process began after publication of the Wickersham Report, which acknowledged that someone needed to police the police. It was at this time that police department began forming **internal affairs bureaus (IABs)**, specialized police units that citizens could register complaints with. These complaints would then be investigated in due course by this unit, which was comprised entirely of police officers. Most complainants were encouraged to withdraw their complaints, and those that were investigated were most often unsubstantiated or the officer was **exonerated** (found not liable for the conduct with which they were charged) (Terrill 1991). By the 1960s, with outbreaks of urban rioting in response to police misconduct, various citizen groups began vocalizing their dissatisfaction with the police complaint process. They claimed that the police cannot effectively police themselves, and that the existing means for seeking redress were ineffective (Goldstein 1977). Therefore, citizen groups, as well as commissions, suggested that external review boards should be set up for civilians to hold the police accountable for their actions.

An external review board will not eliminate misconduct, brutality, or prejudicial discretion, but it can provide one level of **democratic accountability**, or accountability to the community, over a group of individuals with the power to use coercive force. This system of accountability should alert police management to potential problems with officers in the force, thus allowing for actions to be taken to deter future misconduct. IABs also provide **hierarchical accountability**, or accountability to those structurally higher within the department (e.g., accountability to the police chief). Both types of accountability are important and can help to reduce misconduct among officers.

A satisfactory complaint system can help to instill public confidence in the police; those who register complaints are likely to consider the effectiveness of the police complaints system to be based on the way they are treated, as well as the outcome of their cases. Studies have found that individuals who file complaints against the police are more likely to be satisfied with the outcome if they view the process through which the outcome was derived as being fair and impartial. This concept is called **procedural justice**. With procedural justice, the outcome is less important than the procedure by which the outcome is produced (Kerstetter 1995). Maguire and Corbett (1991) and Brown (1987) showed that most individuals do not consider internal investigations about police complaints to be fair and impartial, because they seemingly exist within a closed institution and the police will protect each other from the public. In order to allow a greater public confidence in the police and satisfaction from complainants, some form of external review over police actions is necessary.

Civilian oversight of the police has four goals: to deter future misconduct, to remove deviant officers, to satisfy individual complainants, and to maintain public confidence in the police (Walker 2001). Since external review boards were first implemented in the 1960s, they have varied in their accomplishment of these goals. The fact that a civilian oversight committee exists is not enough to eradicate tensions between the police and the community. The board must be created so that it is suitable for the community it is serving, and it must have adequate powers to ensure that the process is satisfactory to the citizens who make complaints.

History of Civilian Oversight

The first civilian review boards emerged in Philadelphia (The Philadelphia Advisory Board, 1958–1967) and in New York City (New York Civilian Complaint Review Board, 1953–present) (Walker et al. 1996). In order to combat the increasing tension between the police and the community, the Philadelphia branch of the ACLU called for the creation of a civilian review board in 1957. Although the police were strongly opposed to civilian oversight, Mayor Richard Dilworth created an entirely civilian body called the Philadelphia Police Advisory Board. The members of the Board had the responsibility to assess complaints of police brutality, false arrest, discrimination charges, or any other wrongful conduct against citizens. The Board faced many problems, such as a lack of any legal standing, political backing, or cooperation from the police (Goldstein 1977).

The police were dismayed by the fact that their actions would be judged by individuals who were not police officers and who had not experienced what they went through on a daily basis (Brown 1983). They considered these boards to be a type of political interference in their police duties (Brown 1983). The police also believed that they would not be able to use the amount of initiative, aggressiveness, and discretion necessary in their police work for as long as the lay board scrutinized them. Their worst fear was that a civilian board would view those making the complaints as being more credible than the officers (Van Maanen 1978). Most important, they did not believe that lay individuals would be able to understand the necessity of discretion in a police officer's job (Reiner 1993).

Despite police opposition to civilian review boards, more cities began to implement some form of civilian oversight over the next few decades. Most of the early boards eventually disbanded, and individuals began turning to the courts in the 1970s for restitution (Cheh 1995). In turn, the government focused on eliminating the misconduct that led to complaints and limiting police malpractice. The concept of an ombudsman was also introduced in the 1970s. An **ombudsman** was a neutral figure who reviewed complaints against all public servants, not just the police, in an effort to combat organizational or systemic misconduct. Today, the role of mediation is similar to the practice used by an ombudsman in the 1970s.

In the 1970s, a number of prominent review boards were formed. The most influential of these boards were in Detroit (Board of Police Commissioners), Chicago (Office of Professional Standards), Berkeley (Police Review Commission), and Kansas City (Office of Citizen Complaints). The 1980s brought forth a conservative period of law enforcement practice, with a primary focus on crime control instead of due process. Nonetheless, fifteen cities established civilian review boards at this time (Peterson 1991). These boards tended to be sparked by emotionally charged cases of police brutality, such as the case of Arthur Duffie, a black insurance salesman. Four white police officers in Dade County, Florida, all with previous complaints of misconduct, followed Duffie in a high-speed car chase and beat him to death when they caught him (Porter and Dunn, 1974). Following this incident, Dade County established an Independent Review Panel (IRP).

By 1995, 66 police departments had some form of civilian complaint review process and by 2000 the number had increased to 100 (Walker 2001). These were generally found in large and medium-sized cities, but also in some rural areas. Some civilian review boards that had already been in place were modified to incorporate changes suggested by the various commission reports. For example, the Civilian Complaint Review Board (CCRB) in New York City was transformed into an all-civilian review board in July 1993. Prior to 1987, it had been composed solely of nonsworn police personnel (e.g., police dispatchers); from 1987 to 1993 the board consisted of both civilians and nonsworn police personnel. This change resulted from suggestions by the Mollen Commission.

Walker's Typologies of Civilian Oversight

What do civilian oversight committees look like today? Each city is unique, but according to Walker they follow four primary systems: Class I, Class II, Class III, and Class IV (Walker 2001). With Class I systems, an independent body has jurisdiction for receiving and investigating complaints. Though the police chief can make recommendations based on the findings of the independent body, the chief's role is primarily of approval and oversight. New York City, Washington, D.C., San Francisco, and Minneapolis have this type of an external complaint system. In the Class II systems, internal affairs units are in charge of investigations, but an oversight agency reviews the results of the investigation. Kansas City is one city with this type of system. With Class III systems, internal affairs investigate the complaints. The complaint goes on to a civilian oversight agency only if the complainant is dissatisfied with the results of the investigation, at which point the complainant can appeal the decision. Omaha is one city with

TABLE 11.2

Walker's Typology of Civilian Oversight

Class	Description
I	• An independent agency has original jurisdiction for receiving and investigating complaints. • Staff investigators are not members of the police department. • Results of the investigation are forwarded by the oversight agency to the police chief for appropriate disciplinary action, if sustained.
II	• Complaints are investigated by an internal affairs or professional standards unit. • Results of the investigation are then reviewed by an oversight agency. • Decision of the oversight agency is then forwarded to the police chief.
III	• Complaints are investigated by an internal affairs or professional standard unit. • Complainant can appeal decision if not satisfied with the result. • Oversight agency handles appeals.
IV	• Responsibility for investigating complaints lies within the department. • Oversight agency audits or monitors the complaint process (quality control).

Source: From *Police Accountability: The Role of Citizen Oversight*, 1st ed. by Walker. 2001. Reprinted with permission of Wadsworth, a division of Thomson Learning: www.thomsonrights.com. Fax 800-730-2215.

this type of review system. With Class IV systems, the responsibility of reviewing police complaints remains entirely within the department. The only role of the oversight agency is to ensure quality control throughout the complaint process. Portland, San Jose, and the Los Angeles sheriff's department have this type of system. Table 11.2 outlines Walker's four classes.

Problems with the Complaint Process: Is There a "Best Practice"?

Each type of police complaint system has costs and benefits. Walker (2001) explains seven ways in which civilian oversight is both beneficial and problematic, as shown in Table 11.3.

The primary dissatisfaction with any police complaints system is the low number of **substantiated complaints**, or those in which the officer is found guilty of the action alleged. The more serious the complaint is, the less likely it is to be substantiated. This difficulty in substantiating complaints is due to several important factors. First, the charges must be proven "beyond a reasonable doubt," the same standard of proof required in criminal courts. If the evidence does not meet this standard, the charge is dismissed. In order to prove a charge beyond a reasonable doubt, there must be corroborating evidence. The majority of complainants cannot substantiate their statements, because there are rarely witnesses to the officers' actions except perhaps other officers or friends of the complainant. Thus, the only statements that exist are those of the complainant and the officer, which often directly contradict each other.

TABLE 11.3

Walker's Arguments for and Against Civilian Complaint Review Boards

Arguments for Civilian Review	Arguments Against Civilian Review
Police misconduct widespread	Police misconduct not a serious problem
More thorough and fair investigations	Less thorough and less fair investigations
Higher sustain rate	Lower sustain rate
More disciplinary action	Fewer disciplinary actions
Deter police misconduct	Deter effective police work
Improve public attitudes	Less public satisfaction
Promote police professionalism	Undermine police professionalism

Source: From *Police Accountability: The Role of Citizen Oversight,* 1st ed. by Walker. 2001. Reprinted with permission of Wadsworth, a division of Thomson Learning: www. thomsonrights.com. Fax 800-730-2215.

Individuals registering complaints usually are unaware of the high standard of proof required and are subsequently disappointed in the results of the process.

In cases of serious complaints, the corroborating evidence is particularly important because of the potentially serious consequences if the results are substantiated. These allegations are important to substantiate if the charges are true, and they are also the most damaging to the officer's career if they are not. The use of coercive force is a tactic that the police use to maintain social order. There is a delicate balance between the amount of force that is legitimate and

Mediation offers important benefits to both police and citizens, including an increased understanding of the other's perspective.

that which is excessive, and what may be excessive in one circumstance might be necessary in another. Complaints of assault and excessive force are most likely to come about in situations where danger is present and force was a necessary action to protect the officer, the public, or the suspected offender (Cheh 1995; Goldstein 1977).

In most cases, the police conduct complaint investigations, even when civilian review boards exist. The public is likely to be skeptical of investigative outcomes when the police investigate themselves, even when civilian review boards oversee the investigation and outcomes. Unfortunately, the police *and* the public are not likely to be satisfied with any one complaint system; the public views police investigations as unfair, feeling that the police will protect each other (Neiderhoffer 1967; Reiner, 1994), and the police feel that civilian investigations are unfair because the word of the complainant might be accepted over that of the officer (Van Maanen 1978; Walker 2001). Generally, however, the police are able to investigate accusations more thoroughly than civilian boards, and the investigations are thus more likely to be substantiated (Walker 2001). This is because the police have access to more information necessary to conduct a thorough investigation. Boards that employed civilian investigators have almost universally collapsed, and those that still exist regularly utilize police investigators to conduct their investigations (Walker 2001).

Another beneficial system of review is the Early Warning System (EWS), which allows the department to keep track of all complaints against officers, the outcome of the complaints, and repetitive behavior patterns that are potentially problematic (Alpert and Dunham 1992). If problematic behavior is noted or an

Linkages *in Law Enforcement*

Civilian Oversight in the War on Terror

In addition to the USA PATRIOT Act of 2001, Congress also passed the Terrorism Tribunal Act of 2001 in order to "support the President and the United States Armed Forces in their actions to deter and prevent acts of international terrorism by providing appropriate mechanisms for the United States to prosecute individuals suspected of committing or supporting terrorism." As a tool against terrorism, the Act seeks to "put accused terrorists on trial faster and in greater secrecy than in an ordinary criminal court" (Fournier 2001). Although the Department of Justice insists that with a military trial the right to a lawyer and jury will remain, the jury will not be composed of civilians.

QUESTIONS

1. What do you think the rationale is for the executive branch to seek a secret tribunal process? Do you agree or disagree with this rationale?

2. What role should citizen oversight play in the war on terrorism? At what point do you feel citizen oversight would sacrifice public safety interests?

3. How much should law enforcement warn the public about possible terrorist threats? What criteria would you develop?

officer receives multiple complaints, his or her entire record is reviewed and action is taken to address the problem (Gaines et al. 1994). This is an internal procedure, providing a means of assistance rather than punishment for potential behavioral problems. It is based on the assumption that officers will be more likely to respond positively to constructive criticism from their peers rather than from an external review committee.

Another positive development in some larger police agencies is the establishment of **mediation** systems, or alternative dispute resolution. Several departments are implementing mediation systems so that minor complaints (e.g., verbal abuse) can be resolved quickly and with preferred outcomes. Following on the concept of procedural justice, many citizens are more satisfied with the informal resolution than with fully investigated complaints because the process is more satisfactory (Corbett 1991). Maguire and Corbett (1991) showed that for cases that have been resolved informally, over half of the complainants were at least fairly satisfied and 30 percent were very satisfied. This can be compared with only 10 percent of complainants for investigated cases being even fairly satisfied and 68 percent very dissatisfied.

Who should police the police? This is the age-old question that is difficult to answer, because no answer will satisfy all parties involved. Many of the commissions evaluated the issue of police accountability and determined that there must be some system of internal and external review so that officers are held democratically and hierarchically accountable. In the past, the police have opposed the initiation of civilian review over their actions, and yet few forces have increased the amount of hierarchical accountability so that civilian review would not be necessary. As the Christopher Commission stated in its report after the Rodney King beating, "The failure to control these officers is a management issue that is at the heart of the problem" (Skolnick and Fyfe 1993, p. 3).

Chapter Summary

- Officers have the legal power to use coercive force, but the force must be the minimum amount necessary to control the situation.

- There is no clear definition of excessive force. In order to determine whether a police officer's force is excessive, the Supreme Court uses the Fourth Amendment standard of "objective reasonableness."

- Specific rules apply as to when officers are allowed to use deadly force. Generally, the officer or the public must be in imminent danger of life or limb. The Court set out standards for use of deadly force in *Tennessee v. Garner*, a case that also abolished the fleeing-felon rule.

- When a police force experiences a serious case of misconduct (or when misconduct is systematic throughout the department), a commission is appointed to investigate the abuse of power. Several commissions have published recommendations for reducing corruption and brutality, the most common ones being better recruitment and training standards, increased accountability, and better complaint systems.

- By the year 2001, more than 100 departments had implemented a civilian review board. This external oversight system should help to make police accountable to the communities they police. However, many citizens are still not satisfied with the complaint structure.

Linking the Dots

1. What are the different levels of legitimate force that an officer can use? How does the court determine if an officer uses legitimate or excessive force? Can reasonable force be defined?

2. Which is more important, democratic or hierarchical accountability? Explain.

3. What would be a proactive way to combat corruption, force, and brutality? What is currently done to combat these problems?

KEY TERMS

Brutality 268
Commission 271
Deadly force 268
Democratic accountability 276
Excessive force 267
Exonerated 276
Fleeing-felon rule 268
Force continuum 264
Grass eaters 271

Hierarchical accountability 276
Internal Affairs Bureau (IAB) 276
Legitimate force 264
Less-than-lethal force 265
Lethal force 265
Meat eaters 271
Mediation 282
Objective reasonableness 267

Ombudsman 278
Police corruption 271
Procedural justice 277
Pursuit 269
Substantiated complaints 279
Third degree 272
Us versus them 268

REFERENCES

Alpert, G. P., and R. C. Dunham. 1992. *Policing Urban America*, 2d ed. Prospect Heights, IL: Waveland Press.

Alpert, G. P., W. Terrill, R. G. Dunham, and M. R. Smith. 2003. "A Management Tool for Evaluating Police Use of Force: An Application of the Force Factor." *Police Quarterly* 6(2):150–171.

Bittner, E. 1970. *The Functions of Police in Modern Society*. Washington, D.C.: National Institute of Mental Health.

Brown, D. C. 1983. *Civilian Review of Complaints Against the Police: A Survey of the United States Literature*. Home Office Research and Planning Unit. London: H.M.S.O.

Brown, D. C. 1987. *The Police Complaints Procedure: A Survey of Complainants' Views*. Home Office Research Study No. 93. London: H.M.S.O.

Bureau of Justice Statistics. 2001. *Contacts Between the Police and the Public*. Washington, D.C.: Author.

Cheh, M. M. 1995. "Are Lawsuits an Answer to Police Brutality?" In *And Justice For All: Understanding and Controlling Police Abuse of Force*, edited by W. A. Geller and H. Toch, 233–259. Washington, D.C.: Police Executive Research Forum.

Christopher Commission. 1992. Christopher Commission Report. Los Angeles, CA: Independent Commission on the Los Angeles Police Department.

Condon, R.J. 1986. *New York City Report on Deadly Force*. Albany, NY: Department of Criminal Justice Services.

Corbett, C. 1991. "Complaints Against the Police: The New Procedure of Informal Resolution." *Policing and Society* 2(1):47–60.

Dunham, R., G. Alpert, G. Kenny, and P. Cromwell. 1998. "High-Speed Pursuit: The Offenders' Perspective." *Criminal Justice and Behavior* 25(1):30–45.

Fournier, R. 2001. "USA: Bush Orders Terrorist Trials by Military Tribunal." Available at www.yale.edu ./lawweb/avalon/sepCll/hr3564_ih.htm.

Gaines, L. K., V. E. Kappeler, and J. B. Vaughn. 1994. *Policing in America*. Cincinnati, OH: Anderson Publishing Company.

Graves, F. and Connor, G. 1992. "The FLETC Use-of-Force Model." *The Police Chief*, p. 56–57.

Kerstetter, W. A. 1995. "A 'Procedural Justice' Perspective on Police and Citizen Satisfaction with Investigations of Police Use of Force: Finding a Common Ground of Fairness." In *And Justice For All: Understanding and Controlling Police Abuse of Force*, edited by W. A. Geller and H. Toch, pp. 223–232. Washington, D.C.: Police Executive Research Forum.

Klockars, C. 1985. *The Idea of the Police*. Beverly Hills, CA: Sage.

Knapp Commission. 1972. *Knapp Commission Report*. New York: Independent Commission on the New York City Police Department.

MacPherson, W. 1999. *The Stephen Lawrence Inquiry: Report of an Inquiry*. London: The Stationery Office.

Maguire, M., and C. Corbett. 1991. *A Study of the Police Complaints System*. London: H.M.S.O.

Manz, P. W., J. M. MacDonald, G. P. Alpert, and R. G. Dunham. 2003. "Police Use of Force: Examining the Relationship Between Calls for Service and the Balance of Police Force and Suspect Resistance." *Journal of Criminal Justice* 31:119–127.

Marzulli, J., and R. Hoyle. 2003. "A Killing in Dispute." *Daily News*, October 12, 2003, 10.

Mollen Commission. 1994. *Commission Report: Commission to Investigate Allegations of Police Corruption and the Anti-Corruption Procedures of the Police Department*. New York: Mollen.

Morris, N., and G. Hawking. 1970. *The Honest Politician's Guide to Crime Control*. Chicago: University of Chicago Press.

National Advisory Commission on Civil Disorder. 1968. *Report of the National Advisory Commission on Civil Disorder*. Washington, D.C.: Government Printing Office.

National Commission on Law Observance and Enforcement. 1931. *The Wickersham Commission Report*. Washington, D.C.: Government Printing Office.

Niederhoffer, A. 1967. *Behind the Shield: The Police in Urban Society*. Garden City, NY: Doubleday.

Petterson, W. E. 1991. "Police Accountability and Civilian Oversight of Policing: An American Perspective." In *Complaints Against the Police: The Trend to External Review*, edited by A. J. Goldsmith, 259–290. Oxford: Clarendon Press.

Porter, B., and M. Dunn. 1984. *The Miami Riot of 1980: Crossing the Bounds*. Lexington, MA: Lexington Books.

Rayburn, M. 2001. *Advanced Patrol Tactics*. Flushing, NY: Looseleaf Law.

Reiner, R. 1993. *The Politics of the Police*, 2d ed. Sussex: Wheatsheat Books.

Reiner, R. 1994. "Policing and the Police." In *The Oxford Handbook of Criminology*, edited by M. Maguire, R. Morgan, and R. Reiner, 705–772. Oxford: Oxford University Press.

Skolnick, J. H., and J. J. Fyfe. 1993. *Above the Law: Police and the Excessive Use of Force*. Toronto: Free Press.

Swanson, C., L. Territo, and R. Taylor. 2000. *Police Administration: Structures, Processes, and Behavior*. Upper Saddle River, NJ: Prentice Hall.

Terrill, R. J. 1991. "Civilian Oversight of the Police Complaints Process in the United States: Concerns, Developments, and More Concern." In *Complaints Against the Police: The Trend to External Review*, edited by A. J. Goldsmith, pp. 291–322. Oxford: Clarendon Press.

Terry, K. J., and H. B. Grant. 2004. "The Roads Not Taken: Improving the Use of Civilian Complaint Review Boards and Implementation of the Recommendations from Investigative Commissions." *In Policing and Minority Communities: Bridging the Gap*, edited by D. J. Jones-Brown and K. J. Terry, 160–182. Upper Saddle River, NJ: Prentice Hall.

Van Maanen, J. 1978. "The Asshole." In *Policing: A View From the Street*, edited by P. Manning and J. Van Maanen, pp. 21–38. New York: Random House.

Walker, S. 2001. *Police Accountability: The Role of Civilian Oversight*. Belmont, CA: Wadsworth Publishing.

Walker, S., C. Spohn, and T. DeLone. 1996. *The Color of Justice: Race, Ethnicity and Crime in America*. Belmont, CA: Wadsworth.

Welch, M. 2002. "Police Pursuits: Just One Form of Violence." In *Policing and Violence*, edited by R. G. Burns and C. E. Crawford, pp. 147–166. Upper Saddle River, NJ: Prentice Hall.

1. 490 U.S. 386 (1989).

2. Only four officers actually beat King, but twenty-three officers in total responded to the incident. See Skolnick and Fyfe (1993).

3. The identity of the officer who held him down is still an issue of contention. Charles Swartz was accused and tried three times, then after another hung jury he pled out to a lesser offense. It is likely that the identity of the second officer will never be known.

4. 471 U.S. 1 (1985).

5. This is only constitutional if deadly force is not excessive punishment for the prisoner's actions. In other words, it would be excessive force for an officer to shoot an offender convicted of misdemeanor larceny who escapes from jail, because deadly force is not proportionate to the offender's prior act.

6. 523 U.S. 833 (1998).

7. *County of Sacramento v. Lewis*, 523 U.S. 833 (1998).

8. For instance, see *Epps v. Lauderdale County*, 2002 U.S. App. LEXIS 16575.

9. According to Skolnick and Fyfe (1993), the first degree is arrest, the second degree is the transport to a place of confinement, and the third degree is the interrogation. The Wickersham Commission describes the third degree process as a situation that encourages police brutality, equating this process with torture.

10. This ended in 1936 with the case of *Brown v. Mississippi*, 297 U.S. 278 (1936).

11. E.g., *Mapp v. Ohio*, 368 U.S. 871 (1961), *Wong Sun v. United States*, 371 U.S. 471 (1963), *Miranda v. Arizona*, 384 U.S. 436 (1966), *Katz v. United States*, 389 U.S. 347 (1967), *Terry v. Ohio*, 392 U.S. 1 (1968), and *Chimel v. California*, 395 U.S. 752 (1969).

12. King's brother and the civilian who taped the beating attempted to register complaints with the police. Both were dissuaded from doing so, and a formal complaint was only registered after the civilian sent the tape to the media, who played it on national television. See Skolnick and Fyfe (1993), pp. 2–3.

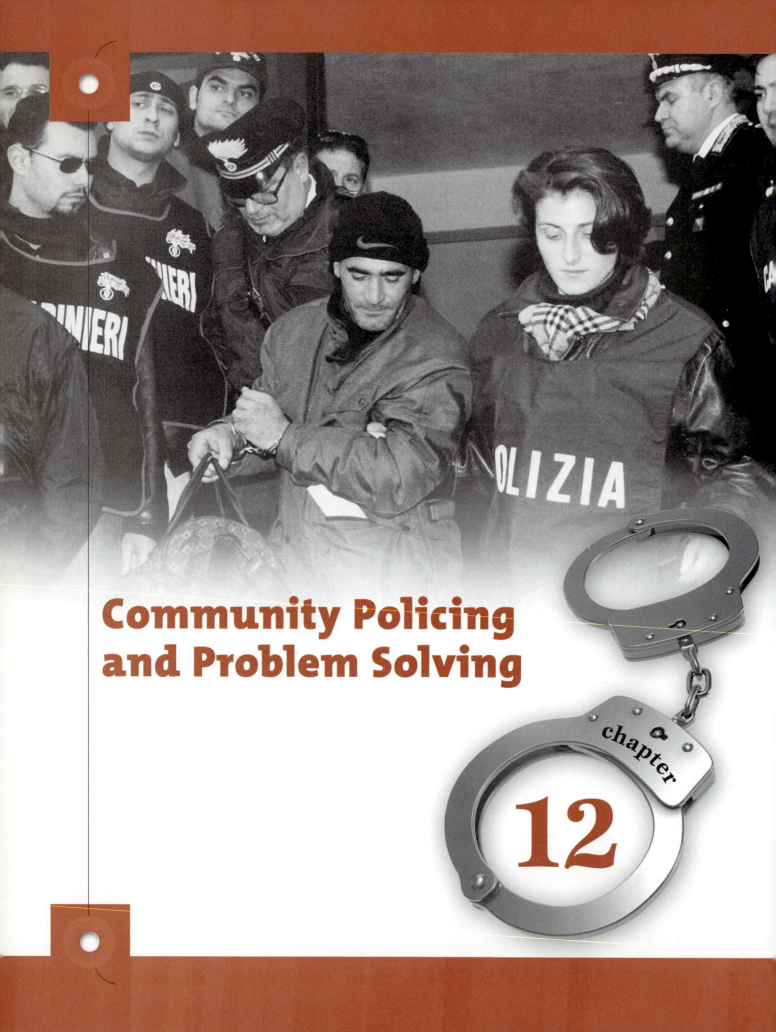

Community Policing and Problem Solving

chapter

12

Chapter Objectives

- Define *community*.

- Understand the theoretical underpinnings of community policing.

- Recognize the key components of community policing as well as their implications on the organization.

- Identify key operational barriers to implementing community policing in practice, as well as be able to articulate ways in which they can be overcome.

- Understand the problem-solving process and its practical relevance the post–September 11 law enforcement context.

- Understand the practical applications of criminological theory on modern law enforcement practice.

Our struggle showed that the law court is only one front in the campaign against violence and lawlessness. The other is culture. An image that occurred to me early in my own fight against the Mafia was of a cart with two wheels, one law enforcement and the other culture. If one wheel turned without the other, the cart would go in circles. If both turned together, the cart would go forward. So, at the same time as brave lawmen were dying in order to establish a rule of law, we were trying to rebuild our civic life (Orlando 2001, p. 7).

Leoluca Orlando,
former Mayor of Palermo, Sicily.

When we think about how law enforcement can respond to a threat as large and subversive as organized crime, many of us think of images direct from Hollywood. Indeed, there is a long history of films about the fight against organized crime, with characters such as the idealistic Eliot Ness of *The Untouchables* being among the most popular. The media is filled with such glamorized portrayals of law enforcement efforts to combat the Mafia, because it has all of the makings of action-packed, romantic entertainment that American audiences crave. These stories often have a kernel of truth (*The Untouchables* was, after all, based on the autobiographical accounts of the real-life Eliot Ness), and organized crime divisions across the country use myriad investigative techniques in their efforts against organized crime.

Few would claim that the community, too, can have an important role in anticrime and anticorruption efforts against an enemy as large as organized crime. However, the success of community policing strategies in Palermo, Sicily, once the "heartland of the Mafia," clearly shows the tremendous role that community participation can play in fighting crime and corruption. Beginning with the example of Palermo, Sicily, this chapter discusses the importance of police partnership with the community in achieving long-term crime reductions.

Hollywood films are rife with dramatic portrayals of law enforcement's efforts to combat organized crime, such as *The Untouchables*.

The important proactive role of the proper application of theory and best practice to law enforcement strategy also is highlighted.

Throughout the 1980s and early 1990s, there were more victims of organized crime violence in Palermo than there were victims of terror in such war-torn places as Palestine and Belfast, numbering into the thousands (Orlando 2001). Palermo's fallen included a general in charge of security forces, the chief of detectives, the chief of police, and two of the most famous magistrates in Europe. Beginning as a struggle for control between Gaetano Badalamenti and Stefano Bontate—the heads of rival organized crime networks of major Sicilian cities—and including new rivals, such as the Corleonisi faction, infighting soon escalated to such a level that it became known as the "Mafia War" (Orlando 2001). Indeed, so fierce was the fighting that many Mafiosi themselves considered the fighting extreme.

Existing as an institution in Sicily since the nineteenth century, the Mafia had come to permeate all aspects of civil society, including social, political, and cultural life. Over time, the established networks eventually began to take on the functions of government, collecting taxes, creating a complex organizational hierarchy, and developing its own groups of "enforcers" to ensure compliance with its demands. It was considered the right of the Mafia families to extort a tax (known as a *pizzo*) on all business activities within their territory, in addition to ensuring that employers hired selected Mafia dependents. The Mafia also served the role as mediator of conflicts, even returning stolen goods (for a fee) on occasion (Orlando 2001).

Former mayor of Palermo Leoluca Orlando notes that the Mafia was able to dominate Sicilian life in such a complete way in part because of its ability to shroud itself in mystique. Its members were portrayed as men of honor who were integral to the smooth functioning of society (Orlando 2001). This mythology allowed them to regard their jobs as a "call to duty" in much the same way as one might think of becoming a police officer or firefighter. As a subculture, Mafia

Known for a time as the "Walking Corpse" for his courageous stand against the Mafia in Sicily, former mayor of Palermo Leoluca Orlanda recognized that long-term, sustainable reductions in crime and corruption required the joint efforts of both the police and the community's cultural centers.

values were transmitted through a rule of secrecy embodied in the word *omerta*, or "silence before the law." So complete was this secrecy that the Mafia was virtually unheard of or openly discussed for many years. In fact, it was not until 1982, after over a hundred years of Mafia domination, that the Catholic hierarchy began to speak out against the "evil institution" on the island (NSIC 2000).

Because political and economic life had adjusted to the presence of the Mafia, law enforcement agencies were faced with a dual challenge in their efforts to control organized crime. In addition to traditional investigative and prosecutorial approaches, agencies such as the police first had to convince the public that members of the mafia were "criminal" (Orlando 2001). Following a particularly violent period in Mafia history, citizens finally began to raise their voices in protest. Eventually, a "Committee of the Sheets" sprung up in some of the worst Mafia-controlled areas, in which housewives hung sheets out of windows denouncing the presence and activities of the Mafia. Teachers began to teach schoolchildren about the negative impact of organized crime on society, and, in an effort to take back the communities that had been allowed to decline under Mafia domination and corruption, began an "Adopt a Monument" program in which children re-

searched decayed monuments throughout the City and took part in their restoration.

As a result of corruption and Mafia domination, Palermo had become a wasteland of sorts, with deteriorating public services, crumbling monuments, overcrowded schools, and high crime. However, the end product of the collaborative efforts of civic organizations (i.e., schools, businesses, and churches) and a revival in fair and effective law enforcement practices, walking the streets of Palermo just ten years later paints an entirely different picture:

> The sidewalks are packed—every day and every night. Underscoring the upbeat tempo, music blares from loudspeakers atop utility poles. Shoppers patronize storefronts that line the streets of a city that has never experienced such prosperity—even though the unemployment rate is 29 percent. (Wood 2001, p. 1)

Further testament to a sea change in such a short time, which has now been characterized as the "Sicilian Renaissance" (Godson 2000), is the fact that the municipal debt rating service, Moody's, upgraded Palermo's bond rating to Triple A, noting the tremendous political, legal, and economic reforms that have helped to restore investor faith in its integrity and potential for economic development.

The story of Palermo clearly demonstrates the importance of community participation in even the most difficult crime reduction efforts. Although many think of community policing as "soft on crime," public support is vitally important, and community involvement when implemented properly can actually have further-reaching, longer-term impact than more traditional attempts to control crime, such as sting operations, undercover operations, and large-scale arrests. Orlando's analogy of the "two wheels of the cart" needing to move forward at the same time in some sense captures the need for both law enforcement and community responsibility in tackling crime and disorder.

What Is Community?

As any resident of a large city knows without having to turn to crime data, crime varies by neighborhood. The correlation between communities and crime has long been recognized by criminologists, beginning with the early work of Shaw and McKay (1931) on the relationship between social disorganization and crime discussed in the next section.

Before we examine the relationship between communities and crime, or the principles of community policing, it is important to have a clear understanding of what is meant by the term **community**. Although this word brings to mind many different ideas and images, defining *community* has proven to be an enormous challenge to both law enforcement agencies trying to implement community policing policies and to researchers trying to evaluate the effectiveness of such policies.

Many police scholars have taken a broad view of the issue, preferring to define community as a population or area affected by some particular problem or a specific police strategy (Goldstein 1990). Although defining community based on the geographical boundaries or police deployment makes immediate sense to the individual police manager, administrator, or researcher, it clearly represents a significant oversimplification that could lead to major difficulties in strategy implementation or understanding why a particular approach to policing is or is not working. Community is clearly much more than a geographic boundary, because a very small area can encompass a diversity of values, cultures, and available resources or problems (Community Policing Consortium 1994).

For this reason, other authors have emphasized the need to view community as a shared sense of ownership and pride in a given place or environment (Miller and Hess 1998). For people living within a distinct geographical area to develop common beliefs and values as represented in such a conception of community, community members must have a common history and a shared process of socialization (Klockars 1991).

Although such distinct communities may exist in suburban areas where there is a significant likelihood that individuals will know and look out for each other, in most large urban centers it is common even for residents of the same housing complex not to know each other's names. It is also true that those areas that are the least well integrated are also most likely to have higher rates of crime, disorder, and poor relations with the police (Skogan 1996). Although such communities stand to benefit most from the practices of community policing (Skogan 1996), it is in these same neighborhoods that such policies are the most difficult to implement.

Sampson and Groves (1989) identify a number of key variables in their effort to define and understand the structure of local communities in the United Kingdom (see also Bursik and Grasmik 1993):

- **Socioeconomic composition**: percent college educated, percent in professional and managerial positions, percent with high incomes
- **Residential stability**: percentage of residents brought up in the area within a fifteen-minute walk from home
- **Racial/ethnic heterogeneity**: index based on percent of each racial/ethnic category

- **Local friendship relational networks**: average number of friends living within a fifteen-minute walk of the respondent's homes
- **Organizational participation**: percentage of residents who participated in meetings in the week before the interview
- **Supervisory capacity**: percentage of residents who reported that disorderly teenagers were a very common neighborhood problem.

On one level, supervisory capacity is a difficult, though essential, gauge of the degree of integration in an area, and thus a sense of community. This can range from direct intervention whereby residents know each other and actively question strangers and other residents about suspicious activities, to casual but active observation of neighborhood activities, to the complete avoidance of areas viewed as unsafe (Greenberg et al. 1982). Of course, community policing benefits from the active participation and monitoring behaviors of area residents—a large factor behind the creation of Neighborhood Watch programs throughout the country. However, over-vigilance of community members does have a downside, as is evident in some cases of racial profiling.

Harris's (2002) important work on the problem of racial profiling, *Profiles in Injustice*, is full of case examples of negative citizen encounters with law enforcement on the basis of race. As in the following example, in some cases citizen participation in the supervision of a community can itself involve elements of racial profiling. Police response is sometimes a reaction to citizen concerns or complaints.

The active engagement of community residents in citizen patrols can play an important role in sending the message that crime and disorder will not be tolerated in a neighborhood.

Suron Jacobs, a construction worker in his twenties who is African American, had a construction job as part of a crew in a nearly all-white suburban area outside of Toledo, Ohio. One day, Jacobs made arrangements to meet his brother on a corner near the construction site during his lunch break to exchange an apartment key. Unbeknownst to Jacobs, a resident who saw him waiting on the corner for his brother called 911 and reported him as a suspicious person. Responding to the call, a police officer drove by, stopped, and began to question Jacobs. What was he doing? Where was his brother, and how long had he been waiting? After a number of these questions, Jacobs became irritated. He refused to answer any more questions and began walking back to the construction site. Jacobs immediately learned the price of defying the police in a place where "he didn't belong"; the officer grabbed him, while another who arrived on the scene handcuffed him. . . . Though charges were eventually dropped, the police responses to the resident's 911 call told Jacobs everything he needed to know about his presence in a white area. (p. 104)

However, although such extreme situations are possible, community policing practices are actually said to minimize such situations due to a greater familiarity between the police and community.

Trojanowicz et al. (2002) provide a useful summary of the eight attributes of a community:

1. It has a particular geographic area or location.

2. It is a recognized legal entity.

3. Social interactions within it include a division of labor and a sense of interdependence.

4. It is composed of citizens with a shared culture, interest, outlook, or perspective.

5. It possesses a moral dimension where values are transmitted.

6. Social interactions within it collectively shape its character.

7. It is defined by the processes of inclusion and exclusion.

8. Its citizens possess a shared sentiment, a sense of belonging, and interdependence.

Police departments will likely have a head start in implementing community policing as a philosophy in an area that meets each of these criteria. However, many communities truly in need of the potential benefits of the model are themselves characterized by crime, disorder, and mistrust of the police, making it very difficult to successfully implement community policing.

Theoretical Underpinnings of Community Policing

Communities can be distinguished by their degree of organization. Geographical areas that are said to be more integrated tend to have the sense of **community ownership** evidenced by self-policing and informal surveillance activities; upkeep of homes, streets, and businesses; and participation in local activities.

In what has now become a classic article in police scholarship, Wilson and Kelling (1982) used the analogy of a broken window to describe the relationship between disorder and crime. One broken window left unrepaired shows others that no one cares about the property. Consequently, others are less likely to respect the property. Over time, more and more of the windows are broken, forcing those in the area who do care about their property to leave. In the words of Kelling and Wilson (1982):

> A stable neighborhood of families who care for their homes, mind each other's children, and confidently frown on unwanted intruders can change, in a few years or even a few months, to an inhospitable and frightening jungle. A piece of property is abandoned, weeds grow up, a window is smashed. Adults stop scolding rowdy children; the children, emboldened, become more rowdy. Families move out, unattached adults move in. Teenagers gather in front of the corner store. The merchant asks them to move; they refuse. Fights occur. Litter accumulates. People start drinking in front of the grocers; in time, an inebriate slumps to the sidewalk and is allowed to sleep it off. (p. 32)

Even though the above activities can be characterized as low-level, nonserious offenses, more serious criminals may be attracted to the area by its minimal self-policing. According to Wilson and Kelling, there is a direct correlation between residents withdrawing from the streets, getting to know less and less of each other, and an increase in crime in an area. The **broken windows theory** suggests that for policing to have a lasting effect on serious crime in a neighborhood, lower-level quality-of-life offenses need to be addressed to restore a sense of community in an area.

Writing in a similar vein, Skogan (1996) describes what he refers to as a **contagion proposition**, whereby certain types of disorders generate more disorder unless they are quickly stamped out. Current levels of disorder thus produce future levels of disorder. Putting this theory to the test, Skogan found that perceived crime problems, fear of crime, and actual victimization were all linked to the extent of social and physical disorder in an area. He also found that disorder was linked to residential satisfaction and commitment, two factors that are indicative of the overall stability of the housing market. As disorder increased, residents were more likely to seek opportunities to leave.

The case example of Palermo, Sicily, appears to provide considerable support for the broken windows theory. As organized crime gradually took control of the city through corruption and violence increased, the city (and certain neighborhoods in particular) began to decline. However, once the residents finally decided that they had had enough and embarked on a campaign of protest and community reclamation, a transformation began to take place that would eventually free Palermo from Mafia domination. In this case, citizen participation, community cooperation, and fair and effective law enforcement eventually brought about the demise of the Mafia in the city.

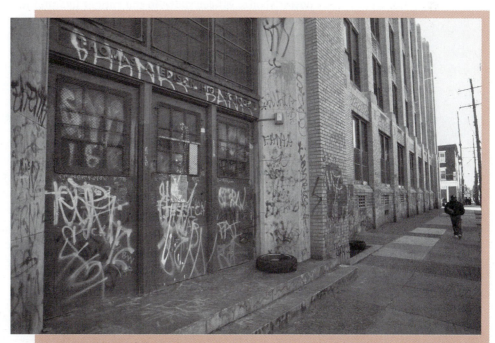

Even small levels of disorder in a community can lead to a spiral of decay over time that might eventually result in high levels of crime.

Although the idea that communities need to participate in the fight against crime and disorder is at the heart of most theories of community policing, this new approach to policy sprang as much from the failure of the professional model to halt rising crime rates during the 1960s and 1970s. Efforts to encourage impartiality and make law enforcement agencies more professional in the Reform Era led to serious rifts between the police and the community (particularly minority citizens) that would reach peak during the riots of the 1960s and 1970s. Although placing patrol predominately behind the wheel of a patrol car may have increased the mobility of police, it failed to reduce crime, or even fear of crime (as was evidenced in the Kansas City Patrol Experiment) (Kelling et al. 1974). Other challenges to the traditional model came from the Rand Study of Investigations, which revealed the reliance of detectives and other officers on information from citizens during preliminary investigations (Greenwood et al. 1977). However, perhaps the most significant push for change came from the police and public realization that despite a renewed focus on crime control, crime continued to rise even though technology and professionalization had transformed the typical police department.

Around the same time, studies of foot patrols in Newark, New Jersey (Police Foundation 1981), and Flint, Michigan (Trojanowicz 1982), began to reveal that the police were more likely to develop a positive attitude toward the community if they spent time on foot patrol and residents were more likely to be satisfied with police services. In accordance with the broken windows theory, the police began to encourage community residents to take a more active role in restoring and revitalizing their communities (Community Policing Consortium 1994).

As a result of these changes, a **public health model** of policing began to emerge, which stood in contrast to the strict emphasis on crime control of the past:

> The doctor (police officer) talks to the patient (community) to identify a problem. Sometimes the solution lies solely with the patient (community), for example, a change of diet (the owner agrees to remove an eyesore or abandoned automobile). Sometimes it calls for the doctor (police officer) and patient (community) to work together, i.e. a change of diet plus medication (organizing the community to shut down a blight establishment). Sometimes only the doctor (police) alone can solve the problem, i.e. surgery (heavy suppression). Sometimes we have to accept the fact that the problem simply cannot be solved, e.g. terminal illness (poverty). (Braiden 1992, p. 21)

The public health perspective encourages law enforcement agencies to look at crime from a preventive standpoint. Just as people are responsible for their own health (e.g., through diet and exercise), communities can take ownership of their neighborhoods and reject disorder and criminality. For example, citizens can become involved in organizing citizen patrols, reporting crime to the police, developing community clean-up activities, as well as numerous other possibilities. A need to focus on the underlying causes of a problem, rather than simply responding to the symptoms, is another central pillar of the public health model.

Community Partnerships and Problem Solving

At the core of community policing strategy is the establishment of mutually beneficial ties between the community and the police, in which both become cooperative partners in crime prevention and reduction. According to the Community Policing Consortium (1994), "the growing trend within communities to participate in the fight against crime and disorder has paralleled a growing recognition by police that traditional crime-fighting tactics alone have a limited impact on controlling crime. Community policing is the synthesis of these two movements" (p. 34).

Although the term *community policing* has been widely used within law enforcement circles over the last twenty years, there has been a great deal of confusion as to what it actually means. As a result of this lack of consensus between practitioners and those in academic circles, the term *community policing* has come to mean many different things (Rosenbaum 1989). Some departments have simply molded the term to encompass more traditional law enforcement strategies, whereas others have taken it to include community relations activities (Bayley 1988). For example, in their in-service training for law enforcement, entitled the *Fundamentals of Community Policing*, the New York State Regional Community Policing Institute (NYSRCPI) proposes its own definition and rejects many of the "myths" of community policing, as summarized in Table 12.1.

Community policing is based on two core beliefs that emerge from a broader perspective than that found in traditional law enforcement efforts: community partnership and problem solving (Community Policing Consortium 1994). Once one recognizes that the police cannot combat crime alone, particularly many quality-of-life concerns, it becomes clear that partnerships with outside organizations must become an important part of policing (community partnership). Partnership does not simply refer to the community residents and organizations becoming the "eyes and ears" of the police, although increasing citizen trust in coming forward to the police is certainly an important first step.

TABLE 12.1

Community Policing: Myth versus Reality

What It Is Not	Reality
It is not a technique or program.	Involves a customer-focus philosophy to provide high-quality services.
It is not a limited or specialized style of policing.	It is full-service policing that provides attention to the old line of business (traditional, call-driven responses) plus proactive prevention. It is a combination of aggressive policing with community-based orientation known as "integrated patrol."
It is not foot patrol or bicycle patrol.	It involves an officer becoming knowledgeable about the area and its businesses/residents. It incorporates problem-solving approaches ranging from working with organized neighborhood associations to making referrals to other community resource services.
It is not soft on crime.	Traditional law enforcement duties continue. Other responsibilities are "in addition to" and not a "substitute for."
It is not a specialized unit.	Each member of the agency needs to be involved, trained, and committed. It is too often relegated to a specific group of officers.

Source: Reprinted by permission of Launcelott Smith.

According to New York State Regional Community Policing Institute (NYS-RCPI) (1999), **partnership** involves several important elements:

- Working together on a common problem
- Identifying common goals
- Steady and consistent communication and information sharing
- Having a shared perception of problems and benchmarks for when problems are solved
- All parties contributing work toward accomplishing shared goals and objectives or solving the problem

Where partnership is really present, the police, residents, and other service agencies are involved in all phases of planning problem resolution (Peak and Glensor 1999). Moreover, a sense of **empowerment** must also be facilitated in which all parties feel they have equal input into the decisions and commitment of needed resources (Eck and Spelman 1987). Given the host of underlying causes of community problems, the police would not be able to deal with them effectively in the absence of such committed partnerships. Depending on the problem being addressed, police can partner with many different community organizations, such as the following:

- Merchant associations
- Neighborhood and civic groups
- Youth-serving agencies
- Tenant associations

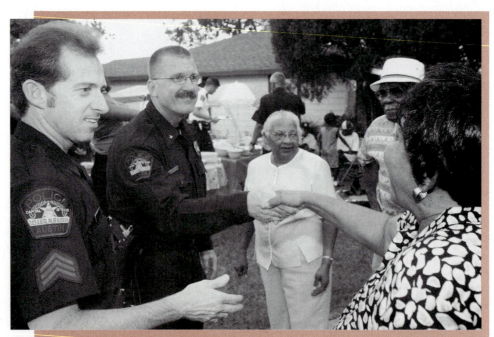

The CAPS community policing model in Chicago has institutionalized the problem-solving process by requiring regular beat officer attendance at community problem-solving meetings.

- Block associations

- Community development corporations

At its most basic, **problem solving** involves the collaborative identification of problems and their underlying causes, rather than simply responding to incidents. In this sense, community policing moves departments beyond the **reactive** stance of waiting for calls for service or citizen complaints to a more **proactive** mode, addressing problems before they occur and attacking the underlying causes of crime.

Eck and Spellman (1987) offer a useful visual representation of the important differences between the reactive, incident-driven focus of traditional policing and the proactive model encompassed within community policing. Incident-driven policing is depicted in Figure 12.1. Just as a flu might be manifested by various disturbing or uncomfortable symptoms, such as a runny nose, fever, headaches, and so on, community problems also have distinctive conditions manifested as incidents that might reflect the nature of the underlying problem.

For example, a late-night gathering of youths in front of a bowling alley could result in repeated calls to the police to deal with unruly behavior and disperse the group. However, if the police were to examine the issue more closely, in an effort to identify underlying conditions and consult with local residents and businesses, they might discover that the bowling alley offers late-night specials that attract the youths, who are subsequently left to walk home due to the lack of public transport. Instead of just continually reacting to incidents, as a

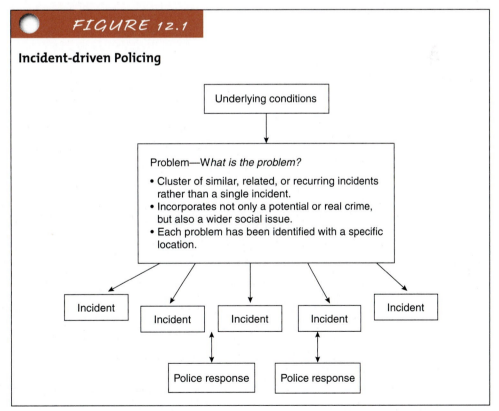

FIGURE 12.1

Incident-driven Policing

Underlying conditions

Problem—*What is the problem?*
- Cluster of similar, related, or recurring incidents rather than a single incident.
- Incorporates not only a potential or real crime, but also a wider social issue.
- Each problem has been identified with a specific location.

Incident   Incident   Incident   Incident   Incident

Police response   Police response

Source: Modified from J. Eck and W. Spelman. 1987. *Problem Solving: Problem-Oriented Policing in Newport News:* Washington, DC: National Institute of Justice.

result of collaboration the police and business leaders may be able to choose an alternative approach, such as arranging for adequate public transportation on those nights with "late night specials," thus reducing the likelihood of future disturbances or incidents. Without adequately addressing the underlying conditions of a problem, incidents will continue to occur. Although reactive police response is required to alleviate the *immediate* issues, it can only be a temporary response to larger, more intractable problems.

Figure 12.2 is based on Eck and Spelman's (1987) summary of the benefits offered by police problem solving. By recognizing that there is a problem, rather than simply a series of unrelated incidents, police can begin to analyze a situation and begin to identify underlying conditions and causes that might be contributing to the problem. In standard policing terminology, **problems** refer to two or more incidents that are capable of causing harm in which there is an expectation that the police and community can do something about it (National Strategy Information Center 2000). Generally, there is no need to go through a detailed problem-solving process in the case of a single incident that is unlikely to be repeated. In such circumstances, a quick police response may be all that is required. However, when there is a series of harmful and related incidents, the only way to ultimately prevent future occurrences is to identify and address the underlying conditions. The recognition that crime problems can be affected

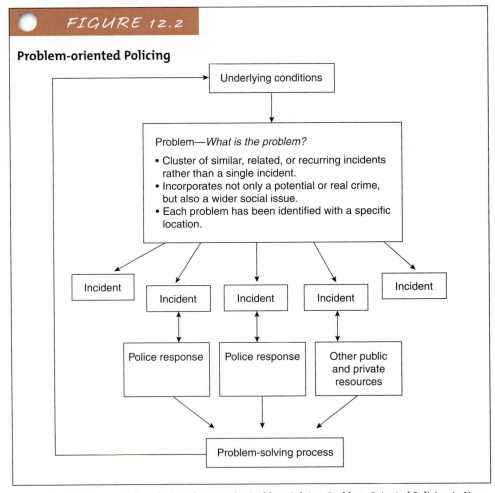

FIGURE 12.2

Problem-oriented Policing

Underlying conditions

Problem—*What is the problem?*

• Cluster of similar, related, or recurring incidents rather than a single incident.
• Incorporates not only a potential or real crime, but also a wider social issue.
• Each problem has been identified with a specific location.

Incident   Incident   Incident   Incident   Incident

Police response   Police response   Other public and private resources

Problem-solving process

Source: Modified from J. Eck and W. Spelman. 1987. *Problem Solving: Problem-Oriented Policing in Newport News:* Washington, DC: National Institute of Justice.

by altering certain precipitating factors is referred to as **crime prevention through environmental design (CPTED)**; it is a direct outgrowth of the problem-oriented policing model (Crowe 2000).

By partnering with other public and private resources, the police also greatly increase the likelihood of success and the chance of finding a permanent solution to a given problem. It is important to recognize that in addition to collaboration, the police and the community must have sufficient resources to attack the identified causes of a problem. No matter how committed and creative a police department and its partners may be to resolving poverty, for example, rarely do they have the means to remedy it. However, while they might not be able to eliminate poverty as a cause of crime, by providing offenders on probation with skills training and job placement schemes, the police and the community may be able to weaken the economic incentive to re-offend.

Networking: Coordination and Collaboration

Collaborative problem-solving through partnership requires a great deal more commitment from both the police and its partners than simply hosting joint meetings or sharing information. Community relations activities introduced by police departments throughout the 1970s and 1980s were important first steps toward building the foundations for community policing, but in many cases these activities amounted to little more than public relations for the department. Examples of community relations activities include citizen academies, neighborhood newsletters, spouse academies, or police athletic leagues (Gaines et al. 2003).

The police must develop positive relationships with the community in order to successfully marshal public support for community policing. In some communities, particularly where aggressive policing strategies have not been well received by residents, the level of trust required as a precondition for such relationships will be absent. Moreover, the path to building relationships is often gradual, requiring a tremendous amount of patience and commitment from both the police and their intended partners. A Department of Justice (1994) monograph depicts the partnership building process as cyclical in nature: trust facilitates increased community contact, which in turn leads to better communication, a key ingredient for increased trust, and so on (see Figure 12.3).

Source: U. S. Department of Justice (1994).

Linkages in Law Enforcement

Collaboration with Courts— Community Prosecution

Prosecutors around the country also are seeing their role as extending beyond the effective and efficient handling of cases. In redefining their methods and their mission with respect to crime, a new approach, known as **community prosecution**, has emerged. According to this approach, prosecutors work with citizens and police to identify high-priority cases and offenders, recognizing that the goal of prosecution should be to eliminate or manage problems rather than simply prosecute cases (Coles and Kelling 1999). In this sense, community prosecution efforts seek to partner with other agencies and resources in the community, including law enforcement, making it a useful complement to community policing strategies.

By focusing on problem reduction or elimination, prosecution partnerships with the police can extend into the use of civil remedies such as nuisance abatement for gang offenders, restraining orders to keep persistent offenders out of certain neighborhoods, trespass statute prosecutions, and health and safety code enforcement (Coles and Kelling 1999).

As an example of a successful community prosecution program, the Buffalo, New York, Weed and Seed initiative created a fifteen-agency Save Our Streets Task Force, which included the Narcotics Division of the Buffalo Police Department, the district attorney's office, probation services, the department of social services, parole services, the U.S. Marshals, and the U.S. Attorney's Office to target houses suspected of drug use and harbor-

ing criminal activity (Grant 1999). Through a creative application of federal asset forfeiture laws, each agency on the task force is responsible for the enforcement of specific ordinance violations within their jurisdictions, holding tenants and owners accountable. In the case of continued problems, the task force seeks prosecution to reclaim the property and place it back into more productive community use, such as through the creation of community gardens or parks.

Another such partnership exists in Washington, D.C., where the Metropolitan Police of the District of Columbia (MPDC) partners with the U.S. Attorney's Office and other private and public agencies to enhance the prosecutorial function (Metropolitan Police District of Columbia n.d.). As a part of their role within this partnership, the Community Prosecution Section of the U.S. Attorney's Office geographically assigns attorneys to assist the police in criminal investigations, the review of arrest warrants, and presentation of arrested cases in court. A major outcome of this partnership has been the increased flow of information between the community, the MPDC, and the U.S. Attorney's Office.

QUESTIONS

1. For what type of crime problems would community prosecution models be most relevant?

2. What are some potential negative effects of community prosecution?

3. What role do the police play in the success of the Drug Court model?

As a mutual trust is developed, community policing can also help to foster increased accountability, with all partners understanding and recognizing their specific roles and tasks that emerge out of the problem-solving process (Peak and Glensor 1999). By identifying the multiple causes of specific problems, it becomes clear to all parties not only that the police cannot be held responsible for remedying all problems, but also that their own agencies can play an essential role in problem resolution.

Linkages *in Law Enforcement*

Collaboration with Corrections—Community Corrections

Over the last several years, the police and correctional agencies have also begun to form mutually beneficial partnerships, based primarily on the goal of enhancing community safety. The push toward establishing such partnerships is a direct response to the community policing movement's recognition of the need to make better use of community resources in order to achieve long-term reductions in crime and disorder.

The National Institute of Justice (NIJ) recently funded a comprehensive study of police–corrections partnerships in the interest of helping administrators and policy makers replicate such models in their jurisdictions. Following an intensive case study review of fourteen police–corrections partnerships across the country, the authors categorized the partnerships into five implementation categories, which are detailed below (Parent and Snyder 1999).

Enhanced-Supervision Partnerships

The most common form of partnerships, enhanced-supervision partnerships, seek to increase the odds of detecting offender violations of the conditions of their probation or parole by conducting joint supervision activities. Random home visits involving police, probation, and parole is a common means of increasing supervision, made famous by the Boston's Operation Night Light successes. Following Night Light and other related projects, homicides decreased form a high of 152 in 1990 to 23 in the first eight months of 1998 (OJJDP 2000). Increased citywide collaborations in response to gang violence were also outcomes of the Boston strategy (OJJDP 2000). An additional benefit of increased supervision is a heightened awareness of offender needs/risks on the part of correctional agencies, allowing them to better match offenders with needed social services.

Fugitive-Apprehension Units

With this model, police and corrections jointly seek to locate and apprehend offenders who have absconded from probation or parole supervision.

Information-Sharing Partnerships

With this model, procedures are implemented that enhance the exchange of information. Formal processes such as shared databases and regular meetings to discuss correctional populations under community supervision within geographic boundaries are examples of partnerships in this category. Sex offender registries and gang intelligence databases are examples of resources utilized in this type of partnership.

Specialized-Enforcement Partnerships

Working together with relevant community agencies, specialized-enforcement partnerships involve collaborative problem-solving efforts related to the individual concerns of particular communities.

Interagency Problem-Solving Partnerships

Both police and corrections identify mutual problems in their jurisdiction and then together prioritize strategy selection and implementation in a mutually beneficial manner.

Police–corrections partnerships produce numerous benefits for the communities in which they are implemented, providing both agencies with more creative means to solve problems than would be the available if each agency acted on its own. For example, whereas a police officer may have no power to stop a gang member from associating with other gang members, a probation officer could arrest the individual and begin revocation hearings for the violation of the conditions of probation (Parent and Snyder 1999). In Baton Rouge,

(continues)

Louisiana, a specialized detail of police officers were familiarized with the members of a hard-core group of probationers and provided with a list of names and photos to take with them when they are out on patrol. If they saw a probationer out on the streets in violation of his or her curfew, the police officer could pass the violation information on to the respective probation officer, thus dramatically increasing the level of available supervision (Sheppard et al. 2000). Other benefits have included an increased ability of police departments to investigate crimes by probationers/parolees, as well as increased information for correctional authorities about the associations of the offenders in their charge provided by the specialized knowledge and contacts offered by the police (Parent and Snyder 1999).

However, police–corrections partnerships are not without risk. For example, there can be a temptation to circumvent many of the constraints of the Fourth Amendment by creatively utilizing the distinct role of the parole or probation officer. Although the police may have reason to suspect that an offender's home might contain evidence of a crime, they may not have sufficient probable cause to obtain the necessary search warrant; however, by having the probation officer search the residence (which is within their authority) and report this information to the police, Fourth Amendment restrictions can be avoided (Parent and Snyder 1999).

QUESTIONS

1. For what types of crime problems do you feel that police–corrections partnerships are most beneficial?

2. What are some potential negative effects of police–corrections partnerships?

3. How can these models be merged with the community prosecution approach to law enforcement?

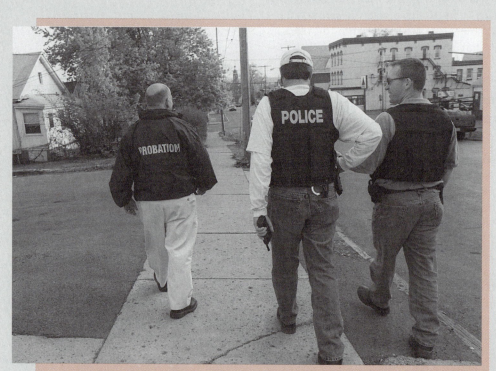

Police–probation partnerships have helped the criminal justice system more effectively monitor offenders without sacrificing the public safety interests of probation officers. These partnerships have also increased information sharing between police and probation in the jurisdictions in which they are implemented.

Community-Oriented versus Problem-Oriented Policing

The term *problem-oriented policing* is generally attributed to the work of Herman Goldstein, who outlined the basic principles of this approach in his book *Policing a Free Society* (1977) and carried it through to his more recent title, *Problem-Oriented Policing* (1990), which is one of the most often cited explanations of the problem-oriented process to date. Many people are initially confused with the distinctions between *community-oriented policing* and *problem-oriented policing*. We have said that the two core components of community policing are partnership and problem solving, so how is it that we are now making a distinction between community-oriented policing (COP) and problem-oriented policing (POP)?

Whereas **community-oriented policing** is meant to be the overriding philosophy guiding departmental change, problem-oriented policing is often viewed as one of the principal means of putting this philosophy into practice (Peak and Glensor 1999). **Problem-oriented policing** involves proactive policing strategies and focuses on the identification of underlying causes of problems and the selection of solutions or remedies to prevent a problem from reoccurring in the future (Goldstein 1990). Problem-oriented policing involves getting police officers and departments to "think outside of the box," recognizing connections across like incidents that they may not have been able to see when responding to a seemingly random incident from an incident-based, reactive perspective.

The SARA Model

In focusing on the resolution of the underlying causes of problems, problem-oriented policing relies on the process of problem solving. Once again, *problem solving* involves the process of moving toward a goal when the path to that goal is uncertain. Eck and Spelman (1987) have developed an acronym for the problem-solving process to facilitate teaching these skills to both law enforcement practitioners and community residents. They coined the term **SARA**, which stands for the four separate components of the problem-solving process: scanning, analysis, response, and assessment. Although usually presented in a linear fashion, Figure 12.4 shows it as a cyclical pattern to provide a more meaningful description of the continuous nature of the problem-solving process.

Scanning involves the clustering of incidents into meaningful problem units. This stage is the recognition that a series of incidents are in fact connected and could be alleviated through common responses. In order to understand the underlying causes leading to the problem, a meaningful **analysis** is then conducted. This stage is often considered the heart of the problem-solving model, because mistakes made here can lead to inappropriate responses or strategies. At this stage, many practitioners use a conceptual framework called the **crime triangle** (provided in Figure 12.5). The crime triangle begins with three known facts derived from studies such as the **Serious Habitual Offender Criminal Apprehension Program (SHOCAP)**,

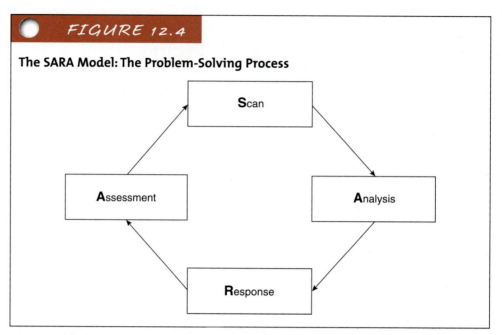

FIGURE 12.4

The SARA Model: The Problem-Solving Process

Source: Modified from J. Eck and W. Spelman. 1987. *Problem Solving: Problem-Oriented Policing in Newport News.* Washington, DC: National Institute of Justice.

developed by the Office of Juvenile Justice and Delinquency Prevention (OJJDP 1995):

1. Ten percent of offenders account for 55 percent of all crimes.

2. Ten percent of victims account for 42 percent of all victimization.

3. Ten percent of all locations account for 60 percent of the call load to the police.

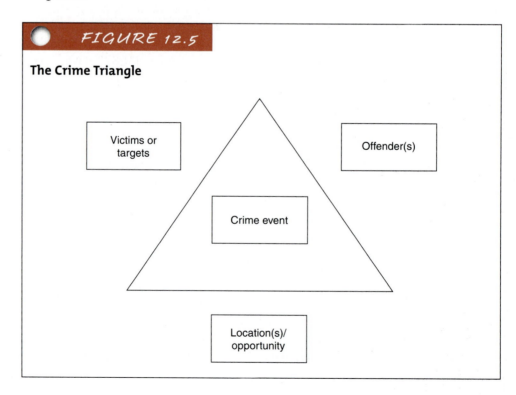

FIGURE 12.5

The Crime Triangle

Thus, by homing in on the specific problem areas, offenders, and victims, police departments and communities can work to identify the true underlying causes of a given problem and be better poised to achieve a successful resolution.

Once a comprehensive analysis has been completed, a strategy (**response**) can be selected based on what is actually causing the problem. However, it is during **assessment** that the community policing practitioner evaluates whether the implemented response actually works. For example, after implementation the community policing practitioner may better understand the problem and recognize the need to reconsider the initial analysis. If so, the practitioner may then have to redesign the current strategy or even select a new approach altogether. In some cases, the practitioner may even come to the conclusion that the nature of the problem was misidentified.

Focusing on Problem Locations

As Pease (1998) has observed, much of the focus on the role of location originated with a number of pioneering studies in the United Kingdom on the phenomenon of **repeat victimization** in crimes ranging from burglary to domestic violence to racial violence. The most significant finding to come from these studies was that repeat victimization may be preventable, especially if the problem-solving process focuses analysis and strategy on repeat locations, victims, and offenders. Moreover, because some locations are responsible for significant amounts of crime, addressing them can also lead to significant decreases in overall crime rates (Davis and Taylor 1997).

These studies also confirmed the importance of **crime analysis**, which involves the statistical review of incident data, calls for service, and so on, to isolate trends and to focus strategy. Chapter 13 will detail advances in technology that have significantly aided proactive policing strategy. When attempting to address a problem such as gun violence within a city (**prevalence** refers to the overall incidence of a problem in a geographical area), the first stage is to identify the particular neighborhood within the city (**target area**) in which the problem is occurring so that the police and community can get a better idea of the underlying conditions that could inform a possible strategy. Focusing analysis even further to specific blocks and locations (**hot spots**) can also be important in gaining an appreciation of the kinds of problem dynamics that can inform strategy.

Figure 12.6 presents the process of location analysis. Once a target area or hot spot is identified, problem solvers can identify possible contextual conditions or those target populations that are responsible for the problem, allowing strategy to be developed, selected, and tailored accordingly.

Management Implications of Community Policing

Even in the most innovative and energetic police departments, implementing community policing policies has proven to be difficult. A major reason for this has been the confusion over what community policing actually is, and the fact that implementation can cause strain or resentment among both line officers and command staff (Gaines et al. 2003). In an effort to address these problems,

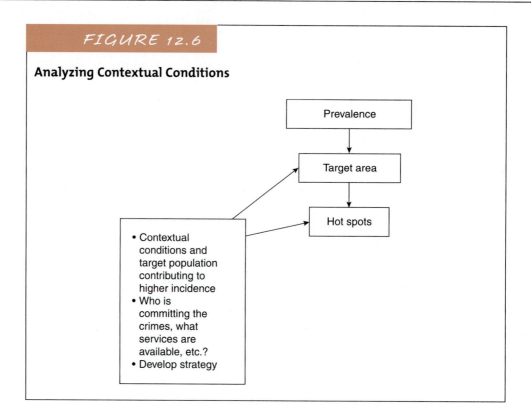

FIGURE 12.6

Analyzing Contextual Conditions

Cordner (1999) provides a comprehensive system involving three important dimensions—philosophical, strategic, and programmatic—that are each necessary in order to adequately implement community policing.

The Philosophical Dimension

In many departments, it is commonly believed that community policing necessarily requires the creation of specialized units whose function it is to act as liaisons with the community, attend meetings, and identify community concerns. However, community policing requires a more fundamental philosophical transformation in policy practices—from a reactive crime-fighting mentality toward a broader approach based on proactive problem-solving and resource deployment (Goldstein 1990). When only a small portion of departmental resources are devoted to community policing, resentment toward the "specialized" group of officers can develop. Moreover, if the majority of officers function within a more traditional model of policing, there will be far less exposure to the benefits of the model within the community. Most of the officers with whom the community continues to interact will remain less committed to incorporating citizen input beyond the most basic of reporting functions. As a result, efforts at implementing community policing policies must begin with a reorientation of officer attitudes and police culture.

The Strategic Dimension

Shifting the focus of policing from responding to incidents to proactive crime prevention has important strategic implications, may of which involve **structural changes**. A key ingredient of successful community policing requires that officers become familiar with the residents and businesses in the area to which they have been assigned and to their particular concerns and problems. As such, an assigned shift structure (based on geographical areas as well as time of day) becomes most desirable. However, even more than this, police operational units must make combined use of foot patrols, directed patrols, and citizen surveys in order to ensure they are able to target the crime and disorder issues judged to be of greatest concern by both the police and community (Gaines et al. 2003).

Additionally, it can be argued that proactive decision making requires that individual patrol officers have increased discretion to respond to problems creatively and quickly, without having to rely on receiving detailed directions through a complex chain of command. As a result, many practitioners argue for **decentralization**, in which the designation of authority and responsibility is widened so as to allow for more independent, localized decision making on the part of the line officers. Similarly, **flattening** the organizational structure reduces the number of hierarchical levels, eliminating unneeded bureaucracy that could stand in the way of proactive policing. Both of these concepts were introduced in Chapter 6.

Pooling officers into **teams** and decreasing the number of specialized units (**despecialization**) also can be compatible with the objectives of community policing. Having officers from patrol, traffic, and the detective divisions working together as a unit can ensure that linkage blindness is minimized and needed resources are brought to bear on a problem. Officers operating under a departmental philosophy of community policing are required to "think outside the box," stay on top of area problems, and constantly interact with residents, businesses, and other agencies. Too much specialization can hamper this process and encourage officers to think that certain issues are "not their concern," even though problems in an area may be interconnected and symptomatic of some of the same underlying issues.

The failed attempts of team policing models in the 1970s suggest the need for police managers to plan ahead before implementing community policing (Walker 1992). Although many of the elements currently touted as essential to community policing have their origins in the **team policing** model (assigned shift structures, increased officer discretion, team management, despecialization), this model proved to be unsustainable, because most of the jurisdictions in which it was piloted failed to first gain the support of middle management within the notoriously hierarchical and militaristic police structure. Consequently, when middle managers began to feel threatened by the increased responsibilities granted to line officers and feared a reduction in their own roles within the department efforts were made to sabotage the viability of the model.

Under community policing, management is based on a **participatory management model**, in which line officers are encouraged to be creative and resolve problems, rather than simply following directives. More freedom is given to officers to interact with the community and work as partners with relevant stakeholders to resolve crime and quality-of-life concerns. However, increased discretion can bring with it certain risks and dangers. Accountability always remains a concern, particularly in light of the corruption that characterized the Political Era of policing. Thus, despite the concern of middle managers over moves toward team policing, such a shift does not necessarily lead to a reduction in their importance within the policing organization. Strong middle managers are needed transmit skills and to provide experience with proactive strategy development. Furthermore, although officers may not be judged solely on arrest quotas and response time, new performance measures will need to be developed that better correlate with the changing expectations of the new model—measures that middle management will be called upon to devise and monitor.

The Programmatic Dimension

The **programmatic dimension** of community policing involves "nuts and bolts" activities, such as problem solving and community mobilization activities. Tied directly into the strategic dimension, programmatic activities need to have a clear, long-term plan for departmental change in mind. Innovative police managers need to think long term with respect to piloting new approaches that will gradually introduce and change everyday policing practices and outlooks in a department. In response to federal youth firearms prevention funding, a former chief of the Bridgeport Police Department in Connecticut sought to instill his officers with proactive problem-solving experience. Although the central objectives of that initiative did not directly target community policing practices, the chief saw the federal money as an opportunity to infuse the department with the concepts of community policing and problem solving by instituting a rotating overtime structure that allowed a significant number of officers to participate in firearms suppression details that would offer the needed exposure and resources to engage in problem solving around firearms violence in the hot spots of the city (Grant and Jacobs 1997). Rather than simply having a small group of officers gaining this specialized knowledge, he had these officers drawn from regular patrol, ensuring that they would return to their regular tours and transmit these new skills to other officers. Moreover, this strategy was just one of numerous complementary pilot initiatives implemented by the chief over a period of years.

Barriers to Implementing Community Policing

Internal departmental resistance to community policing can be overcome through the careful long-term planning efforts of police managers. Techniques that can help to move departments toward a department-wide philosophy and practice of community policing include involving line officer and middle management input into the early planning process and initiating implementation with multiple pilot projects (Sadd and Grine 1996). However, resource demands often lead departments to give community policing a special unit status capable of producing interdepartmental rivalry, defeating any momentum toward true community policing implementation.

In areas where there is a history of mistrust between the community and the police, the requisite **community mobilization** required for partnership can be daunting. Departments must also be aware of residents' own fear of retaliation from area drug dealers as a barrier to participation. Rather than becoming overwhelmed by the need to reach the entire "community," research suggests that police departments wishing to move toward community policing should first target the "critical mass" in a community most likely to engage in civic activities promoting public safety (Correia 2000). This, in combination with collaborations with other city agencies, can slowly build a sense of trust in the department's commitment to change.

The Relationship Between Causes of Crime and Strategy

The community policing movement began with the realization that the police alone could not be expected to bring about long-term reductions in the crime rate. Given the many causes of crime empirically identified throughout the criminological literature, it is important for proactive policing strategy to begin with a **needs assessment** to identify the most likely sources of any local problem. No two communities are the same or have the same crime-producing conditions.

Implications of Criminology Theory for Law Enforcement Practice

A needs assessment is a comprehensive review of the factors underlying a given problem based on multiple data sources. Once community needs have been identified, additional partnering agencies can be selected based on the varying levels of expertise each has in dealing with the factors at hand, as well as the potential resources available to remedy the problem.

Predictor variables found to be associated with delinquent or criminal activity are termed **risk factors** (Hawkins et al. 1995). Hawkins et al. (2000), in their review of the major long-term studies on violence predictors, converted the strength of correlations between risk factors and later violence into odds ratios, highlighting the practical applications of the resiliency-theory literature. Odds ratios "express the degree of increased risk for violence associated with the presence of a risk factor in a population" (Hawkins et al. 2000, p. 2). For example, an odds ratio of 3.0 refers to a tripling of risk due to the presence of a particular risk factor.

The multitude of risk factors can be categorized across five domains: individual, family, school, peer-related, and community/neighborhood factors, as summarized in the following list (Hawkins et al. 2000, p. 2):

Individual Factors

- Pregnancy and obesity complications
- Low resting heart rate
- Internalizing disorders
- Hyperactivity, concentration problems, restlessness, and risk taking
- Aggressiveness
- Early initiation of violent behavior
- Involvement in other forms of antisocial behavior
- Beliefs and attitudes favorable to deviant or antisocial behavior

Family Factors

- Parental criminality
- Child maltreatment
- Poor family management practices

- Low levels of parental involvement
- Parental attitudes favorable to substance use and violence
- Parent–child separation

School Factors

- Academic failure
- Low bonding to school
- Truancy and dropping out of school
- Frequent school transitions

Peer-related Factors

- Delinquent siblings
- Delinquent peers
- Gang membership

Community and Neighborhood Factors

- Poverty
- Community disorganization
- Availability of drugs and firearms
- Neighborhood adults involved in crime
- Exposure to violence and racial prejudice

Several studies (e.g., McKnight and Loper 2002; Rutter 1987; Tiet and Huizinga 2000) provide empirical support for the relationship between these risk factors and violence or other criminal activity, a discussion of which is beyond the scope of this text. Representing the connections across problem behaviors, these risk factors can also play a predictive role in behaviors such as substance abuse and teen pregnancy (Hawkins et al. 1992).

The logic of **resiliency theory** is that the larger the number of risk factors influencing an individual at any given moment, the greater the likelihood of criminal activity or other problem behavior. Thus, programs seeking to reduce or prevent such activities will be most successful if they target multiple risk factors at the same time. A needs assessment clearly documenting the presence of all possible risk factors is an essential ingredient in selecting or tailoring programs to a problem that will have the greatest likelihood of success (Wasserman and Seracini 2001).

The Suppression–Intervention–Prevention Continuum

Once the combination of underlying factors has been identified, a comprehensive plan of action for long-term problem solving can be developed based on matching strategies and activities to particular risk factors. Because most problems have more than one factor contributing to their occurrence, **comprehensive plans** should address as many underlying conditions as both resources and political contexts will allow.

Sheppard et al. (1999) propose a useful framework for the development of comprehensive strategies with police–community partnerships. According to their model, once a needs assessment has been developed, strategy selection occurs within three domains: suppression, intervention, and prevention.

Suppression Strategies   These strategies involve the targeting of specific offenders and locations. Recognizing that problem areas and chronic offenders can be readily identified with criminal justice data and are generally responsible for the majority of crime, strategies identifying key offender and location hot spots are an important component of any comprehensive plan. Suppression strategies generally involve the more traditional law enforcement activities such as directed patrol, intensive supervision, street sweeps, and so on.

Intervention Strategies   Once a chronic group of offenders has been identified, partners will be better equipped to understand the factors influencing offender behavior and location vulnerability. Intervention strategies involve matching offenders to needed services in their community that can help to reduce their likelihood of recidivism.

Prevention Strategies   These strategies attempt to stop a problem before future incidents can occur. Community development techniques addressing the quality of life in an area are important prevention activities. Matching the siblings of gang offenders to needed services prior to their becoming involved in criminal activity is another example.

The OJJDP's (2000) Partnership to Reduce Juvenile Gun Violence program illustrates this continuum and the need to link causes to strategy. Following a review of gun-violence hot spots in the city of Baton Rouge, Louisiana, city planners singled out two high-crime zip codes to serve as pilot target areas for a demonstration project to reduce gun violence. Examination of records of gun violence incidents occurring within these areas indicated that the vast majority of gun offenses were being committed by a small group of repeat juvenile offenders, many of whom were actually being supervised in the community on probation. As a result, a suppression strategy was developed involving intensive and random police–probation supervision of the target group for probation violations, as described in the previous Linkage Box. This hard-core group of juvenile offenders was referred to as "Eigers," named after a mountain in Switzerland that is difficult, though not impossible, to climb.

Although this was a great starting point for a strategy, city planners recognized that it was not enough, particularly as they came to know the target population's needs. A case planner was hired to work with each Eiger and the probation officer to develop an integration plan that would reduce the Eiger's chance of reoffending, including **intervention services** such as job skills training and placement, counseling, conflict resolution skills, and so on. In addition, based on a common service need of the whole target group, a Life Skills Academy was created for skills training for both the Eigers and their families. Moreover, as the city became increasingly knowledgeable about the service needs of this population, new programs and services were identified and/or created to fill in these gaps. Finally, in the recognition that younger children often look up to their older siblings, a special menu of mostly school-based **preventive services** was created in attempt to get to these kids before they, too, made bad decisions in their lives. For more on this and other similar programs, see Sheppard et al. (2000).

Situational Crime Prevention

Routine activities theory states that in order for a crime to occur three elements must intersect at the same time and place (Cohen and Felson 1979):

- A motivated offender
- A suitable target
- Absence of a capable guardianship

These three components also provide a useful framework from which to engage in strategy selection. It follows from routine activities theory that if any one of the three components can be removed, crime will not occur. For example, if a problem analysis indicates that rapes are occurring along a dimly lit section of the city, police strategists might opt to increase surveillance in the area, thereby creating a guardianship that did not exist previously. Such a strategy might include increasing lighting in the area and directing more foot and random patrols to the location during the problem time periods. Altering environmental conditions in the interests of reducing opportunities for crime is referred to in law enforcement as crime prevention through environmental design (CPTED).

Chapter Summary

- The term *community* can mean many things, from geographical boundaries to more complex relationships, including supervisory capacity, interdependence, and shared values. Such distinctions are not arbitrary, because to the extent that there exists a great deal of cohesion, crime and disorder will be less common and police–community partnerships greatly facilitated.

- Broken windows theory and the contagion proposition document the connections between disorder and crime. Police departments need to engage the community in the resolution of even low-level quality-of-life offenses in order to make meaningful, long-term impacts on more serious crime.

- Community policing is not a soft-on-crime approach. Rather, through partnerships and problem solving, community policing can have a serious impact on crime. Community policing involves moving departments from reactive strategies of crime fighting to a proactive commitment to remedying underlying conditions.

- To be effective, community policing requires partnership with all available stakeholders with both knowledge and resources related to a particular problem. Partnerships with both the courts and correctional agencies can be particularly important.

- Problem solving requires the targeting of particular offenders and locations, in addition to gaining a complete understanding of all of the conditions or risk factors perpetuating a given problem. Resulting strategies must be comprehensive, covering the complete spectrum of suppression, intervention, and prevention.

Linking the Dots

1. A commitment to broad social service functions and community interaction were also important ingredients of the Political Era of policing. What factors described in this chapter make community policing different? What are the potential negative implications of community policing approaches?

2. Is community policing still relevant post–September 11 for serious issues such as terrorism? Should law enforcement now be focusing more on public safety than on building police–community partnerships?

3. When a department shifts to community policing, how are average line officers affected? Are any new expectations realistic?

4. Describe the process you would engage in for addressing a gang problem in a high-crime neighborhood. What information would you need? What groups would you partner with? What strategies might be relevant?

KEY TERMS

Analysis 305

Assessment 307

Broken windows theory 295

Community 292

Community mobilization 310

Community ownership 294

Community-oriented policing 305

Community policing 297

Community prosecution 302

Comprehensive plans 312

Contagion proposition 295

Crime analysis 307

Crime prevention through experimental design (CPTED) 300

Crime triangle 305

Decentralization 309

Despecialization 309

Empowerment 298

Flattening 309

Hot spots 307

Intervention services 313

Needs assessment 311

Participatory management model 309

Partnership 298

Prevalence 307

Preventive services 313

Proactive 299

Problem solving 299

Problem-oriented policing 305

Problems 300

Programmatic dimension 310

Public health model 296

Reactive 299

Repeat victimization 307

Resiliency theory 312

Response 307

Risk factors 311

Routine activities theory 314

SARA 305

Scanning 305

Serious Habitual Offender Criminal Apprehension Program (SHOCAP) 305

Structural changes 308

Suppression–intervention–prevention continuum 312

Target area 307

Team policing 309

Teams 309

REFERENCES

Bayley, D. 1988. "Community Policing: A Report from the Devil's Advocate." In *Community Policing: Rhetoric or Reality*, edited by J. Greene and S. Mastrofski, 225–238. New York: Praeger.

Braiden, C. 1992. "Community Policing: Nothing New Under the Sun." In *Community Oriented Policing and Problem Solving*. Sacramento, CA: California Department of Justice.

Bursik, R., and H. Grasmik. 1993. *Neighborhoods and Crime: The Dimensions of Effective Community Control*. New York: Lexington Books.

Cohen, L., and M. Felson. 1979. "Social Change and Crime Rate Trends: A Routine Activity Approach." *American Sociological Review* 44(4):588–608.

Coles, C., and G. Kelling. 1999. "Prevention Through Community Prosecution," *The Public Interest* 136(2):124–137.

Community Policing Consortium. 1994. *Understanding Community Policing*. Washington, D.C.: Bureau of Justice Assistance.

Cordner, G. W. 1999. "Elements of Community Policing." In *Policing Perspectives: An Anthology*, edited by L. Gaines and G. Cordner, 137–149. Los Angeles, CA: Roxbury.

Correia, M. 2000. *Social Capital and a Sense of Community Building: Building Social Cohesion*. Los Angeles, CA: Roxbury.

Crowe, T. 2000. *Crime Prevention Through Environmental Design*, 2d ed. Boston, MA: Butterworth-Heinemann.

Davis, R., and B. Taylor. 1997. "A Proactive Response to Family Violence. The Results of a Randomized Experiment." *Criminology* 35(3):307–333.

Eck, J., and W. Spelman. 1987. *Problem Solving: Problem-Oriented Policing in Newport News*. Washington, D.C.: National Institute of Justice.

Gaines, L., J. Worrall, M. Southerland, and J. Angel. 2003. *Police Administration*, 2d ed. New York: McGraw-Hill.

Godson, R. 2000. "Guide to Developing a Culture of Lawfulness." Unpublished paper presented at the Symposium on the Role of Civil Society in Countering Organized Crime: Global Implications of the Palermo, Sicily Renaissance, December 14, Palermo, Italy.

Goldstein, H. 1990. *Problem-Oriented Policing*. New York: McGraw-Hill.

Goldstein, H. 1977. *Policing in a Free Society*. Cambridge, MA: Ballinger.

Grant, H., and N. Jacobs. 1997. *The Bridgeport Youth Firearms Violence Initiative*. Washington, D.C.: Office of Community-Oriented Policing Services.

Grant, H. 1999. "Buffalo Weed and Seed Initiative." In *Promising Practices to Reduce Juvenile Gun Violence*, edited by D. Sheppard, 34–40. Washington, D.C.: Office of Juvenile Justice and Delinquency Prevention.

Greenberg, S., J. Williams, and W. Rohe. 1982. "Safety in Urban Neighborhoods: A Comparison of Physical Characteristics and Informal Territorial Control in High and Low Crime Neighborhoods." *Population and Environment* 5(3):147–148.

Greenwood, P., J. Chalken, and J. Petersilia. 1977. *The Criminal Investigation Process*. Lexington, MA: D. C. Heath and Company.

Harris, D. 2002. *Profiles in Injustice: Why Racial Profiling Cannot Work*. New York: The New Press.

Hawkins, J., R. Catalano, and J. Miller. 1992. "Risk and Protective Factors for Alcohol and Other Drug Problems in Adolescence and Early Adulthood." *Psychological Bulletin* 112(2):343–427.

Hawkins, J., M. Arthur, and R. Catalano. 1995. "Preventing Substance Abuse." In *Building a Safer Society: Strategic Approaches to Crime Prevention*. Vol. 19, *Crime and Justice: A Review of Research*, M. Tonry and D. Farrington, eds., 343–427. Chicago, IL: University of Chicago Press.

Kelling G., T. Pate, D. Dieckman, and C. Brown. 1974. *The Kansas City Preventive Patrol Experiment: A Summary Report*. Washington, D.C.: The Police Foundation.

Klockars, C. 1991. "The Rhetoric of Community Policing." In *Community Policing: Rhetoric and Reality*. J. Green and S. Mastrofski, eds. New York: Praeger.

McKnight, L., and A. Loper. 2002. "The Effects of Risk and Resilience Factors on the Prediction of Delinquency in Adolescent Girls." *School Psychology International* 23:186–198.

Metropolitan Police District of Columbia, n.d. *Community Prosecution*. Available at http://mpdc.dc.gov/mpdc/cwp/view,a,1238,Q,541614,mpdcNav_GID,1451,mpdcNav,%7C,.asp.

Miller, L., and K Hess. 1998. *The Police in the Community: Strategies for the 21st Century*, 2d ed. Belmont, CA: Wadsworth.

National Strategy Information Center. 2000. *School-Based Curriculum to Counter Crime and Corruption*. Washington, D.C.: National Strategy Information Center.

New York State Regional Community Policing Institute. 1999. *Fundamentals of Community Policing, Module II, Handout 3.2*. New York: New York State Regional Community Policing Institute.

Office of Juvenile Justice and Delinquency Prevention. 1995. *The Serious Habitual Offender Comprehensive Action Program*. Washington, D.C.: Author.

Office of Juvenile Justice and Delinquency Prevention. 2000. "Boston Strategy to Prevent Youth Violence." In *Promising Strategies to Reduce Gun Violence*. Washington, D.C.: Author.

Orlando, L. 2001. *Fighting the Mafia*. New York: Encounter Books.

Parent, D., and B. Snyder. 1999. *Police–Corrections Partnerships: Issues and Practices*. Washington, D.C.: National Institute of Justice.

Peak, K., and R. Glensar. 1999. *Community Policing and Problem Solving: Strategies and Practices*. Upper Saddle River, NJ: Prentice Hall.

Pease, K. 1998. *Repeat Victimization: Taking Stock. Crime Detection and Prevention Series, Paper 90*. London: Home Office Police Research Group.

Police Foundation. 1981. *The Newark Foot Patrol Experiment*. Washington, D.C.: Author.

Rosenbaum, D. 1994. "Community Crime Prevention: A Review of What is Known." In *Police and Policing: Contemporary Issues*. D. Kenny, ed., 203–218. New York: Praeger.

Rutter, M. 1987. "Psychosocial Resilience and Protective Mechanisms." *American Journal of Orthopsychiatry 57*:316–331.

Sadd, S., and R. Grine. 1996. "Implementation Challenges in Community Policing: Innovative Neighborhood-Oriented Policing in Eight Cities." *National Institute of Justice, Research in Brief*, February.

Sampson, R. J., and W. B. Graves. 1989. "Community Structure and Crime: Testing Social Disorganization Theory," *American Journal of Sociology* 94:774–802.

Shaw, C., and H. McKay. 1931. "Social Factors in Juvenile Delinquency." *National Commission on Law Observation and Enforcement*, No. 13, *Report on Causes of Crime*, Volume II. Washington, D.C.: U.S. Government Printing Office.

Sheppard, D., H. Grant, W. Rowe, and N. Jacobs. 2000. *Fighting Gun Violence*. OJJDP Bulletin in Brief Washington, D.C.: Office of Juvenile Justice and Delinquency Prevention.

Skogan, W. 1996. *Disorder and Decline*. Berkeley, CA: University of California Press.

Tiet, Q., and D. Huizinga. 2002. "Dimensions of the Construct of Resilience and Adaptation Among Inner City Youth." *Journal of Adolescent Research* 17:260–276.

Trojanowicz, R. 1982. *An Evaluation of the Neighborhood Foot Patrol Program in Flint, Michigan*. East Lansing, MI: State University Press.

Trojanowicz, R., V. E. Kappeler, and L. K. Gaines. 2002. *Community Policing: A Contemporary Perspective*. Cincinnati: Anderson.

Walker, S. 1992. *The Police in America: An Introduction*, 2d ed. New York: McGraw-Hill.

Wasserman, G., and A. Seracini. 1995. "Family Risk Factors and Interventions." In *Child Delinquents: Development, Intervention, and Service Needs*, R. Loeber and D. Farrington, eds., 165–189. Thousand Oaks, CA: Sage Publications.

Wilson, J. Q., and G. Kelling. 1982. "The Police and Neighborhood Safety." *Atlantic Monthly* (March): 29–38.

Wood, L. 2001. "Palermo Creates a Culture of Legality; Economic Growth Follows." *The Business Journal Online*, January.

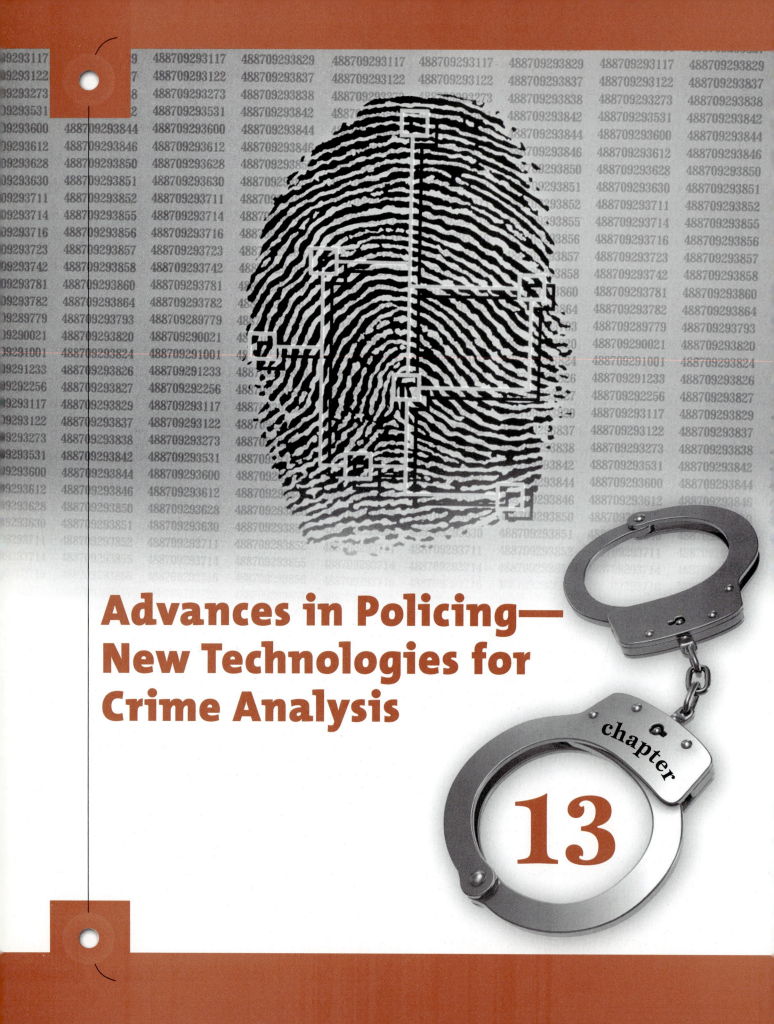

Advances in Policing—
New Technologies for
Crime Analysis

chapter

13

Chapter Objectives

- Identify the stages of technological advancement in policing and the implications of technological utilization in the field.

- Understand the different types of crime analysis and the technologies available for them, such as GIS.

- Know the variety of applications of GIS technology.

- Appreciate the many types of technologies available to modern law enforcement.

Introduction

Throughout its history, the U.S. Border Patrol has faced the seemingly insurmountable task of detecting and apprehending the ever-present stream of drug traffickers and illegal immigrants. The 60-mile area around the U.S.–Mexico border in the San Diego area alone requires the management of more than 2,000 agents and 900 seismic sensors (DeAngelis 2000). To aid them in their efforts, the U.S. Border Patrol San Diego Sector has many high-tech tools at their fingertips, such as geographic information systems (GIS), seismic sensors (more than 900), and infrared night-vision equipment.

The agents use the GIS technology to map the locations of alien apprehensions as a means of determining why certain areas are higher in illegal migration and drug trafficking than others. Using real-time sensor feeds from the Intelligent Computer Aided Detection System (ICAD), agents monitor "hits" corresponding to potential illegal migrant entry into the country. After identifying a possible entry point, agents are able to map out the travel route that has the highest probability of leading to the apprehension of the illegal border crossers.

In addition to the tremendous challenges presented by the region's mountainous terrain, illegal traffic has also found underground avenues of escaping detection. To combat this eventuality, the Border Patrol has used Global Positioning System (GPS) receivers and GIS to plot storm drain and sewer system routes that are facilitating traffic from Mexico into the United States.

The application of such technologies to the practice of law enforcement has revolutionized the capacity of police to both *respond* to crime that is taking place in real time and to proactively identify problems, analyze their causes, and develop strategic plans that truly enhance an agency's *crime prevention* capabilities. For example, the U.S. Border Patrol also targets high-risk areas

The struggle to manage our borders is made increasingly easier through the use of high-tech equipment such as GPS, GIS, and night vision.

with warning signs in Spanish regarding the dangers of crossing the border illegally.

In this technological era, law enforcement has had to evolve to be better equipped to fulfill its mandate of contributing to public safety. Technology has proven invaluable in responding to the problem of linkage blindness across jurisdictions, as well as with other criminal justice agencies and sectors of the community. In an age faced with continuing threats of transnational crime and terrorism, the importance of continued technological advances cannot be overstated.

However, the increasing reliance on and availability of technology to law enforcement can be intimidating. This technology brings with it new legal challenges, particularly in relation to the balance between crime control and the private interests of citizens introduced in the beginning of this book. This chapter will begin with a brief overview of the development of technological advances to law enforcement, followed by a descriptive coverage of key technological applications in policing. Particular attention will be paid to the use of GIS in facilitating proactive police management in the twenty-first century.

The Stages of Technological Advancement in Policing

Soulliere (1999) provides a useful conceptual framework for describing the advancement of technology in policing since its early professional origins. Although there is significant overlap with Kelling and Moore's (1987) three eras of policing (see Chapter 2), she offers four useful stages to help conceptualize technological development in policing. Table 13.1 summarizes **Soulliere's stages of technological advancement**.

The First Stage (1881–1945)

As described in Chapter 3, much of policing's initial technological advances can be attributed to the work of August Vollmer, who headed the early twentieth-century police department in Berkeley, California. Under his guidance, law enforcement increased its mobility through motor vehicle patrol and enhanced officer–precinct communications through telephone and radio. With his establishment of the first forensic laboratory, criminal investigators had access to an increasing array of technological expertise that would continue to increase exponentially throughout the development of law enforcement. For example, Vollmer's crime laboratory pioneered the use of polygraph, as well as fingerprint and handwriting classification systems (Seaskate 1998).

Soulliere (1999) cites several ways in which these early technological advances impacted the police organization, including:

- The development of increasingly complex police organizations through the creation of specialized sections within large police organizations to handle the new technology, such as radio communications and forensic labs

- Increased mobility for patrol activities offered by the use of automobiles

- Increased officer safety made possible with enhanced communications and the use of automobiles

TABLE 13.1

Soulliere's Stages of Technological Advancement in Policing

Stage 1 (1881–1945)	Stage 2 (1946–1959)	Stage 3 (1960–1979)	Stage 4 (1980–present)
• Mobile patrol • Radio communications • Telephone communications	• Traffic-violation-detection instruments	• 911 • Centralized dispatch • Civilian specialists • Research and development organizations • Computer age begins	• Telecommunications advances • Mobile data communications • Expert systems • Imaging • Biometrics • GIS

Source: N. Soulliere. 1999. *Police and Technology: Historical Review and Current Status.* Ottawa Canadian Police College.

The Second Stage (1946–1959)

Roughly corresponding with the beginnings of Kelling and Moore's Reform Era of policing, Soulliere (1999) claims that the second stage of technological advancement facilitated a major portion of the bureaucratization of policing organizations. During this stage, traffic police received a significant boost with the advent of the first instruments to measure both speeding violations and the condition of the driver. Although early instruments were rather crude indicators, they would grow over time to include the significant automobile surveillance mechanisms and blood-alcohol measures briefly discussed in Chapter 7.

The Third Stage (1960–1979)

As society entered the computer age, Soulliere (1999) claims that police technology began to truly emerge. During this stage, call distribution centers, computerized databanks, and computer sections became commonplace in police agencies. Some of the significant technological advancements in this stage can be attributed to President Lyndon B. Johnson. In 1967, he created the President's Commission on Law Enforcement and the Administration of Justice to analyze crime patterns in the country, as well as the resources available to combat them. The Commission's report highlighted the slow infusion of technological advances into the criminal justice system, with particular attention paid to policing. To this end, the report stated (President's Commission on Law Enforcement and the Administration of Justice 1967):

> The police, with crime laboratories and radio networks, made early use of technology, but most police departments could have been equipped 30 or 40 years ago as well as they are today. . . . Of all criminal justice agencies, the police have had the closest ties to science and technology, but they have called on scientific resources primarily to help in the solution of specific serious crimes, rather than for assistance in solving general problems of policing. (p. 125)

A notable gap existed between the technologies that were currently available that had potential law enforcement applications and what police agencies were actually using. In response to this gap, the Johnson administration began "the flow, a trickle at first, of what eventually became billions of dollars in direct and indirect assistance to local and state law enforcement" (Seaskate 1998, p. 2).

The commission argued for the establishment of a single telephone number that citizens across the country could use to contact the police in the case of an emergency. In only a matter of years following AT&T's announcement of the first **911 system** in 1968, 911 became a driving force for police departments across the country (Seaskate 1998). As highlighted throughout earlier chapters, this increasing emphasis on calls-for-service would have both benefits (the seeming ease of access to the police in times of emergency) as well as detriments (this became the principal means of determining police resource deployment and performance evaluation). Skolnick and Bayley (1986) point out that patrol officers can become exhausted by rushing between calls for service, rather than taking the time needed to truly digest and understand the human situations in which they are regularly thrown.

During this third stage of development, large municipalities began the process of centralizing the dispatch of all fire, police, and medical services

(Seaskate 1998). The over-reliance of the average citizen on the use of 911, regardless of the nature or seriousness of the problem, has led to the establishment of **311 systems** in many metropolitan areas to try and decrease the significant burden 911 has had on city emergency resources. The 311 system is available for all calls to police and fire personnel that are not emergencies. Other recent strategies for handling the call volume brought about by 911 include the differential response approaches described in Chapter 6.

Increased research on law enforcement applications and technological development was also a key characteristic of the third stage. The National Institute of Justice (NIJ) was created in 1968, and it continues to play a leading role in enhancing the field of law enforcement internationally (Soulliere 1999). An increasing reliance on civilian specialists within large police organizations also continued throughout this stage with developments in the areas of forensics and communications technologies.

The Fourth Stage (1980–present)

Information access and use characterize Soulliere's (1999) fourth stage of technological development. In addition to simply amassing a large volume of information—a task that law enforcement agencies have been successful at since their creation—technology now focuses on the speed and ease of information use. Moreover, technology developed throughout the fourth stage now provides law enforcement with access to data that would be unavailable to them without these tools. Collaboration in the research and development activities of traditional law enforcement and the military has resulted in many of the technologies introduced in this stage. Examples of such new tools include telecommunications, mobile data computers, expert systems, imaging, and biometric technologies (Soulliere 1999). Each of these areas will be described further throughout the chapter.

The importance of law enforcement access to such technological advancements is in many ways a balancing act between concerns for personal liberties and public security, as illustrated by Cowper (2003) (see Figure 13.1).

Kurzweil (2001) discusses the significant rate of technological development in modern society. He notes that although technology has always increased exponentially, earlier generations were at such an early stage of development that

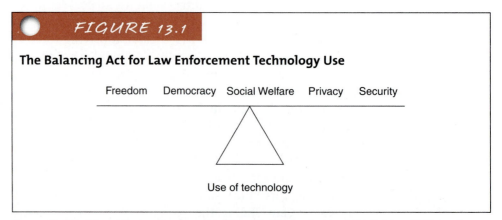

FIGURE 13.1

The Balancing Act for Law Enforcement Technology Use

Freedom   Democracy   Social Welfare   Privacy   Security

Use of technology

Source: Modified from Thomas Cowper. 2003. "Emerging Technology and the Future of Policing," paper presented at the International Police Studies Conference, June 12–15, Eastern Kentucky University, Richmond, KY.

the trends appear flat due to the low baseline. Kurzweil argues that although everyone in society generally expects technological progress to continue at the same pace, the rate of change is accelerating. Rather than just being increased incrementally every year, technological advancement is characterized by exponential growth, doubling every year. He organizes these observations into the **law of accelerating returns**:

- The enhanced methods resulting from one stage of progress are used to create the next stage.

- Consequently, the rate of progress of an evolutionary process increases exponentially over time.

- In addition, the speed and cost-effectiveness of a technological advancement will also increase exponentially over time.

- Finally, current methods of solving a problem in technology (such as shrinking transistors on an integrated circuit as an approach to making more powerful computers) will provide exponential growth until the method exhausts its potential. At that time, a fundamental change will result that will allow the exponential growth to continue.

Cowper (2003) summarizes the law of accelerating returns by stating that we will have 100 years of progress in the next 25 years and 20,000 years of progress in the next 100 years. Applications available to policing now or in the near future might have once seemed the work of science fiction rather than reality.

Certainly the applications of technology to policing have greatly enhanced the ability of law enforcement organizations to meaningfully engage in the problem-solving process. Although many police departments continue to be behind the curve in terms of integrating new technologies into day-to-day operations, the success of many applications to sound policing will make ignoring progress increasingly difficult over time.

Crime Analysis

Integral to the process of problem solving discussed in the previous chapter is crime analysis. **Crime analysis** has been defined as involving "the collection and analysis of data pertaining to a criminal incident, offender, and target" (Canter 2000, p. 4). Ideally, crime analysis will guide police managers in making deployment and resource allocation decisions that are linked to a true understanding of the nature of the problem. The more important data bearing on all components of the crime triangle (see Chapter 12), the better equipped police organizations will be to develop innovative, "out of the box" solutions that include the full spectrum of suppression, intervention, and prevention options.

An important caution must be stressed here. Crime analysis will only be as good as the data or information that is collected. Three **essential criteria for crime analysis** should be used by departments in designing data-collection processes and in interpreting the meaning of information resulting from crime analysis:

1. **Timeliness**. Does the pattern or trend presented reflect a current problem or issue or is it more representative of a previous situation? Deployment decisions with respect to both prevention and offender

apprehension efforts must be based on information that is as current as possible.

2. **Relevancy**. Do the measures used in the analysis accurately reflect what is intended? For example, whether a pattern is based on **calls-for-service data** or **incident data** can be a very important determination depending on what the police manager is trying to understand.

3. **Reliability**. Would the same data, interpreted by different people at different times, lead to the same conclusions?

Canter (2000) categorizes crime analysis into tactical and strategic functions.

Strategic Crime Analysis

The collection and analysis of data spanning a long period of time is **strategic crime analysis**. It is said to be research focused as it includes the use of statistics to make conclusions (Canter 2000). This form of analysis can be useful to departments in terms of **crime-trend forecasting**, or using data to estimate future crime based on past trends (Canter 2000). With crime-trend forecasting, important decisions can be made with respect to the deployment of patrol allocation as a reflection of the changing volume of criminal activity.

Another important benefit of strategic crime analysis is the analysis of changing community dynamics and risk factors that might be contributing to the particular crime trends of a specific area (Canter 2000). Once again, this type of analysis over time can result in more informed decision making that is more likely to lead to police partnership with other city and community agencies that can help create more long-term, sustainable reductions in criminal activity.

Tactical Crime Analysis

Whereas strategic crime analysis involves the review of data spanning generally a year or more, **tactical crime analysis** uses real-time data spanning several days. One of the principal uses of this type of analysis involves problem identification, or the **pattern detection** of multiple offenses over a short period of time that have common characteristics, such as type of crime, modus operandi, and type of weapon used (Canter 2000). One example of tactical crime analysis that will be discussed later in this chapter is geographic profiling, which can be used to suggest the likelihood of where an offender lives based on the pattern of where offenses occur. Tactical crime analysis can occur on as large an area as a department's entire jurisdiction or as small as the few-block-radius of a hot spot.

Linkage analysis involves connecting a suspect to a series of incidents based on commonalities in modus operandi and suspect description, as well as known offenders who live close proximity to a given area (Canter 2000). Following a nationwide effort by state legislatures to implement sex offender registration laws (Terry and Furlong 2004), many police departments regularly search their databases of registered sex offenders when a known series of sexual offenses is identified.

Finally, **target profiling** involves the use of data to determine the potential risks certain areas may have for criminal victimization based on known offense patterns in the area. Following the previous example, some departments have experimented with community risk profiles (i.e., day care centers, presence of parks, etc.) as a means of guiding the community notification process for the presence of registered sex offenders.

Geomapping Crime Patterns: Moving Beyond Push Pins

Based on the previous discussion of the applications of crime analysis to policing, the integral role that **geographic information systems (GIS)** play in the process is readily apparent. A GIS is an automated systems for the capture, storage, retrieval, analysis, and display of spatial data (Clarke 1990). Others have noted that "GIS technology is to geographical analysis what the microscope, the telescope, and computers have been to other sciences" (Cowen 2001, p. 3), By visually representing diverse data sources that can be geographically located, such as crime events, land usage, property values, racial ethnic composition, and so on, GIS enables planners to "manipulate and display geographical knowledge in new and exciting ways" (Cowen 2001, p. 3). Despite its diverse applications across various fields, the common focus of GIS is the enhancement of decision making.

In law enforcement, GIS has revolutionized the practice of electronic **crime mapping**, or visually displaying crime incidents on a mapped surface of a particular jurisdiction. However, the use of crime maps has a long history within policing. For example, the NYPD used pin maps to represent crime patterns at

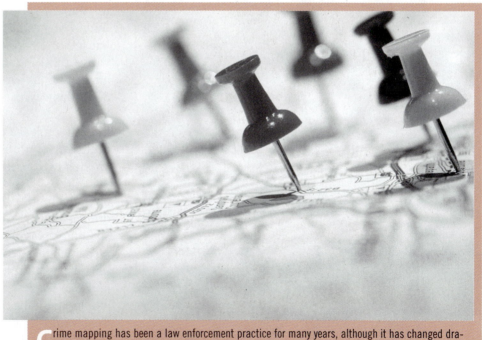

Crime mapping has been a law enforcement practice for many years, although it has changed dramatically with the advent of GIS.

least as far back as 1900 (Harries 1999). Moreover, criminologists and sociologists have examined the spatial trends of crime and delinquency since as far back as mid-nineteenth century France's Quetelet (Phillips 1972) and the Chicago school's **social ecology of crime** efforts pioneered by Shaw and McKay (1942). The difference is, of course, that until the use of GIS became more commonplace in policing practice during the 1990s, crime patterns were literally represented by inserting push pins into the map of a jurisdiction that was usually mounted on the wall.

Although these early crime maps proved to be useful in visually showing where crimes occurred, patterns would be lost over time as more and more pins were added to the map. Additionally, these maps were very difficult to archive for later retrieval and analysis unless they were photographed (Shaw and McKay 1942).

What Crime Maps Do: GIS as a Technical Aid to Problem-Oriented Policing

GIS has revolutionized the way in which problem-oriented policing (POP) is conducted. This is largely due to law enforcement's ability to overlay seemingly diverse types of data that all contribute a true understanding of a particular problem. For example, a series of burglaries taking place between the hours of 1:00 PM and 3:00 PM might be the first thing visually displayed on a crime map. This would correspond with the scanning or problem identification part of the problem-solving model detailed in Chapter 12. However, to get at the underlying causes of the burglary problem requires deeper probing and innovative thinking. In this case, the crime analyst might overlay the burglary incident data with available data about land usage in the area. The analyst might then learn that the burglaries are occurring within walking distance of an area high school.

Although this might seem to be an obvious linkage to many, individuals often overlook such connections. By visually displaying overlays of various potential data combinations, GIS can play a critical role in jump-starting the analysis process. With the current example, the police manager might begin to develop a series of hypotheses related to the fact that the burglaries might be caused by troublemaking youths playing hooky from their after-

One significant advantage of GIS is its capacity to combine many data sources to get a visual understanding of the nature of the problem.

Linkages *in Law Enforcement*

GIS Applications to Sex Offender Management

GIS applications can also help to increase law enforcement's capacity to engage in the collaborative problem solving with other criminal justice and community agencies. The visual representation of information can be a powerful tool in coming to a common understanding of the nature of problems even across planning groups with diverse perspectives.

The authors of this text participated on a citywide task force in New York City composed of representatives from law enforcement, probation and parole, family and criminal courts, mental health, treatment providers, and victim advocates to examine the issue of sex offender management in the community (Grant and Terry 2000). Although New York City had a large registered sex offender population at the time (over 3,000 offenders), there was as yet no comprehensive plan for the

management of these offenders in the community involving collaboration between each of the key stakeholders. Building on the recognition across team members of the clear need for such a collaborative approach to sex offender management, as well as a need to better understand the dynamics of the problem through data collection, the New York City Sex Offender Management Team had tremendous momentum from the start, with agencies opening their doors to facilitate the data collection process.

Beginning at the first team meeting, the partners sought to identify a mechanism for gaining a complete understanding of the sex offender population currently residing in the community. Although it was initially suggested that each of the five district attorneys represented conduct searches on sex offenders within their own databases to form an initial population for study, it became immediately apparent that the most

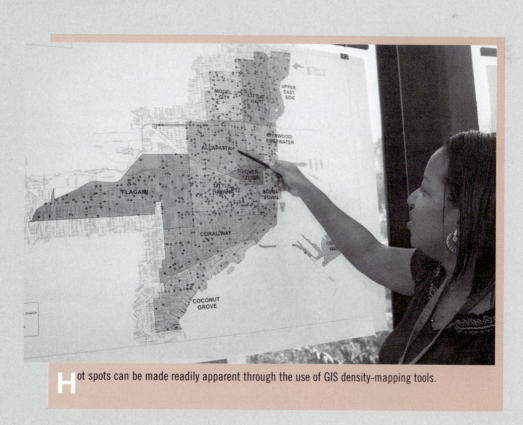

Hot spots can be made readily apparent through the use of GIS density-mapping tools.

(continues)

efficient access to such data would be use a database of all registered sex offenders in the city. Based on this initial database, the team sought to get complete information on probation conditions, employment, treatment, living situation, probation officer contacts, mental status, substance abuse history, and so on. In addition, complete criminal histories on the offenders were requested in order to gain a true understanding of the nature of the population being managed so that accurate, comprehensive strategies could be devised. At all points, ethical considerations were paramount in the use of this information, which was always presented in aggregate form and never published beyond the law enforcement planning team purposes.

In a city the size of New York, and with such a large number of offenders, geomapping of offender residences is essential for two reasons. First, depending on the plan developed by the team, it might have been necessary to pilot the demonstration project within one borough given the tremendous task and resources required for a citywide approach. Second, geomapping had the tremendous ability to demonstrate to the team the scope of the problem, particularly given

the obvious clustering of offenders in several city locations. Mapping enabled researchers to present the planning team with **buffer zones** around each offender, combining offender density in a given area with overlays of key risk factors for re-offending drawn from the relapse-prevention literature and connected to each of the offender residence locations. Examination of this data by school and daycare locations, parks, available treatment resources, and so on were all part of the process for meaningful informed problem solving to which GIS proved the essential core tool.

QUESTIONS

1. How would you go about analyzing a particular problem in your community? Describe the data you would collect to document patterns and arrive at a true understanding of the problem's causes. What role would GIS and hot spot mapping play in this process? How would you use the data to develop a strategic plan? What does the research literature suggest as possible alternatives for dealing with the problem you identified?

noon classes. In addition to providing a large pool of individuals from which investigators might seek to learn information about the incidents, police planners may also begin to collaborate with the school to develop responses that increase truancy enforcement in area schools.

Types of Data with Mapping Applications

The data that can be used for mapping purposes are many, limited only by the creativity of the planning body. Any data that can be **geocoded**, or for which there is geographic reference information, can be used for GIS analysis (Harries 1999). Although early forms of geocoding only permitted street addresses as the geographic unit upon which to map data, now blocks and census tracts can also be used. Crime incidents are readily applicable for geocoding purposes given that they are almost always available as street addresses or otherwise location based (Harries 1999). Crime-mapping applications of GIS include

- mapping incident types and modus operandi, and
- mapping attributes of victims and suspects (Harries 1999)

Based on an initial pattern analysis, overlays with other forms of data can help to develop a broader understanding of a particular problem. For example, pattern analysis might indicate a problem of disorderly conduct and assaults in an area. An overlay with available liquor stores and bars in the area may present the planner with a series of hypotheses as to what factors might be driving the problem. An additional benefit of GIS analyses is that they are directly compatible with statistical analyses to further refine causal projections. Thus, a city planner might be able to statistically link the rate of disorderly conduct and assaults in city jurisdictions with the overall density of alcohol availability or other possibilities. Although such analyses can only show planners the possible relationship between two variables, or **correlations**, rather than saying conclusively that X causes Y (**causation**), there can be no doubt that such findings greatly enhance the level of informed decision making of law enforcement or other key stakeholders in a city.

Mapping and Accountability: GIS in Action

Crime mapping can increase the accountability of a department by visually demonstrating incident patterns for which departmental administrators can hold commanding officers accountable over time. A proactive police manager should use GIS and other problem–solving tools to create sound strategic and tactical decisions for officer deployment, for resource deployment, and for partnering with other agencies to facilitate sustained crime reductions. The CompStat model of the New York City Police Department institutionalized the use of GIS for departmental planning purposes with such apparent success that similar versions of CompStat have been implemented in departments across the country.

The NYPD Crime Control Model, or **CompStat**, cannot be oversimplified to refer simply to quality-of-life policing, aggressive policing, or even simply data-driven policing, as is commonly found in the literature about the model. Rather, as police scholar Phyllis McDonald (2002) emphatically states, "this proliferation of singularly focused descriptors does a disservice to the management principles of CompStat and its potential for use in other jurisdictions. CompStat (the abbreviation for "computer-driven crime statistics") is a comprehensive, continuous analysis of results for improvement and achievement of prescribed outcomes" (p. 7). In other words, CompStat involves managing police operations by institutionalizing accountability and analysis processes that are the embodiment of the problem-oriented policing model.

McDonald (2002) offers a concise overview of the key elements of the CompStat model and issues involved in its replication in other departments. To summarize, these elements include:

- Specific objectives
- Accurate and timely intelligence
- Effective tactics
- Rapid deployment of personnel and resources
- Relentless follow-up and assessment

As we have seen in earlier chapters, police organizations, like any other form of bureaucracy, are often extremely difficult to change. How then did such a seemingly proactive, forward-looking model become implemented in the country's largest police department? In his prior position as head of the New York City Transit Police in the early 1990s, former police commissioner William Bratton had seen tremendous successes in focusing departmental operations on specific measurable objectives and an ongoing review of outcome achievement.

Following a series of complementary strategies in then notoriously dangerous New York City subways, such as increased undercover and uniformed police presence and the removal of graffiti and other signs of disorder, dramatic declines in robberies, fare evasion, and general disorder resulted. New Yorkers once again began to feel safe about riding the subways.

When Bratton came to the helm of the NYPD in 1994, he began a dramatic reengineering effort that included interviews and focus groups involving representatives of every rank and bureau in order to assess the state of command in the department (Silverman 1999). Seven specific objectives were created to guide the future direction of the NYPD (McDonald 2002):

- Get guns off the street.
- Curb youth violence in the schools and on the streets.
- Drive drug dealers out of the city.
- Break the cycle of domestic violence.
- Reclaim the city's public spaces.
- Reduce auto-related crime.
- Root out corruption and build organizational integrity in the NYPD.

To achieve these outcomes, as well as to measure departmental progress toward them, ready access to timely data was essential. However, a significant problem became immediately apparent: The NYPD was not equipped to provide up-to-date crime reports. In fact, there was generally a reporting lag of three to six months for crime statistics, and even then any meaningful analysis on the incident-based level was near impossible (Silverman 1996). Headquarters was not systematically tracking crime activity in the precincts, let alone using such information to evaluate the performance of its commanding officers (Silverman 1999). As a result, precinct commanders did not view crime reduction as a paramount job responsibility. Common to departments across the country, efficiency concerns in responding to crime were seen as being more important. Detective bureaus and other specialized functions thus only rarely collaborated with patrol, and often directly clashed over territorial and other concerns.

CompStat was devised as a means of reforming the NYPD by pushing all precincts to generate weekly crime activity reports so that they could be held accountable for the achievement of the seven specific objectives outlined in the reengineering process (McDonald 2002). In the beginning, Patrol Bureau staff computerized the data and compiled it into the "CompStat Book," which featured year-to-date crime complaints and arrests for every major felony category, in addition to gun arrests (Silverman 1999). This data would then be compared on citywide, patrol borough, and precinct levels. In addition, precinct commanders quickly became accountable not only for the crime activity, but also for any inaccuracies in the data itself. Over time, data became even more readily available by being downloadable directly from the department's On-Line Booking Service (OLBS). Headquarters eventually came to rank order precincts in terms of overall crime changes within their jurisdiction.

By requiring timely and accurate data, it quickly became clear to precinct commanders that their role had changed; they were now being held accountable for the crime under their charges. As such, they began to realize that they had to stop simply responding to crime and had to begin to proactively think about ways to deal with it from all angles: suppression, intervention, and prevention.

To solidify this message, the department began to hold regularly scheduled CompStat meetings in which precinct commanders and their staff met directly with top departmental brass to discuss crime trends and issues in their precincts. In a very intimidating environment, precinct commanders must stand before a lectern in front of three large video screens that flash GIS-generated maps of recent crime patterns (Figure 13.2). Commanders are then asked about what **tactics** they have tried to address the patterns, what resources they have tried or needed, and with whom they have collaborated. The session thus becomes a brainstorming problem-solving session about how better to proactively respond to crime. Suggestions for strategy directives are made and are relentlessly followed up upon at subsequent meetings by top brass to further ensure accountability. Having the top brass available as part of this process ensures that departmental resources will be directed to precinct needs, even across precinct and unit lines. Thus, in addition to implementing accountable problem solving, CompStat seeks to reduce the problems of linkage blindness.

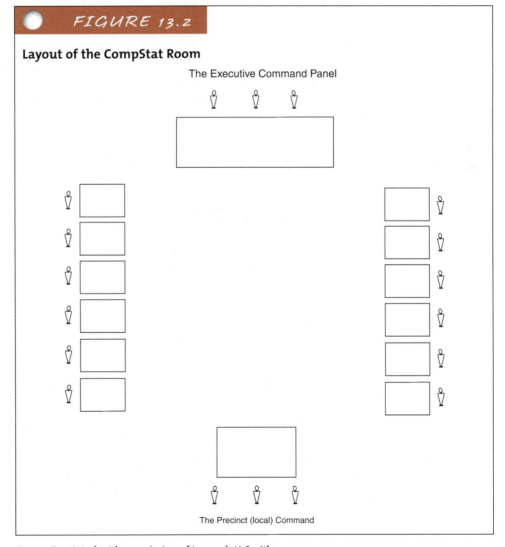

FIGURE 13.2

Layout of the CompStat Room

The Executive Command Panel

The Precinct (local) Command

Source: Reprinted with permission of Launcelott Smith.

In order to be better prepared for the CompStat meetings, each borough implemented **Pattern Identification Modules (PIMs)** composed of hous-ing, transit, patrol, detective, organized crime, and robbery squads to review daily index crime reports and thus identify crime clusters or patterns that need to be addressed. Figure 13.3 provides a conceptual framework of this planning process.

Over time, the CompStat process has evolved to include other data for analy-sis, including census data, arrest and summons activity, available resources, av-erage response time, domestic violence incidents, unfounded radio runs, and personnel absences (Silverman 1999). Former Commissioner Howard Safir also added citizen complaints and charges of officer misconduct to the process. Time-of-day photos might also be presented in CompStat meetings to monitor changes in precinct dynamics by shift period.

Many scholars and practitioners have argued that CompStat has played a critical role in the significant crime reductions witnessed by New York City fol-lowing its implementation (Silverman 1999). Others are more skeptical of these claims, arguing that the crime reduction in New York City can be attributed to larger patterns in society (Karmen 1996). The answer is likely somewhere in the middle; however, the tremendous impact CompStat has had on police manage-ment practices internationally cannot be denied. Although some reports have pointed to the demoralizing effects of the process on precinct commanders and officers who feel a pressure to produce numbers, many others cite the signifi-cant increases in job satisfaction found by those who feel empowered by the problem-solving aspects brought to the job.

An important concern has been whether the pressure to keep crime statis-tics low has led to a zero-tolerance policing style that loses sight of community concerns, further inhibiting police–community relations. The answer to this issue is unclear, and it is probably too soon to come to any concrete conclusions.

FIGURE 13.3

Conceptual Framework of the CompStat Planning Process

- Precinct crime data

- Arrest profiles

Compstat Meetings
- Top brass
- Precinct commanders and staff

- Citizen complaints and charges of brutality

PIMS → **STRATEGY DIRECTIVES**

These questions will have to be tracked by practitioners and academicians alike as the model is implemented across diverse contextual conditions within the United States and abroad.

GIS and the Patrol Officer

As GIS crime mapping became recognized as an important tool in both tracking and responding to crime on a neighborhood level, departments across the country sought to expand its use beyond administrative planning to reach the patrol officers and community residents. For example, the Camden New Jersey Police Department began providing officers with access to crime-mapping information on desktop computers and even wireless laptops in patrol cars (*American City and Country* 2002). The department enabled officers to access crime locations, crime types, and times throughout the city in order to focus patrol efforts. The

Linkages *in Law Enforcement*

GIS Applications to Community Policing

Beginning in 1995, the Chicago Police Department (CPD) implemented one of the most easy-to-use and accessible GIS systems in the country as a complement to its department-wide **Chicago Alternative Policing Strategy (CAPS)** community-policing approach. Called **Information Collection for Automated Mapping (ICAM)**, the program enables departmental personnel to generate maps of reported offenses by type, including charts of the ten most frequently reported offenses, through a series of easy mouse clicks (Rich 1996).

CAPS was implemented in 1993 in pilot districts and has since been expanded to all twenty-five of the city's policing districts. CAPS emphasizes officer problem solving by assigning officers to their beats for at least a year, altering dispatch schedules so that the time spent responding to crime outside of their beats is limited, and requiring officer attendance at community meetings (Rich 1996). Early evaluations of CAPS effectiveness showed significant declines in reported crime, victimization, and fear of crime (Skogan 1996).

ICAM is viewed as a complement to CAPS. CAPS enables officers to better understand the problems in their assigned areas and thus be better facilitators of collaborative problem-solving efforts with community residents (Rich 1996). As part of the ICAM development process, focus groups were held with officers and detectives to seek their understanding and cooperation and ensure that the completed program suited their information needs. Once the department got the officers' buy-in, maps were regularly shared at beat meetings. Because of the success of the ICAM, a Citizen ICAM program has been developed. With Citizen ICAM, citizens can generate much of the same information (without specific identifiers) that an officer can, thereby facilitating joint police–community planning efforts. Initially, confidentiality issues slowed citizen access to ICAM due to the specific details of street locations. However, it is now running for anyone to see at http://citizenicam.chicagopolice.org/ctznicam/ctznicam.asp.

Other departments across the country have produced their own mapping programs, including Web-based citizen crime reports, as will be discussed later.

QUESTIONS

1. Does your local police department have a website? How does it compare to ICAM?

2. Which GIS elements would you include on a department website?

3. What applications of available GIS crime data are there in your community?

maps also enable officers to pinpoint business-contact information when an alarm is sounded, rather than having to call a dispatcher for the information (*American City and Country* 2002).

In 1998, the NIJ awarded the leading GIS software provider, **Environmental Systems Research Institute, Inc. (ESRI),** a $500,000 grant to work with local law enforcement agencies and universities to effectively utilize GIS as a crime-fighting tool (Carney 1998). Collaborating with several local law enforcement agencies, ESRI developed an accessible GIS interface for large-scale departmental needs.

Other Applications: Geographic Profiling

Geographic profiling, the combined use of geography, psychology, and mathematics to identify the location of an offender, is most commonly associated with tracking down serial killers, rapists, and arsonists. However, it is actually useful as an investigative tool in any case in which an individual offender has committed criminal activity across a series of locations (including crimes as diverse as robbery, burglary, theft, and fraud). Building from the significant empirical efforts of Brantingham and Brantingham (1981), geographic profiling suggests investigative alternatives based on the "hunting behavior" of the offender. Leading geographic profiler Kim Rossmo argues that criminals are no different in offending as ordinary citizens are in going about their day-to-day activities (Onion 2002).

Following this logic, geographic profiling uses the **nearness principle**, which means that offenders will remain within a limited range that is comfortable to them when committing their offenses (Rossmo 1998), just as animals will tend to forage within a limited range from their base (Onion 2002). Geographic profiling incorporates all possible methods of transportation available to an offender in providing a calculation of the area in which the offender is most likely to reside.

This research has led to the creation of a computerized geographic-profiling workstation called **Rigel**. Rigel incorporates statistical analyses, GIS, and database management functions to generate investigative suggestions. Crime scenes are broken down into type (i.e., primary and secondary, see Chapter 8), and then entered by location. Based on the theoretical principles of geographic profiling, addresses of suspects can be evaluated by their probability of being the actual offender (Harries 1999). This can help investigators to sort through their existing databases, such as those of registered sex offenders, and other investigative information. When there is not a specific suspect pool, geographic profiling can help to pinpoint the highest probability areas to focus the search. As with the offender-profiling process discussed in Chapter 8, geographic profiling should only be considered an additional tool for investigators; solving the offense will require a sound investigative strategy.

Twenty-First-Century Technologies in Policing

In addition to GIS, over the past decade numerous other technologies have become available to law enforcement, from **record management systems (RMS)** that help departments store and retrieve the immense amount of data they receive on a day-to-day basis all the way to sophisticated weaponry and intelligence technologies that have reached law enforcement by way of the military. Covering all of these advances in significant detail is beyond the scope of this text; however, the remainder of this chapter will provide an overview of some significant technological developments that are becoming part of everyday law enforcement activities.

Closed-Circuit Television

The use of **closed-circuit television (CCTV)** and other forms of public surveillance technology in the United States have witnessed significant growth in recent years as not only police departments, but also airport security and other public entities, have increasingly turned to video surveillance in their efforts to reduce crime and increase public safety. The use of this technology in the United States may not be nearly as prevalent as it is in countries such as England, where there is a camera on nearly every street corner and in every public building; however, it is becoming increasingly popular, particularly following the events of September 11. Law enforcement is now readily turning to surveillance systems such as CCTV as a means of trying to sort through the tremendous traffic at our borders, airports, and dense city streets.

After spending almost two years in CCTV control rooms across England, Goold (2004) concluded that in many cases actual surveillance outcomes have less to do with technological factors than they do with working cultures and

New technology research seeks to merge facial recognition software with CCTV surveillance cameras.

the attitudes of individual camera operators. In particular, Goold found that once established, many surveillance systems in public areas quickly become prone to institutional inertia, with both camera operators and scheme managers being either unwilling or unable to update their systems or change their working practices in response to technological advances. Technology does not exist in a vacuum; it is shaped by social factors and by the attitudes and practices of those who use it (Bijkker et al. 1987). In addition, technical workers, such as CCTV operators, often shape the implementation of new technology by fitting it into their existing routines. Technological change may as often be subsumed into existing organizational structures as it effects organizational change (Barley 1986).

No one can erase the images caught on airport CCTV cameras of the September 11 hijackers boarding their plane in Boston. Certainly such retrospective images can be used as evidence of what transpired in a given incident, but law enforcement has become increasingly more interested in finding better ways to harness CCTV technology to identify known offenders passing through a checkpoint, such as a wanted felon or individual on a terrorist watch list. As such, new advances have sought to merge CCTV systems with promising approaches in the field of biometrics, as will be discussed below.

Some agencies have developed innovative ways of overcoming the limitations of private security systems, which in many cases are useful only for recording crimes in progress rather than providing aid to responding units at the scene. For example, the Seal Beach Police Department installed a network that transmits the output of bank security cameras directly to dispatch and to responding units in real time in a high-robbery-incident suburb of Los Angeles (Garcia 2001). The network transmits video over the air through encrypted wireless communication paths in the same manner that images are sent over the Internet.

Global Positioning Systems

Tracking offenders or patrol officer deployments have also been enhanced by the use of Global Positioning Systems. **Global positioning systems (GPS)** use satellite-based technologies for the purpose of tracking the movement of patrol cars or specially equipped stolen vehicles. In some cases, officers can be equipped with GPS-enabled cellular phones, providing an important alternative to conventional address matching for an officer responding to a call. GPS technology has also significantly enhanced aerial photography of crime-incident locations, allowing for greater visualization of the complete context of a situation (Harries 2001). The State of Iowa has capitalized on the surveillance capacity of GPS to monitor the real-time location of high-risk offenders released from prison. With the use of an offender-monitoring system, law enforcement and correctional agencies can keep offenders away from areas where children are likely to congregate (e.g., schools and daycare centers) (Greene 2003).

The Escambia County Sheriff's Department's SWAT team used a broadband-via-satellite system when responding to an emergency call involving a shooting victim and a barricaded suspect. Through communication with the Mobile Command Center's satellite system, SWAT officers were able to determine that the suspect had fled the scene and that the victim was likely dead (Hughes Network Systems 2002). Pictures of the suspect were immediately obtained via satellite and distributed to patrol, a process that used to take hours or days.

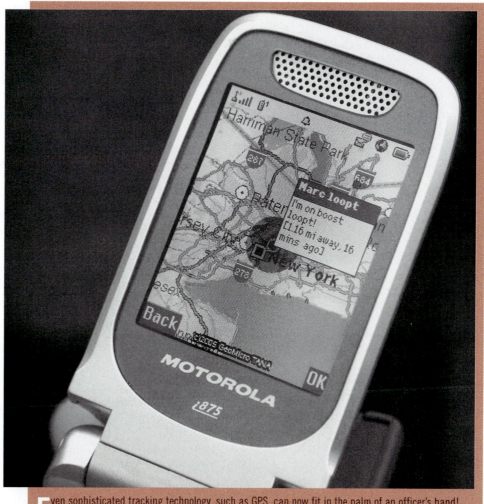

Even sophisticated tracking technology, such as GPS, can now fit in the palm of an officer's hand!

Biometrics

Biometrics involves the automatic, real-time identification of individuals based on their physiology or behavior (Cowper 2003). Biometrics thus encompasses a diversity of technologies, including voice recognition, fingerprint identification, lip movement, retinal scanning, facial recognition software, DNA profiling, thermal imagery, and iris/retinal scanning, to name just a few.

Facial Recognition Software   The field of biometrics, particularly **facial recognition software**, might overcome the limitations of CCTV systems, both by reducing the need for expensive human operators and by making the suspect-identification process faster and more reliable. Several promising studies support the potential applications of facial recognition software; however, little is known about how such systems will function in real-life situations (Norris and Armstrong 1999).

Like any technology, the potential impact of facial recognition technology—from preventing crime to infringing civil liberties—depends on the quality of the database from which possible "hits" are derived. For example, an under-inclusive database might exclude potential terrorists but "catch" a child-support violator; whereas a mistargeted database may send out too large a net that might unnecessarily infringe on people's civil liberties and reduce the effective application of the technology. Cole's (2001) groundbreaking analysis of the history of identification technologies highlights the need for further study of the information elements that comprise biometric databases.

Fingerprint Identification Systems Automated Fingerprint Identification Systems (AFISs) were introduced in Chapter 8. An advanced system to aid in the processing, storage, and matching of fingerprints has been introduced by the FBI. Called the **Integrated Automated Fingerprint Identification System (IAFIS)**, this enhanced technology offers a two-hour turnaround on electronically submitted criminal print searches from federal, state, and local law enforcement agencies (Smith 1998).

Interjurisdictional Communication Technologies

At the core of linkage blindness is minimal amount of critical communication that occurs among different law enforcement jurisdictions as well as other sectors of the criminal justice system and community at large. Given the diversity of criminal justice core functions, the gathering and sharing of criminal justice information is particularly complex (Tomek 2001). The need to build information-sharing capacities, both technological and organizational, is evidenced by the NIJ's decision to make information sharing the number one priority for information technology solutions among state and local agencies, as well as internationally (Tomek 2001).

The need for information continuity and access is key for informed decision making by all criminal justice stakeholders. One of the biggest challenges to larger information-sharing collaborations is the large differences across agencies in terms of agency protocols, standards, and even measures for the collection and utilization of data (Tomek 2001). The Department of Homeland Security is working to reduce this difficulty. In law enforcement's effort to prevent terrorism, the DHS has initiated the **Homeland Security Information Network (HSIN)**. HSIN enables state and urban law enforcement agencies to collect and disseminate information among federal, state, and local agencies in order to prevent terrorist activity. This computer-based communications system was developed by state and local authorities in order to connect all fifty states, Washington, D.C., and major metropolitan areas (DHS 2007).

Offender Databases Efforts have been made in recent years to develop sufficient technologies capable of overcoming many of the barriers involved in cross- and interjurisdictional information sharing. The San Diego County **Automated Regional Justice Information System (ARJIS)** system warrants further description as to the possibilities in interjurisdictional information sharing. ARJIS combines information from thirty-eight state, local, and federal law enforcement agencies into one website that can be accessed by registered police, court, and correctional officials (Walsh 2003). ARJIS includes crime-incident databases that are updated every 24 hours, most-wanted lists, and interactive maps. Similarly, the Pennsylvania Integrated Justice Network (JNET) connects all of its criminal justice agencies together for the sharing of critical information, including offender photos and images of distinguishing marks. In one case, an offender was apprehended based on the victim being able to describe the perpetrator's tattoo to the police (Walsh 2003).

Cross-Jurisdictional Radio Communications

Federal efforts at improving cross-jurisdictional radio communications include the NIJ's **Advanced Generation of Interoperability for Law Enforcement (AGILE)**. AGILE provides direct connections between the radio systems of law enforcement agencies with overlapping or adjacent jurisdictions (Kaluta 2001). The possibilities of such technologies for enhancing national security needs has been demonstrated by early successes of the system as an enhancement to San Diego County's ARJIS (Scanlon 2000). AGILE has also been used to establish an emergency-only radio channel for presidential inaugurations, linking the Secret Service, the FBI, the U.S. Capitol Police, the U.S. Park Police, and the Metropolitan Police Department (Kaluta 2001).

Electronic Warrant Processes

Some jurisdictions have developed solutions to the numerous problems involved in the arrest-warrant process. With the traditional process, courts issue paper warrants that are subsequently used by law enforcement agencies to create a wanted person record in their own systems, which can then be checked by law enforcement officials throughout the country through the use of the FBI's National Crime Information Center (see Chapter 8). One of the problems with this process is the delay between when the court issues or cancels a warrant, creating serious officer safety concerns (Perbix 2001). Additional concerns arise from the lack of synchronization across the systems, in which warrants entered into one system are not entered into another (adding to the linkage blindness problem).

Electronic warrant systems, such as the Colorado Integrated Criminal Justice Information System (CICJIS), link the state's main criminal justice systems (including law enforcement, prosecutors, courts, adult and juvenile corrections) so that data entered by one agency's system is automatically transferred and loaded into another agency's system, thereby reducing linkage blindness and reducing the amount of inconsistent data (Perbix 2001).

Information Security Through Encryption

Given the confidential information being shared by criminal justice agencies through these enhanced technologies, serious privacy concerns inevitably arise. Secure law enforcement communication over the Internet or intranets can be achieved with **virtual private networking (VPN)**. VPN uses encryption software to scramble the contents of communications so that even if the system becomes available to hackers, they are unable to read the information (Taylor 2000). In addition to an advanced encryption algorithm that is virtually impossible to break, VPNs pass encrypted communications through a "tunnel" between communicating agencies, ensuring that users meet a high level of identification to be able to access the information (Taylor 2000). With the establishment of proper identification and access protocols, VPNs offer law enforcement agencies the ability to exchange and track important information, such as gang memberships, enhancing contact between the communicating agencies.

The World Wide Web and Community Policing

With its focus on collaborative problem solving and communication with the public, community policing is even more information intensive than traditional policing methods (Monahan 1998). New communication technologies such as the Internet have proven instrumental in furthering departmental community-policing objectives. Important features that are used by many departmental websites in reaching their constituent audiences include (Hart 1996):

- Officer photo galleries, including photos and biographical sketches
- Libraries devoted to crime prevention
- Safety tips, including information about known scam cases operating within the jurisdiction
- Virtual tours of the department
- Recruitment tool with links to personnel information about the hiring process
- Citywide and neighborhood crime statistics, including crime-mapping capabilities on more advanced sites, such as the Chicago Police Department's Citizen ICAM
- Departmental wanted lists and upcoming court cases
- Capacity for anonymous and/or confidential reporting of crime information or complaints about officer conduct

Department websites move beyond the realm of being public relations tools toward true support for community policing activities to the extent that the department shares important details about activities and arrests rather than the filtered information generally provided to citizens by the media (Price 2001). Departmental posting of such information, however, should be balanced against the privacy needs of victims and nonconvicted offenders.

Improving Accountability—Mobile Communications with Patrol

Radio communications with patrol cars revolutionized the ability of departments to monitor the activities of line officers. Although such technology did not take away the high level of discretion available to officers as part of the nature of the job, enhancements to dispatch communications capabilities had a profound effect on the nature of the job. More recently, cellular phone technology has provided an alternate communication forum for some jurisdictions.

Mobile Digital Communications Mobile digital communications (MDC) offer nonverbal means of communicating information between communication centers and patrol (Thibault et al. 2001). Such communication is achieved through the use of a mobile digital terminal within the patrol car. In some jurisdictions, MDC options allow for electronic submission of reports, thereby reducing the volume of paperwork. More recently, some departments have installed new laptop computers into patrol cars, offering officers instant access to information, such as notes from the communications officer, and even the Internet. Soon officers will not have to leave their cars to write even more detailed reports (Johnson 2003). The Internet also facilitates interjurisdictional information-exchange opportunities immediately available to officers, again providing an important tool in the reduction of linkage blindness.

Automatic Vehicle Monitoring. Through the use of **automatic vehicle monitoring (AVM)** technologies, departments are able to know the location and status of patrol vehicles, including whether the door of the vehicle has been left open and so on (Thibault et al. 2001). AVM systems are thus vitally important in aiding officers in high-speed pursuit situations and in determining whether the officer is in need of backup.

Chapter Summary

- Technology has advanced significantly in the past twenty years, and the application of this technology has benefited law enforcement officers in both proactive and reactive methods of policing.

- The most important factors in crime analysis are timeliness, relevancy, and reliability, all of which are necessary to examine data effectively.

- With GIS crime mapping, a map is created that police officers can use to analyze where and when crime occurs. It has many benefits, particularly with regard to proactive policing. It can help the police develop strategies to combat crime, particularly in crime hot spots.

- Advanced technology allows for the collection of more timely and accurate data, helping patrol officers respond more quickly and effectively to crime.

- One of the leading technologies of the twenty-first century is CompStat, which envelopes the problem-oriented policing model and assists in more effective management of areas where crime occurs.

- Surveillance technology such as CCTV is extremely beneficial in tracking all types of criminals, from shoplifters to terrorists. Through the taped monitoring of movements, combined with emerging biometrics of face recognition technology, there are many potential applications of CCTV.

- GPS is important in facilitating law enforcement operation in both investigatory and deployment capacities.

- Interjurisdictional communication technologies useful to law enforcement include offender databases and electronic warrants systems.

Linking the Dots

1. What have been some of the most significant technological advancements in policing since 1980? Explain their significance.

2. What are some of the dangers associated with the advancement in police technology? How are these dangers balanced with the benefits of such technology?

3. Do you think CompStat is partially responsible for the significant drop in crime in New York City over the past decade?

4. How does law enforcement's use of technology benefit the community?

5. How can technology be used to help combat terrorism?

KEY TERMS

REFERENCES

American City and Country. 2002. "Crime Maps Improve Patrols in Camden." *American City and County*, October 1, 2002. Available at www.americancityandcountry.com/ar/government_crime_maps_improve.

Barley, S. 1986. "Technology as an Occasion for Structuring Evidence from Observations of CT Scanners and the Social Order of Radiology Departments." *Administrative Science Quarterly* 31(1):78–108.

Bijkker, M., T. Hughes, and T. Pinch. 1987. *The Social Construction of Technological Systems. New Directions in the Sociology and History of Technology.* Cambridge, MA: MIT Press.

Brantingham, C., and B. Brantingham. 1981. *Environmental Criminology.* Thousand Oaks, CA: Sage Publications.

Canter, P. 2000. "Using a Geographic Information System for Tactical Crime Analysis." In *Analyzing Crime Patterns: Frontiers of Practice*, edited by V. Goldsmith, P. McGuire, J. Mollenkopf, and T. Ross, pp. 3–10. Thousand Oaks, CA: Sage.

Carney, D. 1998. "Arming Beat Cops with GIS Weapons." *Civic.com*, April 13, 1998. Available at www.civic.com.

Clarke, K. C. 1990. *Analytical and Computer Cartography.* Upper Saddle River, NJ: Prentice Hall.

Cole, S. 2001. *Suspect Identities: A History of Fingerprinting and Criminal Identification.* Cambridge, MA: Harvard University Press.

Cowen, D. 2001. "Why Is GIS Important?" Available at www.env.duke.edullel/enn351/images/uoi.txt!

Cowper, T. 2003. "Emerging Technology and the Future of Policing." Paper presented at the International Police Studies Conference, June 12–15, Eastern Kentucky University, Richmond, Kentucky.

DeAngelis, T. 2000. "GIS: Answering the Why of Where?" *Police Chief*, February. Available at www.iactechnology.orgllibrary/techtal/techtalk0200.htm.

Department of Homeland Security. 2007. Homeland Security. Available at www.dhs.gov.

Goold, B. (2004). *CCTV and Policing: Public Area Surveillance and Police Practices in Britain.* Oxford: Oxford University Press.

Garcia, M. 2001. "Force Protection Using Wireless Internet Technology." *Technology Talk.* Available at www.loronit.com/solutions/casestudies/iactechtalk1201.pdf.

Grant, H., and K. Terry. 2000. *The New York City Sex Offender Management Team: Summary Progress Report.* New York: John Jay College of Criminal Justice.

Greene, K. 2003. "Global Positioning Systems Used for Some Offenders." *Noble News Online*, April 4. Available at www.nonlenatl.orglnews/publish/article_ 501.shtml.

Harries, K. 2001. *Demonstration of Orthophotographic Representation and Analysis*. Washington, D.C.: National Institute of Justice.

Harries, K. 1999. *Mapping Crime: Principle and Practice*. Washington, D.C.: National Institute of Justice.

Hart, F. 1996. "How and Why to Implement the Worldwide Web for Community Policing." *Police Chief 3*(1):55.

Hughes Network Systems. 2002. *Case Study*. Germantown, MD: Hughes Network Systems.

Johnson, M. 2003. "City Vehicles Receive Laptops." *Daytona Beach News Journal*, April 15, 1.

Kaluta, R. 2001. "New Developments in Interjurisdictional Communication Technology." *Police Chief*. Available at www.iacptechnology.org/library/ techtalk/techtalk0401.htm.

Karmen, A. 1996. *New York City Murder Mystery*. New York: NYU Press.

Kelling, G., and M. Moore. 1987. "The Evolving Strategy of Policing." *Perspectives on Policing 4*(1):1–15.

Kurzweil, R. 2001. "The Law of Accelerating Returns." Available at www.kurzweilai.net.

McDonald, P. 2002. *Managing Police Operations: Implementing the New York Crime Control Model: CompStat*. Belmont, CA: Wadsworth.

Monahan, M. 1998. "Technology Management for Community Policing." *Police Chief*, September. Available at www.iacptechnology.orgllibrary/ techtalk/techtalk0998.htm.

Norris, C., and G. Armstrong. 1999. *The Maximum Surveillance Society: The Rise of CCTV*. New York: NYU Press.

Onion, A. 2002. "Coordinates of a Killer: A Mathematical Method Can Help Investigators Locate Killers." *ABCnews.com*, October 8. Available at www .abcnews.com.

Perbix, M. 2001. "Automating Arrest Warrants Between Courts and Law Enforcement." *Police Chief*, October. Available at www.iacptechnology .org/library/AutomatingArrestWarrantsBT CountsandLE.pdf.

Phillips, P. 1972. "A Prologue to the Geography of Crime." *Proceedings, Association of American Geographers 4*(1):86–91.

Presidents Commission on Law Enforcement and the Administration of Justice. 1967. *Final Report of the President's Commission on Law Enforcement and the Administration of Justice*. Washington, D.C.: Presidents Commission on Law Enforcement and the Administration of Justice.

Price, C. 2001. "The Police Web Site as a Community Policing Tool." *Police Chief*, December.

Available at www.iacptechnology.orgllibrary/ PoliceWebsiteasaCommunityPolicingTool.pdf.

Rich, T. 1996. *The Chicago Police Department's Information Collection for Automated Mapping (ICAM) Program*. Washington, D.C.: National Institute of Justice Program Focus.

Rossmo, K. 1998. *Geographic Profiling*. Boca Raton, FL: CRC Press.

Scanlon, P. 2000. "A Successful Partnership: When Police and the Feds Team for Technology." *Police Chief*, October. Available at www.iacptechnology .org/library/techtalk/techtalk/co.

Seaskate, Inc. 1998. *The Evolution and Development of Police Technology*. Washington, D.C.: National Institute of Justice.

Shaw, C., and H. McKay. 1942. *Juvenile Delinquency and Urban Areas*. Chicago: University of Chicago Press.

Silverman, E. 1996. "Mapping Change: How the New York City Police Department Reengineered Itself to Drive Down Crime." *Law Enforcement News*, December 15. Available at www.1ib.jjay.cuny .edu/len96/15Dec/?/htm.

Silverman, E. 1999. *NYPD Battles Crime*. Boston, MA: Northeastern University Press.

Skogan, W., and S. Hartnett. 1996. *Community Policing Chicago Style*. New York: Oxford University Press.

Skolnick, J., and D. Bayley. 1986. *The New Blue Line: Police Innovation in Six American Cities*. New York: The Free Press.

Smith, K. 1998. "Integrated Automated Fingerprint Identification System: Twenty-first-century Technology for Law Enforcement." *Police Chief 62*(6):23.

Soulliere, N. 1999. *Police and Technology: Historical Review and Current Status*. Ottawa: Canadian Police College.

Taylor, B. 2000. "Virtual Private Networking: Secure Law Enforcement Communication on the Internet." *Police Chief 67*(1):13.

Terry, K., and J. Furlong. 2004. *Sex Offender Registration and Community Notification: A "Megan's Law" Sourcebook*, 2d ed. Kingston, NJ: Civic Research Institute.

Thibault, E., L. Lynch, and R. McBride. 2001. *Proactive Police Management*, 5th ed. Upper Saddle River, NJ: Prentice Hall.

Tomek, W. 2001. "Information Sharing: A Strategic Necessity." *Police Chief*, February. Available at www.iacptechnology.orgllibrary/tech talk/ techtalk0201.pdf.

Walsh, T. 2003. "Data Sharing Tightens Net for the Law-Agencies Put Criminal Justice Data On-line for Sharing." *Government Computer News*, July 10. Available at www.gcn.com.

ONWARD AND UPWARD

As a Trooper, your salary will be in excess of $46,000 within five years! And the benefits won't only be financial. You will positiv[...] impact the community where you serve. You'll also receive a m[...] of paid vacation a year, excellent dental and health care covera[...] and a great retirement package. Why settle for a boring job wh[...] you can enjoy an exciting, challenging and rewarding career in [...] Michigan State Police?

YOUR SUCCESS DEPENDS ON YOU!

Tpr. Jill Bennett. 9 years

Sgt. Marva Moore. 15 years

Capt. Marie Waalkes. 22 years

F/Lt. Cheryl Sm[...] years

Insp. D[...] 22

[...]r more information contact the Michigan State Police
[...]cruiting Unit at 517-[...]56-6306 or http://www.msp.state.mi.us

New Standards for
Police Recruitment

chapter

14

Chapter Objectives

- Explain the basic recruitment and selection standards for police officers and how they have developed over the last fifty years.

- Develop an understanding of the difficulties of specific selection requirements on minority populations both historically and presently.

- Explain the effect of legislation on recruitment and selection standards.

- Compare the benefits of academic education and police training from an academy.

- Understand the benefits and problems with affirmative action policies in policing.

- Describe five assessment areas upon which officers are promoted and explain the effect of affirmative action on promotion.

Introduction

Every police department seeks to recruit, select, train, and maintain the best officers possible. However, what characteristics of an officer are "the best"? Ideal qualities of a police officer have evolved and adapted as society has changed. During the Political Era, the only important characteristic of new recruits was that they belonged to a particular political party. Until fifty years ago, the "ideal" police officer was a strong, white male who would listen to commands from superior officers. Both racial and gender minorities were significantly under-represented until the 1970s, when legislation was passed requiring equal opportunities for them in the field of policing. Still, approximately 76 percent of police officers in local departments are white and 89 percent are male (Bureau of Justice Statistics 2002).

This chapter discusses the current standards for recruitment, selection, training, and promotion in police departments and how these standards have evolved. No specific formula exists for recruiting and maintaining the ideal officer, and many of those who were once considered ideal may experience stress, burnout, personal problems, and ultimately may cause more harm than good.

Linkages *In Law Enforcement*

Who Is the "Ideal" Law Enforcement Officer?

Throughout this textbook, the authors have discussed the duties of police officers, the tasks they must perform while on the job, and how their role has changed throughout history. Now it is time to consider who you think would make an ideal police officer. Consider the following questions:

- What would be your ideal composition of police officers in a department with regard to background, age, race, education, agility, and gender? Explain.

- From where would you recruit officers?

- What type of selection process would you have?

- Should police officers be held to higher ethical standards than individuals in other professions?

- How would you retain officers in your police department?

- What would be your standards for promotion?

It is difficult to define the characteristics of an "ideal" police officer. It might be better to ask how departments might recruit, select, and train officers in order to produce an ideal police department, creating opportunities for promotion and encouraging retention. This chapter will help you to analyze these issues while utilizing knowledge gained from the previous chapters.

Recruitment of Candidates

The job of a police officer involves stressful situations and entails interactions with many individuals in the community. It also requires quick decision making and good judgment. Police duties vary from writing reports to maintaining order to responding to criminal situations, all of which require critical thinking skills. Because of the range of duties, officers should possess certain traits: physically agility, the ability to cope with difficult situations, well-developed writing skills, good communication skills, sound judgment, compassion, strong powers of observation, and the ability to both exert and respect commands of authority. Unfortunately, it is difficult to find an ideal candidate with every one of these qualities (Sharp 1994).

Recruitment standards vary depending on the area being policed, and each department will aim to recruit the best person for a particular community. Each department recruits officers in different ways, though there are some standard recruitment techniques. These include passing out flyers in common areas of the community; going to job fairs at universities; advertising with newspaper, radio, or television; and, in larger cities, putting up posters in subways and on billboards (Strandberg 1996). Many of the larger police departments have cadet programs or internships in exchange for college credit, both of which serve as recruitment tools (Leach 1998). The key to recruiting a qualified group of individuals is advertising to a large audience. Within that broad group, each department is likely to find what it is seeking in terms of educational standards, diversity, and residency.

The police department today represents a culturally diverse group of people. This is much different from the early twentieth century, when officers were almost all white males.

Minimum Requirements

There are few articulated standards for officer selection, because every department sets its own standards. Most departments require that the officer, at a minimum:

- Be at least 21 years of age
- Have a driver's license in the state (or be eligible for one)
- Have no prior felony convictions
- Pass a written exam, a medical exam, an interview, a physical agility test, and psychological screening

Individuals who become police officers must have or be eligible to receive a driver's license because their primary duty is patrol, and they must be able to drive to respond to incidents. Police officers must also be able to possess a firearm. In order to qualify to own a firearm, a person must be at least twenty-one years old. For that reason, a police officer will not have full police powers until at least that age, and most police departments do not even allow recruits to enter the police academy until they are at least twenty-one. Convicted felons also are prohibited from possessing a firearm, which thereby bars them from becoming police officers. Individuals with domestic violence convictions are no longer able to possess a firearm, thereby prohibiting them from becoming police officers as well (Clarke 1997).

Education

Many police departments now have educational standards for recruits. Nearly all departments require officers to have at least a high school diploma, and many require at least some college credits. Such high standards in education were not always mandated, however. At the beginning of the twentieth century, the majority of male officers lacked a high school diploma. The male officer was expected to understand English well enough to speak intelligently and to be able to read and write reports (Schulz 1995). The standards for women were different from those for men. The International Association of Policewomen (IAP)—the female equivalent of the International Association of Chiefs of Police that was begun by Alice Stebbin Wells in 1916—suggested that policewomen have minimum educational qualifications equivalent to high school graduates (Schulz 1995). The IAP also suggested that this should be combined with experience in social service or educational work of two years or as a trained nurse. This educational double standard existed until 1972, when Congress amended Title VII of the 1964 Civil Rights Act (discrimination policies). With this legislation, educational standards for men were not raised; rather, educational standards for women were lowered.

Although there was no formal requirement for a college-level education for police officers in most agencies, organizations such as the Wickersham Commission began pushing for higher standards of education as early as 1931. In 1967, the Kerner Commission recommended that police officers should have a four-year college degree. Also around this time, the **Law Enforcement Assistance Administration (LEAA)** began to emphasize the need for police officers to attend college, going so far as to implement a grant system for individuals who were or planned to be police officers upon graduation. The Law Enforcement Education Program (LEEP) lasted for more than a decade and was responsible for a mass increase in degrees in criminal justice.

Despite the efforts of the LEAA, which ended its LEEP program in the early 1980s, the rise of educational standards only became apparent in the 1990s. Table 14.1 shows how educational standards across the United States in 1997 were nearly double the standards in 1990 (Reaves & Goldberg 1999). Still, less than one-quarter (23.8 percent) of all police agencies require their recruits to have some level of college education.

Experts continue to debate whether higher education makes an officer better at his or her job or whether vocational experience (e.g., from the police academy, from being on the street) is all that is necessary. Cao and Huang (2000) found that educational standards did not make a difference in the number of complaints filed against officers. Additionally, some believe that education alone does not make a good police officer; an individual is only a good police officer if

TABLE 14.1

Educational Requirements for New Officer Recruits in City, County, and State Agencies

	1990 (*n* = 584)	1997 (*n* = 651)
Four-year degree	3 (0.51%)	13 (2.0%)
Two-year degree	29 (4.9%)	50 (7.7%)
Some college	41 (7.0%)	92 (14.1%)
Total	73 (12.5%)	155 (23.8%)

Source: Jones-Brown, Delores D.; Terry, Karen J., *Policing and Minority Communities: Bridging the Gap,* 1st ed. Copyright © 2004. Reproduced by permission of Pearson Education, Inc., Upper Saddle River, New Jersey.

he or she possesses all the other characteristics that make a good police officer (e.g., keen powers of observation, physical agility, ability to handle stressful situations), though education can help one who does possess these qualities (Molden 1999). (See also Chapter 3.)

Other researchers, however, believe that education is beneficial to officers in a number of ways. Higher education may increase officers' decision-making skills and help them handle difficult situations through negotiation, as opposed to force. Fewer complaints are filed against officers who have a college degree, and those with some college education have fewer disciplinary problems than those with a high school education (Carter and Sapp 1988). Additionally, well-educated officers, as a whole, seem to have better knowledge of the law, human behavior, and social situations and have better communication and writing skills (Ferriera 1997). Police officers with college degrees believe that they are more prepared for the job those without degrees in many areas, including interpersonal skills, problem solving abilities, and the quality of their work (Krimmel 1996). However, no documented studies have shown that a college education alone makes for more effective police officers or better crime fighters.

Technology

The increasing use of technology in policing is another reason why education is now an important feature of job recruitment. Not only has computer technology been adapted into the daily routine of many police officers, but they must also be able to understand technological advances, such as crime mapping and Comp-Stat. By looking at computerized maps of the city, the police can pinpoint geographic areas where the majority of crime occurs (Bratton and Knobler 1988). This technology is used to hold police officers accountable for crime increases or reductions. Over one-third of all large police departments are using some sort of crime-mapping technology today, it is likely that this number will increase significantly in the near future because of the dramatic drop in crime in some of the cities that use such technology (see Chapter 13).

Technology also is used to assist in criminal identification. Computers are now used to generate composites for identifying suspects, with a library of facial features and accessories to help the witness construct an accurate picture of the perpetrator (Senna and Siegla 2002). Computer technology not only assists in accuracy, but also in efficiency. For instance, an automatic fingerprint system helps identify unique marks and ridges with accuracy and speed. For these reasons, it is important that police officers be knowledgeable about such systems.

Legal Knowledge

Although education may not assist the officer in all aspects of his or her job, it may increase an officer's knowledge of legal issues. Legal knowledge is integral to the job of a police officer. It was argued in Chapter 5 that officers should have an understanding of constitutional law, criminal law, criminal procedure, rules of evidence, and even civil law in case he or she is the subject of litigation. Training in the police academy covers the legal issues central to the duties of a police officer, such as the Fourth Amendment and an individual's right to be free from illegal searches and seizures. Many criminal justice programs in college, however, cover legal issues more extensively and give police officers a broader understanding of the issues they may encounter on a daily basis.

Residency

In addition to education requirements, some departments have residency requirements mandating that officers live within the jurisdiction in which they are policing. This is a recommendation that surfaced from many of the commissions in the hope that by living in the communities they police, officers will be better equipped to understand and thereby interact with its citizenry. There are many benefits to officers living in the community where they police, such as knowing the problems in that community that need to be addressed and being able to identify with residents of that community.

However, there are a few drawbacks to a police officer living in the community that he or she polices. First, the police officer may not be able to live in the area in which he or she is policing if it is an extremely wealthy community. A second drawback to residency requirements is the possibility of corruption. If an officer is patrolling or responds to a situation that involves an acquaintance, he or she is less likely to uphold the law with that individual. Despite these drawbacks, the general consensus is that it is best for an officer to live in or near the area he or she is policing.

Diversity

Perhaps the greatest recruitment push resulting from the various commissions has been toward greater minority representation within law enforcement agencies. Although there has been some improvement in this area, ethnic representation in most police forces is still disproportionate. Racial and ethnic minorities represented 23.6 percent of local police departments in 2003, compared to just 14.8 percent in 1987 (Bureau of Justice Statistics 2006). Specifically, African Americans represented over 10 percent of the population in 2000 (U.S. Census Bureau 2000) and 15 percent of the police officers. However, they are not represented proportionately across the country. Hispanic officers accounted for 11 percent of the police force, although they comprise over 12 percent of the population. Women, who account for 46.5 percent of the U.S. population, accounted for only 14 percent of full-time sworn personnel (Bureau of Justice Statistics 2004).

When recruiting a diverse police force, one must question why an individual seeks to become a police officer. Historically, policing was a job for white males. Women who were hired as police officers worked more as social workers, and it took many decades for them to become crime fighters. Several studies in the late 1970s and early 1980s analyzed why women were interested in entering a male-dominated career such as law enforcement. In 1978, Ermer found that job security was the primary factor in women choosing a law enforcement career, because the starting salaries at the time were higher than for most other equivalent jobs. Meagher and Yentes (1986) also found job security to be an important factor in choosing policing as a career, although they found this to be true for both men and women. They studied whether men and women join the police force for the same reasons, and they found that, contrary to perceptions, there are many similarities between the two groups. Whereas men are perceived to join for reasons of excitement, authority, and the ability to fight crime, they actually claim to join primarily to help people—a reason why women are perceived to (and do) join the force (Meagher and Yentes 1996). Lester (1983) supported these reasons, finding that women tend to join the police force because of the nature of police work, the variety of assignments, and the salary benefits.

Police departments can use a number of methods to recruit ethnic and racial minorities as well as women. Many larger departments have recruiting officers. Ideally, the recruiting officers should represent the minorities that the department is trying to attract (Milgram 2002). Recruiters should attend community meetings in an effort to interact with the individuals they are trying to recruit. Such positive interactions are necessary, because many individuals from minority groups lack trust in the police due to negative personal interactions and negative media attention. Recruiters can also seek out college students and even high school students for internships, cadet programs, youth programs, or other community programs in order to develop their interest in eventually becoming a police officer. In order access a cross section of the community that includes all minority groups, it is necessary to take these additional steps beyond the traditional methods of recruitment.

Selection of Candidates

Once recruited, a candidate must go through an extensive selection process in order to be hired as a police officer. This is a lengthy, competitive process, involving multiple phases. In most police departments, the candidate must pass a written exam, an interview, a physical exam, a psychological exam, a background check, and a polygraph.

The selection process has been modified considerably over the past quarter century, due in large part to equal opportunity criteria. The Court has heard several cases related to hiring standards for police, and it has mandated that the process not be arbitrary or discriminatory in any way but rather focus on job-related criteria. Several selection procedures have been modified as a result of these cases. For instance, the physical agility tests used in the selection process were originally designed in a way that was prohibitory toward women; therefore, very few women were able to pass the physical agility phase of the selection process. Similarly, it was difficult for candidates from other states or who spoke English as a second language to pass the written exam, and so these issues are now addressed in exam preparation courses.

The Written Exam

The written exam is generally the first phase of the selection process once a formal application has been submitted. The test varies by department, but it might be a civil service exam, an exam produced by the individual police department, or one produced by a private testing company. The exam does not test specific legal or criminal justice knowledge, but rather evaluates the candidate's basic reading, writing, and comprehension skills. The exam will likely contain a number of different sections, whereby the candidate must be able to understand and write in English, write a sample essay, understand basic mathematics, memorize facts, show sound reasoning and logic, and analyze potential scenarios. Candidates' scores are ranked, and those who score above a particular benchmark will be able to move to the next phase of selection.

Because of the exam's focus on the ability to read, write, and comprehend the English language, some otherwise-qualified minority applicants may be eliminated from the candidate pool (Rafilson 1997). Some departments have attempted to avoid this predicament by offering exam preparation. One suggestion has been to offer non-native-English speakers extra time to complete the written test (National Crime Prevention Council 1995).

Background Checks

Once a person sends in a formal application to become a police officer, the police department performs a background check on the applicant. The primary purpose of the background check is to determine if the candidate has been convicted of any felonies or serious misdemeanors and to make sure that he or she is of "good moral character" (Fagin 2003). Police departments consider a number of factors in relation to a police candidate's moral character. The candidate should not only be free of prior criminal convictions, but also should not partake in drug use, violent activity, excessive alcoholism, or display prejudicial attitudes of any kind. Though these factors would not necessarily disqualify individuals from attaining other jobs, police officers often are held to higher moral standards than the general population. The reason for this is that police officers must abide by a code of ethics and exhibit moral behavior in their job. When officers lack ethics, they may digress into corruption and mistreatment of the individuals they are policing. Most police departments explain in their recruitment brochures the type of moral behavior that is expected from potential candidates. For instance, the Los Angeles recruitment flyer reads:

> You must have no felony convictions or any misdemeanor conviction which would prevent your carrying a gun. You must not have a history of criminal or improper conduct, or a poor employment, military, or driving record which would affect your suitability for law enforcement work. You must also have a responsible financial history and a pattern of respect and honesty in your dealings with individuals and organizations. A valid California driver's license is required prior to appointment.

The person who is in charge of conducting the background investigation should be professional and unbiased and should exhibit the characteristics the agency is seeking. Although the background investigation will consist of a specified set of questions, such as whether the candidate has ever been convicted of a crime, the background investigator should also be aware of moral and ethical issues that may potentially screen out candidates for a policing job. For instance, the candidate should not express prejudicial views about any particular race, gender, ethnicity, or sexual identity.

The Interview Process

The interview process is designed to evaluate a candidate's suitability for becoming a police officer. The interview panel might consist of three to five skilled interviewers in a variety of fields (e.g., policing, psychology). The interview can be structured, unstructured, or a combination or both. In a structured interview, the candidate is asked a series of questions regarding the job and his or her specific abilities. Structured questions usually require specified answers to direct questions (e.g., do you drink alcohol?). The other alternative is to conduct a semistructured interview, with open-ended questions on particular topics (e.g., how much alcohol do you consume weekly?). Although structured interviews allow for a better comparison of candidates on specific topics, open-ended questions are likely to elicit more information.

Although the interview panel might need to eliminate candidates at this stage because of particular answers they have given (e.g., admitting to drinking excessive quantities of alcohol daily), the purpose of the interview is to assess other issues, such as level of professionalism, social and communication skills, level of reasoning, appearance, composure, and poise. Whereas the written exam is designed to measure basic comprehension skills, the interview attempts to elicit information about the candidate's ambition to become a police officer and how he or she would handle scenarios that a police officer might encounter. The candidate is scored based on his or her answers and compared to other candidates on a range of criteria. Though the candidate must pass all phases of the selection process in order to be hired as a police officer, the interview process is critical in the assessment of the candidate's attitudes, appearance, and demeanor.

Psychological and Polygraph Tests

The purpose of the psychological screening process is to measure intelligence and to identify personality characteristics and any mental disorders that may lead to problematic behavior in the future. Studies show that between 80 and 90 percent of police departments use some sort of psychological screening tool to determine whether the candidate is fit to become a police officer (Langworthy et al. 1995; Reaves and Goldberg 1999). It is important to screen out individuals who may exhibit mental or personality deficits, because police officers interact with individuals on a daily basis and often in high-stress situations.

The most common psychological assessment tool used is the **Minnesota Multiphasic Personality Inventory (MMPI)**. The primary purpose of the MMPI is to assess an individual's psychopathology and determine whether he or she should be diagnosed with a mental disorder. It also identifies problems with social adjustment, neuroses, psychoses, phobias, and delusions; it is used in many occupations to determine whether candidates are suitable for high-risk positions. It has recently been revised and in its second edition, and it consists of 567 true/false questions about attitudes, beliefs and ideas.[1] It is reliable and valid, and it has built-in censors to detect whether the test taker is lying.

Some police departments use multiple psychological tests or tests other than the MMPI. One other common inventory is the California Psychological Inventory (CPI), which contains 434 questions relating to personality that aim to measure individual difference variables. The Rorschach test also is common. Originally published in 1921, it consists of ten inkblots that are meant to identify particular personality traits. This is a controversial test. Some psychologists consider it to be subjective; therefore, it usually is used as a supplement to other screening tools.

Approximately 61 percent of U.S. police departments use a **polygraph**, or lie detector examination, in the selection process (Bureau of Justice Statistics 2004).[2] Information obtained by a polygraph test is not legally admissible in court because it is only 85 to 90 percent accurate (Board on Behavioral, Cognitive, and Sensory Sciences and Education 2003). However, it is used in the assessment process to determine whether the candidate is being deceptive. It works by recording involuntary physiological changes in the body that occur

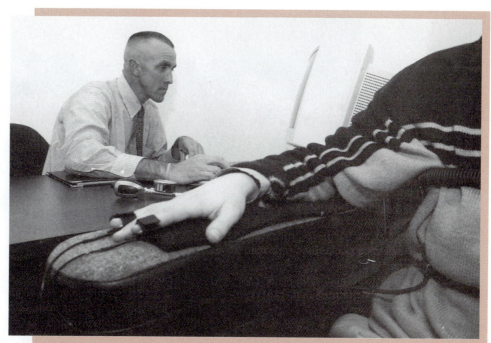

The polygraph is one device used to select police candidates. Integrity and honesty are necessary qualities in a police officer.

when a person is partaking in conscious deceit. It simultaneously measures respiration, changes in blood pressure and pulse rate, and electrical resistance of the skin.

Physical Agility

Measuring a police candidate's level of physical agility is a crucial part of the selection process, although the physical agility test has been controversial and has undergone significant changes since its inception. Until the 1970s, the physical agility test required substantial upper-body strength, which kept many women from passing the test, thereby eliminating them as police candidates. These tests, which consisted largely of pushups, pullups, and situps, measured rapid reflexes, speed and coordination, dexterity, endurance, and strength. The Supreme Court invalidated such tests, however, saying that these were not related to the job as it is performed.

In 1972, Title VII of the 1964 Civil Rights Act declared that all applicants for a position requiring physical strength and agility must be given an opportunity to demonstrate their ability to perform the work in question. The Equal Employment Opportunity Commission (EEOC) guidelines on sex discrimination barred the refusal to hire a female applicant because of characteristics attributed to women as a class. Both of these regulations suggest that women must be given a chance to show that they can do the required duties of the police job and that physical tests must not be applied in a manner that is discriminatory to women. Police agencies must demonstrate the job relatedness of criteria, and for that reason the physical agility tests have changed considerably in the past few decades.

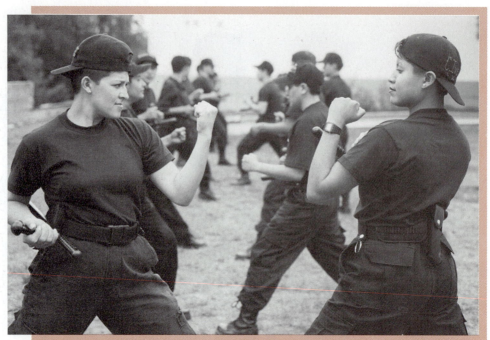

Physical agility tests have changed significantly since the 1970s. At that time, it was difficult for women to pass the agility tests, which required a lot of upper-body strength.

San Francisco is one example of a city that utilized a physical agility test with a substantial disparate impact on the hiring of women. The test, which only about one percent of female candidates passed, consisted of physical skills that were not applicable to the daily situations that an officer would likely face. The tests were considered by the courts to be invalid at measuring the skills of patrol officers. Similarly, the police department in Houston, Texas, had a physical agility test requiring recruits do a pullup on a 7′6″ inch wall, and yet there are no walls 7 feet or higher in Houston. Alternatively, Miami assesses the agility potential of the candidate and gives the candidate training if he or she is unable to pass the test the first time. The majority of women who fail the test the first time later complete it successfully (95 percent). Thus, women are able to pass the test at the same rate as male candidates (Longway et al. 2003).

Most agility tests now consist of an obstacle course that simulates a potential police experience. Throughout the course, candidates must complete activities such as climbing a 4- to 6-foot wall, crawling under a bar that is about 24 inches high, dragging a 150- to 170-pound dummy, sprinting, and climbing stairs, ropes, or ladders within a specified amount of time. Whether this time is the same for all candidates or whether it varies depending on the candidate's characteristics (e.g., male or female, different heights, etc.) depends on the jurisdiction.

The key to passing the physical agility test appears to be in the training. With modifications in training, women are as likely to pass the new agility tests as men. Modification does not mean that standards of physical fitness must be lowered. However, females can emphasize their lower body weight, because they generally have less upper-body strength than men. Women also tend to be weaker with firearms, largely because their hands are smaller, thereby making it difficult to grip the firearm with the same strength as men. With extra training to strengthen their grips, however, they can improve their accuracy and agility with firearms.

Research on the Job Performance of Female Officers

When police departments began to modify their physical agility tests, police officers and researchers alike questioned whether women could perform the duties of a police officer as well as men. In the 1970s, many studies were conducted to study women's performance on the job. These studies showed that in nearly every area of law enforcement, women performed as well as their male counterparts (Bloch and Anderson 1974). By the mid-1980s, studies looked at different issues, including the attitudes of male officers toward female officers and the way that female officers perceived their roles in the department.

Many studies throughout the 1970s focused on how policewomen compared to men in a variety of areas (e.g., urban versus rural) and with a variety of tasks (particularly patrol). Researchers published articles that showed the following results (Fry and Greenfield 1980; Johns and Barclay 1979; Martin 1979):

- Policemen and policewomen perform similarly on patrol, and there is no discernible difference in how they handle incidents.

- Women often are assigned to different types of duties than men. Generally, they are assigned to lighter duties than their male counterparts or they are assigned to lower-crime areas.

- Policewomen are similar to policemen in how they respond to and handle arrests and summons.

- Policewomen and policemen are different in three key areas: policewomen do not draw their weapons as frequently; they use less physical force; and they are better at handling domestic violence and house calls.

Affirmative Action

Physical agility tests were not the only barrier to women becoming police officers, and police departments were strikingly lacking in women and minorities in the 1960s. Because policing was almost universally a white male profession, states and the federal government began enacting laws that created political pressure for law enforcement to hire racial and gender minorities. **Affirmative action** policies required that police departments do more than simply create equal opportunities for everyone. They mandated that the police department take extra steps to hire minorities. Many affirmative action policies established **quotas** for minorities, or a specified number of jobs that a department was required to fill with minorities. The purpose of affirmative action was to ensure that individuals who previously had been excluded from particular types of employment would have access to these jobs. Law enforcement agencies that did not comply with affirmative action policies could face civil suits from the parties being excluded, and they could also face a loss of funding from major grant bodies if their hiring and promotional policies were deemed unlawful. Affirmative action policies are controversial, because despite the positive motivation behind them—equal opportunity in the workplace—they also bring of charges of **reverse discrimination** (hiring of minorities at the expense of those in the majority). In addition, some believe that those of minority backgrounds are hired as "tokens" and that such policies conflict with social integration in the police department.

Legal Issues

Affirmative action policies began appearing in the 1960s and were largely the result of court-mandated legislation. A number of legislative acts were passed in order to assist women and minorities in attaining jobs dominated by white males, one of which was policing. Table 14.2 presents several acts and the purposes of each.

Although these acts set policies mandating that women and minorities have equal access to employment opportunities, it was the case of *Griggs v. Duke Power*[3] in 1971 that firmly established equal opportunity guidelines. The Court stated that jobs that excluded minorities disproportionately were illegal unless the standards for exclusion were job related. For the first time, the Court declared that the burden of proof was on employers, not recruits, to show that exclusion from a job is due to job-related reasons. This burden of proof test has since been swapped, however, and the burden of proof now lies with the person excluded from the job (*Wards Cove Packing Company, Inc. v. Antonio*[4]).

Barriers for Women and Minorities

In the 1970s and 1980s, the percentage of minorities in policing increased significantly. Whereas in 1970 the percentage of African American police officers was 6.35 percent (double the percentage in 1960) (Kuykendall and Burns 1980), by the early 1990s African Americans represented nearly 11 percent of the police force (Bureau of Justice Statistics 1996). This was due to a number of fac-

TABLE 14.2

Acts Requiring Equal Opportunities for Women and Minorities in the Workplace

Act	Purpose
Equal Pay Act, 1963	Passed by Congress, this act prohibited unequal pay for men and women who did the same work. Prior to its enactment, policewomen were paid far less than their male colleagues.
Executive Order, 1969	Passed by President Richard Nixon, this order stated that the federal government could not use sex as a qualification for hiring. This had an impact on federal agencies such as FBI, and the municipal police departments were soon to follow.
Title VII of the 1964 Civil Rights Act, 1972	This prohibited employment discrimination on the basis of race, color, religion, or sex for recruitment, hiring, working conditions, promotion, or benefits in any governmental agency. Prior to this, it was nearly impossible for women and minorities to attain a job in policing.
Crime Control Act, 1973	Ensured that police departments did not discriminate against women in employment practices. It did so by withholding funds from the LEAA, the major funding body of the municipal governments.
Americans with Disabilities Act, 1990	Ensured that agencies did not discriminate against any person otherwise qualified for a job because of a disability.

tors, including the demand for black police officers after the race riots in the 1960s, the civil rights movement, and affirmative action policies (Kuykendall and Burns 1980). This increase in African American police officers was critical in improving police–community relations in minority communities.

The role of affirmative action policies was significant in facilitating this change (Walker 1985). Because of affirmative action policies, police agencies specifically sought out individuals from classes of people who were historically underrepresented or were discriminated against. The rate of racial minorities, particularly African Americans, increased significantly. Although many of these policies became effective in the 1970s, it was the cumulative effect of these policies that made an impact by the 1980s (Lewis 1989).

Affirmative action policies also had a significant effect on the number of women in police agencies at this time. According to Susan Martin (1989), by the late 1980s women comprised 10.1 percent of the force; where there were affirmative action policies but no court order, they comprised 8.3 percent of the force; where there were no affirmative action policies, they comprised 6.1 percent of the force. Today, women make up 20 percent of police applicants, 20.6 percent of persons accepted into training, and 19.2 percent of those who complete training. Thus, the number of women accepted is not disproportionate to the number of women who apply. Minority women comprise 45 percent of women who apply and 44 percent of women who complete training.

However, these employment increases had some negative consequences. Both racial and gender minorities accepted under affirmative action policies were considered **tokens**, the thinking that the department had been legally required to accept them due to affirmative action policies. Had police departments not accepted women onto the force, they would have faced legal repercussions. Unfortunately, those on the force often treated the "tokens" differently from officers from the dominant race and gender. This often led to discrimination in selection, assignments, and evaluations, as well as exclusion from the police culture and harassment.

Policewomen at this time found it particularly difficult to fit it, and they had to change their characteristics in order to socially interact with the male officers. Susan Martin wrote a classic article on the role dilemmas of female police officers in 1979, which also analyzed the effects of affirmative action policies on these officers. She noted two distinct roles of female officers: that of the *police*women, or the defeminized officers who emphasize their physical skills, and the police-*women*, or the deprofessionalized officers who emphasize their femininity.

Martin (1979) explained that the defeminized woman seeks acceptance by acting in an exceptional manner. She does not identify with the other women, but rather with her male counterparts. She tries to fulfill the same work norms as them and not stand out in any way that would allow them to put her down personally or professionally. She shows professional competence above that of many colleagues and closely adheres to the norms of behavior governing male police officers. The defeminized woman adopts coping strategies to maximize her effectiveness as an officer. She acts with self-confidence and tries to not only to meet the production norms of the department, but to surpass them. She accepts the fact that women have to try harder than men, and she goes out of her way to show courage and willingness to take action, even if it is dangerous. She is comfortable on the street and enjoys patrol, is generally ambitious, and tries to make political friends to get ahead. She denies or minimizes the existence of discrimination against women by the department and is likely to blame the other female officers for the problems they encounter. Finally, she does not feel that her work threatens her gender identity outside of the department.

The deprofessionalized woman, in contrast, plays up her femininity. She functions as a junior assistant to the policemen, even though she has an equal title to them. She consistently acts in a feminine manner and is satisfied to do less work that her counterparts. She does not like patrol and is not comfortable on the street. Instead, she prefers the social work aspect of policing. She does not necessarily believe that women are physically equipped to be on patrol and feels that it is better to do work that is not dangerous, because the pay is the same either way. When she is on patrol, she relies on the male partner to do most of the patrol work. Unlike the defeminized officer, the deprofessionalized officer emphasizes her femininity, thereby making police work difficult. She is not interested in a career and promotions within the department, has no desire to supervise men or add additional responsibilities, and does not want more shift work. She has few chances for promotion; however, she knows this and is not disappointed when she does not receive the promotion. Finally, she is critical of the defeminized policewomen because she feels they have objectionable morals, like the policemen.

Policewomen are in a paradoxical situation. If they don't defeminize themselves, they will fit a feminine stereotype and not allow themselves room for promotion. If they do defeminize themselves, they will be competing with men for their promotional opportunities and they become a career threat. Several studies have analyzed this socialization problem. Sherman (1975) showed that if women do not sacrifice at least some of their femininity, they will not be accepted by the male officers. Gross (1984) showed that female academy recruits displayed masculine characteristics and few feminine characteristics. This may be due to the fact that they are subjected to standardized behavior in training, which is essentially masculine.

In their study on women's perceptions of policing, Daum and Johns (1994) found that most policewomen felt accepted by civilians and other female officers. However, 42 percent did not feel accepted by other male officers. Also, 55 percent of the policewomen felt as though their male supervisors did not accept them. On other factors, 76 percent thought they performed the job as well as the policemen, 68 percent felt they had to do more work than their male colleagues to be given the same credit; 58 percent of the women thought they faced tougher standards of conduct than the men (including grooming standards). Fifty-seven percent saw no difference in morale for female or male officers; however, 35 percent thought that morale was lower for women. Some of the women wanted the department to recognize that women have special needs, while at the same time they do the job as well as the men. Others did not want any pampering or special attention at all.

Both African American and white male officers tended to have negative views about policewomen at the outset of the affirmative action selections, marginalizing women on the force. Women tended to be placed on early shifts where the duties were light or they were made to go on dead-end calls, issue tickets, work as dispatchers or desk attendants, or take missing persons reports.

Two major barriers for women in policing is sexual harassment and poor maternity leave policies. Daum and Johns (1994) found that 62 percent of the women they spoke with had experienced some form of sexual harassment in the form of jokes, inappropriate touching, requests for sex, sexually degrading comments, or gestures. Policewomen are generally not happy about their police force's maternity policy, claiming that despite legislation there is discrimination against women who are pregnant. The Pregnancy Discrimination Act was passed in 1978, with an amendment to Title VII of the Civil Rights Act 1964. This prohibited against discrimination "because of or on the basis of pregnancy, childbirth, or related medical conditions," and the purpose of the Act was to allow for women to participate equally in the workforce while still being able to have a child, because the right to a family life is a fundamental right. The police department cannot discriminate against a woman based upon pregnancy, though the department can legally change the policewoman's duties in order to not harm her or her child (Higginbotham 1993).

There has been much litigation concerning the assignment of duties to pregnant women or the leave that these women are forced to take when they are pregnant, and courts have not been consistent in their rulings. The courts often refer to the case of *O'Laughlin v. Pinchback*.[5] In this case, a pregnant corrections officer was told that she was discharged because her work assignments endangered her health and that of her unborn child and because she couldn't perform her duties adequately. The courts said that this was a violation of the Pregnancy Discrimination Act for two reasons: first, because there was no evidence that she couldn't do her duties or respond to security threats just as other employees would; second, because there was no medical evidence that this was dangerous to the health of her unborn child. Though the legislation in this area has come a long way, women still lack equality in a male-dominated field.

Training

Once a police candidate has passed through the selection process, he or she is hired on **probation**, a trial period of one or two years during which the officer is evaluated. This probationary period begins with training at the **police academy**, a school where officers learn on-the-job techniques prior to receiving full police powers. Officers must train at the academy for up to 1,100 hours, and they receive full pay and benefits from the time they enter the academy (Reaves and Goldberg 1999). While in the academy, the officer receives educational as well as practical physical training. The officer must learn constitutional law and criminal law specific to the state in which he or she is policing.

Police academies vary by jurisdiction, although there are certain standard instructional categories. All police academies have lectures from which the officers learn about the law and the criminal justice system. They receive physical training, training in the use of firearms, and training in the systems of patrol and traffic. They must also learn about the police department, its policies, and its relationship to other agencies (e.g., state/county/federal agencies). This training serves a number of purposes; namely, it standardizes the training of all officers in the jurisdiction while encouraging the safety of the officers and the community they will be policing. The extended time in training should aid the officer's confidence in his or her ability to utilize police powers, use quick decision-making skills, and use the appropriate level of discretion when approaching a situation.

Once out of the academy, the police officer is assigned a **field training officer (FTO)**. The FTO assists the new officer in applying the knowledge and skills learned at the academy. The FTO also assists the new officer to acclimate into the police culture, or experience the socialization process. **Socialization** involves

Education is part of the training process for police officers. They must learn about sociological, psychological, and legal issues, as well as critical thinking and writing skills.

learning the values, social processes, and behaviors associated with the police institution. It involves the patterns of interaction that depend on the relations of individuals in particular settings. Because the police culture is so unique, new officers are likely to adapt their personalities to those of other police officers who have experience on the job. It is during the rookie period that officers might develop an "us versus them" attitude. However, FTOs can have a significant influence over new officers and assist them in dealing with the inevitable stress and cynicism of the job.

It is even more difficult for women to adapt to the socialization process, and both women and minorities might be excluded from the police subculture and face harassment. Affirmative action and equal opportunity policies can mandate equal hiring amongst groups, but it does not assist in the socialization process.

Retention

Many individuals are drawn to a policing career because of the job opportunities. These include salary and benefits, job security, and opportunities for promotion, although the job also leads to stress and **burnout** for many of the officers. The key to job retention is to accentuate the positive aspects of the job (e.g., positive community relations, helping people) and provide services that can help to reduce the level of stress experienced by police officers. In studies assessing job strain, Johnson (1991) showed that women experienced more internal burnout whereas men experienced more external burnout. Johnson described *internal burnout* as being emotionally exhausted by the job and *external burnout* as lacking compassion due to emotional hardening. In practical terms, policemen would be more likely to take out the stress of the job on others, such as the individuals they are policing. The tangible result of internal burnout was that policewomen described having difficulty or no desire to wake up each day and face the duties of their job. Despite the problems women face, Daum and Johns (1994) point out that 80 percent of women plan to stay in the department until retirement, and 71 percent said that if they had to do it all over they would again choose to be police officers.

The Bureau of Justice Assistance (2001) has examined the issue of recruitment and retention of female police officers and has issued guidelines for police departments on how to increase retention of female officers. It explains that retention of female officers is more difficult than male officers, because they face additional challenges such as sexual harassment, gender discrimination, and isolation. The guidelines go on to explain, however, the advantages to departments who retain women on the force. These advantages include:

- Women are competent. Female officers are as competent as their male counterparts.

- Women are not likely to use physical force. Subsequently, they are less likely than men to be accused of excessive use of force.

- Women help focus on community-oriented policing tactics. This helps build positive police–community relations.

- Women help in domestic violence incidents. The highest volume of calls to the police is related to domestic violence, and female officers assist in the response to these calls.

- Less discrimination and harassment. The more female officers there are in a department, the less likely female officers will be harassed, because they will have a higher representation in the department.

- Changes in policy. The increasing number of women in departments creates the need for a previously male-only profession to modify outdated policies in relation to selection criteria, performance standards, and supervision.

Standards for Promotion

The promotion process for police officers is very competitive (Garner 1998). Officers may be promoted through several methods. Although promotion processes differ across jurisdictions, officers must typically take a written exam and partake in an interview; they are then assessed on qualities relating to the job. The written exam, although not common across all departments, is particularly common in the larger urban departments, such as those in New York, Los Angeles, and Chicago. The written exam usually is in a multiple-choice format; although it is meant to be objective, there has been a lot of litigation against it for its alleged bias against minorities. For instance, in the case of *Acosta v. Lang*[6] the court stated that if the answers of the candidates are as good or better than the established answers, they must be accepted.

During the interview, a board of several (generally three to six) members asks the candidates a variety of questions. These questions range from information about their background and personal characteristics to judgments about policing situations. After the interview, the candidates are assessed, during which time they are observed, tested, rated, and evaluated. Areas of assessment generally include:

- An "in-basket" exercise, that tests the officer's ability to perform desk tasks and paperwork

- An oral presentation, where the candidate presents an overview of his or her work history and personal strengths

- A creative writing project, where the candidate prepares and delivers a paper on a specialized topic

- A peer-group rating exercise, where the candidate rates his or her peers based on specific criteria

- Group dialogue, where the candidate acts as the leader of a group discussion

The purpose of these assessment tools is to determine how well the candidate would perform at a supervisory level. The promotion is not based on these factors alone, but they are considered in combination with the performance evaluation. Performance evaluations for each candidate look at, among other things, quantity and quality of work, work habits, human relations, and adaptability to new situations.

Until the mid-1980s nearly all of those promoted were white males. However, since then, there has been an increase in the number of women in the ranks above patrol officer. Affirmative action policies helped the promotion of female supervisors considerably. In the 1980s, in departments where there were court ordered affirmative action policies, females comprised 3.5 percent of supervisory positions; where there were affirmative action policies with no court orders, they comprised 2.4 percent; where there were no specific affirmative action policies, they comprised 2.2 percent of the supervisors (Martin 1989). Price and Gavin (1979) noted that promotional opportunities for women at this time were limited, and the police management hierarchy was rigid and restricted at the top. They claimed that the most important indicator for promotion was crime fighting abilities and a good arrest record, qualities associated with male officers.

Many police departments at this time adopted **dual promotion lists**, or separate promotional instruments for white male officers and all other officers. These lists helped women and minorities be promoted, often for the first time, but it negatively affected their levels of integration with the

Although still underrepresented, women are increasingly being promoted into management positions within the police department.

other police officers. These lists generated tension in police departments. The white male and female officers felt resentment toward officers of racial minorities, feeling that they received advancement only because of a court-mandated policy rather than merit. Alternatively, black officers felt that the promotional exams were culturally biased and that was why black officers received lower exam scores. The cultural bias of promotional exams continues to be a contentious issue.

Between 1980 and the mid-1990s, promotional opportunities for women increased. Women continued to be significantly more likely to be eligible for promotion to sergeant in departments with affirmative action. Today, several factors determine whether women apply for, and receive, a promotion. According to Whetstone (2001), the biggest impact on the number of women applicants for promotion was the number of women already serving there. Female officers who were considered to be effective were often given desirable positions above male officers who were similarly qualified. Additionally, many women choose not to apply for a promotion, but decide to remain patrol officers. Reasons for this include poor work conditions, poor assignment and work-hour flexibility, and lack of child care and family concerns (Whetstone 2001).

Chapter Summary

- Standards for recruitment, selection, and training have evolved significantly over the past 100 years. Policing was originally a "white man's job," but legislation in the 1960s began a push for a more representative police force.

- The police began actively recruiting women and minorities, implementing affirmative action policies to help give them equal opportunities to be hired as police officers.

- Though more representative of the community today than ever before, police departments still employ a selection process with controversial requirements.

- Debate continues as to the benefits of higher education, residency requirements, necessary levels of physical agility, and the lengths and types of training.

Linking the Dots

1. How have recruitment and selection standards changed over the past century?

2. Why is it important to have so many selection procedures? Are any of these procedures more important than the others?

3. Compare male and female officers. What are their different strengths and weaknesses?

4. How have legal issues affected the police departments over the last thirty years? How has the law assisted gender and racial minorities? Have these legal requirements hindered minorities in any way?

5. What can police managers do to increase retention?

KEY TERMS

KEY TERMS

Affirmative action 359
Burnout 364
Dual promotion lists 366
Field training officer (FTO) 363
Law Enforcement Assistance
　Administration (LEAA) 351

Minnesota Multiphasic
　Personality Inventory
　(MMPI) 356
Police academy 363
Polygraph 356
Probation 363

Quotas 359
Reverse discrimination 359
Socialization 363
Tokens 361

REFERENCES

Bloch, P. B., and D. Anderson. 1974. *Policewomen on Patrol: Final Report*. Washington, D.C.: The Police Foundation.

Board on Behavioral, Cognitive, and Sensory Sciences and Education. 2003. *The Polygraph and Lie Detection*. Washington, D.C.: National Academies Press.

Bratton, W. W., and P. Knobler. 1988. *Turnaround: How America's Top Cop Reversed the Crime Epidemic*. New York: Random House.

Bureau of Justice Assistance. 2001. "Recruiting and Retaining Women: A Self-Assessment Guide for Law Enforcement." *Bureau of Justice Assistance Bulletin*, Washington, D.C.: NCJ 188157.

Bureau of Justice Statistics. 1996. *Local Police Departments, 1993*. Washington, D.C.: U.S. Department of Justice.

Bureau of Justice Statistics. (2002). *Census of State and Local Law Enforcement Agencies, 2000*. Washington, D.C.: Bureau of Justice Statistics.

Bureau of Justice Statistics. (2004). *Law Enforcement Management and Administrative Statistics, 2000: Data for Individual State and Local Agencies with 100 or More Officers*. Washington, D.C.: Author.

Bureau of Justice Statistics. (2006). *Local Police Departments, 2003*. Washington, D.C.: Author.

Cao, X., and X. Huang, 2000. "Determinants of Citizen Complaints Against Police Abuse of Power." *Journal of Criminal Justice 28*(2):203–213.

California Psychological Inventory (CPI). Palo Alto, CA: Consulting Psychology, Inc.

Carter, D., and A. Sapp. 1988. *The State of Police Education: Critical Findings*. Washington, D.C.: Police Executive Research Forum.

Clarke, J. R. 1997. "Police Careers May Take a Beating from Federal Domestic Violence Law." *Law Enforcement News 23*(1):23–47.

Daum, J. M., and C. M. Johns. 1994. "Police Work from a Woman's Perspective." *The Police Chief 9*:46–49.

Ermer, V. B. 1978. "Recruitment of Female Police Officers in New York." *Journal of Criminal Justice 6*(4):327–338.

Fagin, J. A. 2003. *Criminal Justice*. Boston: Allyn and Bacon.

Ferriera, B. R. 1997. "The Importance of Law Enforcement Education." *Law and Order 26*(1):26, 30–32.

Fry, L., and S. Greenfield. 1980. "An Examination of Attitudinal Differences Between Policemen and Policewomen." *Journal of Applied Psychology 65*(2):123–126.

Garner, G. 1998. "Are You Ready for Promotion?" *Police 28*(1):22–24.

Gross, S. 1984. "Women Becoming Cops: Developmental Issues and Solutions." *Police Chief 51*:32–35.

Higginbotham, J. 1993. "Pregnancy and Maternity Leave Policies: The Legal Aspects." *FBI Law Enforcement Bulletin*, March, 27–32.

Johns, C. J, and A. M. Barclay. 1979. "Female Partners for Male Police: The Effect on Shooting Responses." *Criminal Justice and Behavior 6*(4):327–337.

Johnson, L. B. 1991. "Job Strain Among Police Officers: Gender Comparisons." *Police Studies 14*(1):12–16.

Krimmel, J. T. 1996. "The Performance of College Educated Police: A Study of Self-rated Police Performance Measures." *American Journal of Police 15*(1):85–96.

Kuykendall, J. L., and D. E. Burns. 1980. "The Black Police Officer: An Historical Perspective." *Journal of Contemporary Criminal Justice 1*(4):4–12.

Langworthy, R. H., B. Anders, and T. Hughes. 1995. *Law Enforcement Recruitment and Selection: A Survey of Major Police Departments in the U.S.* Highland Heights, KY: Academy of Criminal Justice Sciences.

Leach, T. 1998. "College Internship: An Aid to Recruitment." *Law and Order 46*(1):57–59.

Lester, D. 1983. "Why Do People Become Police Officers: A Study of Reasons and Their Predictions of Success." *Journal of Police Science and Administration 11*(2):170–174.

Lewis, W. G. 1989. "Toward Representative Bureaucracy: Blacks in City Police Organization, 1975–1985." *Public Administration Review 49*(3):257–267.

Longway, K., K. Spillar, and S. Tejani. 2003. *Tearing Down the Wall: Problems with Consistency, Validity, and Adverse Impact of Physical Agility Testing in*

Police Selection. Washington, D.C.: National Center for Women and Policing.

Martin, C. A. 1979. "Women Police: A Survey of Education, Attitudes and Problems." *Journal of Studies in Technical Careers* 1(3):220–227.

Martin, S. E. 1979. "Policewomen and Equality: Occupational Role Dilemmas and Choices of Female Officers." *Journal of Police Science and Administration* 7(4):314–322.

Martin, S. 1989. *Women on the Move? A Report on the Status of Women in Policing*. Washington, D.C.: Police Foundation Reports.

Meagher, M. S., and N. A. Yentes. 1986. "Choosing a Career in Policing: A Comparison of Male and Female Perceptions." *Journal of Police Science and Administration* 14(4):320–327.

Milgram, D. 2002. "Recruiting Women to Policing: Practical Strategies That Work." *The Police Chief* 69(1):31–34.

Molden, J. B. 1999. "College Degrees for Police Applicants." *Law and Order* 7(1):21–22.

National Crime Prevention Council. 1995. *Lengthening the Stride: Employing Peace Officers From Newly Arrived Ethnic Groups*. Washington, D.C.: National Crime Prevention Council.

Price, B. R., and S. Gavin. 1979. "A Century of Women in Policing." In *Modern Police Administration*, edited by D. O. Schultz, 109–122. Houston: Gulf Publishing Company.

Rafilson, F. M. 1997. "Everything You Always Wanted to Know About Written Exams . . . but Were Afraid (Really) to Ask!" *Law and Order* 45(2):100–102.

Reaves, B. A., and A. L. Goldberg. 1999. Law Enforcement Management and Administrative Statistics,

1997: Data for Individual State and Local Agencies with 100 or More Officers. Washington, D.C.: U.S. Department of Justice, Bureau of Justice Statistics.

Schulz, D. M. 1995. *From Social Worker to Crime Fighter: Women in United States Municipal Policing*. Westport, CT: Praeger.

Senna, J. J., and L. J. Siegal. 2002. *Introduction to Criminal Justice*, 9th ed. Belmont, CA: Wadsworth.

Sharp, A. G. 1994. "Recruiting Quality Applicants: The Ideal Police Officer Candidate Does Not Exist." *Law and Order* 42(2):100–108.

Sherman, L. 1975. "An Evaluation of Policewomen on Patrol in a Suburban Police Department." *Journal of Police Science Administrator* 3(4):434–438.

Strandberg, K. W. 1996. "Police Recruiting: Hiring Strategies." *Law Enforcement Technology* 23(1): 38–42.

Terry, K. J., and H. B. Grant. 2003. "The Roads Not Taken: Improving the Use of Civilian Complaint Review Boards and Implementation of the Recommendations from Investigative Commissions." In *Policing and Minority Communities: Bridging the Gap*, edited by D. Jones-Brown and K. J. Terry, 160–182. Upper Saddle River, NJ: Prentice Hall.

U.S. Census Bureau. 2000. *U.S. Census 2000*. Available at www.census.gov.main/www.cen2000/html.

Walker, S. 1985. "Racial Minority and Female Employment in Policing: The Implications of 'Glacial' Change." *Crime and Delinquency* 31:535–572.

Whetstone, T. S. 2001. "Copping Out: Why Police Officers Decline to Participate in the Sergeant's Promotional Process." *American Journal of Criminal Justice* 25(2):147–159.

NOTES

1. The first edition consisted of 680 questions. It is only meant to be administered to adults, though the MMPI-A is designed for adolescents.
2. Although many departments use the polygraph as an assessment tool, they are prohibited from requiring candidates to submit to a polygraph exam on the basis that the candidate will not be hired without taking this test. The Employee Polygraph Protection Act of 1988, 29 U.S.C.A. § 2001 was enacted because of concerns that employers were using polygraph exams and relying on information that might be inaccurate, inconclusive, or unfounded lie detector results to make employment decisions.
3. *Griggs v. Duke Power Company*, 401 U.S. 424 (1971).
4. *Wards Cove Packing Company Inc. v. Antonio*.
5. 579 So. 2d 788 (1991).
6. 16 N.Y.2d 668.

Sec. 1385. Use of Army and Air Force as Posse Comitatus

Whoever, except in cases and under circumstances expressly authorized by the Constitution or Act of Congress, willfully uses any part of the Army or the Air Force as a posse comitatus or otherwise to execute the laws shall be fined under this title or imprisoned not more than two years, or both.

USA PATRIOT Act of 2001

To deter and punish terrorist acts in the United States and around the world, to enhance law enforcement investigatory tools, and for other purposes. *Be it enacted by the Senate and House of Representatives of the United States of America in Congress assembled,*

SECTION 1. SHORT TITLE AND TABLE OF CONTENTS.

(a) SHORT TITLE–This Act may be cited as the 'Uniting and Strengthening America by Providing Appropriate Tools Required to Intercept and Obstruct Terrorism (USA PATRIOT ACT) Act of 2001'. (b) TABLE OF CONTENTS–The table of contents for this Act is as follows:

Source: Complete text of USA PATRIOT Act of 2001 available at www.epic.org/privacy/terrorism/usapatriot/.

Sec. 904. Temporary authority to defer submittal to Congress of reports on intelligence and intelligence-related matters.

Sec. 905. Disclosure to Director of Central Intelligence of foreign intelligence-related information with respect to criminal investigations.

Sec. 906. Foreign terrorist asset tracking center.

TITLE II—ENHANCED SURVEILLANCE PROCEDURES

SEC. 201. AUTHORITY TO INTERCEPT WIRE, ORAL, AND ELECTRONIC COMMUNICATIONS RELATING TO TERRORISM.

Section 2516(1) of title 18, United States Code, is amended—

(1) by redesignating paragraph (p), as so redesignated by section 434(2) of the Antiterrorism and Effective Death Penalty Act of 1996 (Public Law 104-132; 110 Stat. 1274), as paragraph (r); and

(2) by inserting after paragraph (p), as so redesignated by section 201(3) of the Illegal Immigration Reform and Immigrant Responsibility Act of 1996 (division C of Public Law 104-208; 110 Stat. 3009-565), the following new paragraph:

'(q) any criminal violation of section 229 (relating to chemical weapons); or sections 2332, 2332a, 2332b, 2332d, 2339A, or 2339B of this title (relating to terrorism); or '.

SEC. 202. AUTHORITY TO INTERCEPT WIRE, ORAL, AND ELECTRONIC COMMUNICATIONS RELATING TO COMPUTER FRAUD AND ABUSE OFFENSES.

Section 2516(1)(c) of title 18, United States Code, is amended by striking 'and section 1341 (relating to mail fraud),' and inserting 'section 1341 (relating to mail fraud), a felony violation of section 1030 (relating to computer fraud and abuse),'.

SEC. 203. AUTHORITY TO SHARE CRIMINAL INVESTIGATIVE INFORMATION.

(a) AUTHORITY TO SHARE GRAND JURY INFORMATION-

(1) IN GENERAL–Rule 6(e)(3)(C) of the Federal Rules of Criminal Procedure is amended to read as follows:

'(C)(i) Disclosure otherwise prohibited by this rule of matters occurring before the grand jury may also be made—

'(I) when so directed by a court preliminarily to or in connection with a judicial proceeding;

'(II) when permitted by a court at the request of the defendant, upon a showing that grounds may exist for a motion to dismiss the indictment because of matters occurring before the grand jury;

'(III) when the disclosure is made by an attorney for the government to another Federal grand jury;

'(IV) when permitted by a court at the request of an attorney for the government, upon a showing that such matters may disclose a violation of state criminal law, to an appropriate official of a state or subdivision of a state for the purpose of enforcing such law; or

'(V) when the matters involve foreign intelligence or counterintelligence (as defined in section 3 of the National Security Act of 1947 (50 U.S.C. 401a)), or foreign intelligence information (as defined in clause (iv) of this subparagraph), to any Federal law enforcement, intelligence, protective, immigration, national defense, or national security official in order to assist the official receiving that information in the performance of his official duties.

'(ii) If the court orders disclosure of matters occurring before the grand jury, the disclosure shall be made in such manner, at such time, and under such conditions as the court may direct.

'(iii) Any Federal official to whom information is disclosed pursuant to clause (i)(V) of this subparagraph may use that information only as necessary in the conduct of that person's official duties subject to any limitations on the unauthorized disclosure of such information. Within a reasonable time after such disclosure, an attorney for the government shall file under seal a notice with the court stating the fact that such information was disclosed and the departments, agencies, or entities to which the disclosure was made.

'(iv) In clause (i)(V) of this subparagraph, the term 'foreign intelligence information' means—

'(I) information, whether or not concerning a United States person, that relates to the ability of the United States to protect against—

'(aa) actual or potential attack or other grave hostile acts of a foreign power or an agent of a foreign power;

'(bb) sabotage or international terrorism by a foreign power or an agent of a foreign power; or

'(cc) clandestine intelligence activities by an intelligence service or network of a foreign power or by an agent of foreign power; or

'(II) information, whether or not concerning a United States person, with respect to a foreign power or foreign territory that relates to—

'(aa) the national defense or the security of the United States; or

'(bb) the conduct of the foreign affairs of the United States.'.

(2) CONFORMING AMENDMENT–Rule 6(e)(3)(D) of the Federal Rules of Criminal Procedure is amended by striking '(e)(3)(C)(i)' and inserting '(e)(3)(C)(i)(I)'.

(b) AUTHORITY TO SHARE ELECTRONIC, WIRE, AND ORAL INTERCEPTION INFORMATION-

(1) LAW ENFORCEMENT–Section 2517 of title 18, United States Code, is amended by inserting at the end the following:

'(6) Any investigative or law enforcement officer, or attorney for the Government, who by any means authorized by this chapter, has obtained knowledge of the contents of any wire, oral, or electronic communication, or evidence derived therefrom, may disclose such contents to any other Federal law enforcement, intelligence, protective, immigration, national defense, or national security official to the extent that such contents include foreign intelligence or counterintelligence (as defined in section 3 of the National Security Act of 1947 (50 U.S.C. 401a)), or foreign intelligence information (as defined in subsection (19) of section 2510 of this title), to assist the official who is to receive that information in the performance of his official duties. Any Federal official who receives information pursuant to this provision may use that information only as necessary in the conduct of that person's official duties subject to any limitations on the unauthorized disclosure of such information.'.

(2) DEFINITION–Section 2510 of title 18, United States Code, is amended by—

(A) in paragraph (17), by striking 'and' after the semicolon;

(B) in paragraph (18), by striking the period and inserting '; and'; and

(C) by inserting at the end the following:

'(19) 'foreign intelligence information' means—

'(A) information, whether or not concerning a United States person, that relates to the ability of the United States to protect against—

'(i) actual or potential attack or other grave hostile acts of a foreign power or an agent of a foreign power;

'(ii) sabotage or international terrorism by a foreign power or an agent of a foreign power; or

'(iii) clandestine intelligence activities by an intelligence service or network of a foreign power or by an agent of a foreign power; or

'(B) information, whether or not concerning a United States person, with respect to a foreign power or foreign territory that relates to—

'(i) the national defense or the security of the United States; or

'(ii) the conduct of the foreign affairs of the United States.'.

(c) PROCEDURES–The Attorney General shall establish procedures for the disclosure of information pursuant to section 2517(6) and Rule 6(e)(3)(C)(i)(V) of the Federal Rules of Criminal Procedure that identifies a United States person, as defined in section 101 of the Foreign Intelligence Surveillance Act of 1978 (50 U.S.C. 1801)).

(d) FOREIGN INTELLIGENCE INFORMATION-

(1) IN GENERAL–Notwithstanding any other provision of law, it shall be lawful for foreign intelligence or counterintelligence (as defined in section 3 of the National Security Act of 1947 (50 U.S.C. 401a)) or foreign intelligence information obtained as part of a criminal investigation to be disclosed to any Federal law enforcement, intelligence, protective, immigration, national defense, or national security official in order to assist the official receiving that information in the performance of his official duties. Any Federal official who receives information pursuant to this provision may use that informa-

tion only as necessary in the conduct of that person's official duties subject to any limitations on the unauthorized disclosure of such information.

(2) DEFINITION–In this subsection, the term 'foreign intelligence information' means—

(A) information, whether or not concerning a United States person, that relates to the ability of the United States to protect against—

(i) actual or potential attack or other grave hostile acts of a foreign power or an agent of a foreign power;

(ii) sabotage or international terrorism by a foreign power or an agent of a foreign power; or

(iii) clandestine intelligence activities by an intelligence service or network of a foreign power or by an agent of a foreign power; or

(B) information, whether or not concerning a United States person, with respect to a foreign power or foreign territory that relates to—

(i) the national defense or the security of the United States; or

(ii) the conduct of the foreign affairs of the United States.

SEC. 204. CLARIFICATION OF INTELLIGENCE EXCEPTIONS FROM LIMITATIONS ON INTERCEPTION AND DISCLOSURE OF WIRE, ORAL, AND ELECTRONIC COMMUNICATIONS.

Section 2511(2)(f) of title 18, United States Code, is amended—

(1) by striking 'this chapter or chapter 121' and inserting 'this chapter or chapter 121 or 206 of this title'; and

(2) by striking 'wire and oral' and inserting 'wire, oral, and electronic'.

SEC. 206. ROVING SURVEILLANCE AUTHORITY UNDER THE FOREIGN INTELLIGENCE SURVEILLANCE ACT OF 1978.

Section 105(c)(2)(B) of the Foreign Intelligence Surveillance Act of 1978 (50 U.S.C. 1805(c)(2)(B)) is amended by inserting ', or in circumstances where the Court finds that the actions of the target of the application may have the effect of thwarting the identification of a specified person, such other persons,' after 'specified person'.

SEC. 208. DESIGNATION OF JUDGES.

Section 103(a) of the Foreign Intelligence Surveillance Act of 1978 (50 U.S.C. 1803(a)) is amended by—

(1) striking 'seven district court judges' and inserting '11 district court judges'; and

(2) inserting 'of whom no fewer than 3 shall reside within 20 miles of the District of Columbia' after 'circuits'.

SEC. 209. SEIZURE OF VOICE-MAIL MESSAGES PURSUANT TO WARRANTS.

Title 18, United States Code, is amended—

(1) in section 2510—

    (A) in paragraph (1), by striking beginning with 'and such' and all that follows through 'communication'; and

    (B) in paragraph (14), by inserting 'wire or' after 'transmission of'; and

(2) in subsections (a) and (b) of section 2703—

    (A) by striking 'CONTENTS OF ELECTRONIC' and inserting 'CONTENTS OF WIRE OR ELECTRONIC' each place it appears;

    (B) by striking 'contents of an electronic' and inserting 'contents of a wire or electronic' each place it appears; and

    (C) by striking 'any electronic' and inserting 'any wire or electronic' each place it appears.

SEC. 210. SCOPE OF SUBPOENAS FOR RECORDS OF ELECTRONIC COMMUNICATIONS.

Section 2703(c)(2) of title 18, United States Code, as redesignated by section 212, is amended—

(1) by striking 'entity the name, address, local and long distance telephone toll billing records, telephone number or other subscriber number or identity, and length of service of a subscriber' and inserting the following: 'entity the—

'(A) name;

'(B) address;

'(C) local and long distance telephone connection records, or records of session times and durations;

'(D) length of service (including start date) and types of service utilized;

'(E) telephone or instrument number or other subscriber number or identity, including any temporarily assigned network address; and

'(F) means and source of payment for such service (including any credit card or bank account number), of a subscriber'; and

(2) by striking 'and the types of services the subscriber or customer utilized,'.

SEC. 213. AUTHORITY FOR DELAYING NOTICE OF THE EXECUTION OF A WARRANT.

Section 3103a of title 18, United States Code, is amended—

(1) by inserting '(a) IN GENERAL–' before 'In addition'; and

(2) by adding at the end the following:

'(b) DELAY–With respect to the issuance of any warrant or court order under this section, or any other rule of law, to search for and seize any property or material that constitutes evidence of a criminal offense in violation of the laws of the United States, any notice required, or that may be required, to be given may be delayed if—

'(1) the court finds reasonable cause to believe that providing immediate notification of the execution of the warrant may have an adverse result (as defined in section 2705);

'(2) the warrant prohibits the seizure of any tangible property, any wire or electronic communication (as defined in section 2510), or, except as expressly provided in chapter 121, any stored wire or electronic information, except where the court finds reasonable necessity for the seizure; and

'(3) the warrant provides for the giving of such notice within a reasonable period of its execution, which period may thereafter be extended by the court for good cause shown.'.

SEC. 214. PEN REGISTER AND TRAP AND TRACE AUTHORITY UNDER FISA.

(a) APPLICATIONS AND ORDERS–Section 402 of the Foreign Intelligence Surveillance Act of 1978 (50 U.S.C. 1842) is amended—

(1) in subsection (a)(1), by striking 'for any investigation to gather foreign intelligence information or information concerning international terrorism' and inserting 'for any investigation to obtain foreign intelligence information not concerning a United States person or to protect against international terrorism or clandestine intelligence activities, provided that such investigation of a United States person is not conducted solely upon the basis of activities protected by the first amendment to the Constitution';

(2) by amending subsection (c)(2) to read as follows:

'(2) a certification by the applicant that the information likely to be obtained is foreign intelligence information not concerning a United States person or is relevant to an ongoing investigation to protect against international terrorism or clandestine intelligence activities, provided that such investigation of a United States person is not conducted solely upon the basis of activities protected by the first amendment to the Constitution.';

(3) by striking subsection (c)(3); and

(4) by amending subsection (d)(2)(A) to read as follows:

'(A) shall specify—

'(i) the identity, if known, of the person who is the subject of the investigation;

'(ii) the identity, if known, of the person to whom is leased or in whose name is listed the telephone line or other facility to which the pen register or trap and trace device is to be attached or applied;

'(iii) the attributes of the communications to which the order applies, such as the number or other identifier, and, if known, the location of the telephone line or other facility to which the pen register or trap and trace device is to be attached or applied and, in the case of a trap and trace device, the geographic limits of the trap and trace order.'.

(b) AUTHORIZATION DURING EMERGENCIES–Section 403 of the Foreign Intelligence Surveillance Act of 1978 (50 U.S.C. 1843) is amended—

(1) in subsection (a), by striking 'foreign intelligence information or information concerning international terrorism' and inserting 'foreign intelligence information not concerning a United States person or information to protect against international terrorism or clandestine intelligence activities, provided that such investigation of a United States person is not conducted solely upon the basis of activities protected by the first amendment to the Constitution'; and

(2) in subsection (b)(1), by striking 'foreign intelligence information or information concerning international terrorism' and inserting 'foreign intelligence information not concerning a United States person or information to protect against international terrorism or clandestine intelligence activities, provided that such investigation of a United States person is not conducted solely upon the basis of activities protected by the first amendment to the Constitution'.

  (A) in subparagraph (A)—

    (i) by inserting 'or other facility' after 'telephone line'; and

    (ii) by inserting before the semicolon at the end 'or applied'; and

  (B) by striking subparagraph (C) and inserting the following:

  '(C) the attributes of the communications to which the order applies, including the number or other identifier and, if known, the location of the telephone line or other facility to which the pen register or trap and trace device is to be attached or applied, and, in the case of an order authorizing installation and use of a trap and trace device under subsection (a)(2), the geographic limits of the order; and'.

(3) NONDISCLOSURE REQUIREMENTS–Section 3123(d)(2) of title 18, United States Code, is amended—

  (A) by inserting 'or other facility' after 'the line'; and

  (B) by striking ', or who has been ordered by the court' and inserting 'or applied, or who is obligated by the order'.

(c) DEFINITIONS-

(1) COURT OF COMPETENT JURISDICTION–Section 3127(2) of title 18, United States Code, is amended by striking subparagraph (A) and inserting the following:

  '(A) any district court of the United States (including a magistrate judge of such a court) or any United States court of appeals having jurisdiction over the offense being investigated; or'.

(2) PEN REGISTER–Section 3127(3) of title 18, United States Code, is amended—

  (A) by striking 'electronic or other impulses' and all that follows through 'is attached' and inserting 'dialing, routing, addressing, or signaling information transmitted by an instrument or facility from which a wire or electronic communication is transmitted, provided, however, that such information shall not include the contents of any communication'; and

(B) by inserting 'or process' after 'device' each place it appears.

(3) TRAP AND TRACE DEVICE–Section 3127(4) of title 18, United States Code, is amended—

SEC. 316. ANTI-TERRORIST FORFEITURE PROTECTION.

(a) RIGHT TO CONTEST–An owner of property that is confiscated under any provision of law relating to the confiscation of assets of suspected international terrorists, may contest that confiscation by filing a claim in the manner set forth in the Federal Rules of Civil Procedure (Supplemental Rules for Certain Admiralty and Maritime Claims), and asserting as an affirmative defense that—

(1) the property is not subject to confiscation under such provision of law; or

(2) the innocent owner provisions of section 983(d) of title 18, United States Code, apply to the case.

(b) EVIDENCE–In considering a claim filed under this section, a court may admit evidence that is otherwise inadmissible under the Federal Rules of Evidence, if the court determines that the evidence is reliable, and that compliance with the Federal Rules of Evidence may jeopardize the national security interests of the United States.

(c) CLARIFICATIONS-

(1) PROTECTION OF RIGHTS–The exclusion of certain provisions of Federal law from the definition of the term 'civil forfeiture statute' in section 983(i) of title 18, United States Code, shall not be construed to deny an owner of property the right to contest the confiscation of assets of suspected international terrorists under—

(A) subsection (a) of this section;

(B) the Constitution; or

(C) subchapter II of chapter 5 of title 5, United States Code (commonly known as the 'Administrative Procedure Act').

(2) SAVINGS CLAUSE–Nothing in this section shall limit or otherwise affect any other remedies that may be available to an owner of property under section 983 of title 18, United States Code, or any other provision of law.

(d) TECHNICAL CORRECTION–Section 983(i)(2)(D) of title 18, United States Code, is amended by inserting 'or the International Emergency Economic Powers Act (IEEPA) (50 U.S.C. 1701 et seq.)' before the semicolon.

SEC. 317. LONG-ARM JURISDICTION OVER FOREIGN MONEY LAUNDERERS.

Section 1956(b) of title 18, United States Code, is amended—

(1) by redesignating paragraphs (1) and (2) as subparagraphs (A) and (B), respectively, and moving the margins 2 ems to the right;

(2) by inserting after '(b)' the following: 'PENALTIES–

'(1) IN GENERAL–';

(3) by inserting ', or section 1957' after 'or (a)(3)'; and

(4) by adding at the end the following:

'(2) JURISDICTION OVER FOREIGN PERSONS–For purposes of adjudicating an action filed or enforcing a penalty ordered under this section, the district courts shall have jurisdiction over any foreign person, including any financial institution authorized under the laws of a foreign country, against whom the action is brought, if service of process upon the foreign person is made under the Federal Rules of Civil Procedure or the laws of the country in which the foreign person is found, and—

'(A) the foreign person commits an offense under subsection (a) involving a financial transaction that occurs in whole or in part in the United States;

'(B) the foreign person converts, to his or her own use, property in which the United States has an ownership interest by virtue of the entry of an order of forfeiture by a court of the United States; or

'(C) the foreign person is a financial institution that maintains a bank account at a financial institution in the United States.

'(3) COURT AUTHORITY OVER ASSETS–A court described in paragraph (2) may issue a pretrial restraining order or take any other action necessary to ensure that any bank account or other property held by the defendant in the United States is available to satisfy a judgment under this section.

'(4) FEDERAL RECEIVER–

'(A) IN GENERAL–A court described in paragraph (2) may appoint a Federal Receiver, in accordance with subparagraph (B) of this paragraph, to collect, marshal, and take custody, control, and possession of all assets of the defendant, wherever located, to satisfy a civil judgment under this subsection, a forfeiture judgment under section 981 or 982, or a criminal sentence under section 1957 or subsection (a) of this section, including an order of restitution to any victim of a specified unlawful activity.

'(B) APPOINTMENT AND AUTHORITY–A Federal Receiver described in subparagraph (A)—

'(i) may be appointed upon application of a Federal prosecutor or a Federal or State regulator, by the court having jurisdiction over the defendant in the case;

'(ii) shall be an officer of the court, and the powers of the Federal Receiver shall include the powers set out in section 754 of title 28, United States Code; and

'(iii) shall have standing equivalent to that of a Federal prosecutor for the purpose of submitting requests to obtain information regarding the assets of the defendant—

'(I) from the Financial Crimes Enforcement Network of the Department of the Treasury; or

'(II) from a foreign country pursuant to a mutual legal assistance treaty, multilateral agreement, or other arrangement for international law enforcement assistance, provided that such requests are in accordance with the policies and procedures of the Attorney General.'.

SEC. 318. LAUNDERING MONEY THROUGH A FOREIGN BANK.

Section 1956(c) of title 18, United States Code, is amended by striking paragraph (6) and inserting the following:

'(6) the term 'financial institution' includes—

'(A) any financial institution, as defined in section 5312(a)(2) of title 31, United States Code, or the regulations promulgated thereunder; and

'(B) any foreign bank, as defined in section 1 of the International Banking Act of 1978 (12 U.S.C. 3101).'.

SEC. 320. PROCEEDS OF FOREIGN CRIMES.

Section 981(a)(1)(B) of title 18, United States Code, is amended to read as follows:

'(B) Any property, real or personal, within the jurisdiction of the United States, constituting, derived from, or traceable to, any proceeds obtained directly or indirectly from an offense against a foreign nation, or any property used to facilitate such an offense, if the offense—

'(i) involves the manufacture, importation, sale, or distribution of a controlled substance (as that term is defined for purposes of the Controlled Substances Act), or any other conduct described in section 1956(c)(7)(B);

'(ii) would be punishable within the jurisdiction of the foreign nation by death or imprisonment for a term exceeding 1 year; and

'(iii) would be punishable under the laws of the United States by imprisonment for a term exceeding 1 year, if the act or activity constituting the offense had occurred within the jurisdiction of the United States.'.

SEC. 405. REPORT ON THE INTEGRATED AUTOMATED FINGERPRINT IDENTIFICATION SYSTEM FOR PORTS OF ENTRY AND OVERSEAS CONSULAR POSTS.

(a) IN GENERAL–The Attorney General, in consultation with the appropriate heads of other Federal agencies, including the Secretary of State, Secretary of the Treasury, and the Secretary of Transportation, shall report to Congress on the feasibility of enhancing the Integrated Automated Fingerprint Identification System (IAFIS) of the Federal Bureau of Investigation and other identification systems in order to better identify a person who holds a foreign passport or a visa and may be wanted in connection with a criminal investigation in the United States or abroad, before the issuance of a visa to that person or the entry or exit from the United States by that person.

(b) AUTHORIZATION OF APPROPRIATIONS–There is authorized to be appropriated not less than $2,000,000 to carry out this section.

Subtitle B—Enhanced Immigration Provisions

SEC. 411. DEFINITIONS RELATING TO TERRORISM.

(a) GROUNDS OF INADMISSIBILITY–Section 212(a)(3) of the Immigration and Nationality Act (8 U.S.C. 1182(a)(3)) is amended—

(1) in subparagraph (B)—

(A) in clause (i)—

(i) by amending subclause (IV) to read as follows:

'(IV) is a representative (as defined in clause (v)) of—

'(aa) a foreign terrorist organization, as designated by the Secretary of State under section 219, or

'(bb) a political, social or other similar group whose public endorsement of acts of terrorist activity the Secretary of State has determined undermines United States efforts to reduce or eliminate terrorist activities,';

(ii) in subclause (V), by inserting 'or' after 'section 219,' ; and

(iii) by adding at the end the following new subclauses:

'(VI) has used the alien's position of prominence within any country to endorse or espouse terrorist activity, or to persuade others to support terrorist activity or a terrorist organization, in a way that the Secretary of State has determined undermines United States efforts to reduce or eliminate terrorist activities, or

'(VII) is the spouse or child of an alien who is inadmissible under this section, if the activity causing the alien to be found inadmissible occurred within the last 5 years,';

(B) by redesignating clauses (ii), (iii), and (iv) as clauses (iii), (iv), and (v), respectively;

(C) in clause (i)(II), by striking 'clause (iii)' and inserting 'clause (iv)';

(D) by inserting after clause (i) the following:

'(ii) EXCEPTION–Subclause (VII) of clause (i) does not apply to a spouse or child—

'(I) who did not know or should not reasonably have known of the activity causing the alien to be found inadmissible under this section; or

'(II) whom the consular officer or Attorney General has reasonable grounds to believe has renounced the activity causing the alien to be found inadmissible under this section.';

(E) in clause (iii) (as redesignated by subparagraph (B))—

(i) by inserting 'it had been' before 'committed in the United States'; and

(ii) in subclause (V)(b), by striking 'or firearm' and inserting ', firearm, or other weapon or dangerous device';

(F) by amending clause (iv) (as redesignated by subparagraph (B)) to read as follows:

'(iv) ENGAGE IN TERRORIST ACTIVITY DEFINED–As used in this chapter, the term 'engage in terrorist activity' means, in an individual capacity or as a member of an organization—

'(I) to commit or to incite to commit, under circumstances indicating an intention to cause death or serious bodily injury, a terrorist activity;

'(II) to prepare or plan a terrorist activity;

'(III) to gather information on potential targets for terrorist activity;

'(IV) to solicit funds or other things of value for—

'(aa) a terrorist activity;

'(bb) a terrorist organization described in clause (vi)(I) or (vi)(II); or

'(cc) a terrorist organization described in clause (vi)(III), unless the solicitor can demonstrate that he did not know, and should not reasonably have known, that the solicitation would further the organization's terrorist activity;

'(V) to solicit any individual—

'(aa) to engage in conduct otherwise described in this clause;

'(bb) for membership in a terrorist organization described in clause (vi)(I) or (vi)(II); or

'(cc) for membership in a terrorist organization described in clause (vi)(III), unless the solicitor can demonstrate that he did not know, and should not reasonably have known, that the solicitation would further the organization's terrorist activity; or

'(VI) to commit an act that the actor knows, or reasonably should know, affords material support, including a safe house, transportation, communications, funds, transfer of funds or other material financial benefit, false documentation or identification, weapons (including chemical, biological, or radiological weapons), explosives, or training—

'(aa) for the commission of a terrorist activity;

'(bb) to any individual who the actor knows, or reasonably should know, has committed or plans to commit a terrorist activity;

'(cc) to a terrorist organization described in clause (vi)(I) or (vi)(II); or

'(dd) to a terrorist organization described in clause (vi)(III), unless the actor can demonstrate that he did not know, and should not reasonably have known, that the act would further the organization's terrorist activity.

This clause shall not apply to any material support the alien afforded to an organization or individual that has committed terrorist activity, if the Secretary of State, after consultation with the Attorney General, or the Attorney General, after consultation with the Secretary of

State, concludes in his sole unreviewable discretion, that this clause should not apply.'; and

(G) by adding at the end the following new clause:

'(vi) TERRORIST ORGANIZATION DEFINED–As used in clause (i)(VI) and clause (iv), the term 'terrorist organization' means an organization—

'(I) designated under section 219;

'(II) otherwise designated, upon publication in the Federal Register, by the Secretary of State in consultation with or upon the request of the Attorney General, as a terrorist organization, after finding that the organization engages in the activities described in subclause (I), (II), or (III) of clause (iv), or that the organization provides material support to further terrorist activity; or

'(III) that is a group of two or more individuals, whether organized or not, which engages in the activities described in subclause (I), (II), or (III) of clause (iv).'; and

(2) by adding at the end the following new subparagraph:

'(F) ASSOCIATION WITH TERRORIST ORGANIZATIONS–Any alien who the Secretary of State, after consultation with the Attorney General, or the Attorney General, after consultation with the Secretary of State, determines has been associated with a terrorist organization and intends while in the United States to engage solely, principally, or incidentally in activities that could endanger the welfare, safety, or security of the United States is inadmissible.'.

(b) CONFORMING AMENDMENTS-

(1) Section 237(a)(4)(B) of the Immigration and Nationality Act (8 U.S.C. 1227(a)(4)(B)) is amended by striking 'section 212(a)(3)(B)(iii)' and inserting 'section 212(a)(3)(B)(iv)'.

(2) Section 208(b)(2)(A)(v) of the Immigration and Nationality Act (8 U.S.C. 1158(b)(2)(A)(v)) is amended by striking 'or (IV)' and inserting '(IV), or (VI)'.

(c) RETROACTIVE APPLICATION OF AMENDMENTS-

(1) IN GENERAL–Except as otherwise provided in this subsection, the amendments made by this section shall take effect on the date of the enactment of this Act and shall apply to—

(A) actions taken by an alien before, on, or after such date; and

(B) all aliens, without regard to the date of entry or attempted entry into the United States—

(i) in removal proceedings on or after such date (except for proceedings in which there has been a final administrative decision before such date); or

(ii) seeking admission to the United States on or after such date.

(2) SPECIAL RULE FOR ALIENS IN EXCLUSION OR DEPORTATION PROCEEDINGS–Notwithstanding any other provision of law, sections 212(a)(3)(B) and 237(a)(4)(B) of the Immigration and Nationality Act, as amended by this Act, shall apply to all aliens in exclusion or deportation proceedings on or after the date of the enactment of this Act (except for proceedings in which there has been a final administrative decision before such date) as if such proceedings were removal proceedings.

(3) SPECIAL RULE FOR SECTION 219 ORGANIZATIONS AND ORGANIZATIONS DESIGNATED UNDER SECTION 212(a)(3)(B)(vi)(II)–

(A) IN GENERAL–Notwithstanding paragraphs (1) and (2), no alien shall be considered inadmissible under section 212(a)(3) of the Immigration and Nationality Act (8 U.S.C. 1182(a)(3)), or deportable under section 237(a)(4)(B) of such Act (8 U.S.C. 1227(a)(4)(B)), by reason of the amendments made by subsection (a), on the ground that the alien engaged in a terrorist activity described in subclause (IV)(bb), (V)(bb), or (VI)(cc) of section 212(a)(3)(B)(iv) of such Act (as so amended) with respect to a group at any time when the group was not a terrorist organization designated by the Secretary of State under section 219 of such Act (8 U.S.C. 1189) or otherwise designated under section 212(a)(3)(B)(vi)(II) of such Act (as so amended).

(B) STATUTORY CONSTRUCTION–Subparagraph (A) shall not be construed to prevent an alien from being considered inadmissible or deportable for having engaged in a terrorist activity—

(i) described in subclause (IV)(bb), (V)(bb), or (VI)(cc) of section 212(a)(3)(B)(iv) of such Act (as so amended) with respect to a terrorist organization at any time when such organization was designated by the Secretary of State under section 219 of such Act or otherwise designated under section 212(a)(3)(B)(vi)(II) of such Act (as so amended); or

(ii) described in subclause (IV)(cc), (V)(cc), or (VI)(dd) of section 212(a)(3)(B)(iv) of such Act (as so amended) with respect to a terrorist organization described in section 212(a)(3)(B)(vi)(III) of such Act (as so amended).

(4) EXCEPTION–The Secretary of State, in consultation with the Attorney General, may determine that the amendments made by this section shall not apply with respect to actions by an alien taken outside the United States before the date of the enactment of this Act upon the recommendation of a consular officer who has concluded that there is not reasonable ground to believe that the alien knew or reasonably should have known that the actions would further a terrorist activity.

(c) DESIGNATION OF FOREIGN TERRORIST ORGANIZATIONS–Section 219(a) of the Immigration and Nationality Act (8 U.S.C. 1189(a)) is amended—

(1) in paragraph (1)(B), by inserting 'or terrorism (as defined in section 140(d)(2) of the Foreign Relations Authorization Act, Fiscal Years 1988 and 1989 (22 U.S.C. 2656f(d)(2)), or retains the capability and intent to engage in terrorist activity or terrorism' after '212(a)(3)(B)';

(2) in paragraph (1)(C), by inserting 'or terrorism' after 'terrorist activity';

(3) by amending paragraph (2)(A) to read as follows:

'(A) NOTICE–

'(i) TO CONGRESSIONAL LEADERS–Seven days before making a designation under this subsection, the Secretary shall, by classified communication, notify the Speaker and Minority Leader of the House of Representatives, the President pro tempore, Majority Leader, and Minority Leader of the Senate, and the members of the relevant committees of the House of Representatives and the Senate, in writing, of the intent to designate an organization under this subsection, together with the findings made under paragraph (1) with respect to that organization, and the factual basis therefor.

'(ii) PUBLICATION IN FEDERAL REGISTER–The Secretary shall publish the designation in the Federal Register seven days after providing the notification under clause (i).';

(4) in paragraph (2)(B)(i), by striking 'subparagraph (A)' and inserting 'subparagraph (A)(ii)';

(5) in paragraph (2)(C), by striking 'paragraph (2)' and inserting 'paragraph (2)(A)(i)';

(6) in paragraph (3)(B), by striking 'subsection (c)' and inserting 'subsection (b)';

(7) in paragraph (4)(B), by inserting after the first sentence the following: 'The Secretary also may redesignate such organization at the end of any 2-year redesignation period (but not sooner than 60 days prior to the termination of such period) for an additional 2-year period upon a finding that the relevant circumstances described in paragraph (1) still exist. Any redesignation shall be effective immediately following the end of the prior 2-year designation or redesignation period unless a different effective date is provided in such redesignation.';

(8) in paragraph (6)(A)—

(A) by inserting 'or a redesignation made under paragraph (4)(B)' after 'paragraph (1)';

(B) in clause (i)—

(i) by inserting 'or redesignation' after 'designation' the first place it appears; and

(ii) by striking 'of the designation'; and

(C) in clause (ii), by striking 'of the designation';

(9) in paragraph (6)(B)—

(A) by striking 'through (4)' and inserting 'and (3)'; and

(B) by inserting at the end the following new sentence: 'Any revocation shall take effect on the date specified in the revocation or upon publication in the Federal Register if no effective date is specified.';

(10) in paragraph (7), by inserting ', or the revocation of a redesignation under paragraph (6),' after 'paragraph (5) or (6)'; and

(11) in paragraph (8)—

(A) by striking 'paragraph (1)(B)' and inserting 'paragraph (2)(B), or if a redesignation under this subsection has become effective under paragraph (4)(B)';

(B) by inserting 'or an alien in a removal proceeding' after 'criminal action'; and

(C) by inserting 'or redesignation' before 'as a defense'.

SEC. 412. MANDATORY DETENTION OF SUSPECTED TERRORISTS; HABEAS CORPUS; JUDICIAL REVIEW.

(a) IN GENERAL–The Immigration and Nationality Act (8 U.S.C. 1101 et seq.) is amended by inserting after section 236 the following:

'MANDATORY DETENTION OF SUSPECTED TERRORISTS; HABEAS CORPUS; JUDICIAL REVIEW.

'SEC. 236A. (a) DETENTION OF TERRORIST ALIENS-

'(1) CUSTODY–The Attorney General shall take into custody any alien who is certified under paragraph (3).

'(2) RELEASE–Except as provided in paragraphs (5) and (6), the Attorney General shall maintain custody of such an alien until the alien is removed from the United States. Except as provided in paragraph (6), such custody shall be maintained irrespective of any relief from removal for which the alien may be eligible, or any relief from removal granted the alien, until the Attorney General determines that the alien is no longer an alien who may be certified under paragraph (3). If the alien is finally determined not to be removable, detention pursuant to this subsection shall terminate.

'(3) CERTIFICATION–The Attorney General may certify an alien under this paragraph if the Attorney General has reasonable grounds to believe that the alien—

'(A) is described in section 212(a)(3)(A)(i), 212(a)(3)(A)(iii), 212(a)(3)(B), 237(a)(4)(A)(i), 237(a)(4)(A)(iii), or 237(a)(4)(B); or

'(B) is engaged in any other activity that endangers the national security of the United States.

'(4) NONDELEGATION–The Attorney General may delegate the authority provided under paragraph (3) only to the Deputy Attorney General. The Deputy Attorney General may not delegate such authority.

'(5) COMMENCEMENT OF PROCEEDINGS–The Attorney General shall place an alien detained under paragraph (1) in removal proceedings, or shall charge the alien with a criminal offense, not later than 7 days after the commencement of such detention. If the requirement of the preceding sentence is not satisfied, the Attorney General shall release the alien.

'(6) LIMITATION ON INDEFINITE DETENTION–An alien detained solely under paragraph (1) who has not been removed under section 241(a)(1)(A), and whose removal is unlikely in the reasonably foreseeable future, may be detained for additional periods of up to six months only if the release of the alien will threaten the national security of the United States or the safety of the community or any person.

'(7) REVIEW OF CERTIFICATION–The Attorney General shall review the certification made under paragraph (3) every 6 months. If the Attorney General determines, in the Attorney General's discretion, that the certification should be revoked, the alien may be released on such conditions as the Attorney General deems appropriate, unless such release is otherwise prohibited by law. The alien may request each 6 months in writing that the Attorney General reconsider the certification and may submit documents or other evidence in support of that request.

'(b) HABEAS CORPUS AND JUDICIAL REVIEW-

'(1) IN GENERAL–Judicial review of any action or decision relating to this section (including judicial review of the merits of a determination made under subsection (a)(3) or (a)(6)) is available exclusively in habeas corpus proceedings consistent with this subsection. Except as provided in the preceding sentence, no court shall have jurisdiction to review, by habeas corpus petition or otherwise, any such action or decision.

'(2) APPLICATION-

'(A) IN GENERAL–Notwithstanding any other provision of law, including section 2241(a) of title 28, United States Code, habeas corpus proceedings described in paragraph (1) may be initiated only by an application filed with—

'(i) the Supreme Court;

'(ii) any justice of the Supreme Court;

'(iii) any circuit judge of the United States Court of Appeals for the District of Columbia Circuit; or

'(iv) any district court otherwise having jurisdiction to entertain it.

'(B) APPLICATION TRANSFER–Section 2241(b) of title 28, United States Code, shall apply to an application for a writ of habeas corpus described in subparagraph (A).

'(3) APPEALS–Notwithstanding any other provision of law, including section 2253 of title 28, in habeas corpus proceedings described in paragraph (1) before a circuit or district judge, the final order shall be subject to review, on appeal, by the United States Court of Appeals for the District of Columbia Circuit. There shall be no right of appeal in such proceedings to any other circuit court of appeals.

'(4) RULE OF DECISION–The law applied by the Supreme Court and the United States Court of Appeals for the District of Columbia Circuit shall be regarded as the rule of decision in habeas corpus proceedings described in paragraph (1).

'(c) STATUTORY CONSTRUCTION–The provisions of this section shall not be applicable to any other provision of this Act.'.

(b) CLERICAL AMENDMENT–The table of contents of the Immigration and Nationality Act is amended by inserting after the item relating to section 236 the following:

'Sec. 236A. Mandatory detention of suspected terrorist; habeas corpus; judicial review.'.

(c) REPORTS–Not later than 6 months after the date of the enactment of this Act, and every 6 months thereafter, the Attorney General shall submit a report to the Committee on the Judiciary of the House of Representatives and the Committee on the Judiciary of the Senate, with respect to the reporting period, on—

(1) the number of aliens certified under section 236A(a)(3) of the Immigration and Nationality Act, as added by subsection (a);

(2) the grounds for such certifications;

(3) the nationalities of the aliens so certified;

(4) the length of the detention for each alien so certified; and

(5) the number of aliens so certified who—

(A) were granted any form of relief from removal;

(B) were removed;

(C) the Attorney General has determined are no longer aliens who may be so certified; or

(D) were released from detention.

SEC. 413. MULTILATERAL COOPERATION AGAINST TERRORISTS.

Section 222(f) of the Immigration and Nationality Act (8 U.S.C. 1202(f)) is amended—

(1) by striking 'except that in the discretion of' and inserting the following: 'except that—

'(1) in the discretion of'; and

(2) by adding at the end the following:

'(2) the Secretary of State, in the Secretary's discretion and on the basis of reciprocity, may provide to a foreign government information in the Department of State's computerized visa lookout database and, when necessary and appropriate, other records covered by this section related to information in the database—

'(A) with regard to individual aliens, at any time on a case-by-case basis for the purpose of preventing, investigating, or punishing acts that would constitute a crime in the United States, including, but not limited to, terrorism or trafficking in controlled substances, persons, or illicit weapons; or

'(B) with regard to any or all aliens in the database, pursuant to such conditions as the Secretary of State shall establish in an agreement with the foreign government in which that government agrees to use such information and records for the purposes described in subparagraph (A) or to deny visas to persons who would be inadmissible to the United States.'.

SEC. 414. VISA INTEGRITY AND SECURITY.

(a) SENSE OF CONGRESS REGARDING THE NEED TO EXPEDITE IMPLEMENTATION OF INTEGRATED ENTRY AND EXIT DATA SYSTEM-

(1) SENSE OF CONGRESS–In light of the terrorist attacks perpetrated against the United States on September 11, 2001, it is the sense of the Congress that—

(A) the Attorney General, in consultation with the Secretary of State, should fully implement the integrated entry and exit data system for airports, seaports, and land border ports of entry, as specified in section 110 of the Illegal Immigration Reform and Immigrant Responsibility Act of 1996 (8 U.S.C. 1365a), with all deliberate speed and as expeditiously as practicable; and

(B) the Attorney General, in consultation with the Secretary of State, the Secretary of Commerce, the Secretary of the Treasury, and the Office of Homeland Security, should immediately begin establishing the Integrated Entry and Exit Data System Task Force, as described in section 3 of the Immigration and Naturalization Service Data Management Improvement Act of 2000 (Public Law 106-215).

(2) AUTHORIZATION OF APPROPRIATIONS–There is authorized to be appropriated such sums as may be necessary to fully implement the system described in paragraph (1)(A).

(b) DEVELOPMENT OF THE SYSTEM–In the development of the integrated entry and exit data system under section 110 of the Illegal Immigration Reform and Immigrant Responsibility Act of 1996 (8 U.S.C. 1365a), the Attorney General and the Secretary of State shall particularly focus on—

(1) the utilization of biometric technology; and

(2) the development of tamper-resistant documents readable at ports of entry.

(c) INTERFACE WITH LAW ENFORCEMENT DATABASES–The entry and exit data system described in this section shall be able to interface with law enforcement databases for use by Federal law enforcement to identify and detain individuals who pose a threat to the national security of the United States.

(d) REPORT ON SCREENING INFORMATION–Not later than 12 months after the date of enactment of this Act, the Office of Homeland Security shall submit a report to Congress on the information that is needed from any United States agency to effectively screen visa applicants and applicants for admission to the United States to identify those affiliated with terrorist organizations or those that pose any threat to the safety or security of the United States, including the type of information currently received by United States agencies and the regularity with which such information is transmitted to the Secretary of State and the Attorney General.

SEC. 415. PARTICIPATION OF OFFICE OF HOMELAND SECURITY ON ENTRY-EXIT TASK FORCE.

Section 3 of the Immigration and Naturalization Service Data Management Improvement Act of 2000 (Public Law 106-215) is amended by striking 'and the Secretary of the Treasury,' and inserting 'the Secretary of the Treasury, and the Office of Homeland Security'.

SEC. 416. FOREIGN STUDENT MONITORING PROGRAM.

(a) FULL IMPLEMENTATION AND EXPANSION OF FOREIGN STUDENT VISA MONITORING PROGRAM REQUIRED–The Attorney General, in consultation with the Secretary of State, shall fully implement and expand the program established by section 641(a) of the Illegal Immigration Reform and Immigrant Responsibility Act of 1996 (8 U.S.C. 1372(a)).

(b) INTEGRATION WITH PORT OF ENTRY INFORMATION–For each alien with respect to whom information is collected under section 641 of the Illegal Immigration Reform and Immigrant Responsibility Act of 1996 (8 U.S.C. 1372), the Attorney General, in consultation with the Secretary of State, shall include information on the date of entry and port of entry.

(c) EXPANSION OF SYSTEM TO INCLUDE OTHER APPROVED EDUCATIONAL INSTITUTIONS–Section 641 of the Illegal Immigration Reform and Immigrant Responsibility Act of 1996 (8 U.S.C. 1372) is amended—

(1) in subsection (a)(1), subsection (c)(4)(A), and subsection (d)(1) (in the text above subparagraph (A)), by inserting ', other approved educational institutions,' after 'higher education' each place it appears;

(2) in subsections (c)(1)(C), (c)(1)(D), and (d)(1)(A), by inserting ', or other approved educational institution,' after 'higher education' each place it appears;

(3) in subsections (d)(2), (e)(1), and (e)(2), by inserting ', other approved educational institution,' after 'higher education' each place it appears; and

(4) in subsection (h), by adding at the end the following new paragraph:

'(3) OTHER APPROVED EDUCATIONAL INSTITUTION–The term 'other approved educational institution' includes any air flight school, language training school, or vocational school, approved by the Attorney General, in consultation with the Secretary of Education and the Secretary of State, under subparagraph (F), (J), or (M) of section 101(a)(15) of the Immigration and Nationality Act.'.

'(d) AUTHORIZATION OF APPROPRIATIONS–There is authorized to be appropriated to the Department of Justice $36,800,000 for the period beginning on the date of enactment of this Act and ending on January 1, 2003, to fully implement and expand prior to January 1, 2003, the program established by section 641(a) of the Illegal Immigration Reform and Immigrant Responsibility Act of 1996 (8 U.S.C. 1372(a)).

SEC. 503. DNA IDENTIFICATION OF TERRORISTS AND OTHER VI-OLENT OFFENDERS.

Section 3(d)(2) of the DNA Analysis Backlog Elimination Act of 2000 (42 U.S.C. 14135a(d)(2)) is amended to read as follows:

'(2) In addition to the offenses described in paragraph (1), the following offenses shall be treated for purposes of this section as qualifying Federal offenses, as determined by the Attorney General:

'(A) Any offense listed in section 2332b(g)(5)(B) of title 18, United States Code.

'(B) Any crime of violence (as defined in section 16 of title 18, United States Code).

'(C) Any attempt or conspiracy to commit any of the above offenses.'.

SEC. 504. COORDINATION WITH LAW ENFORCEMENT.

(a) INFORMATION ACQUIRED FROM AN ELECTRONIC SURVEIL-LANCE–Section 106 of the Foreign Intelligence Surveillance Act of 1978 (50 U.S.C. 1806), is amended by adding at the end the following:

'(k)(1) Federal officers who conduct electronic surveillance to acquire foreign intelligence information under this title may consult with Federal law enforcement officers to coordinate efforts to investigate or protect against—

'(A) actual or potential attack or other grave hostile acts of a foreign power or an agent of a foreign power;

'(B) sabotage or international terrorism by a foreign power or an agent of a foreign power; or

'(C) clandestine intelligence activities by an intelligence service or network of a foreign power or by an agent of a foreign power.

'(2) Coordination authorized under paragraph (1) shall not preclude the certification required by section 104(a)(7)(B) or the entry of an order under section 105.'.

(b) INFORMATION ACQUIRED FROM A PHYSICAL SEARCH–Section 305 of the Foreign Intelligence Surveillance Act of 1978 (50 U.S.C. 1825) is amended by adding at the end the following:

'(k)(1) Federal officers who conduct physical searches to acquire foreign intelligence information under this title may consult with Federal law enforcement officers to coordinate efforts to investigate or protect against—

'(A) actual or potential attack or other grave hostile acts of a foreign power or an agent of a foreign power;

'(B) sabotage or international terrorism by a foreign power or an agent of a foreign power; or

'(C) clandestine intelligence activities by an intelligence service or network of a foreign power or by an agent of a foreign power.

'(2) Coordination authorized under paragraph (1) shall not preclude the certification required by section 303(a)(7) or the entry of an order under section 304.'.

SEC. 506. EXTENSION OF SECRET SERVICE JURISDICTION.

(a) Concurrent Jurisdiction Under 18 U.S.C. 1030–Section 1030(d) of title 18, United States Code, is amended to read as follows:

'(d)(1) The United States Secret Service shall, in addition to any other agency having such authority, have the authority to investigate offenses under this section.

'(2) The Federal Bureau of Investigation shall have primary authority to investigate offenses under subsection (a)(1) for any cases involving espionage, foreign counterintelligence, information protected against unauthorized disclosure for reasons of national defense or foreign relations, or Restricted Data (as that term is defined in section 11y of the Atomic Energy Act of 1954 (42 U.S.C. 2014(y)), except for offenses affecting the duties of the United States Secret Service pursuant to section 3056(a) of this title.

'(3) Such authority shall be exercised in accordance with an agreement which shall be entered into by the Secretary of the Treasury and the Attorney General.'.

(b) Reauthorization of Jurisdiction under 18 U.S.C. 1344–Section 3056(b)(3) of title 18, United States Code, is amended by striking 'credit and debit card frauds, and false identification documents or devices' and inserting 'access device frauds, false identification documents or devices, and any fraud or other criminal or unlawful activity in or against any federally insured financial institution'.

SEC. 507. DISCLOSURE OF EDUCATIONAL RECORDS.

Section 444 of the General Education Provisions Act (20 U.S.C. 1232g), is amended by adding after subsection (i) a new subsection (j) to read as follows:

'(j) INVESTIGATION AND PROSECUTION OF TERRORISM-

'(1) IN GENERAL–Notwithstanding subsections (a) through (i) or any provision of State law, the Attorney General (or any Federal officer or employee, in a position not lower than an Assistant Attorney General, designated by the Attorney General) may submit a written application to a court of competent jurisdiction for an ex parte order requiring an educational agency or institution to permit the Attorney General (or his designee) to—

'(A) collect education records in the possession of the educational agency or institution that are relevant to an authorized investigation or prosecution of an offense listed in section 2332b(g)(5)(B) of title 18 United States Code, or an act of domestic or international terrorism as defined in section 2331 of that title; and

'(B) for official purposes related to the investigation or prosecution of an offense described in paragraph (1)(A), retain, disseminate, and use (including as evidence at trial or in other administrative or judicial proceedings) such records, consistent with such guidelines as the Attorney General, after consultation with the Secretary, shall issue to protect confidentiality.

TITLE VII—INCREASED INFORMATION SHARING FOR CRITICAL INFRASTRUCTURE PROTECTION

SEC. 701. EXPANSION OF REGIONAL INFORMATION SHARING SYSTEM TO FACILITATE FEDERAL-STATE-LOCAL LAW ENFORCEMENT RESPONSE RELATED TO TERRORIST ATTACKS.

Section 1301 of title I of the Omnibus Crime Control and Safe Streets Act of 1968 (42 U.S.C. 3796h) is amended—

(1) in subsection (a), by inserting 'and terrorist conspiracies and activities' after 'activities';

(2) in subsection (b)—

(A) in paragraph (3), by striking 'and' after the semicolon;

(B) by redesignating paragraph (4) as paragraph (5);

(C) by inserting after paragraph (3) the following:

'(4) establishing and operating secure information sharing systems to enhance the investigation and prosecution abilities of participating enforcement agencies in addressing multi-jurisdictional terrorist conspiracies and activities; and (5)'; and

(3) by inserting at the end the following:

'(d) AUTHORIZATION OF APPROPRIATION TO THE BUREAU OF JUSTICE ASSISTANCE–There are authorized to be appropriated to the Bureau of Justice Assistance to carry out this section $50,000,000 for fiscal year 2002 and $100,000,000 for fiscal year 2003. '.

TITLE VIII—STRENGTHENING THE CRIMINAL LAWS AGAINST TERRORISM

SEC. 801. TERRORIST ATTACKS AND OTHER ACTS OF VIOLENCE AGAINST MASS TRANSPORTATION SYSTEMS.

Chapter 97 of title 18, United States Code, is amended by adding at the end the following:

'Sec. 1993. Terrorist attacks and other acts of violence against mass transportation systems

'(a) GENERAL PROHIBITIONS–Whoever willfully—

'(1) wrecks, derails, sets fire to, or disables a mass transportation vehicle or ferry;

'(2) places or causes to be placed any biological agent or toxin for use as a weapon, destructive substance, or destructive device in, upon, or near a mass transportation vehicle or ferry, without previously obtaining the permission of the mass transportation provider, and with intent to endanger the safety of any passenger or employee of the mass transportation provider, or with a reckless disregard for the safety of human life;

'(3) sets fire to, or places any biological agent or toxin for use as a weapon, destructive substance, or destructive device in, upon, or near any garage, terminal, structure, supply, or facility used in the operation of, or in support of the operation of, a mass transportation vehicle or ferry, without previously obtaining the permission of the mass transportation provider, and knowing or having reason to know such activity would likely derail, disable, or wreck a mass transportation vehicle or ferry used, operated, or employed by the mass transportation provider;

'(4) removes appurtenances from, damages, or otherwise impairs the operation of a mass transportation signal system, including a train control system, centralized dispatching system, or rail grade crossing warning signal without authorization from the mass transportation provider;

'(5) interferes with, disables, or incapacitates any dispatcher, driver, captain, or person while they are employed in dispatching, operating, or maintaining a mass transportation vehicle or ferry, with intent to endanger the safety of any passenger or employee of the mass transportation provider, or with a reckless disregard for the safety of human life;

'(6) commits an act, including the use of a dangerous weapon, with the intent to cause death or serious bodily injury to an employee or passenger of a mass transportation provider or any other person while any of the foregoing are on the property of a mass transportation provider;

'(7) conveys or causes to be conveyed false information, knowing the information to be false, concerning an attempt or alleged attempt being made or to be made, to do any act which would be a crime prohibited by this subsection; or

'(8) attempts, threatens, or conspires to do any of the aforesaid acts,

shall be fined under this title or imprisoned not more than twenty years, or both, if such act is committed, or in the case of a threat or conspiracy such act would be committed, on, against, or affecting a mass transportation provider engaged in or affecting interstate or foreign commerce, or if in the course of committing such act, that person travels or communicates across a State line in order to commit such act, or transports materials across a State line in aid of the commission of such act.

'(b) AGGRAVATED OFFENSE–Whoever commits an offense under subsection (a) in a circumstance in which—

'(1) the mass transportation vehicle or ferry was carrying a passenger at the time of the offense; or

'(2) the offense has resulted in the death of any person,

shall be guilty of an aggravated form of the offense and shall be fined under this title or imprisoned for a term of years or for life, or both.

'(c) DEFINITIONS–In this section—

'(1) the term 'biological agent' has the meaning given to that term in section 178(1) of this title;

'(2) the term 'dangerous weapon' has the meaning given to that term in section 930 of this title;

'(3) the term 'destructive device' has the meaning given to that term in section 921(a)(4) of this title;

'(4) the term 'destructive substance' has the meaning given to that term in section 31 of this title;

'(5) the term 'mass transportation' has the meaning given to that term in section 5302(a)(7) of title 49, United States Code, except that the term shall include schoolbus, charter, and sightseeing transportation;

'(6) the term 'serious bodily injury' has the meaning given to that term in section 1365 of this title;

'(7) the term 'State' has the meaning given to that term in section 2266 of this title; and

'(8) the term 'toxin' has the meaning given to that term in section 178(2) of this title.'.

(f) CONFORMING AMENDMENT–The analysis of chapter 97 of title 18, United States Code, is amended by adding at the end:

'1993. Terrorist attacks and other acts of violence against mass transportation systems.'.

SEC. 802. DEFINITION OF DOMESTIC TERRORISM.

(a) DOMESTIC TERRORISM DEFINED–Section 2331 of title 18, United States Code, is amended—

(1) in paragraph (1)(B)(iii), by striking 'by assassination or kidnapping' and inserting 'by mass destruction, assassination, or kidnapping';

(2) in paragraph (3), by striking 'and';

(3) in paragraph (4), by striking the period at the end and inserting '; and'; and

(4) by adding at the end the following:

'(5) the term 'domestic terrorism' means activities that—

'(A) involve acts dangerous to human life that are a violation of the criminal laws of the United States or of any State;

'(B) appear to be intended—

'(i) to intimidate or coerce a civilian population;

'(ii) to influence the policy of a government by intimidation or coercion; or

'(iii) to affect the conduct of a government by mass destruction, assassination, or kidnapping; and

'(C) occur primarily within the territorial jurisdiction of the United States.'.

(b) CONFORMING AMENDMENT–Section 3077(1) of title 18, United States Code, is amended to read as follows:

'(1) 'act of terrorism' means an act of domestic or international terrorism as defined in section 2331;'.

SEC. 803. PROHIBITION AGAINST HARBORING TERRORISTS.

(a) IN GENERAL–Chapter 113B of title 18, United States Code, is amended by adding after section 2338 the following new section:

'Sec. 2339. Harboring or concealing terrorists

'(a) Whoever harbors or conceals any person who he knows, or has reasonable grounds to believe, has committed, or is about to commit, an offense under section 32 (relating to destruction of aircraft or aircraft facilities), section 175 (relating to biological weapons), section 229 (relating to chemical weapons), section 831 (relating to nuclear materials), paragraph (2) or (3) of section 844(f) (relating to arson and bombing of government property risking or causing injury or death), section 1366(a) (relating to the destruction of an energy facility), section 2280 (relating to violence against maritime navigation), section 2332a (relating to weapons of mass destruction), or section 2332b (relating to acts of terrorism transcending national boundaries) of this title, section 236(a) (relating to sabotage of nuclear facilities or fuel) of the Atomic Energy Act of 1954 (42 U.S.C. 2284(a)), or section 46502 (relating to aircraft piracy) of title 49, shall be fined under this title or imprisoned not more than ten years, or both.'.

'(b) A violation of this section may be prosecuted in any Federal judicial district in which the underlying offense was committed, or in any other Federal judicial district as provided by law.'.

(b) TECHNICAL AMENDMENT–The chapter analysis for chapter 113B of title 18, United States Code, is amended by inserting after the item for section 2338 the following:

'2339. Harboring or concealing terrorists.'.

SEC. 806. ASSETS OF TERRORIST ORGANIZATIONS.

Section 981(a)(1) of title 18, United States Code, is amended by inserting at the end the following:

'(G) All assets, foreign or domestic—

'(i) of any individual, entity, or organization engaged in planning or perpetrating any act of domestic or international terrorism (as defined in section 2331) against the United States, citizens or residents of the United States, or their property, and all assets, foreign or domestic, affording any person a source of influence over any such entity or organization;

'(ii) acquired or maintained by any person with the intent and for the purpose of supporting, planning, conducting, or concealing an act of domestic or international terrorism (as defined in section 2331) against the United States, citizens or residents of the United States, or their property; or

'(iii) derived from, involved in, or used or intended to be used to commit any act of domestic or international terrorism (as defined in section 2331) against the United States, citizens or residents of the United States, or their property.'.

SEC. 807. TECHNICAL CLARIFICATION RELATING TO PROVISION OF MATERIAL SUPPORT TO TERRORISM.

No provision of the Trade Sanctions Reform and Export Enhancement Act of 2000 (title IX of Public Law 106-387) shall be construed to limit or otherwise affect section 2339A or 2339B of title 18, United States Code.

SEC. 808. DEFINITION OF FEDERAL CRIME OF TERRORISM.

Section 2332b of title 18, United States Code, is amended—

(1) in subsection (f), by inserting 'and any violation of section 351(e), 844(e), 844(f)(1), 956(b), 1361, 1366(b), 1366(c), 1751(e), 2152, or 2156 of this title,' before 'and the Secretary'; and

(2) in subsection (g)(5)(B), by striking clauses (i) through (iii) and inserting the following:

'(i) section 32 (relating to destruction of aircraft or aircraft facilities), 37 (relating to violence at international airports), 81 (relating to arson within special maritime and territorial jurisdiction), 175 or 175b (relating to biological weapons), 229 (relating to chemical weapons), subsection (a), (b), (c), or (d) of section 351 (relating to congressional, cabinet, and Supreme Court assassination and kidnaping), 831 (relating to nuclear materials), 842(m) or (n) (relating to plastic explosives), 844(f)(2) or (3) (relating to arson and bombing of Government property risking or causing death), 844(i) (relating to arson and bombing of property used in interstate commerce), 930(c) (relating to killing or attempted killing during an attack on a Federal facility with a dangerous weapon), 956(a)(1) (relating to conspiracy to murder, kidnap, or maim persons abroad), 1030(a)(1) (relating to protection of computers), 1030(a)(5)(A)(i) resulting in damage as defined in 1030(a)(5)(B)(ii) through (v) (relating to protection of computers), 1114 (relating to killing or attempted killing of officers and employees of the United States), 1116 (relating to murder or manslaughter of foreign officials, official guests, or internationally protected persons), 1203 (relating to hostage taking), 1362 (relating to destruction of communication lines, stations, or systems), 1363 (relating to injury to buildings or property within special maritime and territorial jurisdiction of the United States), 1366(a) (relating to destruction of an energy facility), 1751(a), (b), (c), or (d) (relating to Presidential and Presidential staff assassination and kidnaping), 1992 (relating to wrecking trains), 1993 (relating to terrorist attacks and other acts of violence against mass transportation systems), 2155 (relating to destruction of national defense materials, premises, or utilities), 2280 (relating to violence against maritime navigation), 2281 (relating to violence against maritime fixed platforms), 2332 (relating to certain homicides and other violence against United States nationals occurring outside of the United States), 2332a (relating to use of weapons of mass destruction), 2332b (relating to acts of terrorism transcending national boundaries), 2339 (relating to harboring terrorists), 2339A (relating to providing material support to terrorists), 2339B (relating to providing material support to terrorist organizations), or 2340A (relating to torture) of this title;

'(ii) section 236 (relating to sabotage of nuclear facilities or fuel) of the Atomic Energy Act of 1954 (42 U.S.C. 2284); or

'(iii) section 46502 (relating to aircraft piracy), the second sentence of section 46504 (relating to assault on a flight crew with a dangerous weapon), section 46505(b)(3) or (c) (relating to explosive or incendiary devices, or endangerment of human life by means of weapons, on aircraft), section 46506 if homicide or attempted homicide is involved (relating to application of certain criminal laws to acts on aircraft), or section 60123(b) (relating to destruction of interstate gas or hazardous liquid pipeline facility) of title 49.'.

SEC. 809. NO STATUTE OF LIMITATION FOR CERTAIN TERRORISM OFFENSES.

(a) IN GENERAL–Section 3286 of title 18, United States Code, is amended to read as follows:

'Sec. 3286. Extension of statute of limitation for certain terrorism offenses

'(a) EIGHT-YEAR LIMITATION–Notwithstanding section 3282, no person shall be prosecuted, tried, or punished for any noncapital offense involving a violation of any provision listed in section 2332b(g)(5)(B), or a violation of section 112, 351(e), 1361, or 1751(e) of this title, or section 46504, 46505, or 46506 of title 49, unless the indictment is found or the information is instituted within 8 years after the offense was committed. Notwithstanding the preceding sentence, offenses listed in section 3295 are subject to the statute of limitations set forth in that section.

'(b) NO LIMITATION–Notwithstanding any other law, an indictment may be found or an information instituted at any time without limitation for any offense listed in section 2332b(g)(5)(B), if the commission of such offense resulted in, or created a forseeable risk of, death or serious bodily injury to another person.'.

(b) APPLICATION–The amendments made by this section shall apply to the prosecution of any offense committed before, on, or after the date of the enactment of this section.

'DISCLOSURE OF FOREIGN INTELLIGENCE ACQUIRED IN CRIMINAL INVESTIGATIONS; NOTICE OF CRIMINAL INVESTIGATIONS OF FOREIGN INTELLIGENCE SOURCES

'SEC. 105B. (a) DISCLOSURE OF FOREIGN INTELLIGENCE–(1) Except as otherwise provided by law and subject to paragraph (2), the Attorney General, or the head of any other department or agency of the Federal Government with law enforcement responsibilities, shall expeditiously disclose to the Director of Central Intelligence, pursuant to guidelines developed by the Attorney General in consultation with the Director, foreign intelligence acquired by an element of the Department of Justice or an element of such department or agency, as the case may be, in the course of a criminal investigation.

'(2) The Attorney General by regulation and in consultation with the Director of Central Intelligence may provide for exceptions to the applicability of paragraph (1) for one or more classes of foreign intelligence, or foreign intelligence with respect to one or more targets or matters, if the Attorney General determines that disclosure of such foreign intelligence under that paragraph would jeopardize an ongoing law enforcement investigation or impair other significant law enforcement interests.

'(b) PROCEDURES FOR NOTICE OF CRIMINAL INVESTIGATIONS–Not later than 180 days after the date of enactment of this section, the Attorney General, in consultation with the Director of Central Intelligence, shall develop guidelines to ensure that after receipt of a report from an element of the intelligence community of activity of a foreign intelligence source or potential foreign intelligence source that may warrant investigation as criminal activity, the Attorney General provides notice to the Director of Central Intelligence, within a reasonable period of time, of his intention to commence, or decline to commence, a criminal investigation of such activity.

'(c) PROCEDURES–The Attorney General shall develop procedures for the administration of this section, including the disclosure of foreign intelligence by elements of the Department of Justice, and elements of other departments and agencies of the Federal Government, under subsection (a) and the provision of notice with respect to criminal investigations under subsection (b).'.

(b) CLERICAL AMENDMENT–The table of contents in the first section of that Act is amended by striking the item relating to section 105B and inserting the following new items:

'Sec. 105B. Disclosure of foreign intelligence acquired in criminal investigations; notice of criminal investigations of foreign intelligence sources.

'Sec. 105C. Protection of the operational files of the National Imagery and Mapping Agency.'.

SEC. 906. FOREIGN TERRORIST ASSET TRACKING CENTER.

(a) REPORT ON RECONFIGURATION–Not later than February 1, 2002, the Attorney General, the Director of Central Intelligence, and the Secretary of the Treasury shall jointly submit to Congress a report on the feasibility and desirability of reconfiguring the Foreign Terrorist Asset Tracking Center and the Office of Foreign Assets Control of the Department of the Treasury in order to establish a capability to provide for the effective and efficient analysis and dissemination of foreign intelligence relating to the financial capabilities and resources of international terrorist organizations.

(b) REPORT REQUIREMENTS–(1) In preparing the report under subsection (a), the Attorney General, the Secretary, and the Director shall consider whether, and to what extent, the capacities and resources of the Financial Crimes Enforcement Center of the Department of the Treasury may be integrated into the capability contemplated by the report.

(2) If the Attorney General, Secretary, and the Director determine that it is feasible and desirable to undertake the reconfiguration described in subsection (a) in order to establish the capability described in that subsection, the Attorney

General, the Secretary, and the Director shall include with the report under that subsection a detailed proposal for legislation to achieve the reconfiguration.

SEC. 907. NATIONAL VIRTUAL TRANSLATION CENTER.

(a) REPORT ON ESTABLISHMENT

(1) Not later than February 1, 2002, the Director of Central Intelligence shall, in consultation with the Director of the Federal Bureau of Investigation, submit to the appropriate committees of Congress a report on the establishment and maintenance within the intelligence community of an element for purposes of providing timely and accurate translations of foreign intelligence for all other elements of the intelligence community. In the report, the element shall be referred to as the 'National Virtual Translation Center'.

(2) The report on the element described in paragraph (1) shall discuss the use of state-of-the-art communications technology, the integration of existing translation capabilities in the intelligence community, and the utilization of remote-connection capacities so as to minimize the need for a central physical facility for the element.

(b) RESOURCES–The report on the element required by subsection (a) shall address the following:

(1) The assignment to the element of a staff of individuals possessing a broad range of linguistic and translation skills appropriate for the purposes of the element.

(2) The provision to the element of communications capabilities and systems that are commensurate with the most current and sophisticated communications capabilities and systems available to other elements of intelligence community.

(3) The assurance, to the maximum extent practicable, that the communications capabilities and systems provided to the element will be compatible with communications capabilities and systems utilized by the Federal Bureau of Investigation in securing timely and accurate translations of foreign language materials for law enforcement investigations.

(4) The development of a communications infrastructure to ensure the efficient and secure use of the translation capabilities of the element.

(c) SECURE COMMUNICATIONS–The report shall include a discussion of the creation of secure electronic communications between the element described by subsection (a) and the other elements of the intelligence community.

(d) DEFINITIONS–In this section:

(1) FOREIGN INTELLIGENCE–The term 'foreign intelligence' has the meaning given that term in section 3(2) of the National Security Act of 1947 (50 U.S.C. 401a(2)).

(2) ELEMENT OF THE INTELLIGENCE COMMUNITY–The term 'element of the intelligence community' means any element of the intelligence community specified or designated under section 3(4) of the National Security Act of 1947 (50 U.S.C. 401a(4)).

SEC. 908. TRAINING OF GOVERNMENT OFFICIALS REGARDING IDENTIFICATION AND USE OF FOREIGN INTELLIGENCE.

(a) PROGRAM REQUIRED–The Attorney General shall, in consultation with the Director of Central Intelligence, carry out a program to provide appropriate training to officials described in subsection (b) in order to assist such officials in—

(1) identifying foreign intelligence information in the course of their duties; and

(2) utilizing foreign intelligence information in the course of their duties, to the extent that the utilization of such information is appropriate for such duties.

(b) OFFICIALS–The officials provided training under subsection (a) are, at the discretion of the Attorney General and the Director, the following:

(1) Officials of the Federal Government who are not ordinarily engaged in the collection, dissemination, and use of foreign intelligence in the performance of their duties.

(2) Officials of State and local governments who encounter, or may encounter in the course of a terrorist event, foreign intelligence in the performance of their duties.

(c) AUTHORIZATION OF APPROPRIATIONS–There is hereby authorized to be appropriated for the Department of Justice such sums as may be necessary for purposes of carrying out the program required by subsection (a).

Glossary

311 system (p. 324) due to the many demands on the 911 emergency phone lines for reasons outside of the responsibility of the police, many municipalities have implemented 311 systems for all calls that do not require an emergency response.

911 system (p. 323) the implementation of 911 systems, in which citizens could call in incidents requiring immediate response, not only revolutionized citizen access to police service, but also created many conflicting demands.

actual damages (p. 102) in a civil lawsuit, actual damages refer to a verdict in which the plaintiff receives monetary compensation for the actual losses (e.g., wages, property damage, etc.) resulting from the defendant's actions.

actus reus (p. 98) an essential element in a criminal case, actus reus refers to the commission (or omission of duty) of the act that is prohibited by law.

administrative liability (p. 102) the legal responsibility of an organization or agency (e.g., police department) for the actions of its members. Examples of areas that can bring about administrative liability include inadequate training, and unclear policies.

administrative unit (p. 147) large police departments in the United States are typically divided into two parts: field services and administration. The administrative unit handles all the support functions for the smooth operation of the department. Examples of administrative functions include: human resources, training, research and planning, and internal affairs.

Advanced Generation of Interoperability for Law Enforcement (AGILE) (p. 341) AGILE is a prototype system designed to improve the communication across law enforcement and other criminal justice agencies within a jurisdiction.

affirmative action (pp. 255, 359) a policy of law enforcement or other agencies to correct a history of imbalances in the hiring of personnel through the creation of specific policies or quotas to guide future hiring. Affirmative action policies typically exist on the basis of race or gender, but can include other demographic concerns as well.

agent provocateur (p. 152) a law enforcement officer that has crossed the line between entrapment and encouragement in undercover operations, possibly planting the initial idea for the criminal action in the mind of the accused.

aggressive patrol (pp. 173) similar to directed patrol, aggressive patrol involves the targeting of specific locations, times, and offenders. Aggressive patrol involves the zero tolerance enforcement of selected activities within the defined target area. Also referred to as **aggressive patrolling (p. 248)**.

alternative sanction (p. 29) within criminal justice, many alternative sanctions exist in lieu of the more traditional punishment. Alternative sanctions can include punishments such as community service, fines, or even diversion responses.

American Sign Language (ASL) (p. 251) language used by those who are hard of hearing.

analysis (p. 305) the heart of the SARA problem-solving model, this is the examination of the underlying causes of a particular problem prior to the selection of a response.

arraignment (p. 27) an early stage in the criminal justice process, in which the offender is brought before a judge for the first time, read the formal charges against him or her, and asked to submit a plea to the court. In some jurisdictions a first appearance before the court to hear the charges can occur prior to the arraignment, while in others the two are merged into one appearance.

arrest (pp. 26, 120) the formal taking into custody of an individual upon the establishment of probable cause for the commission of a criminal act.

asocial offender (p. 203) often referred to as a schizoid or withdrawn personality type, according to the FBI's disorganized/organized typology for criminal profiling, this type of offender will often commit spontaneous acts with little regard for the amount of physical evidence left behind capable of incriminating him or her.

assessment (p. 307) the final stage of the SARA problem solving model, assessment is the evaluation of whether or not the selected response achieved the desired outcomes of reducing or eliminating the problem.

assigned shifts (p. 179) the permanent assignment of officers to a specific geographical area and time of day. Assigned shifts are much more common today, and considered an essential ingredient of community policing operations.

associative evidence (p. 200) all evidence used to demonstrate the linkages between offender, victim, and location necessary for the successful prosecution of a crime.

authoritarian (p. 224) a debate often heard within the policing research literature is related to the extent to which police officers have an authoritarian personality type involving higher levels of conservatism, cynicism, and need for power or control. Even among those researchers that believe in the existence of the authoritarian personality type in policing, there is significant debate as to whether or not officers enter the profession with these characteristics, or they are a product of the career socialization process.

automated fingerprint identification system (AFIS) (p. 206) automated computer systems that allow for the comparison of latent fingerprints found at a crime scene to a digitized database of stored fingerprints of known offenders. AFIS has revolutionized the speed and accuracy of fingerprint analysis from the days involving the manual matching of stored paper cards.

Automated Regional Justice Information System (ARJIS) (p. 340) ARJIS is a database that facilitates the sharing of information among San Diego and neighboring criminal justice agencies.

automatic vehicle monitoring (AVM) (p. 343) created to enhance officer safety as well as accountability, AVM systems allow for the tracking of patrol vehicles in a jurisdiction, as well as such factors as whether or not a car door has been left open, etc.

bail (p. 96) allows for the release of a defendant from criminal justice custody while awaiting trial in order to be better able to prepare a defense and minimize interruption in the offender's life prior to the establishment of guilt. Bail can exist in many forms (e.g., ROR, credit, etc.) but is designed to ensure the reappearance of the defendant in court. According to the Supreme Court, the withholding of bail can be based on public safety concerns, but cannot be used as a form of punishment.

behavioral evidence (p. 201) the actions of an offender at the scene of the crime or during the post-crime period of interrogation and trial that can aid in the establishment of guilt. The observation of behavioral evidence is a key factor in criminal profiling.

beyond a reasonable doubt (p. 27) the standard of proof required for conviction in a criminal case involving the almost certainty of an individual's guilt based upon the evidence brought to trial.

bicycle patrol (p. 178) an alternative method of patrol involving officers conducting their patrol activities on bicycles. Bicycle patrol has the advantage of having officers closer to the community for interaction than is the case with automobile patrol, and at the same time as it increases the mobility of officers to respond across distances than is the case with foot patrol.

Bill of Rights (p. 84) the first ten amendments of the United States Constitution that outline the civil rights and liberties guaranteed to all citizens of the country.

biometrics (p. 339) surveillance technology designed for the speedy identification of individuals on the basis of physical characteristics (e.g., fingerprints, facial structure, voice or retinal patterns).

blending (p. 152) potentially the most dangerous of undercover or covert operations, blending involves a law enforcement agent immersing him or herself completely in the criminal environment being investigated.

bobbies (p. 44) an early nickname for officers of the London Metropolitan Police (LMP) that still persists today, on the basis of their founder Sir Robert Peel.

booking (p. 26) an early stage of the criminal justice process in which a suspect is formally entered into the system through fingerprinting, photographing, and the creation of a record.

Bow Street Runners (p. 41) under the guidance of Henry Fielding, the Bow Street Runners were a predecessor of the professional police detective function, charged with investigating larcenies and returning stolen property in a very high crime district of nineteenth century London.

broken windows theory (p. 295) the recognition that even low level misdemeanors or quality of life offenses can breed or foster more serious crimes in a community through their ability to attract more criminally minded individuals and drive out more law-abiding residents or businesses.

brutality (p. 268) a form of police corruption, brutality involves the intent of an officer to cause harm to an individual beyond what is necessary to accomplish a legitimate law enforcement objective. Brutality can take both physical and verbal forms.

buffer zones (p. 330) a form of crime analysis using GIS that visually displays levels of risk around offending populations in a geographic area.

burnout (p. 364) a psychological state of despair, anxiety and/or withdrawal that is the result of excessive stress on the job and in other facets of life.

calls for service data (p. 326) with increasing technology, most major departments keep automated databases of calls for service within their jurisdictions. Such data can be a useful complement to formal arrests and incident reports because they reflect the level of concern or reporting within a jurisdiction. Given that calls-for-service data are by nature geographically based, it is able to be analyzed easily with GIS mapping technology.

canine (K9) units (p. 158) most major departments now have K9 units, or access to specially trained dogs, to support operations, particularly in the areas of drug interdiction and offender/victim tracking efforts.

case law (p. 85) the law that is the result of recorded cases and judicial decisions within a specific jurisdiction.

causation (pp. 331) the proof that a particular act produced the resulting effect or harms that is an important ingredient in both criminal and civil law. Also referred to as **causation of harm (p. 99)**.

chain of evidence (p. 199) the careful documentation of the handling of evidence involved in an investigation from the point of the preliminary investigation (or arrival of the first law enforcement responder to the scene) all the way through to its ultimate presentation at trial.

chains of command (p. 139) the hierarchical lines of authority and communication illustrated in a formal organizational chart.

Chicago Alternative Policing Strategy (CAPS) (p. 335) considered by some experts to be a true example of a department-wide implementation of a community policing strategy, CAPS is the Chicago Police Department's innovative approach involving the fixed assignment of officers to a particular beat, the requirement that beat officers attend community beat meetings, and the training of both officers and residents in problem-solving approaches.

child pornography (p. 126) any visual depiction involving the use of a minor in a sexually explicit manner, whether it is an actual photograph or an image that has been modified or adapted to appear as a minor engaging in sexual conduct.

circadian rhythms (p. 180) the body's biological clock for sleep patterns; circadian rhythms can be seriously disrupted by rotating shift patterns previously common to many law enforcement agencies.

circle of investigation (p. 204) the pool of possible suspects in an investigation.

civil law (p. 83) the law dealing with private rights or wrongs against the individual, as opposed to the public matters embodied in criminal law. Rather than crimes, civil law involves torts.

civil liability (p. 102) liability dealt with under civil rather than criminal law, in which a government agency or individual is legally responsible for damages.

civil liberties (p. 83) an individual's freedom to act in pursuit of their interests.

civil rights (p. 83) the rights guaranteed to all U.S. citizens under the Bill of Rights and other constitutional amendments such as the Fourteenth and Nineteenth.

Civil Rights Act of 1871 (section 1983) (p. 101) a federal statute created to enforce the rights guaranteed by the Constitution; section 1983 holds that any law enforcement officer acting under the color of law that violates the civil rights of a citizen can be held civilly responsible for such action.

clear and present danger doctrine (p. 89) the doctrine that allows for the restriction of First Amendment freedom of speech where such speech can cause imminent and serious danger to the government or other citizens.

clearance rate (pp. 68, 195) the ratio of solved to reported crimes in a particular jurisdiction.

cleared crimes (p. 69) crimes in which an individual has been arrested and held responsible for his or her actions.

closed-circuit television (CCTV) (p. 337) a system of cameras recording actions in both private and public settings for the purpose of security; CCTV can be combined with biometrics, or facial recognition technologies.

Code of Hammurabi (p. 38) the first written legal codes of human history. Originating in Mesopotamia, the Code of Hammurabi is based upon the principle of *lex talionis*, or "an eye for an eye, a tooth for a tooth."

coercive force (p. 8) the use of force to physically stop an individual and/or take him or her into custody.

Co-lateral assignment (p. 154) when officers serve on special assignments, such as on a S.W.A.T. team, at the same time as continuing their regular duties.

Combined DNA Index System (CODIS) (p. 206) a structured DNA database with local, state, and federal levels.

command (p. 139) at the lowest level of the use of force continuum, even an officer's mere **presence** or **voice** is viewed as offering a certain degree of authority.

command discretion (p. 216) the power of a high-ranking police officer to make decisions about the organization.

Commercial Equipment Direct Assistance Program (CEDAP) (p. 20) Run by DHS, this has provided $32 million in material to small communities for hardware such as weaponry and heavily armored transport vehicles.

commission (p. 271) an investigatory body on the federal, state, or local level that is created for the short-term objective of examining the existence or causes of a particular problem or issue (e.g., corruption, use of force, etc.).

Commission for the Accreditation of Law Enforcement Agencies (CALEA) (p. 66) a voluntary accreditation for law enforcement agencies based on a body of standards internationally accepted by the law enforcement community.

community (p. 292) a geographically distinct area that can encompass a number of dimensions, including socioeconomic composition, residential stability, racial/ethnic heterogeneity, local friendship relational networks, organizational participation, and supervisory capacity.

community mobilization (p. 310) techniques utilized by law enforcement to outreach to and involve various sectors of the community (i.e., residents, businesses, faiths, schools, media) in the maintenance of public security.

community ownership (p. 294) the degree to which a community feels responsible for maintaining public security in its area and has a sense of pride and responsibility with respect to its overall quality of life.

community policing (pp. 297) the department-wide philosophy recognizing the need for partnership with the community and proactive problem-solving efforts in order to combat the conditions of crime more effectively.

Community policing involves strategic, philosophical, and tactical elements, including the fixed assignment of officers to a particular shift/time, and the decentralization of decision-making within the department. The term **community-oriented policing (p. 305)** often is used to reflect the entirety of community policing dimensions.

community prosecution (p. 302) complementary to community policing approaches, community prosecution efforts involve the collaboration of prosecutors with other government agencies in the proactive targeting and resolution of the crime and quality of life concerns within a given area.

comprehensive plans (p. 312) in order to effectively combat crime and corruption, a full continuum of services and strategies are necessary, including suppression, intervention, and prevention efforts.

CompStat (p. 331) the strategic and organizational innovation first implemented by the New York City Police Department (NYPD) that includes the regular reporting of precinct commanders to agency top brass, the holding of commanders responsible for the crime in their precincts through timely and accurate information, and the use of GIS mapping to engage in problem-solving efforts for strategic planning.

concealed-carry handgun statutes (p. 92) statutes that allow citizens to apply for permits to carry concealed weapons, usually on the basis of some objective criteria (see also **shall issue statutes (p. 92)**).

concurrence (p. 99) the need to establish in criminal law that the act (*actus reus*) and the intent (*mens rea*) occurred at the same place and time.

constables (p. 40) originally designated to assist the shire-reeve in ensuring the law and order of a community during feudal England, after the Norman conquest constables often would supervise others whose responsibility it was to guard the gates of a community at night. Later the constables answered to the justice of the peace instead of the community itself. Constables would become a professional civilian body following the Metropolitan Police Act in 1829.

constitution (p. 84) the fundamental law of a country or state, organizing the division of powers as well as the balance between government powers and the individual.

constitutional law (p. 83) the body of law resulting from the interpretation of the U.S. Constitution by the Supreme Court, and the outlining of civil rights and liberties in the country.

contagion proposition (p. 295) as disorder increases and the quality of life decreases in a defined geographic area, more fear and crime is generated over time.

contaminants (p. 196) any element that can alter the quality or nature of evidence at a crime scene and thus impede the processes of association and reconstruction.

contempt of cop (COC) (p. 219) the term often used within the police culture to refer to the mistrust, attitude, and even hatred expressed by the community residents they are sworn to protect.

control beats (p. 174) within the Kansas City Preventive Patrol Experiment, these were the beats in which the same amount of patrol services were deployed as prior to the experiment. The control beats were included in the research design as a comparison to the results found in the proactive and reactive beats.

corpus delicti **(p. 99)** literally means the "body of the crime," but in actuality refers to the elements of a crime that must be proven in order to establish guilt; while this refers mainly to the facts of an illegal act (*actus reus*), ultimately the intent (*mens rea*) also must be established for most crimes.

correlations (p. 331) the statistical relationship between two variables in either a positive or negative direction. Correlation alone cannot be used to indicate that one variable causes another.

covert (undercover) operations (p. 150) investigative operations conducted generally in plainclothes that can take several forms: sting operations, buy-back, surveillance, and reverse sting.

crime analysis (pp. 307, 325) the proactive use of technology, research techniques, and triangulated data sources to analyze crime trends and patterns to develop strategy and make operational decisions.

crime control (p. 11) conceptualized as one of the two principal models of criminal justice by Herbert Packer, the crime control model emphasizes quantity and speed of arrests over due process considerations.

crime indices (p. 69) statistical calculations that allow crime trends to be comparable across jurisdictions of differing size and density (e.g., incidents per 100,000 population); a principal means for the reporting and comparison of FBI Uniform Crime Report (UCR) data.

crime mapping (p. 327) the visual display of crime data with a known geographic origin to facilitate pattern recognition and operational decisions. Although originally crime maps existed solely with pushpins on a map, geographic information systems (GIS) have drastically enhanced the ability of law enforcement agencies to engage in crime mapping.

crime prevention through environmental design (CPTED) (p. 300) the recognition that crime can be prevented or managed through the manipulation of guardianship, target vulnerability, and other locational dynamics.

crime scenes (p. 198) areas in which the crime actually took place (primary crime scene) and/or evidence relating to the crime is sound (secondary crime scene).

crime triangle (p. 305) used to facilitate crime analysis and problem solving, the crime triangle visually displays the three elements necessary in order for a crime to take place: victim, offender, and location.

crime-trend forecasting (p. 326) the use of crime analysis techniques to predict the nature and volume of crime in a specific area to aid deployment and strategy decisions.

criminal justice system (p. 23) the interconnected phases of the processing of a suspected individual from the point of arrest through to trial and ultimately the completion of his or her sentence (i.e., police, courts, and corrections).

criminal law (p. 82) the body of law defined in the penal code of a jurisdiction (e.g., federal, state, or local) that defines the actions or omissions that must be complied with by the public or face punishment by the state.

criminal liability (p. 102) being found criminally responsible for a given action.

criminal profiling (p. 201) the combined use of behavioral and physical evidence in order to develop a profile of the most likely offender type given a particular action or series of actions.

criminalistics (p. 200) the use of physical evidence to reconstruct a crime and associate offender, victim, and crime scene together for probative purposes.

critical incident stress debriefings (CISD) (p. 232) a staged system of therapy to help officers cope with the stress and trauma incurred during a crisis situation.

critical stage (p. 95) a stage in the processing of an offender through the criminal justice system in which the fair outcome of the case could be affected by the absence of legal representation, thereby triggering his or her Sixth Amendment right to counsel.

cross-cultural populations (p. 250) populations that are themselves distinct, and yet cross traditionally accepted racial and ethnic categories (e.g., lesbian gay and transgendered–LGBT, mentally ill, and deaf and hard of hearing).

cultural barriers (p. 244) difficulties in communication or interaction across groups that is caused by a lack of understanding or appreciation of another culture.

cultural cues (p. 207) nonverbal body language that can differ and carry significantly different meanings across cultures (e.g., eye contact, body space, and hand gestures).

culture of lawfulness (p. 9) the acceptance of the majority of a particular society in the importance of rules and laws and a belief in the system of justice generally.

curtilage (p. 119) the part of a property adjoining a home (and usually, though not always, enclosed) that is generally protected from Fourth Amendment warrantless searches.

cyber crime (p. 125) any offense that occurs via the Internet as opposed to the real world. This is not the same as computer crime, which is any wrongful act occurring on or directed against a computer, though computer crimes can include cyber crime.

cyber sleuths (p. 125) individuals who regulate Internet use and enforce cyber laws, such as the possession and distribution of child pornography.

D.A.R.E. (Drug Abuse Resistance Education) (p. 157) originally piloted by the Los Angeles Police Department (LAPD), DARE is a school-based program in which police officers teach students about the dangers of substance abuse. The program is now offered by police departments both nationally and internationally.

dark figure of crime (p. 71) the level of unreported crime in an area that is not known to the police or public.

deadly force (p. 268) the use of potentially lethal force by a police officer.

decentralization (pp. 145, 309) the localization of decision-making to a precinct or even neighborhood level.

decoy operation (p. 152) a type of undercover operation in which officers pose as potential victims in order to apprehend offenders.

Defense Intelligence Agency (DIA) (p. 20) Program under DHS that is responsible for creating the Joint Regional Information Exchange that gives them information pertinent to terrorist activity on U.S. citizens, resident foreigners, and others that is collected by local and state police agencies.

defenses (p. 99) the arguments made by the defense in trial to challenge the prosecution's case with regard to the commission of the act itself (alibis), the level of intent required (excuses), or the harm caused (justifications).

democratic accountability (p. 276) mechanisms to improve accountability of the police department to the community, such as an external review board.

Department of Homeland Security (DHS) (p. 17) the result of the largest governmental reorganization in many years, the Department of Homeland Security includes the transfer of the Coast Guard, Customs Service, Border Patrol, Federal Emergency Management Agency, Secret Service, Transportation Security Administration, and border inspection component of the Animal and Plant Health Inspection service.

despecialization (p. 309) the process of restructuring an organization to include less specialized functions, and making line officers take on more of these responsibilities as generalists.

deviance (p. 7) the violation of both formal and informal rules, laws, or customs.

differential response (p. 172) an alternative form of dispatch in which callers in nonemergency situations are informed that an officer might not respond for several hours, the report is taken over the phone, or a non-sworn employee is sent to respond to the call. Differential response strategies are meant to free up line officer resources for more proactive operations or emergency situations.

directed patrol (p. 172) the deployment of patrol to a specific location and/or time on the basis of a review of crime patterns and trends in that area.

discovery crimes (p. 194) crimes that are discovered and/or reported long after the offense took place and the offender is gone. Home burglaries often are discovery crimes in which the resident returns home well after the incident actually occurred.

discretion (p. 9) the decision-making power of any criminal justice official.

disstress (p. 229) stress that is outside of the normal range and very harmful over time.

diversity (p. 249) differences of people within a community.

division (p. 145) a group of police personnel that share responsibility for a particular policing function.

double jeopardy (p. 94) being prosecuted twice for the same offense, circumstances, and evidence. The Fifth Amendment protects U.S. citizens from double jeopardy.

Drug Enforcement Administration (DEA) (p. 16) within the Treasury Department, the primary responsibility of the DEA is to investigate and prepare evidence for the prosecution of major violators of controlled substances laws both domestically and internationally.

dual promotion lists (p. 366) separate promotional instruments for white male officers and all other officers. Such lists were found in many police departments throughout the 1980s to encourage the promotion of women and minorities.

due process (p. 11) the fair processing of an individual through the criminal justice system from the point of arrest through to sentencing. Protected by the Fifth, Sixth, and Fourteenth Amendments to the Constitution.

eight-hour shift structure (p. 179) a common shift structure in contemporary departments in which officers generally work five days a week for eight hours and then get two days off. Following an additional five days, the officer will receive four days off.

electronic surveillance (p. 93) mechanisms to monitor an offender's movements electronically, such as wiretapping, electronic bracelets, and CCTV.

electronic warrant system (p. 341) technological advances that allow the officer to electronically submit the affidavit for a warrant to the judge or magistrate in order to significantly speed up the time to issue.

empowerment (p. 298) the feeling of all parties in a partnership that they have equal input into decisions and the commitment of resources.

entrapment (p. 152) a situation in which a law enforcement officer can be said to have "planted the seed"

for an offense in the mind of the offender, in order to later prosecute him or her for said offense.

Environmental Systems Research Institute Inc. (ESRI) (p. 336) the leading developer of innovative and practical Geographic Information Systems (p. GIS) for both the public and private sectors.

equal protection clause (p. 97) a provision in the Fourteenth Amendment that requires the states to treat all people involved in similar circumstances equally under the law.

equity (p. 84) the principle of fairness under the law; the recognition that the law can be modified in accordance with the changing needs and dynamics of society.

essential criteria for crime analysis (p. 325) in order to have effective crime analysis capacities, departments should ensure that data collection processes are designed with timeliness, relevancy, and reliability concerns in mind.

establishment of religion clause (p. 86) in the First Amendment, this provision prohibits the government from creating or supporting a particular religion.

eustress (p. 229) stress that is normal and good, even providing on the job motivation.

exceptional clearance (p. 69) a category in the FBI's Uniform Crime Reporting procedures to account for those situations in which the law enforcement agency knows that a certain individual committed a particular crime, but for some reason cannot be brought to justice (e.g., death of the offender).

excessive force (p. 267) any amount of force by a law enforcement officer that is beyond the minimum necessary to achieve legitimate law enforcement objectives.

exclusionary rule (pp. 93, 111) the recognition that any evidence that is obtained illegally by law enforcement (or the fruits thereof) will not be admissible in court. Meant to deter illegal law enforcement conduct.

exigent circumstances (p. 114) an emergency or exceptional situation requiring immediate law enforcement action.

exonerated (p. 276) individuals that have been convicted of a crime that later are proven to be innocent on the basis of new evidence.

expressive purposes (p. 88) peaceable assemblies for religious, political, or social reasons, including protests. Protected under the First Amendment.

external authorizing environmental stakeholders (p. 170) any individual, group, or agency outside of the police department that can influence its policies or procedures.

external stressors (p. 230) problems or factors outside of the police department that can cause stress or disequilibrium for police management.

extra-legal factors (p. 10) variables outside of those directly pertaining to the circumstances of a particular incident, such as race or suspect demeanor, that nonetheless influence an officer's decision on how to handle the situation.

facial recognition software (p. 339) technology designed to recognize physical characteristics of an individual in order to enhance the utility of CCTV and related technology.

fatigue (p. 179) excessive tiredness that police officers feel while on the job.

Federal Air Marshall Service (p. 19) The primary law enforcement entity within the TSA.

Federal Bureau of Investigation (FBI) (p. 15) under the Department of Justice, the FBI is responsible for the investigation of all federal crimes, including an international presence related to counter-terrorism training and intelligence.

Federal Law Enforcement Training Center (FLETC) (p. 20) interagency law enforcement organization that provides training to state, local, and international law enforcement agencies.

felony (p. 98) a serious offense that carries a potential sentence of more than a year of incarceration.

field interrogation (p. 110) a law enforcement officer's questioning of an individual that is not officially under police custody.

field training officers (FTO) (pp. 180, 363) once out of the academy, the FTO assists the police officer in applying the knowledge and skills learned to the job.

fighting words (p. 89) a speech that is not necessarily protected by the First Amendment because it is capable of inciting violence.

flat organizations (p. 141) organizations in which many layers of bureaucracy have been reduced in order to facilitate rapid information sharing across ranks.

flattening (pp. 141, 309) the process of reducing layers of bureaucracy or ranks in an organization.

fleeing felony rule (p. 268) prior to the *Tennessee v. Garner* decision, it was acceptable practice in many jurisdictions to use deadly force when a felon fled from an officer regardless of the immediacy of threat involved in the situation.

force continuum (p. 264) used in the training of officers in most departments nationally, the force continuum demonstrates the increasing types of force allowable with the corresponding increase in offender resistance and threat.

formal social control (p. 8) the laws of a society, and the mechanisms for their enforcement.

free exercise of religion (p. 88) the recognition of the ability of individuals to practice whatever faith they so choose under the First Amendment, so long as such practice does not infringe on the rights of others or violate existing criminal law.

frisk (pp. 93, 110) a brief pat-down search of an individual that is restricted to the search for a weapon.

fruit of the poisoned tree (p. 112) the rule that any later evidence resulting from an illegal search or seizure will itself be held inadmissible under the exclusionary rule.

functional structures (p. 142) a modification to traditional organizational structure to allow divisions with overlapping purpose (such as intelligence) to report to multiple divisions; functional structures are created to reduce the problem of linkage blindness.

fundamental attribution errors (p. 246) the tendency of some individuals to explain criminal behavior in terms of internal factors such as race or membership in a particular ethnic group, rather than by reference to external or situational factors, such as poverty or marginal social position.

Gang resistance education and training (GREAT) (p. 157) program model that puts officers into the classroom to discuss the negative implications of gang involvement.

generalists (p. 138) the tendency in some organizations to reduce specialization of functions and have officers readily able to respond to a variety of situations and operational needs. Generalist functions are much more common in rural jurisdictions by necessity.

geocoded (p. 330) the use of data with a geographic locator as a reference for the purpose of mapping relationships across indicators.

geographic information systems (GIS) (p. 327) software designed for the presentation of geographic data as maps to facilitate analysis possibilities.

geographic profiling (p. 336) the combined use of geography, psychology, and mathematics to identify the location of an offender; most commonly associated with tracking down serial killers, rapists, and arsonists.

global positioning systems (GPS) (p. 338) use satellite-based technologies for the purpose of tracking the movement of patrol cars, stolen vehicles, and in some cases even individuals.

good faith exception (p. 113) an exception to the exclusionary rule allowing evidence obtained from a search warrant later found to be invalid still to be admitted in court, if the officer(s) executing it were acting under the belief that the warrant was legal. Also referred to as **good faith immunity (p. 103)**.

good time (p. 29) offenders who abide by the prison rules and receive positive reports from correctional services can be released prior to completion of their maximum sentence.

grass eaters (p. 271) one of two categories of corrupt police officers identified by the Knapp Commission's investigation into the corruption of the New York City Police Department, grass eaters refer to those officers who passively accept tips, bribes, or other corrupt activities.

harbor patrol (p. 178) type of patrol utilized for jurisdictions bordering shorelines, beaches, or lakes.

hearing impaired (p. 250) a continuum of difficulty with auditory perception ranging from mild difficulties to complete deafness.

hierarchical accountability (p. 276) accountability to those structurally higher within the department.

hierarchy (p. 139) chain of command.

hierarchy rule (p. 71) the UCR reporting guidelines that stipulate that only the most serious offense within a series of linked incidents is to be counted.

high-risk traffic stop (p. 183) a traffic stop in which the driver of the pursued vehicle is known to be a wanted felon or extremely dangerous in some known way.

Hoover, J. Edgar (p. 53) former Director of the Federal Bureau of Investigation from 1935 until the 1970s, Hoover was responsible for many efforts to professionalize its agency policies, procedures, and methods.

Homeland Security Information Network (HSIN) (p. 340) Computer-based communication system that enables state and urban law enforcement agencies to collect and disseminate information among federal, state, and local agencies to prevent terrorist activity.

horizontal differentiation (p. 142) the differentiation within the same layer of an organizational structure.

horse patrol (p. 178) patrol conducted on horse is most common in places that are inaccessible to automobiles or motorcycles, such as parks and wild terrain. Also used for increased visibility in urban settings during parades or demonstrations.

hostage-negotiation techniques (p. 156) techniques employed during a hostage situation to minimize the likelihood of having to resort to lethal force.

hot pursuit (p. 115) Any form of chase when the suspect may escape without immediate police action.

hot spots (p. 307) specific areas within a community that have the highest concentration of crime and other forms of disorder.

hue and cry (p. 41) in early England, the hue and cry was the constable's call for help; failure to heed the call by all men between the ages of fifteen and sixty was an offense.

hung jury (p. 28) a jury that is unable to reach a verdict with the acceptable majority.

immigrant communities (p. 249) concentrated areas within which reside a large number of foreign-born populations.

Immigration and Customs Enforcement (ICE) (p. 19) the largest investigative branch of DHS, this agency is responsible for enforcing immigration and customs laws and protecting the United States from terrorist activity.

inchoate offenses (p. 99) a step is taken toward the commission of a crime that is not the complete offense itself, but deserving of punishment.

incident data (p. 326) data pertaining to the specifics of a particular criminal act.

incident to arrest (p. 115) once an officer has probable cause to arrest an individual, he or she is permitted under the Fourth Amendment to conduct a full-body search of the offender.

incident-driven policing (p. 172) is policing that is focused on responding to calls for service.

individual discretion (p. 216) the personal decision-making power of any criminal justice official.

inevitable discovery (p. 113) when the prosecution can demonstrate that they would have found the evidence anyway, it may not be immediately dismissed under the exclusionary rule for being the fruit of an illegal source.

informal social control (p. 7) mechanisms for ensuring compliance with the formal and informal rules, laws, and customs of society that are outside the purview of the formal enforcement role of law enforcement, such as families, schools, peers, churches, media, and businesses.

Information Collection for Automated Mapping (ICAM) (p. 335) the Chicago Police Department's Web-based mapping system that allows both officers and residents to view crime trends in their areas.

initial appearance (p. 26) the first appearance before a judge by a defendant to formally hear the charges being held against him or her.

Integrated Automated Fingerprint Identification System (IAFIS) (pp. 206, 340) an advanced automated fingerprint database kept by the FBI that allows a two-hour turnaround on electronically submitted criminal print searches from federal, state, and local agencies.

Integrated Ballistic Information System (p. 206) the administrative and networking system of technology that gives law enforcement agencies access to the NIBIN firearms identification program.

integrated patrol (p. 174) combining both automobile and foot patrol operations.

intention (p. 99) holding the requisite mental capacity for the commission of a particular crime.

intentional tort (p. 102) within civil law, wrong to another or their property that is based on the knowing and purposeful deliberations of an individual.

interim order (p. 137) the distribution of a change to the formal policies of a department before it can be formally incorporated into the departmental guidelines.

Internal Affairs Bureau (IAB) (pp. 149, 276) a division within large police departments staffed by sworn officers that serves to both investigate the complaints of citizens, as well as to initiate its own investigations.

Internal Revenue Service (IRS) (p. 20) the largest agency within the Treasury Department, the mission of the IRS is to regulate compliance with tax laws and to investigate tax evasion and fraud.

internal stressors (p. 230) factors within a department that can be a source of difficulty.

International Association of Chiefs of Police (IACP) (p. 65) a professional police organization that is committed to the production of materials and technical assistance efforts that can benefit the field both nationally and internationally.

International Association of Policewomen (IAP) (p. 66) a professional organization founded to serve the interests of policewomen, it has since disbanded as its own agency and been folded under the umbrella of IACP.

interrogation (p. 122) formally questioning a suspect under custody with the intention of eliciting a response related to the actions in question.

intervention services (p. 313) services provided to offenders after they have already committed an offense, usually with the intention of rehabilitation.

investigation (p. 26) police operations focused on the solution of previously committed crimes.

involvement crimes (p. 194) crimes in which the police respond to the scene and the offender is still present and/or the crime remains in progress.

Iron Law of Oligarchy (p. 216) suggests that the formal organization of bureaucracies inevitably leads to oligarchy, in which a small group of self-serving individuals seek to maintain their position of power.

jail (p. 28) incarceration on the municipal level for offenses serving time of less than a year. Also used to house offenders awaiting trial, awaiting transfer to prisons, probation or parole violators, etc.

Jim Crow laws (p. 47) the racist laws begun in the 1880s to enforce segregation between whites and blacks in schools, parks, restrooms, and other public facilities.

Joint Regional Information Exchange System (JRIES) (p. 20) Run by the DIA, this enables the exchange of law enforcement information over the Internet.

Joint Terrorism Task Forces (JTTFs) (p. 15) task forces within the FBI field offices that are composed of representatives of local and state law enforcement, FBI agents, and teams from other federal agencies.

judicial review (p. 86) power given to the Supreme Court and the federal judiciary to consider and overturn any congressional and state legislation or other official governmental action deemed inconsistent with the Constitution, Bill of Rights, or federal law.

jurisdiction (p. 12) local, state, federal, and tribal areas of responsibility under which contemporary law enforcement agencies operate.

justice of the peace (p. 14) a magistrate who presides in the justice's court and is of a lesser rank than those in higher courts.

justice's court (p. 14) courts on the county level that only maintain limited jurisdiction as described by statute in civil matters, such as the performance of marriages, and minor criminal offenses.

Kansas City Gun Experiment (p. 173) intensive patrols that targeted an 80-block high crime area, which revealed that aggressive patrol can significantly reduce gun crimes such as drive-by shootings and homicides without a measured displacement effect.

Kansas City Patrol Experiment (p. 174) study in 1972 using proactive, reactive, and controlled patrol beats that showed that random patrol on its own does not significantly affect in criminal activity.

Kansas City Response Time Study (p. 194) study showing that citizens take longer to report crimes to police than it takes police to respond.

kinesics (p. 201) body language.

knock and announce (p. 114) requirement that police officer knock on the door and announce their presence before going into a residence for the purpose of a search and/or arrest.

latent fingerprints (p. 206) an impression of the markings of the inner surface of the thumb or other finger for the purposes of identification.

law enforcement (p. 6) the role of the police in enforcing the existing legislation or rules of society.

Law Enforcement Assistance Administration (LEAA) (p. 351) organization that began emphasizing the need for police officers to attend college at this time as well, going as far as implementing a grant system for individuals who were or planned to be police officers upon graduation.

Law Enforcement Education Program (LEEP) (p. 61) established in 1964 to help provide the impetus for police-related training/courses in academic institutions across the country by offering financing for criminal justice professionals seeking post-secondary educational opportunities.

Law Enforcement Support Center (LESC) (p. 19) located within ICE, this center assists in the provision of information and assistance to federal, state, and local law enforcement.

law of accelerating returns (p. 325) technological advancement is characterized by exponential growth, increasing doubly each year.

legalistic (p. 50) oriented toward the strict enforcement of the letter of the law.

legalistic style (p. 228) style of policing described by James Q. Wilson that emphasizes the importance of law enforcement and maintaining clear and impartial legal standards for both the police and public alike.

legitimate force (p. 264) the minimum amount of force necessary to control a situation.

less-than-lethal force (p. 265) minimal physical force that is not intended to be deadly, but rather to subdue the suspect so as to avoid harm to the officer or anyone in the surrounding area, including use of hands, pepper spray, mace, a taser, a baton, or rubber bullets.

lethal force (p. 265) force with a firearm.

lex taliones **(p. 38)** retributive principle that literally means an "eye for an eye."

line personnel (p. 139) the lowest in the chain of command, usually patrol officers.

linguistic barriers (p. 244) when ethnic minorities in the community do not have a working understanding of the English language, which can prevent minorities from gaining access to justice or taking advantage of important criminal justice services.

linkage analysis (p. 326) connecting a suspect to a series of incidents based on commonalities in *modus operandi* and suspect description, as well as known offenders that live close proximity to a given area.

linkage blindness (p. 5) the inability to analyze and link critical information across or within agencies.

Locard exchange principle (p. 199) states that it is impossible for anyone to enter a location without changing it in some way, either by bringing something to it or removing something from it, which is why offenders can be linked to a crime scene.

mandatory arrest policies (p. 214) elimination of officer discretion and requiring arrest in particular situations (e.g., domestic violence).

Massachusetts Bartley-Fox laws (p. 91) laws that mandate a one-year jail term for individuals caught carrying a handgun outside of the home without a permit.

matrix structures (p. 142) create a team problem-solving environment in which members of different divisions (i.e., detective bureau, patrol, vice/narcotic) are assigned to specific problem areas such as counterterrorism or organized crime.

max out (p. 29) when a prisoner serves his or her entire sentence in prison.

meat eaters (p. 271) when officers aggressively demand bribes in exchange for protection (or lack of) to the person from whom they are seeking the favor.

mediation (p. 282) alternative dispute resolution.

mens rea **(p. 99)** component of crime that literally means "a guilty mind."

Metropolitan Police Act (p. 43) in 1829, this provided funds for the establishment of a 1,000-officer police force in London governed by strict standards of conduct and discipline.

middle management (p. 139) officers such as captains and lieutenants who are not at the top of the command

chain but have ranking power over some officers in the department.

Minneapolis Domestic Violence Experiment (p. 214) study testing the mandatory arrest policies for domestic violence, which showed that mandatory arrests might decrease the escalating violence of those males who could be adversely affected by criminal justice attention, such as the employed or political figures in a community.

Minnesota Multiphasic Personality Inventory (MMPI) (p. 356) most common psychological assessment tool in the screening of police applicants.

minority communities (p. 244) communities consisting largely of racial or ethnic minorities.

minority recruitment (p. 253) the seeking of minorities for positions in the police department.

Miranda **rights (p. 122)** based on the case of *Miranda v Arizona*, police officers are required to explain to suspects prior to custodial interrogation that they have the right against self-incrimination and the right to counsel.

misdemeanor (p. 98) relatively minor crime subject to less than a year in a jail.

mission statement (p. 137) an expression of a police department's overall purpose and goals.

mobile digital communications (MDC) (p. 342) offer nonverbal means of communicating information between communication centers and patrol.

modus operandi (MO) (p. 202) how a crime is committed.

motive (p. 99) why a criminal act is committed.

motorcycle patrol (p. 178) type of patrol that is particularly useful in traffic enforcement activities given their ability to negotiate heavy traffic situations, such as in cases of high-profile police escorts and for parades.

moving violations (p. 181) enforcement of traffic regulations.

National Crime Information Center (NCIC) (p. 205) maintained by the FBI, NCIC makes information from jurisdictions nationally on wanted felons, stolen vehicles, missing children, and other important data available to the patrol officer in the field who can call into the department for a search.

National Crime Victimization Survey (NCVS) (p. 71) survey conducted by the Bureau of Justice Statistics that collects self-report data on all crimes against individuals or households, regardless of whether or not they were reported to the police.

National DNA Identification System (NDIS) (p. 206) maintained by the FBI, the NDIS contains automated DNA information for offenders convicted of certain offenses such as sexual crimes and other crimes of violence.

National Incident Based Reporting System (NIBRS) (p. 72) an incident-based crime reporting system implemented by FBI in 1989 as a means of improving existing statistical reporting and crime analysis standards nationally and eventually intended to replace the UCR.

National Institute of Justice (NIJ) (p. 62) created in 1960 as a research entity specifically targeting advanced study in the areas of policing and other areas of criminal justice reform.

National Integrated Ballistic Information Network (NIBIN) (p. 205) a firearms identification program run by ATF.

nearness principle (p. 336) offenders will remain within a limited range that is comfortable to them when committing their offenses.

needs assessment (p. 311) the identification of problems and sources of the problems in local communities in order to establish a proactive policing strategy.

negligent wrong (p. 102) the breach of a common law or statutory duty to act reasonably toward those who potentially may be harmed by an officer's conduct, for which the officer may be held civilly liable.

Newark Foot Patrol Experiment (p. 177) study showing that increased foot patrol did not appear to have a significant effect on overall crime levels in the community, though it did result in more positive attitudes toward the police as well as reductions in fear of crime.

nolo contendere **(p. 101)** plea in a court of law that literally means "no contest," and in a criminal court is equivalent to a guilty plea.

nominal damages (p. 102) the Court acknowledges that the plaintiff proved his or her allegation but suffered no actual injury.

nonsocial offender (p. 203) an organized offender who is likely to meet the classification of a psychopath.

nonverbal cues (p. 201) changes in tone, pitch, or inflection that are important during interrogations.

objective reasonableness (p. 267) standard based on the circumstances of the case, usually in the use of force. The Court is required to judge whether the force used is legitimate based upon the perspective of a "reasonable officer" on the scene who is required to make quick decisions on the amount of force that may be necessary to use to control a situation.

Office of State and Local Government Coordination (SLGC) (p. 20) facilitates and coordinates DHS programs with state, local, and tribal governments, enabling them to exchange information with homeland security personnel.

ombudsman (p. 278) a neutral figure who reviews complaints against all public servants in an effort to combat organizational or systemic misconduct.

one-officer cars (p. 176) one patrol officer assigned per car.

operating stereotype (p. 247) preconceived ideas about groups of people—such as the belief that individu-als from certain cultures are inherently less law-abiding—that can provide the basis for unwitting but serious discrimination on the grounds of race or ethnicity.

operational unit (p. 147) engaged in activities performed in direct assistance to the public, such as police patrol and traffic, and are typically staffed by sworn police officers.

order maintenance (pp. 50, 74) police duty that is not focused on crime-fighting but rather on preventing disorder in the community.

order of authority (p. 84) a hierarchy of legal authority that exists so that conflicts between different federal, state, and local laws could be resolved, with the U.S. Constitution having the highest authority.

organizational chart (p. 138) formal structure, in terms of both task and authority, that is required to "get a job done."

organized-disorganized typology (p. 202) explanation that helps to correlate crime scene elements with key personality characteristics, with the organized offender taking great care in the planning of his or her offense to ensure that there is little or no evidence remaining at the crime scene and the disorganized offender engaging in a chaotic, unplanned style of attack, in which substantial amounts of evidence are left behind at the crime scene.

parole (p. 29) early release from prison in which the offender is living in the community for the remainder of his or her sentence under supervision from a field agent.

Part I index crimes (p. 69) eight main crimes listed in the UCR, including four violent personal crimes—murder, rape, robbery, and aggravated assault—and four property crimes—burglary, larceny, motor vehicle theft, and arson.

Part II index crimes (p. 69) all crimes in the UCR that are not Part I offenses, including forgery, fraud, embezzlement, vandalism, weapons (carrying/possession), gambling, sex offenses (other than forcible rape, prostitution), drug abuse, and disorderly conduct.

participatory management model (p. 309) policing structure in which line officers are encouraged to be creative and resolve problems, rather than simply following directives.

partnership (p. 298) when community residents and organizations becoming the "eyes and ears" of the police, and also includes working together on a common problem; identifying common goals; steady and consistent communication and information sharing; having a shared perception of problems and benchmarks for when problems are solved; and all parties contributing work toward accomplishing shared goals and objectives or solving the problem.

patrol deployment (p. 179) methods by which the police use officers for patrol, using various shift formats to best resolve crime related problems across diverse contexts.

pattern detection (p. 326) in tactical crime analysis, problem identification of multiple offenses over a short period of time that have common characteristics such as type of crime, *modus operandi*, and type of weapon used.

Pattern Identification Modules (PIMS) (p. 334) group comprised of housing, transit, patrol, detective, organized crime, and robbery squads implemented in each New York City borough to review daily index crime reports and thus identify crime clusters or patterns that need to be addressed for CompStat meetings.

Peel, Sir Robert (p. 43) established the formal system of policing in London with the passing of the Metropolitan Police Act 1829.

penal code (p. 85) body of laws related to criminal offenses.

Pendleton Act (p. 49) a federal bill aimed at eliminating the "spoils system" and the corruption endemic with the federal administration.

Peterloo Massacre of 1819 (p. 41) a political protest in England that turned riotous after the military was brought in to break it up, leaving 11 people dead and hundreds injured, leading up to the formation of a formal policing system.

physical evidence (p. 201) tangible evidence linking a suspect to a crime scene, including type of forcible entry (in a property crime), blood, hair, fibers, fingerprints, and weapons, etc.

plain view (p. 93) immediately apparent by sight.

plain view doctrine (p. 115) if a crime is committed in the immediate presence of an officer, he or she can take the person into custody without a warrant.

plea bargain (p. 28) negotiations of guilty pleas in exchange for reduced charges or lenient sentences.

police academy (p. 363) school where officers learn on-the-job techniques prior to receiving full police powers.

police corruption (p. 271) the misuse of authority by a police officer.

police personality (p. 222) certain core beliefs, values, and behavioral traits that are common to many police officers, and which help to explain how individual officers exercise their discretion, how they deal with members of the public, and how police organizations function.

police policies (p. 137) a specific statement of principle that aims to guide individual decisions and ensure that those decisions reflect the overall objectives of the department.

Police Services Study (PSS) (p. 168) study of how police officers from 24 departments spent their time and their interactions with citizens in 60 residential neighborhoods, with findings that approximately two-thirds of an officer's shift was "unassigned."

police subculture (p. 224) can be the result of history and learned dispositions (socialization) such as cynicism, authoritarianism, and suspiciousness of the general public; these traits often can affect the way in which the police deal with particular groups, such as women and racial minorities.

police–minority tensions (p. 244) poor relationships between the police and the community, often resulting from a highly publicized case of police corruption or brutality in a particular neighborhood.

policing goals (p. 136) an established set of objectives that aim to provide that department with a sense of purpose and direction.

polygraph (p. 356) lie detector test used in the screening of police applicants.

Posse Comitatus Act (p. 41) Act signed in 1878 to separate military functions from local law enforcement in the United States.

posses (p. 40) group of villagers and other members of the community organized by the shire reeve to track down and apprehend offenders.

post-traumatic stress disorder (PTSD) (p. 232) disorder resulting from traumatic incidents, this is diagnosed when the person experiences a traumatic event that involved the actual or threatened death or injury to self or others; the traumatic event is persistently re-experienced through recurrent and intrusive recollections or dreams, acting or feeling as though the event were reoccurring; and intense psychological distress and physiological reactivity upon exposure to internal or external cues resembling an aspect of the traumatic event.

predisposition (p. 246) preformed opinions about groups of individuals that may lead to racist attitudes within the police.

preliminary investigation (p. 196) duties performed by first uniformed officer on arrival at a crime scene, which include determining whether the offender is at the scene or in the area, responding to the victim's needs, and ensuring the general safety of anyone in the immediate vicinity.

preponderance of the evidence (p. 101) the evidentiary standard for civil cases, meaning that the weight of the evidence must be in favor of the complainant.

presentence investigation (PSI) (p. 28) conducted by the office of probation to investigate the background of the offender, this helps the judge to determine what type of sentence is appropriate for an offender, within legislated parameters.

pretextual stops (p. 118) when an officer ostensibly stops a vehicle for some traffic violation (e.g., a broken taillight or speeding) and proceeds to use that stop to conduct a full-scale search of the car.

pretrial motions (p. 27) series of motions to be filed prior to the beginning of trial that can change the place of the trial, suppress evidence, and provide discovery.

prevalence (p. 307) the overall incidence of a problem in a geographical area.

preventive services (p. 313) attempt to stop a problem before future incidents can occur.

primary crime scene (p. 198) the site of the original crime.

Principles of Policing (p. 43) basic rules and principles of the London Metropolitan police, as established by Sir Robert Peel.

prison (p. 28) a state or federal correctional facility that houses offenders serving sentences of one year or more.

proactive (pp. 74, 299) act before the problem occurs as a preventative measure.

proactive beats (p. 175) area in which there is an increase in random patrol activity.

proactive patrol (p. 172) type of patrol, usually directed, that attempts to target problems rather than simply respond to them.

probable cause (pp. 26, 93, 109) evidentiary standard necessary for arrests and searches in which facts of a case lead a reasonable person to believe that an offense was committed and that the suspect committed that offense.

probation (pp. 29, 363) alternative sanction whereby the offender serves a sentence in the community in lieu of prison or jail; a trial period of one or two years during which the officer is evaluated.

problem solving (p. 299) the collaborative identification of problems and their underlying causes, rather than simply responding to incidents.

problem-oriented policing (p. 305) proactive policing strategies that focus on the identification of underlying causes of problems, and the selection of solutions or remedies to prevent a problem from occurring again in the future.

problems (p. 300) in standard policing terminology, this means two or more incidents capable of causing harm, in which there is an expectation that the police and community can do something about it.

procedural due process (p. 94) protects individuals from arbitrary and unfair application of the laws.

procedural justice (p. 277) the outcome is less important than the procedure by which the outcome is produced.

procedural law (p. 97) specifies how the criminal justice system should deal with violations of the substantive laws in a manner that is both efficient and fundamentally fair.

profession (p. 61) occupation consisting of the following seven criteria: an organized body of theoretically grounded knowledge, advanced study, a code of ethics, prestige, standards of admission, a professional association, and a service ideal.

profoundly deaf (p. 250) incapable of any hearing.

programmatic dimension (p. 310) implementing a series of programs to gradually incorporate community policing into departmental operations.

Project Exile (p. 91) a coordinated approach to gun control that began in 1997 in which the U.S. Attorney's office works alongside an assistant commonwealth attorney to review cases involving felons with guns, drug users with guns, guns used in drug trafficking, and gun domestic violence referrals.

property crimes (p. 69) crimes relating to property rather than crimes against a person. The four main index property crimes in the UCR are burglary, larceny-theft, motor vehicle theft, and arson.

psychopath (p. 204) person with an anti-social personality disorder who is able to charm his victims on the one hand, but having a complete void of empathy that is often manifested in sadistic sexual pleasure.

public health model (p. 296) encourages law enforcement agencies to look at crime from a preventive standpoint, saying that just as people are responsible for their own health (through their diet, exercise) communities can take ownership of their neighborhoods and reject disorder and criminality.

public offense (p. 98) felony or misdemeanor committed in the presence of a police officer.

punitive damages (p. 102) the intent of the award is to punish or make an example of the wrongdoer, which often results in significant monetary awards.

pure speech (p. 89) words that are not accompanied by an action and are clearly protected by the U.S. Constitution.

pursuit (p. 269) a situation in which an officer attempts to initiate a stop, but the suspect flees and the officer goes after the suspect.

quasi-military (p. 139) characterized by strict adherence to formal chains of command and the clear division of personnel into ranks.

quotas (p. 359) a specified number of jobs in which the police department was required to hire minorities.

racism (p. 245) bias against racial minorities, resulting in their being treated more harshly than whites.

random (routine) patrol (p. 171) like routine patrol, when officers assigned to a specific area are asked to move around in an "unsystematic" way (usually by motor vehicle) in order to detect crimes in progress and deter crimes through presence.

reactive (p. 299) responding to an incident.

reactive beats (p. 169) when all random patrol activity is suspended and patrol officers only respond to situations.

reactive model (p. 68) model of policing that is incident-based rather than proactive.

reasonable expectations of privacy (p. 119) a person has a reasonable expectation of privacy if it is possible to show that he or she expected privacy, and that that expectation is reasonable.

reasonable suspicion (pp. 26, 93, 110) evidentiary standard, of a lesser degree than probable cause, necessary for frisks in which facts lend an officer to reasonably believe that a person is carrying weapons.

recidivist (p. 29) repeat offender.

reconstruction (p. 197) when the police try to determine exactly what happened and by whom in a crime.

record management systems (RMS) (p. 336) databases for maintaining large amounts of data from the individual incident or offender level to larger organizational concerns.

relevancy (p. 326) when interpreting the meaning of information resulting from crime analysis, it is important to understand whether or not the data used in the analysis accurately reflect what is intended.

reliability (p. 326) when interpreting the meaning of information resulting from crime analysis, it is important to understand whether the same data, interpreted by different people at different times, would lead to the same conclusions.

repeat victimization (p. 307) when individuals are victims of multiple crimes, often property crimes such as burglary, since some locations are responsible for significant amounts of crime.

reported crime (p. 71) crime brought to the attention of the police.

resiliency theory (p. 312) the larger the number of risk factors influencing an individual at any given moment, the greater is the likelihood of criminal activity or other problem behavior.

response (p. 307) fourth component of the SARA model, in which strategy is selected based on what is actually causing the problem.

response time (p. 169) the time it takes an officer to respond to a citizen's call.

reverse discrimination (p. 359) hiring minorities at the expense of those in the majority.

reverse sting operations (p. 152) when officers pose as drug dealers and arrest those who buy drugs from them.

Rigel (p. 336) a computerized geographic profiling workstation that includes statistical analyses, GIS, and database management functions to aid in the process of offering calculated investigative suggestions.

risk factors (p. 311) predictor variables found to be associated with delinquent or criminal activity.

rotating shifts (p. 179) the rotation of officers across either different working hours or different divisions within the department.

routine activities theory (p. 314) in order for a crime to occur three elements must intersect at the same time and place: a motivated offender, the absence of capable guardianship, and a suitable target.

routine patrol (p. 171) in which officers assigned to a specific area are asked to move around in an "unsystematic" way (usually by motor vehicle) in order to detect crimes in progress and deter crimes through presence.

routine traffic stop (p. 183) traffic stop with no unusual circumstances or particularly high degree of risk.

rule of law (pp. 16, 97) Developed over many years through case law, statutes, and scholarly writings, this states that all people in society have the opportunity to participate in establishing the law, the rules apply to everyone, and the rule protect individuals as well as society.

S.A.R.A. (p. 305) term coined by Spelman and Eck related to the four separate components of the problem-solving process: scanning, analysis, response, and assessment.

S.W.A.T. (Special Weapons And Tactics) teams (p. 153) paramilitary units within many police departments that specialize in the use of force and aggressive policing techniques. They are responsible for handling high-risk law enforcement situations that are beyond the capabilities of ordinary patrol officers.

saturation patrol (p. 174) placing extremely high levels of patrol within a narrowly defined geographic area.

scanning (p. 305) the first part of the SARA model, this is the clustering of incidents into meaningful problem units.

schizoid personality (p. 204) a person with a personality disorder characterized by being withdrawn from society.

school liaison officers (p. 157) officers who are permanently assigned to local high schools to investigate juvenile crime and serve as a resource to school staff and students.

search and seizure (p. 92) act that can be carried out by law enforcement officers in order to obtain illegal contraband. Citizens are protected from illegal searches and seizures by the Fourth Amendment, which protects citizens from unwarranted governmental intrusions.

search warrant (p. 114) formal court document obtained by an officer prior to a search specifying where the search will take place and what is to be the basis of the search.

secondary crime scene (p. 198) any subsequent scene of a crime after the primary crime scene.

seizure (p. 111) the taking of a person's property as potential evidence of criminal behavior.

self-incrimination (p. 94) protected by the Fifth Amendment, a person does not have to say anything in a court of law that may implicate his or her guilt.

Serious Habituation Offender Criminal Apprehension Program (SHOCAP) (p. 305) study developed by the Office of Juvenile Justice and Delinquency Prevention that showed that 10 percent of offenders account for 55 percent of all crimes; 10 percent of victims account for 42 percent of all victimization; 10 percent of all locations account for 60 percent of the call load to the police.

service style (p. 228) style of policing described by James Q. Wilson where the police are primarily servants of the community, with particular emphasis placed on maintaining good police-public relations and on the use of informal policing methods aimed at keeping offenders out of the criminal justice system.

shall-issue statutes (p. 92) in which states create a list of objective criteria for obtaining a concealed weapon permit, and if the individual meets that criteria, the state is required to issue him or her a permit.

shire reeves (p. 40) precursor to the modern day sheriff in England.

shires (p. 40) geographic area in England similar to the American county that used to form the basis of an informal policing system.

signature (p. 202) what an offender needs or takes from a crime scene.

slave patrols (p. 46) first established in the South during the mid-1740s, officers on slave patrol were given broad powers to punish slaves who committed offenses or refused to submit to their masters.

social ecology of crime (p. 328) examination of the spatial trends of crime and delinquency by Shaw and McKay of the Chicago school.

socialization (pp. 7, 363) the influences of parents, families, peers, and the community in training individuals about the norms, rules, and customs of a locality with an aim to compel conformity.

solvability factors (p. 197) anything that can potentially affect the probability of successfully concluding the case, such as the presence of witnesses and/or physical evidence.

Soulliere's stages of technological advancement (p. 322) four stages of technological development in policing, consisting of introduction of mobile patrol and basic communications, technology for traffic violations, the development of response technology and an emergency hotline, and advanced technology such as imaging and GIS.

span of control (p. 141) number of people reporting to one commanding officer.

special relationship (p. 82) relationship between the police and a citizen in which litigation can arise if the police fail to protect the citizen.

speech-plus conduct (p. 90) activities such as peaceful picketing, boycotts, and demonstrations that receive some First Amendment protection, though not to the same extent as pure speech.

spoils system (p. 49) system in the political era in which politicians appointed people to civil service jobs predominately based upon patronage, political affiliation, or in return for monetary payments.

stare decisis **(p. 98)** to follow the precedent from previous judicial decisions, this literally means "to stand on decided cases."

statutory law (p. 97) written law as passed by legislature.

sting operations (p. 151) when undercover agents pose as buyers of illegal goods or services.

stop and frisk (p. 110) when the police stop a person and conduct pat-down search of the suspect on the outside of the clothing in order to determine whether the individual is carrying a weapon.

strategic crime analysis (p. 326) the collection and analysis of data spanning a long period of time.

structural changes (p. 308) a shift is the foundation of the departmental structure as the focus of the department changes from one goal (e.g., responding to incidents) to another (e.g., proactive crime prevention).

substantiated complaints (p. 279) when the officer is found guilty of the action alleged.

substantive due process (p. 94) protects against arbitrary or unfair laws.

substantive law (p. 97) defines the specific elements of the crime committed as well as the parameters available for punishment.

suppression-intervention-prevention continuum (p. 312) strategy selection model based on the development of a needs assessment that involves targeting of specific offenders and locations, matching offenders to needed services in their community, and stopping a problem before future incidents can occur.

symbolic speech (p. 89) expression protected by the U.S. Constitution that takes place through tangible items such as signs, buttons, or flags.

systematic stops (p. 118) type of stop based on a particular system, method, or plan, such as a sobriety checkpoint, in which probably cause is not needed.

tactical crime analysis (p. 326) data analysis using real-time data spanning several days.

tactics (p. 333) strategies used to address the patterns of crime data.

tall organizations (p. 141) organizations with many layers in the chain of command.

target area (p. 307) the particular neighborhood within the city in which the problem is occurring most often so that the police and community get a better idea of the underlying conditions that could inform strategy.

target profiling (p. 327) the use of data to determine the potential risks certain areas may have for criminal victimization based on known offense patterns in the area.

team policing model (p. 309) structure of policing consisting of assigned shift structures, increased officer discretion, team management, and despecialization.

teams (p. 309) having officers work together from different units (e.g., patrol, traffic, and the detective divisions) as a single unit to ensure that linkage blindness is minimized and needed resources are brought to bear on a problem.

telescoping (p. 72) phenomenon related to reporting of crimes in which serious incidents might be remembered as more recent to the victim than they really are leading to an over-reporting in the data.

thermal imaging (p. 115) a device used to determine the amount of heat emanating from premises.

thief catcher (p. 193) person in 18th-century England who could be hired to aid in finding lost property.

thin blue line (p. 224) the belief that only the police hold off the dangers of chaos and disorder in society, and thus are themselves often tainted by their mission in society.

third degree (p. 272) an interview technique identified by the National Commission on Law Observance and Enforcement in which officers would inflict pain upon a suspect in order to elicit a confession.

timeliness (p. 325) when interpreting the meaning of information resulting from crime analysis, it is important to understand whether the pattern or trend presented reflects a current problem or issue, or is it more representative of a previous situation.

tithings (p. 40) a group of ten families within a shire, in which every citizen was tied to a particular tithe, and was jointly responsible with all other members of his or her group for the payment of taxes and the maintenance of order (informal policing system).

tokens (p. 361) officers that police departments were legally required to accept due to affirmative action policies.

torts (p. 100) noncriminal restrictions placed on the freedom of individuals that fall under the jurisdiction of civil law.

tour (p. 181) the sector assigned to police officers each shift at roll call.

township police departments (p. 13) police departments within the state that operate similarly to municipal police departments, though they can vary greatly according to level of law enforcement powers and authority.

traditional policing (p. 68) policing in the reform era that was based largely around patrol and incident response time.

Transportation Security Administration (TSA) (p. 19) agency within DHS that is responsible for the security of all modes of U.S. transportation.

twelve-hour plan (p. 179) shift plan in which officers work for three days at twelve hours before having the next four days off.

two-officer cars (p. 176) in which there are two patrol officers assigned per car.

U.S. Bureau of Alcohol, Tobacco and Firearms (ATF) (p. 16) an agency with the Department of Treasury, ATF originally had a taxation and licensing principal focus, but has since evolved to encompass many law enforcement operations both on its own and in collaboration with other law enforcement jurisdictions.

U.S. Coast Guard (p. 19) responsible for the security of U.S. ports.

U.S. Customs and Border Patrol (CBP) (p. 19) a combination and unification of the former U.S. Customs Bureau, the U.S. Immigration and Naturalization services, the Animal and Plant Health Inspection Service, and the U.S. Border Patrol (and now located within Homeland Security), this agency is charged with controlling the continuous flow of goods across the nation's borders.

U.S. Marshal Service (USMS) (p. 15) U.S. agency responsible for the execution of warrants for the federal courts and the handling of federal suspects and prisoners.

U.S. Postal Service (USPS) (pp. 21) agency responsible for the enforcement of over 200 federal laws affecting the U.S. mail and postal system.

U.S. Secret Service (p. 19) agency responsible for protecting the president, the vice president, and the families of each.

Uniform Crime Reports (UCR) (p. 68) report on crime rates compiled by the FBI, based on crime statistics from local and state police departments, which is responsible for measuring and tracking crime trends.

unit (p. 145) within a division, staff may be organized into smaller groups, which deal with a specific aspect of the division's overall function.

us versus them (p. 268) attitude of police officers whereby they believe that non-police officers cannot understand the duties or dangers of their profession.

USA PATRIOT Act of 2001 (p. 4) rushed into implementation immediately following September 11, the PATRIOT Act grants law enforcement significantly increased investigative powers to combat terrorism, such as reductions in the probable cause requirements for certain types of warrants, expansions of the ability to gather internet usage activity, roving wiretaps, etc.

USA PATRIOT Improvement and Reauthorization Act of 2005 (p. 4) a modification of the PATRIOT Act of 2001, which clarifies the powers of the government to combat terrorism.

values (p. 137) the core beliefs and concerns of the department.

vertical differentiation (p. 141) the levels of formal power in an organization.

vigilante (p. 39) a person who takes the law into his or her own hands.

vigilante committees (p. 45) made up of area residents wishing to actively fight crime prior to the establishment of a formal policing system, they would take on all law enforcement duties, ranging from pursuing offenders to trying and punishing them.

vigiles **(p. 38)** first civilian police force in Rome established by the Emperor Augustus.98

violation (p. 98) lesser wrong, such as not obeying a municipal ordinance, that is rarely considered to be part of the criminal law and usually results in fines.

Violent Crime Control and Law Enforcement Act (1994) (p. 181) provided funding for an additional 100,000 officers nationally to increase the availability of officers for foot patrol and other community policing functions.

Violent Criminal Apprehension Program (VICAP) (p. 205) was created by the FBI to help identify national homicide patterns. VICAP is a comprehensive database of solved and unsolved violent crimes that includes significant details related to the crime scene, victim characteristics, and offender characteristics.

violent personal crimes (p. 69) crimes against the person. The four main violent index crimes in the UCR are murder, rape, robbery, and assault.

virtual private networks (VPN) (p. 341) involve the use of encryption software to scramble the contents of communications so that even if the system becomes available to hackers, they are unable to read the information.

voiding (p. 27) when judges dismiss arrests prior to the adjudication process.

Vollmer, August (p. 52) considered one of the pioneers of police reform and professionalization, Vollmer was the Chief of Police in Berkeley, California throughout the early twentieth century. Examples of some of his efforts to professionalize policing include the establishment of crime labs, enhancement of education and training standards, and significant utilization of motor vehicle patrol.

warrant (p. 93) formal court document that usually should be obtained before an arrest is made or a search is conducted.

watch systems (p. 45) consisting of volunteer citizens, these were based on the idea of community responsibility in which members of the community were required by local law enforcement officers to undertake patrols of their neighborhood under the guidance of local marshals or constables to watch for signs of criminal activity.

watchman style (p. 227) policing style described by James Q. Wilson, in which the approach places great emphasis on order maintenance and individual officer discretion.

water patrol (p. 178) types of patrol used by jurisdictions bordering on shorelines, beaches, and lakes given the tremendous amount of illegal activity that can begin on the water.

Wickersham Commission (p. 50) commission formed by Herbert Hoover in 1929 to address concerns with prohibition and the increasing crime rate, as well as problems with the juvenile justice and adult criminal justice processes.

Wilson, O. W. (p. 53) protégé of August Vollmer who focused on use of science and technology in policing in the Reform Era, specifically in relation to response time and efficiency.

wiretapping (pp. 93, 119) electronic "search" of a phone or a computer in which words can be "seized."

working personality (p. 226) resulting from the solidarity within police culture, this is the idea that the police find it acceptable to lie to protect another officer, back up their fellow officers when dealing with the authorities, expect to be backed up in return, and do not support their fellow officers are regarded as "rats," who are not to be trusted and deserve to be excluded from the group.

writ (p. 28) a formal document requesting an appeal.

writ of certiorari (p. 28) a formal document requesting an appeal to have a case reviewed by the U.S. Supreme Court.

zero-tolerance policing (p. 217) when police officers are required to stop anyone they see committing certain offenses, and have little or no discretion as to whether or not to arrest.

Index

Photo Credits